INTERNATIONAL HANDBOOK OF GLOBALIZATION AND WORLD CITIES

International Handbook of Globalization and World Cities

Edited by

Ben Derudder
Ghent University, Belgium

Michael Hoyler
Loughborough University, UK

Peter J. Taylor
Northumbria University, UK

Frank Witlox
Ghent University, Belgium

EE Edward Elgar
PUBLISHING

Cheltenham, UK • Northampton, MA, USA

Published by
Edward Elgar Publishing Limited
The Lypiatts
15 Lansdown Road
Cheltenham
Glos GL50 2JA
UK

Edward Elgar Publishing, Inc.
William Pratt House
9 Dewey Court
Northampton
Massachusetts 01060
USA

Paperback edition 2015

A catalogue record for this book
is available from the British Library

Library of Congress Control Number: 2011930999

This book is available electronically in the **Elgar**online
Economics subject collection
DOI 10.4337/9781781001011

ISBN 978 1 84844 647 2 (cased)
       978 1 78536 068 8 (paperback)

Typeset by Servis Filmsetting Ltd, Stockport, Cheshire
Printed and bound in Great Britain by the CPI Group (UK) Ltd

Contents

PART II   WORLD CITY ANALYSES

II A   *World city infrastructures*

II B   *World city economies*

II C   *World city governance*

Contributors

Michele Acuto, PhD Candidate, Asia-Pacific College of Diplomacy, Australian National University, Canberra, Australia

Arthur S. Alderson, Professor, Department of Sociology, Indiana University, Bloomington, USA

Harris Ali, Associate Professor, Faculty of Environmental Studies, York University, Toronto, Canada

David Bassens, Postdoctoral Research Fellow, Research Foundation – Flanders, Department of Geography, Ghent University, Belgium

Harald Bathelt, Canada Research Chair in Innovation and Governance, Department of Political Science and Department of Geography & Program in Planning, University of Toronto, Canada

Jonathan V. Beaverstock, Professor of Economic Geography, School of Geography, University of Nottingham, UK

Jason Beckfield, Professor, Department of Sociology, Harvard University, USA

Andrew Boulton, PhD Candidate, Department of Geography, University of Kentucky, USA

Stanley D. Brunn, Professor, Department of Geography, University of Kentucky, USA

Lucy C.S. Budd, Lecturer in Transport Studies, Transport Studies Group, School of Civil and Building Engineering, Loughborough University, UK

Tim Bunnell, Associate Professor, Asia Research Institute and Department of Geography, National University of Singapore, Singapore

Kavita Datta, Senior Lecturer in Geography, School of Geography, Queen Mary, University of London, UK

Ben Derudder, Professor of Human Geography, Department of Geography, Ghent University, Belgium

Anneleen De Vos, PhD Candidate, Department of Geography, Ghent University, Belgium

Lomme Devriendt, Production Manager, Orbit GeoSpatial Technologies, Lokeren, Belgium

Ewald Engelen, Professor of Financial Geography, Department of Geography, Planning and International Development Studies, University of Amsterdam, The Netherlands

Yara Evans, Visiting Research Fellow, School of Geography, Queen Mary, University of London, UK

James Faulconbridge, Senior Lecturer in Economic Geography, Lancaster Environment Centre, Lancaster University, UK

Richard Grant, Director of Urban Studies, Professor, Department of Geography and Regional Studies, University of Miami, USA

Tony H. Grubesic, Director, Geographic Information Systems and Spatial Analysis Laboratory, Associate Professor, College of Information Science and Technology, Drexel University, Philadelphia, USA

Carl Grundy-Warr, Senior Lecturer, Department of Geography, National University of Singapore, Singapore

Sarah Hall, Associate Professor, School of Geography, University of Nottingham, UK

Chris Hamnett, Professor of Geography, Department of Geography, King's College London, UK

John Harrison, Lecturer in Human Geography, School of Social, Political and Geographical Sciences, Loughborough University, UK

Joanna Herbert, Visiting Research Fellow, School of Geography, Queen Mary, University of London, UK

Michael Hoyler, Senior Lecturer in Human Geography, School of Social, Political and Geographical Sciences, Loughborough University, UK

Phil Hubbard, Professor of Urban Studies, School of Social Policy, Sociology and Social Research, University of Kent, UK

Roger Keil, Director, The City Institute and Professor, Faculty of Environmental Studies, York University, Toronto, Canada

Anthony D. King, Emeritus Professor, Art History and Sociology, Binghamton University, State University of New York, USA

Robert Kloosterman, Professor of Economic Geography and Planning, Department of Geography, Planning and International Development Studies, University of Amsterdam, The Netherlands

Paul Knox, University Distinguished Professor and Senior Fellow for International Advancement, School of Public and International Affairs, Virginia Tech, USA

Ewa Korcelli-Olejniczak, Assistant Professor, Institute of Geography and Spatial Organization, Polish Academy of Sciences, Warsaw, Poland

Karen P.Y. Lai, Assistant Professor, Department of Geography, National University of Singapore, Singapore

Bart Lambregts, Researcher and Lecturer, Division of Urban and Environmental Planning, Faculty of Architecture, Kasetsart University, Bangkok, Thailand and

Department of Geography, Planning and International Development Studies, University of Amsterdam, The Netherlands

Robert E. Lang, Director, Brookings Mountain West and The Lincy Institute, Professor of Sociology, University of Nevada, Las Vegas, USA

Loretta Lees, Professor of Human Geography, Department of Geography, King's College London, UK

Colin Lizieri, Grosvenor Professor of Real Estate Finance, Department of Land Economy, University of Cambridge, UK

Edward J. Malecki, Professor of Geography, Department of Geography, The Ohio State University, Columbus, USA

Timothy C. Matisziw, Assistant Professor, Department of Geography and Department of Civil & Environmental Engineering, University of Missouri, Columbia, USA

Jon May, Professor of Geography, School of Geography, Queen Mary, University of London, UK

Cathy McIlwaine, Reader in Geography, School of Geography, Queen Mary, University of London, UK

David Murakami Wood, Canada Research Chair (Tier II) in Surveillance Studies, Surveillance Studies Centre, and Associate Professor, Department of Sociology, Queen's University, Kingston, Ontario, Canada

Caroline Nagel, Associate Professor, Department of Geography, University of South Carolina, Columbia, USA

Peter Newman, Professor of Comparative Urban Planning, School of Architecture and the Built Environment, University of Westminster, UK

Christina Nicholas, PhD Candidate, Department of Sociology, University of Nevada, Las Vegas, USA

Jan Nijman, Professor and Director, Center for Urban Studies, University of Amsterdam, The Netherlands

Stijn Oosterlynck, Assistant Professor in Urban Sociology, Centre on Inequality, Poverty, Social Exclusion and the City, Department of Sociology, University of Antwerp, Belgium

Kathy Pain, ALDAR Professor of Real Estate Development, School of Real Estate & Planning, University of Reading, UK

Christof Parnreiter, Professor of Economic Geography, Department of Geography, University of Hamburg, Germany

Andy C. Pratt, Professor of Culture, Media and Economy, Department of Culture, Media and Creative Industries, King's College London, UK

John Rennie Short, Professor, Department of Public Policy, The University of Maryland, Baltimore County (UMBC), USA

James D. Sidaway, Professor of Political and Cultural Geography, Department of Geography, Planning and International Development Studies, University of Amsterdam, The Netherlands

Dennis Smith, Emeritus Professor of Sociology, School of Social, Political and Geographical Sciences, Loughborough University, UK

Richard G. Smith, Senior Lecturer in Human Geography, Centre for Urban Theory, College of Science, Swansea University, UK

Matthew Sparke, Professor of Geography and International Studies, Department of Geography and Jackson School of International Studies, University of Washington, Seattle, USA

Peter J. Taylor, Professor of Human Geography, School of the Built and Natural Environment, Northumbria University, Newcastle upon Tyne, UK

Andy Thornley, Emeritus Professor of Urban Planning, London School of Economics and Political Science, UK

Bert van der Knaap, Emeritus Professor in Economic Geography, Department of Applied Economics, Erasmus School of Economics, Erasmus University Rotterdam, The Netherlands

Herman van der Wusten, Emeritus Professor of Political Geography, Department of Geography, Planning and International Development Studies, University of Amsterdam, The Netherlands

Ronald Wall, Economic Geographer, Institute for Housing and Urban Development Studies (IHS), Erasmus University Rotterdam, The Netherlands

Allan Watson, Senior Lecturer in Human Geography, Department of Geography, Staffordshire University, UK

Jane Wills, Professor of Human Geography, School of Geography, Queen Mary, University of London, UK

Frank Witlox, Professor of Economic Geography, Department of Geography, Ghent University, Belgium

1 Introduction: a relational urban studies

Ben Derudder, Michael Hoyler, Peter J. Taylor and Frank Witlox

Although changing centuries is a purely arbitrary temporal event – it all depends on when you start counting the years – our recent entry into the twenty-first century does coincide with societal recognition of some quite momentous alterations in the condition of, and prospects for, humanity. Critical concerns for climatic change, mega-urbanization, delinquent banks, dwindling energy sources, religious nihilism, anti-social globalization, population growth and/or decline, increasing environmental disasters and new imperialist geopolitics have all come to the fore to jostle for a place on twenty-first century worldwide policy agendas. These are all massive issues that intersect with on-going vital interests within a humanity divided by (in alphabetical order) belief systems, citizenship status, class, ethnicity, gender, nation, race and sexuality. This International Handbook deals with the interface of two of the critical concerns – urbanization and globalization – through which elements of the vital interests will be addressed.

In focusing on globalization and world cities we take a specific approach to urbanization. By treating cities at a global scale we privilege the 'stretching' of their functions beyond their specific place locations. As such we are part of a recent tendency to foreground the role of 'relations' in social research; our relational geographies pivot on cities. Given the scale of their relations we can reasonably refer to them as world cities. As nodes within myriad worldwide networks, these cities may be interpreted as a special spatial organization, the geographical frame of contemporary globalization. In the relational language of Manuel Castells (1996), world cities today are the organizational grounding of spaces of flows in network/knowledge society that is challenging the twentieth century pre-eminence of territorial states as the organizational grounding of spaces of places in mosaic/industrial society.

The genesis of this particular relational approach can be traced back to the founding of the Globalization and World Cities (GaWC) research network in 1998. Organized as an electronic network in cyberspace and grounded at Loughborough University – www.lboro.ac.uk/gawc – the research initiative prospered and grew, quite appropriately, into a worldwide network itself. This was largely because GaWC filled a lacuna in the world cities literature as it existed at the end of the twentieth century. It was noted that for the most part, world cities were studied individually and researchers largely dealt with internal relations rather than cities' external relations. Obviously both sets of relations are equally critical to the success of cities, but in the case of world cities, so named specifically because of their worldwide links and influences, it was particularly inopportune to neglect the latter. This became GaWC's special niche – the external relations of cities in contemporary globalization. Thus if GaWC has any claim to have influenced scholarship on cities, it is that it has contributed to re-balancing the internal and the external in urban studies. This is reflected in this volume: we begin with our initial emphasis – city networks loom large – but we do not overdo our initial niche; internal relations of world cities feature strongly later in the book.

There was a second important criticism of the world city literature in the 1990s that GaWC has also addressed. It seemed to some observers that theoretical ideas concerning world cities were running ahead of any adequate empirical back-up. This evidential deficit was signalled very early in the development of a world city literature (Korff, 1987) but a decade later it was still 'the dirty little secret of world cities research' (Short et al., 1996), leading to sceptics such as Kevin Cox (1997, p. 1) referring to 'so-called "world cities"'. It was a key purpose of GaWC to begin the task of overturning this data problem and we have been reasonably successful in this respect: Cox's adjective and problematizing quotes are unlikely to be repeated a decade or so on, notwithstanding that we now understand all cities to be 'cities in globalization' (Taylor et al., 2007). GaWC's empirical research programme has incorporated two main strands – one extensive, the other intensive (Sayer, 1992) – that were effectively launched by two publications in 2001. In Taylor (2001) the interlocking network model was introduced as a specification of the world city network. This steered new data collection leading to measurement of the world city network (Taylor, 2004). This quantitative research was complemented by a qualitative approach to understanding the relations between London and Frankfurt at the launching of the euro (Beaverstock et al., 2001). This work indicated that this inter-city relation was primarily cooperative rather than competitive with firms using both cities but in different ways. This key finding of intensive research chimed with the extensive measurement exercise in that networks are premised on mutuality: cities in networks need each other. Both strands of GaWC research have mushroomed in the last decade and they constitute much of the content of this book.

But this International Handbook has been designed to be more than a 'working report' on a decade of GaWC research. The topic of cities and globalization is very large, too large for any one research group to cover adequately, but fortunately its study has attracted many researchers beyond the GaWC network. We have selected some researchers whose work we admire and which blends in well alongside mainstream GaWC fare. They cover many important themes that GaWC perforce neglects so that we have taken the opportunity of editing this Handbook to create a much more rounded and comprehensive treatment of world cities. In addition, the interlocking network model, although developed to describe cities in contemporary globalization, has been recently interpreted as a generic model of city networks which has allowed GaWC research to be extended historically (Taylor et al., 2010). Although the dearth of historical context for world city studies has not been widely recognized – the main exception is Anthony King (1990), one of our invited contributors – this new development in GaWC research is featured below alongside the main contemporary concern. In fact, perhaps unexpectedly but rather conventionally, this volume starts with 'history' as part of the 'rounding out' of our subject matter.

We have divided the Handbook into three main Parts:

● Part I covers the antecedents needed for understanding world cities and globalization; it is divided into three sections, starting with four historical chapters focusing on pre-modern city systems, city systems underpinning modern hegemonies, cities in imperialism and political world cities. The other sections have four chapters on the basic concepts used to study cities in globalization, dealing with network modelling, city cooperation, global city and world city concepts, and large city-regions, and chapters on four key examples of empirical measures of inter-city network relations: airlines, the internet, corporate relations and advanced servicing.

- Part II introduces a variety of world city analyses in four sections. The starting point is five chapters on different important infrastructures (airports, offices, fairs, events and smart cities), followed by eight chapters on aspects of world city economies (corporate networks, business knowledge, highly skilled labour, finance, cultural economy, star architects, media and sex), five chapters dealing with questions concerning world city governance (city-region governance, sustainability, planning, surveillance and infectious diseases) and six chapters on the important matter of multiple divisions within world cities (social polarization, gentrification, the super-rich, low-paid migrant labour, cultural diasporas and suburbanization).
- Part III is devoted to case studies, thirteen chapters in all, another indication of our strong commitment to empirical work to sustain the study of an ever-changing subject matter.

These three Parts represent the 'broader GaWC' that constitute this International Handbook.

The case studies are particularly important since they act as a counterpoise to the previous sections covering world city topics in a more general way. First they allow the Handbook to better express the variety of urban outcomes that are found in contemporary globalization. To promote this we have commissioned several different forms of essays – on city-dyads and triads (NYLON and the Indonesia–Malaysia–Singapore Growth Triangle), city comparisons (Shanghai–Beijing–Hong Kong, Berlin–Warsaw and UAE world cities) and multi-nodal city regions (Randstad Holland); on a variety of single cities from different parts of the world (Mexico City, Mumbai, Accra, Brussels, Las Vegas and Sydney); and a non-nodal urbanism (South Florida) – covering different themes from previous chapters but now grounded into a specific geographical context. This is a very important part of the Handbook and not just because of the targeted empirics. Much of the mainstream GaWC research, especially the quantitative extensive work, appears monolithic in its implications and has been criticized as such (Robinson, 2002). However, describing large numbers of cities as nodes in a world city network does not mean that we are reducing every city to being a pale imitation of London or New York. As Castells (1996), and before him Jane Jacobs (1969), have made explicit, cities are best understood as processes. This idea has been at the heart of all GaWC research: every city is constituted of myriad urban processes represented by a particular outcome at the point of study. Thus the world city network process is very strong in London and New York and this is reflected in their network measurements and the fact that they are often applauded as 'global cities' (Sassen, 2001). But both cities encompass so much more than this particular globalization process and this is even more the case for other economically less important cities. In fact all the cities treated in chapters in Part III of this volume do appear as measurements in the world city network (Taylor et al., 2011) and this will be useful information in specific contexts, but we would never claim that such measures represent all that these cities have to offer. Globalization, and the city relations within this meta-process, are essentially complex theoretically, and effectively messy empirically. In much of GaWC's research over the last decade we have tried to make some sense of this complex mess by focusing narrowly on specific processes; in this Handbook we have released ourselves from this constraint through Part III with its wonderful variety. Understanding is an iterative practice alternating order and diversity and both are properly represented below.

REFERENCES

Beaverstock, J.V., M. Hoyler, K. Pain and P.J. Taylor (2001), *Comparing London and Frankfurt as World Cities: A Relational Study of Contemporary Urban Change*, London: Anglo-German Foundation.
Castells, M. (1996), *The Rise of the Network Society*, Oxford: Blackwell.
Cox, K.R. (1997), 'Introduction: globalization and its politics in question', in K.R. Cox (ed.), *Spaces of Globalization: Reasserting the Power of the Local*, New York: Guilford, pp. 1–18.
Jacobs, J. (1969), *The Economy of Cities*, New York: Vintage.
King, A.D. (1990), *Urbanism, Colonialism, and the World-Economy: Cultural and Spatial Foundations of the World Urban System*, London: Routledge.
Korff, R. (1987), 'The world city hypothesis: a critique', *Development and Change*, **18** (3), 483–493.
Robinson, J. (2002), 'Global and world cities: a view from off the map', *International Journal of Urban and Regional Research*, **26** (3), 531–554.
Sassen, S. (2001), *The Global City: New York, London, Tokyo*, Princeton, NJ: Princeton University Press, 2nd edition.
Sayer, A. (1992), *Method in Social Science: A Realist Approach*, London: Routledge, 2nd edition.
Short, J.R., Y. Kim, M. Kuus and H. Wells (1996), 'The dirty little secret of world cities research: data problems in comparative analysis', *International Journal of Urban and Regional Research*, **20** (4), 697–717.
Taylor, P.J. (2001), 'Specification of the world city network', *Geographical Analysis*, **33** (2), 181–194.
Taylor, P.J. (2004), *World City Network: A Global Urban Analysis*, London: Routledge.
Taylor, P.J., B. Derudder, P. Saey and F. Witlox (eds) (2007), *Cities in Globalization: Practices, Policies and Theories*, London: Routledge.
Taylor, P.J., M. Hoyler and R. Verbruggen (2010), 'External urban relational process: introducing central flow theory to complement central place theory', *Urban Studies*, **47** (13), 2803–2818.
Taylor, P.J., P. Ni, B. Derudder, M. Hoyler, J. Huang and F. Witlox (eds) (2011), *Global Urban Analysis: A Survey of Cities in Globalization*, London: Earthscan.

PART I

ANTECEDENTS

I A   Histories

2 Historical world city networks
Peter J. Taylor

INTRODUCTION: BEYOND 'GREAT CITIES'

The modern world is a world of great cities, first recognized as industrial cities in the nineteenth century (Weber, 1899) and most recently identified as world cities (Friedmann, 1986) or global cities (Sassen, 1991). These latter cities constitute a major subject of this volume on cities in globalization and I focus historically on the more important cities in the world in this chapter. The justification for this brief excursion into past urban worlds has been rehearsed in many different contexts many times. Contemporary cities are exciting manifestations of contemporary society and appear to be very new in many different aspects. And this is important and will be elaborated in detail in subsequent chapters. But these world or global cities are also doing things that cities have done since cities were invented. In other words there is a generic base to all cities that should not be neglected in celebrations of the present. World or global cities are first and foremost cities; we need to understand this before explicating their specific world or global characteristics. The latter – the globality of cities – is a particular feature of modern cities and therefore for my historical perspective I use the term 'world cities' only; I provide a generic definition of this term below.

There are many studies that celebrate the great cities of the past, and two recent volumes are especially enlightening. Peter Hall (1998) in his *magnus opus Cities in Civilization* is concerned for the 'unique creativity of great cities' (p. 7); 27 chapters on cities as the primary sites of creativity and innovation are described, starting with Athens in 500–400 BCE and concluding with London in 1979–1993. Although breathtaking in its substantive coverage of social change through cities, its historical and geographical range is impressive but limited due to a focus on 'Western Civilization'. In contrast John Julius Norwich (2009) has edited a volume *The Great Cities in History* that includes cities from the beginnings of urbanization in all parts of the world. It consists of 70 vignettes of cities that have made their mark on history in politics, commerce or culture, starting with Mesopotamian Uruk as the 'world's first city' and concluding with Shanghai today as 'China's super city'. These are wonderful books but they do not represent the way I am going to approach world cities of the past.

Devoting study to great cities one at a time risks losing the geohistorical context through which the cities became great in the first place. Parallel to the now discredited political 'great men history' we are in danger of creating an urban 'great cities history'. This is where a Jane Jacobs (1969, p. 35) intervention is appropriate: 'A city seems always to have implied a group of cities, in trade with one another.' Cities are at all times connected in spaces of flows. It is through networks, orbits, circuits and chains of commodities that information, people, knowledge and all manner of cultural ideas are transmitted within and between cities. Thus a city never occurs on its own, von Thünen-like, with just its hinterland for company; again, as Jacobs tells us, no city has ever grown 'by trading only with a rural hinterland' (p. 35). Cities come in groups because they need each other to be successful. In my studies of contemporary cities in globalization I have modelled inter-city relations as an interlocking world city network (Taylor, 2004) (of which more in later chapters) and this has been subsequently developed as a generic model of city mutualities. Thus the world cities I will describe in this chapter constitute city networks that feature a number of major cities. I identify eight such major city networks that precede the modern world-system as described by Wallerstein (1979). This historical system was constructed in the 'long sixteenth century' (c.1450–c.1650) and I identify a European 'early modern' major city network at the time of its beginnings and before the onset of industrialization in the late eighteenth century. Hence the substance of this chapter is to define and describe these nine major city networks prior to the rise of great industrial cities.

DEFINING WORLD CITIES BEFORE MODERNITY

Current study of world cities traces its origins back to Peter Hall's (1966) *The World Cities* in which he identified six important cities and city-regions with a multitude of important functions. He refers back to Patrick Geddes' use of the term in the early twentieth century. Gottmann (1989, p. 62) traces it back even further to *Weltstadt* as used by Goethe to describe Rome and Paris 200 years ago. More recently, Braudel (1984) has coined the phrase 'world-city' to label the leading financial centres of early modern Europe. There are two things to learn from this brief historical exegis of the concept of world city: first there appears to be no continuous use of the concept, and secondly, none of the uses encompasses any strong notion of inter-city relations. Thus although the term has been recently applied to a particular historical case – Robertson and Inglis (2006) consider imperial Rome as a world city – we can use the term consistent with current usage linking it to network, and project it back historically without causing any particular confusion.

There is one recent scholar who has explicitly projected the world city concept back historically to early cities: George Modelski (2003) in his book *World Cities: –3000 to 2000*. This is both a comprehensive data source and a narrative interpreting his long-term findings. I will follow Modelski in certain respects and will re-analyse his data. He defines world cities as complex centres of organization that are part of wider networks of cities:

> World cities are bases of institutions capable of organizing vast regions of the world into an integrated world system. They might be mighty capitals and centers of wide-ranging international political responsibilities. They might serve world-wide religious institutions. Or else they might function as global centers of learning and stores of knowledge (as in the library of Alexandria). They obviously provide the infrastructure of world trade. (Modelski, 2003, p. 4)

Unfortunately there are no comprehensive historical data for this range of functions and therefore he operationalizes this city 'importance' as demographic size, the assumption being that large urban population is associated with the complex division of labour necessary for world city functions. To illustrate his definition he uses the example of Uruk 5000 years ago:

why should Uruk be called a world city? Well, for one, it was in its time the world's largest city; secondly, it was the center of a nucleus of cities that would expand world-wide, and third, it was also the cradle of writing; in all three respects, a city of worldly import. (Modelski, 2003, p. 4)

Thus although Uruk only reaches a maximum population of 80,000, not particularly large today, it qualifies, for Modelski, as the very first world city because of its contemporary impact and world-changing legacy. I will use this case prominently in my later analyses.

There are two ways I diverge a little from Modelski's (2003) work. First, there is always a danger when using a place-based measure, such as population size, as a surrogate for the complexity of world cities, that the space of flows – the essence of the complexity – is neglected. This is, I fear, what has happened to a degree in Modelski's text. Secondly, and to rectify this, I employ Braudel's (1984) concept of world-economy as a framework for cities in spaces of flows. For Braudel there have been world-economies that exist in tandem with world-empires. For instance, the Roman Empire defined a political space and simultaneously there was a Roman economy that actually extended beyond imperial frontiers (p. 25). In such an example, 'world' does not imply worldwide but refers to a distinctive fragment of the myriad societies in the world, in the sense of the 'Roman world'. I will argue it is city networks that provide the basic organization frame for such 'worlds' as world-economies. Hence for these specific worlds, their cities constitute a world city network just as contemporary cities define the world city network of our globalizing world. I realize this emphasis on economy dilutes Modelski's more comprehensive definition of world city but this can be justified as follows. I will be interested in city networks that are reasonably long lasting, at least 200 years. Such sustainability requires complex commercial transactions across many cities for their mutual benefit. There will be important imperial capitals that depend on simpler patterns of tribute but ultimately city dynamism will be tested through integration into the network rather than just being a site for stacking up capital. However, there will never be a purely commercial network of cities; the degree of political influence will be manifest in different levels of hierarchical tendency in world city networks.

METHODOLOGY

There are two parts to this section, first a description of the data, and secondly, how the data are used to identify world city networks.

Data: Estimating City Populations

There are two main sources of worldwide historical population estimates for cities: Chandler (1987) and Modelski (2003). Modelski's estimates use Chandler's figures as a starting point but there are also important revisions. They are complementary because the two sources do not provide the same coverage and therefore both need to be used. Modelski is best for the early period because he uses a lower threshold (10,000) for inclusion than Chandler, who, in any case, only provides data back to 2250 BCE. Chandler is necessary for the later centuries after 1000 AD because his threshold for inclusion remains at 40,000 whereas Modelski only considers cities with over a million from this date. In the middle period, between 1000 BCE and 1000 AD, the Modelski data use a threshold of 100,000 and Chandler of 40,000; here I use the former supplemented by the latter as necessary.

Early city population measures are derived from the areal size of sites with an urban density multiplier used to provide an estimate. For instance, Modelski (2003, pp. 7–11) uses a site-density formula of 200 persons per hectare (see also Chandler, 1987, pp. 6–7). Otherwise various textual sources are evaluated and used (Modelski, 2003, pp. 12–13; Chandler, 1987, pp. 2–6). However calculated, these populations remain estimates and should never be treated as exact measures. Thus despite the massive amount of work involved in producing estimates for hundreds of cities, Modelski (2003) remains modest in his description of the outcome: 'estimates are necessarily speculative, and basically belong to the category of educated guesses' (p. 9). It is in this spirit that I use this work. I am looking for 'worlds of large cities' using population estimates as notional rather than definitive. I am not carrying out sophisticated numerical analyses with the data; I use the numbers simply to define a category of 'large city'. There may be cities included in a network or others excluded through inaccuracies in the data but within reason this is not a problem: I think Chandler and Modelski have done as good a job as can be expected for such a large and daunting task. My networks of cities are not meant to be definitive; rather they indicate approximately which leading cities constituted world city networks historically.

Identifying World City Networks

World city networks consist of groupings of leading cities. There are no comprehensive data on flows (e.g. trade) and, furthermore, there is no comprehensive information on the agents, people in the city, doing the inter-city networking. Hence the need to use population size as a surrogate for economic and political activities that produce flows. The assumption is that large cities generate large inter-city flows. Two thresholds have to be set: (i) the population size to qualify as a leading city, and (ii) the number of such cities that make a network.

The threshold I use to define a leading city is 80,000, the population of Uruk in 2800 BCE. As noted previously, Modelski used this case to clarify his world city concept: it is truly the world's first great city. Just think of the economic and political logistics for the everyday reproduction of a city of this size some 5000 years ago. Table 2.1 shows Uruk's precociousness in terms of sheer size. The cities in this table are all those with populations of 80,000 or more from 2800 to 600 BCE. Notice for over a millennium after Uruk, only one other city reached this threshold: Ur, the first major imperial capital and the first city of 100,000. In later years there is a mixture of Egyptian and Chinese cities that join the list but, even with these additional regions, cities of such a size remain rare. And most cities are not far above the threshold; only one city in Table 2.1 had a population over twice the size of Uruk: Luoyang was the first 200,000 city in the final century recorded in Table 2.1. Uruk sets the standard for what is a leading city.

How many of these cities are required to indicate a fully flourishing world city network? Such a threshold is obviously very arbitrary and can be manipulated to

Table 2.1   Cities with populations of 80,000 or more, 2800–600 BCE

Date (BCE: Before Christian Era)	Cities with estimated populations of 80,000 or more
2800	Uruk
2700	None
2600	None
2500	None
2400	None
2300	None
2200	None
2100	Ur
2000	None
1900	None
1800	None
1700	None
1600	Avaris
1500	None
1400	Thebes
1300	Thebes, Yin
1200	Pi-Rames, Thebes, Yin
1100	Memphis, Pi-Ramses, Thebes
1000	Babylon, Haoqing, Memphis, Thebes
900	Haoqing, Memphis, Thebes
800	Haoqing, Memphis, Thebes
700	Linzi, Luoyang, Memphis, Thebes
600	Carthage, Gelonus, Linzi, Luoyang, Xiatu

Source: Modelski (2003)

ensure a number that is manageable for purpose. In this case I have set a high threshold of 10 leading cities within a common cultural area ('civilization') to constitute a world city network. Such a grouping of cities provides the network structure of flows that reproduces the world that is a 'civilization'. I search out such places with 10 or more 'Uruks' over a two-century period to reflect sustained reproduction. Operationalizing this generates nine world city networks to describe and discuss in the remainder of the chapter.

Of course, the original Sumerian cities of which Uruk is the head do not qualify as a world city network by the criteria applied here. But this does not mean it was not an important city network. In fact Modelski (2003, p. 28) identifies 15 cities including Uruk in 2800 BCE with populations over 10,000. Clearly not great cities – the second highest population was only 40,000 – but nevertheless they constituted a vibrant city network, possibly the very first (Algaze, 2005). The point I am making is that the world city networks I identify are only the major networks amongst myriad such organizations that were created before modernity. But they are the most impressive, 10-plus Uruks-worth of spatial organization, and they begin to appear in the final half-millennium BCE.

Table 2.2   The first East Asian world city network, 400–300 BCE

Leading cities	Population estimates in thousands
Linzi	350
Xiatu	320
Luoyang	250
Daliang	200
Yiyang	200
Qufu/Lu	180
Yenhsiatu	180
Shangqiu	130
Xinzheng	120
Handan	100
Suzhou	100
Anyi	100
Yong	100
Yianyang	100

Source: Modelski (2003, p. 42) supplemented by Chandler (1987, p. 461)

THE NINE WORLD CITY NETWORKS BEFORE INDUSTRIAL MODERNITY

In my search for world city networks one feature stands out: the majority are found in East Asia, China and surrounding countries. Starting in 400 BCE and only ending as the Chinese Empire is beginning to be absorbed into the modern world-system in 1800 AD, most great city networks of the world have been Sino-centric. In the early period China is rivalled by the Mediterranean world, for which I find two distinctive world city networks, and the other pre-modern network, that of the Moslem world, is partly a legacy of the earlier Mediterranean networks. This leaves another partial progeny of the Mediterranean world, the pre-industrial European world city network of the early modern period. In what follows I introduce these networks briefly in chronological order. For each world city network I have produced a table of qualifying cities with their highest estimated populations over the two centuries of the network's existence. Discussion of each world city network focuses on these tables.

There is one hypothesis to keep in mind when considering these world city networks. Christopher Chase-Dunn in numerous forays into historical city analyses has suggested cities flourish when political structures are weak (e.g. Chase-Dunn and Hall, 1997, p. 90). Thus the impressive world city networks I have identified should occur in periods where there is little or no political centralization by world-empires.

The First East Asian World City Network (400–300 BCE)

This is not just the first East Asian world city network; it is the very first in world history. With 14 leading cities, 5 over 200,000, it is clearly an established network (Table 2.2).

Table 2.3   The first Mediterranean world city region, 200–100 BCE

Leading cities	Population estimates in thousands
Alexandria	1000
Rome	400
Carthage	200
Pergamum	200
Antioch	125
Jerusalem	100
Ephesus	100
Apamea	100
Cibyra	100
Syracuse	100

Source: Modelski (2003, p. 49) supplemented by Chandler (1987, p. 462)

This world city network developed in the Eastern Zhou period before the first Chinese unification in 221 BCE, and therefore seems to reflect the commercial advantages of decentralized politics. According to Shen (2003, p. 290) this was a period when 'the number of cities dramatically increased, and urban population grew rapidly'. He captures the process as follows:

> Production and commerce clearly became a very important part of the urban economy during the Eastern Zhou. Political centers, such as capitals of states, quickly turned into commercial cities that attracted a large number of migrants. (p. 295)

As 'evidence of the extensive trading activities' (p. 304) he refers to one city site where over 30,000 coins have been found, many originating from other city-states. This appears to be a very worthy first world city network in world history.

The First Mediterranean World City Network (200–100 BCE)

There had been important Mediterranean city networks developed first by the Phoenicians and latterly by the Greeks (Gottmann, 1984) but neither grew large enough to become world city networks by my definition. But this changed with the rise of Rome, dominant in the eastern Mediterranean from 188 BCE, at the period when Alexandrian city development remained (Table 2.3). This is reflected in there being more hierarchical tendencies in this network: the city of Alexandria is identified by Modelski as the first 'millionaire city', and Rome is also recorded as very large. This is the world city network of Republican Rome: it consisted largely of cities to the east often in alliance with Rome, incorporated into the Roman world by conquest and trade (Grimal, 1983, p. 6).

The Second Mediterranean World City Network (200–300)

This second Mediterranean grouping is the world city network of Imperial Rome. However, this should not be interpreted as extreme political centralization because, as

Table 2.4   The second Mediterranean world city network, 200–300

Leading cities	Population estimates in thousands
Rome	1200
Alexandria	600
Antioch	400
Carthage	300
Capua	240
Ephesus	200
Pergamum	170
Apamea	120
Caesarea	110
Smyrna	100
Caesarea Mazaca	100
Trier	100
Milan	100
Emerita	100
Nicomedia	100

Source: Modelski (2003, p. 49) supplemented by Chandler (1987, p. 464)

Grimal (1983, p. 109) has pointed out: 'the Roman Empire was, legally and in prac-tice, a federation of city-states' so that 'until the late third century AD, the Roman Empire consisted essentially of cities, each of which had a territory attached to it' (p. 329).

According to Grimal (1983, p. 7), 'the apogee of the Roman cities [occurred] in the first and second centuries of our era.' The leading cities listed in Table 2.4 reflect the subsequent outcome as a network with relatively high hierarchical tendencies, with Rome at the apex easily topping over one million according to Modelski (2003, p. 49). One and a half times larger than the Republican network, the Imperial network also had a larger geographical spread. Although still biased towards the eastern Mediterranean, there are now large cities to the west, two extra in Italy (Capua and Milan), one in Spain (Emerita) and one in Gaul (Trier). However, this imperial urban development to the west was soon made problematic by the movement of the capital from Rome to Constantinople in 330.

The Second East Asian World City Network (700–800)

This world city network occurs during the disintegration phase of the Tang Dynasty (618–907). Strong centralizers, the Tangs created their great new capital at Changan as a forward base for expanding their empire westwards. However, military defeat and internal rebellion changed the situation dramatically after 755. This is how Barraclough (1979, p. 126) describes it:

> The imperial authority was much reduced, and the uniform centralised policies of the 7th century were abandoned. Power passed to the provinces, and many provincial capitals grew into large and wealthy metropolises. There was a massive movement of population into the

Table 2.5   The second East Asian world city network, 700–800

Leading cities	Population estimates in thousands
Changan	1000
Luoyang	500
Guangzhou	200
Suzhou	100
Chengdu	100
Xin Jang	100
Youzhou	100
Kaifeng	100
Nara	100
Kyoto	100
Lsasa	100
Wuchang	84

Source: Modelski (2003, p. 44) supplemented by Chandler (1987, pp. 467–468)

fertile Yangtze valley, where new methods of farming produced large surpluses of grain. Trade boomed, and a network of small market towns grew up everywhere.

But our data, Table 2.5, show much more than 'small market towns'. Barraclough appears to have missed the boom in great cities that Table 2.5 illustrates. Thus this seems to be another case where political weakness has allowed the blooming of a Chinese world city network.

The Moslem World City Network (900–1000)

This is the most impressive world city network to have been developed outside East Asia before modern industrialization. In Table 2.6 there are 16 cities listed, with a geographical spread from Iberia to central Asia. And at the centre there is Baghdad, capital of the Caliphate, which Chandler (1987, p. 527) claims to be the first and only millionaire city before 1800.

The rise of Islam produced what Hourani (1991, p. 110) calls 'a chain of great cities running from one end of the world of Islam to the other', thereby 'linking the world of the Indian Ocean with that of the Mediterranean'. Here is his description of the network processes that ensued:

> The canons of correct behaviour and thought . . . linked cities with each other. A network of routes ran through the world of Islam and beyond it. Along them moved not only caravans of camels or donkeys carrying silks, spices, glass and precious metals, but ideas, news, fashions, patterns of thought and behaviour . . . Merchants from one city settled in others and kept a close and permanent link between them.

In other words this was a classic case of a vast world city network interlocked by teachers and merchants.

Table 2.6   The Moslem world city network, 900–1000

Leading cities	Population estimates in thousands
Baghdad	1200
Cordova	450
Fustat/Cairo	200
Samarkand	200
Alexandria	175
Nishapur	130
Basrah	100
Samarra	100
Kairouan	100
Bokhara	100
Mopsuetia	100
Al Ahsa	100
Seville	100
Isfahan	100
Tinnis	100
Ravy	100

Source: Modelski (2003, p. 55) supplemented by Chandler (1987, pp. 468–469)

The Third East Asian World City Network (1300–1400)

The cities shown in this world city network (Table 2.7) depict a complete change from the previous East Asian network (Table 2.5). Two features stand out: first the retreat from the west in terms of the largest cities, and secondly, a much flatter distribution of cities is indicated. This is a network that flourished in the period of transfer from the Mongol Yuan Dynasty to the domestic Ming Dynasty. In this period of political uncertainty there is no one capital city that dominates before the Ming Dynasty moved back to Peking in 1421.

Three World City Networks Compared: The Fourth and Fifth East Asian World City Networks (1500–1600 and 1700–1800) and the European World City Network (1500–1600)

I deal with these three world city networks together since they cover the period of the rise of the modern world-system. At this time the system was still not global and, in particular, had not deeply penetrated East Asia (Wallerstein, 1979). Thus the two world city networks identified for this region are the last two such networks to have developed outside the modern world-system. The European world city network identified developed right at the beginnings of the modern world-system and represents a network before the consolidation of the system through Dutch hegemony in the early seventeenth century (Wallerstein, 1984).

There are two points to be made on the evidence for these networks (Table 2.8, Table 2.9 and Table 2.10). First, the two East Asian world city networks are quite similar

Table 2.7   The third East Asian world city network, 1300–1400

Leading cities	Population estimates in thousands
Nanking	487
Hangchow	432
Peking	401
Kamakura	200
Canton	150
Kyoto	150
Soochow	129
Sian	118
Seoul	100
Kaifeng	90
Wuchang	90
Yangchow	85
Fuchow	81
Chuanchow	80

Source: Chandler (1987, pp. 73–74)

Table 2.8   The fourth East Asian world city network, 1500–1600

Leading cities	Population estimates in thousands
Peking	706
Osaka	360
Kyoto	300
Hangchow	270
Nanking	194
Canton	180
Sian	138
Soochow	134
Seoul	125
Chengdu	100
Sumpu	100
Changchun	85
Fuchow	83
Kaifeng	80
Yamagushi	80

Source: Chandler (1987, pp. 75–76)

and might be interpreted as a single large network that grew to full fruition in 1800. At this point Peking was still the largest city in the world at the head of what was by far the largest world city network developed before industrial modernity. Secondly, and a corollary of the above, the one and only European world city network is a very poor relation to the East Asian equivalent. It appears to have very little coordinating structure

Table 2.9   The fifth East Asian world city network, 1700–1800

Leading cities	Population estimates in thousands
Peking	1100
Canton	800
Yedo	688
Hangchow	387
Osaka	383
Kyoto	377
Soochow	243
Sian	224
Seoul	194
Kingtehchen	164
Tientsin	130
Fuchow	130
Foshan	124
Chengdu	97
Nagoya	92
Lanchow	90
Shanghai	90
Ninghsia	90
Changsha	85
Ningpo	80
Kaifeng	80

Source: Chandler (1987, pp. 77, 79)

Table 2.10   The European world city network, 1500–1600

Leading cities	Population estimates in thousands
Paris	245
Naples	224
London	187
Venice	151
Seville	126
Prague	110
Milan	107
Potosi	105
Palermo	105
Rome	102
Lisbon	100
Ghent	80
Madrid	80

Source: Chandler (1987, pp. 19–20, 42)

– ranging from a major capital city (Paris) to a key trading city (Venice), an American silver production centre (Potosi) and a precocious manufacturing city (Ghent) – and did not survive into the seventeenth century. The relationship between these world city networks and why East Asia did not experience a 'crisis of the seventeenth century' has been described in detail by Frank (1998, pp. 231–237).

CONCLUSION

We have reached the modern world-system, and this featured a different sort of economic organization determining social change. Instead of these far-flung world city networks the new system created a much more hierarchical core–periphery structure at the centre of which was a hegemonic state created through a local multi-city region of high creativity and innovation. This is the story of the next chapter.

REFERENCES

Algaze, G. (2005), *The Uruk World System*, Chicago: University of Chicago Press.
Barraclough, G. (1979), *The Times Atlas of World History*, London: Times Books.
Braudel, F. (1984), *The Perspective of the World*, London: Collins.
Chandler, T. (1987), *Four Thousand Years of Urban Growth: An Historical Census*, Lewiston, NY: Edwin Mellon Press.
Chase-Dunn, C. and T.D. Hall (1997), *Rise and Demise: Comparing World-Systems*, Boulder, CO: Westview.
Frank, A.G. (1998), *ReOrient: Global Economy in the Asian Age*, Berkeley, CA: University of California Press.
Friedmann, J. (1986), 'The world city hypothesis', *Development and Change*, **17** (1), 69–83.
Gottmann, J. (1984), *Orbits: The Ancient Mediterranean Tradition of Urban Networks*, Oxford: Leopard's Head.
Gottmann, J. (1989), 'What are cities becoming centers of? Sorting out the possibilities', in R.V. Knight and G. Gappert (eds), *Cities in a Global Society*, Newbury Park, CA: Sage, pp. 58–67.
Grimal, P. (1983), *Roman Cities*, Madison, WI: University of Wisconsin Press.
Hall, P. (1966), *The World Cities*, London: Heinemann.
Hall, P. (1998), *Cities in Civilization*, London: Weidenfeld & Nicolson.
Hourani, A. (1991), *A History of the Arab Peoples*, London: Faber & Faber.
Jacobs, J. (1969), *The Economy of Cities*, New York: Vintage.
Modelski, G. (2003), *World Cities: –3000 to 2000*, Washington, DC: Faros 2000.
Norwich, J.J. (2009), *The Great Cities in History*, London: Thames & Hudson.
Robertson, R. and D. Inglis (2006), 'The global animus', in B.K. Gills and W.R. Thompson (eds), *Globalization and Global History*, London: Routledge, pp. 33–47.
Sassen, S. (1991), *The Global City: New York, London, Tokyo*, Princeton, NJ: Princeton University Press.
Shen, C. (2003), 'Compromises and conflicts: production and commerce in the royal cities of Eastern Zhou, China', in M.L. Smith (ed.), *The Social Construction of Ancient Cities*, Washington, DC: Smithsonian Books, pp. 290–310.
Taylor, P.J. (2004), *World City Network: A Global Urban Analysis*, London: Routledge.
Wallerstein, I. (1979), *World-Systems Analysis*, Cambridge: Cambridge University Press.
Wallerstein, I. (1984), *Politics of the World-Economy*, Cambridge: Cambridge University Press.
Weber, A.F. (1899), *The Growth of Cities in the Nineteenth Century: A Study in Statistics*, New York: Macmillan.

3 Cities in the making of world hegemonies
Peter J. Taylor, Michael Hoyler and Dennis Smith

INTRODUCTION: WALLERSTEIN'S WORLD HEGEMONIES

In Immanuel Wallerstein's (1979, 2004) world-systems analysis the modern world-system developed in the 'long sixteenth century' (c.1450–c.1650) as a European–Atlantic world-economy and expanded to become global in scope around 1900. This world-system was different from previous successful historical systems because of the enhanced importance of economic processes. Prior world-empires were political entities, the modern world-system developed as a political economy entity: the capitalist world-economy. It was able to achieve and maintain this political economy because of the fragmented nature of modern political structures. Earlier world-systems had a single over-arching political structure (one sovereignty); in the modern world-system there developed a competitive inter-state system (multiple sovereignties). And among the numerous states within the modern world-system, there were a few that were very special; Wallerstein (1984) calls them 'hegemonic states'.

Hegemonies constitute the prime time and space coordinates of the modern world-system. They are crucial to the on-going development and survival of the system over the half-millennium of its existence. Wallerstein (1984) identifies just three cases: the Dutch (the United Provinces) in the late sixteenth and seventeenth centuries, the British (the United Kingdom) in the late eighteenth and nineteenth centuries, and the Americans (the United States) in the twentieth century. According to Wallerstein, the economic development dimension of hegemony consists of three stages of increasing economic dominance, first in production, followed by commercial prowess, and culminating in financial command. High hegemony, the peak of economic power, occurs when the hegemonic state is leading simultaneously in all three areas – production, commerce and finance. Economic dominance is lost in the same order: other countries 'catch up' first in production and then in commerce, leaving finance as the last vestige of hegemonic power. This rise and fall of hegemonic power is the hegemonic cycle, the prime 'rhythm' of the modern world-system.

But this hegemonic mega-process never went unchallenged. And this is where the political survival dimension of hegemony comes into play. At some time within each hegemonic cycle there has been a 'world war' in which the hegemonic state led an alliance to defeat a military imperial threat to the system. Thus the Dutch defeated the Habsburg threat in the Thirty Years War (1618–1648), the British defeated the French threat in the Revolutionary and Napoleonic Wars (1792–1815) and the USA defeated the German threat in the twentieth century World Wars (1914–45). These three are 'world' wars not just because of their size and scope, but crucially because they determined the future survival of the modern world-system. If any one of the counter-hegemonic threats had succeeded then the world-economy would have reverted to a new world-empire. Hence hegemonic states combine both economic and political powers to develop and reproduce the modern world-system.

BRINGING CITIES INTO THE ARGUMENT

Cities hardly feature at all in this story of the modern world-system. And since one of the unique features of modernity is ever-increasing urbanization far in excess of any previous world-system, this should make us cautious in considering Wallerstein's otherwise ground-breaking account of how modernity came to be. His only important mention of cities is in relation to finance: the hegemonic state's financial prowess is concentrated in a single city: first Amsterdam, then London and finally New York. It is in these primate international financial centres that a remnant of hegemony survives long past their state's dominance. This part of Wallerstein's story derives from an earlier treatment of early-modern Europe by Fernand Braudel (1984). He identifies 'world-cities' as financial control centres from the fifteenth century starting with Venice, Antwerp and Genoa before advancing to Amsterdam, London and New York. He interprets Amsterdam as the transition case from early-modern to modern finance: it is a 'half-way house' between initial city control to later state control of international finance. In other words London's and New York's financial statuses, and to a lesser extent Amsterdam's, are premised on their location within a hegemonic state. Wallerstein diverges from Braudel only in firmly fixing Amsterdam's financial prowess to its state's hegemony.

Braudel brings cities into the argument but in a very limited way. His treatment of cities emphasizes their hierarchical nature with particular emphasis on the apex of the hierarchy. Thus although empirical examples in his work show much evidence of city networks, he is not a source for approaching cities in the modern world-system through their networking processes. Here we will use the generic theories of Jane Jacobs (1969, 1984) that link dynamic cities to economic development. In her account cities come in groups that need each other to prosper; these are city networks. She defines cities by a process that generates new work through interaction between cities, which in turn creates increasingly complex divisions of labour in city economies. When this process operates successfully it produces explosive city growths, which is how she argues that economic development happens. It follows therefore that since the modern world-system is the most successful historical system in terms of economic development, it must be because it consists of more dynamic cities than other historical systems. Thus unique levels of urbanization are not a consequence of the rise and reproduction of the modern world-system, they are its cause. And so we come to the proposition on which this chapter is based: *cities must be central players in the three hegemonic cycles; in the rise of the high hegemony, dynamic cities should be to the fore, in the decline phase their influence should wane.*

A PROJECT TO TEST THE THEORY

That's the theory, how does the empirical evidence stack up? This question has been answered in a large survey of cities in the modern world-system from 1500 to the present (Taylor et al., 2010) and the results are summarized below. Of course, it is impossible to get comprehensive data on city economies for the length of the modern world-system but there are reasonable population estimates of cities available for our period. Historically, economic growth and population growth have changed in tandem: dynamic cities that create much new work attract more migrants than less dynamic cities with fewer jobs on offer. Thus we can use demographic change as a surrogate for economic change. Defining different rosters for each century (cities qualified with populations of 10 per cent or more of the average population of the three most populous cities in each century), population changes were computed for 50-year intervals from 1500. Explosive city growths were then defined as cities with an average annual population increase of 1 per cent over a 50-year period. This method was only used for periods up to 1950 because at this point, in the second half of the twentieth century, the simple relation between demographic and economic change broke down (the massive de-peasantization of poorer countries has produced very large mega-cities in which population growth far out-paced economic growth in terms of (formal) jobs). Thus a search for a different surrogate was undertaken. The most suitable was found to be the change in airline connections per city and these were analysed as above from 1970 to 2005: cities that expanded their connections at an annual rate of 1 per cent or over were deemed to have experienced an explosive city growth.

EXPLOSIVE CITY GROWTHS IN HEGEMONIC CYCLES

From this exercise 184 explosive city growths were identified. They were strictly limited by the bounds of the modern world-system: from 1500 to 1750 only European and American cities were included; Ottoman, Russian and Indian cities were added from 1750; and Chinese and Japanese cities were included from 1850. Our interest is in the changing importance of Dutch, British and US cities within this population of 184 explosive city growths. The results will be shown and discussed for three periods: 1500 to 1700 for investigating Dutch hegemony; 1700 to 1900 for investigating British hegemony; and 1800 to 2005 for investigating US hegemony. Note the overlap in the last two periods. It is unusual to consider US hegemony as early as 1800 but our analysis does lead us back this far: the implications of this will be discussed later.

1500–1700: Holland's Cities and Dutch Hegemony

Dutch cities with economic spurts are highlighted for the period 1500 to 1700 in Table 3.1. This early-modern period shows relatively few economic spurts and they are concentrated in the sixteenth century. The 'crisis of the seventeenth century' is clearly reflected in these results, with only two economic spurts in the second half of the seventeenth century.

Although only four Dutch cities are featured, they experienced eight examples of explosive city growth between them. Led by Amsterdam with three such spurts, the table confirms that the Dutch Republic was not simply 'Amsterdam's city-state', as has been suggested (Barbour, 1963), but was a multi-nodal city-region of several vibrant cities (Taylor, 2005). The most intriguing feature of the sequencing of these spurts is that they are evenly divided between the two centuries despite the fact that the Dutch Republic only comes into being in the last 20 years of the fifteenth century and its hegemonic cycle is usually deemed to begin in 1598 at the earliest. Thus we find Amsterdam's first explosive city growth well before the creation of the Dutch Republic, and there are

Table 3.1   Dutch cities in the Dutch hegemonic cycle

1500–1550 (n = 12)	1550–1600 (n = 11)	1600–1650 (n = 8)	1650–1700 (n = 2)
Lisbon	London	AMSTERDAM	Seville
Seville	AMSTERDAM	LEIDEN	ROTTERDAM
Augsburg	HAARLEM	ROTTERDAM	
Antwerp	LEIDEN	London	
Magdeburg	Bordeaux	Paris	
AMSTERDAM	Cuenca	Lyon	
Hamburg	Vicenza	Hamburg	
London	Milan	Marseilles	
Lecce	Torino		
Rouen	Paris		
Venice	Jerez		
Catania			

Note: n = number of economic spurts.

Source: derived from Taylor et al. (2010)

three explosive city growths that build up Dutch hegemony (Amsterdam, Haarlem and Leiden) before hegemony begins. In the seventeenth century there is the reverse pattern with three economic spurts (Amsterdam, Leiden and Rotterdam) during the period covering high hegemony (1609–1648); but with only the latter city continuing with a final Dutch city spurt in the downside of the cycle.

During this period the Dutch went largely without a serious economic rival; France came the closest with five cities (Rouen, Bordeaux, Paris, Lyon and Marseilles) and six spurts, but all are consistently smaller than the Dutch city growths.

There are three key points to make from these results:

1.   High hegemony is represented by a higher proportion of economic spurts in the modern world-system (three out of eight or 32.5 per cent, discounting 1650–1700 when there were only two spurts). *In other words economic spurts correlate with high hegemony.*
2.   There is a definite front-loading of economic spurts to such a degree that half occur before hegemony itself. *In other words half of all Dutch spurts come before hegemony, which is entirely consistent with cities creating the hegemony.*
3.   All the cities involved are from one of the seven provinces that constituted the Dutch Republic: Holland. *In other words, the creation and reproduction of Dutch hegemony is not state-wide: only Holland was hegemony-making in the period 1500 to 1700.*

Table 3.2   British cities in the British hegemonic cycle

1700–1750 (n = 7)	1750–1800 (n = 6)	1800–1850 (n = 25)	1850–1900 (n = 39)
LIVERPOOL	MANCHESTER	New York	Chicago
BIRMINGHAM	LIVERPOOL	Baltimore	Buenos Aires
Cadiz	GLASGOW	Philadelphia	Leipzig
Cork	BIRMINGHAM	Boston	Pittsburgh
MANCHESTER	Barcelona	LIVERPOOL	New York
GLASGOW	Moscow	MANCHESTER	Berlin
BRISTOL		BIRMINGHAM	NEWCASTLE
		GLASGOW	Dresden
		Bombay	Boston
		Rio de Janeiro	Budapest
		Brussels	Hamburg
		NEWCASTLE	Rio de Janeiro
		Plus	Plus
		LONDON (15)	BIRMINGHAM (15)
			MANCHESTER (19)
			GLASGOW (27)
			LONDON (29)
			LIVERPOOL (37)

Note: n = number of economic spurts; figures in brackets indicate rank of British cities below the top 12.

Source: derived from Taylor et al. (2010)

1700–1900: Northern British Cities and British Hegemony

British cities with economic spurts are highlighted for the period 1700 to 1900 in Table 3.2. The number of spurts remains low in the eighteenth century but there is a rapid expansion in the nineteenth century reflecting the spread of industrialization that is, of course, British hegemony's chief contribution to the modern world-system.

In this period 7 British cities are featured with 21 explosive city growths between them. The key feature is the dominance of the four great cities of northern Britain: Birmingham, Glasgow, Liverpool and Manchester. These four cities dominate the eighteenth century with 8 out of the 13 economic spurts recorded in the modern world-system. These big four cities continue with explosive growth in both nineteenth century periods, although gradually falling down the ranks. Their clustered position just below four US cities in 1800–1850 reflects the fact that the US cities were starting from a lower population base; that is to say, Liverpool, Manchester, Birmingham and Glasgow still dominated the world-economy. In both nineteenth century lists they are joined by Newcastle and London. London was conspicuous by its absence among eighteenth century city spurts and, although featuring in the nineteenth century, its economic spurts are lowly ranked. Newcastle is somewhat like Rotterdam in the Dutch cycle: it arrives late and has its largest spurt at the end of the hegemonic cycle.

It is noteworthy that although France is Britain's main rival during its hegemony its economic competition was severely weak: in Table 3.2 only two French cities are featured, Paris and Lyon, both with lowly ranked spurts in the nineteenth century. Clearly the French were less of an economic rival to the British than they were to the Dutch in the previous cycle.

There are three key points to make from these results:

1. High hegemony (mid nineteenth century) is represented by a higher quantity of economic spurts in the modern world-system (although proportions are lower given the large differences in totals between the two centuries). *In other words, the greatest number of British economic spurts correlate with high hegemony.*
2. There is a very strong front-loading of economic spurts to such a degree that the four leading northern cities account for well over half the economic spurts in the eighteenth century (8 out of 13 or 61.5 per cent). *This shows that multiple spurts come before hegemony, which is entirely consistent with cities creating the hegemony.*
3. The four key cities in northern British cities are consistently found in all four periods and are in the top eight ranks for the first three periods. They are joined by another northern city with two spurts in the nineteenth century: Newcastle. London's economic spurts appear in the nineteenth century but, with one exception, are ranked below the northern cities. *In other words, the creation and reproduction of British hegemony is not state-wide; it is largely the work of the great northern British cities and it is here that we find hegemony-making in the period 1700 to 1900.*

1800–2005: Manufacturing Belt (plus California and Texas) Cities and American Hegemony

US cities with economic spurts are highlighted for the period from 1800 to 2005 in Table 3.3. There is never any discussion in the literature of the US hegemonic cycle going back as far as 1800 but our results strongly suggest that this is where to start.

In this period 15 US cities are featured with 25 explosive city growths between them. This confirms a trend of *absolute* increases in number of economic spurts in cities of hegemonic states but with a trend of *relative* decline in the proportion of such economic spurts within the modern world-system. The surprise is the top four rankings in 1800–1850 for the leading east coast cities: New York, Baltimore, Philadelphia and Boston. These cities continue to feature in the second half of the nineteenth century, albeit with much lower rankings, but now Chicago is ranked first and Pittsburgh fourth, showing important inland explosive city growths. US dominance of spurts is greatest in the first half of the twentieth century, with four of the top five places: explosive city growth has now reached the Pacific coast with Los Angeles ranked first, two Texas cities ranked second and third (Houston and Dallas), and with another inland industrial centre, Detroit, ranked fifth. In addition, San Francisco and Seattle add to the Pacific coast representation and Atlanta to southern representation. Washington also features for the first time and New York, Boston and Philadelphia, but not Baltimore, continue with economic spurts in the new century. In the 1970–2005 period, the US returns to having just four cities in the list. Now it is Washington with the highest ranking (third), Los Angeles and Chicago continue to feature, and Miami makes a first appearance. Although the change of criteria makes comparisons with the final column in Table 3.3 problematic, nevertheless the

Table 3.3   American cities in the American hegemonic cycle

1800–1850 (n = 25)	1850–1900 (n = 39)	1900–1950 (n = 39)	1970–2005* (n = 35)
NEW YORK	CHICAGO	LOS ANGELES	Beijing
BALTIMORE	Buenos Aires	HOUSTON	Shanghai
PHILADELPHIA	Leipzig	DALLAS	WASHINGTON
BOSTON	PITTSBURGH	Hong Kong	Osaka
Liverpool	NEW YORK	DETROIT	Seoul
Manchester	Berlin	São Paulo	Singapore
Birmingham	Newcastle	Shanghai	Budapest
Glasgow	Dresden	Seoul	Madrid
Bombay	BOSTON	SEATTLE	Vienna
Rio de Janeiro	Budapest	Buenos Aires	Berlin
Brussels	Hamburg	ATLANTA	Tokyo
Newcastle	Rio de Janeiro	Toronto	Hamburg
	Plus	Plus	Plus
	PHILADELPHIA (22)	WASHINGTON (14)	LOS ANGELES (15)
	BALTIMORE (25)	SAN FRANCISCO (16)	MIAMI (20)
		NEW YORK (24)	CHICAGO (28)
		BOSTON (32)	
		PHILADELPHIA (33)	

Note: n = number of economic spurts; figures in brackets indicate rank of cities below the top 12.
*   the results for this column relate to spurts on scheduled airline flights

Source: derived from Taylor et al. (2010)

result indicating relatively fewer economic spurt cities towards the end of the hegemonic cycle is consistent with previous results (Tables 3.1 and 3.2).

In this hegemonic cycle the main rival is very clear: Germany has 7 cities with 16 episodes of explosive city growth. Their main challenge was in the second half of the nineteenth century, when there were 5 German cities near the top of the economic spurts: Leipzig (ranked 3rd), Berlin (6th), Dresden (8th), Hamburg (11th) and Munich (14th). Unlike the French in the British cycle, Germany was a very credible economic rival to the USA during its cycle.

There are three key points to make from these results:

1. The highest quantity of economic spurts in the modern world-system, featuring 11 US cities, occurs as high hegemony is being reached (1950). *In other words, economic spurts correlate with the coming of high hegemony.*
2. There is a very unexpected, very early, front-loading of economic spurts featuring east coast cities. *This means that spurts come well before hegemony, which is entirely consistent with cities creating the hegemony.*
3. The key cities are largely from what was generally referred to as the 'manufacturing belt' (east coast plus mid-west cities) with important outliers in California and Texas. *In other words, the creation and reproduction of US hegemony is not state-wide: only select parts of the USA can be considered hegemony-making in the period 1800–2005.*

CONCLUSIONS

From this evidence, it is very clear that the geography of explosive economic growths in the modern world-system is related to the development and reproduction of world hegemonies. Further, the timing of the city spurts is additionally informative. Peaks of Dutch, British and American city spurts are found at the centre of their respective hegemonic cycles approximating their high hegemonies. But the two key results are to be found in the distribution of these city spurts across each of the three time periods and within their respective states. If vibrant cities were merely the result of state hegemonic processes then we might expect them to be relatively evenly spread across different periods of the cycle and across the territory of the state. This is not the case in any of the three world hegemonies. Rather there are two consistent patterns. First, in terms of timing, dynamic cities and their economic spurts are front-loaded in the cycle. This indicates that the cities are hegemony-makers and that portends of hegemony can be found much earlier than Wallerstein's initial framing of hegemonic cycles allows for. Secondly, the dynamic cities are concentrated in just part of the state's territory. This indicates that the hegemony-making occurs in specific vibrant economic regions.

For reasons of resource and manageability, the research exercise upon which this chapter is based has only searched out explosive city growths in the more important cities within the modern world-system. But for the vibrant economic regions of the hegemonic states this is only the tip of the urban-economic dynamism. For instance, each of the following pairs of cities prospered during their relevant hegemonic cycles: in Holland Dordrecht and Hoorn, in Britain Bradford and Preston, and in the US manufacturing belt Cleveland and Buffalo. Quite clearly, hegemonies were created through dense networks of thriving cities generating economic development in three economic core regions of the hegemonic states. Hence this conclusion: *it is these cities generating myriad new work through their networking that create and reproduce hegemony, not territorial states.*

One final point concerning hegemonic states and their territories: this chapter's conclusion is eminently sensible given basic knowledge of the geography of hegemonic state territories in their rise to high hegemony. In the seventeenth century Dutch Republic the outer provinces were economically backward with little or no city dynamism (Taylor, 1994); the nineteenth century United Kingdom included Ireland, which suffered famine causing a mass exodus that indicates a dearth of city dynamism; and in the USA in the twentieth century as far as the 1960s, the 'American South' was another byword for economic backwardness, again indicating little or no city dynamism. And yet the states should not be entirely written out of the story. The dense creative city networks were initially concentrated within a single state; successful diffusion of new economic practices to cities in other states came later. This may be related to the relative economic liberalisms within the hegemonic states. Movement infrastructures are also important for maintaining economic dynamism and their geographical scale and capital expense often require state power and resources. From Dutch canals to British railways to the US inter-state road system, hegemonic states have enabled huge territorial infrastructures to be built by various means, including sponsoring, subsidizing or even building. But ultimately the hegemonic states' key contribution to hegemony has been, as Wallerstein (1984) originally argued, to ensure the survival of the system.

ACKNOWLEDGEMENTS

We acknowledge the support of the Leverhulme Trust for funding the research project of which this chapter is a part.

REFERENCES

Barbour, V. (1963), *Capitalism in Amsterdam in the Seventeenth Century*, Ann Arbor, MI: University of Michigan Press.
Braudel, F. (1984), *Perspective of the World*, London: Collins.
Jacobs, J. (1969), *The Economy of Cities*, New York: Random House.
Jacobs, J. (1984), *Cities and the Wealth of Nations*, New York: Random House.
Taylor, P.J. (1994), 'Ten years that shook the world: the United Provinces as the first hegemonic state', *Sociological Perspectives*, **37** (1), 25–46.
Taylor, P.J. (2005), 'Dutch hegemony and contemporary globalization', in J. Friedman and C. Chase-Dunn (eds), *Hegemonic Declines: Present and Past*, Boulder, CO: Paradigm Publishers, pp. 117–134.
Taylor, P.J., A. Firth, M. Hoyler and D. Smith (2010), 'Explosive city growth in the modern world-system: an initial inventory derived from urban demographic changes', *Urban Geography*, **31** (7), 865–884.
Wallerstein, I. (1979), *The Capitalist World-Economy*, Cambridge: Cambridge University Press.
Wallerstein, I. (1984), *Politics of the World-Economy*, Cambridge: Cambridge University Press.
Wallerstein, I. (2004), *World-Systems Analysis: An Introduction*, Durham, NC: Duke University Press.

4   Imperialism and world cities
Anthony D. King

IMPERIALISM

Examining the relationship of imperialism to world cities depends on how both terms are understood. In its simplest sense, imperialism describes a process by which one state extends its rule, usually by military power, over the territory and population of others, in earlier times, to form a contiguous realm. In modern times, imperialism has more often involved acquiring overseas colonies, the aim being to exploit subjugated populations in order to extract economic and political advantage. Developing as a term and concept in English especially after 1870, imperialism refers to a phenomenon that originates in the metropole; what happens in the colonies, as a result of imperial control, is colonialism, or neo-colonialism (Loomba, 1998). As a corollary, imperial or postimperial cities are in the metropole, colonial or postcolonial cities in the colony.

More sophisticated interpretations of the term link it to the analysis of capitalist accumulation, the periodization of capitalism into successive eras and, related to this, the political division of the world into different countries (Weeks, 1988). As recently as the late nineteenth century, world space was dominated by some 16 (mostly European) empires, each with their imperial capital, other major inland and port cities, and the marine, land and, eventually, aerial transportation links between them. That the six official languages of the United Nations are those of what were historically once the world's largest empires, English, Russian, Qing Chinese, French, Spanish and Arabic, is sufficient evidence of both the past and continuing importance of previous empires and their principal cities, administrative and communication networks in disseminating their languages, forms of law, systems of governance and education, religions, cultures, building and land control regulations, architectures and built environments. That this book is being read in English rather than, say, Mandarin Chinese, Arabic or Hindi is the outcome not only of the historic extent of British imperialism but also of its American successor.

WORLD CITIES

While the current interest in world cities as key nodes in the world economy can arguably be traced back to the 1970s, the term itself is much older. In the eighteenth century, the German poet and thinker, Goethe, used *Weltstadt* to describe the cultural pre-eminence of Paris and Rome (King, 1995, p. 216). In 1915 British planning pioneer, Patrick Geddes, used the term to refer to 'certain great cities in which a quite disproportionate part of the world's most important business is conducted' (Hall, 1984, p. 1). Expanding substantially on Geddes' interpretation, current use of the term represents the world city as a site for capital accumulation and primarily as a business centre, playing a key role in the inter-linked global economy (Friedmann and Wolff, 1982), a site for corporate headquarters, international banks and trading houses, and especially for the presence of key advanced producer service firms (accountancy, advertising, law, real estate). The identification of major cities in the world as specifically named 'world cities' and their hierarchical ranking according to the presence and quantity of advanced producer service firms in each city, as in the 2008 'Globalization and World City Research Network' roster (GaWC, 2008), have emphasized this economic understanding of the term. Other interpretations add political and cultural criteria, as represented by the presence of international organizations of governance and administration, a minimally large and diverse population, media, communications and publishing activities, museums, theatres, educational facilities, religious sites for pilgrimage and tourism, and the capacity to sponsor global sporting or cultural events. Infrastructural criteria include the existence of a major airport and transport hub. Visual and architectural criteria include the presence of skyscrapers and a distinctive skyline (Wikipedia, 2010). In the first phase of research on world city formation (Friedmann and Wolff, 1982), some 30 cities were identified and, drawing on world-system language, were located either in 'core' or 'semi-periphery' countries and arranged hierarchically. Given the absence of a single definition, therefore, and especially a universally agreed list of cities, in the remainder of this chapter, unless otherwise indicated, I take the 2008 GaWC roster of cities as a basis for discussing the relationship between world cities and imperialism. In addition to utilizing the Greek 'alpha, beta, gamma' to classify different levels of world city status, I shall also refer to different tiers, including fourth and fifth tiers, indicating some level of 'world city' qualities.

IMPERIAL CITIES

Compared with the quantity of published literature on the 'world', 'global' and 'colonial city', that on the 'imperial city' is sparse. By imperial cities, I refer in the first instance to imperial capitals, that is, the imperial metropole and seat of the emperor or empress, although the term can also be applied to other major cities in the imperial realm. One of the few studies on this topic (Driver and Gilbert, 1999) takes as its subject the capitals of some of the large European empires of recent times – London, Paris, Rome (and implicitly, though not discussed, also Brussels, Amsterdam, Madrid, Berlin, Lisbon and Vienna), all but one, first tier world cities today (the exception, second tier Berlin). Also considered in their study are examples of significant 'secondary' imperial cities such as Glasgow, Seville and Marseilles, cities also included in the lower two tiers of the world cities listing. Where the first tier cities were those of imperial decision-making and governance, imperial science and knowledge, imperial culture and symbolism, imperial literature, art and architecture (and also imperial producer services, though this term is of relatively recent use), secondary imperial cities are more those of empire-dependent manufacturing and processing of (especially) 'tropical' commodities such as tobacco (in Britain, Glasgow, Bristol), slaves (Bristol, Liverpool), cotton (Manchester, Glasgow), or in France, phosphates (Marseilles – a city that was also the site of colonial labour and the 1922 colonial exposition) (Fletcher, 1999). Again, all are included in the lower tiers of the world cities list.

The evidence for the level of integration of such cities into the imperial network can be found in many different places, dependent on where we look. At the simplest of levels, imperial network connectivity is manifest culturally, in imperial toponymy: in London, in thoroughfares named for places located throughout the imperial and colonial world – Malabar, Penang, Benares, Lucknow, Kabul, Khyber, Kashmir, Borneo, Gibraltar, Toronto, Rhodesia and many more (King, 2004, p. 101); or in Glasgow, Havannah, Jamaica, Tobago, Virginia (MacKenzie, 1999, p. 224), just as, reciprocally, imperial names designated the streets of colonial cities (King, 2004, p. 146 et seq.). At a larger scale there are forms of planning, architecture and built environment where colonial port city forms, functions and styles have more in common with the imperial city than they have with those of the colonial inland town; or in the integration of agriculture and industry in a division of labour across the imperial economy, and continuing postimperial links in banking and elsewhere in the financial sector (King, 1990a).

GLOBALIZATION AND WORLD CITIES IN HISTORY

Compared with the 1990s, subsequent interpretations of globalization have done much to correct the initial Eurocentric and ahistorical focus of that process. As discussed elsewhere (King, 2004, p. 28) scholars have not only examined globalization from the viewpoint of countries (and religions, including Islam) outside the West but have also traced earlier, Islamic phases of globalization, before European hegemony, as well as later ones, including, since 1950, 'postcolonial globalization' (Hopkins, 2002). Despite these theoretical developments, however, the historical origins and later development of what have come to be called world (or global) cities, either individually or in the form of a network or system (Taylor, 2004), are still greatly neglected.

The principal aim of this chapter is to argue that not only are the origins of many of today's world or global cities to be found in their imperial and colonial antecedents but also, to recognize the corollary, that the major European empires – British, French, Spanish, Austro-Hungarian, Portuguese, Dutch, Belgian (and also Ottoman) – energized by capitalism and the adoption of new technologies, have created vast new intercontinental networks which have done much to lay down the foundations for today's globalized world, foundations that are cultural (such as language), institutional (in terms of finance, commerce, law, education, governance) and infrastructural (communications, transport, urban space and function-specific building forms). In the words of empire historian, John Darwin, it was 'the ability of Europeans . . . to draw the commerce of the world into one vast network centred on the port cities of the West . . . [that] was the main dynamic behind the gradual formation between the 1860s and 1880s of a "world economy" – a single system of trade' (Darwin, 2007, p. 237) and eventually, 'a single global market' (p. 7).

EMPIRES AND STATES

Taken for granted in current research on the world city, many of which are national capitals, is the idea of world space or territory organized as a system of nation-states. The dominance of the nation-state as the principal form of polity in the contemporary world has tended to obscure the importance of historic empires – over 200 of which are conventionally recognized – in the political and spatial organization of humankind. The fact that three-quarters of these empires were part of the ancient and medieval, rather than modern worlds, does not detract from the importance of modern empires in influencing the state of our contemporary world.

Currently, the United Nations recognizes some 208 independent nation-states, each with its own national capital. Yet at the end of the eighteenth century, there were only 14 of what today would be accepted as independent nation-states, the increase occurring mainly in the nineteenth and especially late twentieth centuries. In the 30 years between 1959 and 1989, the number of independent states almost doubled, from 84 to 156, following the collapse of different European imperial regimes, especially in Asia and Africa. The leap to 208 largely resulted from the dissolution of the USSR (Cohen and Kennedy, 2007). With the world's population now over 50 per cent urban, with vast numbers living in huge cities, we can say that, over the last century, the identities of some populations have been successively determined to different degrees by imperial, national, urban-city and global identities.

For the purpose of this chapter, the significance of imperialism lies in the impact various empires have had in establishing the infrastructure of present day globalization: making use of and modifying existing cities and transport networks, developing institutions and languages, and, often in collaboration with the local population, creating modern cities (Nasr and Volait, 2003). While the modern empires are clearly of importance here, a much older, but equally instructive, example of the networked infrastructure created by imperialism is that of the Roman Empire (27 BCE–476).

The Roman contribution to the establishment of urban and transportation infrastructure and networks throughout and beyond Europe is unparalleled. Extending from the Mediterranean into Northern Europe, the Middle East and North Africa between 27 BCE and 330, cities were founded from which the new provinces were governed. Fundamental to this new infrastructure were the characteristically straight roads and the innovatory grid form around which Roman towns were developed. New types of building were introduced, essential for economic and social activity: the forum as a market place, barracks for the soldiers, occasionally a circus or race track for leisure activities; other distinctively Roman innovations included an amphitheatre providing space for gladiatorial displays; in larger towns, baths, theatres and gymnasia helped keep the garrison occupied. In addition to the networked roads linking towns and settlements across both province and empire, greatly encouraging trade and hence enlarging the new cities, vast aqueducts were constructed bringing water to the cities, as at Segovia in Spain and Nimes in France (Scarre, 1995).

A major characteristic of imperial space is its reciprocal nature, produced by both centrifugal and centripetal processes. Where people, ideas, language, institutions, building forms and types move outward from the imperial metropole, to be reproduced in often hybridized form in the colony, other ideas and forms are brought back to the metropolitan centre, or are transferred to other nodes in the imperial network. Equally significant is the persistence, over two millennia, of Roman (incorporating Greek) models of urbanism and architecture in the modern world and the architectural elements, language and building typologies which, through different European colonialisms, have been circulated around the world.

Of the European cities included in the GaWC roster, at least 20 can be traced to Roman times, if not before. The network of roads which link them together are routes which – in many cases – still determine present day ground transportation.

IMPERIAL NETWORKS

With the exception of China, which had the highest population, the five largest empires in terms of territory and population in 1900 were those of Britain, Russia, France, the USA and Germany, though the latter had less territory than the Ottomans (Bartholomew, c.1901, p. xiv). Theoretically, it would be possible to make the case for the relationship between imperialism and the development of world cities by reference to any modern empire. While the organization and practices of these various empires clearly differed in many respects, in order to extract the economic surplus from their colonies or provinces, whether grain, metals, timber or labour, imperial governments require a basic urban infrastructure of port cities, docks, inland towns with accommodation, communications and transport facilities, along with administrative, governance and security personnel and institutions among others. Thus, as part of its modernization plan from the 1870s, the Ottoman Empire installed the telegraph from its imperial capital of Istanbul throughout its Arab provinces. For military, economic and religious reasons, an extensive railway network was built from Istanbul, the imperial capital (and potential world city), in the north, taking in Beirut and Jerusalem (to become potential world cities) down to Medina in the south. By 1914, this was to extend to Mecca and Jeddah (another potential world city) on the Red Sea (Çelik, 2008, p. 29). Along with railway stations, its modernization programme included hospitals, schools, post offices, barracks, police stations, bridges, schools and, not least, clock towers, providing a (modern) form of time to compete with that coming from the minaret. Following the collapse of the Ottoman Empire, key cities like Beirut and Baghdad were taken over by French and British successors.

The 'first empire' of the French had taken them to North America in the seventeenth century, where they established new cities that were eventually to become what today are the actual or aspiring world cities of Montreal, Quebec, Detroit and Ottawa. In the 'second empire' of the nineteenth and twentieth centuries, the French were to re-develop the Arab cities in their North African colonies of Morocco, Algiers and Tunisia (Wright, 1991). Between the 1840s and the early twentieth century, they built a railway along the Mediterranean coast, from Oran and Algiers in the west to Tunis and Bizerte in the east, having annexed Tunisia in the 1860s. In towns and cities along the route they introduced strict grid plans, re-planning city centres, separate from the indigenous city, on which they built a modern urban infrastructure. The square was a key central feature, around which were modern institutions: town hall for a municipal government, post offices, schools, theatres, hospitals. The railway was essential for transferring phosphates, olive oil and other products into the docks and onto the steamships back to France. Ports were re-built and cities re-planned on 'dual city' colonial lines (Çelik, 2008). In Morocco, Casablanca formed a major colonial node, and after Moroccan independence matured into what is now classified as a world city. Managing the logistics of these extensive new colonies, millions of French men and women migrated to France's North African possessions. Across the world, Saigon (now Ho Chi Minh City) and Hanoi were France's key colonial cities, totally re-modelled as modern cities (Wright, 1991), both today classed as 'world cities'.

IMPERIALISM AND RELIGION

The connection between imperialism and religion has been a major force affecting the development of both imperial and world cities. Throughout history, emperors and imperial governments – whether Roman, Arab, Spanish or British – have allied with religious institutions, appropriating their values, resources and practices to found cities and, within these, construct spectacular religious buildings – cathedrals, mosques, temples, but also schools, hospitals, madrasas. As a powerful force for social cohesion as well as social conflict, bestowing identity and transforming social practices, religion has also provided mechanisms for the division and ordering of territory, from provinces to parishes. In established or aspiring world cities, the promotion or defence of particular religious identities have, for decades, if not longer, been the defining force in the city's space and politics, for example in Belfast, Jerusalem, Beirut, Rome, Mumbai, Istanbul, Baghdad and Tehran. Religious conflict or cooperation have been key factors affecting a city's economic and political stability, influencing its claims to function as a node in the world economy. Different religious beliefs and practices have influenced economic transactions, governed the nature of interest rates, and affected the accumulation of capital, hours and days of work, and the nature of property ownership.

WORLD AND IMPERIAL CITIES

Is there further evidence to support the hypothesis that imperialism was a major factor in establishing many of what today we designate as world cities, not only individually but also as part of an integrated network? If we take the 2008 GaWC roster as our data base, we can see that, of the 40 alpha world cities, 15 of them (mostly in Europe) at one time or another have been imperial capitals; a further 18 have, at various recent points in time, been major colonial cities, populated and administered as part of a larger empire (whether British, French, Dutch, Spanish, Portuguese, Ottoman). The imperial and colonial histories of these 33 cities, all part of one or more larger networks, would doubtless also help to explain why, already over a century ago, most of them were among the world's largest 80 cities (Bartholomew, c.1901, p. xiv).

If we widen the net to accommodate beta and gamma categories to make 128 cities in all, some additional 55 colonial cities could be included (including those developed in the USA after 1776 and being ultimately dependent on the colonial origins of the state). That is, roughly two-thirds of the 128 cities have some kind of imperial or colonial connection to at least one imperial network. In 1901, for those wishing to travel from the UK around these networks, a table of 126 'Travel Routes All Over the World', indicating port of departure (Southampton, Liverpool, London, Marseilles, Hamburg, New York, San Francisco and others), shipping lines, destination (from Accra to Zanzibar), distance in miles and duration of journey (in days) was easily available – if not yet on the internet – in standard respected atlases (Bartholomew, c.1901, p. xiv).

In the early days of world city research in the late 1980s, I attempted (using UN and World Bank data sets) to predict the development of what Friedmann (1986, p. 72) called 'basing points for capital' in countries of the 'semi-periphery', surmising they could become world cities by the year 2000. The criteria chosen to identify these 'third' or 'fourth order' world cities, to use Friedmann's classifications at that time, included a) state policies oriented towards, or not opposed to, market oriented growth; b) a minimum country population size of 15 million, providing potential market growth; and c) the largest city in the country to have a minimum size of one million, providing a potential market for consumer goods. In the case of states with large populations (India, China), more than one world city was likely to develop d) a continuous average growth rate between 1965 and 1985 in the region of 1 per cent. The list compiled related only to the World Bank's 'middle income' and 'low income' countries and did not include 'industrial market economies' in Europe (King, 1990b, pp. 51–52). On the basis of the 2008 GaWC roster, 16 of the 17 predictions proved to be accurate (Shanghai, Tientsin, Jakarta, Kuala Lumpur, Calcutta, Bombay, Delhi, Karachi, Colombo, Istanbul, Cairo, Casablanca, Lagos, Nairobi, Bogota, Lima). The one exception was Tehran, unsurprisingly, given the unstable political and religio-cultural circumstances which have persisted and which had already been stated in the original listing of 1990. What these 16 cities, national or regional centres, had in common, however, is that all were either strongly influenced by (especially) Western colonialism, were direct colonial products or, in the case of China, colonial 'free ports' (or in the case of Istanbul, a major imperial city).

Among the many factors which might explain this outcome is less the presence in these cities of advanced producer services at that time (about which little is known) but rather the underlying infrastructures necessary for those services: international language knowledge, education, availability of local and expatriate skilled manpower, business connections to the metropole, transnational banks and offices, among others.

IMPERIAL TO WORLD CITY

The reciprocal growth between imperial capital and its overseas empire and its maturation into a world city is best illustrated by the historical development of London (see King, 1990b, from which this much condensed account is taken). The expansion of British military, naval and trading power in the Caribbean and North America and profits from slavery, sugar and tobacco did much to establish an infrastructure for an overseas trading economy in the late seventeenth century. Merchants in this trade were behind the establishment of Lloyd's Insurance (1687), a Stock Exchange (1670s), the Bank of England (1694). Simultaneously, trade with the East had been stimulated by the East India Company (founded 1600). Conquests in India and the Caribbean in the mid eighteenth century and the boom in the Atlantic economy boosted London's role as the largest centre of international trade, demanding extensive new docks 50 years later. Between 1750 and 1910 (the highpoint of British imperial power) London remained the world's largest city. As trade grew, the city was already a world financial centre by 1815, boosted by the Industrial Revolution and with capital flowing into overseas investment. Between 1815 and 1925, over 25 million people emigrated from the British Isles, 10 million of them to British possessions, especially Canada, Australia and South Africa. Between 1808 and 1900, the growth in overseas trade attracted dozens of foreign (including colonial) banks, among others, from Hong Kong, Australia, New Zealand, the Middle East, Canada, Ottoman Empire, France, Switzerland, Germany, Italy, Belgium, Russia, the USA and Japan. The 1861 Census recorded some 29,000 people working in the City, mainly merchants, bankers, stock and commercial brokers, accountants and commercial clerks, the predecessors, in some cases, of workers in advanced producer services firms today (King, 1990b, p. 79). By 1900 London already had a substantial multicultural population. In the words of prominent novelist, H.G. Wells, London was 'the richest city in the world, the biggest port, the greatest manufacturing town, the Imperial city – the centre of civilization, the heart of the world' (Wells, 1908, p. 73). In the late nineteenth century, Britain's empire had been extended by a third with new colonies in Southeast Asia, Southern, Central and West Africa, South America, South Asia and Hong Kong. New buildings were provided for an expanded Foreign Office, Colonial Office and India Office; institutions for scientific research and education were established in the Imperial College of Science and Technology; a School of Hygiene and Tropical Medicine (1899) and, later, a School of Oriental (and subsequently) African Studies catered for the needs of colonial cadres. New centrally located institutions dedicated to the interests of particular colonies – Australia House, India House, Canada House, Africa House – were set up in the 1920s. The British Empire Exhibition of 1924 provided the country's first national sport stadium at Wembley.

The transformation of London from imperial to postimperial, international and, subsequently, world and global city, following the mid twentieth century demise of empire, is most evident in its cosmopolitan, multicultural population. More than half England's ethnic minority population lives in London, where it forms over a quarter of the city's population and speaks over 300 languages. Along with cosmopolitan educational and cultural sectors – museums, universities, libraries, theatres, research institutes, stadiums, architectural and festive spectacles – a bloated financial services industry, including banking, insurance, real estate, law and accountancy, once providing the infrastructure for maintaining an empire, now, massively expanded, serves the interests of a capitalist world economy.

REFERENCES

Bartholomew, J.G. (c.1901), *Twentieth Century Citizen's Atlas of the World*, London: George Newnes.
Çelik, Z. (2008), *Empire, Architecture, and the City: French–Ottoman Encounters, 1830–1914*, Seattle: University of Washington Press.
Cohen, R. and P. Kennedy (2007), *Global Sociology*, Basingstoke: Palgrave Macmillan.
Darwin, J. (2007), *After Tamerlane: The Rise and Fall of Global Empires 1400–2000*, Oxford: Oxford University Press.
Driver, F. and D. Gilbert (eds) (1999), *Imperial Cities: Landscape, Display and Identity*, Manchester: Manchester University Press.
Fletcher, Y.S. (1999), 'Capital of the colonies: real and imagined boundaries between metropole and empire in 1920s Marseilles', in F. Driver and D. Gilbert (eds), *Imperial Cities: Landscape, Display and Identity*, Manchester: Manchester University Press, pp. 136–155.

Friedmann, J. (1986), 'The world city hypothesis', *Development and Change*, **17** (1), 69–84.
Friedmann, J. and G. Wolff (1982), 'World city formation: an agenda for research and action', *International Journal of Urban and Regional Research*, **6** (3), 309–344.
GaWC (2008), 'The world according to GaWC', available at www.lboro.ac.uk/gawc/world2008t.html (accessed 16 January 2010).
Hall, P. (1984), *The World Cities*, London: Weidenfeld & Nicolson, 3rd edition.
Hopkins, A.G. (ed.) (2002), *Globalization in World History*, London: Pimlico.
King, A.D. (1990a), *Urbanism, Colonialism and the World-Economy: Cultural and Spatial Foundations of the World Urban System*, London and New York: Routledge.
King, A.D. (1990b), *Global Cities: Post-imperialism and the Internationalization of London*, London and New York: Routledge.
King, A.D. (1995), 'Re-presenting world cities: cultural theory/social practice', in P.L. Knox and P.J. Taylor (eds), *World Cities in a World-System*, Cambridge: Cambridge University Press, pp. 215–231.
King, A.D. (2004), *Spaces of Global Cultures: Architecture, Urbanism, Identity*, London and New York: Routledge.
King, A.D. (2006), 'Building, architecture and the new international division of labour', in N. Brenner and R. Keil (eds), *The Global Cities Reader*, London and New York: Routledge, pp. 196–202.
Loomba, A. (1998), *Colonialism/Postcolonialism*, London and New York: Routledge.
MacKenzie, J.M. (1999), 'The second city of the Empire: Glasgow – imperial municipality', in F. Driver and D. Gilbert (eds), *Imperial Cities: Landscape, Display and Identity*, Manchester: Manchester University Press, pp. 215–238.
Nasr, J. and M. Volait (2003), *Urbanism: Imported or Exported? Native Aspirations and Foreign Plans*, Chichester: Wiley-Academic.
Scarre, C. (1995), *The Penguin Historical Atlas of Ancient Rome*, London: Penguin Books.
Taylor, P.J. (2004), *World City Network: A Global Urban Analysis*, London: Routledge.
Weeks, J. (1988), 'Imperialism and world market', in T. Bottomore (ed.), *A Dictionary of Marxist Thought*, Oxford: Blackwell, pp. 223–227.
Wells, H.G. (1908), *Tono-Bungay*, London: Odhams Press.
Wikipedia (2010), 'Global city' (also 'world city'), available at http://en.wikipedia.org/wiki/Global_city (accessed 16 January 2010).
Wright, G. (1991), *The Politics of Design in French Colonial Urbanism*, Chicago: Chicago University Press.

5   Political global cities
Herman van der Wusten

INTRODUCTION

Seen from space, cities on the dark side of the globe light up and radiate. In dreary places on Earth city lights have long attracted people to try their luck. Cities radiate in different ways at different ranges. In this chapter I concentrate on cities that radiate politically and at global range: political global cities. It is not the cities themselves that radiate on the satellite images but the concentrated set of bulbs within each city; not necessarily the city as a whole that attracts the aspiring traveller but the opportunities for making a living and for having fun. The external political effects of political global cities result from politically relevant actors and politically meaningful institutions and material establishments present in those cities.

In what follows I explore a smallish literature on political global cities that has developed alongside those aspects of global cities that have drawn most attention during the last decades like corporate headquarters and positions in the global networks of advanced producer services. I first deal with some conceptual issues: the distinction between 'world' and 'global' as indications of range (section 2), and then the various approaches to political global cities that result in a definition (section 3). After an interlude on the relation of these political global cities and the kinds of global cities mostly covered in the current literature (GaWC) (section 4), I concentrate on the ways in which the political global cities fit in with an emerging but still highly contested global polity (section 5), followed by discussion on the politics and policies by which they emerge, are sustained and further evolve (section 6). I end with final remarks on shifting meanings of 'the political' and the most pressing research questions on global political cities at hand.

WORLD AND GLOBAL

For the long historical period in which a human society at global scale was unimaginable and no such society could actually function, it makes sense to call the largest fragments of the global population that somehow hung together 'worlds'. They were worlds apart. This is what Wallerstein (1979) did in developing his model of the development of the world system taking economic links as his yardstick for coherence. At the same time these separate worlds were of course parts of one planet, its material expression always to be conceived as a single System Earth.

This situation radically altered around 1900. The Europeans connected the different worlds on the globe through political and economic links to such a degree that a social world at the global level became at least imaginable and to some extent realized. Mackinder (1904) and Wallerstein (1979, but with a long pedigree) argued the case for a global social level quite strongly from a political and an economic point of view without any agreement on the way this global level would eventually be instituted. Since that time it is no longer very useful to keep a distinction between a world and a global level. The only remaining undisputed world level is the global level, not only with a view to System Earth but also in a social sense.

In the political context, that primarily concerns us here, the centres of earlier empires which did not communicate with external political units on an equal basis are useful examples of world but not global political cities. Moscow and Washington during the Cold War, and perhaps Rome, Berlin and Tokyo during World War II, are late, partial examples of the same type. All contemporary political cities with global radiance are world political cities at the global level, political global cities for short.

THREE APPROACHES AND A THREE-PART DEFINITION

The recent literature suggests three ways to conceptualize political global cities. One aims at the reach of political actors operating from a city or at the availability of political arenas for decisions of global scope in cities (Taylor, 2005; Van der Wusten et al., 2011). These political actors may be state governments with global aims, interests, capabilities and centrality vis à vis other relevant actors (e.g. the US, increasingly China, perhaps also the EU as a pooled state entity) or globally operating political organizations, that is, those of the UN family. Political global cities host the headquarters and major offices of these actors and/or the arenas where relevant decision-making takes place (e.g. Washington, Beijing, Brussels, New York, Geneva). The second approach deals with the presence of civil society hubs providing transnational connections to private actors for public purposes that are globally oriented (e.g. university cities and cities that host a multitude of secretariats of international Non Governmental Organizations (NGOs)) (Van der Wusten, 2004; Taylor, 2005). There are also ambiguous in between cases like the annual Davos event called the World Economic Forum for managers, politicians and commentators, and the countermanifestations of the World Social Forum, first in Porto Allegre and then diffusing across the world to other cities. In these privately instigated settings civil society actors mingle more or less informally with politicians. A third approach concentrates on those cities globally recognized as world political cities through their symbolic significance, notably by means of their townscape (King (1995) is the most prominent author but he refers to a more general notion of global cities). The symbols should refer to globally relevant political content (e.g. Hiroshima and its Peace Monument referring to its destroyed townscape in 1945 and as a plea for the global abolition of nuclear arms, images of places generally recognized as politically significant at the global level like the White House in Washington DC, and the meeting room of the Security Council in the UN building, New York).

We could briefly refer to these three approaches as the boardroom (Alberts, 1974, a short novel on alienating boardroom experiences), the coffeehouse (Ellis, 2004) and the 'city upon a hill' (Matthew 5:14) conceptualizations of global political cities. Should we look at these approaches as different entries to a single phenomenon? It is true that they often come together and are functionally related. Those who govern attract those parts of civil society that want to benefit from and to affect the direction of governmental action. This draws many civil society institutions to close proximity of governmental centres. In addition, those in charge of government also occasionally wish to see their position reflected in the attention of external spectators, a public; and sometimes they need genuine feedback. Governing actors as well as those concerned with civil society foci generally want to underline their presence and their actions by shaping their physical environment in such a way that their actions attract spectators and an audience. Public action always has a theatrical side to it and a symbolically charged material context helps in shaping the optimal conditions for the performances and directly adds to them (Kostof, 1985). London and Paris are perhaps the most persuasive examples of political global cities with the empirical manifestations of the three conceptual approaches still all present. While certainly the concentration of relevant political actors and perhaps also the preponderance of their civil society hubs have diminished lately, the symbolisms are still there in all their power (Hancock, 2003).

The three possible elements of political global city-ness very often come together, but they are only loosely coupled. As we have just seen, cities may well end up as mainly global cities upon a hill in the perception of a global public after their actual roles as global boardrooms or coffeehouses have declined. Some cities only acquire their symbolic content after they have played the role of successful boardrooms and coffeehouses for quite a while. It has been suggested that this increased urge to underline their significance results from growing unease as their actual prominence in the other dimensions starts to decline. On the other hand new political cities have been proposed and built before they had actually played the intended political roles. At a different spatial scale many new political capitals were mainly of symbolic significance before they were anything else, the best example probably being Brasilia. During the belle époque preceding World War I there were some efforts to make one European city into the civil society capital of the world (Bosma, 1993, pp. 47–69). The designs were highly charged with symbolic significance. More cities upon a hill have in recent times been proposed, but their global acceptance seems very much rarer. In sum, the three central elements in the conceptualizations of political global cities come in different combinations and in some cases (Hiroshima) they are even completely limited to a single dimension. Consequently, the provisional definition of these cities considers the three central elements of the different approaches each as sufficient ground to call these cities politically global and recognizes various subcategories according to the strength of the three elements in various cases. The dynamics of these mixes is a research problem still to be tackled.

A political global city thus has at least one of the following attributes:

- it is from here that political actors with global reach operate or it is here that globally relevant decisions are taken;
- it is the site of significant manifestations of a transnational civic society encompassing the globe;
- it is widely considered in all parts of the world as a global political city; its townscape has globally recognized iconic features that connect the city to this particular role.

POLITICAL AND ECONOMIC GLOBAL CITIES

Political global cities are defined in ways clearly different from the global cities identified by economic features like headquarters concentrations of corporations and centres of advanced producer services that are the primary focus of the current literature. But do they in fact indicate different cities or represent different sides of the same cities; to what extent do these politically coloured global cities overlap with their economic namesakes and why?

In the literature on world and global cities published since the 1980s, the emphasis has always been on aspects of their economic profiles and dynamics. At the same time it has repeatedly been stressed that there were political issues to address. From very early on the tone was set. John Friedmann, whose 1982 paper with Wolff is considered the beginning of the current scholarly wave of attention, indicated in a follow-up in 1986 that the interest was in cities as the 'basing points' for global capital and that 'the economic variable . . . is likely to be decisive for all attempts at explanation' (Friedmann, 1986, p. 69). But both papers also indicated the importance of politics based on the increasing polarization and growing social costs that would accompany further development of these world cities. However, that is not our interest here. This chapter is not about the local political issues resulting from shifts in the organization of capitalism, but on the widest external political effects of cities as they host relevant political actors, provide room for political decision-making, make space for civil society manifestations and get characteristic features in their townscapes highlighted. These processes may be related to global capitalism as it unfolds or not.

Would political global attributes of cities tend to be encouraged in general global cities with a more economically driven nature or, the other way round, do general global cities particularly thrive in politically global cities? These questions have still to be studied seriously. If experience on the national level is any indication, they cannot be unambiguously resolved. The old 'law of the primate city' (Jefferson, 1939), suggesting that higher, wider-ranging functions tended to concentrate in the largest city, has long been discarded. It is obvious that national capitals dominating the economy and politics of a country exist but so do many variants. The coalescing cases are to be found in older, European, as well as recently decolonized countries; the diverging cases mostly result from purpose built political capitals after a country had been well established, leaving in place the most internationally oriented cities somewhere else.

Apart from analogies at lower levels we can also consider the different pedigrees of our two kinds of global city and see if there is particular reason for them to mingle. Political global cities have often been the outcome of inter-state negotiations or explicit development of a single political global centre by interested national and local governments. As interested actors tend to reside in the national capital cities and have some say in their government, global political cities are often national capitals. But there are important exceptions that we have already encountered: New York and Geneva as boardroom oriented cases, a few university cities as coffeehouse oriented cases, and finally Hiroshima as a city upon a hill oriented case. There is no question that in the current set of economically oriented global cities, national capitals again are common among the political global but they are by no means limited to these niches in the current capitalist order. Again, it is often the recently purpose built or recently selected capitals that do not act simultaneously as major magnets for headquarters of globally operating firms or globally networked economic functions. Germany's 'provisional' capital in Bonn (before reunification) did not act as such and the return of the major part of Germany's political function to Berlin and the accompanying global significance of its politics have, after some hesitation, not attracted a lot of globally operating economic clout. In China there is some concentration of globally operating economic actors in the nation's capital that also now has some global political radiance, but the emphasis in the hosting of economic global functions is still divided between Shanghai and Hong Kong (Lai, 2009). We conclude again that the different paths of political global presence and economic global functions often cross in capitals but there are significant exceptions where either only one function turns up or none.

Finally, there are various conditions in the general make-up of cities that apparently favour the establishment of global political functions and other globally operating functions. They overlap to a considerable extent and I will come back to them in section 6.

POLITICAL GLOBAL CITIES AND A GLOBAL POLITY

Political global cities presuppose the existence of, or act as stepping stones towards, a global polity, however weak (Held et al., 1999, pp. 49–62). Polities are the entities with which people identify as the base for the conduct of public affairs. These are the frames in which politics play out and policies are shaped. The polity originated in the city (the Greek *polis*). Cities were home to the collectivities implied in the decision-making that was the heart of the polity's existence. The role that individuals play in their relation to the polity/ies of which they find themselves to be part still refers clearly to that origin (citizenship). But polities and citizens have not remained exclusively tied to cities. In different ways the entities that polities embody can shift along scales and can be delimited on the basis of different kinds of attributes. And so does citizenship.

Polities embody the systems of rule in which authoritative decision-making occurs. States are still the dominant polities in the current historical period. But the general agreement on their privileged status is being undermined. As new transnational frames for politics emerge and policy-making is less exclusively arranged in and around state institutions, new polities gradually emerge. While national states still fully function, the concentration of global political action and globally relevant political references signal the emergence of a new higher level polity in the making.

This current arrangement assumes the possibility of simultaneous multiple memberships/allegiances of political actors including citizens in various polities. This is contrary to the predominant sovereign spirit of the national state system, but it reflects, at least, a continuous undercurrent of social reality nonetheless. Robb (2007) describes an earlier example at lower level; Meinecke (1908) is a classic on the German case; and see also the current expanding literature on cosmopolitanism. Into the future we will still be dealing with multiple polities, particularly at different spatial scales, with contested differentiation in salience. A global polity may take multiple forms: from an imperial order dominated by a core state like the American hyper-power dystopia (Védrine, 2000) to a well-regulated, legally backed society of states based on sustained multilateralism (Watson, 1992; Ruggie, 1998), or a series of functionally differentiated global orders, that, however, will be difficult not to fix in some sort of territorial units (Sack, 1986). These different models would result in different configurations of political global cities. They would also differentially affect the further development of the system of national states. The global scale will not likely be the most politically salient any time soon.

This introduces a series of questions about how political actor capability at the global scale and globally relevant political arenas (both based on the ability to act in a legitimate fashion against the preferences of other actors at different scales) affect global polities and their cities of the boardroom, coffeehouse and city upon a hill varieties and mixes.

POLITICAL GLOBAL CITIES, POLITICS AND POLICIES

What about the politics (the practices – rules, roles and their translation in actual behaviour) and policies (the content of what is in the end to be achieved) that help select, maintain and further improve political global cities? The relevant factors for the realization of boardroom, coffeehouse and city upon a hill attributes may well vary. The distribution of roles between relevant political actors differs (public officials versus private citizens, actors at different levels) and the differences in content of the various attributes invite different approaches (negotiations, conversations, prize competitions). At the same time, there is no question that in the current political order, next to the relevant local/ regional governments (often quite a number of adjacent and interlocked entities; see for example Keil and Ronneberger (2000) and Hoyler et al. (2006) on the Frankfurt case), national governments are of the utmost importance in explaining the fate of all varieties of political global cities.

To a large extent due to the important role of existing polities in the emergence of political global cities, the capital cities of their central governments are eminently but not uniquely qualified to perform in this capacity (Abbott, 1996). Capital cities are familiar to those who decide on the allocation of political global city attributes. In addition they are, as a rule, well endowed with the functional, residential and theatrical conditions needed to perform in that role. It is intriguing that the idea that the global political function might rival the existing capital city role and should therefore not be performed by the same city does not seem to have played much of a role in this kind of decision-making. It is not always that political global city roles are performed by capitals. Particularly since World War I and II, Geneva and New York have become spectacular but also fairly unusual examples of other kinds of places in those roles. There has been a lot of contingency in their selection (Van der Wusten et al., 2011).

The policies that aim at global political positions of the boardroom type are mostly in the hands of polities, national governments in the current political order. This can be in the context of a multilateral choice process or as a policy sui generis. In international negotiations and in bid-book based selection competitions, boardroom political global assets may be acquired: a permanent secretariat of an international institution, a heavy diplomatic post, the venue for an important, politically relevant international conference, and so on. These kinds of competition very often involve national governments that then protect and put forward the interests of one of their cities (for the case of The Hague, see Van der Wusten (2006)). Preparations for actually playing this role, and fulfilling the conditions for a successful political global city role once the selection has been made, are more typically in the hands of local governments. For really huge projects they need higher level assistance but the functioning of a powerful and persistent local government is here very important. In many cases the relations between national and local level are very close where the capital city is concerned.

To become a successful political global city as a civic society hub, a locally receptive, cosmopolitan social climate is obviously indispensable. Uninhibited accessibility and tolerance are important. Institutions of higher education, universities as of old but now existing in a number of guises are extremely useful in this respect. They provide captive audiences of students for all sorts of civic society events, and staff and students are active in all sorts of relevant ways. It is probably no coincidence that many university cities have an unusually large number of secretariats of international civil society associations in their midst (Van der Wusten, 2004). Cities may also aim at such roles by hosting key events and attracting the secretariats of important NGOs. Such new centre formation of the coffeehouse type is then ultimately based on private initiative, as in the case of the World Economic Forum, or on movement dynamics, as in the case of the Social Forum. The Davos and Porto Allegre examples are somewhat transitional with the boardroom type because politicians are also present on both occasions although not in an official capacity.

The city upon a hill kind of political global city needs a lot of attention in the world through spectacles and icons that show the townscape as an essential carrier of the role. Apart from a local history that has produced the materials from which such townscapes can be constructed, one needs an entrepreneurial spirit in local circles aimed at the development and maintenance of attractive real estate. Such iconic townscapes will be put forward as wannabe global political cities by patrons, architects and decorative artists. They may sometimes result from shock events that will then give rise to commemorative rituals of all sorts (e.g. Ground Zero for a long drawn out set of disputes). They may also translate the suggestions of certain public groups. Following Hannerz (1992) and King (1995), the most important producers of our current representations of world cities are the transnational management class, Third World populations migrating to these cities, expressive specialists, tourists and the academics that study the phenomenon and write about it. The media have important roles as one major stage where such representations play out and are in the process reconfigured according to the presumed media laws. Those in the business of taste-making, reputation management and public communication strategy will then use their skills to make this imagery readable for this purpose and widely accepted as such. How all this subsequently translates in actual success or failure as a global icon is a big question mark.

Those who want to support the intended political global cities should in any case try to create the conditions for functioning as a prominent political global city. There are several kinds of conditions that count. These conditions overlap to a considerable extent with the conditions needed for a successful role as an economic world city. As mentioned in section 4, this is another reason to find both global city types jointly in a single city.

Cities can be provided with the functional requirements to ideally operate as a political global city. These include a range of services that optimize the working conditions at the place where the global political functions are established. Among them are the intellectual guidance provided by the presence of universities and think tanks; the support facilities for a state of the art execution of bureaucracy-smoothing jobs like ICT support, bookkeeping and accounting; a pool of first class administrative workers; and a superb hosting environment for receiving variable numbers of external guests on short notice with the necessary hotel and restaurant facilities, but also with the leisure facilities that satisfy a continuous flow of high status visitors. Cities could also aim to acquire the residential quality necessary to keep a floating population of expatriates positively linked to their environment. Apart from mundane but very essential assets such as good housing and quality international schools, there is (overlapping with the requirements for short term visitors) the need for leisure facilities ranging from outdoor sports and parks to museums, theatres, opera houses and the like. Finally, to the extent that governing is also a theatrical activity, cities that want to play in the first league of political global cities have to include working place accommodation that assists in the performance of the actors that have to carry the global reputation. Just as in cases of national government, the issue of locating, designing and decorating the buildings and surrounding landscapes of international, globally significant political institutions has always been under intense scrutiny (Van der Wusten, 2007).

Some cities that eventually become global political cities have from an earlier vocation already preserved some of these requirements; in other cases they have to be fulfilled as soon as the trajectory towards a pronounced political global city role starts to develop. Several instances of delayed development and accompanying friction are known. Despite its traditional reputation as a well-equipped city, Geneva suffered from several functional deficits as its role as prominent global political centre started from 1920 (Van der Wusten et al., 2011). The residential quality of The Hague as a political global city hopeful has repeatedly been severely criticized and it is only in the last few years that serious steps to remedy these defaults have been taken. Its competitor, Vienna, has been careful in shaping the conditions for its global political role over time (Van der Wusten, 2006, 2007). The serious lack of maintenance of the UN headquarters building in New York undermines the effectiveness of that institution.

FINAL REMARKS

Political global cities are emerging. They come in different versions. I have drawn thumbnail sketches of three types and their combinations. One major distinction was between government–administrative concentrations dominated by public officials and civil society hubs dominated by the organizations of private citizens. But this distinction is obviously based on the division of political labour in polities that took shape as national states and that have been the predominant political entities of the last few centuries. Even there the recent emphasis on governance instead of government has blurred the distinction between these two kinds of roles. It may well be that new distinctions and new political divisions of labour will crystallize as the global political level becomes more institutionalized in a new polity. What has developed lately in Davos, Porto Allegre and elsewhere may be a first indication of things to come.

From the current perspective four major research questions on political global cities come to the fore. The first is: how, and how closely or loosely, are boardroom, coffee-house and city upon the hill attributes of political global cities coupled under different conditions? Secondly, to what extent and why are political global cities overlapping with more economically oriented global cities? Thirdly, how do political global cities articulate the different possible kinds of global polity? Fourthly, what politics and policies significantly affect the fate of emerging political global cities?

REFERENCES

Abbott, C. (1996), 'The internationalization of Washington D.C.', *Urban Affairs Review*, **31** (5), 571–594.
Alberts, A. (1974), *De vergaderzaal* [The boardroom], Amsterdam: Van Oorschot.
Bosma, K. (1993), *Ruimte voor een nieuwe tijd* [To shape the space for a new era], Rotterdam: NAi.
Ellis, M. (2004), *The Coffee House: A Cultural History*, London: Weidenfeld & Nicolson.
Friedmann, J. (1986), 'The world city hypothesis', *Development and Change*, **17** (1), 69–83.
Friedmann, J. and G. Wolff (1982), 'World city formation: an agenda for research and action', *International Journal of Urban and Regional Research*, **6** (3), 309–344.
Hancock, C. (2003), *Paris et Londres au XIXe siècle. Représentations dans les guides et récits de voyage*, Paris: CNRS éditions.
Hannerz, U. (1992), *Culture, Cities and the World*, Amsterdam: Centrum voor Grootstedelijk Onderzoek.
Held, D., A. McGrew, D. Goldblatt and J. Perraton (1999), *Global Transformations: Politics, Economics and Culture*, Cambridge: Polity Press.
Hoyler, M., T. Freytag and C. Mager (2006), 'Advantageous fragmentation? Reimagining metropolitan governance and spatial planning in Rhine-Main', *Built Environment*, **32** (2), 124–136.
Jefferson, M. (1939), 'The law of the primate city', *Geographical Review*, **29** (2), 226–232.
Keil, R. and K. Ronneberger (2000), 'The globalization of Frankfurt am Main: core, periphery and social conflict', in P. Marcuse and R. van Kempen (eds), *Globalizing Cities: A New Spatial Order?*, Oxford: Blackwell, pp. 228–248.
King, A.D. (1995), 'Re-presenting world cities: cultural theory/social practice', in P.L. Knox and P.J. Taylor (eds), *World Cities in a World-System*, Cambridge: Cambridge University Press, pp. 215–231.
Kostof, S. (1985), *A History of Architecture: Setting and Rituals*, Oxford: Oxford University Press.
Lai, K.P.Y. (2009), 'Global cities in competition? A qualitative analysis of Shanghai, Beijing and Hong Kong as financial centres', *GaWC Research Bulletin*, 313, available at www.lboro.ac.uk/gawc/rb/rb313.html (accessed 10 August 2010).
Mackinder, H.J. (1904), 'The geographical pivot of history', *Geographical Journal*, **23** (4), 421–437.
Meinecke, F. (1908), *Weltbürgertum und Nationalstaat: Studien zur Genesis des deutschen Nationalstaates*, München: Oldenbourg.
Robb, G. (2007), *The Discovery of France*, London: Picador.
Ruggie, J.G. (1998), *Constructing the World Polity: Essays on International Institutionalization*, London: Routledge.
Sack, R.D. (1986), *Human Territoriality: Its Theory and History*, Cambridge: Cambridge University Press.
Taylor, P.J. (2005), 'New political geographies: global civil society and global governance through world city networks', *Political Geography*, **24** (6), 703–730.
Védrine, H. (dialogue with D. Moïsi) (2000), *Les cartes de la France à l'heure de la mondialisation*, Paris: Fayard.
Wallerstein, I. (1979), *The Capitalist World-Economy*, Cambridge: Cambridge University Press.
Watson, A. (1992), *The Evolution of International Society: A Comparative Historical Analysis*, London: Routledge.
Wusten, H. van der (2004), 'The distribution of centrality in the European state system', *Political Geography*, **23** (6), 677–700.
Wusten, H. van der (2006), '"Legal capital of the world": political centre-formation in The Hague', *Tijdschrift voor Economische en Sociale Geografie*, **97** (3), 253–266.
Wusten, H. van der (2007), 'Political world cities: where flows through entwined multi-state and transnational networks meet places', in P.J. Taylor, B. Derudder, P. Saey and F. Witlox (eds), *Cities in Globalization: Practices, Policies and Theories*, New York and London: Routledge, pp. 204–220.
Wusten, H. van der, R.A. Denemark, M. Hoffmann and H. Yonten (2011), 'The map of multilateral treaty-making 1600–2000: a contribution to the historical geography of diplomacy', *Tijdschrift voor Economische en Sociale Geografie*, doi: 10.1111/j.1467-9663.2011.00653.x.

I B Contemporary concepts

6   The interlocking network model
Peter J. Taylor

INTRODUCTION: THE NEED FOR SPECIFICATION

If you have a research interest that covers cities in globalization you have to decide how this new scale of inter-city relations is organized. At first glance this appears to be a fairly simple question to answer: you just go to the literature and see what the experts think. But this exercise actually complicates the situation: as in any new area of research, the conceptualization of the subject is not necessarily agreed. And this is certainly the case for the literature on cities in globalization. In Table 6.1 50 such conceptualizations are listed alphabetically (Taylor and Lang, 2004) and we can see that there is no agreement on how the scale is represented, how the entities are represented and how the relations are represented. Thus although the most common adjective for scale is 'global', 'world' and 'international' are popular as well, with references also to 'transnational', 'cross-border' and 'planetary'. For the entities themselves, as well as 'city' and 'urban' there are references to 'metropolitan', 'nodes', 'lynchpins' and 'strategic places'. And the relations are equally variable: the three main relations are 'system', 'hierarchy' and 'network', with additional references to 'grid', 'web', 'archipelago', 'chain' and 'matrices'. Wow, we appear to be overwhelmed by choice.

Choice is not always a good thing. Although Table 6.1 can be interpreted as reflecting exceptional riches in ingenuity for describing cities in globalization, I prefer to consider it as indicating a basic confusion in how to conceptualize contemporary relations between cities. All the concepts listed above come with theoretical baggage: for researchers this is not a smorgasbord of delights, preferences are not 'neutral', each choice is important because it means something to the research to be conducted. Whether we call the scope of the relations global, world or international implies different ways of looking at scale. Cities mean much more than merely urban, and very much more than just node and lynchpin. And choosing between system, hierarchy and network is critical to the very nature of relations being studied. Among these choices I select 'world city network'. I justify this for individual concepts and because their combination can be theoretically grounded to my satisfaction. This enables a model specification, the world city network, which is the main purpose of this chapter.

The idea of 'world' is much more flexible than both global and international. The latter relates only to modern political organization; global is just a single scope of relations. In contrast, I follow Wallerstein's (1979, 2004) world-systems analysis, where 'world' means a historical-system; for instance, there has been a 'Roman world' based upon the Roman world-empire, a 'Chinese world' based upon a sequence of Chinese world-empires, an 'early modern world' in the 'long sixteenth century' based upon Europe and its Atlantic expansion. (City networks in each of these regions are briefly described in Chapter 2.) Today there is a 'modern world' that is the modern world-system, which has been global only since about 1900. This systemic definition of 'world' means that

Table 6.1   50 ways of describing inter-city relations in globalization

1	Archipelago economy
2	Chain of metropolitan areas
3	Cities in global matrices
4	Cross-border network of global cities
5	Functional world city system
6	Global city network
7	Global city system
8	Global competition among cities
9	Global grid of cities
10	Global metropolitanism
11	Global network of cities
12	Global network of financial centres
13	Global network of major metropolitan management centres
14	Global network of nodes and hubs
15	Global system of cities
16	Global urban hierarchy
17	Global urban network
18	Global urban system
19	Global web of cities
20	Hierarchical global system of urban places
21	International global–local networks
22	International hierarchy of cities
23	International systems of interlinked cities
24	International urban system
25	Internationally networked urban spaces
26	Lynchpins in the spatial organization of the world economy
27	Metropolitan hierarchy exercised throughout the world
28	Neo-Marshallian nodes in global networks
29	Network of world cities
30	Nodal centres of the new global economy
31	Nodes in global networks of institutional arrangements
32	Planetary urban networks
33	System of major world cities
34	System of world cities
35	Transnational system of cities
36	Transnational urban system
37	Transnational urbanism
38	World city actor network
39	World city hierarchy
40	World city network
41	World city system
42	World hierarchy of financial centres
43	World relations of cities
44	World system of cities
45	World system of metropolises
46	World urban hierarchy
47	World urban system
48	World-systems city system
49	Worldwide grid of global cities
50	Worldwide grid of strategic places

Source: derived from Taylor and Lang (2004)

modelling need not be restricted to just contemporary cities. This is important because the entities I am dealing with are cities that are generically highly creative places where key processes, both intra-city (agglomeration) and inter-city (connectivity), generate economic expansion in the way that Jacobs (1969) describes. This use of Jacobs' ideas means that we eschew simple hierarchical patterning of cities that derived from central place theory and the subsequent 'national urban systems' school of urban studies. For Jacobs, cities come in groups and they need each other; this mutuality indicates (horizontal) network relations rather than (vertical) hierarchical relations. And there is no need for portraying inter-city relations as systems; systemic processes are to be found in the broader historical-systems, world city networks are part of the spatial organization within world-systems. Thus the contemporary world city network is global in scope and cooperative rather than competitive in nature (this latter argument is developed further in Chapter 7).

The theoretical basis for treating cities in globalization as a world city network derives from Sassen's (1991) seminal text on the 'global city'. In this work she identified the location of advanced producer services in major cities, notably London, New York and Tokyo, as crucial to their role in organizing contemporary globalization. These major cities were both the production centres and the key markets for this cutting edge development of new business services. But the firms producing these services were not restricted to these major cities. Since their corporate clients were globalizing their activities, the service firms needed to follow them or lose their business. The result was many financial (e.g. wealth management), creative (e.g. advertising) and professional (e.g. commercial law) firms invested in worldwide office networks across a range of cities. It is the work done in these office networks that defines today's world city network. Perched in their ubiquitous office tower blocks, it is the everyday work in these offices in advanced servicing projects (e.g. global advertising campaigns, inter-jurisdictional law contracts) that economically links cities together. Electronic messages (information, knowledge, instruction, data, opinions, ideas, etc.) and inter-personal links (by telephone, by email, tele-conferencing, face-to-face meetings, etc.) 'interlock' cities through advanced producer servicing. There is no possibility of obtaining comprehensive data on such flows, so that direct measurement of inter-city business interlocking is out of the question. Therefore, as in other research contexts, the only solution is to devise means for indirect measurement of the flows using data that are available. To accomplish this it is necessary to model the process that is operating. It is the specification of the world city network as an interlocking network model that is the necessary first step.

WORLD CITY NETWORK ANALYSES

Most network analysis is based upon a two-level structure: nodes and their interrelations as a net. Thus a gang network consists of members as nodes and their interrelations constituting the network. Unusually, the world city network has three levels: nodes and net, plus sub-nodes. The nodes are the cities but these are not the agents, the network-makers. It is the service firms that are the network-makers and these are the sub-nodes that operate within and through the city nodes. Thus the world city network consists of firms as sub-nodes, cities as nodes, and between them they constitute a network at the world-system level.

This unusual triple structure has very important research implications. The basic approach involves studying the firms (agents) in order to identify and describe the relations between cities that are the world city network. Put simply, firms are the objects of study; cities are the subjects of study. In this way the model defines a process of network formation.

Specification

The interlocking network model is specified as follows. There is a set of n service firms with offices across m cities, wherein the activity of firm i in city j is its 'service value', v_{ij}. This defines a service values matrix of n (firms) × m (cities). The simplest measure of importance is the total activity within a city, which defines the size of the node in the network. Thus

$$S_a = \sum_i v_{ia} \qquad (6.1)$$

where S_a is the nodal size of city a. This is a site measure because size incorporates information only on city a and no other city. However, network connectivity is the main measure of importance of a node in this model. It assumes that the quantity of flows between two cities generated by a firm is a function of that firm's activities in each city. Flows between pairs of cities are estimated from the inter-city products of their firms' activities. Summing all such products for all firms in a city with every other city in the network defines network connectivity:

$$C_a = \sum_j \sum_i v_{ia} \cdot v_{ij} \text{ (where } a \text{ does not equal } j) \qquad (6.2)$$

where C_a is the network connectivity of city a. This connectivity of city a is a situation measure because it relates city a to all other cities within the network.

Because C_a is usually a large number and varies with the size of the service values matrix, to ease comparisons network connectivities are usually presented as proportions of the highest connectivity recorded in the analysis:

$$P_a = C_a/C_h \qquad (6.3)$$

where C_h is the highest connectivity measure and P_a is city a's proportion of the latter. For further details of this model specification see Taylor (2001).

Computation of these two measures is illustrated for a simple service values matrix in Table 6.2. Note that the two measures correlate strongly but do not create the same ranking of cities: Sydney has a higher nodal size than Singapore but its network connectivity is lower. Generally network connectivity is the preferred measure because it is relational; it indicates a city's integration into the world city network.

Table 6.2   Nodal size and network connectivity

City	Service firms						Nodal size	Network connectivity
	A	B	C	D	E	F		
London	5	3	5	2	4	5	24	193
Singapore	4	3	2	3	2	3	17	165
Sydney	2	5	2	2	5	2	18	162
Atlanta	1	2	0	5	2	2	12	117
Lagos	2	0	1	1	0	0	4	45

Notes: The numbers in columns 2 to 7 indicate the importance of offices for each firm in each city (service values); for instance, firm A's least important office is in Atlanta with its score of only 1.
Computations for columns 8 and 9 are as follows:
London's nodal size = 5 + 3 + 5 + 2 + 4 + 5 = 24
London's network connectivity =
Service firm A: $(5 \times 4) + (5 \times 2) + (5 \times 1) + (5 \times 2) +$
Service firm B: $(3 \times 3) + (3 \times 5) + (3 \times 2) + (3 \times 0) +$
Service firm C: $(5 \times 2) + (5 \times 2) + (5 \times 0) + (5 \times 1) +$
Service firm D: $(2 \times 3) + (2 \times 2) + (2 \times 5) + (2 \times 1) +$
Service firm E: $(4 \times 2) + (4 \times 5) + (4 \times 2) + (4 \times 0) +$
Service firm F: $(5 \times 3) + (5 \times 2) + (5 \times 2) + (5 \times 0) =$
45 + 30 + 25 + 22 + 36 + 35 = 193

(i)   The products within each bracket are estimated work flows between offices in a specific pair of cities. The assumption is that the more important the office the more flows it generates. Thus firm A's largest flow is between London and Singapore, the cities housing its most important two offices $(5 \times 4 = 9)$.
(ii)   If each column of connectivity calculation above is summed separately, they provide estimates of inter-city work flows; for instance the first column estimates London–Singapore work flows as $(5 \times 4) + (3 \times 3) + (5 \times 2) + (2 \times 3) + (4 \times 2) + (5 \times 3) = 68$.

Operationalization

Operationalizing this model requires creation of a service values matrix. This is done by selecting major service firms with large office networks and investigating how their offices are used across the world. The focus has been on firms in accountancy, advertising, financial services (banking and insurance), law and management consultancy, and the main source has been information available on firms' websites. The information varies greatly between firms but is made comparable using a coding method that scores 5 for the city housing a firm's headquarters, 0 for cities where the firm has no office, and scores 1, 2, 3 and 4 allocated on the basis of the sizes and functions of offices. For further details of this operationalization see Taylor et al. (2002).

Such data collection exercises were carried out in 2000, 2004 and 2008. In 2000 100 firms were studied across 315 cities, creating a 100 × 315 service values matrix carrying 315 × 100 = 31,500 pieces of information. The same firms were studied in 2004 but not all remained or provided adequate data so that their number was reduced to 80, and the matrix to 80 × 315. In 2008 the data were collected on a new basis using the top ranked firms in each sector and included 175 firms across 525 cities, providing 91,875 pieces of information. Each of these three matrices is like that in Table 6.2 and can be interpreted as follows: the columns indicate the locational office strategy of a firm across cities; the rows indicate the service mix available in each city.

SELECTED WORLD CITY NETWORK ANALYSIS RESULTS

This model has been the basis of the main GaWC quantitative strand of research since 2000. In this section some basic results are reported but for a full appreciation of the model's research potential reference should be made to the articles cited and to *Global Urban Analysis*, a major volume of results from analyses of the 2008 data collection (Taylor et al., 2011).

World City Network Connectivities

Network connectivities have been computed for all cities in the data collected in 2000 (Taylor, 2004), 2004 (Taylor and Aranya, 2008) and 2008 (Derudder et al., 2010), and the cities with the top 10 highest connectivities for each year are listed in Table 6.3.

The main feature of these results is the stability at the top of each list. London and New York are the two cities most deeply integrated into the world city network through advanced producer servicing. However, notice the rise of Hong Kong in 2008, suggesting that this 'NYLON' dual city dominance might become a trinity of leading cities in the not too distant future. Paris, Singapore and Tokyo are not much less integrated. The other big story is the relative decline of US cities Chicago and Los Angeles after 2000 and their replacement by Shanghai and Beijing in 2008.

This change-round is confirmed in Table 6.4, where relative changes between 2000 and 2008 are shown: the top 5 'winners' and bottom 5 'losers' are listed. Among the hundreds of cities we deal with, it is the two leading Chinese cities that stand out as the cities integrating furthest into the world city network in the early twenty-first century. In contrast, Los Angeles is the city integrating relatively the least in this period; Miami also is on this bottom list with two other US cities. Obviously the record of Shanghai and Beijing is not a surprise, although it has never been measured in this way before, but the US results do appear a shock since the USA is at the very centre of globalization processes. However,

Table 6.3   Top 10 networked cities in 2000, 2004 and 2008

2000		2004		2008	
Cities	NC	Cities	NC	Cities	NC
London	1.00	London	1.00	New York	1.00
New York	0.97	New York	0.97	London	0.99
Hong Kong	0.73	Hong Kong	0.73	Hong Kong	0.83
Tokyo	0.71	Paris	0.71	Paris	0.80
Paris	0.70	Tokyo	0.70	Singapore	0.76
Singapore	0.67	Singapore	0.67	Tokyo	0.74
Chicago	0.61	Brussels	0.62	Sydney	0.71
Milan	0.60	Toronto	0.61	Shanghai	0.69
Madrid	0.59	Madrid	0.60	Milan	0.69
Los Angeles	0.59	Milan	0.59	Beijing	0.68

Note: NC stands for network connectivity. The results for 2000 and 2004 have been modified from previous publications to make them comparable to the 2008 results – for further details see Derudder et al. (2010).

Table 6.4   Cities experiencing major relative changes in network connectivity, 2000–2008

Top 5 cities (relative positive change)	Change
Shanghai	2.76
Beijing	2.64
Moscow	2.62
Seoul	2.12
Rome	1.89
Bottom 5 cities (relative negative change)	**Change**
Los Angeles	−2.52
Miami	−2.31
San Francisco	−1.91
Cologne	−1.76
St Louis	−1.74

Note: Change is measured as standardized differences between 2000 and 2008.

Source: derived from Derudder et al. (2010)

the conundrum of US cities not being well integrated into the world city network (except for New York) has been noted from the very beginning of this measurement sequence (Taylor and Lang, 2005). It appears to be related to the strength of US domestic producer service markets that operate partially separately from the rest of service markets, so that non-US firms make do with US offices mainly in New York only. For further discussion of this unexpected result see Taylor et al. (2011).

Hinterworld Analyses

For every city the network analysis generates estimated work-flows to every other city (see Table 6.2). This pattern of flows is called a city's hinterworld (Taylor and Walker, 2004). By disaggregating the network connectivity it is possible to measure particular orientations of cities.

In Table 6.5 eight major North American cities are compared in terms of the relative orientation of their integration into the world city network through European and Pacific Asian city connections. Four pairs of cities are listed: two Canadian including its main Pacific coast city; two US east coast cities; two US Pacific coast cities; and two US cities from the centre of the country. Through standardizing the results, under-linkage and over-linkage can be seen as positive and negative results. First, note that most of the results are negative: these major cities are generally under-linked to European and Pacific Asian cities; only New York is over-linked to both. Note also that New York is the most over-linked city in each case, which is no surprise. To help comparison the final column shows the differences between the two orientations. This shows which cities are more strongly orientated to European cities (positive difference) and which to Pacific Asian cities (negative difference). For US cities the results are geographically distinct, although not as clear cut as expected: east coast and central cities show more orientation towards Europe (but New York and Dallas show a slightly stronger orientation to

Table 6.5   East—west orientations of major North American cities

North American city	European orientation	Pacific Asian orientation	Difference
Toronto	−0.02	1.03	−1.05
Vancouver	−1.01	0.02	−1.03
New York	1.39	1.42	−0.03
Washington	−0.24	−0.97	0.73
Chicago	0.61	−0.40	1.01
Dallas	−1.00	−0.74	−0.26
Los Angeles	−0.74	0.68	−1.42
San Francisco	−1.71	−0.10	−1.61

Note: orientations are relative measures in standardized form.

Source: derived from Taylor et al. (2011)

Table 6.6   'Old' and 'new' globalization orientation of major Asian and African cities

City	NYLON orientation	BEIHONSHA orientation	Difference
Dubai	0.78	0.84	−0.06
Mumbai	0.32	0.46	−0.14
Johannesburg	0.35	0.42	−0.07

Note: orientations are relative measures in standardized form.

Source: derived from Taylor et al. (2011)

Pacific Asia); west coast cities are more orientated towards Pacific Asia. But this result does not transfer to Canada, where both cities have stronger orientations to Pacific Asia.

Hinterworld orientation can be more targeted than to just major regions. In Table 6.6 three major Asian/African cities are compared in terms of their orientations towards New York and London (NYLON), which can be considered the traditional centre of globalization, and towards Beijing, Hong Kong and Shanghai (BEIHONSHA), which appears to be becoming the new centre of globalization. In this simple exercise Dubai, Mumbai and Johannesburg are all positively orientated to both globalization centres, as would be expected of major cities. But the interesting result is that they are all slightly more orientated towards the Chinese trio than NYLON. This portends a new geography for the twenty-first century world economy.

EXTENSIONS OF THE MODEL

The descriptions of the contemporary world city network have been supplemented by other applications of the basic model. There are three important developments to report.

Table 6.7   Polycentricity in North West Europe

Mega-city region	Polycentricity
RhineRuhr	0.36
The Randstad	0.36
Paris Region	0.27
South East England	0.24
Central Belgium	0.19
Northern Switzerland	0.17
Rhine Main	0.06
Greater Dublin	0.02

Note: Polycentricity is measured by the average connectivity of the five non-leading cities. (This is interpreted as a proportion of the connectivity of the leading city whose connectivity is set at 1.0.)

Source: derived from Taylor et al. (2008)

Multi-nodal Mega-city Regions

This application represents a change in geographical scales. As well as generating the world city network, contemporary globalization is associated with the rise of large 'global city-regions' (Scott, 2001). These are large multi-nodal regions (Castells, 1996), with multiple cities integrated by myriad business flows. Such regions can be modelled as interlocking networks using advanced producer services; this is recognized by Hall and Pain (2006) in their study of polycentricity in city-regions in North West Europe.

Hall and Pain led a research team that studied the eight city-regions listed in Table 6.7. Logistics and IT design firms were added to the advanced producer services employed for the world city network studies and service values were only coded up to 3, but otherwise research methodology was as described previously. Separate data collection and analysis were undertaken for each region and thereby network connectivities were computed for cities and towns in each region. In order to show how these cities and towns were linked to globalization processes, 25 leading world cities were included so as to measure global connectivities. It is these that are used in Table 6.7 to compute the polycentricity of the city-regions. For each city-region just the leading six cities and towns were considered and the average connectivity of those ranked second to sixth was computed to represent the degree of polycentricity. The limiting cases are an average connectivity of 1.00 indicating that all six cities and towns have equal global connectivities, and an average connectivity of 0.00 indicating that only the leading city has global connections. In Table 6.7 the city-regions are ranked by this measure that ranges from 0.36 to 0.02.

The results in Table 6.7 show both expected results and surprises. The city-regions divide into four pairs. That RhineRuhr and the Randstad have the largest polycentricity is expected – they are the archetypal multi-nodal city-regions. Dublin and Frankfurt dominating their respective regions at the bottom of the ranking is not unexpected. Similarly, the Belgian and Swiss city-regions with Brussels–Antwerp and Zurich–Basle are 'in between' in terms of polycentricity. But the results for Paris and London are surprising; these are usually considered archetypal 'primate cities' and therefore very low polycentricity is expected. But as a pairing, these two cities rank second: cities and towns

Table 6.8   Other world city network-makers

City	Score
UN agencies	
Geneva	1.00
Brussels	0.66
Addis Ababa	0.64
Cairo	0.60
Bangkok	0.58
Diplomatic missions	
Washington, DC	1.00
Tokyo	0.97
London	0.95
Paris	0.88
New York	0.87
NGOs (humanitarian/environmental)	
London	1.00
Geneva	0.93
Washington	0.89
Nairobi	0.82
Manila	0.80
Media conglomerates	
London	1.00
New York	0.74
Paris	0.74
Los Angeles	0.68
Milan	0.65

Source: Taylor (2005a)

around Paris and London have about a quarter of the central cities' global connectivities. It appears that the economic successes of these two cities are spilling over into their respective regions. For further discussion of this interpretation see Taylor et al. (2008, 2009); for more detailed discussion of multi-nodal mega-regions turn to Pain's discussion in Chapter 9.

Other Global Networkers

This application represents a change in the agents, the inter-lockers. Business service firms are not the only institutions that have globalized their work through multi-locational workplaces. There are other contemporary 'global networkers' and in Table 6.8 four are identified. In each case a service values matrix has been constructed based upon how individual institutions use different cities, and from these new network connectivities can be computed. These are shown for the five cities most integrated into their respective networks in Table 6.8.

These results show the variety of world city networks in globalization. The UN agency

Table 6.9   Leading cities in the European world city network, 1300–1400

City	Network connectivity
Bruges	1.00
Florence	0.95
Avignon	0.81
London	0.77
Paris	0.75
Venice	0.75
Genoa	0.74
Naples	0.68
Pisa	0.59
Bologna	0.53

Source: Verbruggen (2010)

network centres on Geneva and reaches out to 'third world' cities. (The absence of New York from this list (it ranks sixth) is because it only houses the one major UN institution, the Assembly and Security Council.) The NGO network is similar to the UN network but here London is the leading city. In contrast the diplomatic city network focuses on the four leading state capitals plus New York as the UN Assembly location. And finally media business networks are very Euro-American; the five cities listed are as would be expected. For further discussion of these alternative world city networks see Krätke and Taylor (2004) and Taylor (2005a, 2005b).

Historical Extensions

This application represents a change away from the focus on contemporary inter-city relations. Cities connected through business and other work links are by no means an invention of globalization. Business houses and financial groups used family members and/or agents, factors and other means to carry out their work in multiple locations across all historical world city networks. These have been delineated in Chapter 2 using simple demographics because systematic research on these agents as macro-network-makers has not been forthcoming. This lacuna in our knowledge of cities has been recti-fied for late medieval and early modern Europe through the doctoral researches of Raf Verbruggen (2010). Table 6.9 is drawn from his PhD dissertation.

In many ways historical research on city networks appears to be more complicated than contemporary study: in this case a nine-point code of service values is used to cover both firms and 'nations' of independent traders. Further, the availability of relevant data is not as straightforward as with contemporary choice of firms. Choice is limited to which firms have been studied and this can lead to biases. For instance, Bruges' rank of first in Table 6.9 is certainly due to the excess of data on Low Countries firms in the fourteenth century. Otherwise the list consists of three major capitals – Avignon (housing the Papacy at this time), London and Paris – plus six Italian cities, the main locale of Europe's medieval commercial revolution. This list indicates the formation of a new Europe-wide city network consequent upon Genoa establishing the first regular link to Bruges in 1277 (Braudel, 1984, p. 114). For further discussion of these historical European city networks see Verbruggen (2010).

CONCLUSION: THE GENERIC ARGUMENT

The interlocking network was devised as a way of describing the world city network in contemporary globalization. But it has turned out to have wider applications than initially intended. This train of thought has led to the notion that the model represents a generic description of what makes cities based on the ideas of Jane Jacobs (1969, 1984).

Inter-urban relations have traditionally been modelled by central place theory where central places and their hinterlands are interlocked into spatial and hierarchical structures (Christaller, [1933] 1966; Taylor, 2009). But as Jacobs (1969) tells it, no city ever became successful by just interacting with its hinterland. She describes cities as a process, cities need each other, they come in groups, and they relate as networks. This is 'city-ness' and the interlocking network model delineates the external relations of city-ness. We call this 'central flow theory' to distinguish it from existing central place theory (Taylor et al., 2010). The latter is now interpreted as a model of 'town-ness', vertical (hierarchical) local urban links that occur simultaneously to the horizontal (network) non-local links of city-ness.

This chapter has shown the GaWC route from quantitative analyses of contemporary inter-city relations to generic understanding of inter-city relations.

REFERENCES

Braudel, F. (1984), *Perspective of the World*, London: Collins.
Castells, M. (1996), *The Rise of the Network Society*, Oxford: Blackwell.
Christaller, W. (1933), *Die zentralen Orte in Süddeutschland*, Jena: Gustav Fischer, translated by C.W. Baskin (1966), *Central Places in Southern Germany*, Englewood Cliffs, NJ: Prentice-Hall.
Derudder, B., P.J. Taylor, P. Ni, A. De Vos, M. Hoyler, H. Hanssens, D. Bassens, J. Huang, F. Witlox, W. Shen and X. Yang (2010), 'Pathways of change: shifting connectivities in the world city network, 2000–08', *Urban Studies*, **47** (9), 1861–1877.
Hall, P. and K. Pain (eds) (2006), *The Polycentric Metropolis: Learning from Mega-City Regions in Europe*, London: Earthscan.
Jacobs, J. (1969), *The Economy of Cities*, New York: Vintage.
Jacobs, J. (1984), *Cities and the Wealth of Countries*, New York: Vintage.
Krätke, S. and P.J. Taylor (2004), 'A world geography of global media cities', *European Planning Studies*, **12** (4), 459–477.
Sassen, S. (1991), *The Global City: New York, London, Tokyo*, Princeton, NJ: Princeton University Press.
Scott, A.J. (ed.) (2001), *Global City-Regions: Trends, Theory, Policy*, Oxford: Oxford University Press.
Taylor, P.J. (2001), 'Specification of the world city network', *Geographical Analysis*, **33** (2), 181–194.
Taylor, P.J. (2004), *World City Network: A Global Urban Analysis*, London: Routledge.
Taylor, P.J. (2005a), 'Leading world cities: empirical evaluations of urban nodes in multiple networks', *Urban Studies*, **42** (9), 1593–1608.
Taylor, P.J. (2005b), 'New political geographies: global civil society and global governance through world city networks', *Political Geography*, **24** (6), 703–730.
Taylor, P.J. (2009), 'Urban economics in thrall to Christaller: a misguided search for city hierarchies in external urban relations', *Environment and Planning A*, **41** (11), 2550–2555.
Taylor, P.J. and R. Aranya (2008), 'A global "urban roller coaster"? Connectivity changes in the world city network, 2000–2004', *Regional Studies*, **42** (1), 1–16.

Taylor, P.J., G. Catalano and D.R.F. Walker (2002), 'Measurement of the world city network', *Urban Studies*, **39** (13), 2367–2376.

Taylor, P.J., D.M. Evans, M. Hoyler, B. Derudder and K. Pain (2009), 'The UK space economy as practised by advanced producer service firms: identifying two distinctive polycentric city-regional processes in contemporary Britain', *International Journal of Urban and Regional Research*, **33** (3), 700–718.

Taylor, P.J., D.M. Evans and K. Pain (2008), 'Application of the interlocking network model to mega-city-regions: measuring polycentricity within and beyond city-regions', *Regional Studies*, **42** (8), 1079–1093.

Taylor, P.J., M. Hoyler and R. Verbruggen (2010), 'External urban relational process: introducing central flow theory to complement central place theory', *Urban Studies*, **47** (13), 2803–2818.

Taylor, P.J. and R.E. Lang (2004), '*The Shock of the New*: 100 concepts describing recent urban change', *Environment and Planning A*, **36** (6), 951–958.

Taylor, P.J. and R.E. Lang (2005), *U.S. Cities in the 'World City Network'*, Washington, DC: The Brookings Institution (Metropolitan Policy Program, Survey Series).

Taylor, P.J., P. Ni, B. Derudder, M. Hoyler, J. Huang and F. Witlox (eds) (2011), *Global Urban Analysis: A Survey of Cities in Globalization*, London: Earthscan.

Taylor, P.J. and D.R.F. Walker (2004), 'Urban hinterworlds revisited', *Geography*, **89** (2), 145–151.

Verbruggen, R. (2010), *World Cities before Globalization: The European City Network, A.D. 1300–1600*, PhD Dissertation, Loughborough University, UK.

Wallerstein, I. (1979), *The Capitalist World-Economy*, Cambridge: Cambridge University Press.

Wallerstein, I. (2004), *World-Systems Analysis: An Introduction*, Durham, NC: Duke University Press.

7 On city cooperation and city competition
Peter J. Taylor

My starting point is that inter-city relations are more complex than is commonly assumed. This is reflected in my title: the key word is 'and', which is used rather than 'versus'. In the more sophisticated studies of competitive cities, it is accepted that the competition exists alongside cooperative relations (e.g. Begg, 1999; Sassen, 1999) and in my own promotion of inter-city mutualities I accept that there are competitive processes present (Taylor, 2004). Given this position, the chapter deals with two related topics. First, there is the matter of careful definition to distinguish the essential differences between the two relations. I will use the excellent work of Powell (1990) and Thompson (2003) on competitive and cooperative processes to guide me. Secondly, there is the question of how the two processes relate to each other. To answer this I develop an argument about generic and contingent inter-city relations. I finish the chapter with case studies that demonstrate the processes in action.

DEFINITIONS

According to Powell (1990) and Thompson (2003) competition and cooperation are directly implicated in two contrasting relational configurations: hierarchies and networks respectively. Hierarchies are there to be climbed (competition); networks are there to be used (cooperation). Translating these ideas to inter-city relations means treating competitive city relations as deriving from hierarchical processes and cooperative city relations as deriving from network processes (Taylor, 2004).

Competition and Hierarchy

All hierarchies involve asymmetric power relations between members at different levels; those above impose their will on those below. This is a particular process and must be specified for identifying a hierarchy – Lukermann (1966) makes this precise point for settlement hierarchies. In other words, simply listing cities by rank order does not define a hierarchy (Taylor, 1997). For instance, in most lists of contemporary cities in globalization, London ranks higher than Paris, but this does not indicate a hierarchy à la Friedmann (1986) unless it is shown that London, in some sense, is imposing its will upon Paris. Without evidence of 'London telling Paris what to do' there is no hierarchy, just a ranked list of cities. There are such asymmetric relations between the two cities but they are rather more complex: for instance banks headquartered in London will be instructing their Paris branch on overall corporate strategy but at the very same time Paris headquartered banks will be similarly instructing their London branch. We can sum the number of such corporate asymmetries and show London has more corporate HQ functions than Paris (Taylor et al., 2002) but to reduce this to London hierarchically above Paris is to simplify too far: there are multiple corporate hierarchies and power flows both ways.

There are simple processes of hierarchy between cities but these are limited to political roles of cities. There are circumstances where London as the UK's capital city has power over Manchester and this may be used to define a national urban hierarchy. It is in this manner that hierarchies are implicated in competitive relations; for instance, Manchester competing with Birmingham for government largesse from London.

However, even political hierarchical processes are more complex than this. Cooley (2005), following Chandler (1969), has suggested a further refinement for understanding international relations. He suggests two organizational forms of hierarchy. Unitary hierarchy is where the lower layers are closely controlled from the centre. An alternative organization, multidivisional hierarchy, provides for more autonomy away from the centre. In his field these are state formation for unitary hierarchy and imperial organization for multidivisional hierarchy. In terms of inter-city relations this translates as national-scale hierarchies (as indicated in the UK cities example above) and world-scale dependency relations. The latter, famously described by Frank (1969) as metropole–satellite relations, is a relative autonomy within an extreme asymmetric relation (informal imperialism): power is held at the centre without the need for overt domination. This relation is consistent with Jacobs' (1984) description of the power of cities over places far away that service its needs for food, raw materials, cheap industrial goods and labour.

The key point is that competition between cities can come in different forms but must always be based upon asymmetric power relations.

Cooperation and Networks

Networks can only operate on the basis of mutuality among nodes (Thompson, 2003). In city networks, cities need each other and all contribute to the wellbeing of the network (Taylor, 2004). Importantly, although she does not explicitly refer to city networks, this process is consistent with Jacobs' (1969, 1984) theorization of cities as sites of economic expansion derived from inter-city relations.

One way of thinking about networks in relation to hierarchies is that the former focus upon 'horizontal' links across all cities whereas hierarchies are only about 'vertical' links between cities at different levels. In the latter case this has been formally derived as central place theory where urban places fit neatly into interlocking spatial hierarchies (Christaller, [1933] 1966; Taylor, 2009). More recently, city networks have been derived as 'central flow theory' (Taylor et al., 2010) based upon the interlocking network model (Taylor, 2001, 2004) whereby firms link cities together through their multi-location office networks.

The question of how these two theoretical approaches, encapsulating cooperation and competition, relate to each other is a matter of ontology. The most common position is a competitive presumption: imbued with central place thinking, how else would cities relate? But central place theory derives from ideas about towns servicing rural populations; its extension to cities comes with no definition of cities except as 'large towns' (i.e. with larger but still bordered hinterlands). Following Jacobs' lead, world city network research refutes this argument using central flow theory. Jacobs (1969) argues that cities do not arrive singly, rather they come in 'packs', in other words as city networks. This is fundamental because it relates to her definition of cities: a city is a process in which these horizontal inter-city relations are central. In other words, cities are generically networked; that is their nature. In this city theory, it follows that hierarchical relations are contingent.

CONTINGENCIES OF INTER-CITY RELATIONS

If city networks are generic and hierarchical processes are contingent, the question arises as to when does contingent pressure for hierarchy occur? In other words, under certain circumstances are there hierarchical tendencies that create competition between specific sets of cities? There are at least three situations where such competition between cities is created.

Process: Political over Economic

The interlocking network model underpinning central flow theory is an economic process but we live in a political economy world. This means that in certain circumstances political process can dominate the generic mutuality of cities to produce powerful hierarchical tendencies. The classic example is in the modern world where nation-states have territorialized social space resulting in strong national urban hierarchies that were prominent in the twentieth century. Because this is the period when most of the literature on inter-city relations was produced, we should recognize that this urban knowledge was created in quite unusual circumstances of politically fragmented space.

With contemporary globalization such territorial pressures towards multiple hierarchies are being lessened. This does not mean that the current world city network is devoid of hierarchical tendencies – firms headquartered in London and New York clearly dominate (Taylor, 2004) – but the evidence is that the network is becoming more horizontal over time (Derudder et al., 2010).

Place: Gateway Battles

There can certainly be competition between cities within a specific bordered area. There will be situations where there is only really economic capacity for one major city so that all local cities are in competition for this position. Such a situation is often referred to as a gateway city, the one place that links a region to the rest of the world (Andersson and Andersson, 2000). Such city/regional relations are traditionally related to transport hubs (Pain, 2008). In contemporary globalization Friedmann's (1986) work treats cities below the top level of his hierarchy in this sort of way: key world cities 'articulate' their national or regional economies into the world economy.

These contingent pressures can be seen in some interesting competitive resolutions: Sydney replacing Melbourne, São Paulo replacing Rio de Janeiro and Toronto replacing Montreal as leading cities in their respective national economies. However, in Castells' (1996) network society gateways are not what they used to be. In the informational age, using electronic communications makes it possible to by-pass so-called 'gateway cities'. In one study this was shown to be happening in Brazil with São Paulo sometimes being by-passed by foreign firms linking back to their own country, organizing insurance through Amsterdam, say, rather than using São Paulo for the service (Rossi and Taylor, 2006).

Time: Cyclical Effects

Historically it has been found that economies appear to be cyclical in nature: there are periods of growth that result in over-production, followed by periods of contraction/ stagnation with under-production. These occur at different time spans and the longer spans will most definitely impinge on inter-city relations. Put simply, in the good times cooperation will be seen as beneficial as the economy produces multiple win–win scenarios but with the downturn prospects of losing will generate a more competitive relation between cities, perhaps even zero-sum games.

Arrighi (1994) has described just such a situation in late medieval northern Italy wherein economic mutuality between cities gave way to political competition so that by the Treaty of Lodz in 1454 only four main cities survived as independent entities: Florence, Genoa, Milan and Venice. A similar process can be found in the rise of contemporary globalization. In the economic downturn of the 1970s and 1980s cities fared badly – they were universally seen as sources of problems in a competitive downward spiral – but their fortunes turned around with later globalization so that by the 1990s they were perceived as economic solutions, with their mutual interests finally modelled as a world city network only in the 2000s (Taylor, 2001).

These three circumstances induce a competitive process that creates strong hierarchical tendencies within city networks. But these are not 'inevitable tendencies'; both generic and contingent processes are reliant on agency: it is the activities of agents that produce networks and hierarchical tendencies.

THE QUESTION OF AGENCY

In something as complex as cities there are innumerable agencies that contribute to making inter-city relations. Here I focus upon the two main agencies that are directly involved in network formation: one political, the other economic.

Government Agency – Mayors, Urban Policymakers and City Planners

From at least the early twentieth century, city governments have formed policy links with each other and these have sometimes evolved into formally organized city networks (e.g. Eurocities). But such city government initiatives are not the reason why cities in networks are considered to be generic. Although these inter-connected local governments can claim to represent their respective cities, such networks are pragmatic and essentially 'simple'. By this I mean that they are the result of a single decision (to join a network) that can be easily rescinded with a change of mayor or party administration. This is not to say that such networks are trivial; they are especially important in diffusing 'best practice' ideas resulting in inter-city flows of policy information. But this is not what cities as generically networked are all about.

However, city governments do have a longer-term relevance for city network formation: maintaining the basic infrastructural space of flows that enables the inter-city connections to prosper. By definition, all successful cities grow to eventually out-strip their existing infrastructure resulting in a threat to their future. To right the situation typically requires large capital projects and these are carried out or underwritten by public authorities. The sort of work I am thinking of here varies over time: enlarging harbours, building new airports, dredging rivers, building canals, building railways, attracting airlines, ensuring smart electronic connections. All such infrastructure, at the least, requires a public subsidy to make the huge new investment viable. But this provides only the bottom layer in Castells' (1996) spaces of flows; such developments are necessary but not sufficient for successful city network formation. Therefore it is not the public supplier but the private agents who create the demand for the infrastructure, and who will be the prime users of new infrastructure, who are the important agents.

Commercial Agency – Trading Houses, International Banking and Business Service Firms

In the interlocking network model it is private agencies that are the key 'interlockers' of cities. They do this through carrying out their everyday commercial business. Where this business covers large geographical distances there has always been a twin problem of trust and information: to carry out distant business you need a presence in a faraway city that you can trust, and who can also be relied on to take advantage of particular local commercial opportunities as they arise in that city. Traditionally this has been accomplished through using extended family links across cities, leading to both large-scale trading houses and international banking. In contemporary globalization the key interlockers are business service firms (financial, professional and creative) that provide advanced transnational knowledge products that enable global capitalism to operate. Typical examples would be a London law firm that sells its inter-jurisdictional legal knowledge and a New York advertising agency that oversees 'global' advertising campaigns.

In order to service their clients in this way such 'advanced producer service' firms have opened offices in numerous cities across the world. It is the business they carry out through their office networks that links the cities together in a world city network (Taylor, 2001, 2004; Taylor et al., 2011). The inter-city relations are constituted by the information, instruction, specialized knowledge, design, planning, strategy, ideas, teleconferencing and face-to-face meetings that flow between city offices when implementing servicing projects for clients. This intra-firm work process is the mutuality that binds the network together. The amalgamation of everyday work carried out by large numbers of business service firms through the myriad flows above generates a world city network that is immensely complex. This is the contemporary representation of generic city networks that I will call primary inter-city relations.

PRIMARY INTER-CITY RELATIONS

Although not usually recognized as such, this contemporary world city network formation equates to Jacobs' (1969, 1984) classic modelling of the economic expansion of cities.

The World City Network and Jacobs' Process of Economic Expansion

In Jacobs' (1969, 1984) argument for 'explosive economic growth', a city replaces imports it had previously relied upon, thereby freeing up resources to obtain new and different imports. Such import shifting has been occurring in contemporary globalization through the making of worldwide office networks by advanced producer service firms. Every time an advanced service firm opens an office in a new city it replaces services that previously had to be imported to that city. For instance, if a major law firm opens a new office in Vancouver, then previous legal services obtained from the firm's existing Toronto office can now be produced locally. This is an example of new work for Vancouver based upon import replacement, which is, for Jacobs (1969, 1984), how cities grow. Thus the world city network can be interpreted as a meta-process of multiple import replacements across the world. Because, for Jacobs (1969), import replacement is an immense economic force that generates the dynamic cities that expand economic life, it follows that the world city network has been an immense power in the massive economic growth in the world economy, the economic globalization covering the last quarter century.

Jacobs (1969) says relatively little about city networks beyond her premise, inherent in the import replacement process, that cities need each other. Her main focus was what went on within city economies and she is generally appreciated in economics as a pioneer of cluster theory (Glaeser et al., 1992; Krugman, 1995). But there is really one mega-process of city-ness: without city clusters there would be no city networks, without city networks there would be no city clusters. This needs exploring further since the literatures on clusters and networks have developed largely independently of each other, post-Jacobs.

Clusters/agglomeration and Networks/connectivity

Cities provide knowledge-rich contexts in which different sectors often cluster together and which overall provide agglomerations of work. All major cities have their financial centres plus, typically, a close grouping of law practices, creative zones in which advertising agencies will be found, and many more local clusters. But even more important is the general agglomeration effect of large size (Glaeser et al., 1992). This makes cities very special places of enhanced communication for development and transfer of ideas within and across clusters. In addition, the agglomeration constitutes a complex division of labour in which new work continually adds to the variety. This provides firms with access to a wide range of employment skills that is necessary when developing new work.

Clusters/agglomeration processes link with networks/connectivity processes because it is the leading firms in the former whose everyday work creates the latter. But this is not a one-way effect; through their work in the net, firms bring new ideas and knowledge into the city, thus enhancing the knowledge-rich environment. Further, the knowledge they bring from the cities of their other offices is non-local, cosmopolitan knowledge. In other words business in the network brings knowledge that makes the clusters and agglomeration all the richer in ideas. In fact most new work derives not from innovation but rather imitation of other cities' innovations. This diffusion process was as true a hundred years ago when all cities electrified their economies (a New York/Newcastle innovation of the late nineteenth century) as today when all cities have their advertising agencies (an early twentieth century innovation emanating from New York).

CASE STUDIES

The argument so far has been quite abstract and I want to take the discussion further by providing two case studies to exemplify the theory. The first illustrates how mutuality is sometimes overlooked until actual processes are researched; and the second reminds us that globalization is an on-going process in which hierarchies are being eroded as the world city network evolves its mutualities.

From Competitive Presumption to Mutuality: London, Frankfurt and the Euro

When the European Union was planning its new currency in the late 1990s, it decided to locate the new European Central Bank in Germany's main financial centre, Frankfurt, rather than London. The problem for London was that although it was by far Europe's chief financial centre, the UK had decided not to join the euro at its launch. With London outside the euro-zone, Frankfurt was the sensible choice. The decision, however, was seen as a political victory for Germany over the UK with the likely outcome being Frankfurt overtaking London to become the new European centre of finance. This sentiment was rife among political and financial commentators. But they collectively misunderstood the relations between London and Frankfurt. In fact this was a classic case of translating inter-city relations as international relations and getting a completely wrong answer; city mutualities were completely overlooked.

Through interviewing practitioners in financial and other services in both cities we were able to show that there was a consensus among practitioners: the embedded financial context of London – its internal and network assets – meant that this city would remain Europe's leading financial centre for the foreseeable future irrespective of the UK being or not being in the euro-zone (Beaverstock et al., 2001). And we found no evidence for inter-city competition; rather London and Frankfurt complemented each other as places in which to do financial work. All firms in our sample had offices in both cities and therefore had a vested interest in both cities being successful. They were located in both cities because they used each city in a different way: the London office was the global platform for each firm; the Frankfurt office covered European business. In other words they were complementary: success in one office was expected to feed into activities in the other office. Put simply, our respondents thought that what was good for London was good for Frankfurt, and vice versa. Locating the European Central Bank was quite trivial compared to this powerful network process.

From Hierarchy to Network: New York Advertisers and New Centres of Creativity

Advertising is the archetypal American service industry and New York, with its famous Madison Avenue cluster, was the main hub throughout the twentieth century. As advertising diffused to other parts of the world, New York became a 'world hub', leading to global campaigns designed and executed in this one city for the rest of the world to consume.

We interviewed advertising practitioners to examine this service industry's changes in use of cities in the twenty-first century (Faulconbridge et al., 2011). The initial 'internationalization' of advertising, as described above, has been termed the imperial model. The firms carrying out worldwide advertising for clients would focus all advanced work from planning through creative design to financial organization on their New York headquarters. Other offices across the world, sometimes derogatorily termed 'post-box' offices, simply took the New York product, made language and minor cultural adjustments, and sold it on to local TV stations. This highly hierarchical framework has not survived; it appears as a temporary evolutionary phase to a network process. With recognition of the need for more nuanced messages reflecting changes in audiences, there has been a transformation to a more cooperative arrangement between offices across cities. Different offices are understood to be composed of different varieties of skills and these have to be brought together for the client. New creative ideas are accepted and expected from offices in certain non-US cities such as Bangkok and São Paulo deriving from their very different cultural contexts. And New York is no longer the automatic lead office; it might be part of a project team led, say, from Los Angeles. The end result is a multi-nodal network approach that harnesses internal and network assets from around the world. Why else, we might ask, would agencies invest in setting up multiple offices in a global network of cities?

CONCLUSION: THE HONG KONG 'SURPRISE'

I will conclude briefly with the best example of a city illustrating the generic nature of the contemporary world city network. When Hong Kong reverted to Chinese sovereignty in 1997, there was a widespread expectation that the city would decline: in Pacific Asia generally Singapore was identified as the main beneficiary, and within China it was assumed that Shanghai would take over Hong Kong's role of linking the country to the rest of the world city network. Here was another supposition of simple competition, a zero-sum game: Hong Kong loses; other cities gain. But surprise, surprise, Hong Kong has gone from strength to strength since 1997, and so too have Singapore and Shanghai. But it is only a surprise for those with simplistic ideas on cities. As noted above, Jacobs' (1969) import replacement process generates win–win scenarios and this is what has been happening in Pacific Asia.

REFERENCES

Andersson, A.E. and D.E. Andersson (eds) (2000), *Gateways to the Global Economy*, Cheltenham: Edward Elgar.
Arrighi, G. (1994), *The Long Twentieth Century*, London: Verso.
Beaverstock, J.V., M. Hoyler, K. Pain and P.J. Taylor (2001), *Comparing London and Frankfurt as World Cities: A Relational Study of Contemporary Urban Change*, London: Anglo-German Foundation.
Begg, I. (1999), 'Cities and competitiveness', *Urban Studies*, **36** (5–6), 795–809.
Castells, M. (1996), *The Rise of the Network Society*, Oxford: Blackwell.

Chandler, A.D. (1969), *Strategy and Structure*, Cambridge, MA: MIT Press.
Christaller, W. (1933), *Die zentralen Orte in Süddeutschland*, Jena: Gustav Fischer, translated by C.W. Baskin (1966), *Central Places in Southern Germany*, Englewood Cliffs, NJ: Prentice-Hall.
Cooley, A. (2005), *Logics of Hierarchy*, Ithaca, NY: Cornell University Press.
Derudder, B., P.J. Taylor, P. Ni, A. De Vos, M. Hoyler, H. Hanssens, D. Bassens, J. Huang, F. Witlox, W. Shen and X. Yang (2010), 'Pathways of change: shifting connectivities in the world city network, 2000–08', *Urban Studies*, **47** (9), 1861–1877.
Faulconbridge, J.R., J.V. Beaverstock, C. Nativel and P.J. Taylor (2011), *The Globalization of Advertising: Agencies, Cities and Spaces of Creativity*, London: Routledge.
Frank, A.G. (1969), *Latin America: Underdevelopment or Revolution*, New York: Monthly Review Press.
Friedmann, J. (1986), 'The world city hypothesis', *Development and Change*, **17** (1), 69–83.
Glaeser, E.L., H.D. Kallal, J.A. Scheinkman and A. Shleifer (1992), 'Growth in cities', *Journal of Political Economy*, **100** (6), 1126–1152.
Jacobs, J. (1969), *The Economy of Cities*, New York: Vintage.
Jacobs, J. (1984), *Cities and the Wealth of Nations*, New York: Vintage.
Krugman, P. (1995), *Development, Geography and Economic Theory*, Cambridge, MA: MIT Press.
Lukermann, F. (1966), 'Empirical expressions of nodality and hierarchy in a circulation manifold', *East Lakes Geographer*, **2**, 17–44.
Pain, K. (2008), 'Gateways and corridors in globalization: changing European global city roles and functions', *GaWC Research Bulletin*, 287, available at www.lboro.ac.uk/gawc/rb/rb287.html (accessed 10 September 2010).
Powell, W.W. (1990), 'Neither markets nor hierarchy: network forms of organization', *Research in Organizational Behaviour*, **12**, 295–336.
Rossi, E.C. and P.J. Taylor (2006), '"Gateway cities" in economic globalization: how banks are using Brazilian cities', *Tijdschrift voor Economische en Sociale Geografie*, **97** (5), 515–534.
Sassen S. (1999), 'Global financial centers', *Foreign Affairs*, **78** (1), 75–87.
Sassen, S. (2001), *The Global City: New York, London, Tokyo*, Princeton, NJ: Princeton University Press, 2nd edition.
Taylor, P.J. (1997), 'Hierarchical tendencies amongst world cities', *Cities*, **14** (6), 323–332.
Taylor, P.J. (2001), 'Specification of the world city network', *Geographical Analysis*, **33** (2), 181–194.
Taylor, P.J. (2004), *World City Network: A Global Urban Analysis*, London: Routledge.
Taylor, P.J. (2009), 'Urban economics in thrall to Christaller: a misguided search for city hierarchies in external urban relations', *Environment and Planning A*, **41** (11), 2550–2555.
Taylor, P.J., G. Catalano and D.R.F. Walker (2002), 'Measurement of the world city network', *Urban Studies*, **39** (13), 2367–2376.
Taylor, P.J., M. Hoyler and R. Verbruggen (2010), 'External urban relational process: introducing central flow theory to complement central place theory', *Urban Studies*, **47** (13), 2803–2818.
Taylor, P.J., P. Ni, B. Derudder, M. Hoyler, J. Huang and F. Witlox (eds) (2011), *Global Urban Analysis: A Survey of Cities in Globalization*, London: Earthscan.
Thompson, G.F. (2003), *Between Hierarchies and Markets: The Logic and Limits of Network Forms of Organization*, Oxford: Oxford University Press.

8 Global city/world city
Ben Derudder, Anneleen De Vos and Frank Witlox

INTRODUCTION

For one thing, the contributions to this book collectively show that in the last few decades researchers have begun to analyse the emergence of a transnational urban system centred on a number of key cities in the global economy. Taken together, the different approaches in this literature are loosely united in their observation that cities such as New York, London and Hong Kong (increasingly) derive their importance from a privileged position in transnational networks of capital, information and people. There is, in other words, a growing consensus that under conditions of contemporary globalization an important city 'is no longer identifiable for its stable embeddedness in a given territorial milieu. It is instead a changing connective configuration with variable actors which can be thought of as "nodes" of local and global networks' (Dematteis, 2000, p. 63).

However, despite this broad agreement, there are equally obvious differences in the way in which this global urban system has been conceptualized. For instance, it is clear that Sassen's influential 'global city' approach is presented as a specific analytical construct rather than as a mere attempt to refine existing approaches. In the revised edition of *The Global City*, Sassen (2001a, p. xxi) states that '[w]hen I first chose to use [the term] global city I did so knowingly – it was an attempt to make a difference.' This attempt to discriminate is most commonly targeted against another important approach in particular, that is, John Friedmann's (1986) 'world cities'. Sassen (2001a, p. xxi) stresses for instance that although it may be the case that 'most of today's major global cities are also world cities' there may just as well 'be some global cities today that are not world cities in the full, rich sense of that term'.

The overall aims of this chapter are (i) to single out the key characteristics of both oft-used approaches to understanding cities in the context of a global urban system, and (ii) to show that it is indeed relevant to distinguish between both (and therefore also other) approaches rather than retreating into sweeping notions of 'the position of cities in global networks'. Obviously, other conceptualizations than world cities/global cities have been devised, including 'global city-regions' (Scott, 2001) and 'global mega-city regions' (Hall and Pain, 2006). As these concepts explicitly incorporate a broader city-regional dimension, they are discussed in the next chapter, which deals with spatial transformations of cities under conditions of contemporary globalization. In addition, it needs to be emphasized that the overall usefulness of *conceptualizing* cities as nodes in transnational networks has been rejected on postmodern grounds (see M.P. Smith, 2001; R.G. Smith, 2003; Robinson, 2006), which has led to the emergence of notions such as 'cities in globalization' (Taylor et al., 2007) and 'ordinary cities' (Robinson, 2006). In this chapter, however, we proceed under the assumption that a proper conceptualization of the key driving forces/processes underlying the formation of global urban networks is both possible and useful, and thereby focus on what have arguably become the two most commonly used concepts (i.e. Friedmann's 'world cities' and Sassen's 'global cities').

The twofold objective of this chapter is reflected in its structure: (i) the next section discusses and compares the key tenets of Sassen's/Friedmann's theoretical work, after which (ii) we emphasize the importance of keeping these analytical differences in mind by comparing the results of empirical analyses of the structure of transnational city networks. In the conclusions, we briefly revisit the implications of our line of argument for the study of the global urban network.

KEY CONCEPTS

Friedmann's 'World Cities'

The world city concept can be traced back to two interrelated papers by Friedmann and Wolff (1982) and Friedmann (1986).[1] Both texts framed the rise of a global urban network in the context of a major geographical transformation of the capitalist world-economy. This restructuring, most commonly referred to as the 'New International Division of Labour', was basically premised on the internationalization of production and the ensuing complexity in the organizational structure of multinational enterprises (MNEs). This increased economic–geographical complexity requires a number of command posts in order to function, and world cities are deemed to be the geographical emanations of these command posts. The territorial basis of a world city is hereby more than merely a Central Business District (CBD), since '[r]eference is to an economic definition. A city in these terms is a spatially integrated economic and social system at a given location or metropolitan region. For administrative purposes the region may be divided into smaller units which underlie, as a political or administrative space, the economic space of the region' (Friedmann, 1986, p. 70).

Friedmann (1986) tries to give theoretical body to his 'framework for research' by (implicitly) framing it in the context of Wallerstein's world-systems analysis, hence the title of Knox and Taylor's (1995) *World Cities in a World-System*. As is well known, Wallerstein (1979) envisages capitalism as a system that involves a hierarchical and a spatial inequality of distribution based on the concentration of relatively monopolized and therefore high-profit production in a limited number of 'core' zones. The division of labour that characterizes this spatial inequality is materialized through a tripolar system consisting of core, semi-peripheral and peripheral zones. The prime purpose of the world city concept is that it seeks to build an analytical framework that searches to deflect attention from the role of territorial states in the reproduction of this spatial inequality (Brenner, 1998, p. 4). Territorial states have, of course, been prime actors in the unfolding of this uneven development, but drawing on the work of Mann (1986) and Dodgshon (1998), it can be put forward that the world-economy is radially rather than territorially managed. This means that the economic and political power of core territories is in fact spatially structured along well-defined routeways that link centres of control via available authoritative and allocative resources. Hence what is commonly labelled as 'core' in world-systems analysis does not necessarily consist of a series of 'strong' territorial states, but of a hierarchy of major and lesser centres (i.e. world cities) that thereupon diffuse their status and function over a wider area and at different scales (Dodgshon, 1998, p. 56).

In other words: despite 'being largely studied through its mosaic of states . . . the modern world-system is defined by its networks' (Taylor, 2000, p. 20), and world cities are the nodes in such networks of power and dominance. Apart from being the economic power houses of the world-system, world cities are also locales from which other forms of command and control are exercised, for example geopolitical and/or ideological–symbolical control over specific (semi-)peripheral regions in the world-system. Miami's control position over Central America is a case in point here (Grosfoguel, 1995). Friedmann (1986, p. 69) reminds us, however, that 'the economic variable is likely to be decisive for all attempts at explanation', whereby major importance attaches to corporate headquarters and international financial institutions and agencies. Although the presence of a business services sector and/or a well-developed infrastructure seems to be required, the latter are conceptually less important, since they are necessary but not sufficient conditions in the formation of a network of world cities.

Global Cities

The global city concept can be traced back to the publication of Saskia Sassen's *The Global City* in 1991. Sassen proposes to look afresh to the functional centrality of cities in the global economy, and she does so by focusing on the attraction of producer service firms to major cities that offer knowledge-rich and technology-enabled environments. In the 1980s and 1990s, many such service firms followed their global clients to become important MNEs in their own right, albeit that service firms tend to be more susceptible to the agglomeration economies offered by city locations. These emerging producer service complexes are at the root of global city-formation, which implies a shift of attention to the advanced servicing of worldwide production. Hence, from a focus on formal command power in the world-system, the

> emphasis shifts to the *practice* of global control: the work of producing and reproducing the organization and management of a global production system and a global market-place for finance (. . .) Power is essential in the organization of the world economy, but so is production: including the production of those inputs that constitute the capability for global control and the infrastructure of jobs involved in this production. (Sassen, 1995, pp. 63–64, her emphasis)

Through their transnational, city-centred spatial strategies, producer service firms have created worldwide office networks covering major cities in most or all world regions, and it is exactly the myriad connections between these service complexes that, according to Sassen (2001a, p. xxi), give way to the 'formation of transnational urban systems'. This urban network, Sassen (1994, p. 4) argues, results in a new geography of centrality that may very well cut across existing North/South divides. Hence, rather than reproducing existing core/periphery patterns in the world-economy, this network may break through these divides.

The focus on urban agglomeration economies has a major implication for the territorial demarcation of global cities. Rather than being structured in mutual dependence to a hinterland, the functional centrality of global cities becomes 'increasingly disconnected from their broader hinterlands or even their national economies' (Sassen, 2001a, p. xxi).

To territorially demarcate global cities, Sassen (2001b, p. 80) opts for 'an analytical strategy that emphasizes core dynamics rather than the unit of the city as a container – the latter being one that requires territorial boundary specification'. This does not necessarily imply that the functional centrality in global cities is a simple continuation of older centrality patterns as in New York City, since the territorial basis can consist of 'a metropolitan area in the form of a grid of nodes of intense business activity, as we see in Frankfurt and Zurich' (Sassen, 2001a, p. 123). It is nonetheless clear that the proper unit of analysis may very well be smaller than the 'metropolitan region'. Tokyo as a global city, for instance, is the 'Tokyo Metropolis' rather than the larger 'Tokyo Metropolitan Region' or the 'National Capital Region' (Sassen, 2001a, p. 371).

SUMMARY

Table 8.1 summarizes the gist of both theoretical approaches. Although each concept has been refined and/or revised in other contributions, it seems fair to state that the table gives a balanced overview of the conceptual core of each term: (i) Friedmann's world cities are centres of dominance and power, while (ii) Sassen's global cities are production centres for the inputs that constitute the capability for global control. These different starting points thereupon give way to diverging perspectives on the main features of a city as node in transnational networks: the city's prime function, the key agents in the urban network, the alleged structure of the network as a whole and the territorial basis of the city-as-node.

One can argue back and forth on the profoundness of the differences summarized in Table 8.1, but it seems clear that there is an unambiguous need to distinguish between both concepts. For instance, one can anticipate that the overall network will have a very different structure. While a network of world cities is expected to reproduce 'traditional' core/periphery patterns across the world-economy, a network of global cities is expected to cut across such divides. In other words: it is not unlikely that erstwhile 'semi-peripheral' cities such as Shanghai, São Paulo and Seoul are well-connected

Table 8.1   Key tenets of Friedmann's 'world cities' and Sassen's 'global cities'

	World cities	Global cities
Key author	Friedmann	Sassen
Function	Powerhouse	Centre for servicing of global capital
Key agents	Multinational corporations	Producer service firms
Structure of the network	Reproduces (tripolar) spatial inequality in the capitalist world-system	New geography of centrality and marginality cutting across existing core/periphery patterns
Territorial basis	Metropolitan region	Traditional CBD or a grid of intense business activity*

Note: * The spatial demarcation depends on the specific form of the territorialization of the core dynamics behind global city-formation. This implies that both the continuation of traditional CBDs (New York) and a new pattern centred on a grid of intense business activity (Zürich) are possible. However, the proper unit of analysis is clearly smaller than the 'metropolitan region' as a whole (see body of text for further elaboration).

global service centres (i.e. global cities) without being major power centres in the world-economy (i.e. world cities). Hence rankings of world cities and global cities may be expected to diverge rather than converge. To further explore this assertion, the next section presents a systematic comparison of the empirical operationalization of both theoretical frameworks.

COMPARING BOTH CONCEPTS

Empirical research into the formation of global urban networks has relied on a wide variety of data sources. Perhaps the most innovative studies in this context have come from the study of transnational urban networks through the lens of globalizing firms. Two often cited examples are the research pursued by the Globalization and World Cities research network (GaWC, www.lboro.ac.uk/gawc) and a series of papers by Alderson and Beckfield (2004, 2010 with Sprague-Jones).

GaWC researchers have developed a methodology for studying transnational urban networks based on the assumption that advanced producer service firms 'interlock' cities through their intra-firm communications of information, knowledge, plans, directions, advice, and so on to create a network of global service centres (Taylor, 2001). Building on this specification, information was gathered on the location strategies of 175 global service firms across 525 cities in 2008 (Derudder et al., 2010; Taylor et al., 2011). Applying the formal social network methodology set out in Taylor (2001), this information was converted in a relational matrix, which can then be analysed with standard network-analytical tools. The key indicator that can be derived from such an exercise is a city's 'global network connectivity' (GNC), that is, a measurement of how well a city is inserted in the office networks of globalized service firms.

Alderson et al. (2010) in turn analyse links between 6308 cities based on the organizational geographies of the 500 largest multinational firms and their subsidiaries for the year 2007. For each firm, the location of the firm's headquarters and subsidiaries was used to create a directional relational matrix. Based on this dataset, a number of connectivity measures can be computed, including 'outdegree connectivity' (the number of ties 'sent' from a city) and 'indegree connectivity' (the number of ties 'received' in a city). Both indicators have a different meaning, but here we assume that a simple combination of both (= aggregation of the number ties sent from/arriving in cities) gives a good indication of a city's degree of insertion in the corporate networks of multinational firms.

Both empirical approaches obviously exhibit a notable parallel in that their analysis of the structure of the global urban network is based on an assessment of the networked location strategies of firms with transnational fields of activity (Derudder, 2006). Put differently: it is suggested that a meaningful measurement of transnational inter-city relations can be derived from intra-firm connections between different parts of a firm's holdings – Alderson and Beckfield (2004, pp. 813–814) consider this to be a 'key relation' in 'an MNE-generated city system', while Taylor (2004, p. 9) argues that it is 'firms through their office networks that have created the overall structure of the world city network'. The main difference between both approaches obviously lies in the type of firms used throughout the analysis: GaWC researches focus on the

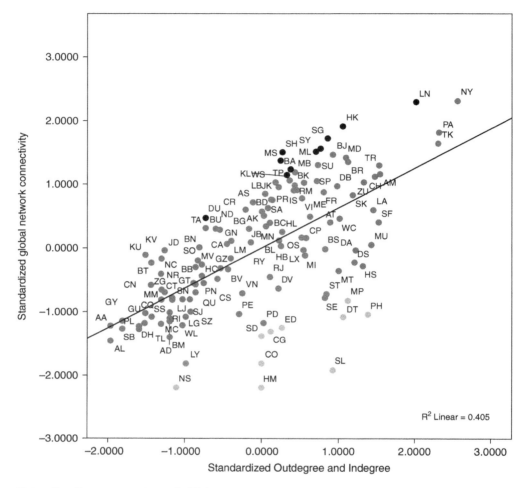

Note: For city names, see Appendix 8A.1.

Figure 8.1   Connectivity in APS networks versus connectivity in MNE networks

location strategies of *producer services firms*; Alderson et al. (2010) use information on the geography of *multinational corporations irrespective of the exact nature of their activities.*

The latter bifurcation is of interest here, as both studies clearly refer to the core tenets of the key analytical constructs outlined before: GaWC papers such as Derudder et al.'s (2010) draw on Sassen's work,[2] while Alderson et al. (2010) primarily work in the spirit of Friedmann. To examine the empirical parallels/differences between both networks, here we focus on the 130 well-connected cities that were singled out in the Derudder et al. (2010) analysis.[3] The results are summarized in Figure 8.1 and Table 8.2. The figure plots cities through a two-letter code (e.g. NY for New York, KU for Kuwait and NS for Nassau; see Appendix) based on their connectivity scores in Derudder et al. (2010) and

Table 8.2   Connectivity in APS networks versus connectivity in MNE networks –
regression residuals

	City			City	
1	Shanghai	1.71	1	St. Louis	−3.22
2	Hong Kong	1.61	2	Hamilton	−2.84
3	Moscow	1.56	3	Philadelphia	−2.46
4	Singapore	1.52	4	Cologne	−2.35
5	Sydney	1.39	5	Detroit	−2.25
6	Milan	1.37	6	Minneapolis	−1.97
7	London	1.33	7	Nassau	−1.95
8	Buenos Aires	1.28	8	Edinburgh	−1.83
9	Kuala Lumpur	1.20	9	Calgary	−1.79
10	Dubai	1.19	10	San Diego	−1.78

Alderson et al. (2010). The X-axis represents the connectivity of a city in the corporate networks of multinational firms (standardized score after logging this connectivity to deal with the skewness of the distribution). The Y-axis represents the connectivity of a city in the corporate networks of globalized Advanced Producer Services (APS) firms (standardized score after logging this connectivity to deal with the skewness of the distribution).

Regressing both connectivity measures shows that although they are clearly related ($R^2 = 40.5$ per cent), there are also notable differences between both networks. Table 8.2 shows some notable examples by listing the 10 largest deviations from the regression line. Large positive values imply that a city is proportionally more connected in the office networks of globalized service firms than in the networks of multinationals per se (and thus exhibit more global city- than world city-formation); large negative values imply that a city is proportionally more connected in the networks of multinationals than in the office networks of globalized service firms (and thus exhibit more world city- than global city-formation).

Taken together, the patterns that emerge from Table 8.2 and Figure 8.1 clearly confirm the split between both approaches. Cities such as St. Louis, Detroit and Cologne are well connected in corporate networks of multinational firms, mainly because of the presence of one or more headquarters of multinational firms with numerous ties across the world (i.e. the traditional 'core' in Wallerstein's scheme). However, this functionality is not matched by its globalized service function. Cities such as Shanghai, London and Dubai, in turn, are well connected service centres that are – in proportional terms – not as well connected in the corporate networks of the world's largest multinational firms. This list consists of cities from the 'traditional core' which have come to assume a key role in the servicing of global capital (e.g. Hong Kong and London), but also 'semi-peripheral cities' that have come to act as major service centres in the global economy (e.g. Buenos Aires and Kuala Lumpur). Referring back to Table 8.1, it is clear that the assumption of a network of world cities reproducing traditional core/periphery patterns and a network of global cities cutting across this divide is indeed noticeable. As a consequence, being precise about the key drivers/processes behind network integration of cities at the global scale does matter.

CONCLUSION

Not that long ago, Taylor (2004, p. 33) argued that the 'world city literature' was characterized by its 'theoretical sophistication and empirical poverty'. One effect of this 'evidential crisis was the failure for there to emerge any agreement on just which cities are world or global cities and which fail to qualify' (p. 39). This clearly comes to the fore in his comparison of 16 different rankings of 'world cities, global cities, and international financial centres from different sources' (pp. 39–41). Taylor (2004, p. 39) noted that there are only 4 cities that all 16 studies agree upon (London, New York, Paris and Tokyo), while there are 78 other cities that at least one source names in its ranking. This profound disagreement, Taylor thereupon suggested, reflects the failure of this literature to provide precise empirical specifications of the various concepts.

In the past few years, different research groups have risen to this challenge. It is, however, clear that despite the innovativeness of their analytical approaches and data collection, the disagreement on the broader structure of the networks has not been resolved. In this chapter, we have argued that at least a part of this enduring empirical disagreement can be attributed to meaningful theoretical differences in the conceptualization of a global urban network. The key point here is that the commonsensical observation that cities such as London, New York, Tokyo and Paris invariably feature at the apex of the various rosters of 'world cities' and 'global cities' does not imply that these (and other) concepts are interchangeable. On the contrary, the differences summarized in Tables 8.1 and 8.2 suggest that a proper specification of the key drivers/processes behind general notions such as 'global urban networks' and 'globalized urbanization' is of the utmost importance.

NOTES

1. There are earlier uses of this term, but Brenner (1998, p. 5) notes that these uses reflected the 'territorialization of the urbanization process on the national scale: the cosmopolitan character of world cities was interpreted as an expression of their host states' geopolitical power'.
2. The straightforward designation of GaWC studies as research into 'global cities' should, however, be somewhat nuanced. It can, for instance, be noted that the empirical rationale of most GaWC research starts from a critique of Sassen's global city concept for its bias towards a limited number of cities, hence the use of the 'cities in globalization' terminology in Taylor et al. (2007). Thus although Sassen's process is used in GaWC studies, it can be said that they do try to by-pass her concept of 'global cities'.
3. In practice, Derudder et al. (2010) focus on 132 cities. However, here we work with 130 rather than 132 cities as the scores for Rotterdam/Amsterdam and Antwerp/Brussels were combined for practical reasons.

REFERENCES

Alderson, A.S. and J. Beckfield (2004), 'Power and position in the world city system', *American Journal of Sociology*, **109** (4), 811–851.
Alderson, A.S., J. Beckfield and J. Sprague-Jones (2010), 'Intercity relations and globalisation: the evolution of the global urban hierarchy, 1981–2007', *Urban Studies*, **47** (9), 1899–1923.
Brenner, N. (1998), 'Global cities, glocal states: global city formation and state territorial restructuring in contemporary Europe', *Review of International Political Economy*, **5** (1), 1–37.
Dematteis, G. (2000), 'Spatial images of European urbanization', in A. Bagnasco and P. Le Galès (eds), *Cities in Contemporary Europe*, Cambridge: Cambridge University Press, pp. 48–73.

Derudder, B. (2006), 'On conceptual confusion in empirical analyses of a transnational urban network', *Urban Studies*, **43** (11), 2027–2046.

Derudder, B., P.J. Taylor, P. Ni, A. De Vos, M. Hoyler, H. Hanssens, D. Bassens, J. Huang, F. Witlox, W. Shen and X. Yang (2010), 'Pathways of change: shifting connectivities in the world city network, 2000–08', *Urban Studies*, **47** (9), 1861–1877.

Dodgshon, R.A. (1998), *Society in Time and Space: A Geographical Perspective on Change*, Cambridge: Cambridge University Press.

Friedmann, J. (1986), 'The world city hypothesis', *Development and Change*, **17** (1), 69–83.

Friedmann, J. and G. Wolff (1982), 'World city formation: an agenda for research and action', *International Journal of Urban and Regional Research*, **6** (3), 309–344.

Grosfoguel, R. (1995), 'Global logics in the Caribbean city system: the case of Miami', in P.L. Knox and P.J. Taylor (eds), *World Cities in a World-System*, Cambridge: Cambridge University Press, pp. 156–170.

Hall, P. and K. Pain (eds) (2006), *The Polycentric Metropolis: Learning from Mega-City Regions in Europe*, London: Earthscan.

Knox, P.L. and P.J. Taylor (eds) (1995), *World Cities in a World-System*, Cambridge: Cambridge University Press.

Mann, M. (1986), *The Sources of Social Power (Volume I: A History of Power from the Beginning to AD 1760)*, Cambridge: Cambridge University Press.

Robinson, J. (2006), *Ordinary Cities: Between Modernity and Development*, London: Routledge.

Sassen, S. (1994), *Cities in a World Economy*, Thousand Oaks, CA: Pine Forge Press.

Sassen, S. (1995), 'On concentration and centrality in the global city', in P.L. Knox and P.J. Taylor (eds), *World Cities in a World-System*, Cambridge: Cambridge University Press, pp. 63–78.

Sassen, S. (2001a), *The Global City: New York, London, Tokyo*, Princeton, NJ: Princeton University Press, 2nd edition.

Sassen, S. (2001b), 'Global cities and global city-regions: a comparison', in A.J. Scott (ed.), *Global City-Regions: Trends, Theory, Policy*, Oxford: Oxford University Press, pp. 78–95.

Scott, A.J. (2001), 'Globalization and the rise of city-regions', *European Planning Studies*, **9** (7), 813–826.

Smith, M.P. (2001), *Transnational Urbanism*, Oxford: Blackwell.

Smith, R.G. (2003), 'World city actor-networks', *Progress in Human Geography*, **27** (1), 25–44.

Taylor, P.J. (2000), 'World cities and territorial states under conditions of contemporary globalization', *Political Geography*, **19** (1), 5–32.

Taylor, P.J. (2001), 'Specification of the world city network', *Geographical Analysis*, **33** (2), 181–194.

Taylor, P.J. (2004), *World City Network: A Global Urban Analysis*, London: Routledge.

Taylor, P.J., B. Derudder, P. Saey and F. Witlox (eds) (2007), *Cities in Globalization: Practices, Policies and Theories*, London: Routledge.

Taylor, P.J., P. Ni, B. Derudder, M. Hoyler, J. Huang and F. Witlox (eds) (2011), *Global Urban Analysis: A Survey of Cities in Globalization*, London: Earthscan.

Wallerstein, I. (1979), *The Capitalist World-Economy*, Cambridge: Cambridge University Press.

APPENDIX 8A.1:   LIST OF ABBREVIATIONS

AA	Amman	DB	Dublin	LX	Luxembourg	RM	Rome
AD	Adelaide	DH	Doha	LY	Lyon	RY	Riyadh
AK	Auckland	DS	Düsseldorf	MB	Mumbai	SA	Santiago
AL	Almaty	DT	Detroit	MC	Manchester	SB	Saint Petersburg
AM	Amsterdam	DU	Dubai	MD	Madrid	SD	San Diego
AS	Athens	DV	Denver	ME	Melbourne	SE	Seattle
AT	Atlanta	ED	Edinburgh	MI	Miami	SF	San Francisco
BA	Buenos Aires	FR	Frankfurt am Main	ML	Milan	SG	Singapore
BB	Brisbane	GN	Geneva	MM	Manama	SH	Shanghai
BC	Barcelona	GT	Guatemala City	MN	Manila	SJ	San José
BD	Budapest	GU	Guadalajara	MP	Minneapolis	SK	Stockholm
BG	Bogota	GY	Guayaquil	MS	Moscow	SL	Saint Louis
BJ	Beijing	GZ	Guangzhou	MT	Montreal	SN	Santo Domingo
BK	Bangkok	HB	Hamburg	MU	Munich	SO	Sofia
BL	Berlin	HC	Ho Chi Minh City	MV	Montevideo	SP	São Paulo
BM	Birmingham	HK	Hong Kong	MX	Mexico City	SS	San Salvador
BN	Bangalore	HL	Helsinki	NC	Nicosia	ST	Stuttgart
BR	Brussels	HM	Hamilton	ND	New Delhi	SU	Seoul
BS	Boston	HS	Houston	NR	Nairobi	SY	Sydney
BT	Beirut	IS	Istanbul	NS	Nassau	SZ	Shenzhen
BU	Bucharest	JB	Johannesburg	NY	New York	TA	Tel Aviv
BV	Bratislava	JD	Jeddah	OS	Oslo	TK	Tokyo
CA	Cairo	JK	Jakarta	PA	Paris	TL	Tallinn
CC	Calcutta	KL	Kuala Lumpur	PD	Portland	TP	Taipei
CG	Calgary	KR	Karachi	PE	Perth	TR	Toronto
CH	Chicago	KU	Kuwait	PH	Philadelphia	VI	Vienna
CN	Chennai	KV	Kiev	PL	Port Louis	VN	Vancouver
CO	Cologne	LA	Los Angeles	PN	Panama City	WC	Washington, DC
CP	Copenhagen	LB	Lisbon	PR	Prague	WL	Wellington
CR	Caracas	LG	Lagos	QU	Quito	WS	Warsaw
CS	Casablanca	LJ	Ljubljana	RI	Riga	ZG	Zagreb
CT	Cape Town	LM	Lima	RJ	Rio de Janeiro	ZU	Zurich
DA	Dallas	LN	London				

9 Spatial transformations of cities: global city-region? Mega-city region?

Kathy Pain

INTRODUCTION

By the turn of the twenty-first century, many of the world's cities were caught up in major economic and social transformation. The 1980s and 1990s informational revolution has facilitated global connectivity on an unprecedented scale compared with previous periods of international economic relations. Ongoing developments in information and communications technologies (ICTs) since the mid 1970s are continuing to upgrade the intensity and speed of communications and transactions between cities across the world. Alongside these dramatic changes, the emergence of a distinctive, enlarged, urban functional space has been observed in a number of world locations. This has been described by Allen Scott as a 'global city-region' (2001a, 2001b) and subsequently by Peter Hall and Kathy Pain (2006) as a global 'mega-city region'. Both these concepts have attracted major policy attention in Europe, North America and East Asia, where city governments are recognizing that something unprecedented is happening around their major urban concentrations.

Globalizing cities are spilling over their metropolitan boundaries, creating challenges for their planning, management and governance. Manuel Castells has gone so far as to proclaim that these changes are making 'the category ("the City") . . . theoretically and practically obsolete' (Castells, 1998, p. 1). Ed Soja has referred to this 'transition if not transformation taking place' as 'Postmetropolis' (2000, p. xiii). New theorization can help inform understanding of what is going on, what processes are involved and the practical implications for governance, but empirical research in Western Europe has shown that we need to be careful about using the same theoretical concepts to describe development patterns being witnessed in different places. Apparently similar urban formations in different continents, and even within the same country, may not be outcomes of the same process. Indeed more than one development process may be occurring in one location at the same time (Taylor and Pain, 2007). This is an extremely important consideration in addressing policy issues for specific city regions.

The impacts of sweeping techno-economic changes at a global scale are impacting everywhere but have distinctive repercussions at the city region scale. The resurgence of interest in regionalism since the turn of the twenty-first century reflects the spiralling concern of nation states around the world for their economic competitiveness in a century which is undoubtedly global (Ward and Jonas, 2004). A key challenge for governments and city planners today, therefore, is engaging with the drivers of contemporary globalization and understanding their implications for economic growth, stagnation or decline; hence there is a need for clarity in the conceptualization of the conditions leading to different emergent city region processes. This chapter examines the two key concepts which have been used to describe this new urban scale – the *global city-region* and the *global mega-city region* – in order to clarify the specific processes they identify and their relevance for policy. First, the conditions leading to the process of city expansion into globalizing city regions now being witnessed in contemporary globalization are briefly examined.

CITY EXPANSION IN GLOBALIZATION

A good starting point is to consider first what the process of city expansion is *not*. Looking back to city regions as described in a pre-globalization era, Walter Christaller's analysis of *Central Places in Southern Germany*, in 1933 (Christaller, [1933] 1966), described very different spatial relations from those being observed today. The industrial revolution had reinforced previous historic international trade, production and consumption patterns but the scale of national social and economic urban relations still predominated. City regions were then seen as having hierarchical relations, with a clear distinction between 'central places', which were clearly defined urban areas where 'higher order' activities were located, and the hinterlands they served. Cities were distinct functional, social and jurisdictional entities. Late twentieth century developments in motorized transportation and virtual communications have made this state-centred and local scale of interaction increasingly irrelevant for understanding contemporary urban relations.

Flows of people, information, goods and finance have stretched and intensified between cities, and across national borders and continents (Cochrane and Pain, 2000), also transforming city regions. The economic growth of cities is now less tied to their national relations and more to the global scale, described by Peter Taylor as city 'hinterworld' relations (Taylor, 2001). Cities are increasingly engaged in world-wide systems of economic exchange and financial flows, and this intense global–local interaction gives rise to new functional relations that cross established urban administrative perimeters. Thus, under conditions of contemporary globalization, certain cities have expanded into larger city regions comprising multiple, functionally interlinked urban settlements. But confusion arises concerning what functional expansion means in theorizing this new city region scale.

The process of city expansion was noted long ago, and prior to present city globalizing tendencies, by Jane Jacobs (1969), who saw the *external* relations of cities, beyond their immediate hinterland, as instrumental in the creation of 'new work', a complex division of labour producing economic vibrancy (Jacobs, 1969, cited in Taylor et al., 2010, p. 7). Given recent heightened concerns for the economic growth of cities in a global context, to what extent does currently observed urban extension represent a new functional scale of economic relations and to what degree are they of a global nature? Research by Janice Perlman, for example, has used the term 'mega-city' to describe the largest contiguous urban areas in the world, irrespective of their overall degree of global economic integration, yet this is now clearly critical in informing local social and economic priorities (Castells, 1998; Perlman and O'Meara Sheehan, 2007). Evidence of city expansion to form a functional city region *in globalization* should relate to integration above the regional scale (e.g. a regional division of labour).

As analyses by John Friedmann (1986, 1995) and Saskia Sassen (1991, 2000) have demonstrated, specific 'world' or 'global' cities have become strategic sites for the operation of the capitalist world-economy and its transnational labour market. Their present-day global economic role has been facilitated by recent major technological and economic transition. But, whereas nineteenth century industrialization set many cities in the Western world up as places of relative prosperity and complacency, the late twentieth century has seen the decline of many once vibrant cities in the new informational economy (Massey, 1983). At the same time, cities in liberalizing countries are catching up with established world cities such as New York and London (Derudder et al., 2010). The economic terms of reference for cities everywhere have thus altered substantially and are more dynamic, giving rise to current territorialist concerns for their competitiveness at the global scale. In this context, attention is focusing on what it is that makes very large urban agglomerations globally integrated economically, and how this can be sustained. The answer lies in the drivers behind the economic globalization of cities.

In spite of predictions of the end of geography by authors such as O'Brien (1992) and Cairncross (1995, 1997a, 1997b), technological developments continue to make cities more important as the locations of global economic activity. As John Kay insisted a decade ago:

> We continue to be told that geography is ceasing to matter and that this will have major implications for the purpose and role of cities, yet cities are increasingly the dominant location of the human population because they are the centres of the contemporary economy. Technology is allowing dispersion but this is building up cities. (Kay, 2001, p. 14)

ICT-enabled financialization of the world economy has given cities a key role in articulating flows in advanced, knowledge-intensive business and professional services. They are the places where value is added to primary and secondary economic sector production and trade in dispersed trans-continental global production networks (Pain 2008a, 2009), but is this role conferred on enlarged city regions?

According to Kay, cities remain the focal points for global centralities, first noted by Sassen (1991), that are the outcome of ICT-facilitated economic dispersal because, as strategic locations of the advanced service economy, 'in a globalised world of freely moving capital and increasingly moving people, it is only social capital that remains tied to specific places' (Kay, 2001, p. 14). Twenty years on from Sassen's original analysis, the geography of knowledge-based economic capital is continuing to centre on cities, but cheaper and improved transportation and ICT applications now allow the formation of enlarged, globalizing city hinterlands which, like global cities, are part of a *hinterworld* space (Pain, 2010a). Potentially, centralities are intensifying to an extent that the global role of some cities is expanding across a proximate urbanized area. This is the spatial dynamic referred to by Scott as a global city-region (Scott, 2001b, p. 814) and it is distinct from the physical extension of very large mega-cities which are focal points of social reproduction but are presently disconnected from economic vibrancy associated with global city expansion.

THE GLOBAL CITY-REGION

It is therefore important to be clear about exactly what an enlarged city region comprises. For example, the 'mega-region' recently identified by the Regional Plan Association on the North East coast of the United States will differ in its scale of external economic relations from that of the 'megalopolis' identified by Jean Gottmann in roughly the same location 50 years ago (Gottmann, 1961; Regional Plan Association, 2006). Likewise, 'mega-city region' functional development identified in the Pearl River Delta and Yangtze River Delta regions of China 20 years ago (Xu and Li, 1990; Hall, 1999), prior to the effects from economic liberalization, will differ from that of today. The key distinction between contiguous built urban development, peri-urbanization and urban 'sprawl', which are marked by local functional connectivities and flows such as daily commuting to work, shopping trips and so on, and the *global* city-region phenomenon identified by Scott, is the presence (or not) of active global economic integration across an area larger than Sassen's global city. As Scott has put it, 'global city-regions' have become the new scale 'at which globalization processes crystallize out on the geographical landscape' (Scott, 2001a, p. 7). They are 'an outgrowth of large metropolitan areas – or contiguous sets of metropolitan areas – together with surrounding hinterlands of variable extent' (2001b, p. 814); furthermore, they constitute 'superclusters' (2001b, p. 820) which are 'spatial nodes of the global economy' (2001a, p. 11). But, if such city regions are more than large morphological and *regionally* interconnected entities, what global activities and flows, precisely, are they nodes for? To consider this question we need to refer back to key sources for Scott's inspiration, principally John Friedmann, Saskia Sassen and Manuel Castells.

Friedmann's (1986) theorization of the *world* city drew attention to major cities as command posts of the world economy in which advanced producer services – financial, legal, advertising, consultancy, and so on – have an important function. Sassen's (1991) concept of the *global* city extended this thesis, shedding light on the world dispersion of these specialized business services provided to multi-national corporations world-wide, and their simultaneous concentration in global cities. This dual dynamic has led strategic decision-making functions in the most knowledge-intensive organizations in the new world economy to centre on specific cities which have taken on the role of 'global service centres' (Sassen, 1991). Scott takes this basic concept and seeks to 'extend its range of meaning so as to incorporate the notion of the wider region as an emerging political-economic unit with increasing autonomy of action on the national and world stages' (2001b, p. 813). This is because such regions are 'dense polarized masses of capital, labour and social life that are bound up in intricate ways in intensifying and far-flung extra-national relationships' (2001b, p. 814). Given Jacobs' understanding of urban economic expansion, if true, this should confer the economic dynamism of global cities on physically larger global city-regions.

Scott sees city region economic dynamism as coming from the role of global cities as 'suitably positioned' for 'massive recent expansion' of 'leading sectors of capitalism'; these are 'organized as dense and intensely localized networks of producers with powerful endogenous growth mechanisms and with an increasingly global market reach' (Scott, 2001b, p. 820). He refers to the need for businesses to cluster to gain competitive advantage, citing the work of Porter and Storper (Porter, 2001; Storper,

1997, referred to in Scott, 2001b, p. 817), and to the 'organizational outcomes' of large-scale agglomeration – 'rich physical infrastructures supplied out of public funds as cities expand', 'dense local labour markets' and 'residential activities', 'consolidation of conventions and cultures' and, 'above all', their role as 'centres for learning, creativity, and innovation . . . new transactional encounters and experiences' (2001b, p. 819). His regional vision incorporates the special significance of advanced producer services both in the globalization of cities and in the rise of their surrounding, globalizing regions (e.g. Cooke and Morgan, 1993).

For Scott, then, globalization is leading to a process which Taylor (2007) has referred to as a 'rescaling . . . in which national domination of social practice is dissipating upwards to the global and downwards to the local'. Furthermore, this makes city regions 'active agents in shaping globalization itself' (Scott, 2001a, p.7), reflecting Kenichi Ohmae's (1995) *The End of the Nation State* thesis. He reiterates Castells' view that, increasingly, economic exchanges between cities are occurring in a global 'space of flows' that is not tied to the 'space of places' (regions and nation states) (Castells, 1996, pp. 376–428). Yet significantly, he sees global city-regions as the important new 'regional social formations' (Scott, 2001a, p. 1).

Rescaling of localized network connections, the development of external urban relations, and the ways in which the latter define and structure city regions, are therefore key determinants of the degree to which global cities are really expanding, functionally. These considerations must inform the question to what extent city regions are simply a new scale of a longstanding process of urbanization and to what extent they are becoming increasingly globally constituted and integrated.

Castells has indicated that the new spatial logic of territorial space, which is increasingly dominated by spaces of flows, is associated with a 'decentralizing trend . . . within the largest metropolitan areas' giving rise to 'multifunctional, multinuclear spatial structures' which are 'complicating the geometry of the corporate structure' (1989, p. 167). Sassen has similarly recognized a 'reconstitution of the concept of region' characterized by 'dense strategic nodes spread over a broader region', which could 'constitute a new form of organizing the territory of the "center"' (2001, p. 85). Potentially, then, the 'rescaling of strategic territories' could also link wider regions, as well as cities, to 'global circuits' (Sassen, 2002, p. 13). These conceptualizations have resonance with Scott's global city-region (Pain, 2008b); however, important definitional and empirical issues remain to be addressed, as Scott acknowledges (2001b, p. 820). For instance: What are the determinants of global economic integration of multinuclear city regions? How should their boundaries be delineated? How fit for purpose are their management and governance structures? These are critically important questions raised by Scott's global city-region thesis.

THE GLOBAL MEGA-CITY REGION

Amidst all the speculation about globalizing city regions, the 2003–06 European Union (EU) funded Polynet study has addressed these questions in the most urbanized area of the world, North Western Europe, where historical development has led to densely populated multinuclear present-day city regions (Hall and Pain, 2006). Recent enlargement of 'old Europe' to include newly liberalizing economies of Eastern member states, coupled with EU-wide demographic changes, have made the competitiveness of European city regions in the advanced global service economy a key concern, as expressed in the Lisbon Treaty (http://europa.eu/lisbon_treaty/index_en.htm). As Castells (1996) has made us aware, increasingly the global economic relations of contemporary cities have become constructed by connectivities and flows, associated with network forms of organization, especially advanced producer services associated with centralities in the world-economy (Sassen, 2000). However, their cross-border network relations cannot be mapped using state-centric official statistics – population, employment, commuting, and so on – as employed in traditional European 'functional urban region' analysis (e.g. Hall and Hay, 1980).

Thus the significant innovation of the Polynet study has been the use of network modelling (Taylor, 2004) to investigate the cross-border structures of advanced producer service firms operating in Europe, and the functional connectivity they confer on multi-nuclear mega-city regions. The unique quantitative results derived from this exercise were supplemented with qualitative data from in-depth interviews with senior personnel working in each region in the service networks surveyed. Four geographical scales of network activity were addressed – regional, national, European and global – in eight regions: South East England, the Dublin Region Ireland, the Randstad Netherlands, Paris Region, Central Belgium, Northern Switzerland, RhineRuhr and Rhine-Main Germany (Pain and Hall, 2006a, 2006b, 2006c; Taylor et al., 2008). Comparative assessments of the results are fully documented in *The Polycentric Metropolis* (Hall and Pain, 2006) and in special editions of *Built Environment* (**32** (2), 2006) and *Regional Studies* (**42** (8), 2008). The results allow new observations to be made about the processes that give rise to, and structure, globalizing city regions. The two key features of global *city relations* – rescaling and complexity – prove critical in determining the spatial relations and functional constitution of multinuclear *city regions*.

What are the Determinants of Global Economic Integration of Multinuclear City Regions?

The first significant observation is that global centralities are focusing most strongly on one city in each region studied; however, spatio-functional differentiation between the city regions is notable. Differences in the degree of advanced producer service network connectivity of the most *globally* connected city in each region are reflected in different functional structures of the city regions (Taylor and Pain, 2007). Cities that are more complex and more strongly integrated in global-scale service networks are conferring complexity on proximate towns and cities which have complementary roles and functions (Pain and Hall, 2006c). London's superior global connectivity therefore has a counter-intuitive spatial effect. Conventional regional analyses based on territorial, space of places statistical data depict London as a primate city within a mono-centric urban region, but the global centralities that are focusing on its densely clustered business milieu, reflecting and reproducing world-wide functional inter-linkages, are also rescaling the functional relations of the city region.

Service networks operating across an extensive area around London are producing 'functional polycentricity' in an enlarged multinuclear urban formation in Southern

England (Hall and Pain, 2006; Pain, 2008c) and are evidence of global city expansion beyond the London metropolitan boundary. This finding adds a new layer to the apparent spatial contradiction associated with the operation of advanced services in globalization. The process of service dispersion and concentration noted by Sassen (1991) now actively involves the city region scale in the case of London (Pain, 2006, 2008c), confirming Sassen's (2002) hypothesis of an emergent new 'territory of the "center"'. Taylor and Pain (2007) have interpreted this new scale of economic integration as a Jacobs (1984) vibrant city-region process that is transforming globalizing mega-city regions (pp. 64–65).

How should their Boundaries be Delineated?

A second important observation is that the geographical extent of functionally polycentric mega-city regions is hard to define because relations conferred on cities by service networks are multi-scalar and fluid; they are determined by markets and organizational operations which are cross-border and dynamic. The regions studied by Polynet are constituted by different intersecting regional to global scales of network organization. In some cases, the regional and national scales of operation remain predominant and, in these cases, functional polycentricity is less evident. However, significantly, in all cases, inter-city relations do not coincide with existing regional administrative and political unit boundaries in North West Europe in spite of EU initiatives to promote a 'Europe of regions' (www.blbe.be/default.asp?V_DOC_ID=1936). This finding concurs with Jacobs' thesis that 'city-regions are not defined by natural boundaries, because they are wholly the artefacts of the cities at their nuclei: the boundaries move outward – or halt – only as city economic energy dictates' (1984, p. 45). Service networks are flexible structures. They comprise dynamic flows of people and knowledge and they use cities strategically to engage with competitive markets at different scales.

How Fit for Purpose are their Management and Governance Structures?

This leads to a third important observation that the structures for contemporary mega-city region management and governance need to be similarly strategic, agile and responsive. They also need to be *non*-competitive across territorial borders in order to be able to engage with inter-city business structures and flows. The major global service agglomerations of all the Polynet regions are inter-linked with proximate towns and cities by regional- and national-scale service networks but, in contrast to London, other global cities are conferring less *global* service network integration on a mega-city region scale. Thus Taylor and Pain (2007) differentiate between two distinct city region processes identified in North West Europe which need to be taken into account in territorial strategic planning and management: first, polycentric regions produced by Jacobs-type global city functional expansion, and second, mega-regions of proximate cities.

London's exceptionally strong *multi-sector* global service network is generating non-dualistic, complementary, functional inter-linkages spanning much smaller proximate, multi-sector service clusters. However, regions consisting of cities of similar size are instead exhibiting *sectoral* specialization between proximate centres which are competing territorially for city users that are predominantly regional or national in network scope; global networks are still centralizing on just one city in these regions. The latter process can be interpreted as a continuation of Sassen (1991) global city centralities as opposed to the Jacobs global mega-city region process associated with London.

Paris is a notable North West Europe exception. Like London, it has very strong multi-sector global service network connectivity but policy interventions have restricted Paris's regional development (Halbert, 2006; Pain and Ardinat, 2011). In terms of mega-city region functional integration, in contrast to the extension of global centralities around London, the Sassen (1991) global city process remains more active and dominant in the Paris Region.

CONCLUSION

These process-based distinctions should be important in informing policies to promote effective regional economic growth; however, the Polynet study found that, in practice, traditional 'space of places' regional analysis has led to what Jacobs (1984) would have regarded as a 'process reducing' European Spatial Development Strategy (ESDP) dating from 1999 (Pain, 2010a). This strategy reflects the concept of 'territorial cohesion' or spatial equity, derived from the French planning philosophy which has limited the development of the Paris Region (Halbert, 2006). Such development control, combined with 'forcible income transfers from productive cities to economically inert regions . . . through regional redistribution schemes', can be interpreted as ineffective regional 'transactions of decline' (Desrochers and Hospers, 2007, p. 120) because suppressing urban functional expansion in one place does not make it reappear in another place to order.

The complex functional geographies that define global mega-city region emergence thus bring forth new challenges for policy in the 'mosaic' space of places (Castells, 1996). Scott sees global city-regions, which are 'the basic motors of a rapidly globalizing production system', as putting much at stake, 'as they steadily sharpen their political identities and institutional foundations' (2001b, p. 820). He speaks optimistically of 'embryonic consolidation of global city-regions into definite political entities . . . as contiguous local government areas . . . club together to form spatial coalitions' (p. 814). Such coalitions seem necessary to inform strategy, but this consolidation is not happening in the European cases Polynet studied.

Despite an illusion of policy cooperation, neither global mega-city regions nor mega-regions of proximate cities have joined-up strategic systems of governance to manage and support multi-scale development processes (Pain, 2010a), illustrating the relevance of the recent scale debate for city regions (e.g. Herod and Wright, 2002; Marston et al., 2006). The most developed European global mega-city region, South East England, is now facing the greatest challenge for joined-up governance of all – management by a mosaic of places under 'localism' which is the new basis for UK sub-national strategy, introduced by the Coalition Government in 2010 (Pain, 2010b).

Even discourse on 'rescaling the state' to counter fragmented governance (Allmendinger and Haughton, 2007; Xu, 2008) does not address the even bigger challenge of managing development processes that flow across multiple *extra*-regional scales within globalizing mega-city regions. Planning tools and investment to boost economic growth and counter uneven economic development require more nuanced, evidence-based conceptual premises that take these complex, multi-scale, functional relations into account. Meanwhile, new institutional arrangements require the involvement of the economic network actors (firms) that use and link cities through their cross-border urban operational practices (Taylor and Pain, 2007; Knox and Pain, 2010; Pain, 2010b). Soja (2000, p. 4) refers to an 'unfolding *postmetropolitan transition*' which signifies an emergence of 'the expansive metropolis' from 'the modern metropolis'. It is the non-dualistic network relations leading to such a transition with which regional territories must engage.

REFERENCES

Allmendinger, P. and G. Haughton (2007), 'The fluid scales and scope of UK spatial planning', *Environment and Planning A*, **39** (6), 1478–1496.

Cairncross, F. (1995), 'Telecommunications: the death of distance', *The Economist*, 30 September.

Cairncross, F. (1997a), *The Death of Distance*, Boston: HBS Press.

Cairncross, F. (1997b), *The Death of Distance: How the Communications Revolution Will Change Our Lives*, New York: McGraw-Hill.

Castells, M. (1989), *The Informational City: Information Technology, Economic Restructuring, and the Urban-Regional Process*, Oxford: Blackwell.

Castells, M. (1996), *The Information Age: Economy, Society and Culture, Vol. I: The Rise of the Network Society*, Oxford: Blackwell.

Castells, M. (1998), 'Why the megacities focus? Megacities in the new world disorder', The Mega-Cities Project Publication MCP-018, available at http://megacitiesproject.org/pdf/publications_pdf_MCP018intro.pdf (accessed 20 February 2010).

Christaller, W. (1933), *Die zentralen Orte in Süddeutschland*, Jena: Gustav Fischer, translated by C.W. Baskin (1966), *Central Places in Southern Germany*, Englewood Cliffs, NJ: Prentice-Hall.

Cochrane, A. and K. Pain (2000), 'A globalising society?', in D. Held (ed.), *A Globalising World?*, London: Routledge, pp. 5–45.

Cooke, P. and K. Morgan (1993), 'The network paradigm: new departures in corporate and regional development', *Environment and Planning D: Society and Space*, **11** (5), 543–564.

Derudder, B., P.J. Taylor, P. Ni, A. De Vos, M. Hoyler, H. Hanssens, D. Bassens, J. Huang, F. Witlox, W. Shen and X. Yang (2010), 'Pathways of change: shifting connectivities in the world city network, 2000–08', *Urban Studies*, **47** (9), 1861–1877.

Desrochers, P. and G.-J. Hospers (2007), 'Cities and the economic development of nations: an essay on Jane Jacobs' contribution to economic theory', *Canadian Journal of Regional Science/Revue Canadienne des Sciences Régionales*, **30** (1), 115–130.

Friedmann, J. (1986), 'The world city hypothesis', *Development and Change*, **17** (1), 69–83.

Friedmann, J. (1995), 'Where we stand: a decade of world city research', in P.J. Taylor and P.L. Knox (eds), *World Cities in a World-System*, Cambridge: Cambridge University Press, pp. 21–47.

Gottmann, J. (1961), *Megalopolis: The Urbanized Northeastern Seaboard of the United States*, New York: Twentieth Century Fund.

Halbert, L. (2006), 'The polycentric city region that never was: the Paris agglomeration, Bassin Parisien and spatial planning strategies in France', *Built Environment*, **32** (2), 184–193.

Hall, P. (1999), 'Planning for the mega-city: a new Eastern Asian urban form?', in J. Brotchie, P. Newton, P. Hall and J. Dickey (eds), *East West Perspectives on 21st Century Urban Development: Sustainable Eastern and Western Cities in the New Millennium*, Aldershot: Ashgate, pp. 3–36.

Hall, P. and D. Hay (1980), *Growth Centres in the European Urban System*, London: Heinemann.

Hall, P. and K. Pain (eds) (2006), *The Polycentric Metropolis: Learning from Mega-City-Regions in Europe*, London: Earthscan.

Herod, A. and M.W. Wright (2002), *Geographies of Power: Placing Scale*, Oxford: Blackwell.

Jacobs, J. (1969), *The Economy of Cities*, New York: Vintage.

Jacobs, J. (1984), *Cities and the Wealth of Nations*, New York: Random House.

Kay, J. (2001), 'Geography is still important', *The Financial Times*, 10 January.

Knox, P. and K. Pain (2010), 'International homogeneity in architecture and urban development?', *Informationen zur Raumentwicklung*, **34** (2), 417–428.

Marston, S.A., J.P. Jones and K. Woodward (2006), 'Human geography without scale', *Transactions of the Institute of British Geographers*, **31** (2), 244–251.

Massey, D. (1983), 'The shape of things to come', *Marxism Today*, 18–27 April.

O'Brien, R. (1992), *Global Financial Integration: The End of Geography*, London: Pinter.

Ohmae, K. (1995), *The End of the Nation State: The Rise of Regional Economies*, London: Harper Collins.

Pain, K. (2006), 'Policy challenges of functional polycentricity in a global mega-city region: South East England', *Built Environment*, **32** (2), 194–205.

Pain, K. (2008a), 'Looking for the "core" in knowledge globalization: the need for a new research agenda', *GaWC Research Bulletin*, 286, available at www.lboro.ac.uk/gawc/rb/rb286.html (accessed 20 February 2010).

Pain, K. (2008b), 'Urban regions and economic development', in C. Johnson, R. Hu and S. Abedin (eds), *Connecting Cities: Urban Regions*, Sydney, Australia: Metropolis Congress, pp. 20–47.

Pain, K. (2008c), 'Examining "core–periphery" relationships in a global city-region: the case of London and South East England', *Regional Studies*, **42** (8), 1161–1172.

Pain, K. (2009), 'Outsourcing and offshoring in business services – new dynamics, new territorial opportunities?', *Regions*, **274**, 11–13.

Pain, K. (2010a), ' "New worlds" for "old"? Twenty-first century gateways and corridors: reflections on a European spatial perspective', *International Journal of Urban and Regional Research*, doi: 10.1111/j.1468-2427.2010.01005.x.

Pain, K. (2010b), 'Local business growth needs an international approach', *The Times*, 16 July.

Pain, K. and G. Ardinat (2011), 'French cities', in P.J. Taylor, P. Ni, B. Derudder, M. Hoyler, J. Huang and F. Witlox (eds), *Global Urban Analysis: A Survey of Cities in Globalization*, London: Earthscan, pp. 231–235.

Pain, K. and P. Hall (2006a), 'Firms and places: inside the mega-city regions', in P. Hall and K. Pain (eds), *The Polycentric Metropolis: Learning from Mega-City Regions in Europe*, London: Earthscan, pp. 91–103.

Pain, K. and P. Hall (2006b), 'Flows and relationships: internal and external linkages', in P. Hall and K. Pain (eds), *The Polycentric Metropolis: Learning from Mega-City Regions in Europe*, London: Earthscan, pp. 104–112.

Pain, K. and P. Hall (2006c), 'People and places: interrelating the space of flows and the space of places', in P. Hall and K. Pain (eds), *The Polycentric Metropolis: Learning from Mega-City Regions in Europe*, London: Earthscan, pp. 113–121.

Perlman, J. and M. O'Meara Sheehan (2007), *The State of the World – Our Urban Future*, available at www.megacitiesproject.org/ (accessed 20 February 2010).

Porter, M.E. (2001), 'Strategy and the internet', *Harvard Business Review*, March, 62–78.

Regional Plan Association (2006), *America 2050: A Prospectus*, New York: Regional Plan Association.

Sassen, S. (1991/2001), *The Global City*, Princeton, NJ: Princeton University Press.

Sassen, S. (2000), *Cities in a World Economy*, Thousand Oaks, CA: Pine Forge Press.

Sassen, S. (2001), 'Global cities and global city-regions: a comparison', in A.J. Scott (ed.), *Global City-Regions: Trends, Theory, Policy*, Oxford: Oxford University Press, pp. 78–95.

Sassen, S. (2002), 'Locating cities on global circuits', *Environment and Urbanization*, **14** (1), 13–30.

Scott, A.J. (ed.) (2001a), *Global City-Regions: Trends, Theory, Policy*, Oxford: Oxford University Press.

Scott, A.J. (2001b), 'Globalization and the rise of city-regions', *European Planning Studies*, **9** (7), 813–826.

Soja, E. (2000), *Postmetropolis: Critical Studies of Cities and Regions*, Oxford: Blackwell.

Storper, M. (1997), *The Regional World: Territorial Development in a Global Economy*, New York: Guilford Press.

Taylor, P.J. (2001), 'Urban hinterworlds: geographies of corporate service provision under conditions of contemporary globalization', *Geography*, **86** (1), 51–60.

Taylor, P.J. (2004), *World City Network: A Global Urban Analysis*, London: Routledge.

Taylor, P.J. (2007), 'Cities, world cities, networks and globalization', *GaWC Research Bulletin*, 238, available at www.lboro.ac.uk/gawc/rb/rb238.html (accessed 20 February 2010).

Taylor, P.J., D.M. Evans and K. Pain (2008), 'Application of the inter-locking network model to mega-city regions: measuring polycentricity within and beyond city-regions', *Regional Studies*, **42** (8), 1079–1093.

Taylor, P.J., M. Hoyler and R. Verbruggen (2010), 'External urban relational process: introducing central flow theory to complement central place theory', *Urban Studies*, **47** (13), 2803–2818.

Taylor, P.J. and K. Pain (2007), 'Polycentric mega-city regions: exploratory research from Western Europe', in P. Todorovich (ed.), *The Healdsburg Research Seminar on Megaregions*, New York and Cambridge, MA: Lincoln Institute of Land Policy and Regional Plan Association, pp. 59–67, available at www.america2050.org/Healdsburg_Europe_pp_59-67.pdf (accessed 20 February 2010).

Ward, K. and A. Jonas (2004), 'Competitive city-regionalism as a politics of space: a critical reinterpretation of the new regionalism', *Environment and Planning A*, **36** (12), 2119–2139.

Xu, J. (2008), 'Governing city regions in China: theoretical discourses and perspectives for regional strategic planning', *Town Planning Review*, **19** (2–3), 157–185.

Xu, X.-Q. and S.-M. Li (1990), 'China's open door policy and urbanization in the Pearl River Delta region', *International Journal of Urban and Regional Research*, **14** (1), 49–69.

I C   Relational empirics

10 World cities and airline networks

Tony H. Grubesic and Timothy C. Matisziw

INTRODUCTION

Global networks, broadly conceptualized, manifest in a variety of ways. Perhaps the most tangible manifestations include infrastructure systems, such as the Internet (Graham and Marvin, 1996; Townsend, 2001; Malecki and Wei, 2009) or other large technical networks such as energy distribution grids (e.g. electricity, oil and gas) (Parsons, 1950; Overbye and Weber, 2000; Sadri and Volkov, 2004). While commercial airline networks share many of the same characteristics as other networked infrastructures, they are somewhat less permanent, changing with variations in consumer demand.

This modest difference aside, airline networks and commercial air service continue to play a significant role in both regional economic development (Debbage and Delk, 2001; Grubesic, 2010) and the larger global economy (Smith and Timberlake, 1995; Derudder et al., 2007a). At the global level, several intriguing aspects of airline networks and their associated levels of service have emerged. With liberalization of the airline industry spreading throughout Europe, Asia, North America and elsewhere, there is increasing interest in the spatial and economic outcomes of markets open to competition. For example, in North America deregulation has generated more frequent service and higher passenger volumes to the most popular destinations (Goetz and Sutton, 1997).[1] More importantly, competition on these routes has reduced average fares. Conversely, deregulation has exacerbated carrier financial instability, generated industry layoffs, reduced the overall quality of service, severely limited the frequency of flights to smaller places and increased their associated fares (Goetz and Vowles, 2009). Against this backdrop of liberalization, the ability to identify winners and losers in a global context is critical (Zook and Brunn, 2006). This is particularly true when considering world cities (Friedmann, 1986), because airline networks represent one of the few viable options for both determining the strength of inter-city relations (Short and Kim, 1999; Smith and Timberlake, 2001; Derudder and Witlox, 2005a, 2005b; Derudder, 2006) and hypothesizing about associated city hierarchies (Taylor, 2005; Grubesic et al., 2009; GaWC, 2010).

The purpose of this chapter is to provide a concise overview of global airline networks and their relationships to world cities. Specifically, three facets are addressed. First, the impact of liberalization in the airline industry is explored, highlighting the implications of Open Skies agreements, route competition and pricing. Secondly, the operational characteristics of airline networks are examined, including a brief discussion on system topology and its impact on commercial air service. Finally, world city connectivity and accessibility are analysed. This includes empirical examples that highlight variations in connectivity through the use of a comprehensive airline schedule database.

AIRLINE INDUSTRY LIBERALIZATION AND OPEN SKIES

While the terms 'deregulation' and 'liberalization' are often used interchangeably, there is an important difference worth highlighting. In the context of the airline industry, deregulation refers to the release of government authority to control the entry and exit, fares, subsidies and mergers of airlines in a given market (Goetz and Sutton, 1997). Liberalization subsumes deregulation and also includes the process of privatization, which is the transfer of ownership and operation of state-controlled airlines to the private sector (Hanlon, 2007). In theory, liberalization represents an effort to increase competition and efficiency and motivate improvements in service, although the results of these policies are mixed (Goetz and Vowles, 2009). One notable benefit of liberalization, however, is its ability to help facilitate growth in air travel. For example, in 1978 there were approximately 254 million air passengers in the United States. In 2008, the number of air passengers increased to approximately 650 million (BTS, 2009), a net gain of 156 per cent. Obviously, not all of this growth can be attributed to the processes of deregulation and liberalization. The demand for air travel has steadily increased with overall gains in wealth, both in the United States and abroad, as well as improvements in aircraft technology (DeNavas-Wale et al., 2004; Hanlon, 2007).

If one sets aside rising affluence and improving aircraft technologies for helping explain growth, it is possible to begin identifying the specific factors associated with liberalization that help fuel increases in air passenger activity. For example, in the early 1990s the United States began to organize a series of bilateral air service agreements (ASAs) with foreign partners for achieving more competition on international routes, better pricing, fewer restrictions on route capacity and frequency, and an increased number of international gateways (Doganis, 2006). Beginning with the Netherlands (1992), the following features were built into these ASAs, better known as 'Open Skies' agreements. First, market access was granted from any point in the U.S. to specified points in foreign countries. This also includes Fifth Freedom rights, which allowed U.S. carriers to transport revenue traffic between multiple foreign countries and break gauge.[2] Second, multiple designations allowed for an unlimited number of designated foreign carriers to compete for passengers over the same routes as incumbent carriers. Third, all frequency and capacity controls were lifted. Fourth, code-shares allowed two airlines to sell seats on the same flight. Finally, virtually all tariff controls were lifted.

From the perspective of a consumer, these are good developments. Route competition, particularly for international flights, often leads to lower itinerary pricing and more options on historically 'thin' routes. Further, Open Skies agreements are not limited to the United States. Today, Europe largely functions as a single market via a series of multilateral agreements and competition rules, including the European Common Aviation Area (ECAA), which covers 28 countries (Doganis, 2006). Countries in Asia, portions of Africa and Latin America are also benefiting from Open Skies agreements with both Europe and the United States (Bowen, 2000; Hanlon, 2007).[3]

Open Skies agreements, however, do not facilitate completely free access to routes. For example, Hanlon (2007) notes that the United States has refused to trade domestic cabotage rights for similar rights overseas because the U.S. has far more to lose (in terms of routes and market share for domestic carriers) than it has to gain.[4] In addition, bilateral Open Skies agreements do not secure Seventh Freedom rights, which is the ability to transport passengers or cargo between two foreign countries without continuing service to the carrier's home country.[5]

Regardless of the short-term fluctuations in capacity or pricing of major international routes, from a network perspective the simple fact that Open Skies agreements allow for increasing levels of interconnection between major markets, including world cities, is important. Further, Open Skies agreements have allowed carriers to better leverage strategic network configurations, such as hub-and-spoke systems, to more efficiently serve geographically dispersed markets. In the next section, several different types of network topologies, including hub-and-spoke, are compared, highlighting their strengths, weaknesses and their implications for world city interaction.

NETWORK TOPOLOGIES

Through the years, many empirical studies have examined commercial airline route structures and their implications for airport service (Reed, 1970; Chou, 1993; Shaw, 1993; Shaw and Ivy, 1994; Bania et al., 1998; O'Kelly, 1998; Burghouwt and Hakfoort, 2001; Burghouwt et al., 2003; Alderighi et al., 2005; Guimerà et al., 2005; Derudder et al., 2007a, 2007b). Route topologies in airline networks generally take one of three forms (Figure 10.1). Aircraft movements on line networks typically consist of several short-haul segments (i.e. with intermediate stops) between an origin and final destination. During these intermediate stops, the aircraft may pick up additional passengers or fuel. As Hanlon (2007) notes, this type of topology is relatively inefficient because the frequency of service is poor (a disincentive to business travellers paying premium ticket prices) and long-haul aircraft are not suited for operation on routes with low load factors (e.g. beginning and ending city pairs) on the line. From an operational perspective, grid networks are more efficient because flights can operate on several different routes without backtracking, minimizing aircraft idle time (Hanlon, 2007). As a result, grid networks benefit from higher rates of utilization for aircraft and crews and are able to maintain a larger geographic footprint for cities served than most line networks. Finally, hub-and-spoke networks, the dominant operational topology for most major commercial airlines, have several major advantages over both line and grid networks. First, hubs are able to leverage greater operational efficiencies because of better equipment and personnel utilization. In addition, for major interhub linkages, economies of traffic density exist. Basically, the cost per passenger decreases as the number of passengers per hub increases. Second, hubs are able to offer many connections over the course of a day (or week) to passengers that are routed through them. This allows hub-and-spoke systems to capture passengers from a much larger geographical area than line or grid networks. A third feature of hub-and-spoke systems, as noted by O'Kelly (1998, p. 175), is that close to full (or completely full) aircraft with a blend of passengers with various elasticities of demand, allows airlines to 'engage in very sophisticated demand management and pricing schemes, effectively micro-managing the yield from the contents of the flight based on the passengers' ability and willingness to pay'. Put more simply, airlines can maximize yields by exploiting variations in the geographic demand and supply of transport between a wider variety of origins, destinations and their associated consumers. For more details on the intricacies of hub-and-spoke systems, see O'Kelly and Miller (1994), Doganis and Dennis (1989) and Hanlon (2007).

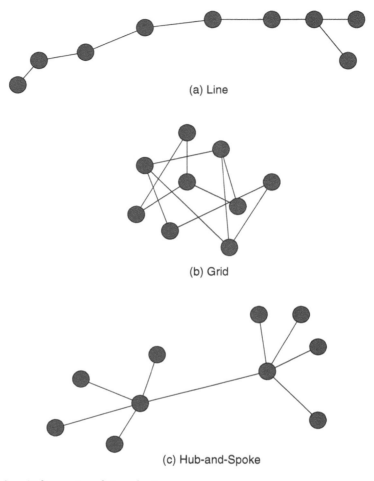

(a) Line

(b) Grid

(c) Hub-and-Spoke

Figure 10.1   Airline network topologies

Given this complex mesh of carrier network topologies, geographical relationships, carrier strategic alliances and deregulation/liberalization policies, how do these factors impact the interaction of world cities? In the next section, we provide an outline of the data and methodologies used for exploring air transport connectivity and service capacities between major world cities.

DATA AND METHODS

Many sources of air transportation data exist and have been used in analysing a variety of regional and global patterns of air movements (Derudder and Witlox, 2005b). In particular, Innovata's Schedule Reference Service (SRS) database has proven to be extremely useful in previous work (Grubesic et al., 2008a; Malighetti et al., 2008; Burghouwt and

Table 10.1   The 2008 Global Cities Index

Rank	City	Rank	City
1	New York	26	Zurich
2	London	27	Dubai
3	Paris	28	Istanbul
4	Tokyo	29	Boston
5	Hong Kong	30	Rome
6	Los Angeles	31	São Paulo
7	Singapore	32	Miami
8	Chicago	33	Buenos Aires
9	Seoul	34	Taipei
10	Toronto	35	Munich
11	Washington	36	Copenhagen
12	Beijing	37	Atlanta
13	Brussels	38	Cairo
14	Madrid	39	Milan
15	San Francisco	40	Kuala Lumpur
16	Sydney	41	New Delhi
17	Berlin	42	Tel Aviv
18	Vienna	43	Bogota
19	Moscow	44	Dublin
20	Shanghai	45	Osaka
21	Frankfurt	46	Manila
22	Bangkok	47	Rio de Janeiro
23	Amsterdam	48	Jakarta
24	Stockholm	49	Mumbai
25	Mexico City	50	Johannesburg

Source: A.T. Kearney (2008)

Redondi, 2009; Grubesic et al., 2009; Malighetti et al., 2009; Grubesic, 2010), and will serve as the foundation for analysis in this chapter. The SRS database contains schedule information for nearly 900 airlines in 4700 cities, representing 99.9 per cent of worldwide commercial passenger schedules for each tabulation quarter (IATA, 2007). As noted by Grubesic et al. (2009), these data represent a 'neutral' schedules database, conforming to global standards put forth by the IATA for quality control.

For the purposes of this chapter, a measure of route capacity (average number of seats per week scheduled between airports) will be used to summarize interaction among world cities. Although the exact definition of what constitutes a world city and its associated global importance is a subject of much debate, rankings of cities are frequently proposed. A good example of this is the 2008 Global Cities Index (A.T. Kearney, 2008). In a joint effort between the consulting firm A.T. Kearney and the Chicago Council on Global Affairs, analysts collected 24 metrics across 5 unique dimensions to develop a ranking of global cities.[6] While this chapter is less concerned with the specific composition of this index, the final rankings are used to generate a subset of world cities for analysis (Table 10.1) (Figure 10.2). For the purposes of this chapter, SRS data will be used to describe the relationships among the top 50 cities identified under this ranking system.

Source: A.T. Kearney (2008)

Figure 10.2 Top 50 world cities

Analytical Challenges

One of the more significant analytical challenges for exploring world city interconnectivity using airline network data is how best to determine the extent that individual airports serve as gateways to world cities (Derudder et al., 2010). For example, consider New York City. While both LaGuardia (LGA) and John F. Kennedy International (JFK) are located within New York City, Newark Liberty International (EWR), located in New Jersey, is also considered a major international gateway to both New York City and the major urban areas in New Jersey and portions of Pennsylvania. As a result, when analysing world city networks, one must carefully consider if, or to what extent, EWR should be associated with New York City. Two basic approaches have been implemented for dealing with this. Derudder and Witlox (2005a), among others, simply aggregate each airport to a metropolitan region. As a result, connections or flows that originate in or are destined for JFK, LGA or EWR are related to New York. A second approach keeps airports in a more disaggregate form, where flows or connections between LGA, JFK and EWR can be tracked separately (Grubesic et al., 2008a, 2009).

The problem with aggregate analysis is that defining exactly what constitutes a metropolitan region/transport hinterland for a city can be difficult, particularly across multiple nation-states and airport catchment areas. In this chapter, a more general approach is taken to catchment area delineation to better accommodate uncertainty and dynamism in airport market areas. For the purposes of this analysis, airports are assigned to a world city's hinterland provided that two criteria are met: 1) the airports are within 70 miles (~112 kilometres) of a city's centre, and 2) they are located in the same country as the world city. While the 70 mile distance constraint is somewhat arbitrary, it does represent a one hour drive (approximately) between locations in the U.S. This is a fairly conservative but realistic geographic threshold (Matisziw and Grubesic, 2010).[7] As a result, while this approach will still include EWR with JFK and LGA as part of New York City's hinterland, it is capable of differentiating between locales that may be geographically proximate but, for other reasons, may not be viable options for air travel. For example, while Detroit is not generally considered a world city, the approach outlined above would preclude the inclusion of Windsor Airport (YQG) (located in Windsor, Ontario) in Detroit's hinterland because of YQG's location in Canada.[8]

Again, Table 10.1 lists the world cities selected for subsequent analysis. Using a geographic information system (GIS), nearly 11,000 airports represented in the SRS database were evaluated with respect to the world cities. As a result, 978 airports (8.84 per cent of the total) were uniquely assigned as serving a world city. Given these derived hinterlands, it is now possible to characterize how these regions are linked through the global air transport system. To do this, each world city was represented as a node in the global air transportation network. The presence of a direct connection between nodes was then identified using seats-per-week (SPW) recorded in the 2006 SRS database. If any scheduled seats existed between a pair of cities in the database, a network linkage between the cities was generated. This process yielded a network consisting of 50 nodes and 662 linkages. All together, interaction among these world cities and their associated hinterlands accounted for an average of 10,487,738 SPW, or 17 per cent of the average weekly scheduled capacity for global air traffic in 2006.[9]

Methodology

In an effort to disentangle the complex matrix of world city interactions, several basic measures are utilized to deepen our understanding of air transport network interconnectivity. First, the number of direct flights originating in or destined for a city (nodal degree) can be better assessed, providing a measure of accessibility with the network (Taaffe et al., 1996). More direct connections are assumed to be indicative of importance in the system, whether through hubbing or gateway functions (Grubesic, 2010), or simply as important origin/destination points. Second, the network representation of world city interaction facilitates the computation of other accessibility metrics such as the minimum cost associated with travelling between any pair of cities on the networks. This includes the calculation of the minimum number of steps (i.e. Shimbel distance) (Shimbel, 1953) or the minimum distance (i.e. L-matrix) (Taaffe et al., 1996). For both of these measures, smaller values suggest higher levels of accessibility or a more efficient set of connections to other network locations.

RESULTS

Figure 10.3 displays the aggregate average SPW (specifically, inflow) for each of the top 50 world cities (from the other world cities) during 2006.[10] Not surprisingly, both London and New York lead the pack, each maintaining an average scheduled inflow of approximately 700,000 SPW. As noted by Grubesic et al. (2008a), scheduled seats for most metropolitan airline hubs are largely symmetric, so the aggregate average SPW (outflow) for each world city are virtually identical. Perhaps the most important feature of Figure 10.3 is the sheer dominance of flow displayed by London and New York, relative to the other world cities. Needless to say, both cities function as major domestic and international airline hubs.

While the flow metric visualized in Figure 10.3 is certainly an important aspect of world city interaction, the number of direct connections that each world city maintains with its peers is equally important. Also known as nodal degree, this measure provides a slightly different landscape of interconnectivity (Figure 10.4). In this instance, the results indicate that Paris (ranked 3rd in the Global Cities Index) maintains the most direct connections (n = 46) between the top 50 world cities, with Frankfurt, Amsterdam, London and New York rounding out the top 5 (Table 10.2). It is interesting to note that the only significant gap in Paris' connections is found within the Pacific Rim (Manila, Sydney and Jakarta). At the opposite end of the spectrum, Rio de Janeiro (ranked 47th in the Global Cities Index) maintains the lowest number of direct connections within the top 50 world cities (n = 8), with direct services primarily to North America and continental Europe.

Evaluating the minimum number of steps required to move between world cities provides a slightly different perspective on world city interconnection and its associated air transport network (Figure 10.5). This metric, also known as the Shimbel Index, is a simple measure of dispersion that tracks the minimum number of intervening arcs or steps between network nodes. By summing the minimum number of steps from each city to all other cities, a metric of a city's overall accessibility can be computed. For example,

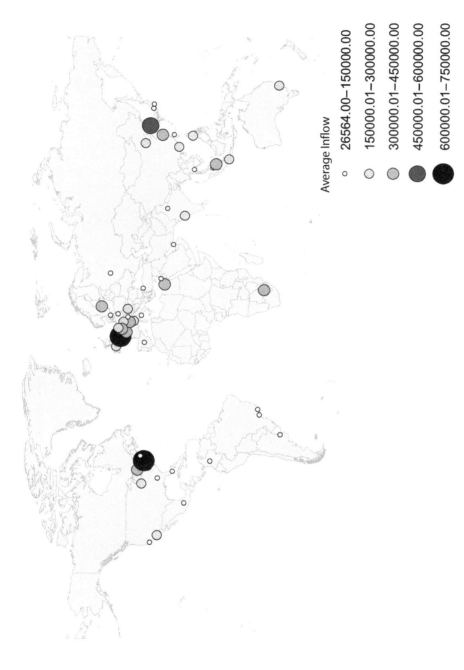

Average Inflow

○	26564.00–150000.00
○	150000.01–300000.00
○	300000.01–450000.00
●	450000.01–600000.00
●	600000.01–750000.00

Note: With the exception of some minor numerical differences in flow totals, the average outflow and average inflow maps are identical in their classifications of world cities.

Figure 10.3   Average inflow (seats per week) (2006)

Figure 10.4   Degree of node: top 50 world cities network (2006)

Table 10.2   Degree of node (>=30) for world cities

City	Country	Degree of node	D-matrix
Paris	FR	46	52
Frankfurt	GM	44	54
Amsterdam	NL	42	56
London	UK	41	57
New York	US	40	58
Zurich	SZ	37	61
Rome	IT	35	63
Munich	GM	35	63
Milan	IT	34	64
Moscow	RS	33	65
Bangkok	TH	33	65
Tokyo	JA	33	65
Chicago	US	32	66
Toronto	CA	31	67
Madrid	SP	31	67
Vienna	AU	31	67
Hong Kong	CH	30	68
Beijing	CH	30	68
Seoul	KS	30	68

given that 50 world cities are represented in the analysis network, a minimum of 49 steps would be involved in moving from one city to all others, if direct connections are the *only* linkages between them. Table 10.2 highlights the results of this analysis and indicates, not surprisingly, that Paris is the most efficiently connected world city (D = 52). Since Paris maintains direct connections with all but three cities, the score of 52 (52–49 = 3) is obviously related to the degree of node measure presented previously. Perhaps the most important facet of this analysis is that the least efficient cities in the top 50 (e.g. Jakarta, Rio de Janeiro, Bogota) only require a maximum of three steps to reach any other world city in the network.[11] This should not be a surprise, given the tremendous significance of these cities in the global economy.

Given a network representation of a system, the actual minimum geographic distance, or cost, involved in travelling between network nodes can also be used as a measure of accessibility and interconnectivity (Taaffe et al., 1996). World cities with lower aggregate values (or shorter paths) indicate greater locational accessibility. The results of this measure are not unexpected. Given the spatial distribution of top 50 world cities, many European cities display the highest levels of accessibility (Table 10.3) (Figure 10.6). However, there are a number of subtleties worth highlighting. While Paris largely dominated the network measures based on direct connections and topological proximity, Frankfurt, Berlin, Munich, Amsterdam, Brussels, Vienna and Copenhagen are all more accessible than Paris when actual distance is incorporated. Conversely, Sydney is the most remote world city, with Buenos Aires and Rio de Janeiro, São Paulo and Bogota rounding out the bottom five.

A final topologically derived metric for describing the interrelationships between

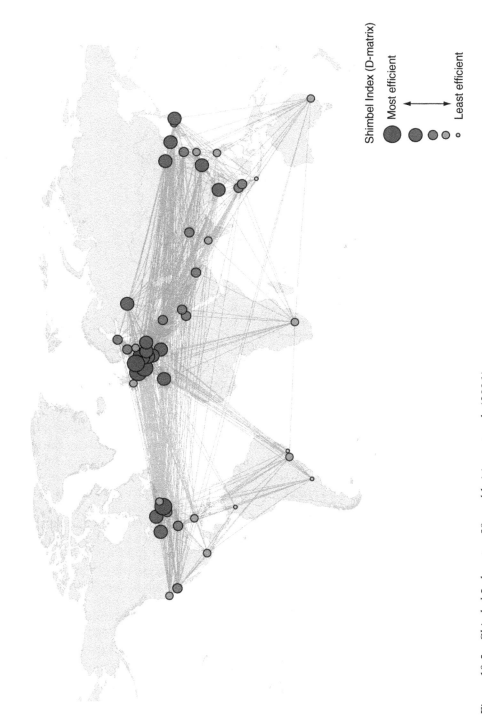

Figure 10.5   Shimbel Index: top 50 world cities network (2006)

Table 10.3   L-matrix for world cities

Most accessible	Miles
Frankfurt	180173.56
Berlin	181156.41
Munich	181172.06
Amsterdam	181180.92
Brussels	181685.39
Vienna	181797.92
Zurich	181965.84
Copenhagen	182131.52
Paris	183276.59
Milan	183857.16
Least accessible	**Miles**
Kuala Lumpur	290499.88
Singapore	295696.59
Mexico City	300694.34
Jakarta	318370.53
Johannesburg	318861.94
Bogota	319197.22
São Paulo	350014.09
Rio de Janeiro	351373.13
Buenos Aires	389408.56
Sydney	410626.09

world cities is derived by averaging the scheduled SPW data across the number of direct connections that each city maintains. For example, if one sums the total inflow and outflow for each city, then divides this by the number of direct connections (i.e. degree of node), an average total flow metric across city connections can be obtained. The resulting distribution of averaged scheduled flow is a compelling one (Table 10.4). Many of the cities that display relatively lower levels of topological accessibility (e.g. Jakarta, Johannesburg and Manila) have a significantly stronger presence for average scheduled flows. In other words, while many of these cities do fail to display a large number of direct connections to other world cities, the air transport linkages which are maintained by these locales display a higher intensity of use. From an operational perspective, this neatly falls in line with many of the strategic economic advantages of operating hub-and-spoke systems. Simply put, serving interhub links with low-capacity flights makes little economic sense because the frequency of service must be increased, effectively off-setting efficiencies gained by operating the interhub links. Further, these results reinforce the dominating role of several major transatlantic hubs (e.g. New York and London).

To provide one last snapshot of world city interaction, Table 10.5 highlights the top 25 interacting pairs of cities on the global air transport network. Not surprisingly, distance decay plays a major role, with high volume of interaction(s) displaying decidedly local characteristics. In fact, the top 11 interacting city pairs are domestic linkages (e.g. U.S. to U.S.).[12] The first significant interaction between international city pairs is Dublin and

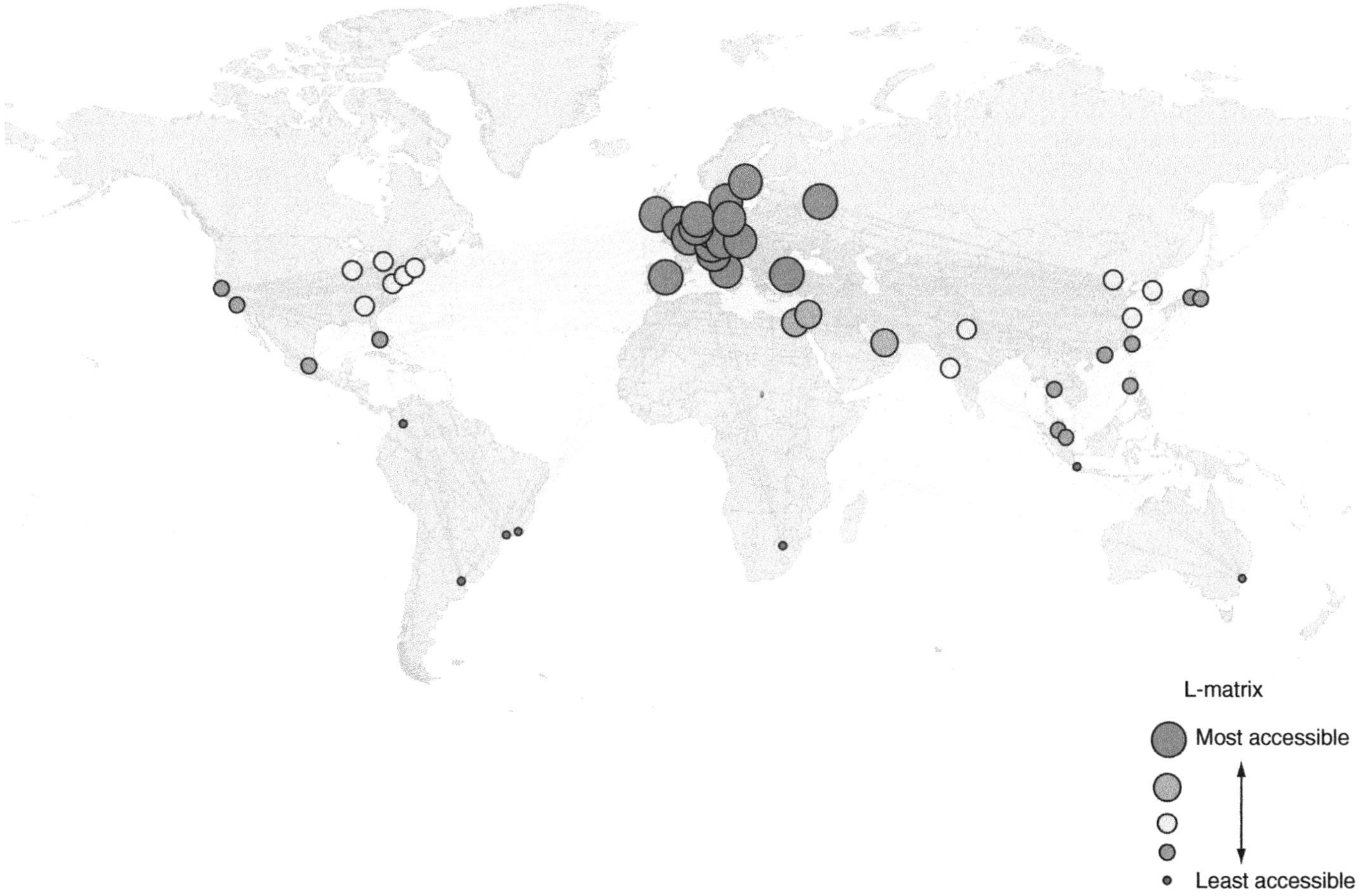

Figure 10.6   L-matrix: top 50 world cities network (2006)

Table 10.4   Average total flows for direct connections

Rank	City	Average flow	Rank	City	Average flow
1	Jakarta	47164.69	26	Bogota	14956.15
2	Johannesburg	42347.92	27	Milan	14193.26
3	Brussels	35767.08	28	Berlin	11731.96
4	Stockholm	35165.93	29	Boston	11241.46
5	Manila	34657.15	30	San Francisco	11015.49
6	London	34268.23	31	Osaka	10953.47
7	New York	34115.95	32	Chicago	10671.26
8	Cairo	30767.53	33	Amsterdam	9436.68
9	Seoul	29997.38	34	Dubai	9211.72
10	Sydney	28737.17	35	Frankfurt	8994.13
11	Shanghai	27224.06	36	Tel Aviv	8353.81
12	Singapore	27147.02	37	Kuala Lumpur	7506.94
13	Rio de Janeiro	26452.53	38	Rome	7155.99
14	Toronto	20714.84	39	Moscow	7064.44
15	Beijing	19739.43	40	Copenhagen	6746.77
16	Zurich	18379.54	41	Bangkok	6711.74
17	Washington D.C.	18288.80	42	Atlanta	6558.59
18	Vienna	17991.47	43	São Paulo	5948.46
19	Hong Kong	17315.58	44	New Delhi	5782.56
20	Bombay	17231.56	45	Istanbul	5719.38
21	Dublin	17214.18	46	Taipei	5453.51
22	Paris	16644.53	47	Munich	5264.32
23	Buenos Aires	16316.50	48	Tokyo	2961.58
24	Mexico City	15598.91	49	Madrid	2634.52
25	Los Angeles	15255.09	50	Miami	2375.89

London (12th), followed by New York and London (15th) and London and Amsterdam (16th) and several others.

DISCUSSION AND CONCLUSION

There are several elements of the empirical results worth further discussion. First, the results of this analysis are limited to the top 50 world cities as a peer group. As noted previously, it is possible that a dramatically different landscape of connectivity and accessibility could emerge if all global airports, cities and/or their hinterlands were included in the analysis. Likewise, if a different distance threshold (e.g. 100 miles) was used for aggregating world city airports and their respective hinterlands, some differences might be evident. For example, Grubesic et al. (2009) highlight the hierarchical structure of major world airports and their hinterlands using a global database of airports and airline schedules – noting significant spatial and temporal dynamism between locales. That said, previous work in this field suggests that the interrelationships between world cities are of the most significance, because they are the primary facilitators for the transnational flow of goods, services, people and ideas (Friedmann, 1986; Keeling, 1995; Knox and Taylor,

Table 10.5   Top interacting world city pairs

Rank	City	City
1	Los Angeles	San Francisco
2	New York	Miami
3	Rio de Janeiro	São Paulo
4	Taipei	Hong Kong
5	New York	Chicago
6	Beijing	Shanghai
7	Washington	Boston
8	New York	Washington
9	New York	Atlanta
10	New York	Boston
11	Miami	Atlanta
12	London	Dublin
13	Milan	Rome
14	Chicago	Washington
15	New York	London
16	London	Amsterdam
17	Washington	Atlanta
18	New York	Los Angeles
19	Shanghai	Hong Kong
20	Tokyo	Seoul
21	New Delhi	Calcutta
22	Los Angeles	Chicago
23	Bangkok	Hong Kong
24	Tokyo	Osaka
25	Singapore	Bangkok

1995). Therefore, while this study is limited to the top 50 world cities with country-specific hinterlands that do not exceed 70 miles, it is likely that this subset accounts for the vast majority of high-level global economic interaction.

A second aspect of the results worth mentioning is associated with data limitations inherent in our analysis. One of the problems with using airline schedule data is that we have no information regarding actual origin/destination information for booked itineraries (Derudder and Witlox, 2005a; Derudder et al., 2008; Grubesic et al., 2009). As a result, SPW data represent the individual legs of trips, rather than complete trips from booked itineraries. The MIDT database used in other studies can circumvent this limitation (Derudder et al., 2007a; Taylor et al., 2007); however, it comprises a relatively limited temporal snapshot of global itineraries (~six months). Therefore, although we cannot say with certainty that network measures capture the true levels of interaction between world cities, there is no doubt that these metrics deepen our ability to reason about the interrelationships between cities and their hinterlands as supported by the global air transport network.

Where the empirical results presented in this chapter are concerned, it is clear that the continental European cities (Paris, Frankfurt, Amsterdam, etc.) display the highest level of accessibility and interconnection within the top 50 world city network. This is not to say, however, that London, New York and Tokyo, the traditional strong-holds for economic, political and cultural activities, are unimportant. All three cities remain critical nodes in the global air transport network, each accommodating millions of passengers each year. However, given the somewhat peripheral locations of New York and Tokyo, relative to the continental European cluster, geography does impact their overall status in the world city network. Similarly, our results indicate that much of the world city interaction facilitated by the air transport network is local in nature, with domestic city-pairs displaying the highest levels of scheduled seating capacity.

In sum, the global airline network is an important component to better understanding the levels of interconnectivity between world cities. However, it is far from the only one. Further, while there are challenges associated with airline data, they still provide one of the more tangible manifestations of relationships between urban agglomerations. Therefore, the ability to identify and describe the dynamics of these networks will be essential in the assessment of how changes to policy (e.g. Open Skies) and organizational structure (e.g. airline mergers) might affect the relationships among world cities. As the global economy continues to evolve, there is little doubt that airlines and their networks will adapt to embrace globalization, the emergence of new world cities and the related dynamics associated with rising or declining demand for air transport service.

NOTES

1. For a recent review of the impacts of liberalization in the airline industry, see the special issue of *Journal of Transport Geography* edited by Bowen (2009).
2. As noted by Doganis (2006, p. 294), 'break of gauge is used in air service agreements to allow an airline that has traffic rights from its own country (a) to country (b), and then Fifth Freedom rights to country (c), to operate one type of aircraft from a to b, and then a different type (usually smaller) from b to c and beyond'.
3. As of the writing of this chapter, the United States and Japan were in the process of negotiating an Open Skies agreement (Kralev, 2010).
4. Cabotage rights allow foreign carriers to operate within the domestic borders of another country without a takeoff or landing in their home country.
5. This is not the case in Europe and the ECAA. In addition, Singapore and the United Kingdom recently agreed to unlimited Seventh Freedom rights (Jomini et al., 2009).
6. These five dimensions include: 1) Business activity; 2) Human capital; 3) Information exchange; 4) Cultural experience; and 5) Political engagement. For more details on the specifics associated with these dimensions, see www.foreignpolicy.com/articles/2008/10/15/the_2008_global_cities_index (accessed 30 July 2010).
7. As noted by Derudder and Witlox (2005a), airport codes often include train and bus stations, particularly when there are direct connections between airports and major regional rail or bus services. For example, while the Brussels International Airport (BRU) maintains a short-haul air transport connection with Paris-Charles de Gaulle Airport (CDG), Air France provides a high-speed train between Brussels and CDG, allowing passengers to 'board' in Belgium.
8. While it is not impossible to live in Windsor and travel out of Detroit, or vice versa, crossing the U.S. and Canada border is time consuming and subject to delays (OCC, 2004), potentially requiring vehicle inspections and the display of a valid passport.
9. These data do not contain unique Origin–Destination segments for individual passenger itineraries.
10. To be clear, this metric represents the average scheduled seats per week for all four quarters (2006), summed between the top 50 world cities. It is likely that the final totals for each origin and destination deviate slightly from these calculated averages. More importantly, this metric does *not* represent the number of passengers enplaned or deplaned at world cities or their hinterland airports.

11. In effect, this is the diameter of the network (Grubesic et al., 2008b).
12. Although the political status of Taiwan as an independent country is the subject of some debate, we view the Taipei to Hong Kong linkage as a domestic interaction.

REFERENCES

Alderighi, M., A. Cento, P. Nijkamp and P. Rietveld (2005), 'Network competition – the coexistence of hub-and-spoke and point-to-point systems', *Journal of Air Transport Management*, **11** (5), 328–334.
Alderighi, M., A. Cento, P. Nijkamp and P. Rietveld (2007), 'Assessment of new hub-and-spoke and point-to-point airline network configurations', *Transport Reviews*, **27** (5), 529–549.
A.T. Kearney (2008), 'Global Cities Index', available at www.atkearney.com/index.php/Publications/global-cities-index.html (accessed 30 July 2010).
Bania, N., P.W. Bauer and T.J. Zlatoper (1998), 'U.S. air passenger service: a taxonomy of route networks, hub locations and competition', *Transportation Research E*, **34** (1), 53–74.
Bowen, J. (2000), 'Airline hubs in Southeast Asia: national economic development and nodal accessibility', *Journal of Transport Geography*, **8** (1), 25–41.
BTS (Bureau of Transportation Statistics) (2009), 'Airlines and airports', available at http://www.bts.gov/programs/airline_information/ (accessed 30 July 2010).
Burghouwt, G. and J. Hakfoort (2001), 'The evolution of the European aviation network, 1990–1998', *Journal of Air Transport Management*, **7** (5), 311–318.
Burghouwt, G., J. Hakfoort and J. Ritsema van Eck (2003), 'The spatial configuration of airline networks in Europe', *Journal of Air Transport Management*, **9** (5), 309–323.
Burghouwt, G. and R. Redondi (2009), 'Connectivity in air transport networks: models, measures and applications', Working paper no. 1/09, Department of Economics and Technology Management, University of Bergamo, Italy.
Chou, Y.-H. (1993), 'Airline deregulation and nodal accessibility', *Journal of Transport Geography*, **1** (1), 36–46.
Debbage, K.G. and D. Delk (2001), 'The geography of air passenger volume and local employment patterns by US metropolitan core area: 1973–1996', *Journal of Air Transport Management*, **7** (3), 159–167.
DeNavas-Wale, C., B.D. Proctor and R.J. Mills (2004), 'Income, poverty and health insurance coverage in the United States: 2003', available at http://www.census.gov/prod/2004pubs/p60-226.pdf (accessed 30 July 2010).
Derudder, B. (2006), 'On conceptual confusion in empirical analyses of a transnational urban network', *Urban Studies*, **43** (11), 2027–2046.
Derudder, B., L. Devriendt and F. Witlox (2007a), 'Flying where you don't want to go: an empirical analysis of hubs in the global airline network', *Tijdschrift voor Economische en Sociale Geografie*, **98** (3), 307–324.
Derudder, B., P.J. Taylor, P. Ni, A. De Vos, M. Hoyler, H. Hanssens, D. Bassens, J. Huang, F. Witlox, W. Shen and X. Yang (2010), 'Pathways of change: shifting connectivities in the world city network 2000–08', *Urban Studies*, **47** (9), 1861–1877.
Derudder, B. and F. Witlox (2005a), 'An appraisal of the use of airline data in assessing the world city network: a research note on data', *Urban Studies*, **42** (13), 2371–2388.
Derudder, B. and F. Witlox (2005b), 'On the use of inadequate airline data in mappings of a global urban system', *Journal of Air Transport Management*, **11** (4), 231–237.
Derudder, B., F. Witlox, J. Faulconbridge and J. Beaverstock (2008), 'Airline data for global city network research: reviewing and refining existing approaches', *GeoJournal*, **71** (1), 5–18.
Derudder, B., F. Witlox and P.J. Taylor (2007b), 'U.S. cities in the world city network: comparing their positions using global origins and destinations of airline passengers', *Urban Geography*, **28** (1), 74–91.
Doganis, R. (2006), *The Airline Business*, London: Routledge.
Doganis, R. and N. Dennis (1989), 'Lessons in hubbing', *Airline Business*, March, 42–47.
Friedmann, J. (1986), 'The world city hypothesis', *Development and Change*, **17** (1), 69–83.
GaWC (Globalization and World Cities Research Network) (2010), available at www.lboro.ac.uk/gawc (accessed 30 July 2010).
Goetz, A.R. and C.J. Sutton (1997), 'The geography of deregulation in the US airline industry', *Annals of the Association of American Geographers*, **87** (2), 238–263.
Goetz, A.R. and T.M. Vowles (2009), 'The good, the bad and the ugly: 30 years of US airline deregulation', *Journal of Transport Geography*, **17** (4), 251–263.
Graham, S. and S. Marvin (1996), *Telecommunications and the City*, London: Routledge.

Grubesic, T.H. (2010), 'Spatial variations in broadband and air passenger service provision in the United States', *GeoJournal*, **75** (1), 57–77.

Grubesic, T.H., T.C. Matisziw, A.T. Murray and D. Snedicker (2008b), 'Comparative approaches for assessing network vulnerability', *International Regional Science Review*, **31** (1), 88–112.

Grubesic, T.H., T.C. Matisziw and M.A. Zook (2008a), 'Global airline networks and nodal regions', *GeoJournal*, **71** (1), 53–66.

Grubesic, T.H., T.C. Matisziw and M.A. Zook (2009), 'Spatio-temporal fluctuations in global airport hierarchies', *Journal of Transport Geography*, **17** (4), 264–275.

Guimerà, R., S. Mossa, A. Turtschi and L.A.N. Amaral (2005), 'The worldwide air transportation network: anomalous centrality, community structure, and cities' global roles', *Proceedings of the National Academy of Sciences*, **102** (22), 7794–7799.

Hanlon, P. (2007), *Global Airlines*, Oxford: Butterworth-Heinemann/Elsevier.

IATA (International Air Transport Association) (2007), Schedule Reference Service, available at http://www.iata.org/ps/publications/srs/Pages/products.aspx (accessed 30 July 2010).

Jomini, P., A. Chai, P. Achard and J. Rupp (2009), 'The changing landscape of air service agreements', available at www.gem.sciences-po.fr/. . ./Jomini_evolution_of_ASAs_062009.pdf (accessed 30 July 2010).

Keeling, D.J. (1995), 'Transport and the world city paradigm', in P.L. Knox and P.J. Taylor (eds), *World Cities in a World System*, Cambridge: Cambridge University Press, pp. 115–131.

Knox, P.L. and P.J. Taylor (eds) (1995), *World Cities in a World-System*, Cambridge: Cambridge University Press.

Kralev, N. (2010), 'When "open skies" are not really open', available at www.washingtontimes.com/news/2010/feb/22/kralev-when-open-skies-are-not-really-open/ (accessed 30 July 2010).

Malecki, E.J. and H. Wei (2009), 'A wired world: the evolving geography of submarine cables and the shift to Asia', *Annals of the Association of American Geographers*, **99** (2), 360–382.

Malighetti, G., G. Martini, S. Paleari and R. Redondi (2009), 'The impacts of airport centrality in the EU network and inter-airport competition on airport efficiency', available at http://mpra.ub.uni-muenchen.de/17673/ (accessed 30 July 2010).

Malighetti, P., S. Paleari and R. Redondi (2008), 'A comparative study of airport connectivity in China, Europe and US: which network provides the best service to passengers?', *ATRS Conference*, 6–10 July, Athens.

Matisziw, T.C. and T.H. Grubesic (2010), 'Evaluating locational accessibility to the US air transportation system', *Transportation Research Part A: Policy and Practice*, **44** (9), 710–722.

OCC (Ontario Chamber of Commerce) (2004), 'Cost of border delays to Ontario', available at http://tinyurl.com/23bwssa (accessed 30 July 2010).

O'Kelly, M.E. (1998), 'A geographer's analysis of hub-and-spoke networks', *Journal of Transport Geography*, **6** (3), 171–186.

O'Kelly, M.E. and H.J. Miller (1994), 'The hub network design problem: a review and synthesis', *Journal of Transport Geography*, **2** (1), 31–40.

Overbye, T.J. and J.D. Weber (2000), 'New methods for the visualization of electric power system information', *Proceedings of the IEEE Symposium on Information Visualization*, Washington, DC: IEEE Computer Society, pp. 131–136.

Parsons, J.J. (1950), 'The geography of natural gas in the United States', *Economic Geography*, **26** (3), 162–178.

Reed, W.E. (1970), 'Indirect connectivity and hierarchies of urban dominance', *Annals of the Association of American Geographers*, **60** (4), 770–785.

Sadri, H.A. and A.Y. Volkov (2004), 'The Russian pipeline system: between globalization and localization', *Eastern European Quarterly*, **38** (3), 383–393.

Shaw, S.-L. (1993), 'Hub structures of major U.S. passenger airlines', *Journal of Transport Geography*, **1** (1), 47–58.

Shaw, S.-L. and R.L. Ivy (1994), 'Airline mergers and their effect on network structure', *Journal of Transport Geography*, **2** (4), 234–246.

Shimbel, A. (1953), 'Structural parameters of communication networks', *Bulletin of Mathematical Biophysics*, **15** (4), 501–507.

Short, J.R. and Y.H. Kim (1999), *Globalization and the City*, New York: Prentice Hall.

Smith, D.A. and M. Timberlake (1995), 'Conceptualising and mapping the structure of the world system's city system', *Urban Studies*, **32** (2), 287–302.

Smith, D.A. and M.F. Timberlake (2001), 'World city networks and hierarchies, 1979–1999: an empirical analysis of global air travel links', *American Behavioral Scientist*, **44** (10), 1656–1678.

Taaffe, E.J., H.L. Gauthier and M.E. O'Kelly (1996), *Geography of Transportation*, New York: Prentice Hall, 2nd edition.

Taylor, P.J. (2005), 'Leading world cities: empirical evaluations of urban nodes in multiple networks', *Urban Studies*, **42** (9), 1593–1608.

Taylor, P.J., B. Derudder and F. Witlox (2007), 'Comparing airline passenger destinations with global service connectivities: a worldwide empirical study of 214 cities', *Urban Geography*, **28** (3), 232–248.
Townsend, A. (2001), 'The internet and the rise of the new networked city, 1969–1999', *Environment and Planning B*, **28** (1), 39–58.
Zook, M.A. and S.D. Brunn (2006), 'From podes to antipodes: positionalities and global airline geographies', *Annals of the Association of American Geographers*, **96** (3), 471–490.

11 Internet networks of world cities: agglomeration and dispersion

Edward J. Malecki

INTRODUCTION

The Internet has become an essential part of the lives and activities of businesses, governments and individual users, who have come to depend on the ready, 24/7 availability of their data and programs. These users are scattered and clustered throughout the world, and to make the programs and files of the Internet always 'there' requires systems and infrastructures whose locations have a material geography (Graham, 2004).

'Far from destroying cities by making place irrelevant, the production and consumption of Internet content, and the infrastructure to support it, are concentrated in cities' (Goldsmith and Wu, 2006, p. 56). Some cities attract greater concentrations of investment and can be identified as *world cities of Internet activity*. Internet infrastructure is concentrated not only in world cities but also in 'new network cities' (Derudder, 2008; Townsend, 2001a). Although the big players in the global Internet infrastructure are giant firms, they fall outside the sectors of advanced producer services on which research has focused (Taylor, 2004; Taylor and Aranya, 2008; Taylor et al., 2009).

As a result, Internet activity in world cities has received relatively little research attention. A prominent exception is the work of Choi et al. (2006), who compare world city networks as defined by Internet backbones and air transport. Research generally has followed the lead of Graham (1999), who describes the attraction of world cities – and their concentrations of transnational corporations and financial service firms – to providers of telecommunications infrastructure. Lack of comprehensive data on actual Internet traffic between cities, however, prevents analysis of flows or relations (Taylor, 2004). Notwithstanding the lack of ideal data, the global hubs of the Internet have been identified by Internet backbone capacity (Townsend, 2001b), number of Internet domain names (Zook, 2001; Sternberg and Krymalowski, 2002) and Internet exchange points (IXPs) (Malecki, 2002; Devriendt et al., 2010).

This chapter reviews what we know about world cities from the perspective of the Internet. In doing so, it focuses on two types of infrastructure identified by Moss and Townsend (2004): the information warehouses (data centers or server farms) and information ports or interconnection points. The chapter proceeds as follows. The following section defines and describes Internet infrastructure and its material geography, particularly in the context of new phenomena such as content distribution and cloud computing. The next section then describes the geography of data centers, which face centripetal forces toward agglomeration and centrifugal forces leading to dispersion. The chapter then identifies the world cities of the Internet, based primarily on IXPs. It concludes with some observations for future research.

INTERNET INFRASTRUCTURE AND ITS MATERIAL GEOGRAPHY

Greenstein (2005, pp. 291–292) defines Internet infrastructure as the capital equipment of large and small users, wireless devices and networks for data transmission, and human capital, a key (often local) input for Internet services. Much of this infrastructure is invisible, buried underground or in tiny devices. Some, however, is massive, attracting the attention of politicians and of local economic developers.

The Internet's links have been the focus of research on network accessibility and bandwidth availability. Identification of a hierarchy of nodes on these links is also common (Wheeler and O'Kelly, 1999; Moss and Townsend, 2000; Malecki and Gorman, 2001; O'Kelly and Grubesic, 2002). Investment in fiber-optic links is attracted not only to large urban markets but also to knowledge centers, such as universities and research institutions (Malecki, 2004; Tranos and Gillespie, 2009).

After the Internet was commercialized, the points of production and consumption became dominant. Notable urban hubs include New York in finance and information, and Los Angeles for the media industry (Kellerman, 2002). In Europe, Munich, Berlin, London and Paris are important media cities (Krätke and Taylor, 2004). Moss and Townsend (2000) note, however, that the three largest urban areas in the US – New York, Los Angeles and Chicago – have less backbone capacity than the San Francisco Bay and Washington areas. These 'new network cities' (Townsend, 2001a) in the US contrast with the urban network in Europe, where bandwidth is concentrated in capital cities and traditional economic centers (Rutherford et al., 2004).

Major centers of production contain agglomerations of data centers or information warehouses (Moss and Townsend, 2004). Data centers housing banks of servers have grown from a disorganized industry of web hosting by local Internet service providers (ISPs) to an industry in which 'cloud computing' utilizes machines in large data centers. In the Web 2.0 world, individual users are both producers (of blogs, videos and web sites) and consumers of Web information. Photos and video place big demands on bandwidth and storage; others, such as blogs and tweets, are small users. Thus the geography of Internet production has begun to disperse and resemble the geography of Internet consumption. Finally, cloud computing is also central to the cyberinfrastructure of geospatial science (Yang et al., 2010).

The 'New Internet'

A 'new Internet' has emerged since 2007, replacing the long-standing 'textbook Internet', with its stable tiers of national backbone operators and regional and local access providers. In the new Internet, traffic is dominated by a small number of large content networks, such as Google, and large cable networks with high levels of video traffic. Both content providers and content distribution networks (CDNs) are increasingly independent of the backbone networks (Labovitz et al., 2009). Content networks and CDNs connect through IXPs directly to regional and tier 2 providers, leading to 'the growing complexity of Internet connection' (Faratin et al., 2008).

Content distribution

CDNs arose in the 1990s to address the problem of users in many places seeking to access the same files simultaneously (Pathan et al., 2008). Akamai, founded in 1998, was a pioneer of content distribution. Akamai remains the market leader, with customers such as Amazon, Apple, CNN and Reuters, accounting for 85 per cent of the CDN market in 2008 and 20 per cent of total Internet traffic (Pathan et al., 2008). Competitors have emerged, largely to distribute video. CDNs 'now make up a critical and central part of the Internet infrastructure' (Huang et al., 2008, p. 1).

Cloud computing

As it has become common to access content from the Internet without concern for the underlying infrastructure, data centers must be maintained and monitored around the clock by content providers. Cloud computing extends this concept beyond storage to business applications, computational resources and services that can be accessed over a network (Buyya et al., 2009; Jaeger et al., 2009).

Like the 'mirror sites' of Akamai and others in the early Internet, data centers in many locations allow content to be located near large numbers of users to minimize latency, or transmission delay. The geography of data centers has assumed far greater importance now that remote storage – of photographs, blogs and other user data – is added to corporate storage and cloud computing on 'virtual machines'. Outages affect greater numbers of people in their personal lives. For example, Facebook stores 80 billion user photos.

THE GEOGRAPHY OF DATA CENTERS AND INTERCONNECTION

Companies such as Google not only own dozens of large data centers, but also lease physical or virtual space in others. That is, colocation firms provide buildings and seek tenants; some firms prefer to construct their own buildings. The geography of the Internet increasingly is the geography of data centers and of interconnection. Whereas IXPs mainly agglomerate, data centers tend both to agglomerate (for interconnection) and to disperse (to seek lower costs).

Demand for data centers is expected to grow faster than capacity. Several firms already have large numbers of servers: Microsoft has approximately 450,000 servers and Google as many as 1 million, and is designing a system for 10 million servers. The geography of data centers is not standardized; many firms and organizations are consolidating their data centers to fewer sites, others continue to add new ones. Companies such as Cisco Systems and IBM provide advice as well as the hardware for data centers.

Data Center Agglomeration

The infrastructure of the Internet evolved from university-based networks. The need for skilled labor led to an attraction to the thick labor markets for specialized engineering talent and supporting services. As the commercial Internet grew, the human capital needed and the likely demand of businesses cemented the attraction of large urban areas (Greenstein, 2005).

At first glance, the spatial distribution of data centers appears to mirror the 'hubs' of the Internet, where bandwidth is most abundant. Accessibility and potential interconnection remain critical, resulting in the 'concentration of strategic resources in giant metropolitan areas' (Graham, 2004, p. 141).

Deglomeration and Dispersion

Both natural and political hazards, such as power shortages and terrorist attacks, have demonstrated the need for data storage facilities in multiple locations (Moriset, 2003). An important trend is data center consolidation to pairs of centers, which means that data are continually backed up in the second facility. Adding a third, remote data center protects against a 'regional' failure, such as a hurricane, that could affect two nearby facilities in the same region. Connection not only to multiple networks, but also to multiple IXPs in separate locations, further reduces risk of failure (Savageau, 2009).

Responding to suggestions that data be backed up in a separate facility, quasi-dispersion has emerged as backup facilities locate in, for example, New Jersey, in an attempt to reduce clustering in Manhattan (Townsend, 2004). Quasi-dispersion provides no resilience against 'regional' events. Dispersion is also limited by the growing priority that data centers have redundant links. The most remote places have few Internet providers, but only two are needed to qualify as redundant.

Risk avoidance and power costs contribute to a new trend: data centers are now being built outside major cities, in remote places, often tapping hydroelectric power. Internet accessibility and adequate bandwidth are no longer in short supply in most places, and this ubiquity renders most actors much more footloose in their location decisions. The cost of cooling equipment is notorious, and can be solved by investing in newer, cooler-running servers or by locating in low-temperature environments which offer free cooling (such as Iceland) and locations with low-cost, hydroelectric energy. As with any mobile investment, governments offer tax breaks and subsidies to attract data centers.

IXPs Public and Private

The Internet's interconnection nodes, IXPs, were once few and far between, and were commonly called network access points (NAPs). However, the number of IXPs has increased substantially (Paltridge, 2006). The largest of these are in Europe; European IXPs comprise 7 of the top 12, and 17 of the top 30, worldwide. Asia is represented in the top 30 only by Hong Kong and Singapore. The number of IXP participants largely mirrors the degree of competition: greater competition spawns a larger number of ISPs that must interconnect.

IXPs are places where interconnection or 'peering' of Internet networks takes place. Most IXPs are large and public, where large and small networks join the Internet. Because the largest IXPs are so large – AMS-IX in Amsterdam, LINX in London and DE-CIX in Frankfurt have over 400 participants – congestion and delay have long been problems. For large firms, the solution has been private peering.

As a result, many IXPs offer both public peering and private peering within their facilities. Some were created to provide both peering and colocation space where content can be distributed throughout the Internet. Less is known about private peering points because they typically are not counted as IXPs (Paltridge, 2006).

The agglomeration of IXPs reflects economies of scale in data interchange and additional economies of scale at public interchange points: all parties benefit more if more of them interconnect at the same location (Greenstein, 2005). Consequently, the number and size of colocation facilities near IXPs continue to increase.

WORLD CITIES OF THE INTERNET

Having set the context for the material geography of the Internet, what does that geography look like? Bandwidth and customers attract networks and firms to large urban areas, as does the presence of IXPs, on which this section focuses.

Using the data of the European Internet Exchange Association (Euro-IX), Devriendt et al. (2008) find that Amsterdam, London and Frankfurt are clearly the top digital cities in Europe. The same result ensues from the global PeeringDB dataset, in which over one-quarter of 1558 networks are content networks. Table 11.1 shows the top-ranked world cities according to number of private peering facilities. San Francisco and London, followed by New York, Amsterdam and Frankfurt, are the only cities with 20 or more facilities. Paris and Los Angeles also join the top ranks, with over a dozen private Internet exchanges.

A similar ranking appears for public Internet exchanges (Table 11.2), with an important difference: European cities rank higher in public exchanges, whereas US cities have larger numbers of private exchanges. This corresponds to a distinction identified by Norton (2009), who notes that in the US IXPs tend to be owned by the colocation facility, whereas in Europe IXPs are separate from the facility. Thus, IXPs

Table 11.1   World cities of the Internet: number of private Internet exchanges

Urban area	Number of facilities
San Francisco	34
London	33
New York	26
Amsterdam	22
Frankfurt	20
Paris	17
Los Angeles	13
Berlin, Prague	10
Atlanta, Brussels, Stockholm	8
Chicago, Düsseldorf, Manchester, Miami, Milan, Zurich	7
Copenhagen, Dallas, Dublin, Kiev, Madrid, Nuremberg, Tokyo, Toronto, Washington	6
Jakarta, Moscow, Seattle, Singapore, Sydney	5

Source: calculated from PeeringDB Facilities List: https://www.peeringdb.com/private/facility_list.php (date of access 17 September 2009)

Table 11.2   World cities of the Internet: number of public Internet exchanges

City/urban region	Number of exchanges	Total participants
London	8	906
Amsterdam	2	598
Frankfurt	3	535
Paris	9	381
Los Angeles	4	330
New York	8	321
San Francisco	6	282
Seattle	2	192
Ashburn, VA (Washington)	2	183
Stockholm	3	163
Chicago	4	127
Tokyo	6	117

Source: calculated from PeeringDB List of Public Exchange Points: https://www.peeringdb.com/private/
exchange_list.php (date of access 17 September 2009)

in Europe are meshed across several different sites, a situation much less common in the US. Consequently, multisite IXPs tend to have larger numbers of participant networks.

As noted above, private peering is increasingly common. Globally, of 9504 peering connections of 1478 networks in the PeeringDB database, 51 per cent are private peering. In other words, although most networks must be present in the large public peering facilities, and small networks must interconnect with them there as well, it is in the private facilities through which one-half of Internet traffic passes, including that of the largest networks.

Examining in detail 23 large networks, which include the new content giants (such as Akamai, Google and Limelight) in addition to traditional tier 1 networks, a pattern emerges that is consistent with the rankings of peering facilities. The peering locations of these networks (Table 11.3) show the top world cities (urban areas) where the Internet exchanges and colocation facilities used by these firms are located. Nearly all of the networks connect in four locations: London, Amsterdam, Frankfurt and San Francisco. Hong Kong matches Tokyo within Asia, with Singapore and Sydney close behind. Finally, São Paulo emerges as the best-linked location in Latin America, still far behind Miami, where the NAP of the Americas (NOTA) continues to function as the hub for Central and South America.

This hierarchy demonstrates the largely transatlantic nature of the Internet. All top-ranked Internet world cities are in Europe or the US. The highest-ranked Asian cities, Hong Kong and Tokyo, rank no higher than 12th by any of the measures in this chapter. After a decade, the Internet world cities identified by Townsend (2001b) and Zook (2001) remain preeminent.

Table 11.3   World cities of the Internet: according to interconnections of 23 networks

Urban area	(Maximum = 23)
London	21
Amsterdam	20
Frankfurt	19
San Francisco	18
Miami, New York, Washington	15
Chicago	13
Los Angeles	12
Dallas	11
Seattle	10
Hong Kong, Paris, Tokyo	9
Milan, Singapore, Stockholm	8
Atlanta, Madrid, Sydney	7
Dublin, Munich, Zurich	6
Toronto	5
Brussels, Geneva, Hamburg, Lisbon, Prague, São Paulo	4

Note: A total of 57 cities are interconnection points for 23 major content and backbone networks. The 31 cities in the table have 4 or more networks interconnecting.

Source: PeeringDB data as of 17 September 2009

CONCLUSIONS AND FUTURE RESEARCH

The empirical findings of this chapter confirm the stability of the top ranks of the Internet world city network. However, a rather different set of cities emerges from the 'big six' identified by Taylor and Aranya (2008), based on the corporate networks of firms in producer services. London and New York are the only cities found at the top in both lists. Amsterdam and Frankfurt are more important in the Internet than in producer services. San Francisco is more prominent than New York, and Miami and Washington are just behind – and ahead of the Asian leaders (Tokyo, Hong Kong and Singapore).

Thus, several years on, we still find notably lower positions of Asian cities in the Internet network, as Choi et al. (2006) found. They suggest that such cities as Tokyo, Taipei, Sydney, Singapore, Beijing and Seoul 'remain heavily dependent on pre-existing thick connections to Los Angeles and San Francisco' (Choi et al., 2006, p. 95). This is likely a result of the dominance of US firms – notably Google, Microsoft and Apple – in cloud computing (*The Economist*, 2009), despite new high-bandwidth connections across the Pacific (Malecki and Wei, 2009).

Future research will need to dig into the increasingly complex world of Internet interconnection. Further, it must look beyond traditional backbone networks to include the new content networks that are responsible for a growing share of Internet traffic. A limitation is the fact that we have no comprehensive data on Internet flows or of interconnection – the relations that would define a world city network. The decentralized nature of the Internet means multiple routes through multiple nodes. However, many of those routes and new networks depend largely on the same few places for their interconnection to the Internet. Agglomeration of activity through the Internet takes place in most of the same world cities as producer services (Taylor, 2004).

A second limitation that future research can address is that lists of IXPs tend to ignore the increasingly massive private data centers that are remote from current clusters as well as those that lease space in colocation facilities. Google, for example, does both. Corporate and government data centers – small, large and mega in size – need to be near IXPs to connect with the major Internet backbones.

Thirdly, research will have to monitor the inevitable rise in importance of Asian cities, as new submarine cables continue to connect the large cities of that region to the global Internet. Finally, further research is needed to distinguish between the various types of network, which now are far more diverse than the simple tiers of national, regional and local providers of the early Internet.

ACKNOWLEDGEMENTS

An earlier version of this chapter was presented at the 56th Annual North American Meetings of the Regional Science Association International, San Francisco, November 2009. Comments from Mat Coleman, Michael Ewers, Jun Koo and Frank Witlox are appreciated.

REFERENCES

Buyya, R., C.S. Yeo, S. Venugopal, J. Broberg and I. Brandic (2009), 'Cloud computing and emerging IT platforms: vision, hype, and reality for delivering computing as the 5th utility', *Future Generation Computer Systems*, **25** (6), 599–616.
Choi, J.H., G.A. Barnett and B.-S. Chon (2006), 'Comparing world city networks: a network analysis of Internet backbone and air transport intercity linkages', *Global Networks*, **6** (1), 81–99.
Derudder, B. (2008), 'Mapping global urban networks: a decade of empirical world cities research', *Geography Compass*, **2** (2), 559–574.
Devriendt, L., B. Derudder and F. Witlox (2008), 'Cyberplace and cyberspace: two approaches to analyzing digital intercity linkages', *Journal of Urban Technology*, **15** (2), 5–32.
Devriendt, L., B. Derudder and F. Witlox (2010), 'Conceptualizing digital and physical connectivity: the position of European cities in Internet backbone and air traffic flows', *Telecommunications Policy*, **34** (8), 417–429.
Faratin, P., D. Clark, S. Bauer, W. Lehr, P. Gilmore and A. Berger (2008), 'The growing complexity of Internet interconnection', *Communications and Strategies*, **72** (4), 51–71.
Goldsmith, J. and T. Wu (2006), *Who Controls the Internet? Illusions of a Borderless World*, Oxford: Oxford University Press.
Graham, S. (1999), 'Global grids of glass: on global cities, telecommunications and planetary urban networks', *Urban Studies*, **36** (5–6), 929–949.
Graham, S. (2004), 'Excavating the material geographies of cybercities', in S. Graham (ed.), *The Cybercities Reader*, London: Routledge, pp. 138–142.
Greenstein, S. (2005), 'The economic geography of Internet infrastructure in the United States', in M. Cave, S. Majumdar and I. Vogelsang (eds), *Handbook of Telecommunications Economics, Vol. 2: Technology Evolution and the Internet*, Amsterdam: Elsevier, pp. 289–373.
Huang, C., A. Wang, J. Li and K.W. Ross (2008), 'Measuring and evaluating large-scale CDNs', paper presented at IMC08, Vouliagmeni, Greece, October.
Jaeger, P.T., J. Lin, J.M. Grimes and S.N. Simmons (2009), 'Where is the cloud? Geography, economics,

environment, and jurisdiction in cloud computing', *First Monday*, **14** (5), 4 May, available at http://firstmonday.org/htbin/cgiwrap/bin/ojs/index.php/fm/article/view/2456/2171 (date of access 5 July 2011).

Kellerman, A. (2002), *The Internet on Earth: A Geography of Information*, Chichester: John Wiley.

Krätke, S. and P.J. Taylor (2004), 'A world geography of global media cities', *European Planning Studies*, **12** (4), 459–477.

Labovitz, J., S. Iekel-Johnson, D. McPherson, J. Oberheide, F. Jahanian and M. Karir (2009), 'ATLAS Internet Observatory 2009 Annual Report', presentation at NANOG 47, Dearborn, MI, October.

Malecki, E.J. (2002), 'The economic geography of the Internet's infrastructure', *Economic Geography*, **78** (4), 399–424.

Malecki, E.J. (2004), 'Fibre tracks: explaining investment in fibre optic backbones', *Entrepreneurship and Regional Development*, **16** (1), 21–39.

Malecki, E.J. and S.P. Gorman (2001), 'Maybe the death of distance, but not the end of geography: the Internet as a network', in T.R. Leinbach and S.D. Brunn (eds), *Worlds of Electronic Commerce: Economic, Geographical and Social Dimensions*, New York: John Wiley, pp. 87–105.

Malecki, E.J. and H. Wei (2009), 'A wired world: the evolving geography of submarine cables and the shift to Asia', *Annals of the Association of American Geographers*, **99** (2), 360–382.

Moriset, B. (2003), 'Les forteresses de l'économie numérique. Des immeubles intelligents aux hôtels de télécommunications', *Géocarrefour*, **78** (4), 375–388.

Moss, M.L. and A.M. Townsend (2000), 'The Internet backbone and the American metropolis', *The Information Society*, **16** (1), 35–47.

Moss, M.L. and A.M. Townsend (2004), 'Moving information in the twenty-first century', in R. Hanley (ed.), *Moving People, Goods, and Information in the 21st Century*, London: Routledge, pp. 63–75.

Norton, W.B. (2009), 'Peering 101', presentation at NANOG 45, Santo Domingo, Dominican Republic, January.

O'Kelly, M.E. and T.H. Grubesic (2002), 'Backbone topology, access, and the commercial Internet, 1997–2000', *Environment and Planning B: Planning and Design*, **29** (4), 533–552.

Paltridge, S. (2006), *Internet Traffic Exchange: Market Developments and Measurement of Growth*, Paris: Organization for Economic Co-operation and Development.

Pathan, M., R. Buyya and A. Vakali (2008), 'Content delivery networks: state of the art, insights, and imperatives', in R. Buyya, M. Pathan and A. Vakali (eds), *Content Delivery Networks* (Lecture Notes in Electrical Engineering Vol. 9), Berlin: Springer, pp. 3–32.

Rutherford, J., A. Gillespie and R. Richardson (2004), 'The territoriality of pan-European telecommunications backbone networks', *Journal of Urban Technology*, **11** (3), 1–34.

Savageau, J. (2009), 'Telecom risk and security part 2 – the carrier hotel supernode', *John Savageau's Technology Topics*, 12 October.

Sternberg, R. and M. Krymalowski (2002), 'Internet domains and the innovativeness of cities/regions – evidence from Germany and Munich', *European Planning Studies*, **10** (2), 251–273.

Taylor, P.J. (2004), *World City Network: A Global Urban Analysis*, London: Routledge.

Taylor, P.J. and R. Aranya (2008), 'A global "urban roller coaster"? Connectivity changes in the world city network, 2000–2004', *Regional Studies*, **42** (1), 1–16.

Taylor, P.J., P. Ni, B. Derudder, M. Hoyler, J. Huang, F. Lu, K. Pain, F. Witlox, X. Yang, D. Bassens and W. Shen (2009), 'Measuring the world city network: new developments and results', *GaWC Research Bulletin*, 300, available at www.lboro.ac.uk/gawc/rb/rb300.html (accessed 20 January 2010).

The Economist (2009), 'Briefing: cloud computing: clash of the clouds', 17 October, 80–82.

Townsend, A.M. (2001a), 'The Internet and the rise of the new network cities, 1969–1999', *Environment and Planning B: Planning and Design*, **28** (1), 39–58.

Townsend, A. (2001b), 'Network cities and the global structure of the Internet', *American Behavioral Scientist*, **44** (10), 1697–1716.

Townsend, A. (2004), 'Learning from September 11th: ICT infrastructure collapses in a "global" cybercity', in S. Graham (ed.), *The Cybercities Reader*, London: Routledge, pp. 143–148.

Tranos, E. and A. Gillespie (2009), 'The spatial distribution of Internet backbone networks in Europe: a metropolitan knowledge economy perspective', *European Urban and Regional Studies*, **16** (4), 423–437.

Wheeler, D.C. and M.E. O'Kelly (1999), 'Network topology and city accessibility of the commercial Internet', *The Professional Geographer*, **51** (3), 327–339.

Yang, C.W., R. Raskin, M. Goodchild and M. Gahegan (2010), 'Geospatial cyberinfrastructure: past, present and future', *Computers, Environment and Urban Systems*, **34** (4), 264–277.

Zook, M. (2001), 'Old hierarchies or new networks of centrality? The global geography of the Internet content market', *American Behavioral Scientist*, **44** (10), 1679–1696.

12 Corporate networks of world cities
Arthur S. Alderson and Jason Beckfield

Research on world cities has been defined by a simple idea, that relations *between* cities are important for what occurs *within* them (e.g. Friedmann, 1986; Sassen, 2001; Knox and Taylor, 1995). Typically situated in relation to the discourse on globalization, this research seeks to address the widespread sense that what happens 'here' is increasingly related to, and even dependent upon, what happens 'there' in the new global economy, polity and culture. Moreover, globalization is held to be fundamentally restructuring the global urban hierarchy, and thus altering the 'there' with which 'here' is linked. In contrast to the comparatively glacial pace at which major cities rose and fell in earlier human history, scholars such as John Friedmann have characterized the present era as one in which 'cities may rise into the ranks of world cities, they may drop from the order, and they may rise or fall in rank' in short order (Friedmann, 1995, p. 26). Thus the rise of Dubai and the decline of Detroit, to note but two dramatic examples, signal the emergence of a novel hierarchy of cities, one that may cut across long-standing North/South and East/West divides in the world system.

Approaching the world city system as a network, what is the *content* of the relation that links cities together within it? Our reading of the literature suggests that the network of world cities is best conceptualized as *multi-relational*, formed by analytically distinct networks in various domains. Ideally, then, in studying the world city system, one would seek to collect data on a range of relevant economic, political, social and cultural linkages between cities. Unfortunately, such data are exceedingly rare. As Taylor (2007) has argued, one consequence of the overriding focus of the social sciences on the nation-state is that there simply are no *intercity* analogues of the large international data sets that can be employed to link nation-states together in international flows.

This state of affairs has begun to change, perhaps decisively. While it may remain the case that 'unrelational' research – research that proceeds in ignorance of the 'connections, links, [and] flows' between cities – 'continues to dominate urban studies even within the world city literature' (Taylor, 2004, p. 2), in the last two decades a number of scholars have begun the painstaking task of gathering data on relations between cities. These data have allowed researchers to address a range of fundamental questions about individual cities in the world system, and about the evolving global urban system itself. In this chapter, we review research on one of the more empirically tractable – and, arguably, central – networks suggested to define the world city system: corporate networks.

CORPORATE NETWORKS AND WORLD CITIES

As firms acquire branches and subsidiaries around the world, they knit cities into a network of ownership, hierarchy and control. If the location decisions of firms are subject to isomorphic pressures, such pressures will tend to produce a hierarchy of cities/

places that mirrors the internal hierarchy of the modal firm. High-level 'command and control' functions, for instance, will cluster in a few key locations and, by tracing out the ties emanating from such centers, one can array cities in a hierarchy in a fashion akin to drawing up a firm's organizational chart, producing a formal representation of the structure of the city system and of the positions occupied, and roles played, by cities.

Developed in different ways by figures such as Cohen (1981) and Hymer (1972), this insight has sparked theory and empirical research on world cities. 'World cities' are typically defined as those that occupy a central position in corporate networks. Friedmann (1986, pp. 70–77), for instance, describes them as 'basing points in the spatial organization of production and markets'. Similarly, Sassen (2001, pp. 3–4) characterizes 'global cities' as 'concentrated command points in the organization of the world economy'. The isomorphic pressures on location decisions that generate such 'peak' cities (i.e. producing a clustering of headquarters in a limited number of cities, rather than a more uniform spatial distribution) are generally assumed to lie in agglomeration economies. This is perhaps given its most sustained theoretical treatment in Sassen's *The Global City* (2001). Sassen argues that the global control exercised by transnational firms depends critically on a wide array of producer and professional services. The global dispersion of production and distribution in the context of the 'new' new international division of labor – which spans multiple political, cultural, linguistic, jurisdictional, and so on boundaries – requires highly specialized and sophisticated external inputs. Because these inputs are subject to agglomeration economies, firms will locate their headquarters or seek to open branches where producer and professional services cluster, further catalyzing the geographic clustering of global control functions.

While there are a range of economies of agglomeration that may emerge from the spatial concentration of corporate headquarters in and of itself, research on corporate networks of world cities typically proceeds in close dialogue with research on producer service networks. As Derudder (2007) has noted, this has caused uncertainty regarding the conceptualization and operationalization of 'world cities' – sites of global command and control – as opposed to Sassen's 'global cities' – sites of the production of the inputs integral to such control. As we detail below, it is best to view work on corporate networks as focused on *already realized* global control and, as such, addressing the world city, rather than global city, problematic.

KEY QUESTIONS

A set of questions common to the broader literature on world and global cities motivates research on corporate networks. First, such research identifies world cities, using various techniques to determine which cities sit atop the urban hierarchy. Second, it seeks to determine the extent to which globalization alters the global urban hierarchy. Third, it is concerned with the spatial distribution of command and control. A key – and distinctive – idea that emerges is that globalization has, in part at least, been a fundamentally implosive, rather than explosive, process. As Sassen describes it, 'the more globalized the economy becomes, the higher the agglomeration of central functions in a relatively few sites' (2001, p. 5). Fourth, research has sought to determine the extent to which the world city system is evolving in ways that cut across long-standing

North/South and East/West divides. In the foundational work of Friedmann and Sassen, there is a strong suggestion that globalization is generating a 'new geography of centrality (and marginality)' (Sassen, 1998, p. 393), raising questions about the nature and trajectory of contemporary global inequality. Finally, this research is concerned with identifying the general structural features of the world city system as a system, the positions and roles that are emerging within it, and the implications of these features for cities and their residents. Smith and Timberlake (1995, p. 293) emphasize placing the question of the 'overall morphology' of the world city system at 'the centre of the analysis', linking the development of the world city system to that of the Wallersteinian (1974) world-system.

DATA AND METHOD

Research in this area begins by defining a sample of firms, always through purposive rather than random sampling. In an early paper exemplary of this approach, Meyer (1986) uses *Polk's World Bank Directory* to identify every city in South America with an international bank office and to link these cities to the 'international financial metropolises' of bank headquarters. Ren (forthcoming) also uses sector-specific data, employing a list of architectural firms identified by *Building and Design* magazine. In another early paper, Rozenblat and Pumain (1993) use a *Dun and Bradstreet* ranking to identify the 300 largest European firms and then survey these firms about their foreign subsidiaries, using the results to link the location of the largest European firms to the location of their European subsidiaries. In our own research (e.g. Alderson et al., 2010), we use rankings such as *Fortune* magazine's Global 500 to identify the world's 500 largest multinationals in various years and then use the *Directory of Corporate Affiliations* to identify the headquarters and branch locations of these firms. Carroll (2007) begins his examination of how firms tie cities together through interlocking directorates in a similar fashion, using *Fortune*'s Global 500.

Having identified a sample of firms and gathered information on location, researchers must decide how to 1) address *internal corporate hierarchies*; 2) generate a network of *cities* from information on *firms*; and 3) code the relations in the network. With notable exceptions (e.g. Rozenblat and Pumain, 2007; Wall, 2009), research in this area typically does not attempt to incorporate detailed information on within-firm hierarchies. As a result, a firm's subsidiaries are treated as equivalent in their relation to each other and to the firm's headquarters. Thus, in contrast to research of the GaWC group on advanced producer service networks, research on corporate networks usually proceeds by 'flattening' internal corporate hierarchies, focusing on headquarters–subsidiary relations. Regarding the transition from firms to cities, when it has been articulated (e.g. Beckfield and Alderson, 2006; see also Neal, 2008), it has been rooted in Simmel's insight, formalized by Breiger (1974), regarding the 'duality of persons and groups'. Just as ties between groups are persons and ties between persons are groups, in this work ties between cities are firms and ties between firms are cities. Thus given data on the network of firms linked by cities, one can readily derive the network of cities linked by firms. While research typically focuses on the latter, both have distinct structural properties worthy of analysis. For instance, using the GaWC data, Neal

(2008) shows that there is greater inequality in the network of cities linked by advanced producer service (APS) firms than in the network of APS firms linked by cities, suggesting that 'place matters' in ways not entirely revealed by a simple summation of the service values of APS firms active in each city. Regarding coding, the central decisions concern whether or not to treat the data as *directional* – to distinguish between senders and receivers (e.g. headquarters and subsidiaries) – and *valued* – to allow multiple ties between two cities. Coding the location of the headquarters and subsidiaries of 446 of the *Fortune* Global 500 in 2000, Alderson and Beckfield (2004), for instance, construct a 3692 × 3692 matrix in which values above the main diagonal of the matrix represent the number of subsidiaries of firms headquartered in City A that are located in City B, and values below the main diagonal represent the number of subsidiaries of firms headquartered in City B that are located in City A. Data can also be coded as undirected. Ren (forthcoming) constructs a symmetric, valued 198 × 198 matrix in which cities are linked by architectural firms, coding the relation as undirected to reflect the idea that headquarters–subsidiary relations in such firms are 'horizontal and collaborative' rather than hierarchical.

An array of methods has been used to analyse such data. Given the interest in identifying world cities and ranking them, research on corporate networks typically devotes a good deal of attention to the *centrality* of cities. Early work attempted to assess the importance of different cities in terms of how many corporate headquarters they hosted. Meijer (1993), for example, traces the 'growth and decline of European cities' by examining the shifting spatial distribution of the headquarters of the 500 largest European firms from 1973–1988. More recent work links headquarters to subsidiaries and assesses the *degree* centrality of cities – the number of ties that a given city has with other cities in the network. Carroll (2007) and Ren (forthcoming) treat the relation between cities as symmetric. In Ren's analysis, the most central cities are those with the largest number of offices (headquarters or branch) and Shanghai emerges as the most central city in the network of architectural firms. Others treat the relation between cities as asymmetric, distinguishing between *outdegree* (number of ties sent) and *indegree* (number of ties received). Rozenblat and Pumain (2007, p. 144) calculate the outdegree of European cities to 'map out a system of control-dependence' between cities that host headquarters and cities that host subsidiaries. Alderson and Beckfield (2004) and Wall (2009) calculate both the outdegree and indegree of the cities in their networks, distinguishing between network power (outdegree) and network prestige (indegree). In the wider literature on world cities, a number of additional measures of network centrality have been employed: *betweenness* (the probability that the paths linking cities j and k contain city i), *closeness* (the inverse average distance between city i and all other cities) and *Bonacich power centrality* (where the centrality of a city is a function of the centrality of the cities it is connected to) (see Wasserman and Faust (1994) for formulae). Each highlights distinct senses of network centrality and power and can be employed to identify and rank world cities.

Examination of these centrality measures also figures prominently in attempts to address the questions of how much the global urban hierarchy is 1) being restructured in the context of globalization, and 2) being restructured in ways that concentrate global command and control functions. Comparing the world city system in 1981 and 2000, Alderson and Beckfield (2007) calculate the *Spearman rank-order correlation* among centrality measures to assess the degree to which cities exchange ranks over the period under investigation and employ a standard measure of inequality – the *coefficient of variation* – to assess change in the distribution of centrality measures.

In the earliest work attempting to assess the extent to which the world city system is evolving in ways that cut across Global North and South (and East and West), scholars note, based on varied data, the rising importance of Southern and Eastern cities (and, correspondingly, the declining importance of cities in the North and West). Sassen (1998, p. 394), for instance, describes a new 'transterritorial "centre"' that includes cities such as New York, London and Tokyo, but also 'cities such as São Paulo and Mexico City'. Similarly, in their taxonomic exercises, Friedmann (1995) and Beaverstock et al. (1999) note the appearance of cities such as Singapore, São Paulo, Beijing and Buenos Aires in their inventories of cities located at the apex of the world city system. The most recent attempt to address this question appears in Alderson et al. (2010). They assign cities in their network to the world region (e.g. Asia, Africa, Latin America) and the circa 1970s world-system position (i.e. core, periphery or semi-periphery) of the nations in which they are located. They then regress change in network centrality on these region and world-system position indicators, reasoning that network centrality should grow increasingly orthogonal to 'old', established divisions in the world city system over the 1981–2007 period as a 'new geography of centrality and marginality' evolves across the era of globalization. Wall (2009) proceeds similarly, using GIS (Geographic Information System) techniques to examine the 'linkage distribution' between cities, nations and regions.

Finally, a number of scholars have been interested in determining what sort of system the world city system is, and with identifying and characterizing the different positions and roles that are emerging within it. Wall (2009) uses *Zipf regressions* to establish that the corporate network of world cities is a scale-free network (i.e. has a degree distribution that follows a power law). This finding has important implications for our understanding of the world city system: scale-free networks, as a class of networks, are known to display small world and Pareto distributions, to prove robust to random interruption (while being at risk of cascading failure), and to exhibit 'rich get richer' and 'winner take all' features as they develop (e.g. Barabási, 2002). Smith and Timberlake (1995) pioneered the use of *blockmodeling* techniques in their research on airline networks. Very generally, blockmodeling abstracts from information on individual cities to identify 'types' of cities that are defined by their relation to other 'types' of cities in the system (i.e. positions and roles). Of the many decisions involved in the course of blockmodeling (see Lloyd et al., 2009), the most fundamental concerns the notion of equivalence employed to join cities into positions. Smith and Timberlake (2001) cluster cities in terms of *structural equivalence*: cities are assigned to sets composed of cities that share the same ties to all other cities. Strict structural equivalence is rarely observed in such data, so researchers, based on substantive and theoretical concerns, typically settle on an approximation of strict structural equivalence to join cities (Wasserman and Faust, 1994). Alderson et al. (2010) join cities in terms of *regular equivalence*. Regular equivalence relaxes the constraint that cities be joined when they have identical (or near-identical) relations with others, joining cities instead based on the degree to which they have relations with *equivalent* others (e.g. abstracting from concrete kinship relations to identify 'fathers', 'daughters', 'cousins', etc.). Having joined cities into equivalence sets, one can then seek to identify the roles played by such cities in the network (see Alderson and Beckfield, 2004, especially Table 5 and Figure 3).

RESULTS

Research on corporate networks of world cities has contributed to debates over which cities sit atop the global urban hierarchy. For instance, it demonstrates the surprising (in light of earlier attribute-based rankings) structural power of Tokyo and Paris. In the case of Tokyo, although it is less prestigious than London and New York in that it receives fewer ties, we find in 2000, for instance, that it sends far more ties (3639) than either London (1955) or New York (2601). Also in terms of outdegree, Paris ranks between London and New York, at 2535 ties sent (Alderson and Beckfield, 2004). Wall's (2009) analysis of the top 100 global firms in 2005 identifies Paris and Tokyo as 2nd and 3rd, respectively, in terms of outdegree. Surprises also appear further down the ranking of cities, as prominent cities such as Miami, Singapore, Mexico City, São Paulo and Sydney do not appear among the top 50 cities on outdegree (in our analysis or in Wall's), while cities such as Basel, Philadelphia and St. Louis – typically absent from rankings of world cities – are among the 50 most powerful cities in the corporate network. Drawing on a selection of *Fortune* Global 500 firms, but focusing instead on interlocking directorates, Carroll (2007, p. 2306) also shows the power of Paris-based firms, along with firms headquartered in Frankfurt and Montréal. Interestingly, although Tokyo exhibits a high degree of activity in the interlock network, directors of Tokyo-based firms are more likely to appear as isolates (p. 2304). This is partly due to the nationalized and regionalized structure of the interlock network (Carroll, 2007). In an investigation of corporate networks in the European region, Rozenblat and Pumain (1993) find that firms locate in cities in ways that reinforce the existing urban hierarchy.

In the corporate network, a city's placement in the hierarchy is multidimensional, and varies according to which aspect of centrality is measured. As noted, Tokyo is more powerful than prestigious in that its outdegree far surpasses its indegree. In the case of Paris, it outranks all other cities on closeness and betweenness centrality, suggesting its strong strategic position in the corporate network. On indegree, cities commonly ranked high in attribute-based urban hierarchies, such as Barcelona, Miami, Vancouver, Johannesburg, Jakarta, Prague and Shanghai, appear as prestigious in that they host a great many subsidiaries, but they are not particularly powerful (Alderson and Beckfield, 2004). This suggests that attention to corporate networks may help to correct a tendency in the literature to mistake prestige for power (cf. Taylor, 2006; Beckfield and Alderson, 2006). Both prestige and power are regionalized in the corporate network of world cities. For instance, Wall (2009) finds that 'North America, Europe and Pacific Asia together claim 98% of all outdegree relations and 82% of all indegree' (p. 180). Tokyo and Paris both stand out as regionally powerful cities (Wall, 2009).

Evidence on change in the urban hierarchy in our research comes from a comparison of the corporate network in 1981 (the first year for which location data are available from the *Directory of Corporate Affiliations*) with the network in 2007 (Alderson et al., 2010). By all four measures of centrality, there is substantial evidence of change: cities' ranks on these measures are only moderately correlated over the nearly 30-year period. Evidence on the *distribution* of centrality in the corporate network reveals that this re-ordering of cities was not random: outdegree centrality became more unequally distributed, as did betweenness. Thus, from the early 1980s there is evidence of increasing concentration of command and control among a re-ordered hierarchy of cities.

Which cities change rank in the urban hierarchy? The evidence to date suggests that, rather than generating a new geography, the recent wave of globalization has reinforced existing divides in the world system (Alderson et al., 2010). These findings are in line with cross-sectional analysis of the corporate interlock network (Carroll, 2007), the European corporate network (Rozenblat and Pumain, 1993) and the top 100 *Fortune* multinationals (Wall, 2009). These inferences are reinforced by regional comparisons, which show that no region outside the Global North grew significantly more central during the 1981–2007 wave of globalization (Alderson et al., 2010), although Shanghai and Beijing have grown in power in the network of architecture firms (Ren, forthcoming). Likewise, analysis of the corporate network using regular-equivalence blockmodeling shows that when cities in the semiperiphery and periphery join the network, they do so as structural isolates, on the passive, dependent and internally disconnected fringes of the world city system. The same results hold for the regional comparisons: cities in Africa, Asia and Latin America are significantly more likely than Global North cities to join the system in a passive, dependent role, and significantly less likely than Global North cities to join the system in an active, primary role.

FUTURE

The collection of relational data on corporate networks is enabling inquiry into the hierarchy of world cities, change in the hierarchy, the concentration of command and control, the (de-)coupling of world city system structure from world-system structure, and the general form of inter-city relations. We see several promising directions for the future of this research. Below, we conclude this chapter by suggesting four unresolved issues that could guide further inquiry.

First, the role of industry and sector in the world city system has received too little empirical scrutiny. In our own work, we are building on sector-specific analysis by Meyer (1986), Ren (forthcoming) and Wall (2009) by disaggregating our multinational corporate network data so that sectoral city systems can be compared. Understanding how cities are embedded in networks that may differ by sector is potentially important for understanding the consequences of inter-city relations. One conjecture is that a city's economic fate may be more closely bound to its position in a rapidly rising (or declining) sector-specific network than to its position in the corporate network as a whole.

Second, longitudinal data on city network formation can be used to address unresolved questions about the mechanisms of world city network formation. For instance, longitudinal data on the locations of producer-services firms in different sub-sectors could be used to examine processes of agglomeration. If such data were available on the locations of corporate subsidiaries and producer-services firms, then one could observe the formation of agglomerated economies in process, and potentially disentangle the sequencing of firm presence in established sub-sectors of producer services such as consulting, finance, real estate, insurance and advertising. Longitudinal data are also necessary to evaluate hypotheses regarding the changing world city system structure. As noted above, many of the central world city hypotheses concern change in the hierarchy of cities and the possibility of new geographies.

Third, although corporate network scholarship attends to organizational structure in that it allows relations of command and control to knit together networks of cities, such research, with a few exceptions (e.g. Rozenblat and Pumain, 2007; Wall, 2009), downplays variation in organizational structure. For instance, information on the level of investment of a firm in its subsidiaries, along with internal corporate reporting relationships, would add considerable richness to depictions of corporate networks – as would attention to 'governance without ownership' through, for instance, global commodity chains (Vind and Fold, 2010). We are currently gathering data on internal organizational hierarchies to complement the location data of the *Fortune* Global 500 sample of firms.

Finally, research on corporate networks of cities should of course directly inform the question of whether and how inter-city relations impact social life in cities. Debates surround how world city-ness impacts various attributes of cities, including migration, employment, economic development and inequality (Wall, 2009). For instance, Timberlake (2006) uses data on U.S. cities to test the hypothesis that world city-ness drives up urban economic inequality, and finds little evidence for the hypothesis. Comparing Amsterdam and Rotterdam, van der Waal and Burgers (2009) reach a similar conclusion. Such work seems likely to drive new debates over the consequences of corporate networks of world cities for urban life.

REFERENCES

Alderson, A.S. and J. Beckfield (2004), 'Power and position in the world city system', *American Journal of Sociology*, **109** (4), 811–851.

Alderson, A.S. and J. Beckfield (2007), 'Globalization and the world city system: preliminary results from a longitudinal data set', in P.J. Taylor, B. Derudder, P. Saey and F. Witlox (eds), *Cities in Globalization: Practices, Policies, and Theories*, London: Routledge, pp. 21–36.

Alderson, A.S., J. Beckfield and J. Sprague-Jones (2010), 'Inter-city relations and globalization: the evolution of the global urban hierarchy, 1981–2007', *Urban Studies*, **47** (9), 1899–1923.

Barabási, A.-L. (2002), *Linked: The New Science of Networks*, Cambridge, MA: Perseus.

Beaverstock, J.V., R.G. Smith and P.J. Taylor (1999), 'A roster of world cities', *Cities*, **16** (6), 445–458.

Beckfield, J. and A.S. Alderson (2006), 'Reply: whither the parallel paths? The future of scholarship on the world city system', *American Journal of Sociology*, **112** (3), 895–904.

Breiger, R.L. (1974), 'The duality of persons and groups', *Social Forces*, **53** (2), 181–190.

Carroll, W.K. (2007), 'Global cities in the global corporate network', *Environment and Planning A*, **39** (10), 2297–2323.

Cohen, R.B. (1981), 'The new international division of labor, multinational corporations and urban hierarchy', in M.J. Dear and A.J. Scott (eds), *Urbanization and Urban Planning in Capitalist Society*, New York: Taylor and Francis, pp. 287–318.

Derudder, B. (2007), 'The mismatch between concepts and evidence in the study of a global urban network', in P.J. Taylor, B. Derudder, P. Saey and F. Witlox (eds), *Cities in Globalization: Practices, Policies, and Theories*, London: Routledge, pp. 271–286.

Friedmann, J. (1986), 'The world city hypothesis', *Development and Change*, **17** (1), 69–84.

Friedmann, J. (1995), 'Where we stand: a decade of world city research', in P.L. Knox and P.J. Taylor (eds), *World Cities in a World-System*, New York: Cambridge University Press, pp. 21–47.

Hymer, S. (1972), 'The multinational corporation and the law of uneven development', in J.N. Bhagwati (ed.), *Economics and World Order*, New York: Macmillan, pp. 113–140.

Knox, P.L. and P.J. Taylor (1995), *World Cities in a World-System*, New York: Cambridge University Press.

Lloyd, P., M.C. Mahutga and J. De Leeuw (2009), 'Looking back and forging ahead: thirty years of social network research on the world-system', *Journal of World-Systems Research*, **15** (1), 48–95.

Meijer, M. (1993), 'Growth and decline of European cities: changing positions of cities in Europe', *Urban Studies*, **30** (6), 981–990.

Meyer, D.R. (1986), 'The world system of cities: relations between international financial metropolises and South American cities', *Social Forces*, **64** (3), 553–581.

Neal, Z.P. (2008), 'The duality of world cities and firms: comparing networks, hierarchies, and inequalities in the global economy', *Global Networks*, **8** (1), 94–115.

Ren, X. (forthcoming), *Building Globalization: Transnational Architectural Production in Urban China*, Chicago: University of Chicago Press.

Rozenblat, C. and D. Pumain (1993), 'The location of multinational firms in the European urban system', *Urban Studies*, **30** (10), 1691–1709.

Rozenblat, C. and D. Pumain (2007), 'Firm linkages, innovation, and the evolution of urban systems', in P.J. Taylor, B. Derudder, P. Saey and F. Witlox (eds), *Cities in Globalization: Practices, Policies, and Theories*, London: Routledge, pp. 130–156.

Sassen, S. (1998), 'The impact of new technologies and globalization on cities', in F.-C. Lo and Y.-M. Yeung (eds), *Globalization and the World of Large Cities*, Tokyo: United Nations University Press, pp. 391–409.

Sassen, S. (2001), *The Global City: New York, London, Tokyo*, Princeton: Princeton University Press.

Shin, K.H. and M. Timberlake (2006), 'Korea's global city: structural and political implications of Seoul's ascendance in the global urban hierarchy', *International Journal of Comparative Sociology*, **47** (2), 145–173.

Smith, D.A. and M. Timberlake (1993), 'World cities: a political economy/global network approach', *Research in Urban Sociology*, **3**, 181–207.

Smith, D.A. and M. Timberlake (1995), 'Conceptualising and mapping the structure of the world's city system', *Urban Studies*, **32** (2), 287–302.

Smith, D.A. and M. Timberlake (2001), 'World city networks and hierarchies, 1977–1997: an empirical analysis of global air travel links', *American Behavioral Scientist*, **44** (10), 1656–1678.

Taylor, P.J. (2004), *World City Network: A Global Urban Analysis*, London: Routledge.

Taylor, P.J. (2006), 'Comment: parallel paths to understanding global intercity relations', *American Journal of Sociology*, **112** (3), 881–894.

Taylor, P.J. (2007), 'A lineage for contemporary inter-city studies', in P.J. Taylor, B. Derudder, P. Saey and F. Witlox (eds), *Cities in Globalization: Practices, Policies, and Theories*, London: Routledge, pp. 1–12.

Timberlake, M.F. (2006), 'A global city hypothesis: an empirical assessment among U.S. cities, 1990–2000', paper presented at the World Congress of the International Sociological Association, Durban, South Africa.

Van der Waal, J. and J. Burgers (2009), 'Unravelling the global city debate on social inequality: a firm-level analysis of wage inequality in Amsterdam and Rotterdam', *Urban Studies*, **46** (13), 2715–2729.

Vind, I. and N. Fold (2010), 'City networks and commodity chains: identifying global flows and local connections in Ho Chi Minh City', *Global Networks*, **10** (1), 54–74.

Wall, R. (2009), 'Netscape: cities in global corporate networks', *ERIM PhD Series in Research in Management 169*, Rotterdam: Erasmus University.

Wallerstein, I. (1974), *The Modern World-System*, New York: Academic Press.

Wasserman, S. and K. Faust (1994), *Social Network Analysis: Methods and Applications*, Cambridge: Cambridge University Press.

13 Advanced producer servicing networks of world cities

Peter J. Taylor, Ben Derudder, Michael Hoyler and Frank Witlox

INTRODUCTION

In Chapter 6 advanced producer services featured crucially in the exposition of the interlocking network model. Drawing on Sassen's (1991) identification of this work as integral to global city formation, the office networks of advanced producer service firms were modelled to generate a world city network. To this end the office networks were aggregated so that differences between different service sectors were lost in the initial modelling. But advanced producer services are of interest in their own right and not just as input in world city network analysis. In this chapter the service categories are 'recovered' and described for their importance in contemporary globalization processes.

The rise of the service sector was one of the most remarkable changes in the twentieth century world economy (Bryson and Daniels, 1998). Industries in this sector can be divided into those servicing individuals and households (e.g. retail firms) and those servicing businesses (e.g. advertising agencies). These are commonly referred to as consumer services and producer services, respectively, although in practice the distinction is often blurred. For instance, most bank branches in cities offer both retail banking for their individual customers and specific financial services for their business customers. Nevertheless this distinction is a useful one because the business services developed in new ways in the last decades of the twentieth century to create a crucial knowledge component of economic globalization. These were very high value-added services through specialized knowledges – professional, creative and financial – that are the advanced producer services, the subject of this chapter.

WHY ADVANCED PRODUCER SERVICES ARE IMPORTANT

As noted in Chapter 6, advanced producer service firms followed their clients from the 1980s onwards to create worldwide office networks. It is worth pondering this astonishing turnaround in the scale of their activities. Service firms have traditionally been very local because they built up the client base through face-to-face encounters. The result was that firms became designated by their city location – a Washington law firm, a Paris advertising agency, a London bank, and so on. But with worldwide offices to service global client bases this simple process has been superseded. With the combining of the computer and communications industries in the 1970s, plus vastly expanded business air travel, the situation has become much more complicated, reflected in new global geographies of servicing. Thus when scholars refer to a new information age and network society (e.g. Castells, 1996), it is advanced producer service firms that are the archetypal generators of this new world. And yet, the city origins do not disappear. Despite globalization, the business culture of firms while becoming more cosmopolitan also remains local and national (Dicken, 2007): for instance, London and New York law firms remain very different even though their work entwines through both cities and beyond, as clearly illustrated by Faulconbridge (2007). It is this 'glocalization' that makes advanced producer service firms so theoretically interesting for understanding contemporary globalization.

But there are also three related practical reasons why these firms demand special attention. First, advanced producer services can be reasonably interpreted as a contemporary 'indicator sector' in the world economy. That is to say, places where this sector is expanding indicate economic success. Thus although firms from this sector, except for banks, remain relatively small compared with other economic sectors – they hardly get a mention in the Forbes 2000 top corporations – their importance lies not in their size but in their relationality. These firms instigate and thrive through their centrality in economic webs that constitute cities and their networks. Just as the vitality of ecologies can be monitored via 'indicator species', so too can city-economies via indicator sectors, and in economic globalization advanced producer services are arguably the best candidate for this role.

Second, and again size notwithstanding, advanced producer service firms are at the cutting edge of contemporary modern economy. As traditional 'knowledge industries', firms in this sector were well placed to take advantage of the rise of Castells' (1996) informational society. Like a limited number of other sectors, notably logistics, these firms have enthusiastically taken up the economic openings made possible by new electronic communication. In this way they have been at the forefront of exploiting the network society to generate worldwide work practices, the cutting edge of economic change over recent decades.

Third, in their worldwide work practices, advanced producer service firms have had a crucial role in enabling economic globalization. This enabling is usually allocated to Castells' (1996) bottom layer of his global space of flows – electronic and transport infrastructure – and there has been a literature that claimed an 'end of geography' in a 'borderless world' (Brown, 1973; O'Brien, 1991; Ohmae, 1999). We know now that this is not how globalization has operated; places are still important and borders remain. Corporations manoeuvre through globalization by using the specialist expert knowledge of advanced producer service firms operating through the real social relations that are Castells' second tier in his space of flows. It is here that contemporary globalization has been made a viable means of production and consumption.

The latter point can be further developed by briefly considering some core functions of the five sub-groups of service firms focused on in Chapter 6. We treat them in an order that traces their distinctive contributions.

1.   Advertising firms were critical to the construction of consumer modernity, ultimately providing contemporary globalization with its essential nature (Taylor, 2008). They emerged in the early twentieth century to convert wants into needs in the birthplace of modern consumerism, the USA. The work diffused to other 'affluent societies' in Western Europe and Japan in mid century, before globalizing in the last decades

of the twentieth century. The final move enabled needs to be converted to wants globally to provide the beginnings of a worldwide demand side to contemporary globalization, its crucial component that distinguishes it from earlier production-only globalizations.

2. For corporations to provide for global consumer demand it would be nice to operate in a borderless world and a key role of global law firms is to help get as close as possible to this ideal. Through their expertise in inter-jurisdictional law practices they ensure business can proceed smoothly in a transnational manner. Anchoring other national law systems to either English common law (initially through London) or New York State law (initially through New York City) in order to translate across myriad jurisdictions, law firms help take the borders out of business.

3. Ultimately it is all about the bottom line: finance. Financial services firms have been some of the most creative within economic globalization through inventing new financial instruments to move, change and expand capital as never before. This was the role they successfully played until 2008. As traditional merchant banks morphed into contemporary investment banks, international financial centres – not least London and New York – generated global financial movements far outpacing traditional international trade in the world economy. It is this 'financial globalization' that some see as contemporary globalization's real nature (Arrighi, 1994).

4. And through all this economic growth, it was accountancy firms that expanded the most. Their key role relates to their core competency in auditing. This might not sound very exciting but as globalization brought in firms from outside the core regions of the world economy it generated new forms of firms, including relatively 'informal' family corporations. In a world where amalgamations and takeovers are commonplace, it is necessary that all firms conform to similar standards of auditing. This is what accountancy firms provide – they were especially active in the late 1990s economic turndown in Asia where their intervention enabled failing local firms to be scooped up by Western corporations.

5. Management consultancy is the new kid on the block, a late twentieth century boom industry built on the back of hundreds of thousands of MBA graduates coming onto the global labour market. Management consultants advise corporations on enhancing the bottom line through savings via reorganizations; effectively this has meant redeploying labour, with the middle rung of management being a favourite target. Their key role is to create a more homogeneous corporate world by bringing all firms down to a common level in labour costs.

These groups of services vary in their relation to cycles in the world economy: in the good times advertising and financial firms tend to prosper, more challenging times are better for law and accountancy firms. Management consultancy work is never done.

FIVE NEW SERVICE GEOGRAPHIES IN GLOBALIZATION

In this section we look at the new geographies of servicing in globalization using the 2008 data and analysis from Chapter 6 broken down into the five groups of services. Thus the analyses below are based upon the original services value matrix of 525 cities × 175

Table 13.1   Advertising network connectivity

Rank	City	NC	Rank	City	NC
1	New York	1.00	20	Madrid	0.60
2	London	0.75	21	Milan	0.60
3	Paris	0.75	22	Seoul	0.59
4	Hong Kong	0.73	23	Budapest	0.57
5	Tokyo	0.71	24	Vienna	0.56
6	Singapore	0.70	25	Istanbul	0.56
7	Moscow	0.65	26	Kuala Lumpur	0.55
8	Shanghai	0.64	27	Helsinki	0.55
9	Warsaw	0.63	28	Dubai	0.55
10	Sydney	0.63	29	Lisbon	0.54
11	Brussels	0.62	30	Mexico City	0.53
12	Buenos Aires	0.62	31	Amsterdam	0.53
13	Taipei	0.61	32	Jeddah	0.53
14	Mumbai	0.61	33	Copenhagen	0.52
15	Toronto	0.61	34	Bucharest	0.52
16	Athens	0.60	35	Chicago	0.51
17	Stockholm	0.60	36	Rome	0.51
18	Beijing	0.60	37	Prague	0.50
19	Bangkok	0.60	38	Caracas	0.50

firms, where a service value (ranging from 0 to 5) indicates the use of a city by a firm. The 175 firms consist of 75 financial service firms and 25 each of accountancy, advertising, law and management consultancy firms. For a detailed description see Taylor et al. (2011).

Each group is analysed separately to produce network connectivities for the cities. These values (ranging from 0 to 1) indicate the degree of integration of a city into the specific networks: how well Washington DC is integrated into law networks; how well Paris is integrated into advertising networks, and so on. All values are given as proportions of the highest connectivity for each group of firms. In the discussion below we consider only the leading cities in the sector networks: those with at least one half of the highest connectivity (i.e. the network connectivity values reported are 0.5 and above). It is these values that define the city geographies described below. They are presented in the order in which the groups of firms were treated above.

Advertising: New York Imperium

It is no surprise that New York dominates the advertising city network (Table 13.1); originally clustered in Madison Avenue, this advanced producer service remains the archetypal American industry maintaining its traditional centre. It is from this locale that first national advertising campaigns and latterly global advertising campaigns were devised and practised through networks of 'subsidiary' cities. However, moving on the global stage meant confronting new levels of national, language and cultural differences across the world that have required additional local inputs to customize the product.

This is reflected in the large number and worldwide range of cities that are integrated into the advertising city network in Table 13.1.

Most advertising is still based upon TV campaigns. Television remains largely a national medium; stations transmit to a 'national audience' within their state's boundaries. Thus a 'global' campaign has to be, in reality, an 'international' campaign with a state by state practice. Thus the 37 important advertising cities below New York in Table 13.1 are from 33 different countries. These cities are the main TV centres for the larger national markets across the world. Usually that city is the capital city but there are also cases where the capital is not the economic and cultural centre of the country: Sydney, Mumbai, Toronto, Istanbul and Jeddah are each non-capital TV centres. There are just three countries with multiple cities in Table 13.1. The special case of China where Hong Kong, Shanghai and Beijing are important advertising cities is partly a size effect but also reflects the triple-city centred nature of China's recent economic rise (Lai, 2009). The second example is Italy where both Milan and Rome are advertising cities; sharing a large to medium national market means that the two cities are relatively lowly ranked.

It is important that omissions from Table 13.1 are also mentioned. The whole of Africa is off the network map; largely a feature of the small size of national markets. But there are large markets not represented. The most obvious case is the USA itself; despite this industry's American origins, after New York only Chicago features, but ranked a lowly 35, and no other important advertising cities are found. And there are two very important national markets missing altogether: Germany and Brazil, which both have relatively 'flat' urban 'hierarchies'. Germany has four main cities servicing its large economy for advertising: Frankfurt, Düsseldorf, Hamburg and Berlin; and Brazil has two: São Paulo and Rio de Janeiro. These examples may indicate more than dividing national markets. The New York 'imperial mode' of advertising was first challenged in the US national market and Faulconbridge et al. (2011) argue that this may well now be happening globally. New York remains the main centre for advertising in the world but other centres are now emerging, some still strongly linked to New York and others more independent. For further discussion of the globalization of advertising see Taylor (2008) and Faulconbridge et al. (2011).

Law: NYLON Duopoly

Law is similar to advertising in having a basic international framework for its practice: every country has its own distinctive legal and associated professional certification for practice. But this internationality is not reflected in cities integrated into global law networks. Legal services have very different global geographies from advertising (Table 13.2). By the definition used here, there were only eight global law cities in 2008. And these were dominated by the duopoly of London and New York. It was in these two cities that law firms developed the expertise for inter-jurisdictional practices, which is still reflected in the use of two basic legal frameworks (as noted previously, English common law and New York State law).

Beyond the duopoly, the next four ranked law cities are also from North West Europe and the USA: Paris and Washington are major national capitals, and Frankfurt and Brussels are major European Union centres for finance and politics, respectively. The

Table 13.2   Law network connectivity

Rank	City	NC
1	London	1.00
2	New York	0.89
3	Paris	0.70
4	Frankfurt	0.59
5	Washington	0.58
6	Brussels	0.54
7	Hong Kong	0.53
8	Moscow	0.50

top six ranked cities confirm the close affinity of leading law firms and their banking and government clients.

The only breakout of the traditional 'North Atlantic' core relates to the opening up of European COMECON and Communist China in the late twentieth century. In both cases the nature and policies of the previous regimes meant there was a commercial law vacuum that London and New York law firms were more than willing to fill. Hong Kong became the 'global legal gateway' to the new commercial China, and Moscow attracted law firms because it was the capital of the country that had the largest turnover in property in COMECON consequent upon the privatization of state assets.

The lesson of this geography of globalization is that networks do not have to be 'horizontal' in nature to facilitate globalization. Since there is no suggestion that this highly restricted geography has limited legal worldwide competence, this case illustrates a global projection of power through extraordinary high value-added work.

Financial Services: Global Trinity

In twenty-four-hour financial markets, there need to be three time-zoned centres for continuous expert attention and capabilities. This was originally provided for by Tokyo, London and New York (Thrift, 1989), Sassen's (1991) initial 'global cities', but since 1990 the stagnation of the Japanese economy and the massive growth of the Chinese economy have meant that Hong Kong has replaced Tokyo. Tokyo was always the 'poor relation' of the first 'big three' (Sassen, 1999) but this does not seem to be the case with Hong Kong. Table 13.3 shows London, New York and Hong Kong almost equally integrated into financial services city networks. This is now a tight global financial trinity at the heart of economic globalization.

But this city network is not part of a sequence-continuality from single (advertising) to dual (law) to triple dominance. Unlike Tables 13.1 and 13.2, Table 13.3 records numerous cities with network integration levels above 0.75; in fact this defines the top eight. And what a curious top eight it is: apart from the top two and Paris ranked 6th, all these highly integrated financial centres are in the western Pacific Rim: Tokyo, of course, now in 4th place, but also Singapore, Shanghai and Sydney recording network connectivities above 0.75. Pacific Asia has long been identified as the world region with concentration of financial services (Taylor, 2004), but this has been remarkably accentuated through

Table 13.3   Financial network connectivity

Rank	City	NC	Rank	City	NC
1	London	1.00	15	Moscow	0.61
2	New York	0.96	16	Frankfurt	0.61
3	Hong Kong	0.93	17	Zurich	0.60
4	Tokyo	0.82	18	Mumbai	0.59
5	Singapore	0.82	19	Brussels	0.57
6	Paris	0.79	20	Kuala Lumpur	0.57
7	Shanghai	0.77	21	Chicago	0.56
8	Sydney	0.77	22	Amsterdam	0.56
9	Seoul	0.70	23	Dublin	0.56
10	Madrid	0.70	24	Jakarta	0.54
11	Milan	0.70	25	São Paulo	0.54
12	Beijing	0.69	26	Bangkok	0.54
13	Taipei	0.64	27	Buenos Aires	0.51
14	Toronto	0.64	28	Warsaw	0.50

to 2008. More recent evidence suggests the 2008 financial crisis has further augmented this trend (Derudder et al., 2011). In addition, Seoul (9th), Beijing (12th), Taipei (13th), Kuala Lumpur (20th), Jakarta (24th) and Bangkok (26th) show further financial power in this region.

But there is more to this global geography than the Pacific Asian cluster. There are 28 cities listed in Table 13.3 and most of the remainder are European (11 to be precise), plus Toronto and 1 Indian city, Mumbai, and 2 Latin American cities, São Paulo and Buenos Aires.

However, perhaps the noteworthy feature of Table 13.3 is to be found in an omission: there is only one other US city – Chicago (21st) – found to be strongly integrated into financial services city networks. This does not mean that the USA has no other major financial centres outside New York but they do not feature large in the city networks of financial services firms. This dearth of US cities with high network connectivities is a common feature in world city analyses – for further discussion see Taylor and Lang (2005), Derudder et al. (2010), Hanssens et al. (2011) and Taylor et al. (2011).

Accountancy: Ubiquitous Globalization

The first point to make about the global geography of accountancy is that there are 45 cities listed in Table 13.4. Accountancy firms (and associations of such firms) tend to have much larger office networks than any other advanced producer service and this leads to the surfeit of global accountancy cities.

Apart from the top three ranking cities being very familiar from other tables – London, New York and Hong Kong – Table 13.4 displays a rather distinctive geography. For instance, Buenos Aires (9th) is ranked above Tokyo (13th), and Tel Aviv (12th) and Auckland (18th) are ranked above Seoul (19th). But this does not indicate a diminution of Pacific Asian representation in global accountancy cities: there are four cities from the region ranked above Tokyo, including Beijing (8th) and Kuala Lumpur (10th).

Table 13.4   Accountancy network connectivity

Rank	City	NC	Rank	City	NC
1	London	1.00	24	São Paulo	0.56
2	New York	0.79	25	Berlin	0.56
3	Hong Kong	0.74	26	Madrid	0.56
4	Sydney	0.69	27	Istanbul	0.56
5	Singapore	0.67	28	Caracas	0.56
6	Milan	0.67	29	Oslo	0.55
7	Paris	0.66	30	New Delhi	0.55
8	Beijing	0.64	31	Kuwait	0.55
9	Buenos Aires	0.63	32	Bogota	0.55
10	Kuala Lumpur	0.62	33	Barcelona	0.55
11	Toronto	0.61	34	Vienna	0.53
12	Tel Aviv	0.61	35	Jeddah	0.52
13	Tokyo	0.60	36	Santiago	0.52
14	Shanghai	0.60	37	Dublin	0.52
15	Jakarta	0.60	38	Warsaw	0.51
16	Moscow	0.60	39	Guadalajara	0.51
17	Brussels	0.59	40	Riyadh	0.50
18	Auckland	0.59	41	Johannesburg	0.50
19	Seoul	0.59	42	Zurich	0.50
20	Lisbon	0.57	43	Chicago	0.50
21	Rome	0.57	44	Hamburg	0.50
22	Mumbai	0.57	45	Athens	0.50
23	Mexico City	0.57			

And the surprises do not end here. There are 17 European cities appearing as strongly integrated into this network, 4 of which appear in these analyses for the first time: Berlin (25th), Oslo (29th), Barcelona (33rd) and Hamburg (44th). Similarly there are new Latin American cities appearing: 3 – Bogota (32nd), Santiago (36th) and Guadalajara (39th) – out of 7 cities from this world region in all. The Middle East is represented, not by Dubai, but by Kuwait (31st), Jeddah (35th) and Riyadh (40th). And finally there is African representation: Johannesburg (41st). Again there is only one US city included in addition to New York: Chicago (43rd). This is the most worldwide of all advanced producer service networks, and is very different from the advertising network which has the second highest number of major integrated cities (Table 13.1). The unexpected in the geography of global accountancy cities suggests a fairly random distribution.

The only process that can be discerned from the list is that it includes cities that have required additional audit capacity to enable increased foreign direct investment. The role of Buenos Aires in the recovery of Argentina's economy after its financial crisis in 2001–2 might account for this city's particularly surprising ranking in Table 13.4. A similar story concerning the South East Asian financial crisis of 1997–8 might account for the relatively high rankings of Kuala Lumpur and Jakarta. But overall what is being shown here is the ubiquity of accountancy in the contemporary world economy: this service has been the big winner of globalization.

Table 13.5   Management consultancy network connectivity

Rank	City	NC
1	New York	1.00
2	London	0.67
3	Paris	0.65
4	Chicago	0.62
5	Hong Kong	0.61
6	Singapore	0.56
7	Tokyo	0.56
8	Zurich	0.55
9	Madrid	0.55
10	Beijing	0.53
11	Mumbai	0.50
12	Atlanta	0.50

Management Consultancy

To some extent global management consultancy was born out of accountancy: some of the major firms are the result of dividing off from accountancy firms because of potential conflicts of interest between auditing and consultancy. But the geography of their service networks could hardly be more different: Table 13.5 lists the second fewest cities.

Like advertising, management consultancy's main origins are in the USA and in Table 13.5 New York is very dominant. Furthermore, two other US cities appear as strongly integrated into this service network: Chicago (4th) and Atlanta (12th). Otherwise the global consultancy cities are all to be found in Western Europe and Pacific Asia with the sole exception of Mumbai (11th).

There are two interpretations of this service geography. First, management consultancy is concentrated in few regions in the world because it is in these places that its work is most needed: down-sizing by stripping out middle management. However, it must be remembered that what we are dealing with are processes and 2008 results are just a cross-section. Secondly, therefore, management consultancy is a relatively new global service and its contemporary concentration just reflects early days before branching out into new horizons.

CONCLUSION: GLOBALIZING EFFECTS OF NETWORKS

The key finding of this chapter is that there are very different geographies of globalization even within just one major economic sector, advanced producer services. In this short conclusion these differences will be compared by treating each network geography as representing a process and then measuring its geographical effect.

The notion of globalization replaced an earlier conceptualization of the world divided into three: a rich 'first world', a communist 'second world' and a poor 'third world'. Although an unsatisfactory taxonomy given very different criteria for differentiations, it became the 'common sense' description of the world until the end of the Cold War

Table 13.6   The globalizing effects of advanced producer service networks

Advanced producer service network	Number of major cities	% old 'first world'	% old 'second world'	% old 'third world'
Advertising	38	60.5	18.4	21.1
Law	8	87.5	12.5	0.0
Financial services	28	64.3	14.3	21.4
Accountancy	45	57.8	8.9	33.3
Management consultancy	12	83.3	8.3	8.3

in 1989–91 and the consequent demise of communism as a major political force. This eliminated the 'second world' and left the idea of 'third world' in somewhat of a limbo, which was 'solved' by Western triumphalism proclaiming the birth of 'one world'. Globalization came to be the label that confirmed the new world order. This timing is interesting because it is in the period after 1990 that advanced producer services really began to expand rapidly in cities across the world to create the networks studied in this chapter. Therefore the 'one world' thesis can be assessed through looking at how each of the erstwhile divisions has fared in contemporary globalization.

In Table 13.6 the major cities integrated into each of the five service networks are distributed across the earlier triplicate categories. The first world includes Northern America (Canada and USA), Western Europe (non-communist countries) and parts of Pacific Asia (Japan, South Korea, Taiwan, Hong Kong and Singapore); the second world includes all communist states before 1989; and the third world includes the three 'continents' – Latin America, Africa and Asia – not including 'first world Pacific Asia' and communist states. The second column in Table 13.6 shows the variation in numbers of major cities in each network; the remaining columns show percentages of cities in each of the initial 'three worlds'.

The first point to make is that all cells are above zero except one showing that major cities strongly integrated into service networks are found in all three worlds with the sole case of legal services not represented in the erstwhile 'third world'. Global law is the most concentrated of networks and therefore this is perhaps not a surprise. On the other hand, again not surprisingly, it is the old 'first world' that has by far the most major network cities, always more than half, in all five services. However, there is a separation of service networks in terms of degree of 'first world' continued dominance: three networks have less than two-thirds of their major network cities in this category (advertising, financial services and accountancy), and for the other two (law and management consultancy) over 80 per cent of major cities are in the old 'first world'. This simple dichotomy directly reflects the total number of major network cities in the different services: the basic globalizing effect is that the more network concentration in cities, the less network diffusion across the world.

The conclusion is that while legal services and management consultancy are sorting out global capital in the richer countries, accountancy is spearheading globalizing effects through getting other regions fit for investment; advertising is expanding the global market resulting in financial services deploying and expanding capital across the world. This was the world in 2008 since when the financial and economic crises may indicate further global effects consequent upon the rise of BRIC (Brazil, Russia, India and China), two erstwhile 'third world states' and two former 'second world states'.

REFERENCES

Arrighi, G. (1994), *The Long Twentieth Century*, London: Verso.

Brown, L.R. (1973), *World without Borders*, New York: Vintage.

Bryson, J. and P.W. Daniels (eds) (1998), *Service Industries in the Global Economy*, Cheltenham: Edward Elgar.

Castells, M. (1996), *The Rise of the Network Society*, Oxford: Blackwell.

Derudder, B., M. Hoyler and P.J. Taylor (2011), 'Goodbye Reykjavik: international banking centres and the global financial crisis', *Area*, **43** (2), 173–182.

Derudder, B., P.J. Taylor, P. Ni, A. De Vos, M. Hoyler, H. Hanssens, D. Bassens, J. Huang, F. Witlox, W. Shen and X. Yang (2010), 'Pathways of change: shifting connectivities in the world city network, 2000–08', *Urban Studies*, **47** (9), 1861–1877.

Dicken, P. (2007), *Global Shift*, New York: Guilford Press, 5th edition.

Faulconbridge, J. (2007), 'Relational networks of knowledge production in transnational law firms', *Geoforum*, **38** (5), 925–940.

Faulconbridge, J.R., J.V. Beaverstock, C. Nativel and P.J. Taylor (2011), *The Globalization of Advertising: Agencies, Cities and Spaces of Creativity*, London: Routledge.

Hanssens, H., B. Derudder, P.J. Taylor, M. Hoyler, P. Ni, J. Huang, X. Yang and F. Witlox (2011), 'The changing geography of globalized service provision, 2000–2008', *The Service Industries Journal*, **31** (14), 2293–2307.

Lai, K.P.Y. (2009), 'Global cities in competition? A qualitative analysis of Shanghai, Beijing and Hong Kong as financial centres', *GaWC Research Bulletin*, 313, available at www.lboro.ac.uk/gawc/rb/rb313.html (accessed 20 September 2010).

O'Brien, R. (1991), *Global Financial Integration: The End of Geography*, London: Thomson Learning.

Ohmae, K. (1999), *The Borderless World*, New York: Harper.

Sassen, S. (1991), *The Global City*, Princeton, NJ: Princeton University Press.

Sassen, S. (1999), 'Global financial centers', *Foreign Affairs*, **78** (1), 75–87.

Taylor, P.J. (2004), *World City Network*, London: Routledge.

Taylor, P.J. (2008), 'Advertising and cities: a relational geography of globalization in the early twenty first century', in E. Kofman and G. Youngs (eds), *Globalization: Theory and Practice*, New York: Continuum, 3rd edition, pp. 205–220.

Taylor, P.J. (2011), 'Advanced producer services in the world economy', in P.J. Taylor, P. Ni, B. Derudder, M. Hoyler, J. Huang and F. Witlox (eds), *Global Urban Analysis: A Survey of Cities in Globalization*, London: Earthscan, pp. 32–39.

Taylor, P.J. and R.E. Lang (2005), *U.S. Cities in the 'World City Network'*, Washington, DC: The Brookings Institution (Metropolitan Policy Program, Survey Series).

Taylor, P.J., P. Ni, B. Derudder, M. Hoyler, J. Huang and F. Witlox (eds) (2011), *Global Urban Analysis: A Survey of Cities in Globalization*, London: Earthscan.

Thrift, N. (1989), 'A hyperactive world', in R.J. Johnston, P.J. Taylor and M.J. Watts (eds), *Geographies of Global Change*, Oxford: Blackwell, pp. 18–35.

PART II

WORLD CITY ANALYSES

II A World city infrastructures

14 Airports: from flying fields to twenty-first century aerocities
Lucy C.S. Budd

INTRODUCTION

I started my travels – where else? – in the airport

(Pico Iyer, 2000, p. 41)

Since the dawn of commercial aviation at the beginning of the twentieth century, airports have played a crucial role in the development and maintenance of a new world order. At their most basic level, airports exist to facilitate international flow and mobility and are routinely classified and judged according to the number of direct flights they host and the volume of passengers, cargo and aircraft they process. Each nation has (with the exception of Andorra, San Marino, Vatican City, Monaco and Liechtenstein, the only countries in the world without an airport) developed a national airport system appropriate to its transportation needs and this has resulted in a global airport system of great complexity. There are currently around 49,000 active airports in the world, ranging in size from tiny airfields that serve some of the remotest regions on earth to mega aerotropoli that handle tens of millions of passengers every year. Yet, irrespective of their particular geographic characteristics, airports have become a common feature of our industrialized landscape and have left indelible imprints on our language, culture and environment.

As the transition points between earth and sky, airports enable people, goods and information to travel around the world. They have brought nations closer together in time and space and have enabled business and personal relationships to be routinely conducted at a distance. They have inspired novelists, artists, architects, politicians, musicians, philosophers, and film and documentary makers and have been the setting for some of the most important moments in recent geopolitical history. Yet they have also provoked controversy and become increasingly criticized for their congestion and delays, their deleterious environmental impacts and strict security. In a little over 100 years, the airport has been transformed from a place of excitement and opportunity into an increasingly maligned aspect of modern culture (Hickman, 2007).

In charting the development of airports, from their origins in the early twentieth century to the present day, this chapter draws on literature from across the social sciences to explore how the creation of a functionally highly differentiated global airport system has enabled and driven processes of globalization in ways that have sometimes been unexpected. Attention is paid both to the development of mega-airport hubs and to the smaller regional or secondary facilities that play an important, but hitherto largely unappreciated, role in the creation of highly dynamic geographies of international trade and mobility. The chapter concludes by speculating on future airport scenarios, including the impact of rescheduling flights away from key hubs into less congested airports located in the hinterland of major world cities and the possibility that airports may ultimately become relics of a bygone age of mass aeromobility.

FROM THE AIRFIELD TO THE AIRPORT

The origins of the airport as a distinct form of public space can be traced back to 1904, when pioneering aviators Wilbur and Orville Wright established a permanent flying ground on Huffman Prairie, a 34-hectare cow pasture at Simms Station, near Dayton, Ohio (Mackersey, 2003). Unlike the fixed infrastructure demanded by modern airports, the requirements for early 'flying fields' were relatively modest. Ideally, they needed to be located on open areas of flat, preferably windswept, land, away from tall buildings and other obstructions to enable pilots to take off and land safely. Depending on one's location, these sites were variously described as 'air stations' (the aeronautical equivalent of railway stations), 'air fields', 'flying grounds' or 'aerodromes' (an adaptation of the Greek word *dromos*, meaning speed).

Throughout the late 1900s and early 1910s, flying exerted an ever-stronger grip on the public imagination. The excitement that accompanied Louis Bleriot's successful flight across the English Channel and the first international air meeting at Reims, France, in 1909, resulted in vast crowds regularly gathering at municipal parks, racecourses and playing fields on the outskirts of major towns and cities to watch pioneering aviators perform daring stunts and feats of aerial speed and endurance. Almost from their inception, these events became fashionable spaces of spectacle and spectatorship and were promoted as places for a curious and potentially 'air minded' population to visit (Wohl, 1996; Adey, 2006). London's first aerodrome, at Hendon, on the northern fringes of the city, opened in 1909 and rapidly evolved into a 'successful and well-organised place for amusement for the entertainment of the public' complete with a spacious grandstand, sightseeing enclosures, an open-air café, tea tents and pavilions (Claxton, 1914, p. 253).

After the outbreak of war in 1914, many airfields were requisitioned for military use and public grandstands were replaced by prefabricated maintenance facilities. When civil flying resumed in Europe in 1919, many demobbed pilots purchased surplus ex-military aircraft and organized themselves into airline companies to begin operating on a commercial basis. The rapid inauguration of regular passenger and airmail services between major towns and cities in Europe and North America during the early 1920s gave renewed impetus to the development of airfields and the provision of a modern landing ground became an issue of municipal pride and prestige that demonstrated 'a city "belongs" in the global net of cities' (Bouman, 1996, p. 193). Significantly, this desire to have an airport exists to this day, with many communities, including the islanders of St Helena in the Atlantic Ocean, believing an airport will integrate them more fully into the global economy (Smith, 2009).

By the late 1920s, the growing number of commercial flights and volume of airline passengers worldwide, combined with the increased size and weight of new purpose-built civilian aircraft, necessitated a fundamental redesign of airfield form and function. In order to entice potential passengers away from the relative comfort and safety of the railways, a number of 'air minded' individuals advocated the construction of a new type of facility to cater to the particular needs of discerning air travellers. Leading architects of the time, including Le Corbusier, Henard and Sant'Elia, designed fanciful 'airports of the future' in which airports were constructed between or on top of another icon of early twentieth century modernity, the skyscraper (Voigt, 1996; Gordon, 2004; Pearman, 2004). However, operational and safety concerns dictated that airports were not suited to downtown urban areas but a city's outskirts.

In order to facilitate the development of regular international air services, it was necessary to provide permanent customs and immigration facilities. The International Convention of Aerial Navigation of October 1919 stipulated that all civil aircraft engaged in international operations must, on leaving or entering a contracting state, depart from or land at a specified customs aerodrome. This regulation necessitated the construction of new and bigger buildings that served not only the operational needs of airlines and the personal requirements of travellers, but also had space in which passports and luggage could be examined. Permanent landing strips were established, paved aircraft parking areas laid, and grand passenger terminals, containing post offices, bookstalls, hotels and restaurants, were provided for the comfort and convenience of passengers (Dierikx and Bouwens, 1997). At Le Bourget airfield near Paris, all commercial aviation activities were housed within a new passenger 'air station' that was considered to epitomize all that was exciting and progressive about modernity (Greif, 1979; Voigt, 2005). In order to distinguish international 'customs aerodromes' from smaller facilities, a new word, 'air-port', entered the English language and was increasingly used from the mid 1920s onwards (Voigt, 1996).

In the 25 years of architectural modernism that followed World War Two, few structures were more functionally modern than the airport. Though international regulations increasingly dictated the practices and procedures that should be followed at every airport (including the separation of arriving and departing passengers and the provision of secure 'airside' areas to separate flying passengers from non-travelling members of the public), terminal buildings became the centrepieces of modern design. Terminals, including Eero Saarinen's TWA building at Kennedy International Airport in New York (1956–1962), attempted to capture the wonder of flight and often featured soaring roofs and cantilevered facades. In order to expedite the timely and efficient flows of increasing numbers of passengers through these terminals, a new global airport logic – which provided continuity of progression from check-in to aircraft and from aircraft to baggage hall – was quickly established and copied around the world. English-language signs and (it was hoped) universally comprehensible pictograms began appearing in passenger terminals to identify the location of key airport facilities and guide passengers through the building.

The introduction of new wide-bodied long-haul passenger aircraft in the late 1960s and early 1970s, combined with the introduction of new 'tourist' or 'economy' class fares, stimulated unprecedented demand for air travel and made flying *the* normal mode of long-distance travel for a significant segment of the population (see Bowen, 2009). The introduction of Boeing's wide-bodied 747 'Jumbo Jet', Lockheed's Tristar and McDonald Douglas's DC-10, which were wider and heavier and could seat over twice as many passengers as existing aircraft, required a fundamental redesign of many airports. Existing sites had to be reconfigured and expanded. On the airfield, runways and taxiways had to be widened, lengthened and strengthened, while passenger terminals had to be expanded to accommodate hundreds of additional passengers and pieces of baggage. At the same time, a growth in the number of terrorist attacks against airports and aircraft necessitated the installation of ever-more stringent and time-consuming security checks. As the time taken to turn around large aircraft and screen hundreds of passengers and bags grew, so too did the time passengers spent waiting in airports before their flight. In order to take advantage of this otherwise unproductive dwell time, airport operators began installing duty-free shops and other retail concessions in their terminals. Airport retailing had the dual purpose of helping to mitigate passenger boredom while raising valuable revenue for the airport operator. However, the development of a universally familiar airport environment led some commentators, including Kaplan (1994) and Wood (2003), to suggest that the once distinctive local spaces of air travel had been subsumed by a global airport system that has a similar form and appearance regardless of physical location.

As a consequence, airports and other spaces associated with mobility, such as motorway service areas and railway stations, have often been described as being 'placeless' or 'non-spaces' of speed. Famously associated with the writings of Edward Relph (1976) and Marc Augé (1995), the idea that spaces of mobility are somehow 'global' spaces of flow, devoid of any local interest or cultural connection, gained widespread currency among some members of the academic community who used the theoretical concepts Relph and Augé advanced to criticize airports for their global 'look-alike' architecture and familiar retail landscapes. The spaces of the departure lounge and arrivals hall, in particular, are often described as being symptomatic sites where place has been sacrificed in the name of mobility (see Kaplan, 1994; Lloyd, 2003; Wood, 2003).

Such accounts have, however, been criticized for glossing over the variegated socialities of air spaces. Merriman (2004, p. 152), in particular, argues that 'frequent flyers, baggage handlers, flight crews, first-time flyers, first class passengers, refugees, air traffic controllers, police officers and the homeless are likely to have very different experiences of movements, dwelling, security, familiarity and belonging' in airports. While Vidler (1998, p. 15) similarly contends that framing airports as 'empty, sterile, non-spaces, determined more by mathematical calculation of times of arrival and departure than by any regard for the human subjects' ignores the rich sociality of air travel, something Cresswell (2001) and Gottdiener (2001) have also been quick to recognize. The supposedly 'placeless' realm of the airport may, therefore, be variously experienced as exciting, stressful, overcrowded, disorganized, frightening, regimented or boring, triggering a remarkably diversified range of inhabitation.

THE RISE OF THE 'AIRPORT CITY': WORLD AIRPORTS AND THEIR CITIES

> The world cities are the site of the great international airports: Heathrow, Kennedy, Orly, Schiphol, Sheremetyevo.
>
> (Hall, 1977, p. 1)

Within academia and civil aviation discourse, the term 'air city' or 'airport city' first emerged in the mid 1940s to describe the growth of an international network of cities connected by air travel. Though a small general aviation facility called 'Air City' had been constructed near the town of Sturtevant, Wisconsin in the 1920s, it was only after the Second World War, when airports gained the ability to function largely independently of the city that they were originally designed to serve, that they began to be conceptualized as modern cities in their own right (Bouman, 1996).

During the mid 1940s it became apparent that the then-leading global aviation nations, Britain and the United States, held radically different views on how post-war civil aviation should develop. While the majority of countries agreed that every state had complete and exclusive sovereignty over the airspace above its territory (including that above all land, territorial waters, colonies, dependencies and mandates), many states were not prepared to grant other countries extensive access rights to their airspace. US proposals for 'open skies' across the Atlantic and unrestricted competition, while supported by some countries, were flatly rejected by Britain and other European nations which advocated a system of strict bilateral regulation (Cheng, 1962). Given that aircraft had no automatic right to 'innocent passage' through sovereign airspace, individual access agreements and airport landing rights had to be negotiated. The exchange or denial of these bilateral agreements had significant implications for the development of the global airline and airport network (Glassner, 1996). In the 1960s, for example, aircraft belonging to the Israeli national carrier, El Al, were prohibited from overflying or landing in Iraq or Syria while other nations were prohibited from overflying what were deemed to be 'unfriendly' countries. The denial of overflying and landing rights has thus been used as a geopolitical tool by countries that have either sought to protect their own national carrier from competition or prevent certain countries from accessing their airports and airspace.

While strict bilateral and multilateral air service agreements largely dictated the structure of the evolving airline network throughout the 1940s, 1950s and 1960s, regulatory changes within the global airline industry, beginning with the deregulation of the US domestic aviation market in 1978 and subsequent liberalization elsewhere, again transformed the patterns of world air services. Deregulation enabled new airlines to enter the marketplace and encouraged competition. In order to protect their market share on lucrative inter-city routes, incumbent US carriers rationalized their route structures and consolidated their traffic at a few key 'hubs' (see Graham, 1995; Button, 2002). The creation of hub-and-spoke networks (or 'hubbing') conferred significant operational advantages for the carriers concerned, but was not always popular with travellers.

The consolidation of flights and passengers at a limited number of major hubs has led to a new phenomenon in which major airports often fulfil many of the roles traditionally performed by the cities they were designed to serve. Large airports have their own security forces, medical units, business centres, hotels, resident press corps, beauty salons, gardens, places of worship and entertainment, and transient homeless populations (Kaplan, 1994). They usually have their own independent systems of power generation and waste disposal, and employ tens of thousands of workers in a bewilderingly diverse range of occupations. Furthermore, at the self-styled 'AirportCity' of Amsterdam Schiphol, it is possible for passengers and the public to shop, eat, sleep, worship, view famous works of art and have a massage, all without leaving the central terminal area. Munich airport boasts a vast conference and hotel complex adjacent to the main terminals, Frankfurt airport contains 222 retail units, while Terminal Five at Heathrow reportedly contains more retail space than central

London's Bond Street. Vancouver International Airport's terminal features indoor rivers, parks and aquaria for the enjoyment of passengers, while travellers using Singapore's Changi airport can wander through tranquil orchid and butterfly gardens. Arguably, the only things cities possess which airports do not are resident populations and permanent residential areas.

For John Kasarda, the influence of the world's major airports is so profound that it is actively reshaping the geography of the airport hinterland. For him, the airport city has become the 'Aerotropolis', consisting of an airport city core and an outlying area of airport-related businesses that can stretch for 15 miles (20 km) or more beyond the airport boundary (Kasarda, 2001, 2008, 2009). The crux of Kasarda's thesis posits that major airports act as 'network magnets' that attract large international businesses, which then cluster along main transportation routes and reshape the airport hinterland creating a new economic geography of the airport periphery. While a number of commentators, including Charles et al. (2007), have sought to critique the aerotropolis model by raising concerns about its long-term sustainability, many others have remarked upon the distinctive geography of car rental lots, access roads, hotels and light industrial units that surround many major airports (Pascoe, 2001; de Botton, 2009).

CLASSIFYING WORLD AIRPORTS

Many measures, including total passenger emplanements, the number of aircraft movements, the type of air traffic and the volume of cargo uplifted, have been used in an effort to classify airports and quantify their relative importance within a global airport hierarchy (Schaafsma, 2003; Derudder and Witlox, 2005a, 2005b; Guimerà et al., 2005; Zook and Brunn, 2006; Derudder et al., 2007a, 2007b). Such rankings help to describe the ways in which individual airports are stitched into local, regional, national and international space-economies, with 'world cities' fully participating in the international economy through international air connections (Keeling, 1995). As a result, much of the existing world cities and globalization literature focuses on the passenger processing capabilities and/or network attributes of the top 20 or so biggest hubs of the estimated 840 airports worldwide that support regular international services. Despite a lack of consensus about what constitutes a 'hub' (Button, 2002), these sites tend to be the focus of sustained academic inquiry. However, while much attention has been paid to these major centres of global aeromobility, there are tens of thousands of smaller sites whose role in the global aviation system has often been overlooked.

Crucially, the hub-and-spoke networks of the post-deregulation era mean that even relatively small airports can be intimately connected into the global airline network via short-haul connections to major hubs elsewhere. For example, Birmingham International Airport (BHX), a regional facility in central England, has daily connections to Emirates' worldwide network via Dubai; Air France/KLM's network via Charles de Gaulle and Amsterdam; Lufthansa's international network via Frankfurt and Munich; Continental Airlines' network via New York; and SN Brussels Airlines via the Belgian capital. Hence, classifying BHX's worldwide connectivity using a metric that only counts direct flights and does not take into account transfer traffic is arguably misleading.

Table 14.1   The connectivity of the top five busiest international airports (2008/2009)

Rank (passenger nos)	Airport	Direct destinations served	Number of countries served	Number of airlines
1	London/Heathrow	180	90	90
2	Paris/Charles de Gaulle	294	106	66
3	Amsterdam/Schiphol (2007 figures)	267	87	98
4	Frankfurt	304	106	119
5	Hong Kong	180	46	85

Source: compiled from individual airport websites, 2009

Table 14.2   International airport hierarchy based on connectivity rankings

Airport	Rank – intl. passengers	Rank – no. of direct destinations served	Rank – no. of countries served	Cumulative score
Paris/Charles de Gaulle	2	2	=1	5
Frankfurt	4	1	=1	6
London/Heathrow	1	=4	3	8
Amsterdam	3	3	4	10
Hong Kong	5	=4	5	14

In terms of passenger numbers, Atlanta airport in Georgia is the world's busiest international airport. Significantly, however, a large proportion of the 90 million passengers it handled in 2008 were US domestic travellers. If domestic passengers are stripped away, the five busiest international airports in the world in 2008 were London/Heathrow (62 million international passengers), Paris/Charles de Gaulle (55 million international passengers), Amsterdam/Schiphol (48 million international passengers), Frankfurt (47 million international passengers) and Hong Kong (46 million international passengers). However, as Table 14.1 shows, the busiest international airports are not necessarily the best connected, with Heathrow serving fewer direct destinations than Paris, Amsterdam and Frankfurt. If these individual attributes are ranked, Paris/Charles de Gaulle emerges at the top of the international airport hierarchy and Heathrow is relegated to third place (Table 14.2).

The progressive worldwide liberalization of the aviation sector has resulted in a new type of carrier entering the marketplace. These low-cost airlines typically eschew the congestion, delays and expense associated with operating from major airports and fly instead from smaller and cheaper facilities in the hinterland of major world cities. Hence these carriers will use London/Stansted, Frankfurt/Hahn and Stockholm/Skavsta in preference to Heathrow, Frankfurt-am-Main and Arlanda. Despite the fact that these secondary airports are often located many miles away from the city they are intended to serve, passenger growth has often been rapid. As a consequence, two discrete networks of passenger aviation have emerged. One is a major international hub-and-spoke system that serves major city airports and the other is a low-cost point-to-point network that operates from smaller secondary airports. Yet in addition to recognizing the existence of different types of passenger airport, it is also important to acknowledge the role major cargo facilities, including Liege (Belgium), Memphis (USA) and East Midlands (UK), and dedicated business aviation airports such as London/Farnborough and Paris/Le Bourget (see Budd and Graham, 2009), play in the global airport system.

FAILED AIRPORTS

While a network of highly functionally differentiated airports developed to meet the needs of multiple air travel users during the twentieth century, the structure of the global airport hierarchy is highly dynamic and individual airports are vulnerable to competition, evolving aeronautical technology and changing international political relations (see Grubesic et al., 2005). Until the introduction of jet-powered commercial aircraft in 1952, much of the strategic importance of certain airports was due not only to the size and/or intrinsic business or tourist attractions of the area they served but also to the limited range of early aircraft. In the mid 1930s, Britain and other European Imperial powers established chains of landing grounds across the Middle East and Africa. These sites enabled aircraft to be refuelled and allowed pilots and passengers time to rest between sectors on long-distance journeys to the Far East and South Africa. However, the introduction of modern longer-range jet-powered aircraft meant that these small intermediate landing grounds could be overflown with ease. As a consequence, many were abandoned or served far less frequently and once busy international air junctions in Africa and the Middle East were relegated to the relative backwaters of commercial aviation. Similarly, the replacement of flying boats and piston-powered aircraft by jet airliners on transatlantic routes in the late 1950s meant that the once busy refuelling stations at Prestwick (Scotland), Shannon (on the west coast of Ireland), Gander (Newfoundland) and Goose Bay (Labrador), and the once important staging posts of the Azores, Bermuda, Sondrestromfjord (Greenland) and Iceland, are now overflown with ease and only used in the case of a technical problem or diversion. In the Pacific Ocean too, the once busy airports of Honolulu, Nadi (Fiji), Papeete (Taihiti), Canton Island, Midway, Guam and Wake Island have lost their status as important trans-Pacific staging posts.

Other airports have become victims of changing aeronautical practice and/or global economic recession more recently. Montreal's Mirabel airport, for example, which opened in 1975, was designed to handle over 6.8 million passengers a year. However, due to its location 45 miles north of Montreal, it was never a commercial success and fewer than 800,000 passengers a year were using the facility when it closed in 2003 (Clark, 2003). In South Korea, several airports have been mothballed owing to challenging trading conditions, while Coventry and Sheffield City airports in the United Kingdom have closed because of a lack of traffic and competition from neighbouring facilities. Liberalization and the rise of low-cost flying have also meant that airlines are free to enter and leave the marketplace as economic conditions dictate. Many airports, which have often invested heavily to attract new services, have found these links withdrawn at short notice, while others have struggled to make a profit in the face of adverse economic conditions.

THE FUTURE

In a little over a century, airports have evolved from rudimentary flying fields into 24-hour a day mobility machines that serve hundreds of thousands of flights and millions of passengers every year. The unprecedented growth in passenger demand during the latter half of the twentieth century not only necessitated a rapid evolution in airport form and function but also resulted in many airports operating close to capacity. This, in turn, has led to congestion and delays and a growing sense of customer dissatisfaction with the airport experience. Anecdotal evidence suggests that the current economic downturn, combined with increased awareness of aviation's environmental impacts and growing concern about the risk of aviation terrorism, are starting to depress passenger demand. It has been suggested that many travellers are now actively avoiding congested hub airports and buying point-to-point tickets between smaller regional airports instead, choosing to holiday within their own country and engaging in teleconferencing rather than business travel. Given current concerns about oil price volatility and 'peak oil', it could be argued that air travel may once again become a luxury obtainable only by the very rich. Under this scenario, commercial airports might become relics of a bygone age of mass aeromobility.

CONCLUSION

Geographers and social scientists have consistently identified air travel as being one of the key drivers of globalization. Airports have enabled business and personal relationships to be conducted at a distance and they have transformed human cultures of movement. However, in addition to being places of excitement and opportunity, airports are also highly contested spaces and have been sites of political protest, opposition and violence. Yet, despite controversy surrounding their development, airports are emblematic spaces of the modern world whose importance to, and influence on, human society are difficult to overstate.

REFERENCES

Adey, P. (2006), 'Airports and air-mindedness: spacing, timing and using Liverpool Airport 1929–39', *Social and Cultural Geography*, **7** (3), 343–363.
Augé, M. (1995), *Non-Places: Introduction to an Anthropology of Supermodernity* (translated J. Howe), London: Verso.
Bouman, M.J. (1996), 'Cities of the plane: airports in the networked city', in J. Zukowsky (ed.), *Building for Air Travel. Architecture and Design for Commercial Aviation*, Munich: Prestel, pp. 177–193.
Bowen, J. (2009), 'Three decades of airline industry liberalization – an introduction', *Journal of Transport Geography*, **17** (4), 249–250.
Budd, L. and B.J. Graham (2009), 'Unintended trajectories: liberalization and the geographies of private business flight', *Journal of Transport Geography*, **17** (4), 285–292.

Button, K. (2002), 'Debunking some common myths about airport hubs', *Journal of Air Transport Management*, **8** (3), 177–188.

Charles, M.B., P. Barnes, N. Ryan and J. Clayton (2007), 'Airport futures: towards a critique of the aerotropolis model', *Futures*, **39** (9), 1009–1028.

Cheng, B. (1962), *The Law of International Air Transport*, London: Stevens and Sons.

Clark, A. (2003), 'Lesson of Canadian airport in terminal decline', *The Guardian*, 23 September, 16.

Claxton, W.J. (1914), *Mastery of the Air*, London: Blackie and Sons Ltd.

Cresswell, T. (2001), 'The production of mobilities', *New Formations*, **43**, 11–25.

Cresswell, T. (2006), *On the Move: Mobility in the Modern Western World*, London: Routledge.

de Botton, A. (2009), *A Week at the Airport. A Heathrow Diary*, London: Profile Books.

Derudder, B., L. Devriendt and F. Witlox (2007a), 'Flying where you don't want to go: an empirical analysis of hubs in the global airline network', *Tijdschrift voor Economische en Sociale Geografie*, **98** (3), 307–324.

Derudder, B. and F. Witlox (2005a), 'An appraisal of the use of airline data in assessing the world city network: a research note on data', *Urban Studies*, **42** (13), 2371–2388.

Derudder, B. and F. Witlox (2005b), 'On the use of inadequate airline data in mappings of a global urban system', *Journal of Air Transport Management*, **11** (4), 231–237.

Derudder, B., F. Witlox and P.J. Taylor (2007b), 'U.S. cities in the world city network: comparing their positions using global origins and destinations of airline passengers', *Urban Geography*, **28** (1), 74–91.

Dierikx, M. and B. Bouwens (1997), *Building Castles of the Air. Schiphol Amsterdam and the Development of Airport Infrastructure in Europe, 1916–1996*, The Hague: Sdu Publishers.

Frankfurt Airport Corporate Website (2009), available at www.frankfurt-airport.com (accessed 12 December 2009).

Glassner, M.I. (1996), *Political Geography*, New York: J. Wiley, 2nd edition.

Gordon, A. (2004), *Naked Airport: A Cultural History of the World's Most Revolutionary Structure*, Chicago: University of Chicago Press.

Gottdiener, M. (2001), *Life in the Air: Surviving the New Culture of Air Travel*, Lanham, MD: Rowman and Littlefield.

Graham, B.J. (1995), *Geography and Air Transport*, Chichester: Wiley.

Greif, M. (1979), *The Airport Book: From Flying Field to Modern Terminal*, New York: Mayflower Books.

Grubesic, T.H., T.C. Matisziw and M.A. Zook (2005), 'Spatio-temporal fluctuations in the global airport hierarchies', *Journal of Transport Geography*, **17** (4), 264–275.

Guimerà, R., S. Mossa, A. Turtschi and L.A.N. Amaral (2005), 'The worldwide air transport network: anomalous centrality, community structure, and cities' global roles', *PNAS*, **102** (22), 7794–7799.

Hall, P. (1977), *The World Cities*, London: Weidenfeld and Nicolson, 2nd edition.

Hickman, M. (2007), 'The world's worst airports', *The Independent Extra*, 28 November, 1–5.

Iyer, P. (2000), *The Global Soul: Jet-Lag, Shopping Malls and the Search for Home*, London: Bloomsbury.

Kaplan, J. (1994), *The Airport: Planes, People, Triumphs, and Disasters at John F. Kennedy International*, New York: Quill William Morrow.

Kasarda, J. (2001), 'From airport city to aerotropolis', *Airport World*, **6** (4), 42–45.

Kasarda, J. (2008), *Airport Cities: The Evolution*, London: Insight Media.

Kasarda, J. (2009), 'Airport cities', *Urban Land*, April, 56–60.

Keeling, D.J. (1995), 'Transport and the world city paradigm', in P.L. Knox and P.J. Taylor (eds), *World Cities in a World System*, Cambridge: Cambridge University Press, pp. 115–131.

Lloyd, J. (2003), 'Dwelltime: airport technology, travel, and consumption', *Space and Culture*, **6** (2), 93–109.

Mackersey, I. (2003), *The Wright Brothers*, London: Time Warner.

Merriman, P. (2004), 'Driving places: Marc Augé, non-places, and the geographies of England's M1 motorway', *Theory, Culture and Society*, **21** (4/5), 145–168.

Pascoe, D. (2001), *Airspaces*, London: Reaktion.

Pearman, H. (2004), *Airports: A Century of Architecture*, London: Laurence King.

Relph, E. (1976), *Place and Placelessness*, London: Pion.

Rosler, M. (1998), *In the Place of the Public: Observations of a Frequent Flyer*, Ostfildern-Ruit: Cantz.

Schaafsma, M. (2003), 'Airports and cities in networks', *disP – The Planning Review*, **154**, 28–36.

Smith, A.D. (2009), 'Angry islanders accuse UK of stalling over £200m airport', *The Observer*, 24 May, available at http://www.guardian.co.uk/uk/2009/nay/24/st-helenas-island-south-africa (accessed 1 July 2011).

Vidler, A. (1998), 'Terminal transfer', in M. Rosler, *In the Place of the Public: Observations of a Frequent Flyer*, Ostfildern-Ruit: Cantz, pp. 12–21.

Voigt, W. (1996), 'From the hippodrome to the aerodrome, from the air station to the terminal: European airports, 1909–1945', in J. Zukowsky (ed.), *Building for Air Travel: Architecture and Design for Commercial Aviation*, Prestel: Munich, pp. 27–50.

Voigt, W. (2005), 'The birth of the terminal: some typological remarks on early airport architecture in Europe', in B. Hawkins, G. Lechner and P. Smith (eds), *Historic Airports: Proceedings of the International 'L'Europe de l'Air' Conferences on Aviation Architecture,* London: English Heritage, pp. 11–22.

Wohl, R. (1996), *A Passion for Wings: Aviation and the Western Imagination, 1908–1918,* New Haven, CT: Yale University Press.

Wood, A. (2003). 'A rhetoric of ubiquity: terminal space as omnitopia', *Communication Theory,* **13** (3), 324–344.

Zook, M.A. and S.D. Brunn (2006), 'From podes to antipodes: positionalities and global airline geographies', *Annals of the Association of American Geographers,* **96** (3), 471–490.

15 Global cities, office markets and capital flows
Colin Lizieri

INTRODUCTION

This chapter examines office markets in global cities and, in particular, international financial centres. The early world city literature focused on classification (Friedmann, 1986) or on a small number of global cities and on inequalities within them (Sassen, 1991). More recent work focuses on linkages between cities, drawing on theoretical approaches such as Castells' (1996) 'Space of Flows'. Empirical work in this tradition is exemplified by the Globalization and World Cities (GaWC) research network, which explores the connections between cities (e.g. Taylor, 2005). Those connections relate to exchange of information and human capital within and across firms and establishment of trust relationships, emphasizing knowledge creation and processing and advanced producer services (Hall and Pain, 2006; Cook et al., 2007).

While the emphasis on flows and relationships is critical, the bulk of the activities that form these linkages takes place in offices – indeed much of the GaWC connectivity measures rely on identification of the office networks of high order service firms. Offices, by their fixity, ground flows in particular locations. They are not simply passive receivers and transmitters: office markets shape cities, direct firms to particular locations and create path dependency (in that a critical mass of office stock creates the breadth of business activities that drive agglomeration economies). Further, they are an investment asset, a store of value and a significant part of institutional and private investment portfolios. As assets, they act as collateral for bank lending and real estate securities. Thus they link global cities to international capital markets and expose cities to the volatility of global finance.

In the global cities literature, financial activity is seen as a key function. What makes a city a financial centre? Kindleberger (1974) provided an early definition of international financial centres, focusing on their role in effecting payments and transferring savings around the economy: 'the specialized functions of international payments and foreign lending or borrowing are typically best performed at one central place that is also (in most instances) the specialized center for domestic interregional payment' (Kindleberger, 1974, p. 6).

An international financial centre (IFC) will have a greater concentration of cross-border activity than a domestic financial centre, but it is not clear where the boundary lies or whether it is the scale or the proportion of international activity that is critical (e.g. Tokyo in the modern era and New York historically were dominated by domestic transactions and capital). It is possible to identify IFC indicators and attributes: global ranking in financial activities, headquarters of multinational financial firms, the presence of foreign financial firms in the city. Research generally leaves the definition open and examines the activities and characteristics of leading cities: a financial hierarchy to mirror the world urban hierarchy.

Table 15.1   Global city classifications, financial cities

GFCI 7			Master Card Centres of Commerce		GaWC 2008	
1	London	775	London	79.2	New York	100
2	New York	775	New York	72.8	London	98.6
3	Hong Kong	739	Tokyo	66.6	Hong Kong	81.3
4	Singapore	733	Singapore	66.2	Paris	77.9
5	Tokyo	692	Hong Kong	63.9	Singapore	74.1
6	Chicago	678	Paris	63.9	Tokyo	72.5
7	Zurich	676	Frankfurt	62.3	Sydney	71.7
8	Geneva	671	Seoul	61.8	Beijing	70.1
9	Sydney	670	Amsterdam	60.1	Shanghai	68.8
10	Shenzen	670	Madrid	58.3	Milan	67.7

Sources: Z/Yen (2010), MasterCard Worldwide (2008), GaWC (2008)

There is ample evidence that international financial activities are strongly concentrated in particular cities. In ranking lists, some cities dominate niche areas (Geneva, Zurich for wealth management, for example) but are less prominent in others; but a handful of key cities are highly ranked in most financial sectors. A number of 'global rankings' exist. In each, rankings vary slightly, depending on criteria used and datasets employed. Those based on survey work may carry cultural or linguistic biases, but there is strong common ground. In this chapter, the rankings produced by Z/Yen using their 'Global Financial Centres' index (GFCI) are used. The GFCI combines quantitative indicators of market share, qualities (labour market, infrastructure, available services) and openness (transparency, regulatory and tax structure, etc.) with survey data on competitiveness as a business location.

Table 15.1 shows the top ten cities in the seventh GFCI (Z/Yen, 2010), alongside the top ten cities in the MasterCard Worldwide 2008 survey and the *World According to GaWC 2008*. The list contains few surprises. Paris is not ranked in the top ten and the high ranking of both Swiss centres (reflecting their private fund management status) may be unexpected. Tokyo – regularly placed alongside London and New York (and sometimes Paris) as a dominant world city – is ranked fifth, reflecting concerns about its openness to foreign businesses operating there and the aftermath of the bursting of the Japanese asset bubble in the 1990s. Shenzen appears over-ranked (and was absent from earlier indices). The full list of financial centres includes offshore centres (Hamilton, Bermuda, for example) whose significance greatly exceeds their size or prominence as cities, and emerging centres such as Dubai.

The remainder of the chapter focuses on commercial real estate investment and on major city office markets. The next section examines global real estate investment flows, demonstrating that they are strongly concentrated in both office markets and global cities. Next, urban office dynamics are examined: it is argued that the linkage between space, investment, supply and finance markets is amplified in international financial centres, which are characterized by their functional specialization. This exposes cities to shocks – a vulnerability coordinated across cities. Evidence for this is provided by examining office market behaviour in the aftermath of the 2007–2008 liquidity crisis. Finally, policy implications are drawn.

CAPITAL FLOWS AND GLOBAL REAL ESTATE INVESTMENT

While advanced producer services have become increasingly international in nature (and concentrated in global cities), real estate investment in developed economies remained predominantly local and domestic for much of the latter decades of the twentieth century. There was cross-border investment – notably by Japanese investors in the 'bubble' era and by mainland-European investors including Dutch and Swedish institutional investors (constrained by the size of their domestic markets) and by German open-ended funds, freed from regulatory constraints. However, information advantages for domestic investors, the additional costs of monitoring and of hedging exchange rate risk and the problems faced in diversifying international holdings limited growth in global markets.

Innovation in real estate investment vehicles from the 1990s transformed the market. Alongside the spread of tax-efficient listed Real Estate Investment Trusts, the late 1990s saw rapid growth of private real estate funds that allowed global investors to pool capital and invest in non-domestic markets. INREV (the European Association for Investors in Non-Listed Real Estate Vehicles) figures show the number of private real estate funds in Europe rising from less than 100 in 1998 to some 650 in 2008, those funds managing assets in excess of €300 billion. Baum (2008) suggests that the value of unlisted real estate funds in Europe grew 10 per cent per annum between 1997 and 2007, with more recent explosive growth seen in Asian and emerging markets. Fund structures and investment styles varied but the net effect was to make it simpler for investors to build global real estate portfolios. Many new global funds utilized debt to increase both assets under management and promised returns for investors. That leverage linked funds to global credit markets and increased investment risk: trading off higher volatility for higher expected returns.

There are few robust statistics of global commercial real estate investment; those sources do not offer long time series. Data become more available from the early 2000s and show the rapid increase in overall volume of investment activity and the share of that activity that is global in nature. For example, Jones Lang LaSalle figures show private commercial real estate transactions rising from $350 billion in 2003 to $759 billion in 2007; within those figures, cross-border deals rose from $90 billion to $357 billion. In the global liquidity crisis, overall transaction volumes dropped: by 50 per cent between 2007 and 2008, and by a further 44 per cent between 2008 and 2009. By 2009, domestic investors were again in the ascendancy. However, in the credit crunch many global real estate recovery funds raised equity, intending to buy as the market turned or acquire distressed assets from banks. As the global market recovers unevenly, international investment levels are likely to be restored.

As an example, Lizieri and Kutsch (2006) reveal a marked shift in global ownership of City of London offices (Figure 15.1). Until the mid 1980s, international ownership remained remarkably stable, at between 10 per cent and 15 per cent. The proportion of non-UK ownership began to increase in parallel with financial deregulation across the late 1980s, reached 25 per cent in the second half of the 1990s and, by 2005, exceeded 45 per cent. The late 1990s saw the appearance of 'international investment' – offices purchased by funds with equity from a diverse mix of nationalities and investor types. It is difficult to obtain comparable figures for other markets but global capital flow increases suggest London was not unique in experiencing a globalization in ownership. Property

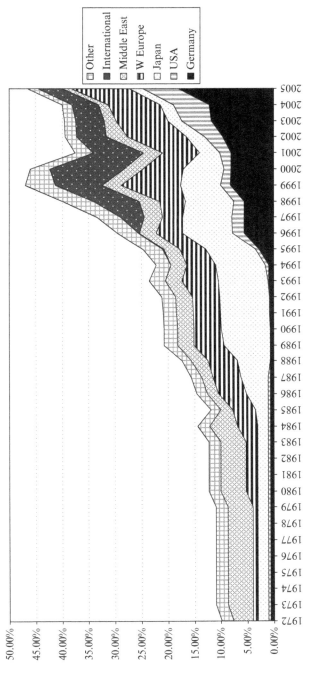

Note: 'International' indicates a fund or ownership vehicle that combines capital from owners of different nationalities – for example, a Limited Partnership with investors from a number of countries.

Source: Lizieri and Kutsch (2006)

Figure 15.1   Non-domestic office ownership, City of London

Funds Research's (2008) survey of global fund managers reports that, of 107 funds surveyed (with over €1 trillion of property assets under management), 38 per cent had 10 per cent or more of their assets spread across more than one continental region.

THE IMPORTANCE OF IFCs IN GLOBAL REAL ESTATE INVESTMENT

In principle, real estate investors should seek diversification in their real estate portfolios. Geographical diversification involves selection of properties in different regions (or countries); sectoral diversification involves acquisition of buildings of different types, industrial, office, retail, apartments or hotels. Again, in principle, the growth of Real Estate Investment Trusts (REITs) and private real estate funds should permit greater diversification, with investors able to gain exposure to, say, Asian industrial markets or emerging Eastern European retail. However, the markets targeted by larger funds appear to be more traditional in nature. To what extent is global real estate capital investment concentrated in office markets – and in global cities?

While it is difficult to obtain accurate data on stock of space, the importance of IFCs in global capital market activity can be gauged from flow data. Real Capital Analytics (RCA) data for the top 1000 commercial real estate deals by value in 2007 and in 2008 demonstrate concentration of investment activity, despite the expanding global arena for investment. The cleaned RCA data contain 1979 deals with a total value of $527 billion. By value, 49 per cent of the deals were office acquisitions, with a value of $257 billion and floor space in excess of 437 million square feet. The RCA data identify the location of each deal. Table 15.2 shows the cities with the most deals for all property and for offices. The concentration is striking: 50.2 per cent of the major deals took place in just ten cities, over 40 per cent in just five cities. Office investment is more concentrated still: 55 per cent of the largest office deals were in ten cities, 44 per cent in five cities and nearly 30 per cent of the deals took place in London or New York.

Table 15.2   Commercial real investment by city: 2007–2008

All property types			Office deals		
City	Value $ m	(% of total)	City	Value $ m	(% of total)
1. Shanghai	81,483.7	15.5	1. New York	38,511.8	14.96
2. New York	45,869.3	8.7	2. London	37,783.4	14.68
3. London	44,188.5	8.4	3. Tokyo	15,589.9	6.06
4. Tokyo	22,171.7	4.2	4. Paris	13,073.5	5.08
5. Singapore	20,654.3	3.9	5. Singapore	8,406.7	3.27
6. Paris	13,703.6	2.6	6. Madrid	6,353.5	2.47
7. Beijing	13,094.2	2.5	7. Seoul	5,782.2	2.25
8. Hong Kong	8,878.5	1.7	8. Washington	5,770.3	2.24
9. Washington	7,283.8	1.4	9. San Francisco	5,282.6	2.05
10. Madrid	6,896.0	1.3	10. Beijing	5,031.3	1.95

Source: Author, from RCA data,

It is evident that many of the cities dominating global real estate investment activity are IFCs. Sixty-four per cent of total deals and 72 per cent of office deals took place in those cities ranked as IFCs by Z/Yen. Excluding highly ranked offshore financial centres such as the Cayman Islands, Jersey and the Isle of Man, 37 per cent of the value of all property deals and 56 per cent of all office deals were located in the top 20 IFCs. Office investment activity is strongly correlated to financial market strength: there is a 0.6 correlation between office investment value and the city's score on the GFCI.

As a further indicator of the globalization of property investment, the top 1000 deals (which, in total, represent over 80 per cent of all sales by value) were analysed and the head office of the acquiring investor identified.[1] Of these large deals, 44 per cent of all trades ($189 billion) and 38 per cent of office sales ($74 billion) were cross-border. Nearly a quarter of all office sales was cross-border *and* took place in a top-ranked IFC. Fifty per cent of buyers were based in top ten international financial centres, a further 10 per cent of buyers were in IFCs ranked 11–20, with less than a third of buyers *not* having a headquarters in a global financial centre.

From these results, it is evident that despite the trend towards global property funds and diversified property holdings, real estate investment activity – and office market activity in particular – remains strongly concentrated geographically in a small number of cities – the majority of which are global financial centres. The leading IFCs dominate office investment, with some $100 billion of major office sales in London, New York, Frankfurt and Tokyo alone across 2007 and 2008. This emphasizes the importance of the IFCs to real estate investment.

UNDERSTANDING OFFICE MARKET DYNAMICS

The behaviour of office markets derives from the interaction of four market types: the occupier or space market; the development or supply market; the investment market; and the market for real estate finance. These markets – notably the space market and the developer market – have tended to be analysed in isolation. However, the linkage between markets is critical to understanding risk–return relationships and the interface with capital markets that assumes critical importance in credit booms and financial crises. In global cities and in financial centres, the markets may be more strongly linked than in second-tier and non-financial cities, with consequences for the volatility of office markets in those cities.

In the space market, occupiers seek offices for their business activities, paying rent that reflects the profitability of operating in a particular location – access to resources, labour markets, customers and the agglomeration economies available from co-location: competition between users determines rent levels. Standard models, however, tend to assume away the supply of that space – property is seen as a derived demand, delivered as required. However, supply of space is more complex. There is path-dependency (the existing stock of space constrains the activities of developers), an institutional context (the role of planning regulation, for example) and a decision-making process that must balance cost of development with the reward, the value of the completed development. Developers face uncertainty, since time to build may be lengthy and demand for space may change over that period. There are asymmetries in the relationships between

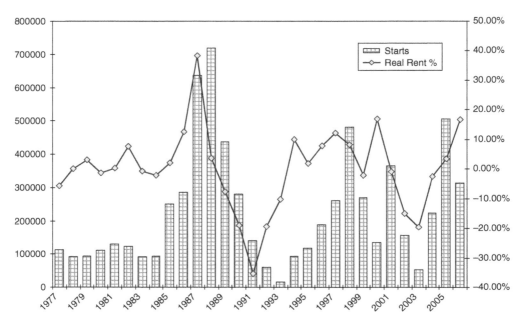

Source: Author, from Corporation of London, CBRE, Office for National Statistics

Figure 15.2   Office construction and real rents

rents and supply, since developers can build more space but, once built, offices cannot simply be 'withdrawn' in response to negative demand shocks (Englund et al., 2008; Hendershott et al., 2010).

In most major office markets, supply of space is not smooth, nor does it seem to react to anticipated rent. Rather, periods of intense building activity surrounded by periods of inactivity are observed (as in Figure 15.2, showing supply in the City of London). Moreover, construction starts *lag* real increases in rent. If fluctuations in demand allied to short term inelasticity in supply produce rental fluctuations, this pronounced building 'cycle' is likely to result in extreme swings in rents and capital values. While the cyclicality of office markets is often cited as indicating irrational behaviour by developers and lenders, a developing body of work seeks to combine real options models and game theory to explain the behaviour of economic agents in the development process. These models focus on the decisions of individual developers faced with future uncertainty and volatility. Perhaps the most complete formulation is found in Grenadier (1995, 1996). Grenadier seeks to explain why development is clustered and why developers develop into recessions, despite declining occupational demand and building values. He shows that strategies adopted by developers depend on starting conditions in the market, on volatility of demand and on time to construct. Development cascades – with developers rushing to develop simultaneously – occur in particular where volatility of demand is high. Volatility increases the option value of waiting – but once conditions favour development, all developers race to build. Developers are prone to build 'defensively' when demand signals falter, for fear of being shut out of the market if competitors do build.

Grenadier's model is theoretical in nature but, nonetheless, captures many of the features observed in real estate development. It also suggests that cycles will be more pronounced in markets characterized by high employment volatility (e.g. where there is strong functional specialization in economic activity); where the time taken from start to completion is long (e.g. in densely developed urban centres); and where there are entry barriers for development (e.g. where the cost of development and access to capital exclude smaller developers). All these characteristics apply to the office markets of global cities.

Developers react to rents and anticipated capital values, providing linkage to the real estate investment market. Investors acquire real estate for its cashflow characteristics – which combine bond-like contractual rental income and equity elements in anticipated rental and capital value growth. Formally, the value of a building is the discounted value of anticipated future cashflows. That discount rate is determined by the cost of capital – required return on equity, marginal cost of debt and the debt–equity ratio. Investment values are thus bound to credit availability. The rise in real asset values seen across mature economies before the credit crunch was, in large measure, driven by a capital glut, competition between lenders driving down interest rates and forcing banks to relax loan terms. Development, too, is linked to credit availability, access to finance for projects.[2] Development activity alters the stock of space, relative to demand, which determines rents, closing the circle.

GLOBAL OFFICE MARKETS AND SYSTEMIC RISK

This section broadly follows the arguments in *Towers of Capital* (Lizieri, 2009) and in Lizieri et al. (2000) in suggesting that office markets in global cities and international financial centres have characteristics that tend to reinforce cyclical behaviour and volatility in rents and capital values. In essence, I argue that development, investment, space and financing markets are locked together *within* financial centres and *across* financial centres, suggesting both greater amplitude in cycle and potential coordination of cycles across cities. This can then feed back into the capital markets, creating systemic risk. Having set out the main arguments, some preliminary evidence from the market corrections following the global liquidity crisis is presented.

Lizieri et al. (2000) argue that the distinction between the funding of real estate development, ownership of real estate as an investment and occupation of property has become blurred. They describe an integration of property and financial markets and argue that this creates systemic risk as shocks in one area of the property market are transmitted throughout the system. This is seen most clearly in global cities and financial centre office markets. The scale of development demands complex finance and funding arrangements provided by major banks, finance houses and institutional investors. Those same financial firms are the *occupiers* of space, as owners or as tenants. Thus rents and capital values are linked to the fortunes of international financial firms and their demand for space. It is those same firms that *invest* in offices in financial centres – directly by acquisition for their investment portfolios, indirectly through investment in real estate funds, by holding shares of property companies owning the buildings or by investing in securitized debt products backed by office values. Those investments are significant parts of the asset base of the financial firms and act as collateral for their operational activities, including property lending. Thus occupier, supply and investment markets are locked together.

Evidence for concentration of financial occupation is not easy to obtain. While global financial centres exhibit high concentrations of financial services activity compared with other cities, detailed employment statistics tend to be available only at metro level, with sub-market data for central business districts rarely available. Further, many specialized business service activities in IFCs are tied into financial activity. Thus in New York City, 'only' 15 per cent of employment is classified to finance, insurance and real estate, with a further 16 per cent in professional or information services; similarly, in metropolitan Frankfurt 15 per cent of employment is in financial and credit institutions, with a further 26 per cent in real estate, leasing and business activities. London is unusual in that its major financial district, the City, forms a separate administrative area. It provides strong evidence of the extent of concentration. In 2008, Corporation of London (CoL, 2010) figures show financial services share of employment at 45 per cent, with 76 per cent of employment in business and financial services (firms such as Reuters and Bloomberg and international law firms focused on financial activity being classified as business services). The Canary Wharf office cluster is similarly concentrated, with the shares of finance and finance and business services being, respectively, 55 per cent and 70 per cent. Lizieri and Kutsch (2006) show that 44 per cent of office space in the City of London is simultaneously owned and occupied by financial service firms and 77 per cent of space simultaneously owned and occupied by financial and business service firms, the majority of which will have an international orientation.

Financial innovation in real estate increases that lockstep. Globalization of financial activity leads to increasing functional specialization in financial centres, with many domestic-focused firms squeezed out of the market by international financial service or associated professional service firms. Globalization of ownership means that professional investors based in one financial centre typically have exposure to real estate in other centres. Innovations in investment make it easier to acquire a global real estate portfolio, with capital from multiple investors pooled to acquire prime property. Greater use of debt in these vehicles, facilitated by securitization and capital market lending, increases gearing and, hence, implicit volatility of real estate. Finally, purchase of debt securities by financial firms brings further exposure to real estate risk.

This process of lockstep is important in the context of the volatility of global capital markets. In many global city office markets, demand for space is driven by the employment needs of financial firms which, in turn, are driven by the behaviour of international financial markets. Demand shocks are thus likely to occur in a coordinated fashion across the major IFCs. Integration of occupational, asset and development markets means that demand shocks (positive or negative) are reinforced. A downturn in global capital markets reduces financial firms' demand for space, putting downward pressure on rents. This affects capital values and returns, damaging the performance of investment portfolios. Falling rents and capital values and rising vacancy rates put pressure on borrowers, increase the risk of debt instruments and depress the value of debt securities held as an asset and used as collateral. This affects the profitability of financial firms, depressing their demand for space. The converse applies to positive shocks driven by booming capital markets. Larger firms based in financial centres capture greater market share and seek to expand, placing upward pressure on rents; rising property prices

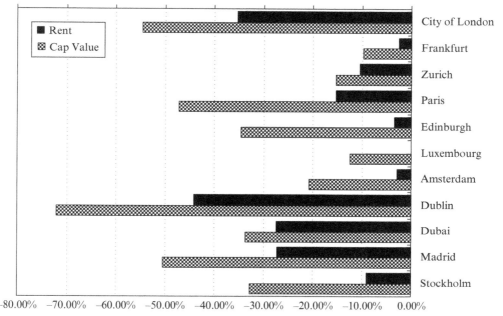

Source: Author, from CBRE data

Figure 15.3   Office value falls, 2005–2009

enhance asset values and encourage lending and development, with the additional activity enhancing short term profitability. By implication, this suggests that the amplitude of cyclical fluctuations in IFCs will be higher and peaks and troughs will be coincident.

Evidence of common movement of office markets across financial centres was provided in *Towers of Capital*. Correlation in rental movements was found to be higher between major financial centres than between cities not dominated by finance, while a component analysis of rental variance identified a strong global factor explaining some 40 per cent of the variation in rents, with major financial centres loading strongly on that factor. Weaker evidence of coordinated development cycles and linkages between employment change was found. The financial turmoil of the credit crunch provides a further opportunity to test the prediction of coordinated crises. Given data issues, analysis is, perforce, exploratory rather than definitive.

Figure 15.3 shows changes in office rental and capital values for those European and Middle Eastern cities tracked by real estate consultants CBRE that are highly ranked in the GFCI. Falls in value are shown from the peak values post-2004 to the lowest value up to Q4 2009. Markets differ in their turning points both entering the downward correction and in showing signs of recovery. However, *all* cities show falls, in most instances substantial. Timings varied: some markets – notably London – fell early and sharply. Others lagged, with appraisers reluctant to mark values down. This, in part, may explain lower apparent falls in Frankfurt, Zurich and Geneva (where there was also a less pronounced rise in values). Capital value falls are greater than rental value falls, emphasizing the importance of investment markets and credit in maintaining and bursting asset bubbles.

It is worth stressing the wider implications of these value falls. Much of the real estate acquisition activity in the period immediately before the credit crunch was by funds using a mixture of debt and equity; much of that activity was in global city offices. For a fund with a mix of 60 per cent debt and 40 per cent equity, a 30 per cent fall in capital values equates to a 75 per cent loss of equity capital. Many real estate funds and property companies breached their loan to value covenants, defaulted or struggled to renegotiate debt.[3] Similar falls are observed in non-EMEA (Europe, Middle East and Africa) markets. CBRE total office occupancy costs for world cities show widespread falls from peak values: –27 per cent in New York, –19 per cent in Shanghai, –33 per cent in Tokyo. Investors who had built international property portfolios focused on major city office markets did not get diversification when they most needed it, when confronted with turbulent market conditions.

It is clear, then, that values fell sharply across most global financial centres. Did they fall *more* in financial centres? Figure 15.4 shows capital value falls reported by CBRE for 64 EMEA cities, grouped by type of city. The largest falls are in financial cities ranked in the top ten by Z/Yen, while unranked cities show lower falls. As striking are the falls arranged by GaWC classification, where GaWC 'alpha plus' cities fall fastest (averaging –44 per cent), with GaWC alpha cities as a whole showing sharper falls (–33 per cent) than lower category cities (–27 per cent).

Figure 15.5 examines capital value volatility in office markets by type of city. Offices in financial centres would be expected to have experienced greater increases in value in the first half of the 2000s, and sharper falls in the market correction. Broad confirmation is provided, with volatility in annual returns between 2000 and 2009, proxied by the standard deviation, being higher in global financial centres. Mid-ranked IFCs exhibit higher volatility than larger cities. This opens up an interesting new area of research. It may be that the sheer scale and critical mass of the largest centres offer some protection, while smaller centres dependent on global financial markets may be more vulnerable to shocks. To some extent, though, higher volatility relates to a small number of cities showing extreme price movements, notably Moscow and Johannesburg. Higher volatility is not compensated by higher average growth rates.

CONCLUSIONS AND POLICY IMPLICATIONS

Office markets are not simply a by-product of demand for space from producer services firms. They are an investment asset and store of value; they help determine demand; and they expose cities to volatility in global capital markets. This will be particularly true for offices in international financial centres, where space, supply, investment and financial markets are locked together by functional specialization in economic activity, financial ownership of space, and the provision of equity and debt for investment and development. Cities specializing in financial activity are likely to exhibit volatility in office rental and capital values that is linked to the credit cycle and the behaviour of global capital markets.

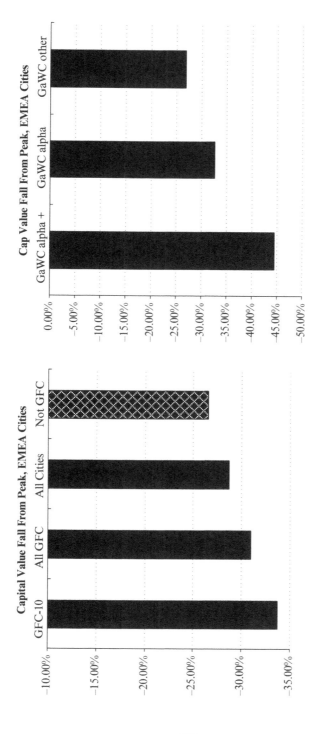

Source: Author, from CBRE data

Figure 15.4   Capital value falls by city type

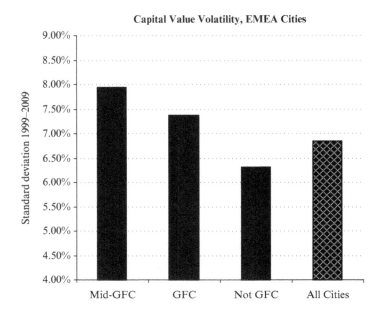

Source: Author, from CBRE data

Figure 15.5   Capital value volatility by city type

For global real estate investors, this has significant implications. A key motivation for an international investment strategy is diversification. However, diversification benefits are generally demonstrated with reference to securitized real estate assets or to national indices of real estate market performance. Direct private real estate investment happens in *cities* and much of that investment takes place in financial centres bound together by the flows and fortunes of global finance. This creates exposure to common patterns of volatility and to systemic risks of contagion in financial crises. An international real estate investment strategy with a significant component of global financial centre exposure may fail to deliver diversification when it is most required.

For investors, then, the key lesson here is the need for 'smart diversification'. Geography alone does not provide diversification. What matters is the factors that drive return and risk – demand for space that determines rents, investment and capital flows that influence the development cycle and property yields. A global investment strategy, then, needs to seek properties in other sectors, in cities with a varied employment base and with a different set of return drivers. Innovations in finance and the growth of international property funds allow investors the opportunity to build portfolios that are efficiently diversified but, with many funds still heavily exposed to big city offices, great care is necessary in choice of vehicles and target markets.

There are wider implications, too, for urban development and city planning. Many city managers, seeking to enhance the competitiveness of their cities, have encouraged redevelopment of CBDs and creation of financial services clusters. In so doing, they tie their cities' fortunes to the ebb and flow of global capital markets. There are benefits from such a strategy, with inflows of capital and employment. Yet there are clear downsides, too, in the inherent volatility that follows – and in the fragmentation of ownership that global property investment often brings. Strategies that emphasize diversity of employment structure, that encourage non-financial clusters as a counterbalance, may help to protect cities from the periodic crises that seem to affect global financial cities.

NOTES

1. This was no easy task, with a number of private funds being impossible to locate while many others were local subsidiaries of non-domestic parent investors. The figures cited here are thus an underestimate.
2. While it falls outside the scope of this chapter, it is important to stress the role that asset values play in credit bubbles. Real estate is used as security in lending: excess lending drives up asset values, which provides collateral for more lending. Once values begin to fall, a downward spiral sets in, creating liquidity and capital crises – see Brunnermeier (2009) for a review.
3. Readers thinking 'serves them right' might recall that these investments could well be in their pension funds.

REFERENCES

Baum, A. (2008), 'The emergence of real estate funds', in A. Peterson (ed.), *Real Estate Finance: Law, Regulation and Practice*, London: LexisNexis.

Brunnermeier, M. (2009), 'Deciphering the liquidity and credit crunch 2007–2008', *Journal of Economic Perspectives*, **23** (1), 77–100.

Castells, M. (1996), *The Rise of the Network Society: The Information Age*, Vol. I, Oxford: Blackwell.

CoL (Corporation of London) (2010), *Employment Trends in the City of London: City Stat Shot*, June, London: CoL.

Cook, G.A.S., N.R. Pandit, J.V. Beaverstock, P.J. Taylor and K. Pain (2007), 'The role of location in knowledge creation and diffusion: evidence of centripetal and centrifugal forces in the City of London financial services agglomeration', *Environment and Planning (A)*, **39** (6), 1325–1345.

Englund, P., Å. Gunnelin, P.H. Hendershott and B. Soderberg (2008), 'Adjustment in commercial property space markets: taking long-term leases and transaction costs seriously', *Real Estate Economics*, **36** (1), 81–109.

Friedmann, J. (1986), 'The world city hypothesis', *Development and Change*, **17** (1), 69–83.

GaWC (Globalization and World Cities Research Network) (2008), 'The world according to GaWC 2008', available at www.lboro.ac.uk/gawc/world2008t.html (accessed 20 March 2010).

Grenadier, S.R. (1995), 'The persistence of real estate cycles', *Journal of Real Estate Finance and Economics*, **10** (2), 95–119.

Grenadier, S.R. (1996), 'The strategic exercise of options: development cascades and overbuilding in real estate markets', *Journal of Finance*, **51** (5), 1653–1679.

Hall, P. and K. Pain (eds) (2006), *The Polycentric Metropolis: Learning from Mega-City Regions in Europe*, London: Earthscan.

Hendershott, P.H., C.M. Lizieri and B.D. MacGregor (2010), 'Asymmetric adjustment in the City of London office market', *Journal of Real Estate Finance and Economics*, **41** (1), 80–101.

Jones Lang LaSalle (various), *Global Market Perspective*, London: Jones Lang LaSalle.

Kindleberger, C. (1974), *The Formation of Financial Centers: A Study of Comparative Economic History*, Princeton Studies in International Finance, 36, Princeton University.

Lizieri, C. (2009), *Towers of Capital*, Oxford: Wiley-Blackwell.

Lizieri C., A. Baum and P. Scott (2000), 'Ownership, occupation and risk: a view of the City of London office market', *Urban Studies*, **37** (7), 1109–1129.

Lizieri, C. and N. Kutsch (2006), *Who Owns the City 2006: Office Ownership in the City of London*, Reading: University of Reading Business School and Development Securities plc.

MasterCard Worldwide (2008), *Worldwide Centers of Commerce Index 2008*, New York: MasterCard Worldwide.

Pain, K. and P. Hall (2008), 'Informational quantity versus informational quality: the perils of navigating the space of flows', *Regional Studies*, **42** (8), 1065–1077.

Property Funds Research (2008), *Global Real Estate Fund Managers' Report 2008*, Reading: PFR.

Sassen, S. (1991), *The Global City: New York, London, Tokyo*, Princeton, NJ: Princeton University Press.

Taylor, P.J. (2005), 'Leading world cities: empirical evaluations of urban nodes in multiple networks', *Urban Studies*, **42** (9), 1593–1608.

Z/Yen (2010), *Global Financial Centres Index 7*, London: Corporation of London.

16 International trade fairs and world cities: temporary vs. permanent clusters
Harald Bathelt

INTRODUCTION

Trade fairs have long been the focus of studies in management and marketing, investigating the importance of such events in attracting new buyers, establishing brands and developing a particular image (Meffert, 1993; Kirchgeorg, 2003). Although the character of these events has changed over time, the negotiation and certification of contracts are still important aspects of many trade fairs today (Power and Jansson, 2008). What we can observe is that while the number of firms making deals during a fair is limited, the number of 'atypical visitors' that are not classical buyers has increased (Borghini et al., 2006). Overall, the goals behind the participation in trade fairs have become more manifold and heterogeneous over time.

In this context, it is important to note that trade fairs are increasingly recognized as important places where knowledge circulation and creation take place in a condensed form over a limited time period. This has been acknowledged in studies that characterize trade fairs as temporary assemblages of human beings (Zelinsky, 1994), periodic events of the social economy (Norcliffe and Rendace, 2003), temporary clusters (Maskell et al., 2004) or temporary markets (Golfetto and Rinallo, 2010) with organized proximity (Rallet and Torre, 2009). They provide information about global developments in markets and technologies and are key in the process of making personal contact with customers. Few studies have, however, focused on the nature of knowledge flows and communication during such events. Only recently has a broader research agenda developed that aims to provide a knowledge-based understanding of these events (Borghini et al., 2006; Maskell et al., 2006; Bathelt and Schuldt, 2008a).

This work has shown that leading international trade fairs have become central nodes which connect the global political economy (Bathelt and Zakrzewski, 2007) and provide a microcosm of an industry for a limited time period (Rosson and Seringhaus, 1995). Leading international business-to-business fairs bring together agents from all over the world and create temporary spaces of presentation and interaction. The global information and communication ecology, or 'global buzz' (Bathelt and Schuldt, 2008b), during these events provides unique opportunities for knowledge generation and stimulates innovation.

Two questions arise which are addressed in this chapter. First, are the interaction processes observed at trade fairs limited to temporary spaces, and what is the relationship to the cities that host them? Second, why do firms not aim to draw permanent advantages from this by (partially) relocating closer to major trade fair centres? This chapter deals with these questions by first conceptualizing a knowledge-based understanding of trade fairs as temporary clusters. Next, the spatial patterns of trade fair places will be discussed, and how these have changed over time. I argue that these events are key venues to reproduce knowledge flows in world cities, but that the most important trade fairs do not necessarily coincide with world cities. This leads to a discussion as to why these events remain temporary in nature, followed by some conclusions.

INTERNATIONAL TRADE FAIRS AS TEMPORARY CLUSTERS

This section argues that international business-to-business fairs can be viewed as temporary clusters which support processes of interactive learning, knowledge creation and the formation of international networks (Maskell et al., 2004). Although knowledge flows during these events are complex and encompass various dimensions, it should be emphasized that the most prominent relationships are vertical in character, linking producers with their respective users (Golfetto and Rinallo, 2010). They generate both vertical and horizontal knowledge flows and are the reasons why trade fairs exist to begin with.

Like permanent industry clusters (Maskell and Malmberg, 1999; Bathelt et al., 2004), trade fairs are characterized by distinct vertical and horizontal communication patterns. Vertical interaction with suppliers and customers consists of information exchange about recent trends, experiences and requirements for future products and services. Firms set up meetings with established suppliers, located in different regions and nations, to discuss technological changes in product specifications, developments in markets and future conditions. At the same time they look out for suppliers that might offer opportunities for new applications.

Systematic customer contact is the key component of the vertical interaction during trade fairs (Golfetto and Rinallo, 2010). Firms intensify social relations with their customers and address new customers to market their products, display new developments and discuss potential contracts (Backhaus, 1992; Meffert, 1993). Scheduled meetings between producers and their customers are a vital source of information for further product improvements.

Trade fairs also bring together firms that compete against one another and normally do not interact. At this horizontal level, they provide multiple opportunities for firms to observe and compare their products and strategies with those of their competitors (Borghini et al., 2004). Firms systematically look through the exhibits of their competitors, make note of product designs, innovations and new fields of application. Part of the screening and observation process is less systematic, as firms try to get an overview of what is going on in their business and what trends exist (Bathelt and Schuldt, 2008a). This information is of great importance because it enables firms to evaluate their products and technological sophistication in relation to what goes on in other parts of the world. Along with the information gathered from customers and suppliers, firms receive a broad overview of state-of-the-art technologies and market trends which helps to review their own practices and strategies (Rosson and Seringhaus, 1995). Sometimes, it is even possible to discuss general technological problems or industry trends with representatives of competing firms during these events (Bathelt and Schuldt, 2008b).

Manifold opportunities for interactive learning and problem solving develop at trade shows, especially when the same specialists from different firms meet regularly during these cyclical events (Power and Jansson, 2008). In trade fairs, members of communities of practice and epistemic communities with partly overlapping and complementary knowledge bases get together (Brown and Duguid, 1991; Wenger, 1998; Knorr Cetina, 1999). This provides a basis for common interpretations and mutual understandings through intense communication during these events (Bathelt and Schuldt, 2008a). As common interpretative schemes and visions about technological trajectories are reproduced through focused communities, the institutional dimension of trade fair interaction unfolds.

Overall, the vertical, horizontal and institutional cluster dimensions enable intensified circulation of information and knowledge between participants. New ideas and projects in an industry or technology field can be identified through scouting and monitoring. This is possible because important information, news, trends and gossip make their rounds through the event. Knowledge exchange occurs in scheduled meetings with business partners, as well as accidental meetings with former colleagues. Just as certain off-work social meeting points seem crucial for knowledge exchange in permanent clusters, the corridors, cafés and bars at trade fairs are sometimes places where important knowledge circulates. During a trade fair, people are surrounded by a thick web of specialized knowledge from which they can hardly escape. The resulting information and communication ecology can be characterized as temporary 'global buzz' (Maskell et al., 2004; Bathelt and Schuldt, 2008b). As a result, knowledge flows at fairs are both planned and intended as well as spontaneous and unplanned in nature.[1]

The fact that firms do not necessarily have to be in direct contact with a specific source of knowledge makes participation in a trade fair extremely valuable. Firms benefit from the decentralized character of knowledge flows and the multiplicity of channels which exist. Since knowledge is constantly being transmitted from one agent to another, it is repeatedly interpreted, evaluated and enriched with additional relevant information and knowledge (Storper and Venables, 2004). This reduces uncertainties and helps firms distinguish important from less important trends and information.

Global buzz helps to identify interesting firms, acquire information about them and make initial contacts with new partners. Over time, through consecutive trade fairs (Power and Jansson, 2008), potential partners get to know one another better and initial trust may develop. This process is supported by the multiplex nature of social relations (Uzzi, 1997) between the people who attend trade fairs and interact with one another as competitors, experts of the same community, long-term partners or 'old trade fair buddies'. In the end, international trade fairs not only help maintain and intensify networks with international customers and suppliers (Prüser, 1997), but also enable firms to identify and select firms from other national contexts that may become partners later on in new 'trans-local pipelines' (Bathelt and Schuldt, 2008a).

THE CHANGING GEOGRAPHY OF TRADE FAIRS

The emerging literature about a knowledge-based understanding of international trade fairs shows that these events are important venues in the context of new geographies of circulation (Thrift, 2000; Amin and Cohendet, 2004) that enable knowledge creation and dissemination over distance. As the interaction patterns and knowledge flows during these events provide strategic information for corporate decision making, research and

Table 16.1   Top 20 world and trade fair cities

Rank[1]	Alpha (A) and Beta (B) world cities	Rank[2]	Leading cities in business service links	Indoor exhibition space[3] (gross m²)	Leading trade fair cities
1	A London	1	London	495,000	Hanover
1	A Paris	2	New York	460,000	Milan
1	A New York	3	Hong Kong	433,000	Paris
1	A Tokyo	4	Paris	368,000	Las Vegas
5	A Chicago	5	Singapore	340,000	Guangzhou
5	A Frankfurt	6	Tokyo	324,000	Moscow
5	A Hong Kong	7	Sydney	322,000	Frankfurt
5	A Los Angeles	8	Milan	315,000	Barcelona
5	A Milan	9	Shanghai	284,000	Cologne
5	A Singapore	10	Beijing	264,000	Düsseldorf
11	B San Francisco	11	Madrid	248,000	Chicago
11	B Sydney	12	Moscow	231,000	Valencia
11	B Toronto	13	Seoul	202,000	Birmingham
11	B Zurich	14	Toronto	200,000	Bologna
15	B Brussels	15	Brussels	200,000	Madrid
15	B Madrid	16	Buenos Aires	194,000	Toronto
15	B Mexico City	17	Mumbai	191,000	Orlando
15	B São Paulo	18	Kuala Lumpur	180,000	Munich
19	B Moscow	19	Chicago	162,000	Basel
19	B Seoul	20	Warsaw	160,000	Berlin/ Nuremberg

Sources: Estimates based on [1]Beaverstock et al. (1999), [2]Taylor (2011), [3]AUMA (2002, 2009a, 2009b)

development, and marketing, it appears logical to expect that such events are clustered in the leading global or world cities that have become major centres of corporate governance and control. These cities are characterized by a high concentration of global financial and advanced business services and headquarters of multinational corporations (Sassen, 1994; Taylor, 2004). They are connected to other cities and production centres by means of sophisticated information technology infrastructure and transportation networks, such as international airports (Beaverstock et al., 2009).

Indeed, international trade fairs are important venues in the economic fabric of world cities such as Paris, Milan and Frankfurt, providing them with strategic knowledge and connecting them with other cities in the global urban hierarchy. If we map the geography of trade fairs worldwide, we can see that the important world cities are indeed important places that host such temporary clusters. They are typically equipped with large convention centres and/or trade fair grounds. However, global hierarchies of trade fair centres and urban regions do not completely overlap (Table 16.1). For instance, while New York is one of the dominant world cities, it does not have a large number of global flagship fairs. In contrast, lower ranked world cities like Frankfurt and Hanover host some of the world's most important trade fairs in various industries. A closer analysis reveals that the geographies of trade fair places are fluid, constantly changing and led by competitive battles in their historical development (Fischer, 1992; Rodekamp, 2003; Golfetto and Rinallo, 2010).

To provide a better understanding of these patterns it is helpful to investigate the historical structures and changes of trade fair geographies. Already in medieval times, commodity fairs in Europe were attended by international traders who would sell their produce at these events. Until the 15th century, Saint Denis near Paris, the Champagne region, Lyon, and other cities in France played a leading role in fostering international trade through fairs (Allix, 1922). Trade fairs in German cities became important later on after religious upheaval and associated conflicts significantly decreased trade fair activity in France. This led to new rivalries between trade fair places such as Leipzig and Frankfurt (Backhaus and Zydorek, 1997; Bathelt and Boggs, 2003). In order to maintain their business, traders had to travel from one trade fair to the next. This created competition between places if they scheduled their fairs during the same time period (Fischer, 1992).

With changes in the importance and location of commodity fairs, it was unusual that a single trade fair location, such as Leipzig, would maintain a central role over several hundred years (Allix, 1922). Even though religious aspects were initially important in the selection of trade fair places, two other criteria were key to the developing geography of trade fairs: (a) a production core in the surrounding region, and (b) a location at the intersection of major trade routes. Shifts in trade fair locations over time were influenced by political hegemonies, disparities in economic development, innovation cycles and shifting markets. To understand these geographical shifts, we must bear in mind that most such events were not deeply embedded in the urban fabrics that hosted them (Allix, 1922).

When traditional commercial fairs were increasingly replaced by permanent market places, the so-called sample fair (*Mustermesse*) was introduced in Leipzig around 1890 as a new fair type (Rodekamp, 2003). In contrast to traditional fairs, these events would only present samples of products, so buyers could make orders of goods that would be shipped at a later stage. This type of trade fair quickly became the standard form across most industries (Backhaus and Zydorek, 1997). In the late 20th century, trade fairs increasingly shifted their focus from places where contracts were made to places where important knowledge about product characteristics, innovations and market trends was exchanged (Borghini et al., 2004; Maskell et al., 2004).

Over time, trade fairs increased their geographical reach and some developed into global events with a large percentage of international visitors and exhibitors. Only a few flagship events were needed, however, to accomplish a global flow of knowledge in an industry, rather than a dense network of similar, smaller events in different places. Golfetto and Rinallo (2010) use the case of European clothing fabric to illustrate the competitive dynamics that developed. In this industry segment, a competitive 'battle' evolved between German, Italian and French trade fairs. While the German fair Interstoff in Frankfurt used to be the dominant event of the industry, it lost ground to its French competitor Première Vision which moved from its original location in Lyon, close to the production core, to Paris to become more accessible for international visitors. In response to increasing rivalry, smaller Italian fairs that originally existed close to regional centres of production (e.g. Florence and Como) merged to form Milano Unico, which now took place in Milan. Frankfurt's Interstoff was unsuccessful in responding to these shifts and eventually disappeared from the international landscape.[2]

Similar developments have led to ongoing rivalries between trade fair locations in different cities and countries across many industries.[3] In contrast to Europe, trade fairs in North America have developed out of a distribution tradition that was reliant on the role of travelling salesmen. Because of this, American fairs are even less attached to particular places, and regularly alternate between different cities (Zelinsky, 1994; AUMA, 2009a).[4] Although this strongly suggests that the overall geography of temporary clusters is fluid and subject to changes over time, it is not clear why industries and their leading actors would not aim to benefit from the key advantages of such settings more permanently by co-locating near these places.

TEMPORARY VERSUS PERMANENT PROXIMITY?

During international trade fairs, participants leave their normal work contexts and socio-institutional milieus to communicate and interact with others in an artificial temporary cluster based around an industry or value chain. Given the enormous advantages in terms of interactive learning and learning by observation that firms can realize from participating in this information and communication ecology, why do firms not turn these events into permanent settings by relocating (at least partially) near these sites?

Of course, permanent industry locations are important configurations of production that provide substantial advantages to local firms due to the development of localized capabilities and specialization effects, as well as representing enormous sunk costs. As argued below, trade fairs complement permanent industry configurations and do not compete against them. It is exactly the temporary nature of these events that triggers intensive processes of knowledge circulation and pipeline creation; and world cities need not necessarily be the best places for this. Three reasons in particular emphasize why it is unlikely that temporary clusters be transformed into permanent ones (Maskell et al., 2004).

(a) Reflexive Specialization and Localized Capabilities

New locations near trade fair sites are unlikely to compete against existing industry settings because the latter already provide an important basis for cumulative learning, collective action and problem solving. This is due to the role of 'localised capabilities' (Maskell and Malmberg, 1999), such as specialized local resources, skills and local institutional structures. In permanent clusters, firms use local resources and existing competencies to specialize production. This impacts existing local supplier relations and leads to adjustments in their production schemes. Over time, a common knowledge base develops which enables firms to continuously recombine shared resources. Day-to-day routines and interactive learning have an important impact on the labour market, organizational routines and best practices at these locations through which localized capabilities develop further.

(b) Sunk Costs and Spatial Persistence

Another reason why traditional industry settings likely remain an important basis for production and innovation is related to the existence of sunk costs (Clark, 1994).

Since it is expensive to relocate plants, machinery and equipment, existing locations with substantial sunk costs are characterized by spatial persistence. This is particularly due to what Clark and Wrigley (1997) refer to as the 'functional value' of capital. The functional value of capital, as opposed to its market value, increases over time because experience-based knowledge about processes, products and markets is incorporated into the machinery and infrastructure. Long-term inter-firm relations and local buzz provide an important basis for solving problems and coping with external challenges (Bathelt et al., 2004). A key feature of the knowledge pools in permanent settings is that they have evolved in a cumulative way to include both tacit and contextualized knowledge which cannot easily be transferred to other regional contexts (Maskell and Malmberg, 1999; Belussi and Pilotti, 2002).[5]

(c) Global Buzz and the Strength of Weak Ties

Most importantly, a relocation of trade fair participants to a new joint agglomeration space would not necessarily be advantageous to these firms in the long term. A relocation has several consequences. First, it would weaken former permanent production contexts and could cause a hollowing out of these locations. Second, the temporary setting would become permanent and eventually grow into a new agglomeration of firms. This trans-formation into a permanent setting, however, might have drawbacks over time. One of the main reasons to relocate production from an existing agglomeration to a new loca-tion would be to provide access to the wider set of knowledge pools and global buzz that characterize trade fairs. If, however, many firms decided to relocate in this way, this buzz would lose some of its original quality over time. Some of the former ties to permanent locations might fade out and knowledge about these locations become more difficult to acquire. Firms would again have to re-connect with other places to gain access to outside knowledge; a process that was originally accomplished through trade fairs. The resulting situation might not be much different from that before and the need to develop trans-local pipelines just as urgent.

This situation resembles the process described by Granovetter (1973) as the strength of weak ties (Grabher, 1993). According to this, strong ties between economic actors in a production network are an important source for efficient communication and allow for the fast diffusion of incremental innovations within the network. But because of the efforts required to maintain strong ties and their self-reinforcing character, they are rarely capable of bridging the gap between different networks. On the contrary, loose couplings in the form of so-called local bridges allow a cluster to source external knowledge that is absent within the network (Granovetter, 1973). Therefore, weak ties at the periphery of networks are especially important for the diffusion of more radical innovations, which would not be easily recognized by strong ties within the network core. The relocation of firms from formerly separate industrial clusters to a joint agglomeration space near the fair grounds could be interpreted as a transformation of weak ties into strong ties. Firms would lose intimate knowledge about their original locations, eventually carrying with it the danger of over-embeddedness and lock-in (Uzzi, 1997).

Although firms would likely not relocate all operations to a new agglomeration space, regular participation in the temporary spaces of a trade fair obviously suffices the cor-porate needs for new knowledge about distant partners, competitors and markets. Such temporary clusters enable important communication and interaction exactly because they are – and only as long as they remain – temporary in character.

CONCLUSIONS

This chapter has developed a knowledge-based conceptualization of trade fairs as temporary clusters emphasizing the knowledge disseminating and creating qualities of these events. The multidimensional structure of information and knowledge flows enables firms to get an overview of the market and scrutinize the trends visible in the exhibits of others. Global buzz at leading international trade fairs enables firms to systematically acquire knowledge about competitors, suppliers and customers and their strategic choices. Through regular attendance at such events, firms are able to find suitable partners to complement their needs, establish trust with distant partners and undertake first steps toward the development of durable inter-firm pipelines in research, production and/or marketing (Bathelt and Schuldt, 2008b).

As the advantages of global buzz are closely related to the face-to-face qualities of trade fairs, one might wonder why firms do not aim to draw permanent advantages from these contexts by relocating near the trade fair sites. Several reasons help explain why this does not take place. In particular, global buzz during international flagship fairs relies on a diverse set of agents with partially different and partially overlapping knowledge bases reflecting the global state of an industry. Regular attendance during such events satisfies a firm's needs for information and knowledge exchange, which are then transformed into practice during the periods in between trade fairs.

Nonetheless, we can conclude that many trade fairs are based in large metropolitan regions. Most world cities have major trade fair facilities which host a variety of different fairs and contribute substantially to maintaining and extending the strategic global knowledge pipelines that are directed to these places. However, closer analysis reveals that the locations of major international trade fairs in different industries do not fully coincide with those of the most important world cities. Furthermore, the geography of trade fairs has historically been fluid, characterized by competitive battles and dynamic changes.

In his early analysis, Allix (1922, p. 541) found that 'the fairs themselves are subject to a sort of migration or displacement. In general they do not prosper for long in the same place'. Further he noted (p. 540) that, '[i]n every epoch it was the fairs at the frontiers [of wider market regions; author's note] that flourished best. Those of Champagne near the Flemish border declined [in the 14th century] when independent Champagne became French, losing its character of a neutral country. Those of Lyon owed their success to proximity to the Swiss and Italian frontiers.' While historical shifts of commercial fairs seemed to be driven by market frontiers, contemporary shifts in trade fair patterns are influenced by a complex mix of strategic decisions, power relationships, competitive battles, and market and/or production changes.

If we assume that contemporary shifts in the geography of trade fairs are driven by a need to gain accessibility and visibility in relation to global markets (Golfetto and Rinallo, 2010), world cities could easily move up in the hierarchy of trade fair places in the future. This would strengthen their position at the top of the urban hierarchy. Given the fluidity of international trade fairs, and possible restrictions in mobility associated with the effects of climate change and peak oil, trade fairs in world cities could develop into major nodes of international knowledge exchange in the future. This is, however, speculative at this point, subject to the strategies and innovative ideas of policy makers, trade fair organizers and industry organizations.

ACKNOWLEDGEMENTS

I would like to thank Rachael Gibson, Francesca Golfetto, Diego Rinallo, Nina Schuldt and Ben Spigel, as well as the editors of this volume, particularly Michael Hoyler, for stimulating comments in preparing this chapter.

NOTES

1. In this context, we have to keep in mind that not all such events generate rich decentralized and self-sustained knowledge ecologies. In the field of fashion, for instance, knowledge flows during trade fairs are highly organised or 'concerted' through industry associations and/or trade fairs organizers (Rinallo and Golfetto, 2006).
2. This was related to several factors. It seemed that Interstoff had become too big and unstructured, and that the organizers were not able to develop a new strategy to make this trade fair more attractive. Furthermore, the German manufacturing base had become too small to sustain Interstoff in a period of increased rivalry.
3. Examples of large flagship fairs in Germany where this has been the case include CeBIT in Hanover, which has become over-crowded (*Frankfurter Rundschau*, 2006); Games Convention, which has created heavy rivalry between the cities of Cologne, Frankfurt and Leipzig (Dietz, 2008), and Heimtextil in Frankfurt, which has decreased in importance over time (Dietz, 2010).
4. LightFair International, the major trade fair of the lighting industry in North America, for instance, alternates every other year between New York and Las Vegas.
5. Over time, however, the existence of sunk costs alone does not exclude a gradual reorientation to other regions, possibly leading to relocation tendencies later on.

REFERENCES

Allix, A. (1922), 'The geography of fairs: illustrated by old-world examples', *Geographical Review*, **12** (4), 532–569.
Amin, A. and P. Cohendet (2004), *Architectures of Knowledge: Firms, Capabilities, and Communities*, Oxford and New York: Oxford University Press.
AUMA – Ausstellungs- und Messeausschuss der deutschen Wirtschaft (2002), *Messemärkte Ausland – Kanada [Foreign Trade Fair Markets – Canada]*, Berlin, AUMA, available at www.auma.de/_pages/d/04_MessemaerkteAusland/0402_Laenderprofile/040215_Kanada/04021501_Uebersicht.aspx, (accessed 10 June 2009).
AUMA – Ausstellungs- und Messeausschuss der deutschen Wirtschaft (2009a), *Messemarkt USA [Trade Fair Market USA]*, Berlin, AUMA, available at www.auma.de/_pages/d/04_MessemaerkteAusland/0402_Laenderprofile/040226_USA/download/Messemarkt_USA.pdf, (accessed 10 June 2009).
AUMA – Ausstellungs- und Messeausschuss der deutschen Wirtschaft (2009b), *Die Messewirtschaft: Bilanz 2008 [The Trade Fair Economy: 2008 Balance]*, Berlin: AUMA.
Backhaus, H. (1992), *Investitionsgütermarketing [Investment Goods Marketing]*, München: Vahlen.
Backhaus, H. and C. Zydorek (1997), 'Von der Mustermesse zur ubiquitären Messe [From sample fairs to ubiquitous trade fairs]', in H. Meffert, T. Necker and H. Sihler (eds), *Märkte im Dialog: Die Messen der dritten Generation [Markets in Dialogue: Trade Fairs of the Third Generation]*, Wiesbaden: Gabler, pp. 134–158.
Bathelt, H. and J.S. Boggs (2003), 'Towards a reconceptualization of regional development paths: is Leipzig's media cluster a continuation of or a rupture with the past?', *Economic Geography*, **79** (3), 265–293.

Bathelt, H., A. Malmberg and P. Maskell (2004), 'Clusters and knowledge: local buzz, global pipelines and the process of knowledge creation', *Progress in Human Geography*, **28** (1), 31–56.

Bathelt, H. and N. Schuldt (2008a), 'Between luminaires and meat grinders: international trade fairs as temporary clusters', *Regional Studies*, **42** (6), 853–868.

Bathelt, H. and N. Schuldt (2008b), 'Temporary face-to-face contact and the ecologies of global and virtual buzz', *SPACES online* (2008–04), Toronto and Heidelberg, available at www.spaces-online.com, (accessed 10 June 2009).

Bathelt, H. and G. Zakrzewski (2007), 'Messeveranstaltungen als fokale Schnittstellen der globalen Ökonomie [Trade fairs as focal intersections in the global economy]', *Zeitschrift für Wirtschaftsgeographie*, **51** (1), 14–30.

Beaverstock, J.V., B. Derudder, J.R. Faulconbridge and F. Witlox (2009), 'International business travel: some explorations', *Geografiska Annaler B*, **91** (3), 193–202.

Beaverstock, J.V., R.G. Smith and P.J. Taylor (1999), 'A roster of world cities', *Cities*, **16** (6), 445–458.

Belussi, F. and L. Pilotti (2002), 'Knowledge creation, learning and innovation in Italian industrial districts', *Geografiska Annaler B*, **84** (2), 125–139.

Borghini, S., F. Golfetto and D. Rinallo (2004), 'Using anthropological methods to study industrial marketing and purchasing: an exploration of professional trade shows', paper presented at the Industrial Marketing Purchasing Conference, Copenhagen, 2–4 September.

Borghini, S., F. Golfetto and D. Rinallo (2006), 'Ongoing search among industrial buyers', *Journal of Business Research*, **59** (10–11), 1151–1159.

Brown, J.S. and P. Duguid (1991), 'Organizational learning and communities of practice: toward a unified view of working, learning, and innovation', *Organization Science*, **2** (1), 40–57.

Clark, G.L. (1994), 'Strategy and structure: corporate restructuring and the nature and characteristics of sunk costs', *Environment and Planning A*, **26** (1), 9–32.

Clark, G.L. and N. Wrigley (1997), 'The spatial configuration of the firm and the management of sunk costs', *Economic Geography*, **73** (3), 285–304.

Dietz, P. (2008), 'Game over für Frankfurt [Game over for Frankfurt]', *Frankfurter Rundschau*, 14 February, D7.

Dietz, P. (2010), 'Kaum Schwund bei Heimtextil [Limited decline at Heimtextil]', *Frankfurter Rundschau*, 13 January, D7.

Fischer, W. (1992), 'Zur Geschichte der Messen in Europa [On the history of trade fairs in Europe]', in K.-H. Strothmann and M. Busche (eds), *Handbuch Messemarketing [Handbook of Trade Fair Marketing]*, Wiesbaden: Gabler, pp. 3–13.

Frankfurter Rundschau (2006), 'IT-Messe: Cebit droht Umsatzeinbruch [IT trade fair: Cebit might face downturn]', 20 December.

Fuchslocher, H. and H. Hochheimer (2000), *Messen im Wandel: Messemarketing im 21. Jahrhundert [Trade Fair Marketing in the 21st Century]*, Wiesbaden: Gabler.

Golfetto, F. and D. Rinallo (2010), 'Competition among temporary clusters: a longitudinal study of the European clothing fabric trade shows (1986–2006)', paper presented in the seminar 'Culture, Competition, and Trade Shows', Toronto, University of Toronto, 22 January 2010.

Grabher, G. (1993), 'Rediscovering the social in the economics of interfirm relations', in G. Grabher (ed.), *The Embedded Firm: On the Socioeconomics of Industrial Networks*, London and New York: Routledge, pp. 1–31.

Granovetter, M.S. (1973), 'The strength of weak ties', *American Journal of Sociology*, **78** (6), 1360–1380.

Kirchgeorg, M. (2003), 'Funktionen und Erscheinungsformen von Messen [Functions and types of trade fairs]', in M. Kirchgeorg, W.M. Dornscheidt, W. Giese and N. Stoeck (eds), *Handbuch Messemanagement: Planung, Durchführung und Kontrolle von Messen, Kongressen und Events [Handbook of Trade Fair Management: Planning, Execution and Control of Trade Fairs, Conventions and Events]*, Wiesbaden: Gabler, pp. 51–72.

Knorr Cetina, K. (1999), *Epistemic Cultures: How the Sciences Make Sense*, Chicago: Chicago University Press.

Maskell, P., H. Bathelt and A. Malmberg (2004), 'Temporary clusters and knowledge creation: the effects of international trade fairs, conventions and other professional gatherings', *SPACES online* (2004–04), Toronto and Heidelberg, available at www.spaces-online.com (accessed 10 June 2009).

Maskell, P., H. Bathelt and A. Malmberg (2006), 'Building global knowledge pipelines: the role of temporary clusters', *European Planning Studies*, **14** (8), 997–1013.

Maskell, P. and A. Malmberg (1999), 'The competitiveness of firms and regions: "ubiquitification" and the importance of localized learning', *European Urban and Regional Studies*, **6** (1), 9–25.

Meffert, H. (1993), 'Messen und Ausstellungen als Marketinginstrument [Trade fairs and exhibitions as a marketing tool]', in K.E. Goehrmann (ed.), *Polit-Marketing auf Messen [Marketing Policy on Trade Fairs]*, Düsseldorf: Wirtschaft und Finanzen, pp. 74–96.

Norcliffe, G. and O. Rendace (2003), 'New geographies of comic book production in North America: the new artisans, distancing, and the periodic social economy', *Economic Geography*, **79** (3), 241–263.
Power, D. and J. Jansson (2008), 'Cyclical clusters in global circuits: overlapping spaces in furniture trade fairs', *Economic Geography*, **84** (4), 423–448.
Prüser, S. (1997), *Messemarketing: Ein netzwerkorientierter Ansatz [Trade Fair Marketing: A Network Approach]*, Wiesbaden: Deutscher Universitäts-Verlag.
Rallet, A. and A. Torre (2009), 'Temporary geographical proximity for business and work coordination: when, how and where?', *SPACES online* (2009–02), Toronto and Heidelberg, available at www.spaces-online.com (accessed 10 June 2009).
Rinallo, D. and F. Golfetto (2006), 'Representing markets: the shaping of fashion trends by French and Italian fabric companies', *Industrial Marketing Management*, **35** (7), 856–869.
Rodekamp, V. (2003), 'Zur Geschichte der Messen in Deutschland und Europa [On the history of trade fairs in Germany and Europe]', in M. Kirchgeorg, W.M. Dornscheidt, W. Giese and N. Stoeck (eds), *Handbuch Messemanagement: Planung, Durchführung und Kontrolle von Messen, Kongressen und Events [Handbook of Trade Fair Management: Planning, Execution and Control of Trade Fairs, Conventions and Events]*, Wiesbaden: Gabler, pp. 5–13.
Rosson, P.J. and F.H.R. Seringhaus (1995), 'Visitor and exhibitor interaction at industrial trade fairs', *Journal of Business Research*, **32** (1), 81–90.
Sassen, S. (1994), *Cities in a World Economy*, Thousand Oaks, CA: Pine Forge Press.
Storper, M. and A.J. Venables (2004), 'Buzz: face-to-face contact and the urban economy', *Journal of Economic Geography*, **4** (4), 351–370.
Taylor, P.J. (2004), *World City Network: A Global Urban Analysis*, London: Routledge.
Taylor, P.J. (2011), 'Advanced producer service centres in the world economy', in Taylor, P.J., P. Ni, B. Derudder, M. Hoyler, J. Huang and F. Witlox (eds), *Global Urban Analysis: A Survey of Cities in Globalization*, London: Earthscan, pp. 22–39.
Thrift, N. (2000), 'Performing cultures in the new economy', *Annals of the Association of American Geographers*, **90** (4), 674–692.
Uzzi, B. (1997), 'Social structure and competition in interfirm networks: the paradox of embeddedness', *Administrative Science Quarterly*, **42** (1), 35–67.
Wenger, E. (1998), *Communities of Practice: Learning, Meaning, and Identity*, Cambridge: Cambridge University Press.
Zelinsky, W. (1994), 'Conventionland USA: the geography of a latterday phenomenon', *Annals of the Association of American Geographers*, **84** (1), 68–86.

17 Mega-events: urban spectaculars and globalization

John Rennie Short

Globalization is constructed and maintained in many ways. One of the most important is through the experience of mega-events hosted in particular cities. The circulation of these events in different cities across the world creates and tightens global urban networks. These spectaculars connect cities and societies in global discourses and shared practices. The host cities also have opportunities for achieving or reaffirming world city status, acting as platforms for globalizing trends and laboratories for future urban forms. The host cities are hubs and exchanges in global flows and networks, the transmission points in the production of a global society (Roche, 2006). In this chapter I will consider two of the most important mega-events of the modern period: the urban spectaculars of World Fairs and the Olympic Games. World Fairs were a vital element in the globalization of modernity in the period from 1850 to around 1940. The Olympic Games, in contrast, were an important staging of the contemporary wave of globalization especially from around 1960 to the present day. Let us consider each in turn.

WORLD FAIRS: THE BEGINNING

1 May 1851 is an important date in the history of the relationship between globalization and cities. On that day the Great Exhibition of the Works of Industry of all Nations (hereafter Great Exhibition) opened in London in Hyde Park. The main building was the Crystal Palace designed by Joseph Paxton. In an innovative design, huge sheets of glass were shaped around an elegantly thin framework of cast iron frames. The effect was to provide a light-filled building that was open to the sky but closed to the elements. It was a supremely self-confident design, befitting the highpoint of British global prominence, an incorporation of nature that also signified the human control over nature. Inside the impressive large building, 563 meters long and 138 meters wide, a total of 13,000 exhibits were displayed. The exhibits came from around the world as countries displayed their technological advancements. The majority of exhibits originated in Britain and reflected the industrial might of the world's largest trading nation and imperial power. Inside the glass cathedral the latest designs and appliances of modern industrial capitalism were displayed and worshipped.

Contemporaries such as Charles Dickens and Charlotte Brontë were amazed at the sheer range of exhibits. But not all contemporaries viewed it with such slack-jawed wonder. Karl Marx, for example, saw it as the ultimate fetishization of the commodity form. The poet Tennyson referred to the 1851 Great Exhibition as the 'world's great fair' and the name stuck. The term 'Expo' was only used in Montreal in 1967. I will use the term World Fair throughout this chapter.

The connection between the Exhibition and a capitalist globalization was apparent in Prince Albert's speech, delivered two years before the Exhibition opened, when he noted:

> The distances which separated the different nations and parts of the globe are gradually vanishing before the achievements of modern invention, and we can traverse them with incredible ease; the languages of all nations are known and their acquirements placed within the reach of everybody; thought is communicated with the rapidity and even by the power of lightning. (Martin, 1880, p. 247)

WORLD FAIRS AND GLOBALIZATION

While there had been World Fairs before 1851 – the first was held in London in 1756 and awarded prizes for improvements in the manufacture of tapestry, carpets and porcelain – the Great Exhibition marked the formal beginning of the modern World Fairs and their association with the globalization of a capitalist modernity. Over 6 million people visited the Exhibition and it was widely considered the leading edge of a capitalist globalization that was sweeping across the world. It was so successful that it was widely copied. Other cities in other countries wanted to host World Fairs. The sheer number is impressive, a total of 265 from 1851 to 2010. The high point or golden era of World Fairs was from 1870 to 1940 when over 20 fairs were held each decade. While the large urban centers hosted Fairs, some multiple times, such as London and Paris, other smaller cities from across the globe also hosted Fairs, including British colonial cities such as Cape Town, Brisbane, Melbourne and Sydney. Host cities were scattered throughout Europe, the Americas and Asia, including Tokyo, Shanghai and Nanking. There were so many World Fairs during the golden era because it was a time of rapid globalization. Hosting a World Fair signaled economic achievement, raised the profile of the city, leveraged national public funds for civic purposes and influenced global public opinion. Indeed the World Fairs were part of the construction of global public opinion and world city maintenance and creation. A smaller number of World Fairs were sanctioned by the Bureau of International Expositions (BIE), an international organization established in 1928; originally consisting of 31 countries, it now has 156 member countries. Table 17.1 lists these larger World Fairs sanctioned, some retrospectively, by the BIE. This list is dominated by, especially in the earlier years, London and Paris, as the two capitals of rival imperial powers competed with each other. It is only in 1970 that an Asian city hosts a BIE sanctioned event. There is an even smaller list of Fairs considered so large and important that they significantly influenced global trends enough to be considered landmark Fairs (Findling and Pelle, 2008). These are also noted in Table 17.1.

The World Fairs embodied a particular form of capitalist modernity and displayed a global world of linked national economies. While each Fair promoted this general message they also had a touch of particularity. The Great Exhibition, for example, gave the promise of a new world, one where human ingenuity could conquer the limitations of nature. It was also a socially encoded promise that comprised a complex set of ideas including British industrial might, free trade, pacifism and what was called universalism. The very form of the Exhibition, in which national products were under one roof, showed how national economies compared and contrasted but also were linked and connected.

Table 17.1 World Fairs 1851–2010

1851	**London, UK**
1855	**Paris, France**
1862	**London, UK**
1867	**Paris, France**
1873	**Vienna, Austria–Hungary**
1876	**Philadelphia, US**
1878	**Paris, France**
1879	Sydney, Australia
1880	Melbourne, Australia
1888	Melbourne, Australia
1888	Barcelona, Spain
1889	**Paris, France**
1893	**Chicago, US**
1897	Brussels, Belgium
1900	**Paris, France**
1904	**St. Louis, US**
1905	Liège, Belgium
1906	Milan, Italy
1909	Seattle, US
1910	Brussels, Belgium
1913	Ghent, Belgium
1915	**San Francisco, US**
1929	Barcelona, Spain
1933	Chicago, US
1935	Brussels, Belgium
1937	**Paris, France**
1939	**New York, US**
1949	Port-au-Prince, Haiti
1958	**Brussels, Belgium**
1962	Seattle, US
1964	New York, US
1967	**Montreal, Canada**
1968	San Antonio, US
1970	**Osaka, Japan**
1974	Spokane, US
1975	Okinawa, Japan
1982	Knoxville, US
1984	New Orleans, US
1985	Tsukuba, Japan
1986	Vancouver, Canada
1988	Brisbane, Australia
1992	**Seville, Spain**
1993	Daejeon (Taejon), South Korea
1998	Lisbon, Portugal
2000	Hanover, Germany
2005	Aichi, Japan
2008	Zaragoza, Spain
2010	**Shanghai, China**

Note: The list only includes Fairs sanctioned by the BIE. Bold indicates landmark Fairs.

Subsequent Fairs had complex, often conflicted, messages as nationalism competed with free market ideologies and government power had to deal with consumer choice.

World Fairs signified a global world, an urban circuitry of regular events through which flowed people, ideas and capital. One dominant idea was the importance of technological innovations and inventions. World Fairs introduced many new goods to large audiences: the Colt revolver and the McCormick reaper (London, 1851); the elevator (Dublin, 1853); the sewing machine (Paris, 1855); the calculating machine (London, 1862); the telephone (Philadelphia, 1876); outdoor electric lighting (Paris, 1878); the gas-powered auto (Paris, 1889); motion pictures (Paris, 1900); controlled flight, the wireless telegraph (St. Louis, 1904); Kodachrome photos (San Francisco, 1915); television (New York, 1939); computer technology, fax machines (New York, 1964). For much of their history Fairs presented futures of technological wonder and a technical fix to social problems. Human ingenuity could overcome not only distance and disease but also want and hunger. Medical technologies such as the incubator and the X-ray machine were first exhibited at World Fairs. The Fairs became sites of technology transfer and adoption wrapped in an ideology of technological triumphalism. However, the past half century has witnessed a corrective to this easy and glib technological optimism. The theme of the Brussels World Fair of 1958 was a *More Human World*, while the theme of the 2005 Expo in Aichi in Japan was *Nature's Wisdom*. While technological accomplishments still figure largely, there has been a more palpable greening of attitudes and a less naïve sense of what technology, on its own, can accomplish. A heady modernity, which asserted ownership and control of the future, has been replaced by more sophisticated post-modernity with a less breezy attitude to the future.

A global discourse was created by the large World Fairs. Let us just consider the early Fairs held in Paris. At the 1855 Paris Fair, for example, the Bordeaux wine classification still in use today was first introduced. At the 1867 Fair, visited by more than 9 million people, the Japanese woodcut prints on display helped to shape the modern art movement of Impressionism. At a meeting held alongside the 1878 Fair international copyright laws were first formulated. The main symbol of the 1889 Fair was the Eiffel Tower, which became an iconic symbol not only of the city of Paris in particular but of contemporary urban design in general. The Eiffel Tower is one of the best modern examples of urban placemaking linked to a particular urban structure (Thompson, 2000). Javanese music played at this Fair also influenced the development of ambient music. More than 50 million attended the 1900 Fair where talking films and escalators were first shown to the public.

The Fairs were not just sites of technology transfer; they were hubs in the global transmission of cultural practices and worldviews that created the aesthetics of modernism. There are connections between the development of modern art and architecture and World Fairs. At the 1929 Barcelona Fair Mies van der Rohe designed an early example of the International Style. At the 1937 Paris Fair Picasso's *Guernica* was displayed. The World Fair of 1939 in New York, for example, is considered a seminal moment in the maturing of an international modernist movement. Alvar Aalto designed the Finnish pavilion. The Fair, the official motto of which was *World of Tomorrow*, presented a model of mass-market modernism (Christie, 2006). Then there were the more incidental connections. For the 1964 World Fair also held in New York, Andy Warhol created a work, *Thirteen Most Wanted Men*, consisting of large silk screens of wanted criminals.

The governor of New York State, Nelson Rockefeller, ordered the piece to be removed. The censorship added to Warhol's fame in the New York art scene and indirectly helped to promote pop art.

In their attempts to display and narrate modernity World Fairs shaped and reshaped ideas about class, race, gender and nationality as well as about progress and development. The contradictions of modernity were also embodied. Harvey (1996) explores Fairs as sites where nation states and multinational corporations compete in representational space as they do in the global economy. Pred (1995) exposes the contradictions in World Fairs in representing the three phases of modernity: industrial modernity, high modernity and hypermodernity. The World Fairs not only reflected a globalizing world, they helped to create it.

The Fairs, especially the large Fairs, gave a glimpse of new forms of urban living, new templates for global and globalizing cities. The new metropolitan spaces depicted at the Fairs were managed and controlled; they gave order and discipline and shape and form in contrast to the chaos of the cities around them. From the Great Exhibition onwards Fairs introduced the notion of the managed urban crowd. Urban tourism was initiated by Thomas Cook in selling the Exhibition to foreign and national visitors, as were forms of commoditized mass eating and drinking for the huge crowds. The World Fairs introduced arcades, escalators, night illumination and mass transit. They imagined cities given over to consumption and entertainment spaces. At the World Fair in 1939 in New York, an exhibit, funded by General Motors, showed a city of high-rise towers and fast, free flowing motorways; it was a tantalizing vision presented to almost 5 million visitors. The plan unveiled at the Fair, which drew upon ideas of urban modernism of the early twentieth century, was the blueprint for postwar urban America. For the Brisbane Fair in 1988 an urban promenade was created along the riverside, a place of play and consumption. An urban modernity has been replaced by visions of urban sustainability. Shanghai 2010 had as its official slogan *Better City, Better Life*.

New ideas of cities were presented at the World Fairs and the hosting of the large World Fairs also was vital in the creation and maintenance of world city status. As new urban forms diffused from the host cities a recognizable metric of world city status was established. Cities needed mass illumination, modern transport and modern technological solutions in order to be considered a world city. World Fairs displayed a modern global world of redesigned and reimagined cities. The Eiffel Tower is just one of the enduring legacies on both the physical form and imaginative geography of a host city that through its hosting solidified its world city status and gave to the world a symbol of both the city in particular and of urban modernity in general. We now have a large body of literature that examines the effect of hosting World Fairs on individual cities (Gold and Gold, 2005).

THE OLYMPIC GAMES

The modern Summer Olympic Games are an interesting case study of some of the more intriguing connections between the city and globalization. There is now a growing body of literature examining these connections (Short, 2004, 2008; Gold and Gold, 2007, 2008). In this chapter I will limit my comments to the Summer Olympics since they have a much wider national participation and larger global reach than the Winter Olympics.

Table 17.2   The Summer Olympic Games

Date	Host city	Participants (women)	Participating countries
1896	Athens	241 (0)	14
1900	Paris	1205 (19)	26
1904	St. Louis	687 (6)	13
1908	London	2035 (36)	22
1912	Stockholm	2547 (57)	28
1920	Antwerp	2668 (77)	29
1924	Paris	3092 (136)	44
1928	Amsterdam	3014 (290)	46
1932	Los Angeles	1408 (127)	37
1936	Berlin	4066 (328)	49
1948	London	4099 (385)	59
1952	Helsinki	4925 (518)	69
1956	Melbourne	3184 (371)	67
1960	Rome	5346 (610)	83
1964	Tokyo	5140 (683)	93
1968	Mexico City	5530 (781)	112
1972	Munich	7123 (1058)	121
1976	Montreal	6028 (1247)	92
1980	Moscow	5217 (1124)	80
1984	Los Angeles	5330 (1567)	140
1988	Seoul	8465 (2186)	159
1992	Barcelona	9634 (2707)	169
1996	Atlanta	10310 (3513)	197
2000	Sydney	10651 (4069)	199
2004	Athens	10625 (4329)	201
2008	Beijing	11028 (4746)	204

The International Olympic Committee (IOC) first met in 1894. The first Games of the modern era, held in Athens in 1896, involved 241 athletes from only 14 countries and limited press coverage. The early modern Games became an integral part of the tradition of city boosterism and city image making inaugurated by the World Fairs. There is a connection between the two spectacles. Two of the early Games overlapped in specific cities with World Fairs: Paris in 1900 and St. Louis in 1904. Over the years, the Games have grown in size, scope and international media coverage (see Table 17.2). In 2008 in Beijing, 11,028 athletes represented 205 countries. The Games are now the most watched event on television, with a truly global audience. The Games' global reach reflects the shrinking and flattening of the world.

While the number of countries participating in the Games has increased, the siting of the Games still reflects the Euro-US bias. Only 19 countries held the Games from 1896 to 2008, five of them twice. It was only in 1964 that the Games were held in Asia and only six have been held outside Europe and North America. Hosting the Games means either existing substantial or proposed infrastructural investments that only a few countries in the world can afford or are willing to undertake.

Table 17.3 lists the cities bidding and hosting the Games from 1976 to 2016. In the

Table 17.3   Olympic Games Candidate and host cities, 1976–2016

Year	Host city	Bid city
2016	Rio de Janeiro	Chicago, USA
		Madrid, Spain
		Tokyo, Japan
		Baku, Azerbaijan
		Doha, Qatar
		Prague, Czech Republic
2012	London	Paris, France
		Madrid, Spain
		New York, USA
		Moscow, Russia
		Leipzig, Germany
		Rio de Janeiro, Brazil
		Istanbul, Turkey
		Havana, Cuba
2008	Beijing	Toronto, Canada
		Paris, France
		Istanbul, Turkey
		Osaka, Japan
		Bangkok, Thailand
		Cairo, Egypt
		Havana, Cuba
		Kuala Lumpur, Malaysia
		Seville, Spain
2004	Athens	Rome, Italy
		Cape Town, South Africa
		Stockholm, Sweden
		Buenos Aires, Argentina
		Istanbul, Turkey
		Lille, France
		Rio de Janeiro, Brazil
		St. Petersburg, Russia
		San Juan, Puerto Rico
		Seville, Spain
2000	Sydney	Beijing, China
		Manchester, United Kingdom
		Berlin, Germany
		Istanbul, Turkey
1996	Atlanta	Athens, Greece
		Toronto, Canada
		Melbourne, Australia
		Manchester, United Kingdom
		Belgrade, Yugoslavia
1992	Barcelona	Paris, France
		Belgrade, Yugoslavia
		Brisbane, Australia

Table 17.3   (continued)

Year	Host city	Bid city
		Birmingham, United Kingdom
		Amsterdam, Netherlands
1988	Seoul	Nagoya, Japan
1984	Los Angeles	
1980	Moscow	Los Angeles
1976	Montreal	Moscow,
		Los Angeles

Note: The cities italicized for the 2004, 2008, 2012 and 2016 bids did not make it to the final round.

immediate post-World War II era US cities, because they had the resources and had avoided war related damage, dominated the pool of candidate cities. Of the seven candidate cities for the 1952 Olympics, five were US cities. As the cost of the Games escalated and revenues stagnated, the number of candidate cities dropped off. There were only four candidate cities for the 1964, 1968 and 1972 Games, three for 1976, two for 1980 and only one for 1984. The financial success of Los Angeles inaugurated a new era of intense city competition to host the Olympic Games. However, as the Games become more elaborate and more expensive, with a greater reliance on existing substantial urban and sporting infrastructure, many cities in small and/or poor countries find it difficult to make it past the early rounds. Witness the early rejection of Havana for the 2008 and 2012 Games, and the fate of Baku compared with Chicago or Tokyo in the bidding process for the 2016 Games. Financial ability to host the Games and commercial 'spin-off' (i.e. the ability to use the Games to penetrate new markets) are principal considerations for the IOC. Beijing was almost certain to win, given the willingness of the Chinese government to fund the Games and the huge commercial potential of the Chinese market to corporate sponsors.

Candidate cities now include global cities at the apex of the global urban hierarchy (Shoval, 2002). Major cities such as New York, London and Paris compete to host the Olympics and National Olympic Committees now increasingly promote the larger cities as their candidate cities.

Hosting an Olympics provides an opportunity to make a global city. Athens, for example, upgraded its infrastructure by installing a new transportation network, including motorways, a tramway and a metro system (Beriatos and Gospodini, 2004). The Chinese government used the 2008 Games as an opportunity to modernize Beijing (Broudehoux, 2007). One plan involved the destruction of the old, high-density neighborhoods of small alleyways in the central part of the city, seen by officials as a remnant of a premodern past. Almost 20 square km were destroyed and almost 580,000 people were displaced in this one program (Fan, 2008).

The creation of a more global city is one of the main goals and consequences of hosting the Games. The Games allow a city to showcase itself to a global audience and become more globally connected. For two weeks the city is constantly mentioned and represented in the world's media. New or greatly expanded international airports are standard requirements, as are new road and mass transit linkages from the airport to the rest of the city. Hosting the Games allows the city to achieve global recognition with the possibility of increased tourism and investment. The business community of Atlanta used the Olympics as one in a long line of civic boosterist projects (Rutheiser, 1996). Barcelona successfully used the Games to reposition itself as a major tourist destination, almost doubling the number of foreign visitors two years after the Games compared with two years prior to the Games (Brunet, 2005).

The Games act as an important tool to literally reshape the city, in both discursive and spatial terms. Hosting the Games involves a massive restructuring of urban space (Essex and Chalkley, 1998). The city is permanently transformed by the spatial restructuring of hosting the Games. In Seoul the Chamsil area was redeveloped; in Barcelona the sea front was opened up; in Atlanta there was a central city gentrification that involved the construction of lofts, telecom hotels and high tech offices. In Sydney, Home Bush Bay was cleaned up. In Athens disused quarries, abandoned waste dumps and old army barracks were reclaimed and reused. There is also the physical legacy of the Olympic villages constructed to house the athletes. In Seoul, Barcelona and Sydney, new Olympic villages were built and became new neighborhoods. The stadia constructed to host the Olympic events also became permanent sites able to be used for subsequent events. The Seoul Olympic stadium was a venue for the 2002 FIFA World Cup. In Atlanta the stadium became the permanent home of the Atlanta Braves baseball team. Perhaps the largest infrastructural legacy is the upgrade of airports, telecommunications, mass transit schemes and road networks that quite literally better connect the city to global flows of people, ideas and commerce.

Hosting the Games provides a significant opportunity to forge new and improved links with the wider world that plug the city more effectively into the global flows of capital, people and ideas. Among the positive effects of recent Games are the clean-up of derelict and abandoned sites, the creation of attractive public spaces, legacies of new spaces and improved athletic facilities, and even an increase in the environmental quality of the city. The improvements in the air quality in Beijing, part of the city's Olympic bid package, will be enjoyed by all the residents of the city. As with most urban social changes there is an unequal distribution of costs and benefits. The poor tend to gain least and pay more. However, for every Atlanta there is also a Barcelona and Sydney where there were general improvements to the quality of urban life that were not entirely regressive. While all cities are rewritten by hosting the Olympics, the particular narrative can vary enormously.

The Summer Olympics are an example of cultural and economic globalization. The number of countries competing has grown steadily until it covers most of the globe. Because of the increasing corporatization of the Games, they have also become a launching site for economic globalization as major corporations use the Games as a platform for global penetration. The Games provide the opportunity for firms to sell their goods and services to a global market. The hosting of the Games in Beijing was in large measure driven by the need to find an entry into the vast Chinese market. The Games have become an important process of globalization, but a process that reinforces rather than undermines nationalism and national identity.

At the city level the hosting of the Games provides one of the most obvious cases of glocalization as the global spectacle is centered in a specific city, while the hosting of the event tends to reconnect the city into a global space of flows. The Games have become an important transformative experience that denotes and connotes global cities. The globality of a city is never given or fixed, or even the result of some inert attribute; it is enacted, performed, spectacularized. This is evident in the bidding and hosting of the Summer Games. They have become the mega-event with the ability to create, reinforce and consolidate global city status. The Olympic Games embody the increasing globalization of the world; they represent a significant regime of international regulation, embody a shared cultural experience and provide an important platform for economic globalization as transnational corporations advertise in and through the Games. The Games are a global event that unfold in a particular city.

While there are an increasing number of urban events (Waitt, 2008) and an increasing number can be called mega-events – some global, such as the World Cup, and some more regional, such as the European Cities of Culture – the history and present reality are dominated by World Fairs and the Summer Olympics. They were and are the largest international events that embody and promote globalization in and through the host cities. Hosting these international mega-events is an important nexus in the connections between the city and globalization.

REFERENCES

Beriatos, E. and A. Gospodini (2004), '"Glocalizing" urban landscapes: Athens and the 2004 Olympics', *Cities*, **21** (3), 187–202.

Broudehoux, A.-M. (2007), 'Spectacular Beijing: the conspicuous consumption of an Olympics metropolis', *Journal of Urban Affairs*, **29** (4), 383–399.

Brunet, F. (2005), *The Economic Impact of the Barcelona Olympic Games, 1986–2004*, Barcelona: Centre d'Estudis Olimpics UAB.

Christie, I. (2006), 'Mass-market modernism', in C. Wik (ed.), *Modernism: Designing A New World*, London: V and A Publications, pp. 375–414.

Essex, S. and B. Chalkley (1998), 'Olympic games: catalyst of urban change', *Leisure Studies*, **17** (3), 187–206.

Fan, C. (2008), 'As Beijing Olympics near, homes and hope crumble', *The Washington Post*, July 12, A6.

Findling, J.E. and K.D. Pelle (eds) (2008), *Encyclopedia of World's Fairs and Expositions*, Jefferson, NC: McFarland.

Gold, J.R. and M.M. Gold (2005), *Cities of Culture: Staging International Festivals and the Urban Agenda, 1851–2000*, Aldershot: Ashgate.

Gold, J.R. and M.M. Gold (eds) (2007), *Olympic Cities: City Agendas, Planning and the World's Games, 1896–2012*, London: Routledge.

Gold, J.R. and M.M. Gold (2008), 'Olympic cities: regeneration, city rebranding and changing urban agendas', *Geography Compass*, **2** (1), 300–318.

Harvey, P. (1996), *Hybrids of Modernity: Anthropology, the Nation State and the Universal Exhibition*, London: Routledge.

Martin, T. (1880), *The Life of His Royal Highness the Prince Consort*, Volume 2, New York: D. Appleton & Co.

Pred, A. (1995), *Recognizing European Modernities: A Montage of the Present*, London: Routledge.

Roche, M. (2006), 'Mega-events and modernity revisited: globalization and the case of the Olympics', *Sociological Review*, **54**, 25–40.

Rutheiser, C. (1996), *Imagineering Atlanta: The Politics of Place in the City of Dreams*, London: Verso.

Short, J.R. (2004), *Global Metropolitan*, London: Routledge.

Short, J.R. (2008), 'Globalization, cities and the Summer Olympics', *City*, **12** (3), 321–340.

Shoval, N. (2002), 'A new phase in the competition for the Olympic gold: the London and New York bids for the 2012 Games', *Journal of Urban Affairs*, **24** (5), 583–599.

Thompson, W. (2000), '"The symbol of Paris": writing the Eiffel Tower', *The French Review*, **73** (6), 1130–1140.

Waitt, G. (2008), 'Urban festivals: geographies of hype, helplessness and hope', *Geography Compass*, **2** (2), 513–537.

18 Cyberinfrastructures and 'smart' world cities: physical, human and soft infrastructures

Andrew Boulton, Stanley D. Brunn and Lomme Devriendt

MAPPING POINTS AND FLOWS

Each Sunday in central Kashgar more than four thousand vendors bring their goods to the International Trade Market of Central and Western Asia. Here, buyers and sellers from the city and its desert hinterlands barter over everything from silk and handicrafts to livestock and vegetables, much as they have since (at least) the days of the Han Dynasty (206–220 BC) when explorers such as Zhang Qian remarked with surprise upon the vibrancy of the urban marketplace in this arid outpost. Much of the architectural character of Old Town Kashgar is no more: wrecked, a small, hyperreal, tourist-friendly 'taste' of the Old excepted, in the first decade of the 21st century in the name of safety, 'modernization' and anti-extremism by a government seeking to bring stability and control to the alleys and warrens of this cold, 'threatening' western city (Sheridan, 2008; Macartney, 2009). An oasis city of 350,000 in the far west of China's Xinjiang region, Kashgar arguably sustains itself as a viable city today on the basis of the same locational advantages that made it a key trading location, staging post and population center on the ancient Silk Road: water supply, relatively fertile land and superior accessibility by land and, today, by air (see Kreutzmann, 2003, on livelihood strategies in the region).

In classic textbook maps of the ancient Silk Road, Kashgar appears as a dot (or node) within a more-or-less coherent system of arrows and dots tracing out seasonal, cyclical and longer-run 'flows' of migrants and goods across a vast, intercontinental network of trading routes. But we wonder: another two thousand years from now, what might an equivalent iconographic mapping of today's intercity relationships in Eurasia, or elsewhere, look like? A map showing flows of capital? Flows of people? Flows of goods? Flows of telecommunications data? Flows . . . Flows . . . Flows.

Recently, the very 'flow' metaphor (Castells, 1996) adopted unreflexively in much world cities work (see Beaverstock et al., 2000; Taylor et al., 2002; Devriendt et al., 2008) has itself come under scrutiny (Smith and Doel, 2011). The question becomes not 'what flows?' – bits, bytes, planes, money, ideas and so forth – but '*what* flows?' (cf. Boulton et al., 2011). Is a flow ontology even an appropriate framework (or plausible metaphor; a discontinuous flow?) to apprehend the relationships existing between places in an Information Age supposedly divested of a necessary or even predominant basis in geographical contiguity (Castells, 2000; Smith and Doel, 2011)?

In one (perhaps glib) reading, Smith and Doel's poststructuralist critique of the ontological assumptions of the 'flow' metaphor, of the 'world cities'[1] category itself and ultimately of the limiting politics thereof, marks the sub-disciplinary coming of age of a world city network geography rooted to date in an avowedly critical realist tradition (ibid.). But, more than that, the critique offers a challenge to and an opportunity for (would-be) world cities scholars. Rather than dismiss, or attempt to co-opt, these timely anti-foundationalist critiques of the world cities literature, there is an exciting opportunity for cyberinfrastructure research in particular, and world cities research more generally, to move beyond a potentially nihilistic deconstructive moment to become vital, multivocal and critical sub-disciplines that address timely and important questions across disciplines and theoretical orientations. Against this backdrop, our purpose in the remainder of this chapter is thus to take stock of the key debates and theoretical and research trajectories in world cities cyberinfrastructure research (Derudder et al., 2007; Zook and Graham, 2007; Smith and Doel, 2011) and to identify promising future research directions on this diversifying terrain of 'smart cities'. First we introduce an expanded notion of 'smartness' that takes into account what we characterize as the (i) physical, (ii) human and (iii) soft moments of cyberinfrastructure. Thereafter, we utilize these three dimensions in order to characterize the open questions and dynamism of current (and potential future) world cities research. These three dimensions of cyberinfrastructure are not intended to be exhaustive or exclusive categories, but merely potential empirical or analytical 'cuts' through the messy and infinitely multiple multiples that are the 'world city' (Smith and Doel, 2011).

CONCEPTUALIZING SMARTNESS

When a rich endowment of 'classic' site and situational advantages is no longer sufficient or even necessary for a city's prosperity and economic dynamism, scholars and policymakers alike are driven to search for new data, new strategies and new narratives to describe, explain and, in the case of policymakers, to affect the relative competitiveness of, and differentiation between, cities. What many of these new logics of, or strategies for, 'competitiveness' – fostering educational 'export' industries (Robertson, 2003); encouraging high-tech clusters; creating a 'climate' suitable for an emerging Creative Class (Florida, 2002) – rely on implicitly, or more often explicitly, is a notion of 'smartness' predicated on, or underpinned by, knowledge, technology and particularly ICTs.

We argue that a more expansive notion of 'smart' cities than those operational definitions common in the economics literature is necessary in order to appreciate the range of research trajectories and conceptual frameworks at the cutting edge of 'smart' world cities research. Where smartness is frequently operationalized as a product of the education level of a population – which is then correlated with employment or GDP growth (Shapiro, 2003; Glaeser and Berry, 2006) – we would draw attention to the ambivalent nature of 'smartness' itself not only as an attribute of places (a 'smart city') or individuals, but simultaneously as a messier, multi-scalar and overlapping set of concerns related to cyberinfrastructure in its 'physical', 'human' and 'soft' moments.

Physical infrastructure refers to cities' locations with respect to the global network of physical infrastructures such as airlines, hotel and conference facilities, and the high-tech fiber optic technologies on which telecommunications depend (Malecki, 2002; Zook and Brunn, 2006; Derudder et al., 2007).

Human infrastructure, by contrast, refers to the more 'traditional' human capital concerns of agglomeration, clustering and economies of scale (Saxenian, 1996; Gorman, 2002).

Soft infrastructure refers to the domains (literally and figuratively) of cyberspace: the informational 'cloud' of Web domains (Zook, 2001), cyberscapes, and user-generated and georeferenced spatial data (Graham and Zook, 2011), which, despite their apparent placelessness, 'touch the ground' with real, material effects (Graham, 2005; Crutcher and Zook, 2009).

This is not to deny the importance of classic notions of 'smartness' to particular kinds of economic analysis, or the value of simple education-level measures of human capital. Indeed, regardless of the merits of the often scathing critiques of Richard Florida's liberal, middle class-centric Creative Class meme (Marcuse, 2003; Peck, 2005), the prevalence of university degrees within a city's population – one of Florida's creativity measures – appears to be directly correlated with incomes of the population in general, including of the least wealthy (Moretti, 2004). As an aside, though, the payoff for mayoral devotees' cities resulting from their 'cultish' adoption of Florida's prescriptions – that is, pandering to 'the lifestyle preferences of yuppies' (Marcuse, 2003, p. 41) – is 'evasive' at best (Peck, 2005, p. 768). The key point to reiterate here is that any normative claim about the nature of or potential futures for world cities/networks is necessarily partial, situated and contextual. Framed differently – and more modestly, perhaps, as contextualized descriptive analyses rather than universal prescriptions – simplistic, quantitative analyses such as Florida's (2000) need not subscribe to or draw on any particular, problematic (critical realist, positivist, or whatever) epistemology. As conceptual interventions, and empirical cuts through the inherent messiness of the city, they may signal interesting trends (however transitory or superficial), productive tensions, or points of intervention towards innumerable – and not necessarily neoliberal, as is the critique of Florida (Peck, 2005) – futures. Thus, to bastardize the words of French philosopher Alain Badiou, the 'situation' (something like reality) *is* infinitely more complex than the 'state', as claimed, as secured, in its re-presentation and in its recounting (Badiou, 2005, p. 85, cited in Smith and Doel, 2011). But the complexity of the situation, we suggest, need not paralyze us from saying *something* – however contingent, partial, tentative – about 'it'.

City planners, private corporations and governments grapple perpetually with the competitiveness problem: how to abstract the 'growth' ingredient from an infinitely complex, multiple and interconnected totality. Perhaps the allure of self-styled gurus and their high-energy, simple (if expensive!) solutions are understandable. Today's world cities are centers of knowledge, innovation and technology, but they are also infinitely complex assemblages of people and things, dynamic and indeterminate both in and of themselves and in their relationships to other places (Smith and Doel, 2011). Recognizing these complex and intrinsic 'networks' of relationships between cities, scholars of world cities, globalization and the knowledge economy have, increasingly, turned their attention to the ways in which cities are positioned differentially in relation to global information 'flows', and specifically in relation to ICT networks. Note that we say cities are 'positioned differentially' rather than 'arranged hierarchically', as this is an important distinction (see also Taylor, 2008). Whereas hierarchy implies relationships of control – literally, of domination by the top 'tier' of subsequent, submissive tiers – the speciously similar concept of 'rank' refers not to relations of power between, but to differential attributes of and within, cities. Thus ranking cities in terms of, for example, headquarters of global producer firms, Web page references (or 'hyperlinks'), conference proceedings and news stories (Williams and Brunn, 2004; Devriendt et al., 2009) does not imply a hierarchical ordering of cities in the sense of command and control. Rather, such rankings – if recognized as transient, partial 'snapshots' (Boulton et al., 2011) –

constitute but one potential point of comparison between cities and their relative experiences of and relationships to the eventfulness of the global economy.

PHYSICAL, HUMAN AND SOFT DIMENSIONS OF CYBERINFRASTRUCTURE

'Smart cities', then, may be used as a shorthand to refer to those cities with high densities of 'cyber' or digital infrastructure and high levels of utilization of ICTs. Operationalizing 'density', and drawing out the implications of relative densities to social/economic life, entails a broad and collective (but diverse) effort towards data gathering/production and theory development. The genealogy of much current research on smart cities and creative cities in geography can be traced to major research agendas of the 1960s and 1970s that focused on the concentrations and diffusion of innovations (see Abler et al., 1971). The pioneering research of Torsten Hägerstrand (1952, 1967), though not focused on cities, sought to explicate the spatial processes underlying innovations in rural areas and small towns of Sweden. His diffusion work was supplemented by that of rural sociologist, Everett Rogers (1962), who identified specific stages in the diffusion of innovations. In Rogers' account, it was the innovators who were the leaders, working on the cutting edge, willing to experiment and taking the necessary risks. At the heart of these diffusion/communication studies were always questions about where a practice or idea originated, what were the distinguishing characteristics of these 'origin' places, and what kinds of spatial processes were operating to produce the resulting patterns of diffusion and concentration. Along with the work of other key 1960s and 1970s geographers, including Peter Gould (1969) and Larry Brown (1968, 1981), this spatial science tradition of mapping innovation offers a strong foreshadowing of the work on creative cities and smart cities conducted three decades later in terms of its focus on the *attributes* of 'smart' places: 'human capital', creativity and agglomeration economies (Florida, 2000, 2002; Gorman, 2002; see also Krueger and Buckingham, 2009, introducing a *Geographical Review* special issue on creative cities).

In a similar vein, Allan Pred's (1966) pioneering work on the social and commercial landscapes of patent awards mirrors in its place-based ontology recent work on the 'human' attributes of successful and/or creative and/or competitive cities. All patents are awarded to a specific individual or firm, at a specific address. Thus one could 'map' the locations of those places that received particular kinds of patent (biotech, automotive, and so forth). By studying the locational patterns of patents over a longer period of time (a decade) or a slice of time (such as one year), one might infer not only the location but some of the characteristics of those 'creative' or innovative places in particular fields. Data on patents awarded in the fields of ICT, fashion design, music and myriad other 'creative' industries (e.g. Watson, 2009) offer a rich potential source by which to test, and/or add conceptual and empirical depth to, broad brush 'creativity' indices (see Chapman, forthcoming).

A crucial task, then, for world cities research is to think about how we might understand the ways in which the contemporary city produces, is produced by and is experienced in relation to cyberinfrastructures: both in terms of aggregate 'human capital' variables such as patents, but also in terms of day-to-day experiences of place in relation to ICT infrastructures. Promising research directions in this respect are diverse, and call for innovative conceptual frameworks as well as new and creative use of data. Here we explore one broad topic: cyberscapes.

CYBERSCAPES AND THE 'SOFT' DIMENSIONS OF CYBERINFRASTRUCTURES

As conceptualized by Zook and Graham (2007) cyberscape refers to the experiential blurring between cyber*space* and material place. That is, places – cities – are experienced as and constituted within 'virtual' and material spaces simultaneously (Graham, 2010). Particularly suggestive is the observed unevenness of cyberspaces (ibid.): that is, the varying density of digital spatial data tied to particular locations. The relatively new phenomenon of user-generated spatial data – the so-called 'crowd-sourced' cloud of cyberspace contributed via platforms such as Google Maps (see Crampton, 2009, for an excellent overview of these 'neogeographies'; see also Graham, 2010 and Boulton, 2010) – raises important questions about the ways in which 'cyberspace' (re)produces extant relations of domination, inequity and racialization (Crutcher and Zook, 2009). Critical geographies of world cities in this 'cyberscape' vein suggest that cyberinfrastructures can scarcely be understood without reference to (at least) the soft (cyberspace/cloud) and the human (discrimination, 'digital divides' and so forth), or their intersections with myriad other dimensions of the social. A related question also arises: if we are prepared to identify 'smart' cities, are we prepared, also, to delineate 'dumb' cities? A broadened conceptualization of 'smartness' suggests a more nuanced reading of 'smart' and 'dumb' than a simple binary, or even numerically ranked, classification. Understandably, world cities research has focused on the 'great' cities (and what makes them so), but there is, arguably, a case for placing other cities – regional cities, national centers, small cities – within the same analytical space, to focus on the 'have nots' as well as the 'haves' of neoliberal globalization.

Hyperbolic claims that distance – and with it, place, the city and geography – is, or soon will be, 'dead' (e.g. O'Brien, 1992) belie an important paradox in cyberspace research: even as ICTs become accessible 'everywhere', demand for transportation between places, and for prime, proximate real estate within 'core' urban locations, continues to grow (Denstadli and Gripsrud, 2010). The vision of so-called 'post-industrial' theorists of a world without distance, where 'everyplace is everyplace' (Abler, 1974), remains unmet in many ways. The ubiquitous 'cloud' of communication is, in fact, underpinned and enabled by a vast, physical (placed) ICT infrastructure of cables, data centers and exchanges. Rather than rendering place irrelevant, cities' economic performance and their prominence within the global urban network become, increasingly, a product of their relative attractiveness vis-à-vis other places, and in relation to ICT networks. As the highly uneven geographies of 'Web factories' and high-tech enclaves suggest, communication has not and cannot be substituted for the social, cultural and economic advantages of agglomeration (Gorman, 2002), Silicon Valley being the paradigmatic case (Saxenian, 1996). Within our conceptual framework of treating the physical (place, material infrastructure), the human and the soft (qua cyberspace) as related intrinsically, one can begin to imagine a plural 'world cities' research agenda concerned both with networks *of* world cities, and with world cities *as networks* or even 'plasmas' (cf. Smith and Doel, 2011) of multiplicity, diversity and indeterminacy.

CONCLUSIONS: INFRASTRUCTURE, INTERCONNECTION AND PLURALITY

(One tooth of) the cutting edge of cyberinfrastructure research is characterized by a two-pronged approach to 'smart' cities: cyberplace approaches, focusing on the material, placed infrastructure underpinning digital 'flows', and cyberspace approaches which focus on the less bounded/grounded 'cloud' of digital information circulating in, about and between places (Devriendt et al., 2008).[2] These in turn correspond most closely with, respectively, the 'physical' and 'soft' dimensions of cyberinfrastructure outlined in this chapter. As a diverse array of work on world cities has noted, the interconnections between cities, however they are measured, are arguably more global, more immediate and deeper than ever before. One has only to look at the pace with which the shockwaves of the 'global financial crisis' (2008) and Greek debt crisis (2010) reverberated monetarily and imaginatively across the globe. For scholars, lending empirical specificity to these alluringly simple and apparently self-evident claims of deepening and quickening interconnection is a different matter entirely.

The ambivalent relationship between the supposed placelessness of cyberspace, and the continued importance of place (qua the city) signals a core concern for world cities research going forward. The lexicon surrounding cyberspace, the Internet and 'new' technologies is replete with spatial metaphors and analogies (Adams, 1997): online *community*, web *site*, information *gateway*, *portal* site, chat *room*. At one level, the reading of this spatial language is straightforward. Spatial/territorial analogy superimposes upon the otherwise intangible (and unintelligible) sphere of bits and bytes a determinate and visible/visualizable *representational* surface. Cyberspace, so imagined, becomes knowable; written in 'geographical language' (Kellerman, 2002, p. 31) it becomes definable, mappable and understandable in terms of standard spatial rubrics of distance and proximity, connection and flow. But an alternative reading of this spatial language suggests a problematization of the supposed separation between underlying reality (intangible/unintelligible) and overlaid representation (tangible/visible) (see Cicognani, 1998). This reading recognizes that the 'virtual' world of cyberspace is already fundamentally imbricated with the 'real', material life of the contemporary city (Crutcher and Zook, 2009).

An expanded conceptualization of cyberinfrastructures as comprising overlapping physical, human and soft dimensions suggests an exciting and (theoretically) broad research agenda targeted towards understanding the complex variations between and within contemporary cities.

ACKNOWLEDGEMENTS

Thanks to Matt Zook for his ideas and discussions on these topics; responsibility for errors and omissions lies with the listed authors.

NOTES

1. In what follows, the term 'world cities' is used advisedly. In common with our sympathetic reading of the poststructural critique of the world cities literature (Smith and Doel, 2011), we reject any necessary a priori category of 'world city'. Rather, in line with our call for an expanded notion of world cities, a reflexive use of 'network' and 'flow' metaphors, and our recognition of the multiplicity of world cities and world city networks, we retain the notion of 'world cities' insofar as it provides a useful heuristic for talking about rankings and qualities of, and relationships between, places (however fleeting, however partial).
2. The discussion of cyberplace and cyberspace approaches builds on our earlier GaWC working paper (Devriendt et al., 2009) and the article by Devriendt et al. (2008).

REFERENCES

Abler, R. (1974), 'The geography of communications', in M. Hurst (ed.), *Transportation Geography*, New York: McGraw Hill.

Abler, R., J. Adams and P. Gould (1971), 'Spatial diffusion: meshing of time and space', in *Spatial Organization: The Geographer's View of the World*, Englewood Cliffs, NJ: Prentice-Hall, pp. 389–451.

Adams, P.C. (1997), 'Cyberspace and virtual places', *Geographical Review*, **87** (2), 155–171.

Badiou, A. (2005), *Being and Event*, London: Continuum.

Beaverstock, J.V., R.G. Smith and P.J. Taylor (2000), 'World-city network: a new metageography?', *Annals of the Association of American Geographers*, **90** (1), 123–134.

Boulton, A. (2010), 'Guest editorial – just maps: Google's democratic map-making community?', *Cartographica*, **45** (1), 1–4.

Boulton, A., L. Devriendt, S.D. Brunn, B. Derudder and F. Witlox (2011), 'City networks in cyberspace and time: using Google hyperlinks to measure global economic and environmental crises', in R.J. Firmino, F. Duarte and C. Ultramari (eds), *ICTs for Mobile and Ubiquitous Urban Infrastructures: Surveillance, Locative Media and Global Networks*, Hershey, PA: IGI Global, pp. 67–87.

Brown, L. (1968), *Diffusion Processes and Location: A Conceptual Framework*, Philadelphia, PA: Regional Science Research Institute.

Brown, L. (1981), *Innovation Diffusion: A New Perspective*, London: Methuen.

Castells, M. (1996), *The Rise of the Network Society*, Oxford: Blackwell.

Castells, M. (2000), 'Materials for an exploratory theory of the network society', *British Journal of Sociology*, **51** (1), 1–24.

Chapman, T. (forthcoming), 'Creative class occupations', in S. Brunn et al. (eds), *Atlas of the 2008 Elections*, Boulder, CO: Rowman and Littlefield, in press.

Cicognani, A. (1998), 'On the linguistic nature of cyberspace and virtual communities', *Virtual Reality*, **3** (1), 16–24.

Crampton, J.W. (2009), 'Cartography: maps 2.0', *Progress in Human Geography*, **33** (1), 91–100.

Crutcher, M. and M. Zook (2009), 'Placemarks and waterlines: racialized cyberscapes in post-Katrina Google Earth', *Geoforum*, **40** (4), 523–534.

Denstadli, J.M. and M. Gripsrud (2010), 'Face-to-face by travel or picture: the relationship between travelling and video communication in business settings', in J.V. Beaverstock, B. Derudder, J. Faulconbridge and F. Witlox (eds), *International Business Travel in the Global Economy*, London: Ashgate, pp. 217–238.

Derudder, B., L. Devriendt and F. Witlox (2007), 'Flying where you don't want to go: an empirical analysis of hubs in the global airline network', *Tijdschrift voor Economische en Sociale Geografie*, **98** (3), 307–324.

Devriendt, L., A. Boulton, S. Brunn, B. Derudder and F. Witlox (2009), 'Major cities in the Information World: monitoring cyberspace in real-time', *GaWC Research Bulletin*, 308, available at www.lboro.ac.uk/gawc/rb/rb308.html (accessed 24 June 2009).

Devriendt, L., B. Derudder and F. Witlox (2008), 'Cyberplace and cyberspace: two approaches to analyzing digital intercity linkages', *Journal of Urban Technology*, **15** (2), 5–32.

Florida, R. (2000), 'The economic geography of talent', *Annals of the Association of American Geographers*, **92** (4), 743–755.

Florida, R. (2002), *The Rise of the Creative Class: And How It's Transforming Work, Leisure, Community, and Everyday Life*, New York: Basic Books.

Glaeser, E.L. and C.R. Berry (2006), 'Why are smart places getting smarter?', Rappaport Institute/Taubman Center Policy Brief, 2006–2, March, Harvard University: John F. Kennedy School of Government.

Gorman, S.P. (2002), 'Where are the Web factories? The urban bias of e-business location', *Tijdschrift voor Economische en Sociale Geografie*, **93** (5), 522–536.
Gould, P. (1969), *Spatial Diffusion*, Washington, DC: Association of American Geographers, Commission on College Geography (Resource Paper No. 4).
Graham, M. (2010), 'Neogeography and the palimpsests of place: web 2.0 and the construction of a virtual earth', *Tijdschrift voor Economische en Sociale Geografie*, **101** (4), 422–436.
Graham, M. and M. Zook (2011), 'Visualizing global cyberscapes: mapping user-generated placemarks', *Journal of Urban Technology*, **18** (1), 115–132.
Graham, S.D.N. (2005), 'Software-sorted geographies', *Progress in Human Geography*, **29** (5), 562–580.
Hägerstrand, T. (1952), *The Propagation of Innovation Waves*, Lund: Gleerup (Lund Studies in Geography Series B, No. 4).
Hägerstrand, T. (1967), *Innovation Diffusion as a Spatial Process*, postscript and translation: A. Pred, Chicago: University of Chicago Press.
Kellerman, A. (2002), *The Internet on Earth: A Geography of Information*, Chichester, England: John Wiley and Sons Ltd.
Kreutzmann, H. (2003), 'Ethnic minorities and marginality in the Pamirian Knot: survival of Wakhi and Kirghiz in a harsh environment and global contexts', *The Geographical Journal*, **169** (3), 215–235.
Krueger, R. and S. Buckingham (2009), 'Creative-city scripts, economic development, and sustainability', *Geographical Review*, **99** (1), iii–xii.
Macartney, J. (2009), 'End of the Silk Road for historic trading hub of Kashgar', *Times Online*, available at www.timesonline.co.uk/tol/news/world/asia/article6525325.ece (accessed 18 June 2009).
Malecki, E.J. (2002), 'Hard and soft networks for urban competitiveness', *Urban Studies*, **39** (5–6), 929–945.
Marcuse, P. (2003), 'Review of *The Rise of the Creative Class* by Richard Florida', *Urban Land*, **62**, 40–41.
Moretti, E. (2004), 'Estimating the social returns to higher education: evidence from cross-sectional and longitudinal data', *Journal of Econometrics*, **121** (1–2), 175–212.
O'Brien, R. (1992), *Global Financial Integration: The End of Geography*, London: Pinter.
Peck, J. (2005), 'Struggling with the Creative Class', *International Journal of Urban and Regional Research*, **29** (4), 740–770.
Pred, A. (1966), *Spatial Dynamics of U.S. Urban-Industrial Growth: 1900–1914*, Cambridge, MA: MIT Press.
Robertson, S. (2003), 'WTO/GATS and the global education services industry', *Globalisation, Societies and Education*, **1** (3), 259–266.
Rogers, E. (1962), *Diffusion of Innovations*, New York: Free Press of Glencoe.
Saxenian, A. (1996), *Regional Advantage: Culture and Competition in Silicon Valley and Route 128*, Cambridge, MA: Harvard University Press.
Shapiro, J. (2003), 'Smart cities: explaining the relationship between city growth and human capital', *Social Science Research Network Working Papers*, available at http://ssrn.com/abstract=480172 (accessed 20 September 2009).
Sheridan, M. (2008), 'Anger turns to uprising along the Silk Road', *Times Online*, available at www.timesonline.co.uk/tol/news/world/asia/article4547322.ece (accessed 17 August 2008).
Smith, R.G. and M.A. Doel (2011), 'Questioning the theoretical basis of current global-city research: structures, networks, and actor-networks', *International Journal of Urban and Regional Research*, **35** (1), 24–39.
Taylor, P.J. (2008), 'World cities in globalization', *GaWC Research Bulletin*, 263, available at www.lboro.ac.uk/gawc/rb/rb263.html (accessed 24 June 2009).
Taylor, P.J., G. Catalano and D.R.F. Walker (2002), 'Measurement of the world-city network', *Urban Studies*, **39** (13), 2367–2376.
Watson, A. (2009), 'The world according to iTunes: creative project ecologies and the global urban networks of digital music production', *GaWC Research Bulletin*, 317, available at www.lboro.ac.uk/gawc/rb/rb317.html (accessed 20 September 2009).
Williams, J.F. and S.D. Brunn (2004), 'Cybercities of Asia: measuring globalization using hyperlinks (Asian cities and hyperlinks)', *Asian Geographer*, **23** (1–2), 121–147.
Zook, M.A. (2001), 'Old hierarchies or new networks of centrality? The global geography of the Internet content market', *American Behavioral Scientist*, **44** (10), 1679–1696.
Zook, M.A. and S.D. Brunn (2006), 'From podes to antipodes: positionalities and global airline geographies', *Annals of the Association of American Geographers*, **96** (3), 471–490.
Zook, M.A. and M. Graham (2007), 'Mapping DigiPlace: geocoded Internet data and the representation of place', *Environment and Planning B: Planning and Design*, **34** (3), 466–482.

II B   World city economies

19 Centrality, hierarchy and heterarchy of worldwide corporate networks
Ronald Wall and Bert van der Knaap

INTRODUCTION

Although globalization has developed for centuries, its magnitude in terms of trade and foreign direct investment (FDI) has increased dramatically (Barba Navaretti and Venables, 2004). Facilitated by reduced transportation costs, advanced technologies, increased market openness and trade liberalization, this inter-organizational system connects firms and cities together. Because only a handful of multinational corporations (MNCs) control most global FDI and trade (Rugman, 2005), their influence on the fate of cities and nations is clear. These investments increasingly concentrate within and between a limited number of nations, creating an international division of labour that corresponds to labour divisions between different levels of corporate hierarchy (Hymer, 1972). However, despite these important global changes, economic geography still presents itself as the science of the meso-scale (Grabher, 2006), leading to an 'overterritorialized' view on regional development. Instead a strategic coupling of global production networks and regional assets should be pursued in which activities are mediated across different geographical and organizational scales (Coe et al., 2004). In this light, the topology of the world city system will be explored, concerning different levels of corporate ownership, centrality, hierarchy and heterarchy of cities within the global network. The chapter starts with a theoretical discussion of hierarchy and heterarchy within networks, followed by an explanation of the data and methodology used. Next, the results are discussed, followed by conclusions.

NETWORK HIERARCHY AND HETERARCHY

Because economic action is fundamentally social (Polanyi, 1944; Grabher, 2006), it can be argued that social network analysis is applicable to understanding firms. In this perspective, the firm is considered as a constellation of relations governed by social actors. Rather than being a mechanistic function of production, the firm is a contested site for discursive and material constructions at various organizational and spatial scales. Furthermore, networks encompass hierarchies of power, in which there would be no incentive for stronger actors to remain in a network if they did not gain disproportionately from the benefits of network participation (Lin et al., 2001). So, considering that hierarchy exists within corporate networks, it is questionable what the structure of this will be.

Hymer (1972) saw the world system as mirroring the organizational structure of the multinationals of his day and assumed that this static, top-down hierarchy would simply be perpetuated at the start of the 21st century. However, because the organizational architecture of today's firms is far more complex than this, it is important to move beyond Hymer's simplistic projection (Dicken and Malmberg, 2001). For instance, the late 20th century has witnessed the emergence of new organizations, such as strategic alliances and inter-firm networks, that are different from previously hierarchical (vertical) forms (Yeung, 2005). Only in recent studies, for example by the Globalization and World Cities Research Network (GaWC), are more complex relationships acknowledged (e.g. Taylor, 2004). More recently, Taylor et al. (2010) postulated the need for 'central flow theory' which concerns the horizontal spatial structure linking non-local interactions. This theory complements Christaller's (1933) 'central place theory', known for its conception of vertical spatial structures that link local scales of interaction. Indeed, today's MNCs do tend to function more horizontally than vertically (Birkinshaw and Morrison, 1995; Taggart, 1997). The dominant vertical form of corporate organization is disintegrating as new economic innovations lead to intricate networks in which vertical and horizontal connections intertwine (Koestler, 1978; Wall, 2009), creating a 'heterarchical' system in which firms become enmeshed in loosely coupled networks of interdependence, reciprocity and unequal power relations (Grabher, 1993, 2006).

Three aspects distinguish heterarchic from hierarchical models of corporate organization. First, resources and managerial capabilities are dispersed throughout the organization, instead of being located only at the top. Second, lateral relationships exist between subsidiaries in terms of products, people and knowledge flows. Third, activities are coordinated along multiple dimensions, typically geography, products and functions (Hedlund, 1994). Hence the multinational has evolved from a comparatively simple set of unidimensionally and vertically controlled processes into a complex system of vertical and lateral intra- and inter-firm relationships (Dunning and Lundan, 2008). Nonetheless, although it may be true that a transformation towards a more integrated network is taking place, the primacy of the vertical, hierarchical dimension should not be neglected (Hedlund, 1986). It is therefore arguable that distinct categories of network structure do not exist, but instead overlap and interpenetrate each other, with networks forming complex combinations of overlapping, juxtaposed and nested governance mechanisms (Grabher and Powell, 2004). So, if hierarchy and heterarchy coexist, then what are their characteristic features? As indicated in the conceptual diagram (Figure 19.1), the topology of a hierarchical, vertically organized network would resemble the star-shaped structure on the left (Hannemann and Riddle, 2005). Alternatively, a heterarchical, horizontally organized structure would resemble the 'universal' network structure on the right, in which all actors are mutually connected (Todeva, 2006).

DATA AND METHODOLOGY

This analysis is based on intra-firm data of the global Fortune top 100 headquarters (2005) and their 9243 ownership relations to subsidiaries in 2245 unique cities worldwide. The firms accounted for 27 per cent of OECD revenue in 2005, indicating their economic importance. The subsidiaries of these headquarters and their different levels of share ownership were extracted from the LexisNexis *Directory of Corporate Affiliations* (2005). Because about 20 per cent of the data is incomplete, the missing information had to be obtained using various internet search engines. Next, it is necessary to explain how differ-

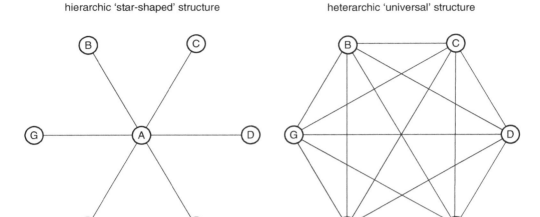

hierarchic 'star-shaped' structure   heterarchic 'universal' structure

Source: based on Todeva (2006, Figure 2.4)

Figure 19.1 Simplified network diagrams to explain hierarchy and heterarchy

ent levels of corporate structure translate into different city network structures. In Figure 19.2a five levels of corporate ownership exist. In the first level, headquarters A owns shares in key subsidiaries B, C, D and E. The second level shows that subsidiaries C and E govern sub-subsidiaries F–J. Firm I, at the third level, holds shares in firms K and L, and so forth.[1] Next, it is seen how the corporate organization in Figure 19.2a translates into a city × city network of corporate relations (Figure 19.2b). Firms in Figure 19.2a are located in any of cities 1–5. For instance, firms B, F, I and N are situated in city 2. Based on this approach, centrality and linkage measures were derived for cities.

The centrality measures of *outdegree*, *indegree* and *diagonal* can be explained as follows. In the matrix (Figure 19.2a), moving from left to right, we see outdegree relations (corporate holdings) stemming from firms in each of the five cities to other firms in these same cities. This is simply a measure of the amount of ownership that firms in a particular city have of firms in other cities. Outdegree can be interpreted as the 'power' of certain cities over others (Alderson and Beckfield, 2004). In this case, city 3 has the most influence over other cities, and it ranks first in terms of outdegree centrality. Furthermore, its strongest holdings are in cities 1 and 2. Inversely, by moving from top to bottom, we can determine the degree to which firms in particular cities are owned by firms in other cities. This is a measure of the indegree or 'prestige' of a city (Alderson and Beckfield, 2004). In this sense, a city is prestigious because governing firms in other cities are dependent on a certain number of its firms. In this case, we see that cities depend most on city 2, making it rank first in terms of indegree centrality. In network analysis, these types of data are called 'directional' because we can measure the direction of corporate ownership between cities. Furthermore, a city can possess more than one ownership linkage to another city. For instance, city 3 has two ties to city 1. The third measure is called the diagonal and is simply a measure of corporate 'self-ties' within a city. Based on these measures, the extent to which a city is dependent on intercity and intra-city ties can be derived.

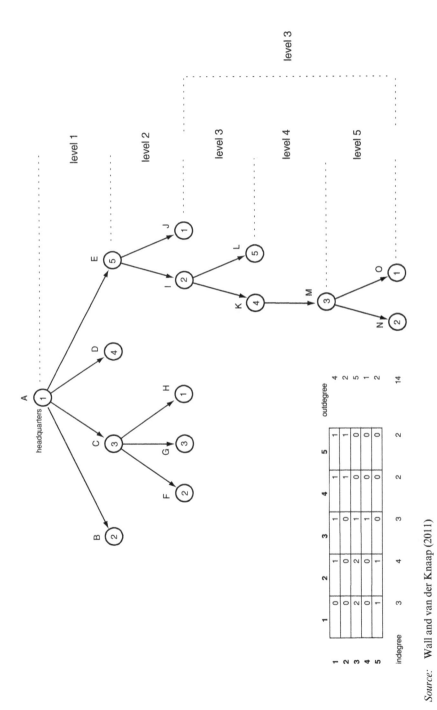

Source: Wall and van der Knaap (2011)

Figure 19.2a Levels of corporate ownership

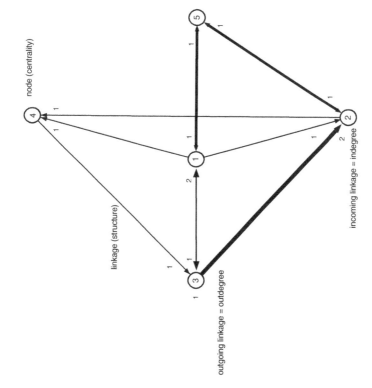

node (centrality)

incoming linkage = indegree

linkage (structure)

outgoing linkage = outdegree

Source: Wall and van der Knaap (2011)

Figure 19.2b   Corporate ownership between city nodes

The centrality measures defined above are 'nodal' measures of the network and concern aggregations of linkages; however, the structure of a network concerns the strengths of the linkages between nodes. For instance, in Figure 19.2b, not only can we observe that the tie between cities 1 and 3 is the strongest but it also indicates the core and the periphery in the network of cities. For instance, city 4, with the weakest combined outdegree and indegree, is seen here as the most peripheral city of this network. To determine the nodal centralities and overall network structures, we used the network analysis software Ucinet/Netdraw (Borgatti et al., 2002). The software reveals the essential nodes, linkages, and core and periphery zones of the data. Because this analysis disregards geographic location, the geographic information systems (GIS) software MapInfo was used to map the spatial distribution of the network.

RESULTS

Table 19.1a concerns the combined five levels of corporate holdings. The grey part shows the intercity centrality values of outdegree and indegree, representing ties 'between' cities, and intra-city diagonal values (self-ties). Because it is arguable that self-ties be included in outdegree and indegree scores, a separate white table is provided with these scores. In the 'outdegree' column, New York evidently has the largest number of corporate shares with other cities, followed by Paris, Tokyo and London. Only 17 per cent of 2259 cities have outdegree scores and all are from developed countries – where New York, Paris, London and Tokyo together hold 25 per cent of outdegree. This verifies that headquarters activity is indeed concentrated in limited developed cities close to capital markets (Hymer, 1972). In the lower group of cities, a strong match with Alderson and Beckfield's (2004) study is seen, that is, Zurich, Düsseldorf, Munich and Amsterdam. Furthermore, the presence of specialized cities like Palo Alto and New Brunswick confirms Alderson and Beckfield's (2004) observation that headquarters functions are not necessarily concentrated in world cities and are often located in the city where the firm originated.

In terms of indegree the top two cities match Alderson and Beckfield's findings, but Singapore and Hong Kong are identified as the second and third most prestigious cities. This is similar to Godfrey and Zhou's (1999) results showing that cities like Singapore, Hong Kong, Mexico City, Buenos Aires, Jakarta and Bangkok (see Table 19.1a), hold important subsidiary functions. Because the indegree list holds cities from both developed and developing nations, it supports Hymer's expectation of a strong diffusion of industrialization to developing countries. Also, cities once conceptualized as 'peripheral', like Bangkok and Mexico City, as discussed by Sassen (1994), have emerged as highly ranked world cities. In terms of diagonal centrality, only 16 per cent of interactions are intra-urban (self-ties). It follows that important cities derive their status from what flows between them rather than what remains fixed within them (Castells, 1996; Amin and Graham, 1999). Hence firms are capable of exercising control and power over other firms 'at a distance' (Yeung, 2005, p. 316). Table 19.1b concerns headquarters to first-order subsidiaries (first level), while Table 19.1c represents first subsidiary to second subsidiary holdings (second level). Table 19.1d shows the combined remaining linkages. The first level accounts for 44 per cent of connections, followed by the second level with

Table 19.1   Differing centrality scores at each level of corporate governance

19.1a   All industrial sectors – across all five subsidiary levels

	City	Outdegree (ED)	City	Indegree (ED)	City	Diagonal	City	Outdegree (ID)	City	Indegree (ID)
1	New York	692	New York	165	New York	186	New York	878	New York	351
2	Paris	491	London	115	Tokyo	113	Paris	581	Tokyo	198
3	Tokyo	367	Singapore	101	Paris	90	Tokyo	480	Paris	182
4	London	326	Hong Kong	93	Düsseldorf	64	London	381	London	170
5	Zurich	293	Paris	92	Houston	63	Zurich	338	Houston	129
6	Düsseldorf	259	Tokyo	85	London	55	Düsseldorf	323	Brussels	123
7	Munich	253	Brussels	80	Zurich	45	Munich	278	Singapore	108
8	Palo Alto	218	Madrid	76	Brussels	43	Amsterdam	229	Hong Kong	102
9	Amsterdam	204	Milan	75	Atlanta	33	Palo Alto	219	Düsseldorf	94
10	Lausanne	191	Houston	66	Dearborn	28	Houston	197	Zurich	92
11	The Hague	165	Toronto	62	Amsterdam	25	Lausanne	197	Madrid	88
12	Irving	148	Mexico City	59	Munich	25	The Hague	170	Milan	82
13	New Brunswick	146	Buenos Aires	57	Omaha	25	New Brunswick	157	Amsterdam	74
14	Houston	134	Dublin	55	Turin	18	Brussels	152	Toronto	73
15	Ludwigshafen	131	Jakarta	50	Vienna	17	Irving	149	Mexico City	71
16	Frankfurt	116	Amsterdam	49	Stamford	13	Ludwigshafen	134	Atlanta	68
17	Brussels	109	Vienna	49	Madrid	13	Frankfurt	125	Vienna	62
18	Gerlingen	85	Bangkok	49	Mexico City	13	Stamford	92	Buenos Aires	62
19	Stamford	79	Frankfurt	48	Toronto	12	Gerlingen	85	Munich	59
20	Chicago	78	Zurich	47	Seoul	12	Detroit	84	Frankfurt	57
21	Detroit	74	Barcelona	47	Osaka	11	Dearborn	82	Dublin	55
22	Toyota	71	São Paulo	47	Cincinnati	11	Chicago	82	Barcelona	53
23	Wolfsburg	71	Sydney	40	New Brunswick	11	Wolfsburg	80	São Paulo	52
24	Northfield	69	Hamburg	39	Hamburg	11	Cincinnati	75	Bangkok	52
25	Cincinnati	64	Montreal	36	Detroit	10	Northfield	75	Jakarta	52
26	Calgary	59	Taipei	36	Glendale	10	Toyota	72	Hamburg	49
27	Cupertino	55	Atlanta	35	Hong Kong	10	Atlanta	65	Seoul	45
28	Osaka	54	Munich	34	Frankfurt	9	Osaka	65	Sydney	42
29	Alpharetta	54	Chicago	34	Minneapolis	9	Calgary	64	Luxembourg	39
30	Dearborn	54	Seoul	34	Wolfsburg	9	Omaha	59	Chicago	38

Table 19.1 (continued)

19.1b All industrial sectors – but only headquarters to first subsidiary level

	City	Outdegree (ED)	City	Indegree (ED)	City	Diagonal	City	Outdegree (ID)	City	Indegree (ID)
1	New York	443	New York	53	New York	67	New York	510	New York	120
2	Zurich	205	Paris	42	Düsseldorf	56	Düsseldorf	238	London	72
3	Munich	202	Houston	41	London	35	Munich	215	Düsseldorf	70
4	Palo Alto	186	Tokyo	40	Brussels	33	Zurich	214	Brussels	66
5	Düsseldorf	182	Milan	40	Atlanta	27	Palo Alto	187	Houston	59
6	London	134	Frankfurt	38	Amsterdam	19	London	169	Milan	47
7	Paris	121	London	37	Dearborn	19	Paris	124	Amsterdam	46
8	The Hague	112	Madrid	36	Houston	18	New Brunswick	115	Paris	45
9	Irving	110	Singapore	34	Turin	14	The Hague	113	Frankfurt	40
10	New Brunswick	104	Mexico	34	Munich	13	Irving	111	Tokyo	40
11	Amsterdam	91	Brussels	33	Vienna	11	Amsterdam	110	Vienna	40
12	Brussels	72	Toronto	29	Seoul	11	Brussels	105	Madrid	40
13	Frankfurt	67	Vienna	29	Omaha	11	Frankfurt	69	Singapore	38
14	Chicago	62	Zurich	28	New Brunswick	11	Chicago	64	Zurich	37
15	Lausanne	60	Amsterdam	27	Zurich	9	Houston	61	Atlanta	37
16	Gerlingen	51	Dublin	27	Wolfsburg	9	Lausanne	60	Toronto	36
17	Wolfsburg	50	Hong Kong	27	Detroit	8	Wolfsburg	59	Mexico	34
18	Detroit	48	Hamburg	26	Milan	7	Detroit	56	Seoul	32
19	Calgary	44	Buenos Aires	26	Toronto	7	Atlanta	55	Munich	30
20	Houston	43	Bangkok	25	Schaumburg	7	Gerlingen	51	Bangkok	28
21	Stuttgart	40	Barcelona	24	Bloomington	7	Calgary	49	Hamburg	28
22	Toyota	40	Berlin	22	Nicosia	6	Stuttgart	44	Dublin	27
23	Ludwigshafen	40	Taipei	22	Luxembourg	5	Toyota	41	Hong Kong	27
24	Tokyo	39	São Paulo	22	Rome	5	Ludwigshafen	40	Barcelona	26
25	Stavanger	35	Seoul	21	Saint Louis	5	Tokyo	39	Buenos Aires	26
26	Cincinnati	32	Luxembourg	19	Calgary	5	Stavanger	38	Luxembourg	24
27	Philadelphia	32	Montreal	19	Cincinnati	5	Cincinnati	37	Berlin	22
28	Atlanta	28	Kuala Lumpur	19	Trieste	5	Schaumburg	35	Taipei	22
29	Schaumburg	28	Athens	19	Ingolstadt	5	Philadelphia	33	São Paulo	22
30	Chesterbrook	28	Istanbul	18	Madrid	4	Trieste	31	Turin	20

19.1c All industrial sectors – but only first subsidiary level to second subsidiary level

#	City	Outdegree (ED)	City	Indegree (ED)	City	Diagonal	City	Outdegree (ID)	City	Indegree (ID)
1	Paris	290	New York	65	New York	89	Paris	350	New York	154
2	Tokyo	177	Hong Kong	57	Paris	60	Tokyo	231	Paris	94
3	London	133	London	43	Tokyo	54	New York	217	Tokyo	78
4	New York	128	Singapore	40	Zurich	34	London	145	Hong Kong	57
5	Amsterdam	84	Paris	34	Houston	20	Zurich	106	London	55
6	Zurich	72	Brussels	30	London	12	Amsterdam	90	Zurich	48
7	Lausanne	59	Buenos Aires	26	Munich	11	Munich	60	Singapore	43
8	Düsseldorf	53	Tokyo	24	Brussels	10	Lausanne	59	Brussels	40
9	Ludwigshafen	52	Madrid	24	Stamford	10	Houston	58	Houston	33
10	Munich	49	Milan	24	Osaka	10	Düsseldorf	56	Buenos Aires	30
11	Edinburgh	40	Atlanta	20	Dearborn	9	Ludwigshafen	52	Madrid	29
12	Alpharetta	39	Dublin	18	Amsterdam	6	Edinburgh	45	Milan	24
13	Houston	38	Barcelona	17	Madrid	5	Brussels	42	Amsterdam	21
14	Frankfurt	38	Amsterdam	15	Auburn Hills	5	Frankfurt	42	Barcelona	21
15	Brussels	32	Toronto	15	Santiago	5	Dearborn	41	Munich	20
16	Dearborn	32	Melbourne	15	Edinburgh	5	Alpharetta	39	Atlanta	20
17	Southfield	27	Vienna	14	Richmond	5	Osaka	32	Dublin	18
18	Auburn Hills	26	Zurich	14	Utrecht	5	Auburn Hills	31	Melbourne	17
19	Detroit	25	Kawasaki	13	Buenos Aires	4	Stamford	29	Stamford	16
20	Osaka	22	Houston	13	Barcelona	4	Southfield	29	Toronto	16
21	Morristown	22	São Paulo	13	Frankfurt	4	Detroit	27	Vienna	16
22	Round Rock	22	Geneva	13	Los Angeles	4	Richmond	25	Kawasaki	14
23	Greenwich	21	Mexico	13	Louisville	4	Greenwich	24	Sydney	14
24	The Hague	21	Sydney	12	Cheshunt	4	The Hague	24	São Paulo	14
25	Richmond	20	Jakarta	12	Evansville	4	Morristown	22	Johannesburg	14
26	Glendale	20	Budapest	12	Singapore	3	Round Rock	22	Jakarta	13
27	Stamford	19	Luxembourg	11	Johannesburg	3	Glendale	21	Geneva	13
28	Toyota	18	Bogota	11	Düsseldorf	3	Toyota	18	Mexico	13
29	Voorhees	17	Irvine	11	Minneapolis	3	San Ramon	17	Frankfurt	13
30	Wolfsburg	17	Istanbul	11	Baltimore	3	Northfield	17	Los Angeles	12

Table 19.1 (continued)

19.1d All industrial sectors – but only second subsidiary level to fourth subsidiary level

	City	Outdegree (ED)	City	Indegree (ED)	City	Diagonal	City	Outdegree (ID)	City	Indegree (ID)
1	Tokyo	151	New York	47	Tokyo	59	Tokyo	210	Tokyo	80
2	New York	121	London	35	New York	30	New York	151	New York	77
3	Paris	80	Singapore	27	Paris	27	Paris	107	Paris	43
4	Lausanne	72	Tokyo	21	Houston	25	Houston	78	London	43
5	Stamford	60	Jakarta	20	Mexico	12	Lausanne	78	Houston	37
6	London	59	Toronto	18	Hong Kong	9	London	67	Singapore	27
7	Cupertino	55	Brussels	17	Glendale	9	Stamford	63	Mexico	24
8	Houston	53	Paris	16	London	8	Northfield	56	Toronto	21
9	Northfield	51	Madrid	16	Honolulu	8	Cupertino	56	Jakarta	21
10	New Brunswick	42	Bangkok	15	Culver City	8	Ludwigshafen	42	Madrid	19
11	Ludwigshafen	39	Shanghai	15	Hamburg	7	New Brunswick	42	Hong Kong	18
12	Irving	34	Chicago	14	Minneapolis	6	Portland	36	Brussels	17
13	Portland	33	Cleveland	14	Cincinnati	6	Irving	34	São Paulo	16
14	Osaka	32	Houston	12	Atlanta	6	Osaka	33	Bangkok	15
15	The Hague	32	Mexico	12	Hartford	6	The Hague	33	Shanghai	15
16	Naperville	31	São Paulo	12	Lausanne	6	Omaha	31	Düsseldorf	14
17	Amsterdam	29	Los Angeles	11	Düsseldorf	5	Naperville	31	Chicago	14
18	Omaha	27	Markham	11	Wilmington	5	Düsseldorf	29	Cleveland	14
19	Irvine	26	Milan	11	Washington	5	Irvine	29	Hamburg	13
20	Palo Alto	25	Sydney	11	Northfield	5	Amsterdam	29	Los Angeles	12
21	Düsseldorf	24	Mississauga	10	São Paulo	4	Glendale	28	Minneapolis	12
22	Dallas	24	Dublin	10	Omaha	4	Greenwich	25	Cincinnati	11
23	Warrendale	24	San Jose	10	Bentonville	4	Dallas	25	Atlanta	11
24	Gerlingen	23	Osaka	9	San Antonio	4	Warrendale	25	Beijing	11
25	San Diego	22	Düsseldorf	9	Torrance	4	Palo Alto	25	Markham	11
26	Greenwich	22	Hong Kong	9	Maryville	4	Hong Kong	24	Milan	11
27	Los Angeles	20	Lima	9	Toronto	3	Gerlingen	23	Sydney	11
28	Auburn Hills	20	Montreal	9	Madrid	3	Cincinnati	22	Osaka	10
29	Glendale	19	Petaling	9	Beijing	3	San Diego	22	Charlotte	10
30	Providence	17	Prague	9	Charlotte	3	Los Angeles	21	Honolulu	10

Notes: ID - including diagonal ED = excluding diagonal

Source: Wall and van der Knaap (2011)

218

30 per cent and the remaining levels with 26 per cent. From this it is clear that corporate governance is strongest at the top of the system, possibly because higher-end functions require more control at this level.

At the first level (Table 19.1b), the strongest outdegree cities are New York, Zurich and Munich. London and Paris play weaker roles at this level than in aggregate (Table 19.1a), and Tokyo's outdegree drops significantly from the 3rd to the 24th position within these higher economic functions. However, as shown in Tables 19.1c and 19.1d, Tokyo's outdegree is more important at the production-oriented levels. It is also clear that Hong Kong and Singapore do not play strong outdegree roles at any corporate level. Even in terms of specific producer service data (see Wall and van der Knaap, 2011), Singapore and Hong Kong do not play significant roles in terms of outdegree centrality. Concerning indegree scores at the first level (Table 19.1b), there are only minor divergences from the top cities (Table 19.1a). More interestingly, both Singapore and Hong Kong drop significantly in rank, indicating that their strengths as subsidiary cities are weaker at this level of high-end functions. In Table 19.1c, the positions of Hong Kong and Singapore rise significantly within the lower subsidiary levels. In terms of self-ties, New York, London, Paris and Tokyo dominate the upper echelons of the list.[2]

In the network of combined corporate levels (Figure 19.3a), a hybrid between hierarchical and heterarchical interdependence exists. Star-shaped structures, in which for example New York, Paris and London exercise corporate governance over others, epitomize Hymer's (1972) hierarchical, vertically organized interaction. Triangulated structures, for example the London, Hong Kong and Singapore triad, characterize heterarchical interactions between cities (Hedlund, 1986). Furthermore, Singapore and Hong Kong not only form part of London's network but also share positions in other networks. For example, Singapore is part of Tokyo's and Zurich's system. Furthermore, New York and Tokyo are effectively connected to cities within their proximate regions. In the sub-network (Figure 19.3b) representing corporate level 1, the primary linkage between New York and London is seen (Derudder et al., 2003). Furthermore, unlike New York, London is essentially connected to transnational cities. Notably, Paris plays a moderate role at this level of interaction. Furthermore, Singapore and Hong Kong are not important at the top of the system. Zurich, Munich, Düsseldorf and Milan form important European centres. At level 2 (Figure 19.3c), Paris, Tokyo, London and New York are important central cities, holding both hierarchical and heterarchical structures. Paris is the primary city at this level, with strong links to Brussels, New York and London. At this level, Hong Kong and Singapore play important roles. At level 3 (Figure 19.3d), the hierarchy of Tokyo, New York, London and Paris is clear, where heterarchy proves weak. Tokyo is strongly connected to London and proximate Japanese and Asian cities. At this level, Tokyo performs a strong national and regional function verifying the role of Japanese integrated trading companies or 'Sogo Shosha'[3] (Edgington and Haga, 1998), which are essentially nationally oriented. It is therefore questionable whether Tokyo can be considered a world city (Hill and Kim, 2001).

In Figure 19.4, the white dots depict firm locations and are scaled according to the sum of their centralities. The black and grey lines illustrate the aggregate corporate shares between cities. The east/west triad (Carroll, 2007) between North America, Europe and Pacific Asia is evident. Seventy per cent of Europe's connections are trans-European, and only 30 per cent take place within Europe. For North America, 65 per cent of its

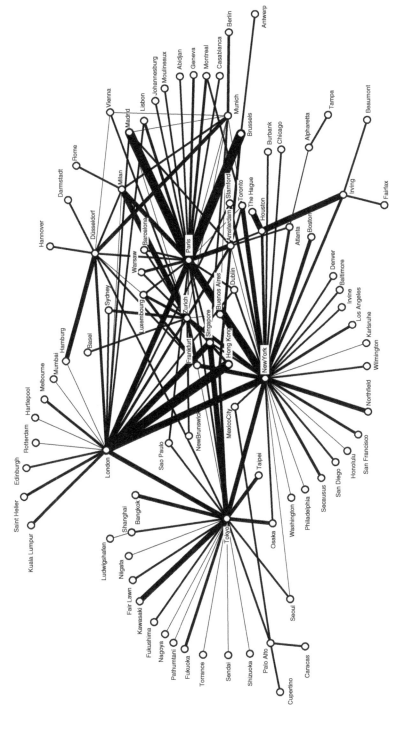

Source: Wall and van der Knaap (2011)

Figure 19.3a   All industries – all headquarters to subsidiaries (levels 1–5)

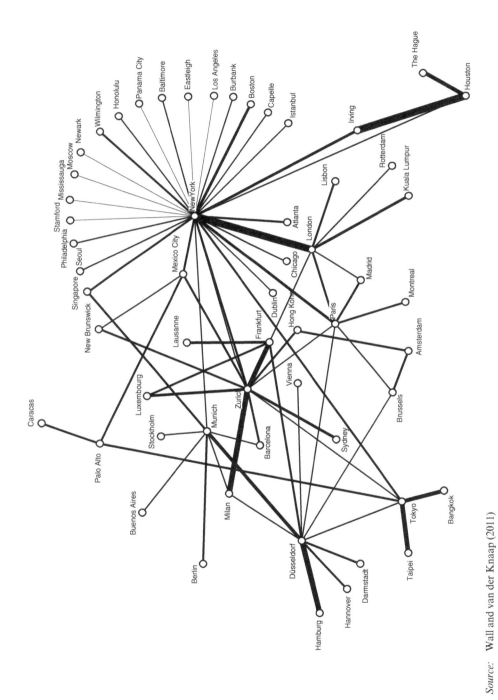

Source: Wall and van der Knaap (2011)

Figure 19.3b All industries – headquarters to first subsidiaries (level 1)

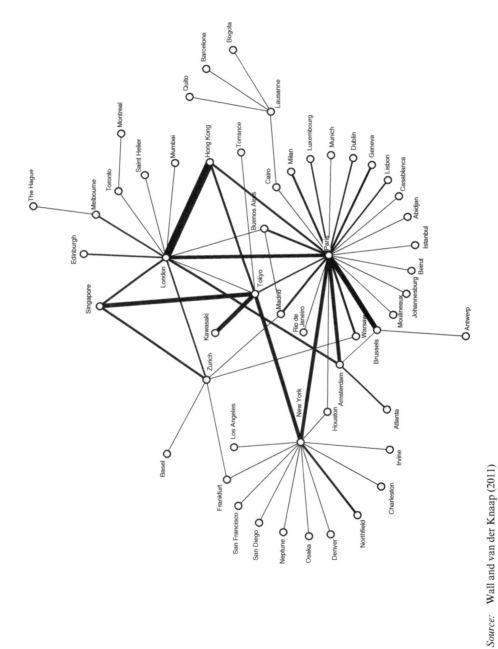

Source: Wall and van der Knaap (2011)

Figure 19.3c   All industries – first subsidiaries to second subsidiaries (level 2)

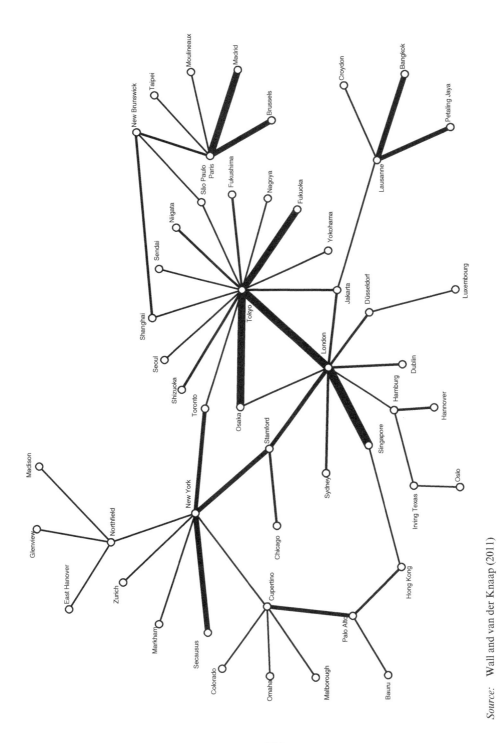

Source: Wall and van der Knaap (2011)

Figure 19.3d All industries – second subsidiaries to remaining subsidiaries (levels 3–5)

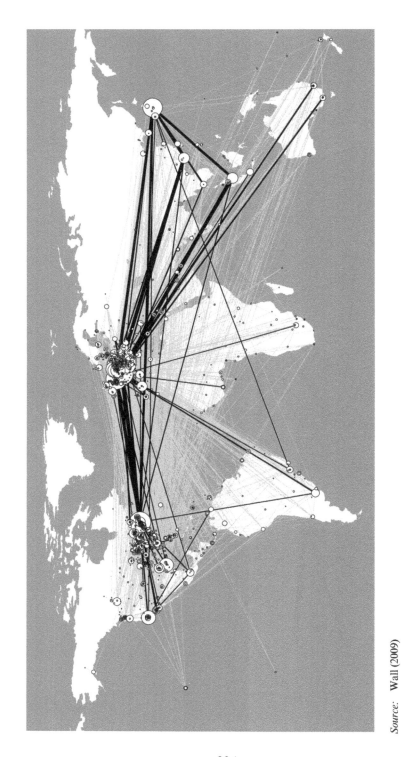

Source: Wall (2009)

Figure 19.4 Geographic information system map of the all-industries multinational network

connections are global. These results verify the existence of a strong coupling of regions and global production networks (Coe et al., 2004). Because 30 per cent of economic ties are localized it shows that many firms depend on geographical agglomerations achieved through territorial embeddedness (Hall and Soskice, 2001). However, because 70 per cent of ties operate 'at a distance', it verifies warnings of fixating too much on local and regional embeddedness (see Bathelt et al., 2002). The southern hemisphere linkages are mainly to Commonwealth countries, and South America and Africa's share of connectivity is sparse (1 per cent of the total). Although the map gives a clear overview, it is unclear how many of a city's ties are intra-national or transnational. Therefore, a close examination of New York, Paris, London and Tokyo was made (Table 19.2). New York is essentially connected to US cities and its transnational ties are sparse.[4] The second most intra-national city is Tokyo, emphasizing the nationally oriented character of Japanese Shogo Shoshas (Hill and Kim, 2001). Paris is the third most nationally oriented city and has the highest number of unique city connections (87 per cent), making it the most integrated of the four. London is the most 'global' of the cities due to its strong transnational ties to Canada (17 per cent) and other countries.

CONCLUSIONS

By showing that 84 per cent of the network occurs between and not within cities and that 70 per cent of European and North American ties extend beyond their supra-regions, it is shown that cities have become dissociated from their local geographies (Friedmann, 1986). Furthermore, differences in corporate ownership substantiate Friedmann's (1995) postulation that world cities can be organized according to the economic relations that they command. For example, although Hong Kong and Singapore are 'important' subsidiary cities, they are not strong in terms of headquarters. Also, Hong Kong and Singapore are less important at the first level of the corporate connectivity than at lower levels. Furthermore, it is shown that high-level economic activities are concentrated in limited cities (e.g. Hymer, 1972; Sassen, 1991). The maps reveal the complex duality of 'spatially dispersed, yet globally integrated organization of economic activity' (Sassen, 2001, p. 3), where a 'vast territory' exists that is excluded from the vital processes of the global economy (Sassen, 1994).

Unlike Friedmann's strictly vertical definitions, where primary cities articulate at the global scale, secondary cities at the supra-regional scale and tertiary cities at the periphery, it is found that cities like New York, London and Tokyo top the lists at all levels of analysis. This signifies the ability of world cities to simultaneously articulate between global, regional and local networks. Linkages between cities are therefore not passed down in a 'tree-like' hierarchy, but instead reciprocated, horizontal interactions exist between levels. Hence the interaction between cities is both hierarchical and heterarchical, confirming the coexistence of different organizational principles. Because New York, Paris, London and Tokyo have hierarchical 'hub-and-spoke' structures, it reveals the 'aristocratic' functions of these cities over subsidiary cities (Watts, 1999). Furthermore, the strongest evidence of 'horizontalization' (heterarchy) is found between the top-ranked cities, especially at the top level of corporate ownership. Because the majority of ties are neither reciprocated nor triangulated, it is evident that in terms of the 'variety

Table 19.2 Outdegree and indegree shares of four major cities to various nations

	City	Country	Links	%	City	Country	Links	%	City	Country	Links	%	City	Country	Links	%
Top 5																
All industrial sectors outdegree																
1	New York	United States	406	59	Paris	France	122	21	London	Canada	64	17	Tokyo	Japan	224	47
2	New York	Canada	43	6	Paris	United States	69	12	London	United Kingdom	45	12	Tokyo	United States	71	15
3	New York	Germany	25	4	Paris	Spain	34	6	London	China	24	6	Tokyo	China	27	6
4	New York	United Kingdom	18	3	Paris	Canada	33	6	London	United States	22	6	Tokyo	Canada	21	4
5	New York	Switzerland	10	1	Paris	Belgium	27	5	London	Germany	19	5	Tokyo	Thailand	13	3
Total links			692				581				381				480	
Destinations			82				87				66				36	
All industrial sectors indegree																
1	New York	United States	260	74	Paris	France	97	52	London	United Kingdom	61	36	Tokyo	Japan	124	63
2	New York	Germany	20	6	Paris	United States	28	15	London	United States	39	23	Tokyo	United States	26	13
3	New York	France	20	6	Paris	Germany	17	9	London	Japan	16	9	Tokyo	Germany	18	9
4	New York	Japan	16	5	Paris	The Netherlands	16	9	London	France	13	8	Tokyo	United Kingdom	11	6
5	New York	United Kingdom	12	3	Paris	United Kingdom	8	4	London	Germany	10	6	Tokyo	France	7	4
Total links			351				187				170				198	
Destinations			13				12				15				9	

Advanced producer services Outdegree

	City	Country			City	Country			City	Country			City	Country		
1	New York	United States	293	65	Paris	France	35	14	London	Canada	44	18	Tokyo	Japan	47	47
2	New York	Canada	30	7	Paris	United States	34	14	London	United Kingdom	34	14	Tokyo	United States	13	13
3	New York	Germany	19	4	Paris	Spain	15	6	London	China	21	9	Tokyo	China	6	6
4	New York	United Kingdom	8	2	Paris	Canada	14	6	London	United States	16	7	Tokyo	Canada	5	5
5	New York	Switzerland	5	1	Paris	Belgium	12	5	London	Germany	16	7	Tokyo	Thailand	4	4
Total links			453				247				244				100	
Destinations			60				66				49				21	

Advanced producer services indegree

	City	Country			City	Country			City	Country			City	Country		
1	New York	United States	112	71	Paris	France	35	58	London	United Kingdom	44	42	Tokyo	Japan	29	63
2	New York	Germany	12	8	Paris	United Kingdom	6	10	London	United States	25	24	Tokyo	Germany	6	13
3	New York	France	11	7	Paris	Belgium	5	8	London	Japan	6	6	Tokyo	United Kingdom	4	9
4	New York	United Kingdom	8	5	Paris	Switzerland	4	7	London	Germany	6	6	Tokyo	The Netherlands	3	7
5	New York	Switzerland	8	5	Paris	Germany	4	7	London	France	6	6	Tokyo	Switzerland	2	4
Total links			157				60				106				46	
Destinations			11				9				12				7	

Source: Wall and van der Knaap (2011)

of connections', the system is essentially hierarchic. However, these ties are generally weak. Alternatively, although reciprocated, triangulated ties are limited, these linkages are disproportionately stronger. Hence, in terms of 'strength of connections', the system is essentially heterarchic.

ACKNOWLEDGEMENT

This chapter is based on R.S. Wall and G.A. van der Knaap (2011), 'Sectoral differentiation and network structure within contemporary worldwide corporate networks', *Economic Geography*, **87** (3), 267–308.

NOTES

1. The subsidiary levels 3, 4 and 5 were condensed into one level because these levels hold low counts of shares (roughly 5 per cent each of the total), and the individual ties are not strong.
2. This is confirmed later in the correlational analysis, which shows a strong coherence between a city's global and local economic functions.
3. Sogo shosha refers to a specific type of Japanese firm: the general trading company, which is a complex agglomeration of diversified firms.
4. Although New York's world city-ness is questionable, the immense scale of the US should be taken into account, where the size of its regional network roughly equals that of all European countries combined.

REFERENCES

Alderson, A.S. and J. Beckfield (2004), 'Power and position in the world city system', *American Journal of Sociology*, **109** (4), 811–851.
Amin, A. and S. Graham (1999), 'Cities of connection and disconnection', in J. Allen, D. Massey and M. Pryke (eds), *Unsettling Cities*, New York: Routledge, pp. 7–38.
Barba Navaretti, G. and A.J. Venables (2004), *Multinational Firms in the World Economy*, Princeton, NJ: Princeton University Press.
Bartlett, C.A. and S. Ghoshal (1986), 'Tap your subsidiaries for global reach', *Harvard Business Review*, November–December, 87–94.
Bathelt, H., A. Malmberg and P. Maskell (2002), 'Clusters and knowledge: local buzz, global pipelines and the process of knowledge creation', Working Paper 2002-12. Copenhagen: Danish Research Unit for Industrial Dynamics.
Birkinshaw, J.M. and A.J. Morrison (1995), 'Configurations of strategy and structure in subsidiaries of multinational corporations', *Journal of International Business Studies*, **26** (4), 729–753.
Borgatti, S.P., M.G. Everett and L.C. Freeman (2002), *UCINET 6 for Windows: Social Network Analysis Software*, Needham, MA: Analytic Technologies.
Carroll, W.K. (2007), 'Global cities in the global corporate network', *Environment and Planning A*, **39** (10), 2297–2323.
Castells, M. (1996), *The Rise of the Network Society*, Oxford: Blackwell.
Christaller, W. (1933), *Die Zentralen Orte in Süddeutschland*, Jena: Gustav Fischer.
Coe, N.M., M. Hess, H.W.-C. Yeung, P. Dicken and J. Henderson (2004), '"Globalizing" regional development: a global production networks perspective', *Transactions of the Institute of British Geographers*, **29** (4), 468–484.
Derudder, B., P.J. Taylor, F. Witlox and G. Catalano (2003), 'Hierarchical tendencies and regional patterns in the world city network: a global urban analysis of 234 cities', *Regional Studies*, **37** (9), 875–886.
Dicken, P. and A. Malmberg (2001), 'Firms in territories: a relational perspective', *Economic Geography*, **77** (4), 345–363.

Dunning, J.H. and S.M. Lundan (2008), *Multinational Enterprises and the Global Economy*, Cheltenham: Edward Elgar.

Edgington, D.W. and H. Haga (1998), 'Japanese service sector multinationals and the hierarchy of Pacific Rim cities', *Asia Pacific Viewpoint*, **39** (2), 161–178.

Friedmann, J. (1986), 'The world city hypothesis', *Development and Change*, **17** (1), 69–84.

Friedmann, J. (1995), 'Where we stand: a decade of world city research', in P.L. Knox and P.J. Taylor (eds), *World Cities in a World-System*, Cambridge: Cambridge University Press, pp. 21–47.

Godfrey, B.J. and Y. Zhou (1999), 'Ranking world cities: multinational corporations and the global urban hierarchy', *Urban Geography*, **20** (3), 268–281.

Grabher, G. (1993), 'The weakness of strong ties: the lock-in of regional development in the Ruhr area', in G. Grabher (ed.), *The Embedded Firm: On the Socioeconomics of Interfirm Relations*, London: Routledge, pp. 255–278.

Grabher, G. (2006), 'Trading routes, bypasses, and risky intersections: mapping the travels "networks" between economic sociology and economic geography', *Progress in Human Geography*, **30** (2), 163–189.

Grabher, G. and W.W. Powell (2004), 'Exploring the webs of economic life', in G. Grabher and W.W. Powell (eds), *Networks*, Cheltenham: Edward Elgar, pp. 1–36.

Hall, P. and D. Soskice (2001), *Varieties of Capitalism: The Institutional Foundations of Comparative Advantage*, Oxford: Oxford University Press.

Hannemann, R. and M. Riddle (2005), *Introduction to Social Network Methods*, Riverside, CA: University of California Press.

Hedlund, G. (1986), 'The hypermodern MNC-A heterarchy?', *Human Resource Management*, **25** (1), 9–35.

Hedlund, G. (1994), 'A model of knowledge management and the N-form corporation', *Strategic Management Journal*, **15**, 73–90.

Hill, R.C. and J.W. Kim (2001), 'Reply to Friedman and Sassen', *Urban Studies*, **38** (13), 2541–2542.

Hymer, S.H. (1972), 'The multinational corporation and the law of uneven development', in J.N. Bhagwati (ed.), *Economics and World Order from the 1970s to the 1990s*, London: Collier-Macmillan, pp. 113–140.

Koestler, A. (1978), *Janus – A Summing Up*, New York: Random House.

Lin, N., K.S. Cook and R.S. Burt (2001), *Social Capital: Theory and Research*, New York: Aldine de Gruyter.

Polanyi, K. (1944), *The Great Transformation: The Political and Economic Origins of our Time*, Boston, MA: Beacon Press.

Rugman, A. (2005), *The Regional Multinationals*, Cambridge: Cambridge University Press.

Sassen, S. (1991), *The Global City: New York, London, Tokyo*, Princeton, NJ: Princeton University Press.

Sassen, S. (1994), *Cities in a World Economy*, Thousand Oaks, CA: Pine Forge Press.

Sassen, S. (2001), *The Global City: New York, London, Tokyo*, 2nd edition, Princeton, NJ: Princeton University Press.

Taggart, J.H. (1997), 'Autonomy and procedural justice: a framework for evaluating subsidiary strategy', *Journal of International Business Studies*, **28** (1), 51–76.

Taylor, P.J. (2004), *World City Network: A Global Urban Analysis*, London: Routledge.

Taylor, P.J., M. Hoyler and R. Verbruggen (2010), 'External urban relational process: introducing central flow theory to complement central place theory', *Urban Studies*, **47** (13), 2803–2818.

Todeva, E. (2006), *Business Networks: Strategy and Structure*, New York: Routledge.

Wall, R.S. (2009), *Netscape: Cities and Global Corporate Networks*, Rotterdam: Haveka.

Wall, R.S. and G.A. van der Knaap (2011), 'Sectoral differentiation and network structure within contemporary worldwide corporate networks', *Economic Geography*, **87** (3), 267–308.

Watts, D.J. (1999), *Small Worlds*, Princeton, NJ: Princeton University Press.

Yeung, H.W.-C. (2005), 'The firm as social networks: an organisational perspective', *Growth and Change*, **36** (3), 307–328.

20 Business knowledges within and between the world city
James Faulconbridge and Sarah Hall

INTRODUCTION

The production of knowledge relevant to business services such as accountancy, advertising, law and finance has been identified as a central factor shaping both the economies *within* world cities and the relations *between* cities. Two strands of research can be identified that emphasize such different, yet complementary, geographies of knowledge and learning. First, research has explored world cities as sites of knowledge production. Both through a combination of dense networks of interactions between individuals working in business services which create 'buzz' (Bathelt et al., 2004), and through more formalized institutions such as universities (Thrift, 1997; Sassen, 2006), knowledge is said to be generated within the agglomeration and localization economies of world cities. Second, research has explored the way world cities form part of a space of knowledge flows (c.f. Castells, 2000). Using examples ranging from the trans-local mobility of workers and skilled international migration (Beaverstock, 2005), to organizational communities of practice (Amin and Cohendet, 2004; Faulconbridge, 2006) and trade fairs that are held in world cities (Maskell et al., 2006; Power and Jansson, 2008), it has been shown that 'global pipelines' (Bathelt et al., 2004) originate and pass through world cities, leading to the circulation of business knowledge and expertise and the production of knowledge in spaces in between cities.

As a result, recent research has moved away from local versus global binaries in conceptualizations of the geographies of business knowledge (see Allen, 2000). Instead of emphasizing the localness of tacit knowledge because of the need for face-to-face contact to transmit such knowledge, and the trans-local qualities of explicit knowledge because of the ease with which codified understandings can be transmitted using information–communication technologies, studies have begun to explore the overlapping and simultaneous roles of tacit and explicit knowledges produced both by city- and network-based processes (see Bathelt et al. (2004) and Faulconbridge (2007a) for summaries of this idea).

In this chapter, we explore the multiple ways that such city- and network-based knowledge production occur and the importance of both for the success of business services that operate in world cities. In particular we draw on examples relating to finance and law. The main argument of the chapter is that the successful world city is one in which business knowledges are generated, first, within the city as a result of effective informal and formal institutions of knowledge production and, second, as a result of the intersection of different processes of inter-city knowledge flow and production. The next section of the chapter, therefore, examines the processes of knowledge production going on within world cities before the subsequent section reviews the nature of the network connectivity and flow which allow knowledge to be produced and move in spaces between cities. Through both sections, we couple findings of empirical work reported in published articles with our own original empirical studies of financial and legal business services.

WORLD CITIES AS SITES OF KNOWLEDGE PRODUCTION

There is a well-established literature in geography and the wider social sciences that builds on work on 'learning regions' to explore the ways in which successful city and regional economies are frequently underpinned by processes of knowledge production, learning and circulation (see Asheim, 1996; Maskell and Malmberg, 1999; Morgan, 2004). Particular attention has focused on the importance of trust-based relations between actors that facilitate the successful production and circulation of tacit knowledge associated with processes of innovation. A range of institutional infrastructures have been identified as being important in inculcating such cultures and the associated (re)production of tacit knowledge. Four are particularly significant: first, formal rules and regulations at a range of spatial scales from the city or region, through national to international governance regimes (Tickell and Peck, 1992); second, dense networks of intra- and inter-firm relations (MacLeod, 2001); third, informal rules and socio-cultural norms that shape and are conducive to inter-firm interaction (Knight, 1992); and fourth, 'organisational structures' such as trade and professional associations that facilitate knowledge circulation, co-production and learning (Amin and Thrift, 1995).

Much of this work was initially developed through case studies of dynamic regional economies, most notably the hi-tech economy of California (see Saxenian, 1994; Storper, 1997). Whilst this literature on the dynamics of knowledge creation and circulation has continued to be developed in a regional context (e.g. Henry and Pinch, 2000; Saxenian, 2006), it has also been used to understand the development of successful, rapidly growing clusters within world cities. Three empirical areas are particularly important in this respect: first, work on knowledge creation and 'buzz' (Bathelt et al., 2004) associated with dense networks of firms and associated face-to-face interaction within cities; second, research into the role of 'organisational structures' associated with learning processes aimed at circulating new forms of both technical know-how and embodied ways of knowing and learning; and third, the role of the consultants, business schools and the media – a group of actors that Thrift (2005) terms the 'cultural circuit of capital' – in shaping processes of learning and knowledge circulation within cities. Below we consider each of these in turn.

CITY MECHANISMS OF KNOWLEDGE PRODUCTION AND FLOW

Reflecting the dominance of a relatively small number of financial centres in shaping the nature of the international financial system, much of the work examining institutional factors in processes of knowledge production and flow within cities has focused on the case of finance (see French, 2000; Clark and Wójcik, 2007). Particular attention has been paid to the role of regulation and firm and inter-personal networks in shaping knowledge production. Beginning with regulation, research has emphasized the ways in which different regulatory regimes are interpreted and understood by financial communities, something that can either enhance or limit processes of knowledge production. Geographers have emphasized the ways in which such regulation needs to be studied not on a city-by-city basis but by considering the regulatory environment of one financial district in relation to others. This is because it is the relative qualities of regulation that are important in shaping the production of innovative knowledges within financial districts. In this respect research has examined: the continued dominance of London over Frankfurt despite the introduction of the Euro (Faulconbridge, 2004); the rise of London at the expense of New York throughout the 2000s that has been explained partly through New York's tighter regulation in both financial and non-financial spheres, particularly following 9/11 (Moran, 1991; Hall, 2007); and the relative demise of some previously dominant financial centres – notably Amsterdam in the European context (Engelen, 2007).

However, it is important not to consider regulation in isolation since research reveals how financial innovation relies on the combination of a favourable regulatory environment with dense networks of interaction between individuals and firms within financial districts. Through the creation of 'buzz' (Bathelt et al., 2004), such networks are argued to help overcome the significant knowledge asymmetries and uncertainties that typify client–provider relations within finance, in common with other advanced producer services (Clark, 2005). Research has identified the importance of a degree of shared history and understandings of work-placed culture in order to facilitate such networks. For example, Thrift (1994) emphasizes the role of shared backgrounds at a small number of public (fee paying) schools and at Oxbridge in facilitating the creation of trust-based relationships between financiers that have been labelled 'gentlemanly capitalists' in the City of London in the 1980s (see also Augar, 2001). More recently, attention has focused on how shared backgrounds and inter-personal networks have been important in developing and legitimating new forms of technical know-how, particularly the advanced mathematics associated with the financial economics that has underpinned financial innovations such as derivatives and securitization (Tickell, 2000; Hall, 2006; MacKenzie, 2006).

However, it is not only in relation to finance that understandings of knowledge creation and circulation within cities have been developed. Research has also focused on other rapidly growing sectors, particularly the creative industries. For example, Rantisi (2002) examines the role of 'organisational structures', notably local industry-specific associations and other institutions, in facilitating the design innovation process in women's wear within the New York City Garment District (see also Vinodrai, 2006). This work emphasizes the ways in which relationships between firms may be competitive as well as supportive and shows that associations and institutions play an important role in shaping the knowledge production process. Meanwhile, Faulconbridge (2007b) develops this argument a stage further by considering the role of 'organisational structures' in the form of professional associations in creating networks of individuals *beyond* firm boundaries that facilitate collective learning and knowledge circulation. In particular, he argues that in the case of legal services and advertising, such associations allow like-minded individuals to come together and learn from one another such that solutions can be co-developed in the face of sector challenges that exist beyond the level of one particular firm.

This focus on the organizational structures within cities that facilitate learning and knowledge production has also been developed recently by specifying the role of formal education and associated education providers in reproducing successful city economies. In some ways, this emerging literature develops one strand of earlier work on learning regions that identified universities based within that region as being important 'anchors' fostering the exchange of knowledge and learning more generally (see Gertler, 1995, 2003; Malmberg, 1997). For example, we have been working on research in legal and financial services to reveal how and why the majority of individuals working in these sectors combine situated learning experiences within firms (often facilitated by informal networks) with other forms of learning provided by different kinds of more formal educational institutions. As such, we suggest that these education providers are an important, yet comparatively neglected, set of institutions in facilitating knowledge production and circulation within city economies (Faulconbridge and Hall, 2009; Hall, 2009).

For example, in the case of finance, our research reveals the ways in which business education temporarily anchors financiers into particular places as education is used to inculcate individuals into the regulatory requirements and cultural norms associated with working in one particular financial district (Hall and Appleyard, 2009). Moreover, the alumni associations created through such educational experiences continue to act as an important vehicle through which knowledge is circulated through a series of networks that are institutionally, temporally and geographically differentiated (Hall, 2011) rather than being understood as one homogeneous 'transnational capitalist class' (Sklair, 2001). In the case of law, our research reveals that a range of both not for profit university style education providers (e.g. The College of Law) and for profit providers (e.g. BPP) have now developed a stranglehold over professional training that all new recruits to law firms in the City of London complete (see Faulconbridge and Muzio, 2009). The education these providers offer ensures new recruits to the legal profession both develop the technical competency needed to be a world city corporate lawyer in London *and* the right identity, defined as an understanding of who a world city corporate lawyer in London is and how such a lawyer should act, and the associated attitudes, values and behaviours.

This emerging interest in the role of business education in shaping processes of knowledge production also follows recent work on the increasingly reflexive nature of work within city economies associated with what Thrift (2005) has termed soft or knowledgeable capitalism. Thrift uses this term to refer to the constant processes of knowledge production and circulation that take place within and between firms as they seek to survive in an increasingly complex and uncertain business environment. In particular, Thrift identifies the importance of business schools, management consultants and business gurus and the media in producing and circulating knowledge into business through a process that he labels the cultural circuit of capital. He suggests that this group of actors has become increasingly important in both responding to and circulating a new managerial discourse that emphasizes the need for flexibility, adaptability and reflexivity (from both organizations and individuals) in post-Fordist economies. This literature is important for the purposes of our arguments in this chapter for three main reasons. First, it highlights the porous boundaries between different sites of knowledge production within city economies, as institutions such as business schools increasingly act as corporate organizations and firms develop their educational and research operations, for example. Second, and following on, knowledge does not only circulate from these institutions into firms but also circulates from firms back into the cultural circuit of capital such that the demands of corporate customers, for instance, are becoming increasingly important in the content of business school degree programmes and even the location of university campuses (Faulconbridge and Muzio, 2009; Hall, 2009). Third, this literature emphasizes the increasing importance attached to embodied, subjective and affective ways of knowing within contemporary city economies (Hinchliffe, 2000; Hughes, 2006), thereby building on earlier work that has sought to break down a binary between local, tacit knowledge and explicit knowledge that has greater potential to circulate trans-locally. It is to these geographically variegated processes of knowledge circulation between cities that we now turn.

WORLD CITIES IN SPACES OF KNOWLEDGE FLOWS

Reflecting the fundamental debates about the importance of relationality, network connectivity and flows in defining the nature of world cities (see Taylor, 2004; Sassen, 2006), an important body of recent work has emphasized how business knowledges are also generated by processes that, to use the language of Amin (2002), 'perforate' scales (Allen, 2000; Amin and Cohendet, 2004; Faulconbridge, 2007a). Specifically, networks are said to take the form of a combination of information–communication technology enabled circulation of documents, such as media reports and business briefings (see Thrift, 1997; Asheim et al., 2007), flows of people (see Castells, 2000; Sklair, 2001) and the creation of transnational communities that connect together spatially distributed business elites (see Hannerz, 1996; Amin and Cohendet, 2004). All of these are said to produce topological geographies of learning and knowledge that cannot be described using scalar terminologies such as local or regional, nor using terminologies that differentiate between embodied (face-to-face) and virtual (technologically enabled) co-presence. Rather these topological geographies are best described using a language that emphasizes the role of non-Euclidean relational proximity in enabling knowledge production and flow. Empirically, the role of such relational proximity in generating networked spaces of knowledge is best demonstrated with reference to three forms of flow and interconnectivity: trade fairs and conferences; migrant and expatriate skilled labour; and organizational communities of practice. The nature of the role of all three of these is reviewed below.

RELATIONAL MECHANISMS OF KNOWLEDGE PRODUCTION AND FLOW

Trade Fairs

Increasing attention has been paid over recent years to the role of trade fairs and conferences in generating flows of business knowledge. For example, Bathelt and Schuldt (2008) highlight how trade fairs result in flows of knowledge being generated as firms, customers and the industry-specific media congregate in one city, bringing with them knowledge about new products, customer needs and industry trends respectively. At the same time trade fairs are shown to generate new knowledge because of the way face-to-face contact between firms, their competitors, customers and members of the media generate conversations – what is often termed 'buzz' (see Bathelt et al., 2004) – which result in new understandings of key industry trends, customer needs and the way products are designed and work. Trade fairs are, therefore, exemplary of the way relational networks between cities allow both flows of knowledge – when understanding held by an individual or group of individuals in a firm is disseminated – but also the production of knowledge – forms of social interaction that generate new understandings.

Power and Jansson (2008) argue that so valuable is such knowledge flow and generation that a global circuit of trade fairs has now developed with events moving from world city to world city, with firms, customers and the media following them because of the knowledge resources they provide. Indeed, reflecting this idea, Maskell et al. (2006) claim that trade fairs represent mechanisms by which world cities become 'hotspots' of business knowledge. Trade fairs are said to form 'temporary clusters' in cities that mimic the city-based cluster described above because of the way they temporarily pin down various flows of knowledge embodied in people and firms. But trade fairs are not the only mechanism that allows world cities to become hotspots of such technical business knowledge.

One of the most empirically significant phenomena leading to flows of knowledge between cities is the role of skilled and mobile labour forces employed by the business services operating in and through world cities. Accountants, advertisers, financial institutions and law firms have all been shown to use either temporary secondments, where an employee moves from one world city to another for a few weeks or months, or expatriation, where an employee relocates for one year or more, to ensure the knowledge and expertise generated in one city are shared with and reproduced in other cities worldwide (see Beaverstock, 2002, 2004, 2005; Millar and Salt, 2008). Such mobile labour provides a mechanism for the embodied flow of knowledge, with individuals being moved by their employers between world cities so as to allow them to deploy and reproduce their knowledge within other offices of a global firm's network.

The embodied knowledge flows enabled by mobile labour are on many occasions technical in nature. For example, an investment banker with knowledge of particular portfolio management techniques may be relocated to train workers in other offices. However, equally important, and differentiating flows generated by expatriates from those generated by trade fairs, are the flows of tacit, encultured and practice-related knowledge (c.f. Blackler et al., 1998) generated by expatriates. For example, both Beaverstock (2004) and Faulconbridge (2008) show how law firms use secondments and periods of expatriation to allow knowledge about a firm's culture, ways of working and expectations in terms of employee behaviour to be reproduced in every office worldwide. Specifically this involves expatriates socializing workers in offices located away from the Anglo-American heartlands of global law firms into ways of working which are based on English and US norms. As a result, this is leading to what might be described as world city-specific lawyering cultures and practices which are produced in and spread between cities (see also Hall and Appleyard (2009) for similar arguments in the case of finance). The role of organizational communities of practice further exemplifies the nature of such flows of tacit, encultured and practice-related knowledge.

There is now an extensive body of work that examines the way communities of practice that 'perforate' (c.f. Amin, 2002) scalar boundaries and metaphorically but not physically 'bring together' individuals in different world cities allow both flows of and the generation of knowledge (see Amin and Cohendet, 2004; Faulconbridge, 2006, 2007a; Hall and Appleyard, 2009). Organizational communities of practice are broadly defined in these literatures as groups of individuals that share a common interest and way of working (a joint enterprise and shared repertoire) and which interact face to face or virtually to share existing and generate new knowledge (c.f. Wenger, 1998; Wenger et al., 2002). Such communities, being formed of individuals located in multiple world cities and 'meeting' in virtual (e.g. information–communication technology enabled) and material (e.g. airport hotels) spaces, mean that knowledge is actually produced in the spaces *between* world cities.

At one level, studies of organizational communities of practice have highlighted the role of communities in allowing flows of and the generation of technical knowledge. For example, Faulconbridge (2006) details the way that advertisers working in the London and New York City offices of global agencies' networks interact by telephone, video-conference and occasional face-to-face meeting to share insights into ways of designing effective advertising campaigns. This allows knowledge to move between the two world cities, thus enhancing the ability of advertisers in each city to develop effective campaigns, something which in turn enhances the competitiveness of the advertising industry in each city. However, at another level an emerging body of work also suggests that organisational communities of practice allow more tacit, encultured and practice-related knowledges to be generated and flow between cities. As Jones (2008) argues, the business practices of elites working in world cities are defined by interactions with fellow employees that are members of the same scale perforating organizational communities of practice. The business practices developed through these communities relate to everyday ways of working and doing business and relate to cultural norms and values associated with the practice of finance, law, and so on. Faulconbridge and Muzio (2009) show, for example, that global law firms use organizational communities of practice to regulate the identity of lawyers and help shape the way lawyers employed in different offices worldwide by English and American firms understand their role as a lawyer and their responsibilities to clients. This involves using various training programmes that allow lawyers in different offices to interact with one another, learn from one another's ways of working and, most importantly, learn from the senior, usually English or American, partners of the firm about the norms and expectations of the firm in terms of the way lawyers behave and act in the office. The effect of such organizational communities of practice is to diffuse English or American understandings of legal practice to world cities in Europe (e.g. Frankfurt, Milan) and Asia (e.g. Singapore, Beijing) and, just like seconded and expatriated workers do, produce transnational, world city-specific forms of legal practice.

CONCLUSIONS

In this chapter we have explored two of the most important dimensions of recent debates about business knowledge in world cities. First, we have argued that knowledge is produced in cities (e.g. in clusters and universities), by flows between cities (e.g. by trade fairs and expatriates) and in spaces in between cities (organizational communities of practice). Second, we have argued that business knowledges produced within and between world cities are both technical in nature and tacit, encultured and practice-based. In so doing, our arguments underscore the importance of understanding the often messy entanglements between different kinds of knowledge that are produced and circulated in different ways within and between cities in the contemporary global economy (Allen, 2000).

However, whilst the literatures we have used to make these arguments have developed significantly in recent years, there are still certain blind spots that need addressing in future research in order to more fully understand such processes and the way they play out in and through world cities. Three such issues are particularly important. First, whilst it is increasingly acknowledged that research needs to consider the complex inter-weaving between technical business knowledges and embodied, encultured and practice-based ways of knowing, how this is researched methodologically remains more problematic. In particular, it appears important that researchers interested in such questions move beyond a reliance on semi-structured interviews to explore more innovative research methods, most notably forms of observation, in order to more fully understand the ways in which embodied ways of knowing are produced, learnt and shared. Second, recent work has begun to explore such issues beyond established world cities, notably London and New York, where much of this work has taken place to date. There is considerable scope to explore issues of knowledge production and flow more fully in emerging, highly dynamic city economies that operate in very different political, economic and cultural contexts, such as those found in Asian cities. Third, more careful study of the power relations influencing knowledge production within and between world cities is needed. These power relations are likely to determine which knowledges are valued and become part of the 'circuits' Thrift (2005) describes and are also likely to determine which knowledges produced in which cities gain global hegemony, as Anglo-American financial practices did before the 2008 financial crisis. Responding to these challenges will achieve a better understanding of the intricate ways in which different types of knowledges are produced and circulated in dynamic cities in the contemporary global economy.

ACKNOWLEDGEMENTS

James Faulconbridge gratefully acknowledges the support of the ESRC (RES-000–22–2957) for his research into knowledge and learning within legal services. Sarah Hall gratefully acknowledges the support of the ESRC (RES-061–25–0071) for her work into business education in London's financial district.

REFERENCES

Allen, J. (2000), 'Power/economic knowledge: symbolic and spatial formations', in J. Bryson, P.W. Daniels, N. Henry and J. Pollard (eds), *Knowledge, Space, Economy*, London: Routledge, pp. 15–33.
Amin, A. (2002), 'Spatialities of globalization', *Environment and Planning A*, **34** (3), 385–399.
Amin, A. and P. Cohendet (2004), *Architectures of Knowledge: Firms, Capabilities and Communities*, Oxford: Oxford University Press.

Amin, A. and N. Thrift (1995), 'Globalisation, institutional "thickness" and the local economy', in P. Healey, S. Cameron, S. Davoudi, S. Graham and A. Madani-Pour (eds), *Managing Cities: The New Urban Context*, Chichester: Wiley, pp. 91–108.

Asheim, B.T. (1996), 'Industrial districts as "learning regions": a condition for prosperity', *European Planning Studies*, **4** (4), 379–400.

Asheim, B., L. Coenen and J. Vang (2007), 'Face-to-face, buzz, and knowledge bases: sociospatial implications for learning, innovation, and innovation policy', *Environment and Planning C: Government and Policy*, **25** (5), 655–670.

Augar, P. (2001), *The Death of Gentlemanly Capitalism*, London: Penguin.

Bathelt, H., A. Malmberg and P. Maskell (2004), 'Clusters and knowledge: local buzz, global pipelines and the process of knowledge creation', *Progress in Human Geography*, **28** (1), 31–56.

Bathelt, H. and N. Schuldt (2008), 'Between luminaires and meat grinders: international trade fairs as temporary clusters', *Regional Studies*, **42** (6), 853–868.

Beaverstock, J.V. (2002), 'Transnational elites in global cities: British expatriates in Singapore's financial district', *Geoforum*, **33** (4), 525–538.

Beaverstock, J.V. (2004), '"Managing across borders": knowledge management and expatriation in professional service legal firms', *Journal of Economic Geography*, **4** (2), 157–179.

Beaverstock, J.V. (2005), 'Transnational elites in the city: British highly-skilled inter-company transferees in New York City's financial district', *Journal of Ethnic and Migration Studies*, **31** (2), 245–268.

Blackler, F., N. Crump and S. McDonald (1998), 'Knowledge, organizations and competition', in G. Krogh, J. Roos and D. Kleine (eds), *Knowing in Firms: Understanding, Managing and Measuring Knowledge*, London: Sage, pp. 67–86.

Castells, M. (2000), *The Rise of the Network Society*, Malden, MA: Blackwell.

Clark, G.L. (2005), 'Money flows like mercury: the geography of global finance', *Geografiska Annaler Series B – Human Geography*, **87** (2), 99–112.

Clark, G.L. and D. Wójcik (2007), *The Geography of Finance: Corporate Governance in the Global Marketplace*, Oxford: Oxford University Press.

Engelen, E. (2007), '"Amsterdamned"? The uncertain future of a financial centre', *Environment and Planning A*, **39** (6), 1306–1324.

Faulconbridge, J.R. (2004), 'London and Frankfurt in Europe's evolving financial centre network', *Area*, **36** (3), 235–244.

Faulconbridge, J.R. (2006), 'Stretching tacit knowledge beyond a local fix? Global spaces of learning in advertising professional service firms', *Journal of Economic Geography*, **6** (4), 517–540.

Faulconbridge, J.R. (2007a), 'Exploring the role of professional associations in collective learning in London and New York's advertising and law professional-service-firm clusters', *Environment and Planning A*, **39** (4), 965–984.

Faulconbridge, J.R. (2007b), 'London's and New York's advertising and law clusters and their networks of learning: relational analyses with a politics of scale?', *Urban Studies*, **44** (9), 1635–1656.

Faulconbridge, J.R. (2008), 'Negotiating cultures of work in transnational law firms', *Journal of Economic Geography*, **8** (4), 497–517.

Faulconbridge, J.R. and S. Hall (2009), 'Educating professionals and professional education in a geographical context', *Geography Compass*, **3** (1), 171–189.

Faulconbridge, J.R. and D. Muzio (2009), 'Legal education, globalization, and cultures of professional practice', *Georgetown Journal of Legal Ethics*, **22** (4), 1335–1359.

French, S. (2000), 'Rescaling the economic geography of knowledge and information: constructing life assurance markets', *Geoforum*, **31** (1), 101–119.

Gertler, M.S. (1995), 'Being there: proximity, organization, and culture in the development and adoption of advanced manufacturing technologies', *Economic Geography*, **71** (1), 1–26.

Gertler, M.S. (2003), 'Tacit knowledge and the economic geography of context, or the undefinable tacitness of being (there)', *Journal of Economic Geography*, **3** (1), 75–99.

Hall, S. (2006), 'What counts? Exploring the production of quantitative financial narratives in London's corporate finance industry', *Journal of Economic Geography*, **6** (5), 661–678.

Hall, S. (2007), 'Knowledge makes the money go round: conflicts of interest and corporate finance in London's financial district', *Geoforum*, **38** (4), 710–719.

Hall, S. (2009), 'Ecologies of business education and the geographies of knowledge', *Progress in Human Geography*, **33** (5), 599–618.

Hall, S. (2011), 'Educational ties, social capital and the translocal (re)production of MBA alumni networks', *Global Networks*, **11** (1), 118–138.

Hall, S. and L. Appleyard (2009), '"City of London, city of learning"? Placing business education within the geographies of finance', *Journal of Economic Geography*, **9** (5), 597–617.

Hannerz, U. (1996), *Transnational Connections*, London: Routledge.

Henry, N. and S. Pinch (2000), 'Spatialising knowledge: placing the knowledge community of Motor Sport Valley', *Geoforum*, **31** (2), 191–208.

Hinchliffe, S. (2000), 'Performance and experimental knowledge: outdoor management training and the end of epistemology', *Environment and Planning D: Society and Space*, **18** (5), 575–595.

Hughes, A. (2006), 'Learning to trade ethically: knowledgeable capitalism, retailers and contested commodity chains', *Geoforum*, **37** (6), 1008–1020.

Jones, A. (2008), 'Beyond embeddedness: economic practices and the invisible dimensions of transnational business activity', *Progress in Human Geography*, **32** (1), 71–88.

Knight, J. (1992), *Institutions and Social Conflict*, Cambridge: Cambridge University Press.

MacKenzie, D. (2006), *An Engine, Not a Camera: How Financial Models Shape Markets*, Cambridge, MA: MIT Press.

MacLeod, G. (2001), 'Beyond soft institutionalism: accumulation, regulation, and their geographical fixes', *Environment and Planning A*, **33** (7), 1145–1167.

Malmberg, A. (1997), 'Industrial geography: location and learning', *Progress in Human Geography*, **21** (4), 573–582.

Maskell, P., H. Bathelt and A. Malmberg (2006), 'Building global knowledge pipelines: the role of temporary clusters', *European Planning Studies*, **14** (8), 997–1013.

Maskell, P. and A. Malmberg (1999), 'Localised learning and industrial competitiveness', *Cambridge Journal of Economics*, **23** (2), 167–185.

Millar, J. and J. Salt (2008), 'Portfolios of mobility: the movement of expertise in transnational corporations in two sectors – aerospace and extractive industries', *Global Networks*, **8** (1), 25–50.

Moran, M. (1991), *The Politics of the Financial Services Revolution: The USA, UK and Japan*, Basingstoke: Macmillan.

Morgan, K. (2004), 'The exaggerated death of geography: learning, proximity and territorial innovation systems', *Journal of Economic Geography*, **4** (1), 3–21.

Power, D. and J. Jansson (2008), 'Cyclical clusters in global circuits: overlapping spaces in furniture trade fairs', *Economic Geography*, **84** (4), 423–448.

Rantisi, N. (2002), 'The local innovation system as source of "variety": openness and adaptability in New York City's garment district', *Regional Studies*, **36** (6), 587–602.

Sassen, S. (2006), *Cities in a World Economy*, Thousand Oaks, CA: Pine Forge Press, 3rd edition.

Saxenian, A. (1994), *Regional Advantage, Culture and Competition in Silicon Valley and Route 128*, Cambridge, MA: Harvard University Press.

Saxenian, A. (2006), *The New Argonauts: Regional Advantage in a Global Economy*, Cambridge, MA: Harvard University Press.

Sklair, L. (2001), *The Transnational Capitalist Class*, Oxford: Blackwell.

Storper, M. (1997), *The Regional World*, New York: Guildford Press.

Taylor, P.J. (2004), *World City Network: A Global Urban Analysis*, London: Routledge.

Thrift, N. (1994), 'On the social and cultural determinants of international financial centres: the case of the City of London', in S. Corbridge, N. Thrift and R. Martin (eds), *Money, Power and Space*, Oxford: Blackwell, pp. 327–355.

Thrift, N. (1997), 'The rise of soft capitalism', *Cultural Values*, **1** (1), 29–57.

Thrift, N. (2005), *Knowing Capitalism*, London: Sage.

Tickell, A. (2000), 'Finance and localities', in G.L. Clark, M.P. Feldman and M.S. Gertler (eds), *The Oxford Handbook of Economic Geography*, Oxford: Oxford University Press, pp. 230–252.

Tickell, A. and J.A. Peck (1992), 'Accumulation, regulation and the geographies of post-Fordism: missing links in regulationist research', *Progress in Human Geography*, **16** (2), 190–218.

Vinodrai, T. (2006), 'Reproducing Toronto's design ecology: career paths, intermediaries, and local labor markets', *Economic Geography*, **82** (3), 237–263.

Wenger, E. (1998), *Communities of Practice: Learning, Meaning, and Identity*, Cambridge: Cambridge University Press.

Wenger, E., R. McDermott and W.M. Snyder (2002), *Cultivating Communities of Practice: A Guide to Managing Knowledge*, Boston, MA: Harvard Business School Press.

21 Highly skilled international labour migration and world cities: expatriates, executives and entrepreneurs
Jonathan V. Beaverstock

INTRODUCTION

Highly skilled international labour migration is a pre-eminent process for world city growth, competitiveness and network building (Friedmann, 1986; Beaverstock and Boardwell, 2000). The burgeoning economies of world cities have created unprecedented conditions for the demand of highly skilled labour in both private and public sector employment (Sassen, 2006). For individuals, world cities have become the 'global elevators' for career development and wealth creation (Beaverstock, 2002). Over the last three decades, the highly concentrated, geo-economic reach and connectedness of world city corporate economies, particularly in banking, finance and professional services, have created the demand conditions for a new breed of highly skilled, talented and mobile worker who is required to engage in transnational working practices within the firm and its client relationships (Beaverstock, 2007a; Jones, 2008). For employers and policy-makers, in the race to be highly competitive on a global stage, the requirement to attract and retain highly skilled, transnational experienced labour has never been so important in the global 'war for talent' (Faulconbridge et al., 2009). Highly skilled labour is the conduit through which capital is accumulated, networks built, connections made and cosmopolitanism reproduced through its embodied knowledge systems, social relations and spatialities of 'cliquey-ness'. These workers are the 'dominant managerial elites' in the so-called third layer of the space of flows (Castells, 2000, p. 445). Following a brief discussion of the significance of highly skilled international labour migration and the firm in the (re)making of the world city, the remainder of the chapter will use the exemplar of Singapore: first to show how highly skilled immigrant labour, so-called 'foreign talent', has been used in economic policy to overtly enhance the city's world city competitive status; and, secondly, to illustrate how a particular spatiality within the city, Holland Village, has become influenced by a critical mass of 'foreign talent' to produce an overtly 'expatriate ambience' through a process known as 'expatriatisation' (Chang, 1995).

HIGHLY SKILLED INTERNATIONAL MIGRATION AND THE WORLD CITY

In a metropolitan context, highly skilled international labour migration, whether permanent or sojourn, is an essential pre-requisite for world cities to remain competitive in a global urban hierarchy or world city network (Beaverstock, 2007b). Such migration is a precursor for the continual making and re-making of the world city (Beaverstock and Boardwell, 2000; Sassen, 2006; Ewers, 2007). It is the agency of the transnational corporation (TNC) that has had a significant role in both 'pulling' and 'pushing' professional, managerial and scientific/technical labour, in intra- or inter-company transfers (ICTs) within or between world cities' international office networks, subsidiaries or affiliates in hyper-mobile expatriation programmes or external recruitment (Koser and Salt, 1997; Beaverstock, 2007b). The process of expatriation, therefore, has not only become an important driver for the world city to secure 'global talent' from the transnational capitalist (Sklair, 2001) or creative class (Florida, 2002), but it is also an important organizational strategy for the firm to succeed in the economic processes of internationalization and market penetration set in a metropolitan context. To further pursue these labour market demand-side arguments about the role of highly skilled international migration and the (re-)making of the world city, the rest of this section of the chapter will focus on unpacking world cities and labour market demand, and the role of the firm in ICTs.

World Cities and Labour Market Demand

As we know from those early writers on the spatial organization of multinational enterprise and the New International Division of Labour (Hymer, 1972; Cohen, 1981; Friedmann, 1986), the concentration of professional and managerial, and technical and scientific occupations within world cities has made these places the strategic nodal points within the world economy. The high concentration of TNC headquarters, regional offices and other fee-earning capabilities within a small number of cities around the globe (Table 21.1) has not only created an unprecedented concentration of corporate 'command and control' (Sassen, 2001) but also 'global reach' in leadership, innovation, creativity and entrepreneurialism (Florida, 2002; Sassen, 2006). World cities are the centre-piece of an international spatial division of labour, where the high-value corporate economy relies on a continuing supply of highly skilled professional and managerial, technical and scientific, and creative labour to meet labour market demand and, ultimately, create value for the firm.

In world cities, the now well documented structural change in internal economies from manufacturing to services and high-value manufacturing and R&D, coupled with the rapid internationalization of producer services and technological change (Bryson et al., 2004), has resulted in great employment change. For example, in London employment in manufacturing has declined by 53 per cent (-0.345 million) from 0.649 to 0.304 million between 1981 and 2008, and during the same period the number of jobs created in the service sector rose by 46 per cent ($+1.184$ million), from 2.439 to 3.623 million (Gordon et al., 2009, p. 12). The growth of the service economy, and especially of producer services, has created the conditions for rapid labour market demand for highly skilled professionals, from the boardroom (presidents, vice-presidents, CEOs, managing partners) to fee-earners on the office 'shop-floor' (e.g. advertising executives, accountants, bankers, consultants, lawyers, media specialists), and in the constellation of 'freelancers' and entrepreneurs who feed into, and on, the world city complex (Mould, 2008). Moreover, such labour market demand has spurred much internal migration to world cities. For example, the high incidence of internal migration from UK regions to the south-east of

Table 21.1 Top-ranking city locations for Fortune Global 500 companies

2009			2006		
Rank	City	No. of Global 500 companies	Rank	City	No of Global 500 companies
1.	Tokyo	51	1.	Tokyo	52
2.	Paris	27	2.	Paris	27
3.	Beijing	26	3.	New York	24
4.	New York	18	4.	London	23
5.	London	15	5.	Beijing	15
6.	Seoul	11	6.	Seoul	9
7.	Madrid	9	7.	Toronto	8
=8.	Toronto	7	=8.	Madrid	7
=8.	Zurich	7	=8.	Zurich	7
=8.	Osaka	7	=10.	Houston	6
=8.	Moscow	7	=10.	Osaka	6
=8.	Munich	7	=10.	Munich	6
13.	Houston	6	=10.	Atlanta	6
=14.	Mumbai	5	=14.	Rome	5
=14.	Atlanta	5	=14.	Düsseldorf	5
=14.	Amsterdam	5			

Source: author's adaptation from CNNMoney.com (2009)

England, including London, in the 1980s has been referred to as movement to an 'escalator' region (Fielding, 1992).

The wider processes of globalization and technological and regulatory change have created the circumstances for the development of a global division of professional and managerial labour, or a transnational elite, composed of highly talented migrants, from a range of nationalities, who move frequently between world cities to fill job vacancies, accumulate personal wealth and maximize career opportunities (Beaverstock, 2002). This is particularly the case in knowledge intensive sectors of the world economy like banking, finance and professional services, creative industries and high-value industries (life sciences, biotechnology, etc.), where knowledge, expertise and skills can rarely be substituted by ICT, and labour market demand has to be filled from the global pool of talent, involving both international and internal migration within and between the internal labour markets (ILMs) of firms (Beaverstock, 2007a). For example, the competitive index of Global Financial Centres makes it very clear that the availability of intellectual capital (well-qualified, experienced professionals), the flexibility of labour markets and the quality of business education are 'the single most important factor in financial service competitiveness' (Z/Yen, 2007, p.11) (Table 21.2). For international financial centres, the rankings of competitiveness are closely aligned to the depth of the talent pool. As Wigley's (2008, p. 6) recent study of the global competitiveness of London's financial centre concluded, it was its 'deep talent pool and welcoming culture' that was a significant factor for its leadership in the global market for banking and finance, and professional services.

Table 21.2   Global financial centres index rankings, ranked by 'people'

2007		2009	
Rank	GFCI1	Rank	GFCI6
1.	London	1.	London
2.	New York	2.	New York
3.	San Francisco	3.	Hong Kong
4.	Chicago	4.	Singapore
5.	Hong Kong	5.	Tokyo
6.	Toronto	6.	Sydney
7.	Singapore	7.	Zurich
8.	Zurich	8.	Frankfurt
9.	Montreal	9.	Toronto
10.	Boston	10.	Chicago

Note: GFC = Global Financial Centre.

Source: author's compilation of data provided by Z/Yen (2007, 2009)

The Firm: Inter- and Intra-company Transfers

The firm, both TNC and small and medium-sized enterprise, plays an essential role in facilitating the movement of labour (of all nationalities) between world cities. Highly skilled citizens of the European Economic Area (EEA) are 'free' to seek jobs in all member states. For EEA citizens moving outside of the EEA and non-EEA citizens moving into the EEA, mobility is regulated through individual state immigration legislation and work permit arrangements, which are often closely aligned to sponsorship by the firm (e.g. the UKs Highly Skilled Migrant Programme). The firm facilitates highly skilled labour migration through ICTs, which is mobility between and within ILMs. ICTs fulfil three generic organizational roles: to fill vacancies that cannot be supplied from the local labour market because qualified locals are not available or cannot be easily trained (knowledge transfer); to develop the global credentials of international managers and fee-earning personnel (knowledge acquisition); and for 'organisational development', which is essentially to disseminate the cultural ethos or 'corporate memory' of the firm (Perkins, 1997) from its headquarters to its subsidiaries (Edstrom and Galbraith, 1977).

As technological advancements in transportation and communication (internet, wireless technologies, video-conferencing) have made radical changes to the workplace and working practices, the rise of so-called 'transnational' or 'global' work (Beaverstock, 2007a; Jones, 2008) has had major effects on the dynamics of ICTs. ICTs have become very fluid in strategic capabilities and, importantly, duration. Millar and Salt's (2008) analysis of ICTs in IT, aerospace, pharmaceuticals, electronic engineering, consulting and extractive industries identified 'portfolios of mobility' within/between firms, which included long-term assignments, short-term-assignments, commuting assignments, rotations, extended business travel (30 to 90 days), business travel (up to 30 days) and virtual mobility. Millar and Salt's (2008) 'portfolios of mobility' mimics almost exactly the

Table 21.3   Global Mobility Programmes for the top four accounting firms (ranked by fee income $m)

PricewaterhouseCoopers (fee income $28.2m; in 153 countries; with 117,000 partners and professional staff)[1]
The Global Mobility Programme (GMP)[2] 'allows us to offer our clients, wherever they are in the world, the right expertise at the right time. It also develops the skills and international perspective of our people.' In 2009, 2866 partners and professional staff were on the programme from members' firms in 100 countries, either involved in short- or long-term transfers or assignments (compared with 3228 in 103 countries in 2008). PwC expect the number of GMP staff to increase worldwide from 2010.

Deloitte (DTT) ($27.4m; 140 countries; 124,000 partners & professional staff)[1]
The International Mobility Program (IMP)[3] actively encourages staff to 'apply for positions through the various international assignment programs . . . to expand their skills and experience . . . [as the firm] . . . recognize[s] the value of having individuals with global skill sets'. Assignments are short-term client service projects and long-term strategic roles, which are open to all levels, with the intended outcomes of enhancing global knowledge, building cross-cultural capabilities and developing leadership competences.

Ernst & Young ($24.5m; 140 countries; 99,000 partners & professional staff)[1]
The Global Exchange Programme (GEP)[4] is intended to broaden 'technical and/or industry skills while working abroad for 18 months', for knowledge transfer and cross-cultural experience. Professionals also move on: short- or long-term international engagements, tailored to client requirements; international assignments programmes, from London to New York and Sydney are popular destinations; and international secondment opportunities.

KPMG ($22.7m; 145 countries; 93,000 partners & professional staff)[1]
The Global Opportunities Program (GO)[5] provides a platform for professionals to move from one member firm to another worldwide. The firm has 'global clients with a global outlook', and it uses the GO to facilitate its professionals 'to be global thinkers too'. KPMG had 2400 assignees involving 90 countries in 2009, and it aims to have 5000 on the GO Program in 2010. The GO has a number of highly flexible time-scales for assignments, organized by area of expertise (e.g. KPMG's Tax Trek Program offers various short-term assignments).

Sources:
1. International Financial Services London (2009)
2. PricewaterhouseCoopers (2009, 52)
3. Deloitte (2009) and www.deloitte.co.uk (accessed 11 January 2010)
4. www.ey.com (accessed 11 January 2010)
5. www.kpmg.com (accessed 11 January 2010)

corporate rationale for ICTs within banking, finance and professional services, and high technology (Beaverstock, 2007a,b; Harvey, 2008; Jones, 2008).

For example, in a sector like accounting, which is crucial to the capabilities and competitiveness of the world city 'new production complex' (Sassen, 2006), the top four firms not only each employ hundreds of thousands of highly skilled, fee-earning staff (partners, qualified accountants, professionals), of all nationalities, in office networks which reach a hundred plus worldwide, but are also responsible for the circulation of thousands of fee-earners between world cities in ICT assignments and secondments (to member firms and clients) (Beaverstock, 2007a) (Table 21.3). For example, Deloitte member firms had 2500+

partners and professional international vacancies that could be filled through their Global Mobility Programme (GMP) in 2008 (5 per cent of all professional staffing) (Deloitte, 2009). If the magnitude of international secondments to clients were added to staffing their GMP, it could be estimated that upward of 10–15 per cent of their global professional staff were working outside of the 'home country' office in a cross-border capacity.

'FOREIGN' TALENT IN SINGAPORE

At the 2009 mid-year estimate, Singapore had a total population of 4.988 million, of which a quarter (1.254m) were non-residents (immigrants) (Singapore Statistics, 2010). All immigrants compete with locals for employment on every rung of the job ladder (*Economist*, 2009). Price and Benton-Short (2007) ranked Singapore as the 10th top total-foreign born immigration world city, second to Hong Kong in the Asia-Pacific region. Singapore's 2009 demographic trend, where one in every four of the total population is foreign born, has not come about by accident. With few natural resources, a mainstay of Government economic policy has been to seek foreign labour to drive an industrialization policy of export-led growth in the Pan-Asian region since independence in 1965 (Sim et al., 2003). Importantly, since the early 1990s, the luring and retention of 'foreign talent' have become institutionalized in overt strategic economic and immigrant policies to maximize competitiveness on a global stage, which would transform Singapore from a regional city into a truly cosmopolitan global city (Yeoh, 2004, 2006). The aim has been to attract highly skilled foreign workers into high-value-added sectors, like banking and financial services, technology and R&D. The state has promoted a 'Foreign Talent Programme' to specifically attract expatriates to work for both domestic and foreign companies, with a skilled-immigration legislative procedure, the Employment Pass schema, that is particularly liberal for both employees and employers. The Singapore Government has been very clear in many high-profile Prime Minister Pronouncements (Yeoh, 2004) that the city's aspiration to become a truly cosmopolitan, global city is founded on the mantra of being able to 'win the global war for talent' to achieve its ambition of becoming a knowledge-based economy (Lim, 2002). As Senior Minister Lee Kuan Yew said in a speech in February 2003:

> if we do not attract, welcome and make foreign talent feel comfortable in Singapore, we will not be a global city and if we are not a global city, it doesn't count for much. The days of being a regional city, that's over. (quoted in Chong, 2003)

It is difficult to report exact data on the magnitude and residency of 'foreign talent' because these data are not released by Singapore Statistics. In 2006, there were an estimated 144,500 expatriates in Singapore, which was a record number in the workforce and, for the first time, deemed to be a 'critical mass' in the city (Lewis, 2008), representing about 17 per cent of the total foreign born population (Table 21.4). Many of these expatriates would have been citizens of North America (e.g. USA), Europe (e.g. UK, Netherlands, Germany, Switzerland, France), Middle East (e.g. UAE), Asia (e.g. India, Japan, South Korea, China) and Australasia (Australia and New Zealand). Comparing the 2006 figures with estimates of the expatriate population from 1990 (15,000) (Chang, 1995) and 2000 (80,000) (Yeoh, 2004), there has been a phenomenal growth in the

Table 21.4   Singapore's estimated expatriate population

Year	Expatriate population	Non-resident population[1]	Expatriate share of all immigrants (%)
1990	15,000[2]	311,200	4.5
1996	50,000[3]	602,600	8.3
2000	80,000[4]	754,500	10.6
2006	144,500[5]	875,500	16.5

Sources: author's own analysis of the data compiled from:
1. Singapore Statistics (2010)
2. Chang (1995)
3. Yeoh and Chang (2001)
4. Yeoh (2004)
5. Lewis (2008)

residency of these talented workers, representing an eight-fold increase (+863 per cent) from 1990 to 2006, a four-fold increase (+433 per cent) between 1990 and 2000, and a +80 per cent change between 2000 and 2006 (Table 21.4).

The international structure and composition of Singapore's world city economy, as an Asian-Pacific centre for regional headquarters of multinational corporations (Yeung et al., 2001), thriving international maritime centre (Lee et al., 2008), major international financial centre (Beaverstock, 2002) and world-class education 'hub' (Olds, 2007) have created significant demand for highly skilled labour from both national and global labour pools. Between 1991 and 2008, employment increased by +0.779 million in manufacturing and 1.1 million in the service sector, with +0.322 million jobs created in financial services, real estate, and leasing and professional services (Ministry of Manpower, 2009). It is impossible to obtain official data from Singapore Statistics on the proportion of expatriates employed in each occupational group or employment sector. However, Beaverstock's (2008) survey of the city's executive search industry indicated that the major European, US and local executive search firms (like Boyden, Egon Zehnder, GT SJ MGT Amrop Hever, Heidrick & Struggles, Korn Ferry, Russell Reynolds and Spencer Stuart) were regularly employed by Singaporean based clients to bring knowledge-rich employees into the city at senior executive (e.g. CEO), managing and senior partner, and fee-earning levels (e.g. accountants, foreign exchange dealers), and for occupations which require high scientific expertise (e.g. biotechnology). Further evidence from this survey suggested that the highest activity in executive search was in banking, finance and professional services, high-value industrial manufacturing and engineering (e.g. maritime, chemical), and high technology (e.g. biotechnology, life sciences, health). For example, in banking, finance and professional services, executive search firms brought in 'foreign talent' from Hong Kong, Tokyo and Sydney, and it was not untypical for labour to be attracted from New York, London, Paris and Frankfurt.

Living the Expatriate Life

Expatriates, of many nationalities, live a privileged life in Singapore. Many work in the knowledge-based economy located downtown, like the financial or civil districts, or are clustered in 'state of the art' industrial/technological complexes, like the Biopolis biotechnology cluster (www.one-north.sg/hubs_biopolis.aspx). Along the Singapore River, the numerous restaurants, bars, coffee and sandwich shops, and hotels (like the Fullerton) that litter Boat and Clarke Quays are important places for expatriates to meet and socialise during and after work. 'British' pubs like Harry's Bar (infamous in the life-story of Nick Leeson) and Penny Black remain very important for the life-worlds of British, Australian and New Zealand expats in the city. Outside of downtown, 'work-place' Singapore, the central Island suburb of Holland Village has been identified as a major expatriate enclave that caters almost exclusively for 'foreign talent'.

Holland Village is a 'home away from home' for many expatriates. The suburb, which developed in close proximity to a former British military base, has always been an important residential preference for the British. Chang's (1995) study of Holland Village used the term 'expatriatisation' to explain how the suburb had become an identifiable expatriate enclave, which catered exclusively to the resident, 'expatriate market' (p. 141). Chang (1995) yielded several interesting factors which contributed to the 'expatriatisation' of Holland Village, including: the majority of merchandizers and food outlets catering specifically for 'Western' expatriates' fashions and tastes; its reputation as an 'expatriate enclave' being built upon informal recommendations within expatriate networks and advertising in expatriate handbooks; the majority of expatriates visiting the Village were women (housewives) in the 31–50 age group; and the reproduction of the Village's expatriate ambience was influenced by its co-location with expatriate residences, luxury condominiums and private houses, and international schools (six within a 4 km radius). Recently, studies by Beaverstock (2011) and Faulkner (2009) have both reiterated the 'expatriatisation' of Holland Village. Beaverstock's (2011) survey of British patronage of 'expatriate clubs' noted that over half of the 24 interviewees lived in or in close proximity to the Village, shopped and socialized there and sent their children to nearby schools. Faulkner's (2009) survey of 100 British expatriates reported that 47 per cent of the sample lived in the Village, with 95 per cent stating that they visited the Village 'always' or 'often'. Hence the pull of Holland Village for an expatriate clientele, whether resident or living nearby, is still fundamentally constructed by its 'expatriate' ambience, cosmopolitan retail outlets, restaurants, wine bars, coffee shops and fashion, and socializing node for various informal networks, especially expatriate spouses. In short, Holland Village has a distinctive 'expatriate sense of place'.

The Fall-out of the Global Economic Crisis

Despite the fall-out of the global economic crisis, the Singapore Government has maintained its overtly liberalized immigration policy towards seeking foreign 'talent', and the 'talented' themselves continue to rank Singapore as one of the best international locations in which to live and work. HSBC's *Expat Explorer Survey* (2009) ranked the country as the second most lavish established market destination in 2009 (behind Hong Kong [1st], but ahead of Japan [3rd], Switzerland [4th] and the USA [5th]). However, expatriation remains a very expensive business for firms when remuneration and relocation packages are calculated. Since the bursting of the dot.com bubble in the early 2000s, expatriate postings to Singapore have become shorter in duration and the contractual focus has been shifting away from the luxurious 'expatriate package' to 'foreign talent' being employed on local packages, partially commensurate to local nationals

(PricewaterhouseCoopers, 2004). The final outcome of the current economic recession in Singapore may result in an exodus of 200,000 highly paid foreigners and permanent residents (Adam, 2009).

CONCLUSIONS

In this chapter, the main argument has been that highly skilled international labour migration is one of the pre-eminent processes which account for world city growth, their competitiveness in the world economy and their ability to build and sustain networks in both material and immaterial flows and connections. Firms have vital agency in the process of pulling highly skilled migrants into the city, from a global labour pool of professional and managerial, scientific and technical, and creative labour, as they seek the most knowledgeable, experienced, technically able and creative workers to add value to their business operations. The world city's 'new production complex' (Sassen, 2006), whether that be financial centres or clusters of creativity, functions at its greatest competitive edge when it continues to attract the *creme de la creme* of the global elite. It is no surprise, therefore, that nation-states adopt relatively liberal immigration regulation for highly skilled workers to make certain that the knowledge intensive industries in their world city or world cities remain highly competitive on a global scale. The Singapore Government is an exemplar of such a strategy, as discussed, where its overt programme of attracting and retaining 'foreign talent' has become a central focus of its wider goals to become a truly cosmopolitan world city.

Throughout the chapter, the argument has been focused on demand-side factors, which pull highly skilled migrants into the world city. It must be acknowledged that supply-side factors are just as critical in the making of the world city's global elite, cosmopolitan workforce. Highly skilled labour, from recent graduates to seasoned executives, search for employment opportunities in the world city complex because its transnationally orientated industrial structures and networks offer the most significant career opportunities, highest levels of remuneration and most cosmopolitan lifestyle choices. Places like Wall Street, the City of London and Singapore's 'Golden Shoe' will continue to be global magnets for bankers, corporate lawyers, accountants and hedge fund managers if they can command 'high-flier' career paths and the most lucrative remuneration packages, whilst living life to the full in truly cosmopolitan world cities.

In the aftermath of the global financial crisis the global 'war for talent' is going to be more intensive than ever. As firms in all different sectors of the economy strive to seek efficiencies and higher market share and profitability, a fundamental strategy will be to employ (and retain) the most talented and gifted. As learnt from the aftermath of the economic downturns of the late 1980s and early 1990s, it is the availability of global talent that will be the key factor in the creation of economic growth and wealth, not office networks or other fixed capital. Moreover, this talent will continue to function as part of a global labour market, where an important attribute of this market will be *hypermobility* between world cities. In short, those world cities which continue to be atop the urban hierarchy or world city network will be those which continue to attract and retain highly skilled labour and 'win the war for talent'.

ACKNOWLEDGEMENTS

I would like to thank The British Academy (Small Grant No. 36613) and The National University of Singapore's Overseas Attachment Programme (2007) for funding the Singapore research reported in this chapter.

REFERENCES

Adam, S. (2009), 'Singapore may see 200,000 foreigners leave, Credit Suisse says', 19 January 2009, available at www.bloomberg.com/apps/news?pid=20601080&sid=aDUTELnSlccU&refer=asia (accessed 14 January 2010).

Beaverstock, J.V. (2002), 'Transnational elites in global cities: British expatriates in Singapore's financial district', *Geoforum*, **33** (4), 525–538.

Beaverstock, J.V. (2007a), 'Transnational work: global professional labour markets in professional service accounting firms', in J. Bryson and P. Daniels (eds), *The Handbook of Service Industries*, Cheltenham: Edward Elgar, pp. 409–431.

Beaverstock, J.V. (2007b), 'World city networks from below: international mobility and inter-city relations in the global investment banking industry', in P.J. Taylor, B. Derudder, P. Saey and F. Witlox (eds), *Cities in Globalization: Practices, Policies, Theories*, London: Routledge, pp. 52–71.

Beaverstock, J.V. (2008), 'The globalization and regionalization of executive search firms in Singapore and the Asia-Pacific', *Association of American Geographers Annual Meeting*, Boston, USA, April 2008 (copy available from the author).

Beaverstock, J.V. (2011), 'Servicing British expatriate "talent" in Singapore: exploring ordinary transnationalism and the role of the "expatriate" club', *Journal of Ethnic and Migration Studies*, **37** (5), 709–728.

Beaverstock, J.V. and J.T. Boardwell (2000), 'Negotiating globalization, transnational corporations and global city financial centres in transient migration studies', *Applied Geography*, **20** (3), 227–304.

Bryson, J., P.W. Daniels and B. Warf (2004), *Service Worlds: People, Organizations, Technologies*, London: Routledge.

Castells, M. (2000), *The Rise of the Network Society*, Oxford: Blackwell.

Chang, T.C. (1995), 'The "expatriatisation" of Holland Village', in B. Yeoh and L. Kong (eds), *Portraits of Places: History, Community and Identity in Singapore*, Singapore: Times Editions, pp. 140–157.

Chong, V. (2003), 'Foreign talent policy here to stay: Lee Kuan Yew', *The Business Times*, 19 February. Singapore, available at http://yaleglobal.yale.edu/content/foreign-talent-policy-here-stay-lee-kuan-yew (accessed 14 January 2010).

CNNMoney.com (2009), 'Fortune Global 500' (from 24 July 2006 and 20 July 2009), available at http://money.cnn.com/magazines/fortune/global500/2006/cities/; http://money.cnn.com/magazines/fortune/global 500/2009/cities/ (accessed 19 January 2010).

Cohen, R.B. (1981), 'The new international division of labour, multinational corporations and urban hierarchy', in M. Dear and A.J. Scott (eds), *Urbanization and Urban Planning in Capitalist Society*, London: Methuen, pp. 287–319.

Deloitte (2009) *The Deloitte DDT 2008 Annual Review*, available at www.deloitte.com/annualreview2008 (accessed 11 January 2010).

Economist (2009), 'Singapore and immigration: a PR problem', *The Economist*, 14 November, 73.

Edstrom, A. and J. Galbraith (1977), 'Transfer of managers as a coordination and control strategy in multinational corporations', *Administrative Science Quarterly*, **22** (2), 248–263.

Ewers, M.C. (2007), 'Migrants, markets and multinationals: competition among world cities for the highly skilled', *GeoJournal*, **68** (2–3), 119–130.

Faulconbridge, J.R., J.V. Beaverstock, S. Hall and A. Hewitson (2009), 'The "war for talent": the gatekeeper role of executive search firms in elite labour markets', *Geoforum*, **40** (5), 800–808.

Faulkner, D. (2009), *Transnational Elite Communities in the Global Cities: Expatriate Spaces in Singapore*, Nottingham: University of Nottingham (unpublished BA thesis, available from the author).

Fielding, A. (1992), 'Migration and social mobility: South-East England as an escalator region', *Regional Studies*, **26** (1), 1–15.

Florida, R. (2002), *The Rise of the Creative Class*, New York: Basic Books.

Friedmann, J. (1986), 'The world city hypothesis', *Development and Change*, **17** (1), 69–84.

Gordon, I., T. Travers, C. Whitehead and K. Scanlon (2009), *London's Place in the UK Economy 2009–2010*, London: The Corporation of London.

Harvey, W. (2008), 'British and Indian expatriate scientists finding jobs in Boston', *Global Networks*, **8** (4), 453–473.

HSBC (2009), *HSBC Bank International Expatriate Explorer Survey 2009*, available at www.offshore.hsbc. com/1/PA_1_4_S5/content/international/2g_pdfs/expat/expatresults09.pdf (accessed 15 January 2010).

Hymer, S. (1972), 'The multinational corporation and the law of uneven development', in J.N. Bhagwati (ed.), *Economics and World Order from the 1970s to the 1990s*, New York: Collier-Macmillan, pp. 113–140.

International Financial Services London (2009), *Accounting Services 2009*, available at www.ifsl.org.uk/ output/Research.aspx (accessed 12 January 2010).

Jones, A. (2008), 'The rise of global work', *Transactions of the Institute of British Geographers*, **33** (1), 12–26.

Koser, K. and J. Salt (1997), 'The geography of highly skilled international migration', *International Journal of Population Geography*, **3** (4), 285–303.

Lee, S.-W., D.-W. Song and C. Ducruet (2008), 'A tale of Asia's world ports: the spatial evolution in global port cities', *Geoforum*, **39** (1), 372–385.

Lewis, L. (2008), 'The "little red dot" intent on becoming the hub that Asia cannot live without', *The Times*, 11 October, 64–65.

Lim, R. (2002), 'External challenges facing the economy', in D. De Cunha (ed.), *Singapore in the New Millennium: Challenges Facing the City-State*, Singapore: Institute of South-East Asian Studies, pp. 26–49.

Millar, D. and J. Salt (2008), 'Portfolios of mobility: the movement of expertise in transnational corporations in two sectors – aerospace and extractive industries', *Global Networks*, **8** (1), 25–50.

Ministry of Manpower (2009), *Data Extracted from the Annual Employment Change by Industry*, available at www.mom.gov.sg/publish/momportal/en/communities/others/mrsd/statistics/Employment.html (accessed 19 January 2010).

Mould, O. (2008), 'Moving images: world cities, connections and projects in Sydney's TV production industry', *Global Networks*, **8** (4), 474–495.

Olds, K. (2007), 'Global assemblage: Singapore, foreign universities and the construction of a "global education hub"', *World Development*, **35** (6), 959–975.

Perkins, S.J. (1997), *Internationalization: The People Business*, London: Kogan Page.

Price, M. and L. Benton-Short (2007), 'Immigration and world cities: from the hyper-diverse to the bypassed', *GeoJournal*, **68** (2–3), 103–117.

PricewaterhouseCoopers (2004), *Expatriate Localisation Survey – Singapore 2004*, Singapore: PricewaterhouseCoopers.

PricewaterhouseCoopers (2009), *Global Annual Review 2009 – Global Mobility*, available at www.pwc.com/gx/ en/annual-review/facts-figures/index.jhtml (accessed 11 January 2010).

Sassen, S. (2001), *The Global City: New York, London, Tokyo*, Princeton, NJ: Princeton University Press, 2nd edition.

Sassen, S. (2006), *Cities in a World Economy*, Thousand Oaks, CA: Pine Forge Press, 3rd edition.

Sim, L.L., S.E. Ong, A. Agarwal, A. Parsa and R. Keivani (2003), 'Singapore's competitiveness as a global city: developing strategy, institutions and business environment', *Cities*, **20** (2), 115–127.

Singapore Statistics (2010), *Monthly Digest of Statistics, Singapore December 2009*, available at www.singstat. gov.sg/pubn/reference.html (accessed 15 January 2010).

Sklair, L. (2001), *The Transnational Capitalist Class*, Oxford: Blackwell.

Wigley, R. (2008), *London: Winning in a Changing World. Review of the Competitiveness of London as a Financial Centre*, London: Merrill Lynch Europe Limited.

Yeoh, B.S.A. (2004), 'Cosmopolitanism and its exclusions in Singapore', *Urban Studies*, **41** (12), 2431–2445.

Yeoh, B.S.A. (2006), 'Bifurcated labour: the unequal incorporation of transmigrants in Singapore', *Tijdschrift voor Economische en Sociale Geografie*, **97** (1), 26–37.

Yeoh, B.A.S. and T.C. Chang (2001), 'Globalising Singapore: debating transnational flows in the city', *Urban Studies*, **38** (7) 583–602.

Yeung, H.W.C., J. Poon and M. Perry (2001), 'Towards a regional strategy: the role of regional headquarters of foreign firms in Singapore', *Urban Studies*, **38** (1), 157–183.

Z/Yen (2007), *Global Financial Centres Index 1*, available at www.cityoflondon.gov.uk/Corporation/LGNL_ Services/Business/Business_support_and_advice/Economic_information_and_analysis/GFCI/ (accessed 21 January 2010).

Z/Yen (2009), *Global Financial Centres Index 6*, available at www.cityoflondon.gov.uk/Corporation/LGNL_ Services/Business/Business_support_and_advice/Economic_information_and_analysis/GFCI/ (accessed 21 January 2010).

22 Grasping the spatial paradoxes of finance: theoretical lessons from the case of Amsterdam
Ewald Engelen

INTRODUCTION

Mapping the hierarchy of financial centers is a staid parlor game played by a small number of social scientists. While spatial to the bone, geographers have never succeeded in vesting a monopoly on this topic. In fact, the first post-war scholars interested in the dynamics of financial centers came from economic history. Kindleberger's booklet of 1974 on the rise of financial centers is still the starting point for many scholars (Kindleberger, 1974). And even in the 21st century the most impressive work has come from economic historians such as Cassis (2006) and Michie (2006).

The renewed interest in the fate of financial centers can be traced back to the 'second wave of globalization' that started in the mid 1970s. The effects of globalization 2.0 on the field of geography are hard to overestimate. Without exaggeration one could claim that without it there would have been no neo-Marshallian cluster theory, no rediscovery of industrial districts, no relational geography, no creative industry research as well as no 'World City Hypothesis' in its many manifestations.

In this chapter, I zoom in on recent attempts to come to grips with the spatial dynamics of financial centers, focusing on the spatial paradoxes thrown up by those dynamics. In the next section I give a brief overview of the extant explanations for these dynamics. I end the section with highlighting some problems linked to these explanations. The subsequent section presents the empirical case around which this chapter is construed and explains why the recent fate of Amsterdam serves as a critical case for theory development. The final section embarks upon a theoretical discussion, arguing for theoretical pluralism to do justice to the complexity of the field of finance and the position of financial centers in that field.

EXPLAINING FINANCIAL CENTERS

Cities are as old as the Neolithic revolution. When people shifted to agriculture as their main source of livelihood, they simultaneously discovered the advantages of congregating in larger communities and the division of labor it made possible (Braudel, 1982; Bairoch, 1988; but see Taylor, 2010a, 2010b for an alternative account). The rise of financial centers, though, is closely linked to the incremental development of regional and global trading networks that connected different economies and allowed the processing of surpluses through long distance trade relationships that were managed by traders located in specific urban settings that specialized in providing the infrastructure and networks needed for those managerial tasks (Braudel, 1982; Arrighi, 1994; Cassis, 2006).

While more widespread than suggested by the Eurocentric literature, the European city-state is still the ideal typical example of such a trading center. According to Braudel and Arrighi, the first 'World Cities' developed among a band of European city-states that connected the trading circuits of the North and Baltic seas with the Mediterranean. Cities like Genoa, Amsterdam and, later, London started their careers as centers of physical trade management that over time transformed into the processing of trade contracts and the financial flows linked to those contracts (Cassis, 2006).

The question why some cities developed such specialties while others did not was traditionally answered by highlighting geophysical contingencies. Kindleberger, Cassis and Michie (2006) stress the importance of a natural harbor to develop an entrepôt-function for a larger 'hinterland', on the back of which a specialization in trade finance, shipping finance and insurance could develop. These financial functions, after they reach a certain threshold, may even survive the disappearance of the trading and storing of valuable commodities, and even the complete disappearance of the nearby harbor, as is demonstrated by London, New York and Amsterdam.

A second set of explanation builds on geopolitical observations. Arrighi in particular links the rise and demise of financial centers to the global dominance and hence the size of the 'national' economy in which the financial center is embedded (1994). This suggests a genealogy that has a center start out as coordinator of national trading and capital flows, transform itself into a center that allocates capital over an expanding area as 'national' agents start dominating extra-national economic spaces and back again to the national level as the dominance of those agents starts to wane. In Arrighi's narrative, size is all. Genoa and Amsterdam could only make their claim to world fame in a context of fragmented national economies and underdeveloped nation-states. As soon as England had succeeded in integrating its national markets, its much larger 'hinterland' rapidly turned the British Isles into the Empire of the late 19th/early 20th century, with London as its global control center. The next phase in capitalist history started when the US, after the Civil War, integrated a continent sized economy, generating sufficient returns to serve as the armament manufacturer for the allies during the Second World War. The ensuing 'Empire' quickly developed its own control center, in the form of New York, whose advantage over competitors was built on the back of a large harbor and the trade related financial specializations that required.

Geographers have been much more interested in reproduction over time of financial centers than in their rise (or decline). Reading off from the urban concentration of financial activities underlying causal variables such as dedicated infrastructures, specialized labor markets and the knowledge generating or knowledge dispersing advantages of proximities, economic geographers have simply viewed those centers as cases of neo-Marshallian clusters (Thrift, 1994; Engelen, 2007; Karreman and Van der Knaap, 2009). As such, economic geography clearly starts from the assumption of path dependency, suggesting that decline and change are a theoretical anomaly, especially endogenous change. Less contested is exogenous change, caused by war, geopolitical shifts or technological change. Hence there have been some spatially inclined observers who have claimed that the virtualization and digitalization of trade would lead to despatialization (O'Brien, 1992; Castells, 1996; Cairncross, 1998).

A fourth explanation is provided by New Economic Geography (NEG), an attempt by economists to apply a micro-economic perspective to spatial behavior (Krugman,

1991; Fujita et al., 1999). In this view, clusters are the outcome of individual cost–benefit decisions over where to set up shop. Given an economic universe with friction – that is, in which transactions are costly, contracts are incomplete and markets are not automatically clearing – firms will rationally decide to co-locate. The beauty of this lies not only in parsimony but also in the dynamic theoretical predictions it generates. Due to declining transaction costs and rising co-location costs, location decisions will follow a U-shaped pattern: under conditions of high transaction costs firms will cluster to minimize those costs, while decreasing transaction costs result in dispersal (Grote, 2007).

A final strand of theorizing is known as 'relational geography'. Both Sassen and Taylor claim parenthood to this approach (Sassen, 1991; Taylor, 1997, 2004). While the emphasis is on tracing relations between 'world cities' in order to theorize the contextual dynamics between those cities, the implicit assumption is that urban centers serve as nodes for coordination and control of economic/financial activities in different regionalized economies and hence follow a spatial division of labor. As such, the implicit conceptualization of globalization in the relational approach is one which sees the increasing linkages between 'world cities' located in different regions as reflecting economic development along 'our' historical lines.

EXPLANATORY CAVEATS

While covering a wide variety of aspects, each of these approaches suffers from different explanatory limitations, inviting geographers to break new theoretical territory. The geophysical and geopolitical explanations favored by economic historians are unable to deal with the much stronger historical continuity than their emphasis on exogenous shocks warrants. The top eight financial centers identified by Cassis around 1780 (London, Paris, Amsterdam, Brussels, Frankfurt, Hamburg, Geneva, New York) are still in the top ten more than 200 years later (Cassis, 2006). In other words, decline is never absolute and seems to leave a 'residue' of contacts, expertise and infrastructure which, under precipitous circumstances, does serve as a springboard for new growth.

Initially relational geography was criticized for data deficiency (Short et al., 1996) and its economistic and Eurocentric view of globalization (Robinson, 2002). GaWC was explicitly established by Peter Taylor and collaborators to address these deficiencies (see www.lboro.ac.uk/gawc/index.html). Less discussed is the absence of an explanatory mechanism, resulting in a body of literature that is strong and ingenious in description and operationalization but weaker in explanation and conceptualization. What causes the dynamics between world cities? Why do some decline and others rise relative to one another? Why do linkages between world cities become denser or looser over time? Is it merely an effect of development? Or do we observe new divisions of labor and new modes of interconnectedness coming into existence? Because of its empirical ambitions, relational geography has not developed the theoretical resources to answer these why-questions.

In a curious twist, this is true too for the causal narrative underlying neo-Marshallian cluster theory and NEG. Here the problem is not theoretical humility but the reverse;

a too mechanical application of one causal mechanism to a too complex object. What is cause and what effect? Do firms follow the labor market or vice versa? This is a long standing bone of contention between cluster theorists. The same is true for dedicated institutions. Are they the cause of firm clustering or its effect? If, as empirical research suggests, the causal arrow runs from firm to institution, cluster theory is only able to explain reproduction not the genesis of a cluster. Further causal indecisiveness concerns the underspecified nature of the claim that proximity matters. Co-location is often seen as a proof of the salience of proximity. But there is increasing evidence that in many instances co-located firms do not interact (Kloosterman, 2008; Engelen and Grote, 2009), raising deep and troubling questions about the extent to which causal explanations can be read off from empirical observations. A final unresolved issue is whether it makes sense to reframe location decisions in cost–benefit terms. While intentionality surely plays a role in location decisions, it is bad metaphysics to project it at the cluster as a whole.

Given these caveats, there is a pressing need for more theoretical openness in studies of financial centers. Below, I use data on the Amsterdam financial center to demonstrate that.

THE CASE OF AMSTERDAM

The Amsterdam financial center has strong historical roots which reach back to the 17th century, when, on the back of rapidly developing trading networks and shipping routes, it developed specialties in trade and finance that turned Amsterdam into one big information processing entity (see Lesger, 2001). These linkages, networks and circuits of information processing proved strong enough to withstand large geopolitical and geo-economic shifts (Arrighi, 1994; Cassis, 2006). While its heyday was in the mid 17th century, it lost its position as location of choice for emitting sovereign bonds only at the beginning of the 19th century, after the blockade of its harbors during the Napoleonic wars. Even then, the dormant infrastructure only needed a small dose of pollination, which came in the second half of the century with the 'first wave of globalization' spawned by the 'Hundred year's peace' (Polanyi, 1944).

During the 20th century, Amsterdam underwent the same fits and starts as other European financial centers. Over time, the Netherlands had developed an open, strongly trade oriented economy, harboring a relatively large number of MNCs (Katzenstein, 1985), strong, internationally oriented banks that were managed from Amsterdam based head offices, markets for equities, bonds and derivatives that were unique on the European continent and a pre-funded pension system, as well as the dedicated institutions, specialized labor force and the well developed linkages between financial firms and other producer services identified by cluster theory as crucial (Engelen et al., 2010).

Given these starting conditions, we would have expected a growth trajectory of Amsterdam during the 2000s much in line with developments in other financial centers. In other words, decline after the bursting of the ICT bubble in 2001, strong growth again on the back of the structured finance bubble between 2003 and 2007, followed by a new phase of decline from the outbreak of the crisis.

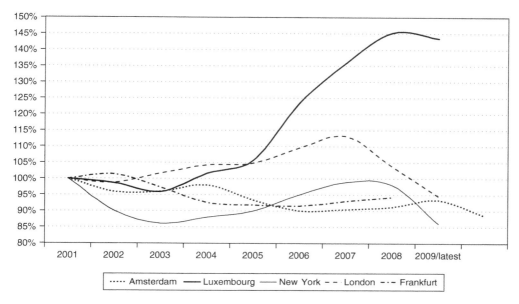

Source: O+S Amsterdam; City of London Corporation; Deutsche Bundesbank; Luxembourg Financial Center

Figure 22.1   Financial service employment in five international financial centers

Disconfirming Observations

The empirics suggest otherwise. First there is the relative drop of Amsterdam on the Global Financial Centres Index, a bi-annual meta-index that was launched in March 2007 by the City of London Corporation. In its first edition, Amsterdam ranked 23rd, just below Dublin (22nd) and Edinburgh (15th) but well above Dubai (25th), Luxembourg (26th) and Brussels (31st) (GFCI, 2007). In the edition of March 2010, Amsterdam reached just number 35, below Luxembourg (10), Dublin (31) and Munich (33), and only just above Brussels (39), suggesting a drop in relative ranking during the bursting of the bubble of 2007 (GFCI, 2010).

A second set of disconfirming observations comes from employment development in the Amsterdam financial center. While the age of 'financialization' brought a dramatic shift in the main sources of value for households, firms and national economies, it did not result in a growing share of financial services in overall employment (Krippner, 2005). Nevertheless, 'financialization' did affect the intra-sectoral and spatial distributions of financial services workers. To put it bluntly: employment decline in retail was largely offset by employment gains in wholesale (investment banking, asset management, proprietary trading), especially in strongly financialized economies.

This is demonstrated by Figure 22.1 that gives indexed employment figures for five financial centers. The biggest winner is Luxembourg, which broke its record of 2001 in 2005 and has since booked strong growth before falling slightly during the crisis. While the pattern of New York and London looks similar – loss on the back of the

2001 crisis, rapid uptake from 2003 onward, strong growth between 2003 and 2007, big losses over the latest crisis – the main difference concerns the size of the 2001 losses; big in New York, slight in London. Frankfurt and Amsterdam betray a different employment pattern. While employment is much less volatile, reflecting the much stronger legal employment protection offered in these countries, what is striking is the absence of any serious rise in employment since the stock market crisis of 2001. While decline in Frankfurt is to be expected, given the adversity of Germany to Anglo-American finance, Amsterdam is located in a strongly financialized national economy and hence should have experienced a growth pattern similar to London and New York. Instead it experienced decline. Why?

Explaining Decline

To answer that question, we need to disaggregate between different segments of the financial services. Since growth is in wholesale financial activities, which, in the Amsterdam context, boils down to trading (exchange related activities), asset management and investment banking, it is these activities that we will zoom in upon.

Trading

As Figure 22.2 demonstrates, Amsterdam has experienced strong losses in employment in exchange related activities. The rapid rise in the second half of the 1990s has turned into its opposite after the 2001 meltdown. The employment trends in trading stand in stark contrast to the revenues earned by the Amsterdam based exchange operator, NYSE Euronext, which over the investment cycle has seen year-on-year increases, mainly because of the rise of daily trades as a result of the growing popularity of automated trading. How come?

During the late 1990s exchanges and their operators underwent a dramatic transformation, with dramatic consequences for some financial centers. Before the 1990s, trade in exchange based financial products took place on physical trading floors, which almost everywhere resulted in concentric location patterns of brokers, banks, and clearing and settlement organizations around the building where the trading floors were located. With the digitization of trading data – the rise of the Bloomberg interface, instant news provision and the launch of the Blackberry smartphone in 1999 – and the dematerialization of shares, bonds and derivative contracts, these physical anchors were gradually lifted. Firms that used to play the physical floor resorted to electronic remote access gates, resulting in an outflow of foreign banks, a merger wave among Dutch brokers, and a movement from the city center to new locations on the outskirts of Amsterdam.

These developments were nested in a wider narrative, of the transformation of equity exchanges from national trading venues to transnational electronic platforms that serve as nodes in a networked flow of digital orders that is currently in the process of fragmenting as a result of the rise of new venues made possible by new regulation (MiFiD in Europe (Posner, 2009)) and new technologies (see Michie, 2006). This is indicated by the strong penetration of foreign investors in Amsterdam. Over 80 percent of shares traded in the secondary equity market are 'owned' by foreign investors, while over 70 percent of all new listings in Amsterdam between 2004 and 2008 were by foreign firms (Engelen and Grote, 2009).

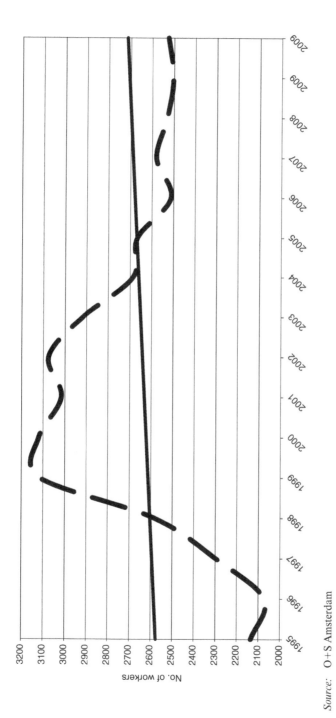

No. of workers

Source: O+S Amsterdam

Figure 22.2 Exchange related employment

Asset management
The employment trend of the Amsterdam asset management industry is even more pronounced. As Figure 22.3 shows, Amsterdam has lost approximately half of its employment in asset management. This trend too appears to be unrelated to the overall investment cycle, although the downward swing since 2008 does suggest some cycle related volatility. So what happened?

The size of employment in asset management is not so much determined by investment opportunities as by the size of the pools of capital to be managed. In the Netherlands the biggest pools of capital by far are those managed by pension funds. Being roughly equal to Dutch GDP these mandatory savings are managed by more than 600 small to very large pension funds, the largest three of which control more than half.

While they used to function as subsidiaries of the budgetary machinery of the Dutch state the largest three public pension funds were privatized in the mid 1990s to grant them access to a larger set of investment opportunities in a context of declining state debt. Initially this spawned a shift from sovereign bonds to shares, traded on the Amsterdam exchange. This generated a surge in transactions for Amsterdam based brokers and asset managers, largely explaining the growth of employment in these two fields of activity in the second half of the 1990s (see Fernandez, 2010). However, as pension funds professionalized they shifted their mandates increasingly to big foreign asset managers like Blackrock, State Street, Barclays and Goldman Sachs. Currently two thirds of Dutch pension savings are managed by Anglo-American asset managers, resulting in a decimation of the Amsterdam asset management industry.

Banking
The employment developments in banking are hardest to interpret, predominantly because banks combine so many different activities. When capital was unleashed in the mid 1970s, banks responded with an unprecedented merger wave, leading to national consolidation and, in the 2000s, hesitant attempts at cross border mergers. In the Netherlands consolidation was actively stimulated by the regulator, who feared that the small size of the Dutch home market would disadvantage Dutch banks in the integrated European banking market to be. According to data from the G10, the Netherlands has one of the most concentrated banking markets; the top five banks have a market share of 76 percent (G10, 2001).

Second, the business model of banking has radically changed over the last decades. ICT has eradicated many routine tasks. The ATM is of course a case in point. In an overbanked country like the Netherlands, this has rapidly shrunk banking networks. While banks still had 6152 branches in 2000, 6 years later that number had declined to 3100 (De Jong, 2009).

Finally, banking has undergone a true 'financial services revolution' since the early 1980s (Moran, 1991). While banks traditionally absorbed excess capital and allocated it to firms and households with capital needs, since finance was unleashed they have increasingly been banking for themselves. This is visible both in their source of funding, which came increasingly from the short term interbank money market (Gorton, 2010), as in their main source of profits, which increasingly came from fees and commissions.

The root cause of this was excessive financial innovation, resulting in an increased hiring of academically trained and highly paid workers, which stood at the cradle of

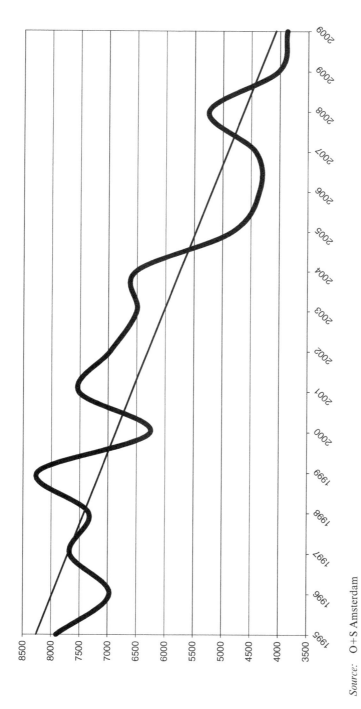

Source: O+S Amsterdam

Figure 22.3 Asset management employment: Amsterdam, 1995–2009 (2nd Q)

the sharply rising income and wealth inequalities in a small number of international financial centers (Duménil and Levy, 2004; Kaplan and Rauh, 2007).

According to OECD data, Dutch banks have undergone similar developments, albeit not to the same extent as UK, US and Swiss banks, suggesting a much milder 'banking revolution' in the Netherlands itself and a similar spatial distribution of fee revenues to Swiss and German banks, that is, nationally based commercial banks with London based investment bank-units generating well over half of total revenues.

How did this affect Amsterdam? As Figure 22.4 demonstrates it is hard to tease out a clear trend from the available employment data. Rapid growth between the mid 1990s and the early 2000s was followed by a steep fall in the wake of the bursting of the ICT bubble in 2001. However, in contrast to trading and asset management, 2003 saw a quick uptake in banking employment. It was only in 2009 that employment started to fall again, mainly due to the takeover and breakup of ABN Amro, resulting in thousands of job losses, especially in its Amsterdam head office (Engelen and Musterd, 2010).

In short, Amsterdam was hit by a triple whammy. First, the retail part of Amsterdam banking experienced similar decline as banking elsewhere, due to labour replacing capital investments in the form of ATMs, automated processing, offshoring and out-sourcing and Internet banking. Moreover, Amsterdam failed to compensate these losses by gains in wholesale employment. Bypassing the Amsterdam financial center, Dutch banks and pension funds tapped directly into the financial networks provided by London. Secondly, Amsterdam, like financial centers elsewhere, was hit by the crisis of 2007–2009. Nevertheless, the marginally smaller employment losses compared with larger financial centers corroborate the claim that most fee revenues were earned in London, not Amsterdam. Finally, Amsterdam was hit by the unique event of the take-over and breakup of ABN Amro, its largest, most ambitious and most interconnected universal bank. While not unrelated to the wave of deregulation that ignited the banking revolution, the takeover and breakup of ABN Amro is still a contingency hard to fit into any theoretical framework.

DISCUSSION

How to make theoretical sense of these different narratives? Neo-Marshallian cluster theory clearly fails. Despite excellent starting conditions, Amsterdam experienced pro-nounced losses of employment in financial services. To frame this in cluster theoretical terms: the centripetal forces of proximity that used to hold the Amsterdam financial center together have clearly lost their powers vis-à-vis London. Both asset management and banking were vulnerable to capture by London based traders, bankers and firms, suggesting a hierarchical financial market structure that is dominated by London and New York, allowing local players to simply bypass smaller national financial centers, which, before the virtualization of finance, used to serve as pipelines between global and national capital circuits.

The second candidate, NEG, at first sight has more to offer. The causal mechanisms stipulated by NEG clearly are at work in the Amsterdam case. Declining transaction and information costs have lowered the threshold for foreign financial service providers to tap Dutch based capital pools, while simultaneously allowing Dutch banks to insert

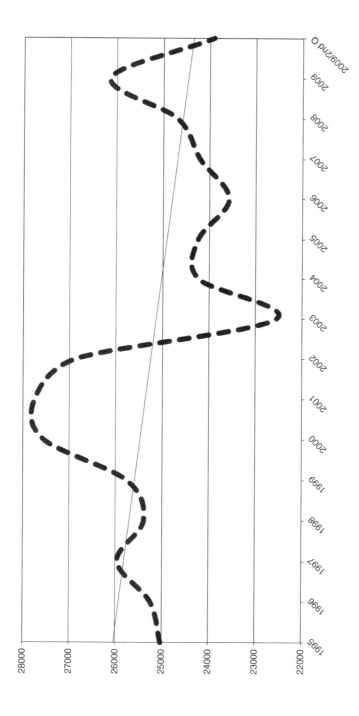

Figure 22.4   Banking employment: Amsterdam, 1995–2009/2nd Q

themselves into foreign networks and expertise elsewhere. Increasing standardization, transparency and deregulation also made comparisons of the value added of the positive externalities generated by proximity in different financial centers more easy. The more flows of capital, firms and expertise left Amsterdam for London, the harder it became for Amsterdam to maintain its position. This is clearly captured by NEG. However, NEG has nothing to say about timing or about the London ability to withstand the centrifugal forces of decreasing transaction and information costs.

Relational geography, the third candidate, has something to offer the Amsterdam case too. The emphasis that relational geography puts upon the proximity of London to Amsterdam in a hierarchically ordered market field clearly is relevant for explaining why Dutch capital pools were increasingly using the London interface to break into global capital flows. Moreover, Dutch banks increasingly resorted to a similar 'satellite' strategy as Swiss and German banks had followed, shifting their wholesale activities lock, stock and barrel to London. This again suggests a 'space of flows' that is hierarchically structured on the back of an internationalizing division of labor, as is stressed by relational geography. That being said, the theoretical caveats mentioned above still stand.

So, in order to explain the Amsterdam case we apparently have to resort to different theoretical perspectives that stress different causal mechanisms and use different data sources and techniques of analysis. In particular, I would like to claim, we need a *comparative* political economy that acknowledges the *cultural turn* (Jessop, 2007) and is able to make sense of institutional unevenness and hybridity (Yeung, 2004; Engelen et al., 2010), of variegated social linkages (Brenner, 2004), of unequally distributed resources and resource coalitions (Helleiner et al., 2009), and of the homogenizing and differentiating effects of shared socio-technical assemblages, devices and discourses (Djelic and Quack, 2007).

Applied to Amsterdam this suggests an historical reconstruction of elite action, informed by political conceptualizations of reality, at the supranational, national and subnational levels. The wave of regulation that kick started the global financial services revolution came from a targeted attempt of a global shadow elite to integrate financial markets (Abdelal, 2007; Wedel, 2009), speed up cross border transactions, shift from pay-as-you-go to prefunded pension systems, enhance the ability of banks to securitize assets, expand the number of products available and speed up financial innovation; projects that were largely informed by a vernacularized version of a body of theory that became known as the Efficient Market Hypothesis and that originated from libertarian scholars based at new US MBAs (Whitley, 1986; MacKenzie, 2006).

These cognitive principles were slowly dispersed over space and were taken up by a growing number of local elites, who used its premises to initiate local changes that were seen to serve their perceived interests, resulting in different forms of hybrid applications of what were seen as universal principles and techniques. Amsterdam was no exception. The Amsterdam financial elite responded to the 'financial services revolution' framed by the Big Bang in London in 1986 with a desperate attempt to transform the conservative, laid back ethos of the Amsterdam financial community into a vibrant pipeline between the US and the European continent. The 1978 derivative exchange was a first attempt at regulatory and organizational renewal. But so were the early initiatives of the Amsterdam broker community to integrate the Amsterdam exchanges, turn the operator into a publicly quoted limited liability corporation, rework itself into a high tech service provider rather than an exchange, and initiate mergers with other European and finally US exchange operators. Together these changes, in a mere decade, have transformed the Amsterdam exchange from a national trading platform into a virtual transnational helicopter platform for mobile capital that is part of a continent crossing conglomerate, namely NYSE Euronext (Fernandez, 2010).

These are the meta-narratives underlying the decline of Amsterdam sketched in this chapter, that we as financial geographers need to tell. There is nothing simple about these narratives, as they betray the fascinating paradoxes of financial spatialities that have been thrown up anew by the financial crisis of 2007–2011. But complexity should not deject us. Rather it is a cue that we are chasing something important and less well understood.

REFERENCES

Abdelal, R. (2007), *Capital Rules: The Construction of Global Finance*, Cambridge, MA: Harvard University Press.

Arrighi, G. (1994), *The Long Twentieth Century: Money, Power, and the Origins of our Time*, London: Verso.

Bairoch, P. (1988), *Cities and Economic Development: From the Dawn of History to the Present*, Chicago: University of Chicago Press.

Braudel, F. (1982), *Civilization and Capitalism, 15th–18th Century. Volume II. The Wheels of Commerce*, London: Fontana Press.

Brenner, N. (2004), *New State Spaces: Urban Governance and the Rescaling of Statehood*, Oxford: Oxford University Press.

Cairncross, F. (1998), *The Death of Distance: How the Communications Revolution will Change our Lives*, London: Orion Business Books.

Cassis, Y. (2006), *Capitals of Capital: A History of International Financial Centres, 1780–2005*, Cambridge: Cambridge University Press.

Castells, M. (1996), *The Information Age: Economy, Society, and Culture. Vol. 1: The Rise of the Network Society*, Oxford: Blackwell.

De Jong, F. (2009), 'Kredietcrisis en tussenpersonen', *ESB* 94, 20 March, pp. 170–172.

Djelic, M.-L. and S. Quack (2007), 'Overcoming path dependency: path generation in open systems', *Theory and Society*, **36** (2), 161–186.

Duménil, G. and D. Levy (2004), *Capital Resurgent: Roots of the Neoliberal Revolution*, Cambridge, MA: Harvard University Press.

Engelen, E. (2007), 'Amsterdamned? The uncertain future of a financial centre', *Environment and Planning A*, **39** (6), 1306–1324.

Engelen, E. and M.H. Grote (2009), 'Stock exchange virtualisation and the decline of second-tier financial centres – the cases of Amsterdam and Frankfurt', *Journal of Economic Geography*, **9** (5), 679–696.

Engelen, E., M. Konings and R. Fernandez (2010), 'Geographies of financialization in disarray; the Dutch case in comparative perspective', *Economic Geography*, **86** (1), 53–73.

Engelen, E. and S. Musterd (2010), 'Amsterdam in crisis: how the (local) state buffers and suffers', *International Journal of Urban and Regional Research*, **34** (3), 701–708.

Fernandez, R. (2010), 'The rise of the global investor and the demise of the local stock exchange: the case of Amsterdam 1970–2008', chapter, Ph.D. thesis, University of Amsterdam.

Fujita, M., P. Krugman and A.J. Venables (1999), *The Spatial Economy – Cities, Regions, and International Trade*, Cambridge and London: MIT Press.

G10 (2001), *Report on Consolidation in the Financial Sector*, Geneva: Bank for International Settlements, available at www.bis.org/publ/gten05.htm (accessed 1 June 2010).

GFCI (2007), *The Global Financial Centres Index, March 2007*, London: Z/Yen/City of London.

GFCI (2010), *The Global Financial Centres Index, March 2010*, London: Z/Yen/City of London.

Gorton, G.B. (2010), *Slapped by the Invisible Hand: The Panic of 2007*, Oxford: Oxford University Press.

Grote, M.H. (2007), 'Foreign banks' attraction to the financial centre of Frankfurt – an inverted "U"-shaped relationship', *Journal of Economic Geography*, **8** (2), 239–258.

Helleiner, E. (1994), *States and the Reemergence of Global Finance: From Bretton Woods to the 1990s*, Ithaca, NY: Cornell University Press.

Helleiner, E., S. Pagliari and H. Zimmermann (eds) (2009), *Global Finance in Crisis: The Politics of International Regulatory Change*, London: Routledge.

Jessop, B. (2007), *State Power: A Strategic Relational Approach*, Cambridge: Polity Press.

Kaplan, S.N. and J. Rauh (2007), 'Wall Street and Main Street: what contributes to the rise in the highest incomes?', *NBER Working Paper*, No. 13270, available at www.nber.org/papers/w13270 (accessed 1 June 2010).

Karreman, B. and B. van der Knaap (2009), 'The financial centres of Shanghai and Hong Kong: competition or complementarity?', *Environment and Planning A*, **41** (3), 563–580.

Katzenstein, P.J. (1985), *Small States in World Markets: Industrial Policy in Europe*, Ithaca, NY: Cornell University Press.

Kindleberger, C.P. (1974), *The Formation of Financial Centers: A Study in Comparative Economic History*, Princeton, NJ: Princeton University Press.

Kloosterman, R.C. (2008), 'Walls and bridges: knowledge spillover between "superdutch" architectural firms', *Journal of Economic Geography*, **8** (4), 545–563.

Krippner, G.R. (2005), 'The financialization of the American economy', *Socio-Economic Review*, **3** (2), 173–208.

Krugman, P. (1991), *Geography and Trade*, Cambridge: MIT Press.

Lesger, C. (2001), *Handel in Amsterdam ten tijde van de Opstand. Kooplieden, Commerciële Expansie en Veranderingen in de Ruimtelijke Economie van de Nederlanden, ca. 1550–ca. 1630*, Hilversum: Verloren.

MacKenzie, D. (2006), *An Engine, Not a Camera. How Financial Models Shape Markets*, Cambridge: MIT Press.

Michie, R. (2006), *The Global Securities Markets: A History*, Oxford: Oxford University Press.

Moran, M. (1991), *The Politics of the Financial Services Revolution: The USA, UK and Japan*, London: Macmillan.

O'Brien, R. (1992), *Global Financial Integration: International Capital Markets in the Age of Reason*, London: The Royal Institute of International Affairs.

Polanyi, K. (1944), *The Great Transformation*, Boston: Beacon Press.

Posner, E. (2009), *The Origins of Europe's New Stock Markets*, Cambridge, MA: Harvard University Press.

Robinson, J. (2002), 'Global and world cities: a view from off the map', *International Journal of Urban and Regional Research*, **26** (3), 531–554.

Ruggie, J.G. (1982), 'International regimes, transactions, and change: embedded liberalism in the postwar economic order', *International Organization*, **36** (2), 379–415.

Sassen, S. (1991), *The Global City: New York, London, Tokyo*, Princeton, NJ: Princeton University Press.

Short, J.R., Y. Kim, M. Kuus and H. Wells (1996), 'The dirty little secret of world cities research: data problems in comparative analysis', *International Journal of Urban and Regional Research*, **20** (4), 697–717.

Taylor, P.J. (1997), 'Hierarchical tendencies amongst world cities: a global research proposal', *Cities*, **14** (6), 323–332.

Taylor, P.J. (2004), *World City Network: A Global Urban Analysis*, London: Routledge.

Taylor, P.J. (2010a), 'Extraordinary cities I: early "city-ness" and the invention of agriculture', *GaWC Research Bulletin*, 359, available at www.lboro.ac.uk/gawc/rb/rb359.html (accessed 5 September 2010).

Taylor, P.J. (2010b), 'Extraordinary cities II: early "city-ness" and the invention of states', *GaWC Research Bulletin*, 360, available at www.lboro.ac.uk/gawc/rb/rb360.html (accessed 5 September 2010).

Thrift, N. (1994), 'On the social and cultural determinants of international financial centres: the case of the City of London', in S. Corbridge, N. Thrift and R. Martin (eds), *Money, Power and Space*, Oxford: Blackwell, pp. 327–355.

Wedel, J. (2009), *Shadow Elite: How the World's New Power Brokers Undermine Democracy, Government, and the Free Market*, New York: Basic Books.

Whitley, R. (1986), 'The rise of modern finance: its characteristics as a scientific field and connections to the changing structure of capital markets', *Research in the History of Economic Thought and Methodology*, **4**, 147–178.

Yeung, H.W.-C. (2004), *Chinese Capitalism in a Global Era: Towards Hybrid Capitalism*, London: Routledge.

23 The cultural economy and the global city
Andy C. Pratt

INTRODUCTION

The aim of this chapter is to examine the relationship between the cultural economy and the global city; it considers the conceptual as well as empirical aspects of the relationship. Implicitly, work on the global city considers culture: in fact one may go so far as to say that culture is presumed in the global city. This presumption has tended to render culture (in its broadest sense) either invisible to analysis, or positioned it in a dualistic relation to the 'real deal': the economic. Such a dualistic relationship is not presented as equal; culture is implicitly or explicitly rendered in all its forms as inferior or dependent: traditional modalities of economic analysis simply harden such conceptions. The empirical focus on the 'power of finance' that characterizes much work on the global city, directly or indirectly, further intensifies the problem. This chapter does not seek to recover all of culture with respect to the global city; instead it focuses upon one particular aspect: arguably the most troubling one, the cultural economy. However, if anything will trouble, or destabilize the relationship between the economy and culture then it is likely to be the cultural economy.

GLOBAL CITIES AND CULTURE

Culture figures as a significant but relatively minor aspect of debates about global cities. In its simplest form the city is represented as backdrop: heritage and cultural artefact that visitors can consume. Much of recent debate has been how to manage the city to maximize tourist income, and minimize adverse and degrading impact (Judd and Fainstein, 1999; Ashworth and Tunbridge, 2000). It is clear that in this sense, the city is a site for consumption of heritage, with a huge hope that visitors will leave behind foreign currency in the form of purchased goods and services.

More central to the global cities debate is a more complex form of cultural representation activity. On the one hand we can point to the seminal work of Anthony King (1989, 1995, 2004) that has been a significant outlier highlighting both the power of culture and representation, especially through the means of architecture and design, as well as questioning the articulation of colonial and imperial power and place. King's work has without doubt opened up the analyses of global cities to those of the global South, as well as tracing their cultural lineages to the old Northern hemisphere city power bases, and to the recursive impacts of both (see also writers such as Simon (1989), McGee (1995), Hannerz (1996), Smith (2001), Pieterse (2004)); and the significance of the cosmopolitanism, creolization and hybridization of culture and the city.

On the other hand, there is a significant body of work that attends to the marketing and selling of cities to attract foreign direct investment (FDI). It is a well documented, and increasingly important way in which cities have sought to project themselves, or maintain their position as global cities. A large literature now plots the different trends and practices in this essentially zero-sum game. Increasingly cultural activities have played a role in place marketing and place branding for both tourist purposes and those of attracting FDI. Major cultural events, world events (such as the Olympic Games or the World Cup) have become embroiled in a globalization of culture and sport, place marketing and place promotion (Hall and Hubbard, 1998; Short and Kim, 1998; Short, 2008). The 'Guggenheim effect' is a hoped for visibility and tourist boom achieved by the establishment of the franchise of the popular art gallery in a location (Plaza, 1999, 2000, 2006). There is of course, in all cases, a significant debate about the possibility of the sustainability of such investments, let alone their (lack of) social redistribution effects (see for example Zukin, 1982, 1995). Culture and the city, especially the global city, are close companions. A further iteration to this argument is provided by Richard Florida's (2002, 2004, 2005, 2008) notion of the creative city, essentially a cultural consumption 'honey trap' for a particular labour pool; which it is hoped will attract employers seeking out this labour.

There are many questions that can be raised here about implicit assumptions and the direction of causality. Specifically that culture attracts other activities: in effect it is a 'loss leader' as it is assumed that the 'real investment' – financial services, or any mobile investment attracted by the improved quality of life registered with each new cultural investment – will follow and hence create the jobs and economic income. And/or any demand for cultural goods will be *derived* from the 'real economy'. The core assumption here is that culture is secondary and dependent: it will not generate activity or income on its own, let alone any secondary activity. It is a doubly-dependent 'service service'.

However, as I will note below, this is not the whole story, and it is a partial representation of the contribution of culture to the global city, in particular the role of the cultural economy. The cultural economy is one of the fastest growing segments of the economy, in particular urban economies and especially global cities. Perhaps the global city economy has just grown so much that it can sustain so much culture; or perhaps the cultural economy is developing in its own semi-autonomous way: commentators do not seem to know which; in part this is a conceptual confusion. One way in which the cultural economy could be 'bolted on' to existing conceptualizations of the global city would be to characterize it as a (new) advanced producer service (APS). Indeed, the existing literature on APSs and the global city would support this, in particular seeing advertising as a regular APS; moreover, this has been extended to 'media' as well. This chapter takes this challenge seriously; it considers the case for the cultural economy as an advanced APS and evaluates the adequacy of this framework for future research. We begin with clarification of what is understood by the notion of the cultural economy.

THE CULTURAL ECONOMY

I have adopted a general usage of the term 'cultural economy' in this chapter: namely the economy of cultural products and services (Pratt, 2009a). This meaning should be differentiated from those definitions that exclusively deal with textual production (see Hesmondhalgh, 2002), or those that focus on the cultural aspects of economic action, or a cultural analysis of the (cultural) economy (see Amin and Thrift, 2004). Specifically, I draw on the lineage of work of French communications studies writers who coined the term 'the cultural industries'. A term that differentiates itself from the singular, and narrowly commodified referent, derived from Adorno's work.

In particular the notion of plural and differentiated cultural industries has been articulated with notions of production networks and production chains (Pratt, 1997). This gives the concept considerable 'depth': that is, running across the process of cultural or creative idea, through prototype and mass production, or simply manufacture, to distribution and consumption. This is complemented by the multiplicity of industries: the breadth of scope from fine art, to film and music, to computer games and sport. Analytically, there are two important issues to acknowledge in this formulation: first, that it is focused on process not simply outputs; second, that it transcends the traditional analytical boundaries of formal–informal, production–consumption and commercial–non-commercial. Superficially, there is much confusion over terminology which has specific political and policy nuances: however, the term 'cultural economy' as deployed here covers popular usage of the cultural industries, creative industries and creative economy.

Using an analytical approach now codified by UNESCO (2009) it is possible to collate employment and value added data on the cultural economy at both a national and urban scale. Analysts have been surprised to note that the rate of increase in activity in the cultural economy is outstripping that of the rest of the economy; moreover, that in some places it is becoming a more significant employer and economic actor than traditional manufacturing industries (DCMS, 2001; KEA European Affairs, 2006; UNCTAD, 2008). One of the characteristics of the cultural economy is the extent to which it is an urban, and a global city, phenomenon (Scott, 2000). For example, analyses from one global city, London, showed that in the early years of the 21st century the cultural economy was the third largest component of the economy (GLA Economics, 2002, 2004). Thus the question we now need to address is: what relation does the cultural economy have to the global city? Should it be added to the list of APSs; or does it have a different relationship?

ADVANCED PRODUCER SERVICES

As Sassen (2001, chapter 6) crisply summarizes, the relationship between global cities and producer services rests on three legs. First, the dispersal of production from the economic and spatial core. Secondly, the functional and spatial concentration of management and regulation functions; a process that itself has agglomeration effects. Thirdly, that services have a role in transforming economic activity more generally, and the concentration of such expertise favours those cities and regions where it is located. The literature on global cities suggests that the financial sector, or Sassen's FIRE industries (Finance, Insurance and Real Estate), are the core of the advanced producer services. Two questions fall out of this argument relevant to both London and the media: first, which industries comprise the advanced producer services; second, are there specific intra-regional locational factors for the advanced producer services?

Strictly speaking, advanced producer services provide critical intermediation between production and consumption (Marshall and Wood, 1995), or the extension of production into consumption (Walker, 1985). Beyond the FIRE group the usual list includes accountancy and management consultants, plus design and advertising (Beaverstock et al., 2000); additionally Sassen (2001) cautiously points to new media, and Krätke (2003, 2006; Krätke and Taylor, 2004) to media.

The general notion of producer services' role in economic development is underpinned by the assumption of their role as intermediaries between consumer services and manufacturing. Indeed, they are viewed in the world cities literature as 'basing points' (spatial and organizational) for the global economy. Such an argument implies evidence of interaction rather than simply location, or function.

Thus the research hypothesis points to the need to explore the balance of internal trade and linkages to external ones, with the expectation that the latter is more important than the former. Second, that one might find dependent producer services that provide inputs to local production (for local or global markets). If we consider the case of the cultural industries we may expect three types of finding. First, that they are dependent on local up-stream production links, or, second, that they are nodes in an international production system. Third, that they are simply dependent on the growth in consumer spending of the city. Only in the second case might the cultural industries be classified as advanced producer services.

In terms of the general literature on advanced producer services the picture is not very clear. Coe and Townsend (Coe, 1998; Coe and Townsend, 1998) examining producer services in the Outer Metropolitan Area of London failed to identify linkages at the local level, or strong local social networks (see also Gordon and McCann, 2000). In some ways, this might be expected, as the London region is being characterized as a global city location in, and with, which international linkages are critical. This is an argument that does not concur with the general literature on agglomeration economies that are sometimes used in tandem to support the nature and location of industries (or services) in global cities. Agglomeration economies imply economies of scale and minimization of transactions costs (usually associated with movement of goods, but sometimes of 'untraded' knowledge 'spillovers') (Amin and Thrift, 1992, 1994; Storper, 1997). Thus if there are few inter-linkages apparent then agglomeration economies would appear not to be the prime explanation of clustering.

On the other hand, numerous studies of aspects of the financial services suggest a rich social and cultural embeddedness, despite the shift to on-line trading activity (Amin and Thrift, 1992; Leyshon and Thrift, 1997; McDowell, 1997). There is evidence that perhaps financial services are different from other advanced producer services. However, Sassen (2001, p. 147) makes the important point – in particular in the case of media activities – that further differences *within* producer services may be confounding such analyses. Thus the cultural economy may also be a special case that is not covered by the general theory.

THE CULTURAL ECONOMY AS AN EXCEPTION

There are a couple of *a priori* reasons for expecting a degree of exceptionalism in the position of the cultural economy in global cities. First, that culture covers many activities from film, to radio, television and new media; they all have different regulatory and organizational dynamics, as well as unique markets. Second, it is difficult to conceive of exactly in which way cultural activities are an 'intermediate' service, and for what?

One might, for example, make such a case for advertising being an intermediate stage between producers and consumers; indeed, it is a paradigmatic advanced producer service of world cities. However, research on the organization of advertising shows clearly that it does not conform to a Hymer-like organizational form (Hymer, 1976). Although it has an international presence and networks, it is in fact strongly bounded by national markets. Moreover, the organizational structure is that of triple agency structures in each market place (so that firms can 'compete' against one another in single product markets. If an agency cannot act for a product's competitors in an oligopolistic market it must limit its potential share). Furthermore, advertising agencies have a relatively vertically disintegrated practice (Grabher, 2002; Pratt, 2006). A second line of argument has been explored recently by researchers looking at the locational clustering of advertising in cities; here organizational forms, especially the preponderance of project working and project companies, have given rise to strong co-locational benefits in competition for labour (Grabher, 2001, 2004). In addition, there is also evidence, echoing that of the financial services, of local knowledge and reputation playing an important role in labour market and firm participation in networks. In this case these agencies are 'world class' but may be physically small and not a member of one of the five big advertising 'groups' (Pratt, 2006).

In a second example film might be assumed to fit the paradigmatic case well. However, generally film production comes from an individual source, Hollywood for example, and is distributed internationally (see Scott, 2005). There is a stronger case for film to be seen more as equivalent to manufacture, with the distributors playing the role of local service agents. Within the industrial model of film there has been considerable debate about the relocation of film production (so-called runaway production). But once again, one has to look closely at the film value chain for evidence of the significant and vital added value of post-production as opposed to location shooting work (Shiel and Fitzmaurice, 2001; Pratt, 2007). Again, in the case of film it is difficult to see the model of advanced producer services, or a simply dependent activity on urban consumption growth.

Recent work by Coe has highlighted the local *and* global nature of film production networks (Coe, 2000a, 2000b, 2001). Bathelt and colleagues (Bathelt et al., 2004; Bathelt, 2005) refer to it as local buzz and global pipelines. There is a sense in which cities are being 'basing points' for an international industry as the APS argument suggests, but the social relations of the organization of production (at both a micro- and a macro-scale) are very uneven and complex, and certainly seldom equate with the head/branch office ideal type of a trans-national corporation.

Finally, we can turn to a third example, that of new media. There have been remarkably few studies of the location and operation of new media work, much of the literature focusing on the (disproven) hypothesis of the footloose and virtual character of the industry (Pratt, 2000; Hutton, 2004; Indergaard, 2004). Again, what is striking is the distinctive and strong clustering effect in a few cities – mainly global – across the world. Clearly, new media products are not those that suffer from large transport costs, and hence a major argument for urban agglomeration is undermined. Research has again pointed to significant labour market issues, work organization (project working), and the significant knowledge exchange, reputation and networking of workers (Grabher,

2002; Jarvis and Pratt, 2006; Pratt, 2006). In the case of London, for example, world city hypotheses would see new media as dependent on the financial services and hence sub-contractors for those industries. The research evidence does not support such an interpretation, with companies *not* trading with financial services, but leading a transformation of the media sector, a role that has helped to maintain London's position in these markets (Pratt, 2009b).

Thus we are led to the conclusion that media, and other cultural economies, may have a *relatively autonomous* role in global cities. It is certainly questionable that the cultural industries are simply dependent. The evidence suggests that the cultural industries may in fact play a more 'propulsive' role. As Sassen (2001, p. 148) observes, 'it is yet another instantiation of the importance of agglomeration effects and the more complex notion of place as crucial to the most advanced sectors of our economies'. The media, and broader cultural industries, are global but local; they are services but require and mediate production of intellectual property and an infrastructure (playback equipment) that stimulates manufacturing. In this relatively autonomous sense it seems reasonable to hypothesize that media and the cultural industries more generally do indeed have local linkages linked to specific social and labour market factors. Moreover, that their role and import cannot be adequately captured by trade alone.

THE CULTURAL ECONOMY AND THE GLOBAL CITY REVISITED

The evidence with respect to the cultural economy does suggest that the APS/Global City hypothesis is not entirely applicable to all parts/industries that comprise the cultural economy; we have to agree with Sassen's judgement that the relationship is a more complex one.

Foremost of the complexities is the relationship between production and consumption (Pratt, 2004), and whether it makes conceptual sense to separate them out into 'services' and 'manufacture' as they are clearly related. Recent work on the nature and organization of production (see Hippel, 2005), especially in respect to innovation, has highlighted the co-construction of both production and consumption, hence questioning the notion of a simple one-way dependency (that underpins much urban economics from Economic Base Analysis onwards). The example of the cultural industries is perhaps a more complex case than others, but it certainly points up some weaknesses of such normative and generic conceptualization and measurement of industrial activities. This problem is being resolved at least in the case of the cultural economy. However, statistical output measures are only the first step in this analysis: the greater impact will be found in qualitative and network analyses.

Research has pointed to two spatial dilemmas of the cultural industries. First, they are not evenly distributed across the world, or cities, but are in fact concentrated in a small number (many, but not all, of which are world cities); moreover, they are concentrated in particular neighbourhoods of these cities. As noted above, researchers have pointed to the complex embodied nature of cultural labour markets and the role of knowledge exchange, fast turnover and extreme competition (Gill and Pratt, 2008; Pratt and Jeffcutt, 2009). Added to this is the complex organizational character of many cultural industries. First, that there are significant differences within organization of production; and second, of the institutional forms of cultural industry markets. Thus it is difficult to make generalizations and more attention might be paid to particular industries.

Furthermore, it is one of the characteristics of the cultural industries that they are heavily concentrated in the hands of a few trans-national companies which are able to generate huge monopoly profits (Hesmondhalgh, 2002); this is counterbalanced by a myriad of often self-employed content creators. Clearly this particular hierarchical structure has an impact on the location of cultural industries in world cities.

A further complicating factor is the fact that global city and advanced producer services roles are based upon a Hymer model, with clear vertical integration and hierarchy in decision making such that there is a clear division between 'control' and 'production' functions. It is clear that divisions of this character do exist in the cultural industries but they are complex, obscured and sometimes dominated by other factors. The first aspect of this is the very tight feedback between production and consumption, and control and production, that may reduce the possibility or effectivity of governing at a distance. The preponderance of social networks and close coupling of cultural industries are evidence of this (Bathelt et al., 2004; Storper and Venables, 2004; Asheim et al., 2007). The second aspect is that many cultural industries are regulated (either in terms of distribution, sale or intellectual property) on the basis of national markets. Thus the particular forms of national market may require a different degree of participation and autonomy from producers.

This leads us back to a critical point: can we see the cultural economy as an intermediate or dependent service? This is clearly an issue for further work; however, we raise the issue here as it is germane to the role that different industries, such as those of the cultural economy, play in global cities. As we have noted, this is an increasingly pertinent question as the cultural sector plays a greater role in urban and international economies.

These issues touch not only on basic economic models, but also policy making. The role of cultural economy in world cities has thus far either been relatively neglected or relegated to a support role. As noted above, the cultural economy is empirically important in many cities. However, policy makers are still primarily engaged in a debate and policy formation around the notion of cultural economy as peripheral or dependent; or as a 'honey pot' with which to attract key labour or prestigious investment. What we are seeing is that the cultural sector can be used in this way, and without a doubt does play such a role. However, it is not the *only one*, and perhaps in some cities it is not the most important one.

This new role concerns the economic vitality of the cultural economy. Here it becomes more important than ever to examine the relationships that flow in both directions between the APS and the cultural sector. Moreover, we need to further examine the nature, organization and functioning of the cultural economy as distinctive industries rather than as instruments of a social or economic multiplier. The implication is a thorough re-conceptualization and analysis of the cultural industries, their role and locational characteristics (locally and globally).

In particular, analyses will have to move beyond measuring co-location and into measuring flows not only of material goods, but of non-material and un-traded knowledge. This is a challenging research agenda. This will involve a more subtle analysis of the processes and outputs of the sector, the changing markets and institutions (as well as the diversity within the sector).

CONCLUSION

Whereas initial analyses characterized the cultural economy as one that stood between city and economy, or represented the city to the world, now we can see that the cultural economy is developing into a more hybrid and complex relationship with the city, and to the global city in particular. Specifically, in this chapter we have interrogated the notion of the cultural economy, and the industries that comprise it, as being advanced producer services.

The challenge to analysts of global cities is to keep up with such empirical changes, and to adopt new and more appropriate lenses and tools to register them adequately. One salient example that was touched upon in this chapter concerned the 'non-Hymer' organizational forms of the cultural economy. Hence the use of analytical tools that register headquarters and connectivity may miss some important issues. The complex organizational forms, the multiple outsourcing, temporary firms, and working across and outside firms are just as challenging as the economic forms that Hymer sought to capture in an earlier manifestation of globalization. Tracing the actions and flows of the cultural economy is very complex; the flows of ideas and concepts are even more difficult to trace than the flows of finance. However, the cultural economy can no longer be ignored. As we have shown, in many places it is one of the fastest growing providers of jobs and income: the cultural economy is clearly transforming the global city. It is important that we don't miss this profound change by either looking in the wrong place or not using sufficiently sensitive tools.

REFERENCES

Amin, A. and N. Thrift (1992), 'Neo-Marshallian nodes in global networks', *International Journal of Urban and Regional Research*, **16** (4), 571–587.

Amin, A. and N. Thrift (1994), *Globalization, Institutions, and Regional Development in Europe*, Oxford: Oxford University Press.

Amin, A. and N. Thrift (eds) (2004), *The Blackwell Cultural Economy Reader*, Oxford: Blackwell.

Asheim, B., L. Coenen and J. Vang (2007), 'Face-to-face, buzz, and knowledge bases: sociospatial implications for learning, innovation, and innovation policy', *Environment and Planning C: Government and Policy*, **25** (5), 655–670.

Ashworth, G.J. and J.E. Tunbridge (2000), *The Tourist-Historic City: Retrospect and Prospect of Managing the Heritage City*, Amsterdam and Oxford: Pergamon.

Bathelt, H. (2005), 'Cluster relations in the media industry: exploring the "distanced neighbour" paradox in Leipzig', *Regional Studies*, **39** (1), 105–127.

Bathelt, H., A. Malmberg and P. Maskell (2004), 'Clusters and knowledge: local buzz, global pipelines and the process of knowledge creation', *Progress in Human Geography*, **28** (1), 31–56.

Beaverstock, J.V., R.G. Smith, P.J. Taylor, D.R.F. Walker and H. Lorimer (2000), 'Globalization and world cities: some measurement methodologies', *Applied Geography*, **20** (1), 43–63.

Coe, N.M. (1998), 'Exploring uneven development in producer service sectors: detailed evidence from the computer service industry in Britain', *Environment and Planning A*, **30** (11), 2041–2068.

Coe, N.M. (2000a), 'On location: American capital and the local labour market in the Vancouver film industry', *International Journal of Urban and Regional Research*, **24** (1), 79–94.

Coe, N.M. (2000b), 'The view from out West: embeddedness, inter-personal relations and the development of an indigenous film industry in Vancouver', *Geoforum*, **31** (4), 391–407.

Coe, N.M. (2001), 'A hybrid agglomeration? The development of a satellite-Marshallian industrial district in Vancouver's film industry', *Urban Studies*, **38** (10), 1753–1775.

Coe, N.M. and A.R. Townsend (1998), 'Debunking the myth of localized agglomerations: the development of a regionalized service economy in South-East England', *Transactions of the Institute of British Geographers*, **23** (3), 385–404.

DCMS (2001), *Creative Industries Mapping Document*, London: Department of Culture, Media and Sport.

Florida, R.L. (2002), *The Rise of the Creative Class and how it's Transforming Work, Leisure, Community and Everyday Life*, New York, NY: Basic Books.

Florida, R.L. (2004), *Cities and the Creative Class*, London: Routledge.

Florida, R.L. (2005), *The Flight of the Creative Class: The New Global Competition for Talent*, New York: Collins.

Florida, R.L. (2008), *Who's Your City? How the Creative Economy is Making Where to Live the Most Important Decision of Your Life*, New York: Basic Books.

Gill, R.C. and A.C. Pratt (2008), 'In the social factory? Immaterial labour, precariousness and cultural work', *Theory, Culture & Society*, **25** (7–8), 1–30.

GLA Economics (2002), *Creativity: London's Core Business*, London: Greater London Authority.

GLA Economics (2004), *Measuring Creativity: 2004 Update of the GLA's Creative Industry Economic Data*, London: Greater London Authority.

Gordon, I.R. and P. McCann (2000), 'Industrial clusters: complexes, agglomeration and/or social networks?', *Urban Studies*, **37** (3), 513–532.

Grabher, G. (2001), 'Locating economic action: projects, networks, localities, institutions', *Environment and Planning A*, **33** (8), 1329–1331.

Grabher, G. (2002), 'The project ecology of advertising: tasks, talents and teams', *Regional Studies*, **36** (3), 245–262.

Grabher, G. (2004), 'Learning in projects, remembering in networks? Communality, sociality, and connectivity in project ecologies', *European Urban and Regional Studies*, **11** (2), 103–123.

Hall, T. and P. Hubbard (1998), *The Entrepreneurial City: Geographies of Politics, Regime, and Representation*, New York: Wiley.

Hannerz, U. (1996), *Transnational Connections: Culture, People, Places*, London: Routledge.

Hesmondhalgh, D. (2002), *The Cultural Industries*, London: Sage.

Hippel, E.V. (2005), *Democratizing Innovation*, Cambridge, MA and London: MIT Press.

Hutton, T.A. (2004), 'Post-industrialism, post-modernism and the reproduction of Vancouver's central area: retheorising the 21st-century city', *Urban Studies*, **41** (10), 1953–1982.

Hymer, S. (1976), *The International Operations of National Firms: A Study of Foreign Direct Investment*, Cambridge, MA: MIT Press.

Indergaard, M. (2004), *Silicon Alley: The Rise and Fall of a New Media District*, New York: Routledge.

Jarvis, H. and A.C. Pratt (2006), 'Bringing it all back home: the extensification and "overflowing" of work: the case of San Francisco's new media households', *Geoforum*, **37** (3), 331–339.

Judd, D.R. and S.S. Fainstein (1999), *The Tourist City*, New Haven, CT: Yale University Press.

KEA European Affairs (2006), *The Economy of Culture in Europe*, Brussels: European Commission DG5.

King, A.D. (1989), *Global Cities: Post-imperialism and the Internationalisation of London*, London: Routledge.

King, A.D. (1995), *Re-presenting the City: Ethnicity, Capital and Culture in the Twenty-First Century Metropolis*, Basingstoke: Macmillan.

King, A.D. (2004), *Spaces of Global Cultures: Architecture, Urbanism, Identity*, London: Routledge.

Krätke, S. (2003), 'Global media cities in a world-wide urban network', *European Planning Studies*, **11** (6), 605–629.

Krätke, S. (2006), 'Global media cities: major nodes of globalizing culture and media industries', in N. Brenner and R. Keil (eds), *The Global Cities Reader*, London: Routledge, pp. 325–331.

Krätke, S. and P.J. Taylor (2004), 'A world geography of global media cities', *European Planning Studies*, **12** (4), 459–478.

Leyshon, A. and N. Thrift (1997), *Money/Space: Geographies of Monetary Transformation*, London and New York: Routledge.

Marshall, J.N. and P.A. Wood (1995), *Services and Space: Key Aspects of Urban and Regional Development*, Harlow: Longman.

McDowell, L. (1997), *Capital Culture: Gender at Work in the City*, Oxford and Malden, MA: Blackwell.

McGee, T. (1995), 'Eurocentrism and geography: reflections on Asian urbanisation', in J. Crush (ed.), *Power of Development*, London: Routledge, pp. 192–211.

Pieterse, J. (2004), *Globalization and Culture: Global Mélange*, Lanham, MD and Oxford: Rowman & Littlefield.

Plaza, B. (1999), 'The Guggenheim–Bilbao Museum effect: a reply to Maria V. Gomez' reflective images: the case of urban regeneration in Glasgow and Bilbao', *International Journal of Urban and Regional Research*, **23** (3), 589–592.

Plaza, B. (2000), 'Guggenheim museum's effectiveness to attract tourism', *Annals of Tourism Research*, **27** (4), 1055–1058.

Plaza, B. (2006), 'The return on investment of the Guggenheim Museum Bilbao', *International Journal of Urban and Regional Research*, **30** (2), 452–467.

Pratt, A.C. (1997), 'The cultural industries production system: a case study of employment change in Britain, 1984–91', *Environment and Planning A*, **29** (11), 1953–1974.
Pratt, A.C. (2000), 'New media, the new economy and new spaces', *Geoforum*, **31** (4), 425–436.
Pratt, A.C. (2004), 'The cultural economy: a call for spatialized "production of culture" perspectives', *International Journal of Cultural Studies*, **7** (1), 117–128.
Pratt, A.C. (2006), 'Advertising and creativity, a governance approach: a case study of creative agencies in London', *Environment and Planning A*, **38** (10), 1883–1899.
Pratt, A.C. (2007), 'Imagination can be a damned curse in this country: material geographies of filmmaking and the rural', in R. Fish (ed.), *Cinematic Countrysides*, Manchester: Manchester University Press, pp. 127–146.
Pratt, A.C. (2009a), 'Cultural economy', in R. Kitchen and N. Thrift (eds), *International Encylopedia of Human Geography (Volume 2)*, Oxford: Elsevier, pp. 407–410.
Pratt, A.C. (2009b), 'Urban regeneration: from the arts "feel good" factor to the cultural economy: a case study of Hoxton, London', *Urban Studies*, **46** (5–6), 1041–1061.
Pratt, A.C. and P. Jeffcutt (eds) (2009), *Creativity, Innovation and the Cultural Economy*, London: Routledge.
Sassen, S. (2001), *The Global City: New York, London, Tokyo*, Princeton, NJ: Princeton University Press.
Scott, A.J. (2000), *The Cultural Economy of Cities: Essays on the Geography of Image-Producing Industries*, London: Sage.
Scott, A.J. (2005), *On Hollywood: The Place, the Industry*, Princeton, NJ: Princeton University Press.
Shiel, M. and T. Fitzmaurice (eds) (2001), *Cinema and the City: Film and Urban Societies in a Global Context*, Oxford: Blackwell.
Short, J.R. (2008), 'Globalization, cities and the Summer Olympics', *City*, **12** (3), 321–340.
Short, J.R. and Y.-K. Kim (1998), 'Urban crises/urban representations: selling the city in difficult times', in P. Hall and P. Hubbard (eds), *The Entrepreneurial City: Geographies of Politics, Regime and Representation*, London: John Wiley and Sons, pp. 55–75.
Simon, D. (1989), 'Colonial cities, postcolonial Africa and the world economy: a reinterpretation', *International Journal of Urban and Regional Research*, **13** (1), 68–91.
Smith, M.P. (2001), *Transnational Urbanism: Locating Globalization*, Malden, MA and Oxford: Blackwell.
Storper, M. (1997), *The Regional World: Territorial Development in a Global Economy*, New York: Guilford Press.
Storper, M. and A.J. Venables (2004), 'Buzz: face-to-face contact and the urban economy', *Journal of Economic Geography*, **4** (4), 351–370.
UNCTAD (2008), *The Creative Economy Report*, Geneva and New York: UNCTAD/ UNDP.
UNESCO Institute for Statistics (2009), *Framework for Cultural Statistics*, Paris: UNESCO.
Walker, R.A. (1985), 'Is there a service economy? The changing capitalist division of labor', *Science & Society*, **49** (1), 42–83.
Zukin, S. (1982), *Loft Living: Culture and Capital in Urban Change*, Baltimore, MD: Johns Hopkins University Press.
Zukin, S. (1995), *The Cultures of Cities*, Cambridge, MA: Blackwell.

24 Starchitects, starchitecture and the symbolic capital of world cities
Paul Knox

One of the consequences of contemporary globalization has been a transformation of the structural composition of architectural practice. Following an increasingly international clientele, more and more firms have developed a global portfolio of design work. Some of them are transnational corporations in their own right, huge architecture and engineering ('A&E') firms that have grown from what Robert Gutman (1988), in his pioneering study of the sociology of architecture, called 'strong delivery firms', commercial firms that rarely win awards but build a great deal. Others have grown from what he called 'strong-service firms', practices that are design-oriented but business-centred. A third group of global practices consists of what Gutman called 'strong-idea firms'. Some of these strong-idea firms are now global brand names within the industry, and a few of them have senior partners whose individual celebrity and marketability have made them rich and famous: they are 'starchitects' (McNeill, 2005).

These celebrity architects and their product – 'starchitecture' – must be understood in the context of contemporary processes of globalization and the political economy of globalizing cities (Jencks, 2005). Leslie Sklair (2005) emphasizes the role of various fractions of what he calls the 'transnational capitalist class'. Specifically, these fractions include politicians and bureaucrats at all levels of administrative power and responsibility (who actually decide what gets built where and how changes to the built environment are regulated) and a consumer-oriented fraction (retailers and media responsible for the marketing and consumption of architecture), as well as distinctive class fractions drawn from architecture and affiliated design professions with an international clientele. These key groups, in turn, operate within complex global networks and sub-networks of businesses, non-profit organizations and governments. They also operate within – and contribute to – a globalized consumption-, celebrity- and brand-oriented culture and a neoliberal political economy.

CONSUMPTION, CELEBRITY AND ARCHITECTURE

Campbell (1987) has written of the 'spirit of modern consumerism' and the way that people's lives have become infused with illusions, daydreams and fantasies about consumer objects. This is the basis of a 'romantic capitalism' that blossomed in the 1950s with a post-war economic boom that was boosted by the widespread availability of credit cards and that has evolved into a 'dream economy' (Jordan, 2007). Traditional identity groups based on class, ethnicity and age began to blur as people found themselves increasingly free to construct their identities and lifestyles through their patterns of consumption. Thanks to Fordism, consumers' dreams could be fulfilled more quickly and more easily. But this led inevitably and dialectically to disenchantment as novelty, exclusivity, distinction and the romantic appeal of goods were undermined by mass consumption. To counter this tendency, product design and niche marketing, along with the 'poetics' of branding, have become central to the enchantment and re-enchantment of things (Frank, 1998). George Ritzer (2005), following Baudrillard, Debord and others, points to the importance of spectacle, extravaganzas, simulation, theming and sheer size in contemporary material culture, and argues that they are all key to enchantment and re-enchantment in the consumer world. Joseph Pine and James Gilmore, meanwhile, write of the emergence of an 'experience economy' where consumer experiences are increasingly the locus of profitability (1999). All this is overlaid by a celebrity culture (Boorstin, 1971; Turner, 2004; Cashmore, 2006; Da Marshall, 2006) that now extends to 'starchitects' – as verified in an episode of *The Simpsons*, where Marge Simpson tells fellow members of the Springfield Cultural Advisory Board that a sure way to win respect is to hire Frank Gehry to design a concert hall along the lines of his Disney Hall in Los Angeles.

The net result is the aestheticization of everyday life, with architecture implicated in consumption at many levels. The design of the built environment has become intimately involved with many aspects of consumption, especially those involving an explicit design premium, such as fashion and luxury products. Endorsement by association, observes Martin Pawley, 'is one of the things that architecture does best, and also one of the things that fashion, the industry, needs most – the new car parked outside the manor house, the classical revival office building, the corporate headquarters campus, the view from the castle, the minimalist interior . . . All of them can be borrowed . . . to make or remake a reputation' (2000, p. 7). In other words, fashion and architecture use one another, not simply as backdrops or as ecologies for celebrity-laden events, but as guarantees of cultural acceptability and valorization of symbolic capital. The spa designed by Peter Zumthor in Vals, Switzerland, for example, has been used as a backdrop for fashion shoots, music videos and advertising in order to create a rarefied atmosphere and at the same time to appeal to a certain target group with architectural knowledge. High-end architecture and high-end fashion also have an affinity for one another because both require great precision in fabrication and construction, high levels of finish quality and carefully controlled lighting. Commodified, the relationship has produced a distinctive luxo-minimalism in interior design, with celebrity architects like Rem Koolhaas and John Pawson furnishing minimalist backgrounds for contemporary fashion brands like Armani, Boss, Jigsaw, Calvin Klein, Mango, Issey Miyake and Prada (Knox, 2010).

In more general terms, the connections between consumption and design, including the marketability of the work of brand-name architects, are maintained and reinforced by what Sharon Zukin (2004) has termed the 'critical infrastructure' of consumption: consumer guides, the Sunday supplements, lifestyle magazines like *Architectural Digest*, *Elle Décor*, *Living*, *Metropolis*, *Metropolitan Home*, *World of Interiors*, and *Wallpaper**, and large-format coffee-table 'look books'. The understanding of architecture derived from these books and magazines is decidedly narrow and usually framed around the persona of a particular designer or the visual aesthetics (read: spectacle, luxury) of a particular building or setting. A similar fixation with aesthetics and personalities is evident in professional magazines, especially the so-called 'showcase' or 'portfolio' magazines such as *Abitare, Communication Arts, Domus* and *I.D.*, all of which are high-gloss productions that use sumptuous photography and printing techniques to show off the latest starchitecture, interior design, furniture design and product design. The profits of trade magazines and the architectural press, and the livelihood of architecture critics and editors depend, in part, on sustaining the international star system. Celebrity is also propagated through major professional awards like the Pritzker Prize; while the pervasive emphasis on the cult of the individual in architectural education (with its almost unquestioned reverence for big names and emphasis on great exemplars and heroic architecture) also plays to the advantage of contemporary signature architects with a global brand.

ARCHITECTURE IN A NEOLIBERAL POLITICAL ECONOMY

Although the collective professional self-image of architects generally emphasizes their independent, socially progressive, environmentally sensitive and holistic perspectives, the practical reality is that they must operate within a starkly neoliberal political economy in which progressive notions of the public interest and civil society have been eclipsed by the bottom line in corporate and public–private investment. Design solutions have to be commercially attractive; projects have to be hustled, commissions have to be won. Similarly, urban governance has become increasingly concerned with providing a 'good business climate' that might attract investment. The increasing entrepreneurialism of urban governance (Harvey, 1989) has made rebuilding, repackaging and rebranding the urban landscape a common priority among large cities. Flagship cultural sites, signature skyscrapers, conference centres, big mixed-use developments, warehouse conversions, waterfront redevelopments, heritage sites, and major sports and entertainment complexes have appeared in many cities. Often geared toward consumption rather than production, these settings are designed to provide a new economic infrastructure suited to the needs of a post-industrial economy: business services, entertainment and leisure facilities, and tourist attractions: an 'ecology of commodified symbolic production and consumption' (Scott, 2001, p. 17). They are, invariably, closely woven into the narratives of city branding. In this context, the would-be iconic buildings of starchitects have become increasingly important as cities compete for world city status through the promotion of signature buildings and the affect of celebrity and spectacle (Doel and Hubbard, 2002).

The net result is the appearance of what Guy Julier (2005) calls 'designscapes': distinctive ensembles of new buildings, cultural amenities, heritage conservation projects, renovated spaces, landscaping and street furniture with, inevitably, an associated programme of planned events and exhibitions. One of the earliest examples in the United Kingdom was Salford Quays on the Manchester Ship Canal, initially developed in 1982 through public–private partnerships on the site of Salford Docks following the closure of the dockyards. As regeneration proceeded, Salford Quays duly acquired starchitecture: the Imperial War Museum North (designed by Daniel Libeskind) and the Lowry arts complex (designed by James Stirling and Michael Wilford). Graeme Evans (2003) uses the term 'hard-branding' to describe the impact of iconic buildings and major events on urban regeneration and place identification.

STARCHITECTURE IN WORLD CITIES

The ability of an iconic building to put a city on the global map was demonstrated by Sydney Opera House, designed by Danish architect Jørn Utzon in the late 1950s and completed in 1973. Utzon was not a star architect – indeed, he was relatively unknown and the Opera House was his first project outside Denmark and Sweden. But the structure, initially very controversial, is now recognized by UNESCO as a World Heritage Site and has become iconic of both Sydney and, indeed, of Australia as a whole. In spite of massive cost overruns in the construction of the building, the return on investment for Australia's government has been extraordinary. The lesson was not lost on the leadership of Bilbao, Spain. Seeking to turn Bilbao into a flourishing international hub of culture, tourism and advanced business services, Bilbao City Council embarked on an ambitious revitalization process featuring signature structures by celebrity architects as symbols of modernity and an affect of economic revitalization. The master plan was devised by César Pelli, Diana Balmori and Eugenio Aguinaga and the centrepiece of the redeveloped riverside site is the Guggenheim Museum (promptly pronounced as a 'miracle' by the *New York Times'* architecture critic Herbert Muschamp), designed by Frank Gehry. Other key elements include a 35-storey office tower (César Pelli); the Euskalduna Juaregia conference centre and concert hall (Federico Soriano and Dolores Palacios); the Bilbao International Exhibition Centre (César Azcárate); a new metro system with striking fan-shaped entrances (Norman Foster); a new airport (Santiago Calatrava); a footbridge spanning Nervión River (also Calatrava); and the 'Gateway' project, a mixed-use quayside development containing luxury flats, cinemas and restaurants (Arata Isozaki). The strategy – and in particular Gehry's museum building – was highly successful in re-branding Bilbao and elevating its perceived status within the global economy. Its success has prompted many other cities to engage starchitects in attempts to replicate what has come to be referred to as the 'Bilbao effect'. As Dejan Sudjic observes (2005, p. 296), 'Sometimes it seems as if there are just thirty architects in the world. . . . Taken together they make up the group that provides the names that come up again and again when another sadly deluded city finds itself labouring under the mistaken impression that it is going to trump the Bilbao Guggenheim with an art gallery that looks like a train crash, or a flying saucer, or a hotel in the form of a twenty-storey high meteorite.' Similarly, the pool of architectural firms that are regularly invited to compete in major architectural competitions is relatively small. Rybczynski (2008) notes that a survey of two architectural journals between 1994 and 2003 turned up 71 invited international competitions, and of the 548 invitations that were issued to 332 firms, 30 per cent went to the top 20 firms and fully 20 per cent were to the top 10 firms.

The names that come up again and again include Will Alsop, Mario Botta, Santiago Calatrava, Pierre de Meuron, Peter Eisenman, Norman Foster, Massimiliano Fuksas, Frank Gehry, Michael Graves, Zaha Hadid, Jacques Herzog, Steven Holl, Arata Isozaki, Rem Koolhaas, Daniel Libeskind, Richard Meier, Jean Nouvel, César Pelli, Dominique Perrault, Renzo Piano, Christian de Portzamparc, Richard Rogers, Robert A.M. Stern, Rafael Viñoly and Peter Zumthor. Most, as Donald McNeill (2009) observes, have an identifiable persona and a flair for self-promotion, whether through book authorship, television appearances or simply personal style: just looking the part. Some, like Mario Botta, Richard Meier, Zaha Hadid and Frank Gehry, have a recognizable oeuvre or 'look', based on striking shapes, surfaces or concepts. Others, like Norman Foster, Renzo Piano, Herzog and de Meuron, develop their brand through sophisticated technological or aesthetic responses to programmatic requirements (Rybczynski, 2008).

All are involved in shaping the designscapes and skylines of world cities. While their work is in demand in these settings, it is also important for starchitects to have a portfolio of work that extends to a variety of world cities, in order to reinforce their reputation. Based in (or frequent visitors to) world cities, starchitects can also become public intellectuals, involved in discourse on a wide range of topics, contributing to influential cultural ideas and trends, and fuelling and reinforcing economic and cultural globalization. The global portfolio of starchitects is heavily weighted toward world cities. Of 165 building and planning projects listed on the web site of Foster + Partners, for example (www.fosterandpartners.com/Projects/ByLocation/Default.aspx), almost two-thirds are located in one or other of the world cities identified by Taylor et al. (2009); and fully 44 per cent of the total are located in Alpha-level world cities.

STARCHITECTS: THE POWER OF BRANDING

Celebrity, branding and brand extension are central to the success of starchitects. It is rooted in the profession's fixation with the cult of personality, something that can be traced back to the role of the Modernist avant-garde and the emergence in the early twentieth century of 'hero' designers who saw themselves as pathfinders in the march of Reason that would bring creativity, enlightenment and a progressive sensibility to a confused and reactionary world. Their manifestos and aphorisms reflected a strongly idealistic, utopian and deterministic attitude, while their individual careers thrived on a radical egocentricity that was often carefully cultivated to enhance their 'heroic' image. The most celebrated example is Le Corbusier. A determined self-publicist, even his signature was designed, while his distinctive spectacles were to become a global shorthand for 'architect'. His North American rival for celebrity, Frank Lloyd Wright, was, like Le Corbusier, a genius at branding himself as well as a gifted designer. Wright adopted a signature cape and cane outfit as props to his hauteur.

After World War II, the professional ideology within architecture was heavily influenced by an optimistic sci-fi futurism that helped to establish outrageous and spectacular proposals as the hallmark of a new avant-garde. By the late 1970s (after the OPEC cartel's four-fold increase in the price of crude oil in 1973 and the subsequent recession) optimistic futurism had been displaced by entrepreneurialism, consumerism and the culture of celebrity. From the early 1980s, just as architecture was becoming a global service profession (Knox and Taylor, 2005), an emerging group of architects began to build in radical and spectacular fashion. Peter Eisenman, Rem Koolhaas, Zaha Hadid and Daniel Libeskind, for example, gained notoriety in the 1980s for 'deconstructivist' buildings that featured non-rectilinear shapes, improbably intersecting volumes and geometric imbalance. (Their work coincided with interest in the humanities and social sciences in Deconstructivist philosophy, but had no real connection except that the opaque writings of Jacques Derrida were handy in lending an apparent intellectual weight to their projects. A similar parallel can be drawn in relation to postmodern architecture and postmodern theory.) It was a short step from the notoriety derived from such radical approaches to international celebrity status, first in the architectural press and then, through careful branding, in a wider context. Freed from the canon of Modernism, starchitects could produce novel, unique and sculptural architecture that almost automatically became instantly 'iconic' (Jencks, 2005, 2006; Sklair, 2006). In a globalizing economy, with booming real estate markets in world cities, many developers came to see the prestige associated with celebrity architects as key to marshalling public consent for big projects, to putting together the necessary amounts of risk capital, to ensuring the exchange value of their products, and to selling the interior space of the building to prospective commercial tenants (McNeill, 2007).

To maintain celebrity, as Jencks points out, starchitects need to keep the media interested, with a judicious mixture of fame and controversy. They are thus encouraged to take risks, break the rules, upstage competitors and shamelessly grab the spotlight. This is where branding comes in. Leading designers, increasingly, are designing themselves, creating distinctive identities that are amenable to corporate branding and the global consumer economy. Rem Koolhaas is the exemplar, an architect whose celebrity derived initially not from novel built work but from the novel style of his book on New York (1978): breathless, iconoclastic and atheoretical, filled with fascinating (but often disconnected) facts and striking and unusual images, and studded with catchy new labels ('architectural mutations', 'utopian fragments') for the established landmarks of New York's built environment. The later success of his built work coincided with an unprecedented amount of branding and self-promotion. Much of this was facilitated through the creation in 1999 of a sister company, AMO, a 'think tank' and research studio for design that allowed Koolhaas to claim intellectual territory and expertise in areas well beyond the boundaries of architecture. In this vein, he has produced a series of publications that have raised his profile. Drawing on the successful affect of *Delirious New York*, with splashy graphics, grainy photoreportage, an assortment of demographic and economic statistics, and essays that pivot around catchy labels ('Generica', 'Junkspace') and would-be profundities ('World Equals City'), these publications have contributed to his image as both star designer and insightful public intellectual. In October 2008 he was invited to become a member of a European 'Council of the Wise' under the chairmanship of former Spanish Prime Minister Felipe Gonzalez to help 'design' the future European Union in relation to long-term challenges such as climate change, globalization, international security, migration, modernizing the European economy and strengthening the European Union's competitiveness. Critics point out that Koolhaas has surfed (rather than challenged) contemporary economic and cultural trends. His forays into the 'dirty realism' of 'Generica', 'Junkspace' and the wild and unrestrained urbanism of Lagos and the Pearl River Delta (Koolhaas et al., 2001) serve only to mask the structural forces that underpin the visual and social outcomes of global capitalism. His design work, meanwhile, unequivocally embraces the dominant economic and cultural flows of the global consumer economy. But such criticism only provides the controversy to sustain celebrity.

Starchitects' broader celebrity status also allows them to engage in 'brand extension'. This is part of the new interdependence among fashion, retail and architecture that has been prompted in part by the acquisition of elite couture houses by retail conglomerates, which quickly realized architecture's marketing and branding potential. Celebrity architects have been drawn increasingly into product lines – from kitchenware and tableware to fountain pens and desk accessories – that are central to the 'habitus' of certain class fractions, especially the 'consumerist fraction' of Sklair's 'transnational capitalist class'. Examples include Michael Graves' kitchenware for Target stores; Aldo Rossi's kitchen- and tableware for Alessi; Mario Botta's Caran D'Ache fountain pen (retail: $2100); Norman Foster's desk accessories for Helit; and Robert A.M. Stern's designs for everything from door levers and bath accessories (for Valli & Valli), to carpets (Bentley Prince Street), carpet tiles (Crossville), fabrics (HBF Textiles, Atelier Martex), furniture (David Edward, HBF), wallcoverings (Innovations), lighting (Baldinger) and jewellery (Acme).

Celebrity has also helped starchitects to rebrand themselves as mega-scale planners (Ockman, 2008). Examples include Frank Gehry's $4 billion project for Atlantic Yards in Brooklyn, New York, and his $1.8 billion 'arts district' around Walt Disney Concert Hall in Los Angeles; Daniel Libeskind's planning projects include a 420,000 square metre, 'skyline-creating' waterfront development in Busan, South Korea; a master plan for a 5–kilometre development corridor south of the historic centre of Copenhagen, and a huge shopping and entertainment complex on the west side of Bern, Switzerland. Norman Foster has been retained as master planner for the historic centre of Duisburg, Germany and for the $22 billion project for Masdar City in Abu Dhabi.

ARCHITECTURE AND THE WORLD CITY BRAND

Just as starchitects derive some of their standing through the visible presence of their built work in major cities, so the potency of the symbolic capital of world cities is derived in part from their association with starchitects, starchitecture and the associated nexus of fashion, design and luxury consumption. Stardom and city branding become mutually self-reinforcing as real estate developers realize that celebrity architects can add value to their projects, world city leaders compete to acquire the services of the top names to design signature buildings that will keep their city on the map, and the signature buildings of star architects provide the backdrop for fashion shoots, movie scenes, TV commercials, music videos and satellite news broadcasts.

World cities derive a kind of monopoly rent as a result of the image they acquire from their 'front regions': the financial districts, cultural quarters, design districts, entertainment districts and 'semiotic districts' (Koskinen, 2005) that are the principal settings for starchitecture and for business activities with international connections. Favourable images of these settings, reinforced and amplified by the media (Doel and Hubbard, 2002; Krause and Petro, 2003), help major world cities to become global tastemakers, the 'valorization of milieu' extending to all sorts of products and activities through branding that simply invokes the city's name (Molotch, 2002; Breward and Gilbert, 2006).

On the other hand, architecture critics like Charles Jencks (2005) point to the serial reproduction of would-be iconic buildings by celebrity architects in world cities, arguing that it will eventually homogenize the visual identities of cities and attenuate any advantage accruing to their competitiveness. Starchitects themselves, meanwhile, may be faced with the conundrum of how not to upstage their own buildings as they win more commissions in the front regions of major world cities. Nevertheless, as Jencks concedes

(2006), starchitects and iconic buildings are here to stay. And as Deyan Sudjic points out (2005), the iconic power and cultural authority of architecture have a long history. Starchitecture is not a new genre associated with a stylistic movement or a cultural sensibility but, rather, the most recent iteration of the 'edifice complex' in the context of economic and cultural globalization.

REFERENCES

Boorstin, D. (1971), *The Image: A Guide to Pseudo-Events in America*, New York: Athenium.
Breward, C. and D. Gilbert (eds) (2006), *Fashion's World Cities*, London: Berg.
Campbell, C. (1987), *The Romantic Ethic and the Spirit of Modern Consumerism*, Oxford: Blackwell.
Cashmore, E. (2006), *Celebrity Culture*, London: Routledge.
Da Marshall, P. (2006), *The Celebrity Culture Reader*, London: Routledge.
Doel, M. and P. Hubbard (2002), 'Taking world cities literally: marketing the city in a global space of flows', *City*, **6** (3), 351–368.
Evans, G. (2003), 'Hard-branding the cultural city – from Prado to Prada', *International Journal of Urban and Regional Research*, **27** (2), 417–440.
Frank, T. (1998), *The Conquest of Cool: Business Culture, Counter Culture and the Rise of Hip Consumerism*, Chicago: University of Chicago Press.
Gutman, R. (1988), *Architectural Practice: A Critical Review*, New York: Princeton Architectural Press.
Harvey, D. (1989), *The Condition of Postmodernity*, Oxford: Blackwell.
Jencks, C. (2005), *The Iconic Building*, New York: Rizzoli.
Jencks, C. (2006), 'The iconic building is here to stay', *City*, **10** (1), 3–20.
Jordan, P.W. (2007), 'The dream economy – designing for success in the 21st century', *CoDesign*, **3** (S1), 5–17.
Julier, G. (2005), 'Urban designscapes and the production of aesthetic consent', *Urban Studies*, **42** (5–6), 869–887.
Knox, P.L. (2010), *Cities and Design*, London: Routledge.
Knox, P.L. and P.J. Taylor (2005), 'Toward a geography of the globalization of architecture office networks', *Journal of Architectural Education*, **58** (3), 23–32.
Koolhaas, R. (1978), *Delirious New York*, New York: Monacelli Press.
Koolhaas, R., S. Boeri, S. Kwinter, N. Tazi and H.U. Obrist (2001), *Mutations*, Barcelona: ACTAR, Bordeaux: Arc en rêve centre d'architecture.
Koskinen, I. (2005), 'Semiotic neighborhoods', *Design Issues*, **21** (2), 13–27.
Krause, L. and P. Petro (eds) (2003), *Global Cities: Cinema, Architecture and Urbanism in a Global Age*, New Brunswick, NJ: Rutgers University Press.
Marshall, R. (2003), *Emerging Urbanity: Global Urban Projects in the Asia Pacific Rim*, New York: Spon Press.
McNeill, D. (2005), 'In search of the global architect: the case of Norman Foster (and Partners)', *International Journal of Urban and Regional Research*, **29** (3), 501–515.
McNeill, D. (2007), 'Office buildings and the signature architect: Piano and Foster in Sydney', *Environment and Planning A*, **39** (2), 487–501.
McNeill, D. (2009), *The Global Architect*, London: Routledge.
Molotch, H. (2002). 'Place in product', *International Journal of Urban and Regional Research*, **26** (4), 665–688.
Ockman, J. (2008), 'Star cities', *Architect*, available at www.architectmagazine.com/design/star-cities.aspx?printerfriendly=true (accessed 17 March 2008).
Olds, K. (1995), 'Globalization and the production of new urban spaces: Pacific Rim megaprojects in the late 20th century', *Environment and Planning A*, **27** (11), 1713–1743.
Pawley, M. (2000), 'Fashion and architecture in the 21st century', in H. Castle (ed.), *Fashion + Architecture*, London: Wiley-Academy, pp. 6–7.
Pine, J. and J. Gilmore (1999), *The Experience Economy*, Cambridge, MA: Harvard Business School Press.
Ritzer, G. (2005), *Enchanting a Disenchanted World*, Thousand Oaks, CA: Pine Forge Press, 2nd edition.
Rybczynski, W. (2008), 'Architectural branding', *The Appraisal Journal*, Summer, 279–284.
Scott, A.J. (2001), 'Capitalism, cities, and the production of symbolic forms', *Transactions of the Institute of British Geographers*, **New Series**, **26** (1), 11–23.
Sklair, L. (2005), 'The transnational capitalist class and contemporary architecture in globalizing cities', *International Journal of Urban and Regional Research*, **29** (3), 485–500.
Sklair, L. (2006), 'Iconic architecture and capitalist globalization', *City*, **10** (1), 21–47.
Sudjic, D. (2005), *The Edifice Complex: How the Rich and Powerful Shape the World*, London: Allen Lane.

Taylor, P.J., with P. Ni, B. Derudder, M. Hoyler, J. Huang, F. Lu, K. Pain, F. Witlox, X. Yang, D. Bassens and W. Shen (2009), 'Measuring the world city network: new developments and results', *GaWC Research Bulletin*, 300, available at www.lboro.ac.uk/gawc/rb/rb300.html (accessed 20 October 2009).
Turner, G. (2004), *Understanding Celebrity*, London: Sage.
Zukin, S. (2004), *Point of Purchase*, London: Routledge.

25 How global are the 'global media'? Analysing the networked urban geographies of transnational media corporations
Allan Watson

INTRODUCTION

World cities research has predominantly focused on the role of advanced producer services in the formation of world city networks. However, global networking processes involve a wider variety of economic activities than advanced producer services alone. This chapter studies an alternative dimension of world city network formation, one in which transnational media corporations (TNMCs), rather than advanced producer services, perform the central role. TNMCs play a central role in globalization. First, giant TNMCs now rank amongst the largest firms in the world, with economic and cultural networks that extend throughout the world city network. In recent years, globalization, digitization, networking and deregulation have acted to remove most of the limits to their corporate media expansion, resulting in the rapid growth of the global commercial media market (Warf, 2007; Castells, 2009). Second, media organizations play a central role in the development of a global communications infrastructure that facilitates global flow of information and cross-border commercial activities. The ability of TNMCs to network globally has been enhanced by this infrastructure, in particular the Internet, which has arguably given media firms the potential to compete in a market space that is potentially borderless and global (Flew, 2007).

However, for Flew (2007), one of the traps in the literature on media globalization is to assume, based upon the global reach of media technologies and the rapid growth of TNMCs, that there has been a seamless change in the system over a short period of time from being based upon locally or nationally based media to one based on global media. For Sreberny (2005) in the context of the media it is not clear if it is the diffusion of technology, the production process, the construction of audiences, the product or the flow of the product, or all of these, or indeed none of these, that are 'global'. Through a consideration of the networked urban geographies of TNMCs, this chapter critically evaluates the extent to which the urban networks of media cities formed by TNMCs through their transnational office networks are truly 'global'. The discussion is based around an empirical analysis of data on the transnational office networks of 25 of the world's largest TNMCs.

TRANSNATIONAL MEDIA CORPORATIONS

By the end of the 1990s, concentration and conglomeration had given rise to the oligopolistic control of media by a small number of giant TNMCs (Warf, 2007), which

Table 25.1   Top 20 media companies by total sales

Rank	Company	Country	Sales ($billion)
1	Time Warner	United States	46.98
2	Walt Disney	United States	36.99
3	Vivendi	France	35.34
4	Comcast	United States	34.26
5	News Corp	United States	32.72
6	Dentsu	Japan	20.62
7	DirecTV Group	United States	19.69
8	Toppan Printing	Japan	16.74
9	Dai Nippon Printing	Japan	16.19
10	Viacom	United States	14.63
11	CBS	United States	13.95
12	Omnicom Group	United States	13.36
13	Lagardère SCA	France	12.53
14	Thomson Reuters	Canada / United Kingdom	11.71
15	DISH Network	United States	11.62
16	WPP	United Kingdom	10.92
17	Liberty Global	United States	10.56
18	British Sky Broadcasting	United Kingdom	9.86
19	RTL Group	Luxembourg	8.33
20	Reed Elsevier	United Kingdom / Netherlands	7.78

Source: Forbes 2000, April 2009, www.forbes.com

have continued to develop a major economic and cultural presence on nearly every continent (Held et al., 1999) and which now rank amongst the largest firms in the world. Digitalization and the associated convergence of media and technology have led to these corporations developing a range of interests across a variety of different media, information and telecommunications sectors (Flew, 2005), including publishing, television, radio, movie studios, music companies, games and electronics. This corporate growth has resulted in the transnational media system being extremely economically non-competitive. As McChesney (1998) notes, many of the largest firms share major shareholders, have interlocking boards of directors and own pieces of each other. Furthermore, in key markets these firms establish multiple joint ventures where risk is reduced and the chance of profitability is shared. This effectively reduces the number of viable entrants into these markets. As McChesney notes:

> The global media is one where the dominant firms compete aggressively in some concentrated oligopolistic markets, are key suppliers to each other in other markets, and are partners in yet other markets. (1998, p. 32)

Writing in 1997, Herman and McChesney suggested that US based firms would continue to dominate the global media market 'for a long time to come', based on the historic competitive advantage of the largest indigenous media market and a new business model of transnational production and distribution. Table 25.1 shows the top 20 media companies by total sales in early 2009. Indeed, US firms do continue to dominate the global media market, at least in terms of sales. Ten of the top 20 corporations listed are US companies. In comparison, only four are UK companies, three are Japanese and two are French.

As Flew (2007) suggests, media organizations compete in particular geographical markets, which may be local, national or international. However, while the global reach of communication technologies, in particular the Internet, enables media organizations to compete in a market space that is potentially borderless and global, almost no media organizations in themselves are truly global. As Gershon (1997) notes, very few TNMCs operate in all markets of the world, but rather they operate in preferred markets, especially their home market, and remain territorially anchored to these main markets (Arsenault and Castells, 2008). As Castells (2009) argues, what are global are the networks of interlocked multimedia businesses organized around strategic partnerships, cross-investments, personnel, production and distribution. As such, he argues that the major transformation we observe in the media is the 'formation of global networks of interlocked multimedia businesses organized around strategic partnerships' (p. 72). Castells asserts that the dominant nodes lying at the core of these global media networks are the small number of TNMCs, which form the 'backbone' of the global network of media networks, connecting locally and nationally focused media organizations across the globe. Chalaby (2005) outlines how media conglomerates are adopting a new organizational structure and management mentality, mutating from global to transnational media companies. In these new structures, headquarters give foreign subsidiaries and affiliates increased autonomy and decision making responsibility, encourage specialization and link them up into an independent corporate network. Such a structure allows global reach and efficiency with responsiveness to the needs and tastes of local markets (see also Gershon, 2000). For Castells (2009) only global networks can master the resources of global media production, but their ability to conquer market share depends on their ability to adapt content to the taste of local audiences. For Herman and McChesney (1997), the widening of the international bases of TNMCs is at least partly due to the need to 'localize' their content.

ANALYSING THE NETWORKED URBAN GEOGRAPHIES OF TNMCs

As Krätke and Taylor (2004) suggest, this trend towards market differentiation is a driving force for the organization of global production networks in the media industries. Media TNMCs however, as Krätke (2003) suggests, not only occupy a prominent position in the cultural economy of individual countries, but are also creating an increasingly global network of branch offices and subsidiaries. These networks are anchored in urban centers, key centers of cultural production which act both as 'local anchoring points' in the 'cultural metropolises' of the global urban network (Krätke, 2003) and as command points for the control of increasingly transnational corporate networks (see Sassen, 2001). Thus we find that one of the main characteristics of the global production networks of the media industries is concentration in and around the key cities of global capitalism (see Morley and Robins, 1995; Robins, 1995). As Krätke (2003) outlines, TNMCs located in urban centers of cultural production interact locally with small specialist producers and service providers, linking them into their global networks of branch offices and subsidiaries, stretched across the global urban network. This not only allows TNMCs to draw on the creativity that resides in these production centers, but also results in the global linking of the urban centers of cultural production through established global networks. Therefore, firms in urban media clusters are not only embedded locally, but also integrated more widely with firms in other clusters in cities throughout the world.

The increase in the level and intensity of supra-regional linkages between local media industry clusters is resulting in the emergence of a system of *global media cities* (Krätke, 2003), characterized by geographical links at both the local and global level. This emerging system can be illustrated by analysing the network connectivities of these media cities, through an examination of the transnational locational networks of media TNMCs. These networks can be interpreted as tangible working connections between cities. Network connectivities can be calculated by applying an interlocking network model, as specified by Taylor (2004), to a data matrix. This interlocking network for world cities is unusual when compared with other networks in that it has three levels. At the nodal level of the network are cities, while at the net level is the global economy, consisting of all the nodes and links (connected cities). The additional level is a *sub-nodal* level comprising firms. This level is critical because it is firms that are the agents of world city network formation rather than cities. As firms have become worldwide under conditions of contemporary globalization, networks of offices have become central to providing a seamless global service and brand. It is the working flows between these offices – communications, knowledge transfer, and the movement of information and people – that constitute the world city network (Taylor, 2001, 2004). Therefore the main measure of importance in this model is *network connectivity*. The formal specification of the model is given by Taylor (2001). The data used in this analysis were collected by researchers of the Globalization and World Cities (GaWC) research network based at Loughborough University, UK and Ghent University, Belgium, in collaboration with the Chinese Academy of Social Sciences (CASS). A data matrix was constructed consisting of 525 cities and 25 firms. The matrix holds data on which firms have offices in which cities and how important each individual office is in the office network of the firm. The level of importance is coded between 0 (no office in the city) to 5 (headquarters). This importance is termed the *media value* of a city based on all firms present. The 25 firms included in the data are the 25 largest media companies, by total sales as given in the Forbes 2000 listing for 2008, for which locational data were available. Table 25.2 displays a list of the top 20 most connected media cities, calculated through application of the interlocking network model, along with their gross network connectivity values. These connectivities are calculated as proportions of the highest city connectivity – in this instance New York.

London and New York are shown to dominate the media rankings as the pre-eminent global cities dyad. New York is the most connected media city, with gross network connectivity far ahead of that of London. As shown in Table 25.3, New York also completely dominates the media 'value' rankings, which are based on the total value of media offices located within the city, with a value of 71 compared with London's value of 50.

Paris is ranked as the number three city for media connectivity, with gross network

Table 25.2   Gross connectivities for the top 20 most connected media cities

Rank	City	Gross connectivity
1	New York	100.0
2	London	71.7
3	Paris	56.7
4	Tokyo	54.8
5	Washington DC	52.5
6	Beijing	51.6
7	Hong Kong	48.9
8	Shanghai	48.1
9	Seoul	47.6
10	Taipei	45.8
11	Bangkok	44.7
12	Madrid	41.2
13	Moscow	40.4
14	Milan	40.1
15	Singapore	40.0
16	Los Angeles	38.5
17	Chicago	36.6
18	Mumbai	35.5
19	Mexico City	34.2
20	Toronto	33.6

Table 25.3   Top 10 cities ranked by total media value across 25 firms

Rank	City	Total
1	New York	71
2	London	50
3	Washington DC	37
4	Beijing	28
5	Los Angeles	25
6	Tokyo	25
7	Chicago	24
8	Paris	22
9	Hong Kong	21
10	Shanghai	20

connectivity well below that of both New York and London, despite having a relatively low media value. This demonstrates that while media offices based in Paris have a relatively low importance within corporate networks (i.e. they are largely not corporate or regional headquarters), they are well connected to other media offices across the world. Six of the top ten ranked media cities are Pacific Rim cities: Tokyo, Beijing, Hong Kong, Shanghai, Seoul and Taipei. These are separated by the US city of Washington DC, ranked at number 5 in terms of connectivity and with the third highest media value. The remaining 10 of the top 20 ranked media cities include a mixture of other Pacific Rim cities (Bangkok, Singapore), European cities (Madrid, Milan) and US and Canadian cities (Los Angeles, Chicago, Toronto). US cities are relatively under-represented, with just two cities in the top 10 (New York, Washington DC) and two more in the top 20 (Los Angeles and Chicago). European cities are also relatively under-represented, also with just two cities in the top 10 (London, Paris) and two more in the top 20 (Madrid, Milan). The rankings given here differ considerably from those of a previous study of media cities undertaken by Stefan Krätke and Peter Taylor (2004). Although the data used in the two studies differ significantly, comparison is interesting. Their finding of a 'privileged Europe' within their rankings is not mirrored in this analysis, with just four European cities present in the top 20 ranked media cities. Rather, the rankings presented here show a different focus for dominance – the Pacific Rim. While Table 25.1 demonstrates that the majority of the top ranking TNMCs have headquarters in the US (10 of the top 20) or Europe (7 of the top 20), the connectivity rankings for these media cities demonstrate that the global production networks of these TNMCs are most intensively anchored in the Pacific Rim region. It is the Pacific Rim, then, that is the 'privileged' region, with Pacific Rim cities functioning as key anchoring points in global media networks.

The above discussion on the connectivity of global media cities has begun to uncover some of the global–spatial configuration of the networks of TNMCs. Four of the top 20 most connected media cities are in the United States, four are in Europe and eight are in the Pacific Rim. It is possible to uncover more of the global–spatial configuration of global media networks by looking at the common variations in the ways in which global media firms use global cities. By employing a Principal Components Analysis, it is possible to examine these common variations and to identify a set of global media 'fields'. Each of these fields represents a group of TNMCs employing similar strategies when locating their offices across the globe. Each of the fields is constituted by a group of media companies, and each contains a number of cities in which the offices of these firms are located. The discussion below draws out the three most significant media fields based on an analysis undertaken on the data matrix of 25 TNMCs located across 526 cities. The analysis provides scores for cities in each field. The larger the score for a given city, the more significant its role in articulating media services in the field.

THE MEDIA FIELD OF THE PACIFIC RIM

The strongest media field emerging from the analysis is centered on the Pacific Rim. The field is made up of eight major media firms including the Fuji Television Network and Toppan Printing with headquarters in Tokyo. Also included in the field are a number of firms headquartered in the US or Europe that have a Pacific Rim focus to their business, including News Corporation, Thompson Corporation and McGraw-Hill (New York); Vivendi and Lagardère SCA (Paris); and Reuters Group (London). The media field which these firms create is orientated towards Pacific Rim cities, but is global in its nature. Table 25.4 shows the ten highest scoring cities from the Pacific Rim, along with comparatively high scoring cities from outside the region. The field is articulated through Tokyo, the highest scoring of all cities, although the city is far from completely dominant in the field. Other cities, including major cities from outside the Pacific Rim, score highly,

Table 25.4   Tokyo articulated media field

Pacific Rim cities	Score	Non-Pacific Rim cities	Score
Tokyo	4.01	New York	3.55
Hong Kong	3.25	Paris	3.11
Beijing	2.33	London	2.68
Shanghai	2.25	Los Angeles	2.22
Taipei	2.11	Toronto	1.70
Seoul	1.97	Washington DC	1.33
Bangkok	1.75	Milan	1.24
Singapore	1.61		
Mumbai	1.09		
Sydney	1.08		

especially Paris, Hong Kong and New York, along with Beijing, London, Shanghai and Taipei. The Pacific Rim orientation is further displayed by the inclusion in the field of Bangkok, Seoul, Singapore and Sydney.

Central to the rise of the Pacific Asian media field has been the rapidly growing Japanese media, home to three of the world's top 20 TNMCs. This importance is highlighted in the role of Tokyo as articulating city for the field. The rapidly expanding East Asian media markets provide Japanese media with their largest export market (Iwabuchi, 2007). This is in turn reflected in the importance of East Asian cities in the media field, in particular the Chinese cities of Hong Kong, Beijing and Shanghai, as well as Taipei, Seoul, Bangkok and Singapore. All of this has been driven by the activation of regional media flows in the Pacific Rim, with greater synchronization between markets meaning that media products produced in these cities find a broader transnational acceptance across the region (Iwabuchi, 2007) and, particularly in the case of Japanese media, are also making inroads into the global markets in some areas (Chan, 2005). As Chalaby (2005) notes, international reach is no longer the preserve of Western-based conglomerates, and now an increasing number of media companies from other areas of the world are expanding overseas.

However, for Iwabuchi (2007), despite the importance of Japanese and East Asian media production, no center has emerged to take the place of the US. Although national and regional conglomerates control much of the mass media market, American and European media remain a pivotal presence in the region, through a web of corporate alliances. US and other Western media conglomerates have allied with domestic and regional business and other TNMCs to gain substantial holdings in the region and share in the profitability of Asia's vast potential media audiences (Sussman and Lent, 1999). US and European media firms have anchored their organizational networks in the Pacific Rim, reflected in the importance of the connections between the Pacific Rim cities and New York, Los Angeles, London and Paris, as identified in this media field. The US-based News Corporation has the strongest foreign presence in Asia. The Corporation, which derives 44 per cent of its revenues from outside North America (Flew, 2007), has for example large equity stakes in eight Indian television networks, and owns six networks in China and seven channels in Taiwan (McChesney, 1998).

THE MEDIA FIELDS OF THE US

The next most significant media field is focused on the US. The field contains six major media firms, predominantly headquartered in the US and with an American focus to their business. They include Viacom and CBS (New York), RR Donnelley & Sons and Tribune (Chicago), as well as Wolters Kluwer (Amsterdam) and Reed Elsevier (London). Table 25.5 shows the ten highest scoring cities from the US, along with comparatively high scoring cities from outside the US. New York is the articulator of this field, dominant above all other cities. A city from outside the US, Amsterdam, is the next highest scoring city, predominantly due to the US business links of the Wolters Kluwer Corporation, followed by Chicago. These are followed by a number of other US cities, including Denver, Dallas, Miami and Sacramento. Amsterdam aside, European cities are relatively unimportant in this field, as are Pacific Rim cities with the exception of the Chinese cities of Beijing and Shanghai.

The US also has a second media field, consisting of five media firms with headquarters in the US and which have a strong US focus to their business. These firms are EchoStar Communications (Denver), Gannett (Washington DC), Comcast (Philadelphia), Tribune (Chicago), and DirecTV Group (Los Angeles). Table 25.6 shows the ten highest

Table 25.5   New York articulated media field

US cities	Score	Non-US cities	Score
New York	7.14	Amsterdam	5.36
Chicago	4.89	Santiago	1.34
Denver	1.10	Shanghai	1.22
Dallas	0.98	Beijing	0.75
Miami	0.95	Alexandria	0.63
Sacramento	0.92		
Seattle	0.87		
Los Angeles	0.86		
Boston	0.78		
Indianapolis	0.54		

Table 25.6   Washington DC articulated media field

US cities	Score	Non-US cities	Score
Washington DC	7.50	St Petersburg	1.22
Denver	4.07		
Philadelphia	3.17		
Atlanta	2.14		
Los Angeles	1.87		
Phoenix	1.58		
San Antonio	1.32		
San Francisco	1.29		
Chicago	1.23		
Sacramento	0.83		

scoring cities in this field from the US, along with comparatively high scoring cities from outside the US. The city of Washington DC is the articulator of this field, with Denver, Philadelphia and Atlanta also important. These are followed by a number of other US cities including Los Angeles and Phoenix. European cities are relatively unimportant in this field, and Pacific Rim cities even less so.

Both of these media fields consist of large TNMCs with headquarters in US cities and with business networks anchored firmly within the US domestic media market. This is reflective of both the size of media markets within the US, and of the importance of these home base markets for US TNMCs. The importance of these domestic markets effectively ensures that US TNMCs will not stray too far from their 'home culture' (Chan, 2005), predominantly producing media products to meet the demands and tastes of US media consumers. In a study of diversification amongst the leading media conglomerates, Chan-Olmsted and Chang (2003) found that, partially due to the importance of North American media markets, US media corporations were less geographically diversified than non-US corporations. The US TNMCs Time Warner, Disney and Viacom for example derive only 20–25 per cent of their total operating revenues from outside North America (Flew, 2007). This is illustrated in the relative unimportance of both European and Pacific Rim cities in this field, with only a few exceptions. As such, both of these US media fields are far less global in nature than the media field focused on the Pacific Rim.

A GLOBAL MEDIA?

The above analysis of global media city connectivities and media fields reveals much about the urban networks of TNMCs and about the globality of media production. First, the global focus of media production emphasizes two dominant centers – the Pacific Rim and the US. This is not to say that there are not other important centers of media production, but rather that the activities of the world's largest media corporations are focused in these two regions. These findings support Rugman's (2000) assertion that the concept of a single global market is an illusion, and that what exists instead is a series of regionalized production and market blocs. The 'global' expansion of TNMCs is then, in reality, regional in its focus. This is due to the way in which the core tendencies of the global market produce a highly uneven worldwide media system (Herman and McChesney, 1997), with commercial media markets arising in regions where people have the money to purchase the products which the media corporations create and advertise. Thus the geography of the media fields highlighted in this chapter can be seen to focus on the wealthiest regions of the world. The 'missing' region from the analysis in this respect is Europe, for which no strong media field emerges from the analysis. This does not mean however that Europe is not an important center for media production. Indeed, seven of the top 20 TNMCs are headquartered in European cities. Rather, it would suggest that European TNMCs are less regionally concentrated and more global than either their American or Pacific Rim counterparts. The identification of two media fields with a strong US-domestic focus suggests that US TNMCs are actually amongst the least global of the giant media corporations, predominantly focusing on the large US domestic media markets (see also Chan-Olmsted and Chang, 2003).

Secondly, it suggests that the dominant flows of Western-based media (Herman and

McChesney, 1997; Sparks, 2005) are being challenged in at least one other region of the world – the Pacific Rim. US-centric views of media globalization have tended to disregard the increase in non-Western exports and intraregional non-Western flows (Iwabuchi, 2007), multiple and horizontal flows which challenge the dominant one-way vertical media flow of 'Americana' (Thussu, 2007). Furthermore, it suggests that we should not assume that the global expansion of TNMCs is undermining local media industries and cultural production. As Flew (2007) argues, as the corporations attempt to expand their markets they are forced to compete with well established and highly competitive local media organizations. However, it is important to recognize that US and European TNMCs have managed to gain substantial holdings in the region through alliances with these local media organizations. This is illustrated by the key role played by a select group of Western global cities in the Pacific Rim media field.

So what of a 'global' media? If the current dominant trends of TNMC diversification and global expansion were to continue, we might envisage a scenario where the logic of trade and liberalization permeates the entire media and communications sphere globally, and in which TNMCs reign supreme (Siochrú, 2004). However, the analysis presented here is demonstrative of the fact that the major TNMCs are presently far from being truly global in terms of their focus for media production. It has demonstrated that much of the world's media production is focused on two media fields – the US and the Pacific Rim. The first of these demonstrates both a local challenge to US media dominance and cultural hegemony, and the expansion of a relatively small number of Western TNMCs into the region. The second demonstrates that some of the world's largest TNMCs in terms of total sales remain extremely domestically focused. Flew (2007) notes that, with a few exceptions, media corporations are less globalized than major corporations in other sectors of the economy, and are globalizing comparatively more slowly.

Cities play a central role in the development of media networks. It is cities that anchor the transnational production networks of TNMCs in particular countries and regions, acting both as key centers of media and cultural production and as command points for the control of increasingly transnational corporate networks. In these cities, in which many TNMCs and smaller media organizations are based, there is an overlapping of a multitude of locational networks. Thus these cities are more global than any one TNMC network alone. These multiple networks link cities to other cities across the globe in a complex pattern of connections and flows. It is these cities, the *global media cities*, characterized by geographical links at both local and global levels, which are the truly 'global' element of the global media.

REFERENCES

Arsenault, A.H. and M. Castells (2008), 'The structure and dynamics of global multi-media business networks', *International Journal of Communication*, **2**, 707–748.

Castells, M. (2009), *Communication Power*, Oxford: Oxford University Press.

Chalaby, J.K. (2005), 'From internationalization to transnationalization', *Global Media and Communication*, **1** (1), 28–33.

Chan, J. (2005), 'Global media and the dialectics of the global', *Global Media and Communication*, **1** (1), 24–28.

Chan-Olmsted, S.M. and B. Chang (2003), 'Diversification strategy of global media conglomerates: examining its patterns and determinants', *Journal of Media Economics*, **16** (4) 213–233.

Flew, T. (2005), *New Media: An Introduction*, Oxford: Oxford University Press, 2nd edition.

Flew, T. (2007), *Understanding Global Media*, Basingstoke: Palgrave Macmillan.

Gershon, R.A. (1997), *The Transnational Media Corporation: Global Messages and Free Market Competition*, Mahwah, NJ: Lawrence Erlbaum Associates.

Gershon, R.A. (2000), 'The transnational media corporation: environmental scanning and strategy formulation', *Journal of Media Economics*, **13** (2), 81–101.

Held, D., A. McGrew, D. Goldblatt and J. Perraton (eds) (1999), *Global Transformations: Politics, Economics and Culture*, Cambridge: Polity Press.

Herman, E.S. and R.W. McChesney (1997), *The Global Media: The New Missionaries of Global Capitalism*, London: Cassell.

Iwabuchi, K. (2007), 'Contra-flow or the cultural logic of uneven globalization? Japanese media in the global agora', in D.K. Thussu (ed.), *Media on the Move: Global Flow and Contra-Flow*, Abingdon: Routledge, pp. 67–83.

Krätke, S. (2003), 'Global media cities in a worldwide urban network', *European Planning Studies*, **11** (6), 605–628.

Krätke, S. and P.J. Taylor (2004), 'A world geography of global media cities', *European Planning Studies*, **12** (4), 459–477.

McChesney, R.W. (1998), 'Media convergence and globalization', in D.K. Thussu (ed.), *Electronic Empires*, London: Arnold, pp. 27–46.

Morley, D. and K. Robins (1995), *Spaces of Identity: Global Media, Electronic Landscapes and Cultural Boundaries*, London: Routledge.

Robins, K. (1995), 'The new spaces of global media', in R.J. Johnston, P.J. Taylor and M.J. Watts (eds), *Geographies of Global Change*, Oxford: Blackwell, pp. 248–262.

Rugman, A. (2000), *The End of Globalization*, London: Random House.

Sassen, S. (2001), *The Global City: New York, London, Tokyo*, Princeton, NJ: Princeton University Press, 2nd edition.

Siochrú, S.Ó. (2004), 'Global institutions and the democratization of media', in P.N. Thomas and Z. Nain (eds), *Who Owns the Media? Global Trends and Local Resistances*, Penang, Malaysia: Southbound, pp. 23–42.

Sparks, C. (2005), 'The problem of globalization', *Global Media and Communication*, **1** (1), 20–23.

Sreberny, A. (2005), 'Contradictions of the globalizing moment', *Global Media and Communication*, **1** (1), 11–15.

Sussman, G. and J.A. Lent (1999), 'Who speaks for Asia: media and information control in the global economy', *Journal of Media Economics*, **12** (2), 133–147.

Taylor, P.J. (2001), 'Specification of the world city network', *Geographical Analysis*, **33** (2), 181–94.

Taylor, P.J. (2004), *World City Network: A Global Urban Analysis*, London: Routledge.

Thussu, D.K. (2007), 'Mapping global media flow and contra-flow', in D.K. Thussu (ed.), *Media on the Move: Global Flow and Contra-Flow*, Abingdon: Routledge, pp. 11–32.

Warf, B. (2007), 'Oligopolization of global media and telecommunications and its implications for democracy', *Ethics, Place and Environment*, **10** (1), 89–105.

26 World cities of sex
Phil Hubbard

Conventionally, the literature on world cities describes them as the global hubs that organize ever-more complex flows of information, money and people. Within this literature, it is advanced producer services that are considered of crucial importance in articulating this space of flows, often to the neglect of other cultural and social practices that give world cities their distinctive character. This chapter redresses this balance by focusing on sex as one of the drivers of the global economy, arguing that world cities are not merely major markets for sexual consumption, pornography and prostitution but are the hubs of a global network of sexual commerce around which images, bodies and desires circulate voraciously. As such, this chapter brings the body into discussions of globalization not merely as a vector of disease transmission, an agent of cultural diffusion or a repository of tacit business knowledge, but as a sexualized and desiring body whose intimate geographies are integral to the reproduction of global economic systems which thrive on the commodification of desire.

WORLD CITIES AS SITES OF SEDUCTION

While world city rosters and league tables can reveal the most powerful world cities – rather than those which merely boast a large population – we need to be mindful of the basis on which these are constructed given that most prioritize particular types of work and ignore the embodied dimensions of urban life. Little attention has been paid to those 'whose paid work involves the care, pleasure, adornment, discipline and cure of others' bodies', such as beauticians, hairdressers, nurses and sex workers (Wolkowitz, 2006, p. 147). The neglect of such forms of body/work, and related forms of emotional labour, is perhaps not surprising given that much of this service sector work is gendered, with world city research often privileging the masculine worlds of finance, banking, insurance and law, seeing these as more 'skilled occupations' and more important in driving the global economy. Yet even those accounts seeking to reintegrate elite migration in the study of world cities (e.g. Malecki and Ewers, 2007) have rarely considered sex, love and intimacy as factors impinging on decisions to migrate, and hence as integral to the making of world city networks.

An exception here is the work by Walsh (2007) which considers the heterosexualities performed by young British expatriate workers in Dubai. Having massively expanded since the discovery of oil in the 1960s, Dubai has become one of the most important cities on the Arab peninsula, its emergence as a world city associated with its growing role as a centre for financial services as well as its reputation as a luxury tourist resort. Significantly, it is also a city where 80 per cent of the resident population are transnational migrants, including both low wage workers employed in construction and tourism work and higher paid workers in finance and advanced producer services. Focusing on the latter, Walsh reports a tendency for young British expats to reject notions of coupledom and instead perform a transient heterosexuality focused on play, freedom and the pursuit of sexual pleasure. Significantly in a city where the consumption of alcohol is not publicly tolerated, this means that a series of hybrid bars/clubs have become important in the social lives of the expats, with dressing up, dancing and flirting being almost daily activities for many of them. Walsh argues that most of the young (heterosexual-identified) expats she interviewed saw their time in Dubai as 'a working holiday', behaving differently from how they might when at 'home'.

To suggest that some transnational workers perform different sexualities when working in foreign contexts is to highlight the importance of sexuality both in decisions to migrate and in migrant lifestyles within world cities. It is also to underline that sites of sociality and sexuality ('landscapes of desire', as Walsh terms them) are integral to world city formation, providing spaces where transnational elites can cement friendships with business contacts and work colleagues at the same time that they pursue sexual pleasures. It is no coincidence, therefore, that leading world cities are known for red light districts and sexual entertainment aimed at business visitors as much as at 'local' consumers (e.g. London's Soho, the Times Square area of New York and Tokyo's Kubukicho). Even Dubai, where prostitution is illegal, has a thriving sex work scene focused on expatriate hotels and clubs, becoming known as the 'prostitution centre of the Arab world' in the process.

The extent to which the governors of Dubai turn a blind eye to sex work in the interest of cultivating a reputation that their city is a 'fun' place in which to live and work is debatable. However, the connection between sex and the economic growth of post-industrial cities is made explicit in the work of globalization 'guru' Richard Florida. Put simply, his thesis is that cities require a critical mass of creatives to thrive, a class of workers whose job is to create meaningful new forms of work (Florida, 2002). According to Florida, for a city to become a magnet for the creative class, it must provide Talent (have a highly talented, educated and skilled population), Technology (have the technological infrastructure necessary to fuel an entrepreneurial culture) and Tolerance (have a diverse community, which has a 'live and let live' ethos). One way that Florida operationalizes the latter is by a diversity index based on the proportion of coupled gay households in a region, which he sees as a good predictor of creativity and urban productivity, noting that 11 of the top 15 high tech metropolitan areas in the US also appear in the top 15 of his gay index (Florida, 2002).

Despite critiques of the equation made between gay (male) coupledom and creativity, the idea that there may be some connection between sexuality and world city formation is not easily ignored, and feeds into numerous policy initiatives designed to market 'wannabe' world cities as hip and happening gay capitals (Markwell, 2002; Hughes, 2003). Moreover, a rising number of city governors acknowledge the importance of adult entertainment in attracting business tourists and conference travellers of all kinds (Sanchez, 2004). Unsurprisingly, few surveys suggest sex is a motivation for business travel, but anecdotal evidence for this is legion, suggesting an important connection between business travel and sexual consumption, especially when such travel allows individuals to escape the confines of an existing, coupled relationship (Wonders and Michalowski, 2001). While this can apply to women travellers, much commentary fixates on the business*man*, who is assumed to be a significant and sometimes voracious consumer of sexual services. For example, Marttila (2008) suggests that around 50 per cent of clients of prostitutes in Estonia are Finnish men drawn to the city not so much because of the presence of sex work but because of its pivotal role as a 'crossroads' between Eastern and Western Europe (Marttila, 2008). In Tokyo, visits to massage parlours and hostess bars appear to be as much a part of corporate hospitality as banqueting and karaoke are (Allison, 1994), while in London female employees have complained about the culture of entertaining foreign visitors by taking them to lap dancing and strip shows (Rutherford, 1999). Drawing connections between sex entertainment and corporate cultures, Holgersson and Svanstrom (2004) likewise allege that visits to strip clubs in Stockholm are homosocial occasions where men together confirm their gender identity, allowing them to develop forms of intimacy between men in a space of heteronormal consumption which effectively guarantees the men's heterosexuality (Liepe Levinson, 2002). Beyond this, it is clear that hotels catering to business travellers are important sites for escort work and prostitution, while sexual consumption is normalized in the provision of hard-core porn on the pay-to-view channels that constitute part of the in-room entertainment. As Pritchard and Morgan (2006) argue, the 'very liminality of hotels – as crossing points into the unknown, as places of transition and anonymity, hidden from familiar scrutiny – makes them attractive as venues for sexual adventure'.

All of this is to insist on the importance of sex in the making of transnational business networks, and to problematize any neat distinction between business and sex tourism: Oppermann (1999) argues that the vast majority of tourists who visit prostitutes or sites of adult entertainment do not travel for that purpose alone. In most cases, this is a byproduct or side attraction rather than the main and sole purpose of travel. O'Connell Davidson (2001) describes these as *situational* sex tourists. Dispensing with clichés of the sex tourist as a predator, travelling solely to exploit and dominate economically subordinate young people, this notion of situational sex tourism suggests that sex and business entwine in a multitude of ways.

EROTIC CITIES: GLOBALIZATION AND THE SHADOW ECONOMY

Acknowledging that business travel is (partly) motivated by sex provides one perspective on the importance of sex in the making of world cities. But to suggest the sex industries simply follow existing flows of finance and business is to downplay the importance of the sex industry as one of the drivers of the global economy. Historically, the sex industry has been associated with centres of trade and finance, with sex workers catering to the wealthy, but sex tourism and adult entertainment have also developed in tourist areas, areas of seasonal employment, in border zones and in centres of conflict (such as occupied zones): in short, any areas where men have been present but where their normal partners have been absent (Ryder, 2004). As such, there are many cities whose importance as centres of sexual commerce is disproportionate to their significance as centres of finance. This implies that while all world cities are seductive, some cities are more seductive than others, becoming de facto *erotic cities*.

Bangkok is a case in point. Positioned within East–West flows of tourism, a context of rural deprivation, gendered inequality and a predominant Buddhist attitude which is tolerant of many forms of sex working, Thailand has been a notorious centre for sex tourism since at least the 1960s, when US military en route to Vietnam stopped there for rest and recreation (Askew, 1998). In some senses, this reputation is undeserved, for much sex work in Thailand caters for local populations, and the country has sought to discourage the package tour 'sex holidays' that were evidentially popular with German and Japanese tourists in the 1980s. But if sex is not the motivation for all tourists to visit the country, Bangkok remains known as 'the brothel of the world' where Thai sex workers perform in a bewildering range of go-go bars, sex shows and karaoke clubs where they do not merely sell sex but a fantasy of an Oriental woman who is not only physically beautiful and sexually exciting but also caring, compliant, submissive and non-Western. Between them, the key 'red light areas' of Bangkok – Patpong Road, Nana Plaza and Soi Cowboy – offer over 300 bars and clubs, with some estimates suggesting that there are as many as 200,000 employed in the city's adult entertainment sector (Babb, 2007).

If Bangkok is the sexual playground of South East Asia, Las Vegas can certainly claim that title in North America. Las Vegas' remarkable expansion in the twentieth century relied upon the popularity of its nighttime economy, meaning that it now boasts a unique high-wage, low-skilled economy based on gambling and tourism. The fact that Las Vegas is in the only state of the US where prostitution is legal has been an important factor in maintaining this growth, allowing Las Vegas to market itself as 'Sin City', a place where sexual fantasies and adult pleasures can come true. While prostitution per se is not (officially) part of the Las Vegas experience (all the licensed brothels are more than an hour's drive from the city) the resort industry has always relied upon sexual promise, embodied in the form of the Vegas showgirl, an idealized and glamorous dancer whose provocative form has entertained visitors since burlesque was introduced to the Strip in the 1950s at celebrated venues such as Minskys, Stardust and the Desert Inn.

Commenting on the iconic status of the Vegas showgirl, Reichl (2002) contends that the economy of Las Vegas depends not so much on the selling of sex but the production of desire, which draws people to the city in the pursuit of pleasure. Gambling remains the cornerstone of the economy, but even conservative estimates suggest there are more employed in the sex industry than in the casinos. While street prostitution has long since been displaced from the Strip, a few blocks away from the main resort hotels, striptease and gentleman's clubs like Spearmint Rhino, Déjà Vu, Sapphire and Crazy Horse Too prosper (with something like 15,000 dancers having the sheriff's licence needed to work such venues). Today, Las Vegas offers a sex-soaked world of lap dancing, stripping, swinging and big casino topless showgirl revues, and it is perhaps unsurprising that up to 3500 illegal prostitutes work in Las Vegas at any given time (Brents and Hausbeck, 2007). While some ply their trade discreetly on the casino floor, escort work is massively important, and the majority of hotels appear complicit in arranging 'personal services'.

Examples such as Bangkok and Las Vegas imply that if we were to draw up a roster of erotic cities, it would appear somewhat different from conventional rankings of world cities. Cities including Bangkok and Las Vegas, as well as the European 'stag capitals' of Tallinn, Hamburg, Riga, Prague and Amsterdam, would all figure strongly, alongside tourist destinations like Havana and border cities such as Tijuana. However, the likelihood of being able to acquire reliable data on the size of these cities' sexual economies is slim, as much of what occurs in the sex industries remains in the shadow economy given that the majority of sex sold worldwide occurs within a context of quasi-legality. Penttinen (2004) has accordingly used the concept of *shadow globalization* when referring to the global flows of migrants who are employed in the sex industry. The extent to which sex markets are dominated by migrant workers varies massively, but there is certainly plentiful evidence to suggest that non-native and/or illegal migrant workers make up the majority of sex workers in major world cities. For example, Tokyo's sex market is dominated by indentured Thai and Filipino workers, while Amsterdam's licensed windows have large numbers of migrant workers from Dutch colonies (e.g. Indonesia, Surinam and Antilles). In the UK, some reports suggest that 80 per cent of those in London's off-street brothels and massage parlours are migrant workers from Latin America, South East Asia and principally Eastern Europe (Dickson, 2003).

Given the feminization of poverty, gender discrimination and emerging 'migration cultures' in the countries of origin (Mai, 2009), the increasing involvement of Eastern European women in Western European sex markets is not hard to understand. These migratory factors are not only confined to women, with the male sex work scene in London populated by significant numbers of migrant men who arrive from places such as South America and Eastern Europe to become involved in the male sex work industry (Sanders, 2008). In a contemporary context, there is much concern that a large proportion – and maybe even a majority – of these men and women will have been trafficked for the express purpose of sexual exploitation. This is tied into the identification of trafficking as a significant byproduct of the thickening of global networks, with 'the growth of shadow economies and transnational criminal networks' a 'negative manifestation of globalization, arising from expanding economic, political and social transnational linkages that are increasingly beyond local and state control' (Goodey, 2003, p. 417). Sex trafficking is obviously not a new phenomenon, yet contemporary commentators accordingly suggest it far exceeds the levels that prompted (for example) the formation of a League of Nations Committee in 1933 to address 'a certain movement of occidental prostitutes to the Orient' (Self, 2003, p. 78). Indeed, it is estimated that somewhere between 400,000 and 1,000,000 people are trafficked globally annually, with a significant – but ultimately immeasurable – number ending up sex working (see Hubbard et al., 2008).

Such estimates are highly suggestive of global patterns of trafficking, but a major issue clouding the trafficking debate is the uncertainty about the proportion of prostitutes who have been trafficked and those migrating voluntarily. Particularly problematic is the distinction between migration via smuggling networks and enforced migration at the hands of traffickers – a distinction many human rights organizations claim is irrelevant given those seeking to migrate with the aid of people smugglers do so in desperate circumstances and with little knowledge about employment opportunities (Hughes, 2002). However, others reject this to posit a more complex range of scenarios situated at different points on a continuum of voluntary and involuntary migration. For example, Agustin (2007) argues that the poor pay and conditions in caring and servicing work means that many migrants prefer to sell sex or sell it as a second job, despite the stigma attached to it. The sex industry thus provides a paid occupation for many millions of people worldwide, offering much higher wages and often more freedom and flexibility than other jobs available: Mai (2009) found that migrant sex workers in London reported better working and living conditions than those they encountered in other sectors (mainly in the hospitality and care sectors). Tellingly, only a handful (around 6 per cent of female interviewees) in his sample felt that they had been deceived and forced into selling sex in circumstances in which they had no share of control or consent.

In spite of such evidence, the conflation of migrant sex work and trafficking continues. Trafficking panics, such as those associated with major urban spectacles and sporting events such as the 2006 World Cup in Germany, the 2010 Winter Olympics in Vancouver and 2010 World Cup in South Africa, have proved unfounded (see Hennig, 2006; Bird and Donaldson, 2009) but this has certainly not prevented the introduction of highly symbolic acts designed to prevent the 'penetration' of Western cities by a seemingly unstoppable influx of 'Eastern girls' (Berman, 2003). Irrespective, movements of men and women employed in the sex industries is a form of 'globalization from below' (Benton-Short et al., 2005), albeit one that is unacknowledged in world cities research, which has fixated on the service rather than the servicing class.

PORNOECONOMIES AND WORLD CITIES

Irrespective of moral arguments about the uses and consequences of pornography, its *availability* has changed in profound ways thanks to the growth of the worldwide web. Even in nations where governments have sought to block adult content and prevent peer-to-peer file sharing, it remains relatively easy to access sites where sexual imagery can be freely viewed (and posted), while there are thousands – perhaps hundreds of thousands – of sites where video content is available to download on a subscription or a pay-to-view basis. The rise of the Internet and the putative pornification of society are hence intimately connected, with pornography producers being early innovators in the use of online and visual technologies to disseminate adult content. Industry statistics suggest that around one-third of Internet users are now regular visitors to online porn sites, and that although the majority visit free-to-view websites (such as Pornhub, the 50th most popular website in the world, and YouPorn, the 57th), subscriptions create annual revenues in excess of $2.5 billion (Edelman, 2009). Such figures may well be unreliable given the tendency for the adult industry to exaggerate its own importance, but are indicative of the importance of pornography as a virtual business given it accounts for around 70 per cent of all purchases of online Internet content, outstripping sports, news and video games.

Within porn studies there is thus much talk of the 'end of geography' as barriers to the consumption of pornography are effectively obliterated. The public space of the Internet is characterized by (relative) anonymity, affordability and accessibility, allowing those in peripheral and poorer regions – especially those outside major metropolitan cores – to become active consumers of adult content (Jacobs, 2004). This implies that pornography has undergone a shift towards decentralization and heterogeneity as a wider variety of producers and consumers participate in globalized sex markets. Adult content has been effectively 'democratized' (McNair, 2002), the sexual marketplace becoming more global as it extends its 'sticky web' to capture the 'curious clicker' (Johnson, 2008). For Jacobs (2004), any contemporary study of pornography needs to capture this dispersal, recognizing that the form, content and meaning of pornography result from 'a network of different factors including (but not limited to) porn performers, producers and distributors, legislation, media, economy, research and various forms of expertise, politics, popular culture and hierarchies of taste' (Paasonen, 2009, p. 564) which can stretch across time and space.

Yet even if pornography is consumed as a transnational commodity, this should not imply the geographies of pornography are disorderly or amorphous (Jacobs, 2004). Indeed, any notion of geographic disembedment is illusionary, as the Internet adult industry operates in a space of flows that offers new possibilities for pornographic distribution but remains anchored in a space of places. In this sense, it is possible that some of the arguments deployed in economic geography about the embedded nature of production and the importance of tacit knowledge are relevant to pornography production. Voss (2007) suggests that within this relatively stigmatized sector, it is extremely difficult for individuals and firms to negotiate trust with people who work outside the industry, suggesting that the construction of strong ties is vital *within* the industry to create new packages of adult entertainment. To some extent this explains why the adult industries have tended to be innovators in the use of online and IT technologies: unable to access existing media channels, they have developed their own platforms of dissemination. Inter-firm knowledge flows have been vital here, with adult entertainment trade fairs (e.g. Venus Berlin, the AVN Expo held in San Francisco, Erotica LA and Shanghai's Adult Toys Exhibition) being important spaces where reputations and trust are negotiated between individuals in the industry, and where knowledge about varying facets of the industry and its markets is shared (Comella, 2008). A key role of such fairs is to encourage *global* copycatting: firms display their latest products, only for other companies to seek to imitate these – something that firms see as inevitable and even beneficial given the lack of patented protection in the sector (Voss, 2007).

To date there have been few studies of these economic geographies of pornography. The pioneering work of Zook (2003, 2007), however, shows it is possible to 'map' the Internet adult industry by specifying the interaction between three sites. The first of these relates to the content that adult websites buy to host on their websites (the most common practice for pay-to-view providers). Though the creation of content is now relatively easy (in the sense that it merely requires relatively cheap camcorder and willing participants), the acknowledged centre of porn has, since the 1970s, been San Fernando (or Silicone Valley, as it is sometimes dubbed), which currently accounts for around two-thirds of listed adult entertainment production studios (being home to around 150 companies). This remarkable agglomeration economy developed by virtue of the fact that San Fernando offered abundant low-rent industrial spaces and warehouses where Hollywood wannabee actors and directors utilized ex-studio equipment and expertise to create the first wave of adult videos (as distinct from *films* – see Simpson, 2004). Today, it persists in spite of higher rentals because it represents a notable cluster in which technical know-how and embodied knowledges are shared through established networks and inter-firm socialities (notably, the industry newsletter Adult Video News is based in the Valley). Emphasizing the continued dominance of the US in studio-produced pornography, Danta (2009) notes that an additional 12 per cent of adult film studios worldwide are located in other parts of Los Angeles; 15 per cent are found in other cities (notably New York, Miami and Las Vegas); and only 2 per cent of studios are located in other countries (mainly Russia, Czech Republic and Hungary). The 'off-shoring' of pornography production to Budapest has certainly been a noted phenomenon, its dominance in

European porn production thought to relate to the availability of 'camera-compatible women' and low production costs in the aftermath of the collapse of the Eastern bloc (see Milter and Slade, 2005 on 'Budaporn'). Irrespective, the geography of porn production remains distinctive in terms of its highly uneven nature (at least in terms of that content sourced from 'professional' studios).

The second location considered by Zook is the website itself. While these can be fee paying, by far the largest number are free, sometimes offering limited or low-res content as a bait to encourage the 'curious clicker' to explore. Perhaps paradoxically, much free online content is more hard-core and 'gonzo' than that available through subscription services: paid websites like Penthouse, Hustler and Playboy have relatively soft-core content and make claims to corporate social responsibility so that they can be accessed via as many search engines as possible, and their content downloaded to iPhones and third generation mobiles. Such sites are also massively important for Internet providers, given that on-line high-res content uses up vast amounts of bandwidth, at great cost to the website providers. Mapping domain names of membership websites, Zook (2003, p. 1272) concludes that the 'UK, Germany, France, and Spain all have a relatively small number of top membership sites compared with their overall presence [on the web] whereas other countries such as the US, Canada, the Netherlands, Denmark, and Australia have a specialization in adult sites': in absolute terms, the US dominates with around 60 per cent of all paid membership sites, though this figure declined by around 5 per cent between 2001 and 2006 (Zook, 2007). One particularly interesting finding here is that a number of adult content sites are registered in locations (such as Antigua, Saint Kitts and the Turks and Caicos Islands) that are otherwise unimportant in domain hosting terms. This points to an off-shoring tendency that might bear some comparison to trends in banking for high net worth individuals (and perhaps reflects a desire to escape intrusive governmental surveillance).

The third site mapped by Zook is the location of the website itself. In theory, this is the easiest location to map as it can be traced via identification of the IP address of the computer on which the website is hosted. While these could in theory be anywhere in the world, Zook (2007) again suggests that most are hosted in the US, the nation through which the majority of the world's Internet traffic passes. The map of the top 100 Internet websites (measured in terms of Internet traffic, 2009) confirms Zook's observations, and reveals a continuing clustering of IP addresses on the West coast of the US, with other significant hubs in Europe (Amsterdam, Budapest, Paris, London and Brussels): in the Americas beyond the US, only Havana and Buenos Aires feature (see Figure 26.1).

While analyses based on searching for domain names and IP addresses need to be treated with caution given the regional packaging of IP addresses, it is possible here to discern a global geography of porn that remains resolutely routed through particular world cities in the US globalization arena. The evident inertia in the geography of pornography is surprising given the rapid technological changes in the sector as well as the low start-up costs associated with pornographic production and uploading. However, the shifts that Zook (2007) discerns, in terms of a gradual movement away from US cities towards European cities, suggest there are specific 'pull' factors diffusing the adult industry into world cities in other globalization arenas. What is of course missing here are reliable data on the real flows of Internet traffic that constitute this form of underground globalization: we need to know more about who is viewing what, when and where.

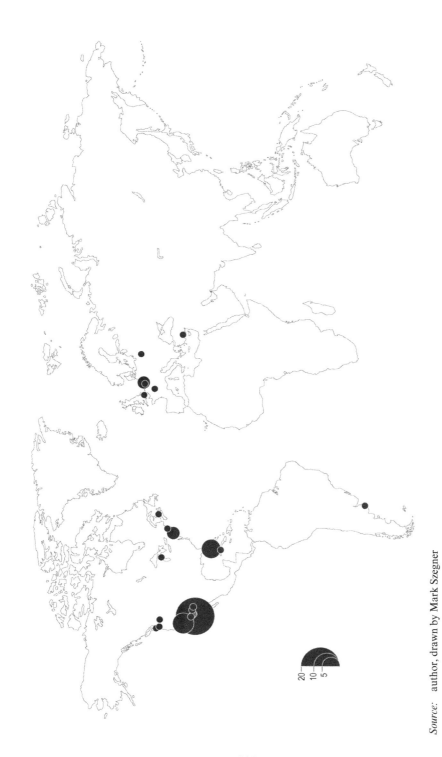

Source: author, drawn by Mark Szegner

Figure 26.1   Location of IP addresses of top 100 adult websites, 2009

303

CONCLUSION

World city research has said little about matters of sexuality, despite the evidential importance of sex to the economies of world cities and, conversely, the importance of world cities in articulating networks of sex. In this chapter, I have offered a broad overview of some of the ways in which world cities research might further engage with themes of sex and sexuality, suggesting that both licit and illicit commercial sex markets have been stimulated by the enhanced flow of people, goods and images between cities across the world. Cities are, perhaps more than ever, contact zones where people of different social and cultural backgrounds mix. In such cities, sex and bodies become 'commodities that can be packaged, advertised, displayed, and sold on a global scale' (Wonders and Michalowski, 2001, p. 117). The visibility of commercial sex at the heart of those world cities most central to global flows of business and finance (i.e. the major 'decision making centres' of the global economy) is thus connected to their status as spaces in which migrants constitute a significant share of the workforce, whether as members of the transnational elite class or as those who work in the brothels, clubs, bars, discotheques, cabarets, peepshows, sex shops, parlours, saunas, hotels, flats, parks and streets which act as sites of sexual-economic exchange.

REFERENCES

Agustin, L. (2007), *Sex at the Margins: Migration, Labour Markets and the Rescue Industry*, London: Zed Publishing.

Allison, A. (1994), *Nightwork: Sexuality, Pleasure and the Performance of Masculinity in a Tokyo Hostess Club*, Chicago: University of Chicago.

Askew, M. (1998), 'City of women, city of foreign men: working spaces and re-working identities among female sex workers in Bangkok's tourist zone', *Singapore Journal of Tropical Geography*, **19** (2), 130–150.

Babb, F.E. (2007), 'The intimate economies of Bangkok: Tomboys, Tycoons, and Avon ladies in the global city', *GLQ: A Journal of Lesbian and Gay Studies*, **13** (1), 111–123.

Benton-Short, L., M. Price and S. Friedman (2005), 'Globalization from below: the ranking of global immigrant cities', *International Journal of Urban and Regional Research*, **29** (4), 945–959.

Berman, J. (2003), '(Un)popular strangers and crises (un)bounded: discourses of sex-trafficking, the European political community and the panicked state of the modern state', *European Journal of International Relations*, **9** (1), 37–86.

Bird, R. and R. Donaldson (2009), '"Sex, sun, soccer": stakeholder-opinions on the sex industry in Cape Town in anticipation of the 2010 FIFA Soccer World Cup', *Urban Forum*, **20** (1), 33–46.

Brents, B. and K. Hausbeck (2007), 'Marketing sex: US legal brothels and late capitalist consumption', *Sexualities*, **10** (3), 425–437.

Comella, L. (2008), 'It's sexy. It's big business. And its not just for men', *Contexts*, **7** (3), 61–63.

Danta, D. (2009), 'Ambiguous landscapes of the San Pornando Valley', *Yearbook of the Association of Pacific Coast Geographers*, **71**, 15–30.

Dickson, S. (2003), *Sex in the City: Mapping Commercial Sex across London*, London: POPPY Project.

Edelman, B. (2009), 'Red light states: who buys online adult entertainment?', *Journal of Economic Perspectives*, **23** (1), 209–220.

Florida, R. (2002), 'The economic geography of talent', *Annals of the Association of American Geographers*, **92** (4), 743–755.

Goodey, J. (2003), 'Migration, crime and victimhood: responses to trafficking in the EU', *Punishment and Society*, **5** (4), 415–431.

Hennig, J. (2006), *Trafficking in Human Beings and the 2006 World Cup in Germany*, Geneva: International Organization for Migration.

Holgersson, C. and Y. Svanstrom (2004), *Lagiga och oligaga affarer – om sexkopoch organizartioner*, Stockholm: NorFa.

Hubbard, P., R. Matthews and J. Scoular (2008), 'Regulating sex work in the EU: prostitute women and the new spaces of exclusion', *Gender, Place and Culture*, **15** (2), 137–152.

Hughes, D. (2002), 'The use of new communication and information technologies for the sexual exploitation of women and children', *Hastings Law Review*, **13** (1), 127–146.

Hughes, H.L. (2003), 'Marketing gay tourism in Manchester: new market for urban tourism or destruction of "gay space"?', *Journal of Vacation Marketing*, **9** (2), 152–163.

Jacobs, K. (2004), 'Pornography in small places and other spaces', *Cultural Studies*, **18** (1), 67–83.

Johnson, J.A. (2008), 'To catch a curious clicker?', unpublished paper, Porn Cultures: Regulation, Political Economy and Technology Conference, September, Athens.

Juffer, J. (1998), *At Home with Pornography: Women, Sex, and Everyday Life*, New York: New York University Press.

Liepe Levinson, K. (2002), *Strip Show: Performances of Gender and Desire*, New York: Routledge.

Mai, N. (2009), *Migrant Workers in the UK Sex Industry*, London: Institute for the Study of European Transformation.

Malecki, E.J. and M.C. Ewers (2007), 'Labor migration to world cities: with a research agenda for the Arab Gulf', *Progress in Human Geography*, **31** (4), 467–484.

Markwell, K. (2002), 'Mardi Gras tourism and the construction of Sydney as an international gay and lesbian city', *GLQ: A Journal of Lesbian and Gay Studies*, **8** (1–2), 81–99.

Marttila, A.M. (2008), 'Desiring the "Other": prostitution clients on a transnational red-light district in the border area of Finland, Estonia and Russia', *Gender, Technology and Development*, **12** (1), 31–51.

McNair, B. (2002), *Striptease Culture: Sex, Media and the Democratization of Desire*, London: Routledge.

Milter, K.S. and J.W. Slade (2005), 'Global traffic in pornography: the Hungarian example', in L.Z. Sigel (ed.), *International Exposure: Perspectives on Modern European Pornography, 1800–2000*, New Brunswick, NJ: Rutgers University Press, pp. 173–204.

O'Connell Davidson, J. (2001), 'The sex tourist, the expatriate, his ex-wife and her "Other": the politics of loss, difference and desire', *Sexualities*, **4** (1), 5–24.

Oppermann, M. (1999), 'Sex tourism', *Annals of Tourism Research*, **26** (2), 251–266.

Paasonen, S. (2009), 'Healthy sex and pop porn: pornography, feminism and the Finnish context', *Sexualities*, **12** (5), 586–604.

Penttinen, E. (2004), 'Corporeal globalization: narratives of subjectivity and otherness in the sexscapes of globalization', *Tapri Occasional Paper 92*, Tampere.

Pritchard, A. and N. Morgan (2006), 'Hotel Babylon? Exploring hotels as liminal sites of transition and transgression', *Tourism Management*, **27** (5), 762–772.

Reichl, A.J. (2002), 'Fear and lusting in Las Vegas and New York: sex, political economy, and public space', in J. Eade and C. Mele (eds), *Understanding the City: Contemporary and Future Perspectives*, New York: Routledge, pp. 363–378.

Rutherford, S. (1999), *Organizational Culture, Patriarchal Closure and Women Managers*, Bristol: Policy Press.

Ryder, A. (2004), 'The changing nature of adult entertainment districts: between a rock and a hard place or going from strength to strength?', *Urban Studies*, **41** (9), 1659–1686.

Sanchez, L.E. (2004), 'The global e-rotic subject, the ban, and the prostitute-free zone: sex work and the theory of differential exclusion', *Environment and Planning D: Society & Space*, **22** (6), 861–883.

Sanders, T. (2008), 'Selling sex in the shadow economy', *International Journal of Social Economics*, **35** (10), 704–716.

Self, H. (2003), *The Fallen Daughters of Eve*, London: Frank Cass.

Simpson, N. (2004), 'Coming attractions: a comparative history of the Hollywood studio system and the porn business', *Historical Journal of Film, Radio and Television*, **24** (4), 635–652.

Voss, G. (2007), 'The dynamics of technological change in a stigmatised sector', paper presented at DRUID Winter Conference 2007, Aalborg, Denmark, January 2007, available at www2.druid.dk/conferences/viewpaper.php?id=1072&cf=10 (accessed 20 January 2010).

Walsh, K. (2007), '"It got very debauched, very Dubai!" Heterosexual intimacy amongst single British expatriates', *Social & Cultural Geography*, **8** (4), 507–533.

Walsh, K., H. Shen and K. Willis (2008), 'Heterosexuality and migration in Asia', *Gender, Place and Culture*, **15** (6), 575–579.

Wolkowitz, C. (2006), *Bodies at Work*, London: Sage.

Wonders, N.A. and R. Michalowski (2001), 'Bodies, borders, and sex tourism in a globalized world: a tale of two cities – Amsterdam and Havana', *Social Problems*, **48** (4), 545–571.

Zook, M. (2003), 'Underground globalization: mapping the space of flows of the Internet adult industry', *Environment and Planning A*, **35** (7), 1261–1286.

Zook, M. (2007), 'Report on the location of the Internet adult industry', in K. Jacobs, M. Janssen and M. Pasquinelli (eds), *C'lick Me: A Netporn Studies Reader*, Amsterdam: Institute of Network Culture, pp. 103–121.

II C   World city governance

27 Global city-region governance, ten years on
John Harrison

INTRODUCTION

It is exactly ten years since Allen Scott's (2001a) edited collection *Global City-Regions – Trends, Theory, Policy* became the antecedent to a resurgent interest among academic and policy communities in the 'city-region' concept. In the book, Scott, along with fellow contributors Saskia Sassen, Peter Hall, John Friedmann, Kenichi Ohmae, Michael Porter, John Agnew, Ed Soja and Michael Storper among others, conceptually map and empirically demonstrate how at the beginning of the twenty-first century there is a new and critically important kind of geography and institutional phenomenon on the world stage – the *global city-region*. Furthermore, they use the concept of the global city-region to set out how processes of global economic integration and accelerated urbanization – the defining features of globalization – are serving to make traditional planning and policy strategies 'increasingly inadequate'. It is apt then that ten years on we should revisit, first, the concept of the global city-region, and secondly, the governance of these pivotal social formations in this *International Handbook of Globalization and World Cities*.

What follows constitutes a necessarily brief synopsis of some of the key arguments on the governance of global city-regions. This focus on governance is particularly important given that while global city-regions have been identified as a new scale of urban organization, the pace of change – particularly in relation to their unrelenting expansion in size, scale and number – means these pivotal social formations are often reliant upon outdated and inadequate institutional structures, frameworks and supports. This was noted by Scott ten years ago, prompting him to raise the important question: *What main governance tasks do global city-regions face as they seek to preserve and enhance their wealth and well-being?* (Scott et al., 2001a, p. 12). A decade on we can argue that this question remains as important as ever – maybe even more so? For despite having more information and more knowledge of what mechanisms are in place, and how different policymakers, strategists and jurisdictions are attempting to construct new city-regional governance arrangements, by the very nature of academic inquiry this has raised as many new questions as it has provided answers.

THE WHAT, WHERE, WHEN AND HOW OF GLOBAL CITY-REGIONS AND THEIR GOVERNANCE

Against the backdrop of accounts heralding the transition to a 'borderless world', the city-region concept has been rejuvenated as part of a wider 'new regionalist' literature documenting how in globalization place-based and site-specific scales of intervention can both anchor and nurture nodes of dense economic, social and political activity. By focusing on heterodox and endogenous ways of doing economic development alongside supply-side innovation strategies, it is argued that actors can capitalize on this increasingly localized agglomeration and intense clustering of socioeconomic activity. For the most part, this has helped cities and regions prosper in globalization. Yet this was not always the case.

In the early stages of globalisation, the prospects for cities looked bleak. Under threat globally from increased foreign competition, capital mobility and labour migration, and undermined locally by labour–management disputes and stagflation, cities that were once the epicentre of Fordist mass accumulation were now on the verge of bankruptcy. A serious drag on national economies, the consensus from the mid 1970s through the 1980s and on into the early 1990s was that advances in technology and communication were inducing an era of global deconcentration. The prospect of a diminishing role for cities has, however, been dispelled in recent years by an increased recognition that although new technologies have indeed extended our capacity to interact across space, the propensity of economic activity to coalesce in dense clusters/agglomerations is being demonstrated by a distinct group of cities, that is, metropolitan clusters of socioeconomic activity, forging ahead as important staging/command posts in an increasingly globalized world economy.

A measure of the degree to which global economic integration and accelerated urbanization have gone hand in hand is that today, for the first time, more than 50 per cent of the world's population live in cities (UNFPA, 2007). Spatially, this rapid urbanization sees the functional economies of large cities (the so-called 'economic footprint') extend beyond traditional boundaries to capture physically separate but functionally networked cities and towns in the surrounding (regional) hinterland – to give three pertinent examples, the city population of Tokyo is 12.8 million but the metropolitan population is 31.7 million, for New York City it is 8.3 and 29.9 million and London 7.6 and 21 million respectively.[1] From this we can clearly see how despite a resurgence of cities in globalization, the city as traditionally conceived is becoming an increasingly outdated entity.

For many, this new spatiality is best captured by the concept of the city-region. At its most basic, a city-region comprises two distinct but interrelated elements: first, the city, which possesses some specified set of functions or economic activities; and secondly, a surrounding territory which is exclusive to that city (Parr, 2005). However, this definition can be traced back through most of the twentieth century to Christaller's (1933) central-place theory, and while useful for describing the spatiality of these emerging social formations, it cannot help uncover, let alone explain, the processes by which city-regions are actively produced in contemporary globalization. It is here, at the conceptual level, that attention has been directed toward so-called 'global city-regions' – which, extending the logic that sees global cities defined by their *external* linkages, are defined by their corresponding *internal* linkages (Hall, 2001). Presented in this way, global city-regions are showcased as a new scale of urban organization: one that is simultaneously networked externally on a global scale, and internally is expanding to cover areas in excess of thousands of square kilometres – in some cases extending across national boundaries (e.g. Copenhagen–Malmo, San Diego–Tijuana, Singapore–Johor–Batam). According to Scott and others then, global city-regions amount to a new phase in capitalist territorial development. As places where globalization crystallizes out on the ground, global city-regions are seen to have a 'deepening role' in the economy, while socially, culturally and politically they are extolled as 'increasingly central to modern life' (Scott et al., 2001a, p. 11).

Following on from this, and perhaps not surprisingly, this rhetoric captured the imagination of academic and policy communities alike at the beginning of the twenty-first century. At one level, policymakers have sought to accelerate their city's path to economic competitiveness in and through strategies designed to construct flexible and responsive frameworks of city-regional governance. The result of this is how, today, the task of devising city-regional policies is firmly established as an officially institutionalized task not only across North America and Western Europe, but large parts of Pacific Asia and Latin America also. At another level, the enthusiasm of policymakers the world over to adopt city-regional strategies has seen the notion of a new city-regionalism in economic development and territorial representation become self perpetuating. To borrow Lovering's (1999) terminology, the policy tail can once more be seen wagging the analytical dog, with the construction of tiers of city-regional governance being used as further evidence of city-regions acting as autonomous political and economic spaces, elevating city-regionalism to a position of orthodoxy, and fuelling further rounds of policy intervention (Harrison, 2007).

GLOBAL CITY-REGION GOVERNANCE: SOME CONTINUING AND EMERGING CHALLENGES

The past ten years have brought into sharp focus a number of continuing and emerging challenges for academics and policymakers when considering the major governance tasks posed by city-regionalism more generally, and by global city-region development in particular. Albeit a partial and inevitably personal take on this, this section identifies three major challenges which, when taken together, outline a research agenda for future inquiry into global city-region governance. The first of these centres on how we define, delimit and designate city-regions.

City-region: Object of Mystery

In his chapter of *Global City-Regions*, Peter Hall (2001) focuses his effort on defining, first, what do we mean by a 'global city', and secondly, what do we mean by a 'global city-region'? Perhaps not surprising given the rich tradition of work developing Sassen's concept of the global city during the 1990s, Hall dedicates 14 pages to this task, but just 2 pages to defining what we mean by a 'global city-region'. Why is this important you might ask? Well ten years on we still do not have the answer. What we have is more definitions, but no commonly accepted one. Take the following examples. For Allen Scott (2001b, p. 814), city-regions constitute 'dense polarised masses of capital, labour, and social life that are bound up in intricate ways in intensifying and far-flung extra-national relationships. As such, they represent an outgrowth of large metropolitan areas – or contiguous sets of metropolitan areas – together with surrounding hinterlands of variable extent which may themselves be sites of scattered urban settlements.' In contrast, Mark Tewdwr-Jones and Donald McNeill (2000, p. 131) define the city-region as 'a strategic and political level of administration and policy-making, extending beyond the administrative boundaries of single urban local government authorities to include urban and/or semi-urban hinterlands'. And as for how this translates into policymaking, to take the UK government as an example, a city-region is 'a functionally inter-related geographical area comprising a central, or core city, as part of a network of urban centres and rural hinterlands. A little bit like the hub (city) and spokes (surrounding urban/rural areas) on a bicycle wheel' (ODPM, 2005, no pagination).

What we have in all three definitions is the 'reach' or 'footprint' of the city emerging as the key determinant of a city-region, but very different interpretations of how this manifests itself conceptually, but also spatially. So where is the connection to governance I hear you ask? It is worth remembering, as Nigel Thrift (2002, p. 205) reminded us nearly a decade ago, that 'to govern it is necessary to render the visible space over which government is to be exercised. And this is not simply a matter of looking: space has to be represented, marked out.' In other words, the important question that arises is how to render an analytical concept, the global city-region, into a visible space over which government can be exercised. All of which suggests that, at one level, we still face the most fundamental challenge – how to define, delimit and designate city-regions. But at another level, it puts into sharp focus the need to examine how city-regions are being constructed politically. For the major issue in city-regional governance today is not how and whether to draw lines around city-regions, but to examine the process through which they are (re-)produced (Hudson, 2007).

Making City-regions Visible: a Question of Politics and Economics

Like the global city, the global city-region is used principally as an analytical concept. As such it does not translate easily into a well defined political jurisdiction with clear territorial boundaries over which political control can be exacted. But it has also seen discourses pertaining to a new city-regionalism constructed around a narrow set of empirical and theoretical issues relating to exchange, interspatial competition and globalization – the 'new economics of city-regions'. Defined in economic terms (travel to work areas, functional economic ties, labour market geographies), all too often what has been missing from city-regional accounts over the past decade is how city-regions are constructed politically and, more specifically, the process by which they are rendered visible spaces. What has resulted from this is a tendency for those promoting the city-region concept to reify the city-region as an agent of wealth creation and redistribution. In response to this, Andrew Jonas and Kevin Ward have argued that having overlooked how city-regions are constructed politically, there is now heightened intellectual urgency around the need to conceptualize the emergence of city-regions as the 'product of a particular set of economic, cultural, environmental and political projects, each with their own logics . . . to discover for which interests city-regions are necessary and for whom this new territoriality is merely contingent' (2007, p. 176). In particular, they outline how there is need for a 'new politics of city-regionalism' centred on important, yet un(der)-represented, aspects of city-regional theory: a politics of governance and state reterritorialization; the role of democracy and citizenship in city-region politics; and tensions around social reproduction and sustainability across city-regions. Not surprisingly this too sparked a flurry of research, this time aimed at illuminating the new politics of city-regionalism. However, while interventions in this area have been doing much to advance debates in recent years on how city-regions are constructed politically, work examining how city-regions are rendered visible spaces has appeared somewhat pre-occupied with their increased visibility in political discourse – often being framed as part of a wider neoliberal agenda. What has been missing is due consideration of the struggle to spatially define, delimit and designate city-regions, with city-regions all too often scripted unreflectively and with little regard for how they have been historically constructed, culturally contested and politically charged (Harrison, 2010a).

The Limitation of City-region Imitation

An officially institutionalized task throughout most parts of the world, the task of building city-regional governance is underpinned not only by a strong theoretical rationale but a strong policy rationale. Indeed, while acknowledging that each has its own localized agenda, there are four commonly accepted elements to this policy rationale. First, and despite what can best be described as inconclusive evidence of whether devolution brings about an economic or democratic dividend, there continues to be a recognition globally that devolution of power, resource and authority to the most appropriate level is a desired outcome. In other words, as the *in vogue* spatial scale the city-region is identified as 'the most appropriate level' and is the main benefactor from this continuing global trend toward devolution. Secondly, the shift from spatial Keynesianism and policies of redistribution toward neoliberal workfare has offered little or no indication of narrowing regional disparities and/or tackling uneven development. With over half the world's population now living in cities, the city is increasingly seen to be an important site of struggle and strategy around the connection between economic growth and quality of life. Moreover, for many proponents of city-regions, collective provision, redistribution and the narrowing of inequality is something which is actively talked up and championed (Jonas and Ward, 2007). Thirdly, studies of governance suggest that the success of leading cities like New York and Tokyo is underpinned by a history of strong political integration resulting from strong metropolitan government. And finally, fourthly, there is general recognition that the best performing cities are those where local government boundaries are most closely matched to the functional geography of the local economy (Cheshire and Magrini, 2009).

With many cities finding themselves under-bounded due to rapid urbanization in the past twenty years, city authorities are increasingly seen as too small, regions too large and city-regions ideal for effective governance. Alongside and somewhat related to this, political praxis has been dominated by a belief in four normatively charged policy assumptions: that, first, a necessary link exists between economic competitiveness and the city-region scale; secondly, a necessary link also exists between city-regions and increased social participation, accountability and stakeholder democracy; thirdly, *all* city-regions can benefit and accelerate their economic growth and raise competitiveness; and fourthly, that both points one and two can be secured by establishing city-regional institutions, frameworks and supports. Presenting a multi-sided argument for establishing city-regional governance, it is not surprising how policymakers worldwide have found themselves captivated by the strong theoretical and policy rationale for city-regions. Indeed, the success enjoyed by certain city-regions has led policymakers in less prosperous cities and regions to cast increasingly envious eyes toward these growth economies, and enticed them to seek greater engagement with these assumptions through state policies aimed at increasing institutional capacity through an empowered city-regional tier of governance. But having said that, the onset of globalization and the emergence of a strong institutionalist literature – highlighting the importance of hard (organizations, agencies) and soft (trust, loyalty, social capital) institutions to local and regional development – has led to much critical thought being given over to the potential dangers of fast policy transfer and policy mobility. To illustrate this, I want to use the remainder of this section to focus on the case of England to highlight some of the difficulties faced by policymakers as they endeavour to copy the success of leading city-regions by imitating their governance arrangements.

At present there are no less than five clearly defined models of city-region governance in England, each of which has appeared in the past decade, in light of the orthodoxy surrounding city-regions. The first, and most obviously recognizable, are the new city-regional governance structures for London. When Scotland, Wales, Northern Ireland and the eight English regions were being afforded new regional institutions as part of the UK government's programme of Devolution and Constitutional Change (1997–1999), London, as the only true global city-region, was afforded new city-regional governance arrangements centred on the new Greater London Authority (GLA), consisting of a directly elected Mayor of London and an elected twenty-five member London Assembly. Formally established on 3 March 2000, the GLA is responsible for the strategic administration of London's thirty-two boroughs and has responsibility primarily for transport, housing, policing, fire and rescue, tackling climate change, health and culture, waste, development and strategic planning. This is then delivered through four functional bodies – Transport for London, the London Development Agency, the Metropolitan Police Authority and the London Fire and Emergency Planning Authority. However, while London has the greatest powers and most closely maps onto Scott's concept of the global city-region, it is noteworthy how even here the institutions of city-regional governance only have jurisdiction over Greater London. Noteworthy is how the boundary of Greater London has remained fixed since 1963, and thus the new governance arrangements only have jurisdiction over an area of 1579km^2 and a population of 7.6 million. Thus when it comes to governance, London's current 'city-region' frameworks are working to boundaries established for the GLA's predecessor, the Greater London Council (established in 1963 and abolished by Margaret Thatcher in 1986), not the global city-region and its population of 21 million that Scott identifies.

In contrast, the four remaining models of city-region governance have emerged as much in locally rooted responses to London's status as a leading global city-region as they have the global policy orthodoxy surrounding city-regions. Moreover, they bear even less resemblance to the concept of the global city-region. For example, the second model of city-region governance centres on the Northern Way Growth Strategy, established in 2004 as the UK government's response to widespread criticism that they were prioritizing growth in and around London, and thereby increasing regional disparities between the London city-region and the rest of the UK. Centred on eight interacting but hierarchically differentiated city-regions, the Northern Way had ambitious aims: to maximize the growth potential of city-regions to drive forward the economy in the north of England, act as a northern counterweight to the economy of London and the south east, and cut the £30 billion north/south productivity gap. However, while on the surface indicative of the new city-regionalism in action, the dovetailing of the Northern Way to the city-region agenda came about more by coincidence than grand design. Initially designed around two growth corridors, the Northern Way was actually formulated to be part of England's post-1997 regional policy. Indeed, it was only after England's regional policy collapsed in November 2004 that the Northern Way was repackaged and branded as a city-region initiative, but even so, there is still clear evidence of its regional ancestry (Harrison, 2010a).

Following on from this, the third model of city-region governance centres on City Development Companies (CDCs). First announced in 2006, CDCs are city- or city-region-wide economic development companies formed to drive economic growth. The premise for CDCs is that international evidence from *inter alia* Toronto, Baltimore, Greater Washington and Stuttgart shows that economic transformation of a city or city-region requires an arm's length organization, distanced from local and central government. However, the extent to which CDCs are 'giving added impetus to the development of city-regions' remains unproven (DCLG, 2008, p. 11). This is because, at root, CDCs are not a new initiative; they are a locally rooted response to a desire to amplify the geographical coverage of sub-city Urban Regeneration Companies (established in 1999) to improve effectiveness and efficiency over a wider geographical area. In other words, the UK government looked at what was going on organically in a number of cities, captured the concept of CDCs from international evidence of what appeared to work in successful metropolitan areas, and then branded it as part of its formative city-region agenda. Indeed, what is more noticeable is how the metamorphosis of sub-city Urban Regeneration Companies (URCs) into city-regional CDCs has in fact not taken place – most CDCs are city-wide, while one covers two cities, one is polycentric and, ironically, a number are not based on cities at all. As a result CDCs were rebranded as Economic Development Companies in 2007.

Announced at the same time as CDCs, the fourth model of city-region governance focuses on establishing Multi-Area Agreements (MAAs) – a framework through which adjoining local authorities work in partnership to facilitate greater cross-boundary collaboration on economic development issues. To incentivize MAAs the government committed to action to devolve more power and reduce barriers to delivering better outcomes in return for groups of local authorities which set out a convincing case for how they could boost economic growth and tackle deprivation and financial inequalities together across a functional economic area – in other words, a city-region. In contrast to CDCs there has been more appetite for establishing city-regional MAAs, but like CDCs they also exhibit incredible spatial and scalar flexibility – the 15 MAAs established to date cover populations ranging from 330,000 people (<5 per cent of the region) through to 2.76 million (>50 per cent of the region), and areas from 384km^2 to 5716km^2. And finally, fifthly, the latest in what is already a long line of models for city-regional governance is seeing Leeds and Manchester established as the first city-regions outside London to receive statutory powers.

So what does this tell us? It illustrates how, despite the rhetoric used to justify their existence, many models of city-regional governance are not city-regional *per se* (Harrison, 2010b). In part this is enabled by the lack of a workable definition for city-regions, but more broadly it is symptomatic of a wider trend where much of what is branded as 'city-regional' bears little resemblance to what Scott and others were imagining when conceptualizing the global city-region and global city-region governance a decade ago. What we have seen over the past ten years then is the city-region, as the *in vogue* spatial scale, promoted as necessarily contingent to accessing global circuits of capital; a process which both encourages and forces those areas which might at first appear marginal to the city-region agenda to be seen to be politically engaged and attempting to keep up with the major cities and city-regions. What remains as an open question is whether the city-region concept is doing significant work for those places and/or initiatives which have forged links to it by identifying as a city-region or attaching the city-region label.[2]

CONCLUSION

This chapter set out to explore global city-region governance, ten years on from Scott's (2001a) identification of global city-regions as the pivotal social formation in contemporary globalization. It started from a recognition that, as an analytical concept, the global city-region is relatively straightforward to define and make distinct from other concepts. However, it has been argued that in policy and governance terms this task is much more difficult because it has become increasingly tempting to overlook the reality whereby: (i) in many cases 'new' city-region governance frameworks actually represent a 'scalar amplification or contraction' of previous entities (Lord, 2009); and (ii) 'new' governance arrangements often 'sit alongside' rather than replace extant institutional frameworks and supports (Harrison, 2010a, 2010b). Often reliant upon outdated and inadequate institutional structures, frameworks and supports, to go back to Scott's question of *what main governance tasks do global city-regions face as they seek to preserve and enhance their wealth and well-being*, this chapter emphasizes the need to understand how city-regions are constructed politically. For when it comes to governance and the rescaling of state power, in this case to city-regions as the *in vogue* spatial scale, there is no blank piece of paper upon which new governance arrangements can be established. Rather, as evidenced by attempts to build a tier of city-region governance in England, new rescaling strategies collide with, are constrained by and can only partially rework inherited landscapes of state scalar organization (Brenner, 2009). In other words, the major challenge going forward lies in developing more concrete examples of the barriers to institutional reorganization and how extant institutions working at or across multiple scales enable and constrain processes of state rescaling: a view that would seem to lend support to Allmendinger and Haughton's (2009, p. 626) contention that in future work:

> it is important to examine how rescaling works across multiple scales . . . rather than simply privileging specific scales of governance. It is how the many scales of governance intersect and interact which matters, not simply the scales which are perceived to be the primary 'beneficiaries' or 'losers' in rescaling.

NOTES

1. A notable exception to this rule is Shanghai, where the city and city-region population are equivalent at 18.2 million and, therefore, the governance arrangements cover the larger metropolitan area.
2. A similar trend has been identified in academic circles, with the concept of the city-region now increasingly

used by authors as a vehicle to push their own particular (often unconnected) agenda, rather than doing significant work (Harding, 2007).

REFERENCES

Allmendinger, P. and G. Haughton (2009), 'Soft spaces, fuzzy boundaries, and metagovernance: the new spatial planning in the Thames Gateway', *Environment and Planning A*, **41** (3), 617–633.

Brenner, N. (2009), 'Open questions on state rescaling', *Cambridge Journal of Regions, Economy and Society*, **2** (1), 123–139.

Cheshire, P. and S. Magrini (2009), 'Urban growth drivers in a Europe of sticky people and implicit boundaries', *Journal of Economic Geography*, **9** (1), 85–115.

Christaller, W. (1933), *Die Zentralen Orte in Süddeutschland*, Jena: Gustav Fischer.

DCLG (2008), *Review of Economic Assessment and Strategy Activity at the Local and Sub-regional Level*, London: Department of Communities and Local Government.

Hall, P. (2001), 'Global cities and global city-regions: a comparison', in A.J. Scott (ed.), *Global City-Regions: Trends, Theory, Policy*, Oxford: Oxford University Press, pp. 59–77.

Harding, A. (2007), 'Taking city regions seriously? Response to debate on "city-regions: new geographies of governance, democracy and social reproduction"', *International Journal of Urban and Regional Research*, **31** (2), 443–458.

Harrison, J. (2007), 'From competitive regions to competitive city-regions: a new orthodoxy, but some old mistakes', *Journal of Economic Geography*, **7** (3), 311–332.

Harrison, J. (2010a), 'Networks of connectivity, uneven development, territorial fragmentation: the new politics of city-regionalism', *Political Geography*, **29** (1), 17–27.

Harrison, J. (2010b), 'Life after regions? The evolution of city-regionalism in England', *Regional Studies*, doi: 10.1080/00343404.2010.521148.

Hudson, R. (2007), 'Regions and regional uneven development forever? Some reflective comments upon theory and practice', *Regional Studies*, **41** (9), 1149–1160.

Jonas, A. and K. Ward (2007), 'An introduction to a debate on city-regions: new geographies of governance, democracy and social reproduction', *International Journal of Urban and Regional Research*, **31** (1), 169–178.

Lord, A. (2009), 'Mind the gap: the theory and practice of state rescaling: institutional morphology and the "new" city-regionalism', *Space & Polity*, **13** (2), 77–92.

Lovering, J. (1999), 'Theory led by policy: the inadequacies of the new regionalism (illustrated from the case of Wales)', *International Journal of Urban and Regional Research*, **23** (2), 379–395.

ODPM (2005), *Planning Glossary*, London: Office of the Deputy Prime Minister.

Parr, J. (2005), 'Perspectives on the city-region', *Regional Studies*, **39** (5), 555–566.

Scott, A.J. (ed.) (2001a), *Global City-Regions: Trends, Theory, Policy*, Oxford: Oxford University Press.

Scott, A.J. (2001b), 'Globalisation and the rise of city-regions', *European Planning Studies*, **9** (7), 813–826.

Scott, A.J., J. Agnew, E.W. Soja and M. Storper (2001), 'Global city-regions', in A.J. Scott (ed.), *Global City-Regions: Trends, Theory, Policy*, Oxford: Oxford University Press, pp. 11–30.

Tewdwr-Jones, M. and D. McNeill (2000), 'The politics of city-region planning and governance', *European Urban and Regional Studies*, **7** (2), 119–134.

Thrift, N. (2002), 'Performing cultures in the new economy', in P. Du Gay and M. Pryke (eds), *Cultural Economy*, London: Sage, pp. 201–234.

UNFPA (2007), *State of the World Population*, New York: UNFPA.

28 Cities and sustainability: reflections on a decade of world development
Kathy Pain

INTRODUCTION

This chapter revisits the key themes addressed by Blowers and Pain in their contribution to the Open University's (1999) *Understanding Cities* book series – 'The unsustainable city?'. The intention of their paper, which was written for the final volume of the series, subtitled *Unruly Cities?*, was to provide a 'turn of the twenty first century' overview of major governance challenges posed for the sustainability of the world's largest cities from a specifically geographical and *spatial* perspective. At a time when discourse on the relationship between sustainability, development and cities was dominated by positivist approaches, the authors' analysis focused on the growing significance of the relational and social nature of cities as key determinants of sustainability. But, in spite of the upsurge of interest and policy rhetoric on this critically important subject during the past decade, inter-city relations, as discussed by Blowers and Pain (1999), still generally lack attention in the growing multidisciplinary literature.

Empirical research undertaken by the Globalization and World Cities (GaWC) research group in the intervening period indicates that the need to adopt a relational approach to understanding cities, and the juxtaposition between their development and sustainability, has become more necessary than ever. Thus the case for contextualizing debate through engagement with the increasingly complex relations of cities in contemporary 'globalization' is revisited in the present chapter. Whereas it is customary to begin the discussion of cities and sustainability by defining the term 'sustainable development', which is broadly concerned with the impact of development on future global sustainability, here I deliberately come to this later. Instead I begin by considering recent empirical evidence and theorization of changes affecting cities worldwide. This is because sustainability and development are relative and contested concepts which cannot be defined independently of cities.

CITIES IN TRANSITION – MEGA-CITIES, WORLD CITIES

The beginning of the twenty-first century has marked a key transition in world development. By 2008, 3.3 billion people (more than half the global population) were living in cities (UNFPA, 2007). A total of 58 cities in the world are expected to have a population size over 5 million by 2015 (Liotta, 2009). Not only do United Nations forecasts indicate that 5 billion people (two-thirds of the global population) will be urban by 2030 (UNFPA, 2007) but the most dramatic year-on-year increase in urbanization involves some of the world's poorest cities. While major migrations are not a new phenomenon, what is new is that very large cities became the dominant foci of migration in the late twentieth century.

This spatial reorganization is tailing off in 'developed' countries but is ongoing in 'developing' countries. Recent estimates indicate that world urban population will double to 2050 and in Africa it will increase from 40 to 60 per cent (UNDP, 2009, p. 32).

Very large cities with a population over 10 million have generally been described as 'mega-cities' in the policy and academic literature (see for example Perlman and O'Meara Sheehan, 2007) but cities of this size actually include different kinds of cities. Their estimated size is dependent on how the boundaries of a metropolitan area are defined, which is a matter of academic debate (see Hall and Pain, 2006), and their social, economic, political and spatial constitution differs considerably. Developed world cities such as New York, London and Tokyo are widely referred to as mega-cities alongside cities in the developing world such as Guangzhou, Mexico City and Mumbai. But these examples illustrate very different development processes occurring in different cities, and different reasons for population growth including natural increase. In the developing world, a present cause of urbanization remains major intra-state, rural–urban migration, whereas in the developed world the causes are more diverse but often include transnational migration (UNDP, 2009). In both cases, however, cities are now the present foci of production and employment which are socially essential, and this is the principal driver of ongoing urbanization. As Tacoli et al. (2008, p. 50) have emphasized:

> Attempts to limit urban growth by controlling migration are misguided – in part because migration flows are logical responses to changing economic opportunities and in part because most urban population growth is actually from natural increase, not net rural-to-urban migration.

The spatial reorganization of human habitation into cities is taking place alongside the technological, informational and communications revolution which began in the late twentieth century, commonly referred to as *globalization* (Cochrane and Pain, 2000). In the late twentieth century, this gave developed 'world cities' (Friedmann, 1986) a critical role as the source of people, knowledge and talent required to support the development of the modern 'world economy'. The concentration of intelligence-based, creative resources and the capacity for innovation and economic growth in such cities have made them central to the functioning of the economies of states and wider political regions, for example the European Union. Importantly, they are the world locations for post-Fordist specialized knowledge-intensive sectors of the new tertiary economy known as advanced producer services, such as finance, law and accountancy, which are now key articulators of the world economy but cluster in 'global city' service centres (Sassen, 1991). They continue to draw in talent from around the world but have come to have a critically important role in adding value to primary and secondary sector economic activities in world-wide global production networks (Pain, 2010). The ongoing importance of human interaction and clustering of complementary skills are still driving the transnational migration of skilled and professional labour to these cities, aided by reduced travel and communication costs (UNDP, 2009, pp. 27, 33).

In general, migration to large cities is driven by income inequalities within and between countries, the divergence between developing and developed world regions and the divergence between world, or global, cities and mega-cities. However, the Pacific Asia region, especially China, which was discussed in detail by Blowers and Pain (1999), is the recent exception to a longstanding geography of regional/city divergence, with national per capita income increasing from 3–14 per cent of the developed country average between

1960 and 2007 (UNDP, 2009, p. 33). Although there are no accurate official statistics, intra-national and intra-regional migration are still an important feature in the developing world, including in China, because cities are the location of work which can dramatically improve livelihoods. As a recent United Nations report states, 'no country in the industrial age has ever achieved significant economic growth without urbanization. Cities concentrate poverty, but they also represent the best hope of escaping it' (UNFPA, 2007, p. 1); however, migrations are frequently constrained for the poor and unskilled by policy and economic barriers (UNDP, 2009, p. 46). Contrary to cities operating within a neo-liberal framework, China has raised a major swathe of its population out of poverty by introducing its 'open door' strategy and this is being articulated through major rural–urban population migration into vast mega-cities (Lo and Yeung, 1998; Lin, 2005).

Despite his dystopic mega-city vision, Manuel Castells (1998a, 1998b) has also identified the connectivity of all cities to value-adding advanced producer services networks as crucial for the economic survival and livelihood of the world population, but for many cities this has not been achieved thus far. Mushrooming mega-cities in less economically developed world regions (termed 'peripheral' in world systems theory and late twentieth century development studies) can be considered world cities which are disconnected from these key networks which are channels for global economic growth. While historic uneven geographies of world economic development may be expected to be replicated in present divergences between cities, new empirical evidence indicates that they are in fact changing and this sheds light on recent developments in China.

Quantitative analysis of global advanced producer service networks between the years 2000 and 2008 by the GaWC Research Network shows a remarkable shift in the connectivity of Chinese cities (Derudder et al., 2010). There has been a dramatic increase in global service network connectivity for cities in Pacific Asia, and in particular Chinese cities. Economic liberalization and powerful state intervention in China have quite deliberately reversed a previous policy of de-urbanization. The development of the major cities Shanghai, Beijing and Guangzhou, since the Blowers and Pain (1999) paper, has effectively connected China to the capitalist world economy leading to major economic expansion in just one decade (Lin, 2005; Yeh, 2005; Pain, 2008b). The analysis also shows that other cities in many places around the world are upgrading their 'World City Network' connectivity (Taylor, 2004; Derudder et al., 2010), indicating a significant shift in world city relations. This is not to say that disconnection can be eradicated easily – disconnection remains in fragmented and spatially specific locales in all cities, regardless of their overall economic development, as theorized in Manuel Castells' 'Fourth World' (1998a). However, the latest empirical evidence on global service network organization supports Allen Scott's (2001) tentatively optimistic vision of a change in established economic relations by which 'core' capitalist countries have so far maintained their global dominance through their world cities. The global servicing role of world cities appears to be mobile in evolving business network structures (Pain, 2008b).

CONCEPTUALIZING CITY DEVELOPMENT AS A PROCESS

There are two main conclusions from the assessment of how cities are changing at the start of the twenty-first century. First, cities are becoming increasingly important as global social and economic interactional entities (the places where most people will in future live and work). Second, two different development processes are happening in cities world-wide – here termed *a global city process* and *a mega-city process*. These two processes can both be present in the same time and space but, overall, more cities are becoming more 'well connected' in the global service economy – China's global connectivity spurt is exceptional. I turn next to consider how the conceptualization of cities can inform the distinction between these two development processes.

As the present era of global technological, economic and urban restructuring started to be felt in developed Western countries, Ray Pahl (1986, p. 10) made a criticism of Peter Hall's 1986 J.R. James Memorial Lecture 'From the unsocial to the social city' that (in spite of its title) its analysis mistakenly rested on economic theories and 'not enough social theory'. As a long line of urban theorists had previously insisted, cities are primarily socially constituted and it still proves vitally important not to forget this. Urban sociologists in the US urban ecology 'Chicago School', for example Ernest Burgess and Robert E. Park, emphasized the importance of both the 'social' and the 'political' in the construction of cities long before contemporary globalization was envisaged. Lewis Mumford emphasized the social interrelations between the 'economic' and 'ecological' dimensions of cities: the city is the 'point of maximum concentration for the power and culture of a community . . . the form and symbol of an integrated social relationship . . . a product of the earth' (Mumford, 1938, p. 1) . . . and a 'social division of labour, which serves not merely the economic life but the cultural process' (Mumford, 1937, republished in LeGates and Stout, 1996, p. 94). At a time when 1960s and 1970s urban geography and planning were still focusing on the classification of urban development based on locational analysis (e.g. Walter Christaller's earlier 1933 'Central Place Theory'), Jane Jacobs developed this reasoning, interpreting cities as the sites of social reproduction, diversified divisions of labour and complexity which create economic expansion and stimulate new work (Jacobs, 1969; Taylor, 2007). Thus city development is in practice structured both by social and economic reproduction.

As discussed by Peter Taylor, this complexity and consequent 'new work' attach to 'cities' as opposed to smaller urban formations, that is, 'towns'. However, Jacobs' insights suggest that large urban populations do not always give rise to city economic vibrancy and expansion. The reason relates to the constitution of cities, hence city economies, as inherently the expression and outcome of social relationships. Thus in 1970 Henri Lefebvre discussed 'urbanism' as a 'social practice' and, together with David Harvey, linked the notion of the 'production of urban space', its political organization and uneven geographies, to social practices (Harvey, 1973; Lefebvre, 1991). This line of argument underpinned Manuel Castells' later (1996) conceptualization of cities in the globalizing 'informational' and 'network society' as a process which has been stimulated by, and also stimulates, technological innovation and constructs business connectivity and flows between cities world-wide, analysed empirically by GaWC (Taylor, 2004).

GaWC qualitative research on the global strategies and practices of advanced producer service networks suggests that without connectivity to the flows conveyed by them, mega-cities (which are the location of the world's poorest expanding population) are unsustainable socially, politically and environmentally (Lachman, 1997; Castells, 1998b; Segbers, 2007) and there are implications for the sustainability of smaller cities too, even in the Western world where structural adjustment is needed (Taylor and Aranya, 2006). Specialized, knowledge-intensive work or 'net-work' (Taylor, 2007; Taylor and Pain, 2007), which is conducted through cities by network forms of business organization, is now generally recognized as critical to support wider regional and national economies in the developed as well as the developing world (Pain, 2008a). Although inequalities persist between high-paid/specialized and low-paid/non-specialized service skills and pay, employment is shown to be fundamentally important to inter-generational progress towards greater economic and social equity (Perlman and O'Meara Sheehan, 2007). Services create a city environment that is conducive to beneficial flows of knowledge and finance between globalizing cities and to innovation and investment in less environmentally damaging city infrastructures (Knox and Pain, 2010). They also mark a transition from labour-intensive and environmentally detrimental forms of employment, to 'cleaner, hi-tech' economic production.

The degree of relative connection/disconnection from global service networks can thus be understood as defining the different development processes of global and mega-cities. Although Manuel Castells' attention to the Fourth World (1998a) must not be overlooked, the astonishing upward economic trajectory of liberalizing Chinese cities in less than ten years, and the upgrading of global service connectivity in far more cities elsewhere, are indicative of a major world city restructuring process which seems to herald a new manifestation of development which Allen Scott has referred to as a 'new social grammar of space' (Scott, 2001, p. 814), raising his question posed in 2001, whether this can override 'in important ways the spatial structure of core–periphery relationships that has hitherto characterized much of the macro-geography of capitalist development' (2001, p. 817). Based on the recent insights into the contemporary global city development process from empirical analyses, how should this inform consideration of the sustainability of very large cities?

SUSTAINABLE DEVELOPMENT AS POLITICAL STRATEGY

The concept of 'sustainable development' remains value-laden and contested, as discussed by Blowers and Pain (1999). 'Sustainability' is a generalized and normative goal which can refer to almost anything (Mitlin and Satterthwaite, 1996); hence sustainable development can be a means of achieving many different things. Following the work of the 1987 Brundtland Commission (WCED, 1987), Blowers and Pain interpreted the goal of sustainability as needing to include cities as a social outcome as well as productive of economic and bio-physical environmental and eco-sphere impacts in their analysis. They interpreted the dominant neo-liberal world economic strategy as reinforcing spatial inequities; thus they saw the term 'sustainable development' as constituting a self-contradictory oxymoron, noted also by Rees (1997). They identified the tensions between Chinese urbanization and wider global environmental issues, but the dramatic rise in the global service economy connectivity of its mega-cities and their economic and social implications were then unanticipated. Viewing 'development' as a potentially non-spatially dualistic process, albeit tempered and shaped by political and governance strategies for cities, brings to the fore interesting questions about the prospects for more sustainable patterns of development.

In 1999, the 'green' agenda had only recently moved from its representation as a fringe, radical interest (e.g. Meadows et al., 1972; Devall and Sessions, 1985) to a mainstream international policy issue. The urban and environmental justice movements were generally associated with radical political activism (Harvey, 1973, 1996), and urban–rural/city–nature dualisms (Tuan, 1978) were only beginning to be challenged by new relational discourses (e.g. Macnaghten and Urry, 1998; Castree, 2000; Swyngedouw and Kaika, 2002; Kaika, 2005; Heynen et al., 2006). Thus Blowers and Pain emphasized the need for a co-evolutionary approach to the relationship between sustainability and cities in which social development must be considered alongside anthropogenic environmental impacts. Since then, widespread publicity and the scientization and popularization of environmental debate (Cochrane and Pain, 2000; Hinchliffe and Woodward, 2000) have turned widespread attention towards biocentric 'deep ecology' concerns (Johnston et al., 2002). Attempts to quantify and model environmental risk have gained prominent media attention. Social concerns and risks which relate to cities, such as poverty, malnutrition, disease, war and urban environmental degradation, gain less attention. This tilting of the global debate begun at Brundtland has implications for green, as well as human, ecological priorities since the former cannot be realized in isolation from the latter in an increasingly urban world.

Institutional approaches to conflicting international priorities remain subject to competing scientific and political claims and debate, and are in consequence often misguided and/or contradictory. While policy is framed by an international institutional context, this is constituted by government, non-governmental organizations and commercial interests that reflect powerful territorial, political and stakeholder objectives. For all these reasons policy agendas have tended to veer away from sensitive and conflictual social and economic issues and towards less contentious environmental issues, including bio-diversity and climate change. As in 1999, less palatable yet fundamental underlying issues concerning spatialities of economic reproduction and consumption remain sidelined. Analytical devices such as the urban 'footprint' and sustainability indicators and toolkits have communicated a range of issues to a wide audience in line with the Local Agenda 21 emphasis on changing individual lifestyle practices, however they oversimplify complex social, economic and political urban issues. The scale of poverty and social and environmental degradation in mega-cities is unsustainable. Forty per cent of the world's urban population is predicted to be slum dwellers by 2030 (Davis, 2006; UNDP, 2009, p. 30). City economic expansion, for which global service connectivity is essential, could help to avert this but what would be the wider environmental outcomes of such development?

This depends on how city development is managed as a process (see for example Humphreys and Blowers, 2009). Agglomeration has substantial environmental as well as economic advantages over more thinly spread urban development patterns. Satellite images indicate that the present world urban space (including urban green space) covers just 2.8 per cent of the Earth's land area, which means that the whole world urban population would fit on less than half of Australia (UNFPA, 2007, p. 45). As already discussed, global connectivity stimulates innovation and investment in cities, which can result in improved technologies to support efficient resource use, such as water and energy and communications systems such as public transportation and ICT. It is not building design and construction in high-density new development which are the principal challenge in places where finance capital flows strongly through globalizing cities but institutional arrangements governing regulation and financing (especially for retrofit in mature cities). Thus although the ecological modernization thesis, discussed in the Blowers and Pain (1999) paper, has been a product of neo-liberal strategy, the capacity for globalizing cities to innovate and create less environmentally compromising robust development strategies is now substantial.

An even greater challenge is the problem of lower-density development which now characterizes developing as well as developed world regions. Suburbanization, urban sprawl and peri-urbanization are differently constituted functionally, economically and socially; however, they share a common problem of a lack of adequate spatial governance arrangements. Even mature polycentric urban regions with a dispersed pattern of 'deconcentrated concentration', regarded as a sustainable urban form in European policy since 1999, have been shown to compromise agglomeration economies and generate intense cross-cutting movement which cannot be supported effectively by public transport (Kloosterman and Musterd, 2001; Hall and Pain, 2006). These new city spaces (variously referred to as 'mega-regions', 'global-' and 'mega-city regions') comprise conflictual territorial, political relations and are effectively ungoverned (McGee and Robinson, 1995; Lang and Dhavale, 2005; Laquian, 2005; Hall and Pain, 2006; Regional Plan Association, 2006).

CONCLUSION

In writing 'The unsustainable city?' Blowers and Pain were at pains to reflect the complex interrelations of cities that are structuring contemporary sustainability tensions. This complexity has increased as a result of the intensification of service network connectivity. The uneven world geography of development that the authors noted in 1999 is beginning to be countered to an extent with regard to their case study on China's development challenges in economic 'liberalization', but this dynamic Chinese capitalist city strategy is unusually embedded in an ideological framework of Communism, strong state intervention and investment. The authors' questioning of the long-term sustainability of a neo-liberal strategy for cities remains open. Knowledge-intensive economic activity seems good news for cities because it promotes creative global intercity flows of knowledge, cultural diversity and finance that can feed a more sustainable development process. As David Harvey (1996, pp. 437–438) has claimed, 'Cities that cannot accommodate diversity, to migratory movements, to new lifestyles and to political, religious, and value heterogeneity, will die either through ossification and stagnation or because they will fall apart in violent conflict.'

Dense cities are centres of education, and cultural, social, health and work opportunities; they can also constitute a more environmentally sustainable development form than dispersed settlements. They can encapsulate what Edward Soja (2000, pp. 13–14) has termed 'generative' and 'innovative', 'synekistic agglomeration' – a 'behavioural and transactional as well as political and economic concept' similar to Jane Jacobs' (1969) 'spark of economic life'. However, as Manuel Castells has cautioned (1998a), these urban assets are unequally shared even within the richest of the world's cities, and city–non-city relations are now polarizing (see for example Neuwirth, 2005; Humphreys, 2006), leading to ongoing rural–urban economic migrations. What seems clear however is that nuanced governance approaches *can* facilitate 'a progressive transformation of economy and society' (Wheeler and Beatley, 2004, p. 56) by 'opening up' to globalization. The politics of governance remains as important as it was in 1999 in shaping the strategies of large cities which can lead to a more, or less, sustainable development process.

REFERENCES

Blowers, A. and K. Pain (1999), 'The unsustainable city?', in S. Pile, C. Brook and G. Mooney (eds), *Understanding Cities: Unruly Cities? Order/Disorder*, London and New York: Routledge, pp. 247–298.
Castells, M. (1996), *The Information Age: Economy, Society and Culture, Vol. I: The Rise of the Network Society*, Oxford: Blackwell.
Castells, M. (1998a), *The Information Age: Economy, Society and Culture, Vol. III: End of Millennium*, Oxford: Blackwell.
Castells, M. (1998b), 'Why the megacities focus? Megacities in the new world disorder', The Mega-Cities Project, Publication MCP-018, available at www.megacitiesproject.org/ (accessed 20 February 2010).
Castree, N. (2000), 'The production of nature', in E. Sheppard and T. Barnes (eds), *A Companion to Economic Geography*, Oxford: Blackwell, pp. 275–289.
Christaller, W. (1966 [1933]), *Central Places in Southern Germany*, translated by C.W. Baskin, Englewood Cliffs, NJ: Prentice-Hall.
Cochrane, A. and K. Pain (2000), 'A globalising society?', in D. Held (ed.), *A Globalising World? Culture, Economics, Politics*, London: Routledge, pp. 5–45.
Davis, M. (2006), *Planet of Slums*, Brooklyn: Verso.
Derudder, B., P.J. Taylor, P. Ni, A. De Vos, M. Hoyler, H. Hanssens, D. Bassens, J. Huang, F. Witlox, W. Shen and X. Yang (2010), 'Pathways of change: shifting connectivities in the world city network, 2000–08', *Urban Studies*, **47** (9), 1861–1877.
Devall, B. and G. Sessions (1985), *Deep Ecology: Living as if Nature Mattered*, Salt Lake City, UT: Gibbs M. Smith.
Friedmann, J. (1986), 'The world city hypothesis', *Development and Change*, **17** (1), 69–83.
Hall, P. and K. Pain (eds) (2006), *The Polycentric Metropolis: Learning from Mega-City Regions in Europe*, London: Earthscan.
Harvey, D. (1973), *Social Justice and the City*, London: Edward Arnold.
Harvey, D. (1996), *Justice, Nature and the Geography of Difference*, Oxford: Blackwell.
Heynen, N., M. Kaika and E. Swyngedouw (2006), *In the Nature of Cities: Urban Political Ecology and the Politics of Urban Metabolism*, London: Routledge.
Hinchliffe, S. and K. Woodward (2000), *The Natural and the Social: Uncertainty, Risk, Change*, London: Routledge.
Humphreys, D. (2006), *Logjam: Deforestation and the Crisis of Global Governance*, London: Earthscan.
Humphreys, D. and A. Blowers (eds) (2009), *A Warming World*, Milton Keynes: The Open University.
Jacobs, J. (1969), *The Economy of Cities*, New York: Random House.
Johnston, R.J., P.J. Taylor and M.J. Watts (2002), 'A burden too far?', Introduction to Part V, Geoenvironmental Change, in R.J. Johnston, P.J. Taylor and M.J. Watts (eds), *Geographies of Global Change: Remapping the World*, Malden, MA: Blackwell, pp.357–363.
Kaika, M. (2005), *City of Flows: Modernity, Nature and the City*, New York: Routledge.
Kloosterman, R.C. and S. Musterd (2001), 'The polycentric urban region: towards a research agenda', *Urban Studies*, **38** (4), 623–633.
Knox, P.L. and K. Pain (2010), 'Globalization, neoliberalism and international homogeneity in architecture and urban development', *Informationen zur Raumentwicklung*, (5/6), 417–428.
Lachman, B.E. (1997), *Linking Sustainable Community Activities to Pollution Prevention: A Sourcebook*, Santa Monica, CA: Critical Technology Institute Rand.
Laquian, A.A. (2005), *Beyond Metropolis: The Planning and Governance of Asia's Mega-Urban Regions*, Baltimore, MD: Johns Hopkins University Press.
Lang, R.E. and D. Dhavale (2005), *Beyond Megalopolis: Exploring America's New 'Megapolitan' Geography*, Alexandria, VA: Metropolitan Institute at Virginia Tech (Metropolitan Institute Census Report Series, Census Report 05:01, July 2005), available at www.mi.vt.edu/publications/otherresearch/document-pdfs/megaopolis.pdf (accessed 20 February 2010).
Lefebvre, H. (1991), *The Production of Space*, Oxford: Blackwell.

Lin, G.C.S. (2005), 'Service industries and transformation of city-regions in globalizing China: new testing ground for theoretical reconstruction', in P.W. Daniels, K.C. Ho and T.A. Hutton (eds), *Service Industries and Asia Pacific Cities: New Development Trajectories*, New York: Routledge, pp. 283–300.

Liotta, P.H. (2009), 'The rise of the 21st century megacity: why it matters, and what could be done', paper presented at the annual meeting of the ISA–ABRI Joint International Meeting, Rio de Janeiro, Brazil, 22 July 2009, available at www.allacademic.com/meta/p381166_index.html (accessed 20 February 2010).

Lo, F. and Y. Yeung (eds) (1998), *Globalization and the World of Large Cities*, Tokyo: United Nations University Press.

Macnaghten, P. and J. Urry (1998), *Contested Natures*, London: Sage.

McGee, T. and I. Robinson (eds) (1995), *The Mega-Urban Regions of Southeast Asia: Policy Challenges and Response*, Vancouver: University of British Columbia Press.

Meadows, D.H., D.L. Meadows, J. Randers and W.W. Behrens III (1972), *The Limits to Growth*, New York: Universe Books.

Mitlin, D. and D. Satterthwaite (1996), 'What is to be sustained, what developed? Sustainability and sustainable cities', in C. Pugh (ed.), *Sustainability, the Environment, and Urbanization*, London: Earthscan, pp. 135–177.

Mumford, L. (1937), 'What is a city?', in R.T. LeGates and F. Stout (1996) (eds), *The City Reader*, London: Routledge, pp. 92–96.

Mumford, L. (1938), *The Culture of Cities*, New York: Harcourt Brace & Company.

Neuwirth, R. (2005), *Shadow Cities: A Billion Squatters, A New Urban World*, New York: Routledge.

Pahl, R. (1986), 'On Hall's social city', *The Planner*, March, 10.

Pain, K. (2008a), 'Urban regions and economic development', in C. Johnson, R. Hu and S. Abedin (eds), *Connecting Cities: Urban Regions*, Sydney, Australia: Metropolis Congress, pp. 20–47.

Pain, K. (2008b), 'Looking for the "core" in knowledge globalization: the need for a new research agenda', *GaWC Research Bulletin*, 286, available at www.lboro.ac.uk/gawc/rb/rb286.html (accessed 20 February 2010).

Pain, K. (2010), 'Emerging cross-border metacity in the Pan Yellow Sea Region', in C. Mo and Y.H. Kim (eds), *The Emerging Cross-border Mega-city Region and Sustainable Transportation*, KOTI-EWC 2010 Special Report, Hawaii, US and Korea: East-West Center/The Korea Transport Institute, pp. 12–37.

Perlman, J.E. and M. O'Meara Sheehan (2007), 'Fighting poverty and injustice in cities', in The Worldwatch Institute (ed.), *State of the World 2007: Our Urban Future*, London: Earthscan, pp. 172–190.

Rees, W. (1997), 'Is "sustainable city" an oxymoron?', *Local Environment*, **2** (3), 303–310.

Regional Plan Association (2006), *America 2050: A Prospectus*, New York: Regional Plan Association.

Sassen, S. (1991), *The Global City: New York, London, Tokyo*, Princeton, NJ: Princeton University Press.

Scott, A.J. (2001), 'Globalization and the rise of city-regions', *European Planning Studies*, **9** (7), 813–826.

Segbers, K. (ed.) (2007), *The Making of Global City Regions: Johannesburg, Mumbai/Bombay, São Paulo, and Shanghai*, Baltimore, MD: Johns Hopkins University Press.

Soja, E. (2000), *Postmetropolis: Critical Studies of Cities and Regions*, Oxford: Blackwell.

Swyngedouw, E. and M. Kaika (2002), 'The environment of the city . . . or the urbanization of nature', in G. Bridge and S. Watson (eds), *The Blackwell City Reader*, Oxford: Blackwell, pp. 567–580.

Tacoli, C., G. McGranahan and D. Satterthwaite (2008), 'Urbanization, poverty and inequity: is rural–urban migration a poverty problem, or part of the solution?', in G. Martine, G. McGranahan, M. Montgomery and R. Fernández-Castilla (eds), *The New Global Frontier: Urbanization, Poverty and Environment in the 21st Century*, London: Earthscan, pp. 37–53.

Taylor, P.J. (2004), *World City Network: A Global Urban Analysis*, London: Routledge.

Taylor, P.J. (2007), 'Space and sustainability: an exploratory essay on the production of social spaces through city-work', *The Geographical Journal*, **173** (3), 197–206.

Taylor, P.J. and R. Aranya (2006), 'Connectivity and city revival', *Town & Country Planning*, **75** (11), 309–314.

Taylor, P.J., P. Ni, B. Derudder, M. Hoyler, J. Huang and F. Witlox (eds) (2011), *Global Urban Analysis: A Survey of Cities in Globalization*, London: Earthscan.

Taylor, P.J. and K. Pain (2007), 'Polycentric mega-city regions: exploratory research from Western Europe', in P. Todorovich (ed.), *The Healdsburg Research Seminar on Megaregions*, New York: Lincoln Institute of Land Policy and Regional Plan Association, pp. 59–67, available at www.america2050.org/Healdsburg_Europe_pp_59–67.pdf (accessed 20 February 2010).

Tuan, Y.-F. (1978), 'The city: its distance from nature', *The Geographical Review*, **68** (1), 1–12.

UNDP (United Nations Development Programme) (2009), *Human Development Report 2009*, New York: UNDP, available at http://hdr.undp.org/en/reports/global/hdr2009/ (accessed 20 February 2010).

UNFPA (United Nations Population Fund) (2007), *State of the World Population: Unleashing the Potential of Urban Growth*, New York: UNFPA, available at www.unfpa.org/swp/2007/ (accessed 20 February 2010).

WCED (World Commission on Environment and Development) (1987), *Our Common Future*, Oxford: Oxford University Press.

Wheeler, S.M. and T. Beatley (eds) (2004), *The Sustainable Urban Development Reader*, New York: Routledge.
Yeh, A.G.O. (2005), 'Producer services and industrial linkages in the Hong-Kong Pearl River Delta Region', in P.W. Daniels, K.C. Ho and T.A. Hutton (eds), *Service Industries and Asia Pacific Cities: New Development Trajectories*, New York: Routledge, pp. 150–172.

29 Planning for world cities: shifting agendas and differing politics
Peter Newman and Andy Thornley

At the heart of the debate about world cities has been the question of whether cities are just riding the waves of economic globalization or whether they are able to steer development and make real choices about social and environmental futures. Strategic planning of one form or another aims to guide the development of world cities. Planning, as defined by its professional associations across the world, has objectives that seek to balance the aims of economic efficiency, environmental sustainability, social welfare and local needs. It is therefore at the forefront of managing global/local tensions. In our view, the balance between these aims expresses the pressure of different interests and lobby groups. Planning priorities and the strategic policy response to economic globalization will therefore be shaped to a greater or lesser extent by urban politics and the processes of governance. On the ground economic globalization will be mediated by differing political traditions and we should expect styles of strategic planning to be shaped by these different contexts.

How do we define strategic planning? We are interested in planning policy that is city-wide. Secondly, we are concerned with policy that has a spatial dimension and has implications for specific geographical areas within the city. This strategic, city-wide, spatial policy can take a number of forms. These vary from city-region plans, city master plans or strategic policy frameworks, through vision or mission statements, to a perhaps less coherent approach based around major key developments. Thirdly, we focus on the establishment of priorities: we are more interested in the aims and objectives and overall balance of the strategic plan than the details of the individual policies. In our work we explore the influence of different pressures and interests in determining the relative importance of economic, environmental and social objectives. In other words we examine how the strategic urban planning agenda is constructed.

There is also an important issue of scales of intervention as governments struggle to manage city-regions or even mega-regions. For the most part in this chapter we will be focusing on world cities that are also defined political units but much has been written, especially by economic geographers (e.g. Storper, 1997; Scott, 2001), on how the economic activity of world cities expands out into the surrounding region. There has been a growing interest in recent years in city-regional plans as a necessary contribution to the competitive advantage of a world city. For example in North America the Province of Ontario has recently taken an interest in the wider Toronto region instituting green belt and growth pole policies. At an even broader scale America 2050 has emerged as a national lobby of regional interests making a case for infrastructure planning across State boundaries (Regional Plan Association, 2006). In Asia in 2008 the Chinese government produced a plan for the whole Pearl River Delta – a region of around 150 million people – as part of its strategy for integrating Hong Kong into the mainland. In Tokyo there is an ongoing debate about how to plan for the broader region with both Tokyo city and the national government developing their ideas. Barcelona, after many years of trying, has recently approved a plan for their city-region. One of the issues for all cities is that these broader economic regions seldom have a matching political entity. Thus creating a city-regional planning approach is usually caught up in struggles between levels of government.

As we can see from other contributions to this volume, a key aspect of the debate on globalization and world cities has been the role of the state. Has there been a reduction in the power of the nation state? Have cities gained more autonomy? Has the relationship between different levels of the state undergone transformation? In our view these questions are best answered through a detailed analysis of particular cities and particular policy areas. Strategic city planning is a very good case to explore. Planning is given legitimacy by being a state activity but has to operate through intervention into, and modification of, the market. Therefore variation in the balance between state and market will provide the 'positioning' of planning. It is therefore at the centre of the state–market relationship. In most cases strategic city planning has also to interact with national and local policy. National concerns provide a framework within which city planning has to operate. The local level is where most detailed implementation takes place and where people participate most in decision-making. Such grass roots activity feeds upwards into the strategic level. Thus strategic planning is also a good case to examine any reformulation of the state between its different levels and the tensions this might create.

Our aim in this chapter is to review some changes in strategic planning priorities in world cities over the past twenty years or so. Our contention is that although globalization creates certain common pressures on cities there is scope for a variation in the policy response. To what extent is globalization accepted, steered, modified or blocked? Has the strategic planning agenda simply translated the forces of economic globalization into land use and development requirements or has it been used to introduce alternative aims and objectives? Variation stems from the opportunities provided by the specific local political conditions in a city. City mayors seem to have become much more visible but they do not have a free hand. They, and other public agencies, are conditioned by the national political culture concerning the role of the state and public intervention. Other interests also influence city politics. Some international businesses, for example, will want to prioritize world city issues and persuade politicians to accommodate economic global forces. On the other hand social movements, from within the city or transnational, may also arise to oppose such views. Strategic planning decisions may, in some cities, offer an arena in which such conflicts can be played out. Cities will differ in the degree to which civil society is active and in the range of participatory opportunities that are available. There is a world of difference between referendums in Los Angeles on city finances and structures of government and the strong central hand that guides the development of cities in many Asian countries.

In this contribution we will draw on our analysis of strategic planning across world cities (Newman and Thornley, 2011) to review two aspects. We focus on established world cities that are highly placed on the various world city hierarchies (e.g. Friedmann, 1986; Taylor, 2004) and those that are rising fast, such as Chinese cities, or playing a strong regional role. The two questions we pose here are:

1. Has there been a change in the priorities of the strategic planning agenda over the last twenty or so years that can be observed across most world cities?
2. Notwithstanding any general trend, is it also possible to detect significant variation in planning approach dependent on political traditions?

A CHANGING PLANNING AGENDA?

Globalization has led to the increased mobility of both economic enterprises and the labour force, both highly skilled and unskilled. As a result local city economies are volatile. Over the last thirty years the economic sectors that epitomize world cities, such as finance, business services, media and tourism, have seen considerable growth. Cities therefore have usually seen themselves in competition with each other to attract inward investment from these sectors. This affects all cities as no position in the world city hierarchy can be considered sacrosanct. City politicians see their own electoral futures as being closely tied to the economic success of their city and they promote the positive world city attributes of their city. They are all engaged in city marketing. National government will often also argue that the success of their major cities will have a positive spinoff for the nation as a whole and will provide their support. This means that in all major cities the strategic planning agenda includes world city promotion as an important element. Globally oriented economic policies will often be the top priority. City business interests will usually encourage politicians to develop this aspect of the planning agenda – sometimes they will actually take the lead. In London for example in the 1990s, when there was no strategic government for the city, it was the business lobby, London First, that represented the globally oriented firms such as the banks, major property companies, British Airways and the airport authority, that pushed for leadership and vision. They, and other business organizations, subsequently had a strong influence on the London Plan published in 2004 with the overarching aim of maintaining London's world city status. In the contrasting city of Mumbai, business leaders noted London's approach and decided to create their own organization called Bombay First. The aim of Bombay First is to mobilize a partnership of business to develop Mumbai as a world-class city. Bombay First commissioned a report from the consultants McKinsey with the support of the central government of India, the state government and the World Bank, and this was published in 2003 with the title *Vision Mumbai: Transforming Mumbai into a World-Class City* (Bombay First and McKinsey, 2003).

Prioritizing this world city aim means prioritizing the provision of certain facilities. The desire to attract global companies and specialist service functions will lead to the provision of attractive, well-serviced and well-located sites for 'state of the art' office development, often utilizing old port areas with potential waterfront amenity. In the world cities this has produced Battery Park (New York), Canary Wharf (London), Pudong (Shanghai), the Tokyo Waterfront, Marina Bay (Singapore) and similar centres in all cities. Luxury housing and eating and entertainment provision are also required to attract the personnel for these global activities. Tourism, whether for business or pleasure, has also become a major economic growth sector in the global economy. As a result, many of the recent urban projects have included trade centres, conference centres, hotels, casinos, urban theme parks and sports complexes. Outside the centre all world cities have been prioritizing international airports. Beijing built a new airport at the time of the Olympic Games that was claimed to be the biggest building in the world, and Delhi opened a new terminal in 2010 that was India's biggest public building. The Indian Prime Minister said at the opening that 'a good airport will signal a new India, committed to joining the ranks of modern industrialised nations' (Burke and Jethra, 2010, p. 20). Even in cities such as London or Tokyo where such projects are lacking, increasing airport capacity and accessibility is a highly contentious political issue.

So such economic aims are central to world city strategic plans. However, prioritizing this aim still leaves scope for variation in how much the economic dimension dominates other objectives. There is a common trend for strategic planning to focus on the central areas or 'world city spaces'. The degree to which the planning agenda gives importance to the more peripheral parts of the city introduces an element of variation and is subject to the characteristics of local or national politics. Outer London has recently come in for more attention, and debate about Grand Paris includes concern about integrating less favoured localities into the world city.

Higher urban quality has come onto the planning agenda in most world cities, from New York to Singapore. This 'high quality' can mean a better physical environment but also a more varied and exciting cultural life. Even in a highly networked society place is still important. The emphasis on urban quality puts a special importance on the management of space and strategic planning can potentially play a major role in this. Paris has always been at the forefront in emphasizing the quality of urban life, with its restaurants, cultural activities and attractive built environment. New York's Hudson riverside, London's South Bank and Shanghai's Expo 2010 are further evidence of a trend towards creating interesting areas of good environment and cultural opportunity. There are differences in the degree to which such schemes cater for outsiders, such as tourists or global elites, or local citizens. Environmental aims also include congestion relief, pollution control and mitigating global warming. For example both London and Tokyo have set themselves up to be exemplary world-leaders in relation to global warming.

Overcoming spatial inequality and regenerating areas of poverty have always been key aims of planning. Globalization and the development of world cities is said to increase social polarization. One question that might be asked is whether in prioritizing world city development cities also develop policies to mitigate the social effects. Generally though cities do not make the direct connection between polarization, poverty and world city growth and simply rely on 'trickledown'. However, there is probably more variation between cities in how much they prioritize social policy compared with economic or environmental aims. For example managing polarization through housing policies can exhibit local differences. In Paris, London and New York there is a common concern for housing affordability, but each city has struggled in its own way to deliver sufficient numbers of social housing units.

The degree to which social issues are directly included in the strategic agenda is also to some extent affected by the degree of polarization and poverty. Singapore and Tokyo are examples of cities were polarization is low. On the other hand cities in developing countries with world city aspirations, such as Mumbai and Johannesburg, have to develop their globally oriented economic aims alongside strong social policies. The extent of poverty means that it is a political necessity to appear to be addressing the issue. Some cities have specific social issues to manage. The policy of attracting migrant workers to the booming Chinese cities has created a problem in the 'urban villages' where they live in poor conditions and without citizenship rights.

Singapore is a useful case to look at in terms of the shifting planning agenda. The city has a long history in promoting itself as a world city. The state has consciously sought to steer this process and adapt the city strategy to ensure that it remains competitive. It constantly monitors the city economy and seeks advice from business and international experts on how to adapt to global changes. In the 1980s the state realized that its manufacturing economy was under threat from competitors and so re-launched the city as an 'international business hub' and changed the priorities in its strategic plan. As other cities in the region moved in this direction it focused on computing and telecommunications with the slogan of the 'intelligent island'. The most recent strategy in 2010 aims to make the city 'new Asia's hub for design innovation and creative enterprise' and a 'leading cultural capital in Asia' (Economic Strategies Committee, 2010). Education, innovation and the development of the arts are now central features. Alongside this the quality of life and environmental policies have been increasing in importance over the last twenty years and in 2009 the government produced its 'Sustainable Development Blueprint' to take a more comprehensive and integrated approach.

THE INFLUENCE OF DIFFERENT POLITICAL TRADITIONS

We now turn to our second question – the extent to which political tradition can lead to different planning approaches. To explore this we believe it is useful to consider cities across the three sub-global regions of North America, Europe and Pacific Asia. There is an argument that in looking at economic globalization it is worth considering differences between these regions as they organize themselves in separate trade blocs. In investigating the varying political cultures and institutional arrangements these differences are even more pronounced. Economic liberalism dominates in North America, the traditions of the welfare state and the role of the EU give Europe a distinctive flavour and the 'developmental state' orchestrating economic growth from the centre dominates in Pacific Asia. These dominant regional cultures of governance are important but the story is rather more complex. These dominant cultures provide the main framework for cities within each global sub-region but variation can still be found. For example, Europe's 'social welfare' tradition has less relevance for the more liberal economic ideology behind the development of London than in Paris. The developmental state takes on different forms across Asian cities, and in China the central state has a particular history and in recent years has initiated a decentralization of urban policy. Meanwhile in North America Canada, the USA and Mexico offer different traditions of intervention. Despite these distinctions the cities of North America clearly differ from European models or those within Asian developmental states.

In the European case we see a complex interplay of European national and sub-national scales in 'multi-level governance'. Out of such multi-level working the idea of a polycentric network of cities is emerging, an image of 'territorial cohesion' and future urban development in Europe that confounds the idea of a world of a few global cities (Hall and Pain, 2006). In Europe nation states still impact on their cities but in a changing institutional context. In Asia strong states have been very consciously developing their strategic urban assets. Nowhere can this be more clearly seen than in city-state Singapore. The pace of change has been most marked in Asia, and in China in particular with the prospect now of 180 'international great cities' (Wu and Ma, 2006).

In addition to governmental structures urban politics clearly differs across cities and regions and influences the planning agenda. Again we can see some common trends – for example the active involvement of business interests in trying to influence the urban policy agenda. The priorities, social, environmental or economic, of many of the cities we examined are associated with political personalities. Leadership, and even the personal preferences of city mayors, has become an important factor in explaining city policies – former mayor Livingstone's enthusiasm for tall buildings, for example. Global forces meet individual preferences. However, behind this overt display of strong leadership we can also detect, across the three regions, a pattern of coherent urban regimes in which these leaders cooperate with other interests in shaping the 'big picture' (Stone, 2005) and setting the strategic planning agenda. However, the actual actors involved and their relative influence vary and this can largely be linked to the broader political culture of the global sub-region in which the city is located. The conservative city politics of most North American cities – the Toronto 'progressive conservatism' and republican-led LA and NYC shared an agenda of low taxes and weak social planning – contrasts with, for example, the socialist mayor of Paris prioritizing social housing. In London the mayor worked closely with business in formulating the strategic agenda and lobbying for world city infrastructure. In New York it was a question of 'business as usual' with the mayor brokering a range of interests including a powerful property development sector. In Paris the governing regime is public sector-led with a strong city role, although other regional and national government actors play sometimes conflicting parts. Tokyo has relaxed planning rules for the benefit of some private investors. In Shanghai and Beijing a form of urban regime can be detected in which economic and local governmental interests cooperated, although within a particular framework set by history and central state regulations.

In all cases international competitiveness drives planning but the character and mix of governing institutions vary. We see more or less involvement of higher-level governments and more or less involvement of the private sector in planning. Business may either be present in key agencies or have its interests expressed by public bodies. Higher-level governments can, as we see in the European cases, mediate social and economic demands. Cooperation at the EU scale can provide the potential for region-wide strategic planning. The idea that the future would consist of a global network of world city states, superseding national powers, emerged in the 1990s. But our cases show cities still shaped by, and dependent on, the national context. Cities may have much greater consciousness of their international rivals but so do higher-level governments and in all three regions we see these governments involved in enhancing the world city status of their cities.

Finally we will illustrate the influence of these political factors by looking in a little more detail at the strategic planning approach in Tokyo. The Tokyo Metropolitan Government (TMG) with a directly elected mayor (governor) is responsible for most urban services and prepares regular strategic plans. However, national government, following the developmental state approach of prioritizing national economic development, has overall control. It prepares its own plans for the Tokyo region to which the city must conform. The last twenty years have seen an increasing tension between central and city government. During the 1980s Tokyo was economically buoyant and most world city analysts placed it at the top of the hierarchy with London and New York. However, even then the city was not 'international' but globally linked because of the strength of Japanese companies. The strategic planning agenda at that time was oriented to facilitating its economic growth and enabling the expansion of office development, including the mega-project of the Tokyo Waterfront. An enormous development boom followed with very weak planning controls and a detrimental impact on the quality of the urban environment. The state, at both city and national levels, was utilizing the rhetoric of 'world city' to justify the real estate expansion. The economic bubble burst in the early 1990s and recession followed. There was no adequate political response to this and the period was called 'the lost decade'. The city's strategic agenda at this time reflected a reaction against the previous property-led approach and stressed quality of life issues but there were no resources to do anything and a lack of steer from central government that was embroiled in political crisis.

However, there was a significant change at the national level from around 2000. National politicians began to react to the imperatives of globalization and saw the need for new national policies, including at the city level. A committee, chaired by PM Koizumi, called 'Headquarters for the Rejuvenation of Cities' was set up in 2001 with the aim of improving the international competiveness of Japanese cities. The 'Urban Renaissance' policy followed in which national government could designate areas for redevelopment and where developers could suggest changes to official plans. The relaxation of regulations, and the higher densities allowed, led to a boom of major mixed use projects across central Tokyo. Some commentators talk of the reassertion of the national state over urban policy on Tokyo (Sorensen et al., 2010) while others stress the fact that the balance between private and public sector has shifted as private consortia take more of a leading role in the new projects (Waley, 2007). Meanwhile at the city level a new governor, Ishihara, was elected in 1999. His first strategic plan in 2000 focused on the need to make Tokyo more competitive especially in competition with other Asian cities. Some leading global companies had been moving their regional offices to Hong Kong or Singapore. In the 1980s the planning agenda had been reacting to the demand for growth but now it was used as a positive tool to make the city more attractive in the face of competition, with a need to improve the CBD. In the later 2006 plan there was an increasing emphasis on quality of life, with environmental policies on climate change, congestion, pollution, leisure and the riverside. The slogan of 'welcoming world city' also indicated an approach that is more open to the world, promoting new policies for tourism and cultural activity. The city made a bid for the 2016 Olympics as they wanted to use it as a way of conveying this more global attitude as well as a vehicle to attract more resources for the necessary infrastructure projects. Although the city plans reflect the national approach as they are required to do, there has also been considerable tension between the governor and the national state. Ishihara has developed policies that go beyond his remit as a way of pressurizing the state. These have involved developing regional policies and airport proposals, and opposing the policy of central government to remove the capital city functions away from Tokyo.

This outline of the planning approach in Tokyo shows that, although the central state has been gradually decentralizing power to cities, it still retains a controlling role. The developmental state focusing on national economic development has been slow to adapt to the pressures of globalization. The governor of Tokyo has been at the forefront of promoting the competitiveness of the city, and the need to take a regional approach and improve airports. However, once the central state decided that cities needed invigorating to compete more effectively it has intervened very directly to open up opportunities for the private sector in mega-project development. This state-led approach is typical of the Pacific Asia region and contrasts with that in North America, which generally lacks such a strategic planning approach and relies on more ad-hoc projects implemented by appointed boards. There are perhaps more similarities between the planning approach in European cities and Tokyo. In both cases there is the involvement of government at different levels with the possible tensions and arrangements for cooperation. However, most European cities have more autonomy over the preparation of their strategic planning agenda and control of major projects. This creates more debate and lobbying at the city level. Central government, however, often maintains its power in other ways, for example in London this is done through financial controls.

The competitive imperative to produce world city spaces makes for similarity in the strategic planning agenda. Over the past twenty years or so this agenda has been changing, adapting more to concerns about quality of life for example, and we can see this shift as a broadly based trend in world city-making. But to understand how priorities emerge and how different interests come to the fore we need to appreciate the very different institutional structures of world cities and the different governing traditions through which planning operates.

REFERENCES

Bombay First and McKinsey (2003), *Vision Mumbai: Transforming Mumbai into a World-Class City*, New Delhi: Galaxy Offset.

Burke, J. and A. Jethra (2010), 'New airport, new India says PM as terminal opens', *Guardian*, 5 July, 20.

Economic Strategies Committee (2010), 'Subcommittee on making Singapore a leading global city. Singapore Government', available at www.esc.gov.sg (accessed 29 May 2010).

Friedmann, J. (1986), 'The world city hypothesis', *Development and Change*, **17** (1), 69–83.

Hall, P. and K. Pain (eds) (2006), *The Polycentric Metropolis: Learning from Mega-City Regions in Europe*, London: Earthscan.

Newman, P. and A. Thornley (2011), *Planning World Cities: Globalisation and Urban Politics*, Basingstoke and New York: Palgrave Macmillan, 2nd edition.

Regional Plan Association (2006), *America 2050: A Prospectus*, New York: Regional Plan Association.

Scott, A.J. (ed.) (2001), *Global City-Regions: Trends, Theory, Policy*, New York: Oxford University Press.

Sorensen, A., J. Okata and S. Fujii (2010), 'Urban renaissance as intensification: building regulation and the rescaling of place governance in Tokyo's high-rise Manshon Boom', *Urban Studies*, **47** (3), 556–583.

Stone, C.N. (2005), 'Looking back to look forward: reflections on urban regime analysis', *Urban Affairs Review*, **40** (3), 309–341.

Storper, M. (1997), *The Regional World: Territorial Development in a Global Economy*, New York: Guilford Press.

Taylor, P.J. (2004), *World City Network: A Global Urban Analysis*, London and New York: Routledge.

Waley, P. (2007), 'Tokyo-as-world-city: reassessing the role of capital and the state in urban restructuring', *Urban Studies*, **44** (8), 1465–1490.

Wu, F. and L.J.C. Ma (2006), 'Transforming China's globalizing cities', *Habitat International*, **30** (2), 191–198.

30 Surveillance in the world city
David Murakami Wood

INTRODUCTION

Surveillance has often been portrayed as a pervasive global phenomenon but it is now being recognized that there are major differences in its character, scope and reception in specific places (Bennett and Lyon, 2008; Arteaga Botello, 2009; Murakami Wood, 2009; Zureik et al., 2010). As spaces where interactions between globalizing forces and local cultures are expected to be of a particularly intense nature, 'global' or 'world cities' offer a key test case for claims about the ubiquity of surveillance, and in particular those arguments that treat surveillance as a global or globalizing phenomenon.

Rather than deal overmuch with theoretical arguments about surveillance or world cities, this chapter will set surveillance in its global urban context and draw on the results of research conducted in three major world cities: London, Tokyo and Rio de Janeiro, and consider the commonalities and differences between the kinds of surveillance practices, processes and technologies found in each place. The focus will largely be on video surveillance; however, it should be recognized that this is just one of a plethora of surveillance processes in contemporary world cities.

A GLOBAL, URBAN SURVEILLANCE SOCIETY?

Surveillance is the systematic collection, classification and sorting of information about subject populations for the purposes of behavioural adjustment or control (Dandeker, 1990; Lyon, 2001). It is a mode of ordering (Law, 1994), and has become perhaps the predominant one in contemporary urban societies (Lyon, 2007). One could argue that the city itself evolved partly as a mechanism for surveillance (Coaffee et al., 2009), but recent sociotechnical development with the advent of computing, and particularly the database, has not just resulted in the possibility of intensified state control, but also the private sector gathering personal data on a vast scale.

However, contemporary urban surveillance is not uniform. It is as unevenly developed as any other phenomenon in the current situation of globalizing neoliberal capitalism. Surveillance is complex and contradictory, involving 'synopticism' (the many watching the few) (Mathiesen, 1997), lateral (or mutual) surveillance (Andrejevic, 2007) and pleasure and performance (McGrath, 2004) in addition to monitoring and control. A 'surveillance society' therefore is not a society of total control, and as such may perhaps be defined not by any totalizing model, whether based on the Panopticon (Foucault, 1977) or any other exemplary mechanism, or even an amorphous 'surveillant assemblage' (Haggerty and Ericson, 2000), but as an 'oligopticon' (Latour, 2005), an environment which fluctuates from the most intense scrutiny and knowledge to none at all.

SURVEILLANCE IN THE WORLD CITY: LONDON, RIO DE JANEIRO, TOKYO

World cities have always been at the heart of this new mode of ordering, not least because the same combination of computing and communications that underlies the new surveillance also underpins the new global economy (Graham and Marvin, 2001). Largely due to the work of investigators like Mike Davis (1990) and the geographers of the 'LA School', Los Angeles is seen as the *ur*-surveillance city, its neoliberal urbanism giving rise to public space video surveillance and contributing to a divided cityscape of homogenized theme-park centres, increasingly gated private suburbs and the exclusion of the poor, a technologically enabled expression of what Mollenkopf and Castells (1992) called a 'dual city'. Such tendencies are to be found at their most extreme in the cities of the newly developing world, including Brazil (see Caldeira, 2001). In the new inward investment zones of the Middle East, India and China, entire private towns are being created, after the model of emerging world cities like Singapore and Dubai, where there is not even the pretence of a liberal democratic state to temper the combination of capitalist exploitation and total surveillance (Davis and Monk, 2007).

London

However, it is London that has come to be known as the surveillance capital of the world and this was indeed the world city where CCTV initially spread most rapidly into public space. The first reason for this was the liberalization of urban planning in the 1980s combined with long-term urban economic decline, which led to British urban centres being abandoned as shopping spaces in favour of out-of-town developments or malls (Norris and Armstrong, 1999). The response was to make cities more like those malls, with neoliberal urban governance and (semi-)privatization through initiatives like Town-Centre Management and Business Improvement Districts (Coleman, 2004). This was only accelerated by Tony Blair's New Labour administration from 1997 with the renewed involvement of the state in urban security (particularly in providing large subsidies for CCTV) (Fussey, 2004; Webster, 2004) and a moralistic socio-economic management of cities with the rise of a new actuarial model of justice (Simon and Feeley, 1994), based on risk.

Secondly, there were a series of trigger events, involving football hooliganism, child abduction and the contemporaneous terrorist attacks by the Provisional IRA (PIRA) on the financial heartlands of the City of London and Docklands (Coaffee et al., 2009). This would have remained a British peculiarity were it not for London's central place in the 'world city network' (Taylor, 2004; Massey, 2007), when, following 9/11, the British 'example' as a supposedly successful urban security policy helped spread open-space CCTV throughout the world, and particularly to mainland European and US cities (Murakami Wood and Webster, 2009).

Around the financial heartlands of the City of London and Docklands, along with the physical 'ring of steel' of closable barriers and checkpoints, a 'ring of surveillance' was established following the PIRA attacks in the early 1990s, that was based around not just public space video surveillance but also Automatic Number-Plate / Licence-Plate Recognition (ANPR/ALPR) (Coaffee, 2003). The City system has been through several changes, expanding and morphing into traffic control (the Congestion Charge Zone) in the late 1990s and now back into a security perimeter as well (Coaffee et al., 2009). This is being extended and modified still further in the run-up to the 2012 Olympic Games. The development can be seen very much as 'revanchism' in the style described by Neil Smith (1996) in which private capital is essentially colonizing what was a liminal, out-of-control area with a strong working class culture and shifting populations of Roma and Irish travellers. There could not, perhaps, be a clearer example of surveillance supposedly installed to ensure the safety of a mega-event and its visitors and participants, acting in fact as a disciplinary advance party for global capital exploitation and taming of a 'wild zone' (Lash and Urry, 1994) in the heart of one of the greatest world cities.

London has also been the site of experiments in high-tech policing. The Metropolitan Police's Police Information Technology Organisation developed strong links into research and development and the security and surveillance industry, heavily promoting biometrics (recognition software), for example (Elliot, 2005). In the borough of Newham, face-recognition software was pioneered in the early 2000s and attracted much media coverage despite its manifest ineffectiveness (Introna and Wood, 2004). Other more recent experiments have linked video surveillance, entertainment and the neoliberal management of social housing, with schemes like the Shoreditch Digital Bridge, a short-lived project which linked CCTV cameras and police mugshot databases and a locally made police 'reality television' show to a special cable television system for residents, providing residents with 'digital lace curtains' (Ballard, 2007). This was not simply a local curiosity but a logical conclusion of the panoptic communitarian tendencies of the New Labour governance; for example, the National Identity Register and card, new databases for health, childcare, DNA, facial images and more, and new powers to allow multiple methods of covert surveillance for many different public authorities under the Regulation of Investigatory Powers Act 2004 (SSN, 2006; House of Lords Constitution Committee, 2009).

However, video surveillance in London is far from a systematic endeavour. Most of the CCTV cameras are either under the control of the city's many different local authorities, as well as the private owners of offices, banks, shops and malls, and there is still very little connection or overall management. This continues to be the case despite recent attempts to systematize urban surveillance systems under complex new national, regional and local 'civil contingencies' management systems in the 2000s, and in the 'Secure by Design' programme designed to integrate security into the infrastructure of new public buildings and spaces (Coaffee et al., 2009).

Rio de Janeiro

If global cities are 'dual cities', then in Rio it is more obvious than in most. Unlike in São Paulo where the favelas (informal settlements) are peripheral, in Rio they exist cheek by jowl with richer, more formal communities, and Rio's Gini Coefficient is one of the worst in Latin America (and the world). Proximity can lead to understanding, but at present the mood is one of fear and defensiveness, despite growing national optimism in Brazil as a whole.

From 2008, Mayor Eduardo Paes and State Governor Sergio Cabral reversed previous progressive policies, including the effective *Favela Bairro* programme of former Mayor Cesar Maia (Moreno-Dodson, 2005), in favour of *Choque de Ordem* (shock of order).

This involves demolition of illegal buildings, walling some favelas, removal of unlicensed street vending and high-profile occupations of favelas by police *Unidades Pacificadores* (Pacification Units/UPs). Three favelas were occupied in 2008: Santa Marta, Cidade de Deus and Batan (since expanded to seven).

In Santa Marta, for example, drug traffickers were expelled and some trust has been built between UP leader and the local community association. However, several developments are undermining this success. The first is the police themselves. Policing in Rio is complex, with several more-or-less independent police forces or groups, and police corruption and violence remain pervasive. The second factor is the numerous unofficial armed groups. Many favelas are controlled by criminal gangs associated with cocaine-trafficking (Arias, 2006). These gangs are frequently in conflict with each other, the police and various militias (*Autodefesas Comunitárias*/ADCs), supported by elements in the army, police and rightist political parties. There are also 80,000 registered private security organizations in Brazil and many more unregistered (Kanashiro, 2008). Police officers moonlight as private security guards and some private security firms are owned by relatives of senior police officers. Police, private security, militias and gangs reinforce each other in a spiral of criminality and securitization. In wealthier neighbourhoods, residents are employing private security to illegally gate several (public) dead-end streets, where guards check ID and restrict access (c.f. Caldeira's work on São Paulo, 2001).

The third factor is the growth of surveillance. Existing official video surveillance systems in Rio are sparse, and traffic control is a key priority, although there is nothing like ANPR in the UK or Japan's N-system (see below). A national government programme, SINIAV, is developing a Radio Frequency Identification microchip-enabled car licence-plate tracking scheme, but so far it has seen only very limited trials. Senior police and government officers are divided between those who see video surveillance as a mere supplement, dismiss it on grounds of cost or are in favour of it as 'intelligence-led' policing. For the latter, video surveillance is essential for the city's preparedness for the 2014 FIFA World Cup and the 2016 Olympics. The pre-conditions and preparations for these mega-events now appear to be reinforcing and intensifying the crackdown on unruly favelas. There is general agreement in official circles that currently Rio is not ready, and the architect of 'Zero Tolerance', ex-Mayor of New York and inspiration for *Choque de Ordem*, Rudy Giuliani, has now been appointed as Security Advisor (*Globo. com*, 2009).

In late 2009, nine networked surveillance cameras were installed in the 'pacified' favela of Santa Marta and it was made clear that it would be introduced into the other 'pacified' favelas too. This was in addition to the wall being built along the west side of the favela, one of many such schemes, particularly along the highway from the international airport. In addition, the fatal landslides that hit the Rio favelas in early 2010, prompted not sympathy but orders from the Governor that favelas be razed (Melo, 2010). By invading, walling and installing video surveillance against local wishes, community representatives argued that the state is operating like a gang, and it does seem the Rio administration is moving increasingly towards what Steven Graham (2010) calls 'military urbanism'.

However, many favelas are already subject to intimate micro-authoritarian internal control by gangs and it is not just the police who have been installing surveillance cameras. In September 2008, the police found a system of 12 cameras and a hidden control room in Parada de Lucas, a favela in the north of the city (*UOL.com.br*, 2008), and in 2009 another was discovered in Morro dos Macacos (*O Globo*, 2009). *Traficante* video surveillance systems therefore predated those of the state in the favelas.

Tokyo

Unlike in Rio where surveillance is clearly about policing class boundaries or London where it has become an all-purpose, mutating tool of state control, in Tokyo it is the fear of *gaikokujin* (foreigners) that currently drives the growth of state surveillance (Murakami Wood and Abe, 2011). Despite longstanding xenophobia in Japanese society and government (see for example Clammer, 2001), this has not always been the rationale for surveillance. Tokyo had its own history of surveillance, much of which was built into the structure of the city with narrow gated streets and monitored bridges (Murakami Wood et al., 2007), and more recently Japanese state institutions have promoted hi-tech surveillance. The most notable is the N-system, an ANPR/ALPR system. This was introduced in the early 1980s, part of an early wave of 'information society' initiatives, and gradually expanded to cover most national expressways and strategic urban locations in Tokyo and Osaka. For example, Kabukicho, the entertainment district in Shinjuku, is surrounded by N-system cameras.

In addition, much of the surveillance on the privatized railways and the Tokyo Metropolitan Government-run Metro system derives not from concern over the foreign other, but internal threats: the growth of mass transit surveillance in Tokyo can be traced directly to responses to the Sarin gas attacks on the transport system by the apocalyptic religious cult, Aum Shinrikyo, in 1996 (Cybriwsky, 1999; Goold, 2002; Murakami Wood et al., 2007). However, this did not prompt a surge in video surveillance in public streets.

Video surveillance systems in Japan have however been expanding since the 1990s. There are just 363 *Keisatsuchou* (National Police Agency/NPA) cameras; however, there are more owned by local municipal authorities, particularly in Tokyo, but as in London there are thousands more outside national state control, operated by the transport networks and quasi-public bodies, for example *choukai* (neighbourhood associations) and *shoutenkai* (shopkeepers' associations).

The direct trigger for the state to become involved in non-traffic public street surveillance (and airport face recognition systems) was the 2002 FIFA World Cup, which targeted European hooligans and illegal vendors, largely from the rest of Asia, and Africa (Abe, 2004). In the same year, the Tokyo Metropolitan Government installed 50 CCTV cameras in Kabukicho, in response to an alleged increase in violence from Chinese gangs. This was later expanded to four other areas: Ikebukuro, Shibuya, Roppongi and Ueno.

The expansion was connected to the introduction, in 2003, of an *Anzen anshin machi-zukuri* ('community safety development'/AAM) *jourei* (ordinance) by long-time Tokyo Governor, Ishihara Shintaro, an independent 'tough on crime' xenophobic populist. This made community safety the responsibility of the *choukai* with co-ordination, information and encouragement from the *Seikatsu Anzen Bu* (Everyday Safety Divisions SAB) of the *ku* (city wards).

There are very different versions of AAM practised in different wards. In the commercial and administrative centre, Shinjuku, the main effort is directed towards co-ordinating state video surveillance systems with *shoutenkai* systems, because at present the latter systems are generally not monitored. Both *shoutenkai* and *choukai* are being encouraged to install video surveillance, and there is a Tokyo grant scheme: one third of capital costs from the city, one third from the *ku* and one third from the *kai*. This means that coverage is uneven and generally restricted to wealthier areas like Shinjuku.

In wealthy residential Suginami, citizen community safety patrols, organized through the local Parent–Teachers' Associations, *shoutenkai* and *choukai,* are prioritized, with 9600 people actively involved. They, in common with many other wards, also have several *ao patoka* (blue patrol cars): miniature police-style cars and bikes, driven mainly by retired police officers. A new system is thus emerging, prioritizing local volunteerism and video surveillance over direct community policing. Suginami does have some experimental video surveillance help points introduced by the Metropolitan Police Department (*keishicho*) after 2002; however, these cameras only cause problems because children tend to press the alarms and run away.

Marginal Arakawa, in contrast, has only a handful of video surveillance systems. But it also has consistently the second or third lowest crime rates of the 23 Tokyo wards. The ward SAB concentrates on using the natural surveillance capacities of local communities, including *wan-wan* ('woof-woof') patrols involving mainly older female residents and their dogs, but with much lower levels of participation than in Suginami. Arakawa also has *ao patoka*, but has gone further with *anzen anshin sutashion* ('security and safety stations'), repurposed traditional *koban* (neighbourhood police boxes). Staffed by ex-police officers, they deal with security holistically, offering help for older people with benefits, for example, as well as physical security.

Now, the NPA is installing new cameras costing ¥597m (around £3.85 million) in 15 residential areas across Japan, starting in January 2010. These small systems of around 25 cameras each will be on streets used by children going to and from school, and operated by local volunteers.

REACTIONS TO SURVEILLANCE

The reaction from Rio's Santa Marta Community Association to the introduction of cameras in their community was shock. Posters called Santa Marta 'the most watched place in Rio', lamented the loss of trust and described the wall as turning the favela into 'a ghetto'. However, outside of these local objections, there is little indication that surveillance is even considered to be an issue by *cariocas* (Rio residents). Among the marginalized there are contradictions. Concern about surveillance is often seen as a frippery of the privileged; however, there is also a strong post-authoritarian sense of freedom – however unfair Brazil remains, there is a strong sense of idealism about what it should be (Holston, 2008).

The police are divided between the 'new breed' who recognize 'limits' and rights, hard-nosed pragmatists and technocratic 'intelligence-led policing' – one senior officer even argued for microchipping all Brazilians, were it possible. However, the complex multilevel, uncoordinated structure of the federal state mitigates against such totalizing surveillance. Brazil is not a total surveillance society and the changes that it would take to become one would be almost inconceivable. When Brazil has been through periods of authoritarianism, it has been of the arbitrary, military form rather than totalitarian. This provides a good basis for understanding why there is so little opposition and why some forms of state surveillance (like ID) might be seen as providing guarantees against arbitrary treatment, anonymity and disappearance (Murakami Wood and Firmino, 2009; see also Fischer, 2008).

In Tokyo, the attention paid to surveillance also seemed small, but there were concerns expressed by a much wider range of people and groups. Video surveillance now seems to be highly normalized in Tokyo and this has happened in a short period. In a meeting with a local community group in 2005, for example, female members expressed concerns that the presence of video cameras made them feel more unsafe and trust other unknown members of the public less; however in mid 2009 the same community group had just installed its own CCTV cameras.

Suginami-ku was the first Japanese local government to introduce a *bohan kamera jourei* (security camera ordinance), in 2004, which is based on data protection and privacy. The ordinance followed public consultation showing that although 95 per cent considered video surveillance effective, 72 per cent wanted regulation to protect privacy. Until neighbouring Setagaya-ku introduced its own ordinance in 2008, this remained the only one in Japan. The Mayor of Suginami is also part of a small but growing right-wing libertarian movement that objects to surveillance (Interview with the Mayor of Suginami, Tokyo, August 2009). Academic and civil society critics have collaborated with the right on issues like the opposition to *juki-net*, the state scheme for linking government databases (see Tajima et al., 2003), but are generally more left wing in orientation, linking the introduction of video surveillance to urban restructuring and control. Japanese left-wing objectors also have particular reactions grounded in the history of social conformity in Japan (see for example Ogura, 2003) – to which they object almost entirely – thus anti-surveillance group, *Kanshi-No!* sees little difference between *mini-patoka* and *wan-wan* patrol initiatives and the expansion of video surveillance. Privacy is mentioned, but the main concern appears to be that surveillance measures are being used to compensate for lost social trust and community.

Finally in London, while one of the most commonly asked questions is 'how did we let this happen?', there has been a growing reaction against the intensification of surveillance from civil society (with groups like Privacy International, No2ID and Big Brother Watch), academia (e.g. the Surveillance Studies Network, which produced the *Report on the Surveillance Society* in 2006), regulatory bodies like the Information Commissioner's Office and parliament. This resulted in surveillance and 'liberty' becoming a national electoral issue, and the Conservative/Liberal Democrat coalition government which took office in 2010 had at the time of writing announced numerous initiatives to halt or roll back surveillance, including the complete abolition of the National Identity Register and card scheme and the (belated) regulation of CCTV (Cabinet Office, 2010).

DIRECTIONS

The idea of the 'surveillance society' describes a highly bureaucratized modern nation-state in which surveillance practices constitute a dominant mode of social ordering. The starting hypothesis was that the concept needed greater engagement with geography (surveillance in place, in different places, at different scales, and its globalization) and the historical development of different non-western and northern cultures.

The first question to ask is whether there was any evidence of linking these different domains, which might indicate a move to a more totalizing surveillance society. In London, this was clearly the case; it was the study of the development of surveillance in Britain that gave rise to recognition of the 'surveillance society' as an actually existing phenomenon rather than an ideal type (see SSN, 2006). One can trace many connections between the growth of video surveillance, new police and governmental powers, growth and centralization of databases and much more, and it is easy to argue, as the SSN did in 2006, that '[W]e live in a surveillance society. It is pointless to talk about surveillance society in the future tense' (SSN, 2006, p. 1). And despite the new government, much of this increasingly integrated architecture of surveillance, especially that around policing, is likely to remain: for example the national extension of ANPR or the connection of ANPR to the Metropolitan Police's database of protestors and terrorist suspects.

In Japan, despite *juki-net*, there is no general connection between the *anshin anzen machizukuri* agenda and other government agendas – except towards those who do not fit. Video surveillance in Shinjuku, for example, and accompanying police crackdowns are now used largely to curb illegal migrant workers, mainly South-east Asian women working in bars and massage parlours. Now the inclusion of foreigners on the *jyuminhyo* (residents' registry) from 2012, combined with the sharing of that information through *juki-net*, means the state will be able to correlate residency and immigration status, entry records, fingerprints and facial photos.

Japan in general has seen a *decline* in traditional forms of surveillance, of mutual social regulation accompanied by state 'moral suasion' (Garon, 1997); however, some like Suginami *ku* perhaps see the possibility of revitalizing this 'suasive surveillance' (Murakami Wood and Abe, 2011) while protecting privacy, and without an impersonal 'technocratic surveillance society'. Such a society however is undoubtedly already here, just inhabited now only by marginal foreigners.

In Rio, in contrast, divisions of class, wealth and physical force predominate, particularly the favelas, those zones of 'advanced marginality' (Wacquant, 2008). Surveillance in Rio remains secondary to physical security. Despite reminders of its authoritarian past, Brazil is not a 'security state' and most of the security is private, part of a market sector growing at between 10 and 15 per cent per annum (e.g. MSAO, 2008).

This is not just part of a global trend towards privatization. James Holston (2008) argues that the delegation of policing functions to large landowners (a process known as *coronelismo*) early in the 18th century built elite private interests into the Brazilian state structure. Since then there has been a continual struggle to bring what was private from the start into the public sphere. Massive underlying inequalities are also a product of what Holston (2008) terms the inclusive but inegalitarian nature of Brazil's citizenship, and it is the ongoing lack of the positive inclusionary surveillance of welfare, health and education which is keenly felt.

However, Brazil's generalized lack of concern for issues of human rights, including data protection (Doneda, 2006), could still open a space, as in Japan, for the strengthening of technocratic surveillance. The youth of the democratic system and persistence of strong anti-democratic attitudes in police, local government and the wealthy are also a serious concern as the state begins to collect and collate more data.

The technocratic surveillance emergent in Tokyo and Rio was visible in London over a decade ago. But this globalizing trend does not mean local reception and socio-cultural results are identical everywhere, nor does emergence mean inevitability. London, Tokyo and Rio today all have aspects of their governmentality that make them partially surveillance societies, but only in London could one argue that 'surveillance' is approaching being a 'dominant' mode of social ordering, and even there it is fractured, uneven, incomplete, and perhaps now in partial retreat.

ACKNOWLEDGEMENTS

Much of the information in this chapter comes from original research conducted by the author in 2008–9 in the UK, Brazil and Japan funded by a UK Economic and Social Reseach Council (ESRC) Fellowship, Cultures of Urban Surveillance. I would also like to thank all my interviewees and contacts in the UK, Japan and Brazil, and in particular in Brazil: Rodrigo Firmino, Paola Barreto Leblanc, Marta Mourão Kanashiro and Fernanda Bruno, and the Pontifical Catholic University of Paraná, Curitiba; and in Japan: Abe Kiyoshi, Hijikata Masao, Ogasawara Midori, Murakami Kayo and Ryu Yuki.

REFERENCES

Abe, K. (2004), 'Everyday policing in Japan: surveillance, media, government and public opinion', *International Sociology*, **19** (2), 215–231.
Andrejevic, M. (2007), *iSpy: Surveillance and Power in the Interactive Era*, Lawrence, KS: University Press of Kansas.
Arias, E.D. (2006), *Drugs and Democracy in Rio de Janeiro: Trafficking, Social Networks, and Public Security*, Chapel Hill, NC: University of North Carolina Press.
Arteaga Botello, N. (2009), *Sociedad de la Vigilancia en el Sur-Global: Mirando América Latina [Surveillance Society in the Global South: Looking at Latin America]*, México, D.F.: Miguel Ángel Porrúa.
Ballard, M. (2007), 'Home snoop CCTV more popular than Big Brother', available at www. theregister. co.uk/2007/11/11/home_tv_cctv_link/ (accessed 14 June 2010).
Bennett, C.J. and D. Lyon (eds) (2008), *Playing the Identity Card: Surveillance, Security and Identification Regimes in Global Perspective*, London: Routledge.
Cabinet Office (2010), *The Coalition: Our Programme for Government*, available at www.cabinetoffice.gov.uk/media/409088/pfg_coalition.pdf (accessed 14 June 2010).
Caldeira, T. (2001), *City of Walls: Crime, Segregation, and Citizenship in São Paulo*, Berkeley, CA: University of California Press.
Clammer, J. (2001), *Japan and Its Others: Globalisation, Difference and the Critique of Modernity*, Melbourne: Trans Pacific Press.
Coaffee, J. (2003), *Terrorism, Risk and the City: The Making of a Contemporary Urban Landscape*, Aldershot: Ashgate.
Coaffee, J., D. Murakami Wood and P. Rogers (2009), *The Everyday Resilience of the City*, Basingstoke: Palgrave Macmillan.
Coleman, R. (2004), *Reclaiming the Streets: Surveillance, Social Control and the City*, Cullompton UK: Willan.
Cybriwsky, R. (1999), 'Changing patterns of urban public space: observations and assessments from the Tokyo and New York metropolitan areas', *Cities*, **16** (4), 223–231.
Dandeker, C. (1990), *Surveillance, Power and Modernity*, Cambridge: Polity Press.
Davis, M. (1990), *City of Quartz: Excavating the Future in Los Angeles*, London: Verso.
Davis, M. and D.B. Monk (eds) (2007), *Evil Paradises: Dreamworlds of Neoliberalism*, New York: New Press.
Doneda, D. (2006), 'Os direitos da personalidade no Código Civil [The rights of personhood in the Civil Code]', in G. Tepedino (ed.), *A parte geral do novo Código Civil: Estudos na perspectiva civil-constitucional. 3ª edição [The General Part of the New Civil Code: Studies from the Civil-Constitutional Perspective, 3rd edition]*, Rio de Janeiro: Renovar.

Elliot, J. (2005), 'Biometrics roadmap for police applications', *BT Technology Journal*, **23** (4), 37–44.

Fischer, B. (2008), *A Poverty of Rights: Citizenship and Inequality in Twentieth-Century Rio de Janeiro*, Stanford, CA: Stanford University Press.

Foucault, M. (1977), *Discipline and Punish: The Birth of the Prison*, Harmondsworth: Penguin.

Fussey, P. (2004), 'New Labour and new surveillance: theoretical and political ramifications of CCTV implementation in the UK', *Surveillance & Society*, **2** (2/3), 251–269.

Garon, S. (1997), *Molding Japanese Minds: The State in Everyday Life*, Princeton, NJ: Princeton University Press.

Globo.com (2009), 'Governo do Rio contrata ex-prefeito de Nova York para ajudar na segurança' [The Governor of Rio appoints the ex-mayor of New York to advise on security], available at http://g1.globo.com/Noticias/Rio/0,,MUL1402463-5606,00.html (accessed 14 June 2010).

Goold, B. (2002), 'CCTV and public area surveillance in Japan', *Hosei Riron [The Journal of Law and Politics, Japan]*, **34**, offprint – no pagination.

Graham, S. (2010), *Cities Under Siege: The New Military Urbanism*, London: Verso.

Graham, S. and S. Marvin (2001), *Splintering Urbanism*, London: Routledge.

Haggerty, K. and R. Ericson (2000), 'The surveillant assemblage', *British Journal of Sociology*, **51** (4), 605–622.

Holston, J. (2008), *Insurgent Citizenship: Disjunctions of Democracy and Modernity in Brazil*, Princeton, NJ: Princeton University Press.

House of Lords Constitution Committee (2009), *Surveillance: Citizens and the State* (2 volumes), London: HMSO.

Introna, L. and D. Wood (2004), 'Picturing algorithmic surveillance: the politics of facial recognition systems', *Surveillance & Society*, **2** (2/3), 177–198.

Kanashiro, M.M. (2008), 'Surveillance cameras in Brazil: exclusion, mobility regulation, and the new meanings of security', *Surveillance & Society*, **5** (3), 270–289.

Lash, S. and J. Urry (1994), *Economies of Signs and Space*, London: Sage.

Latour, B. (2005), *Reassembling the Social: An Introduction to Actor-Network-Theory*, Oxford: Oxford University Press.

Law, J. (1994), *Organising Modernity*, Oxford: Blackwell.

Lyon, D. (2001), *Surveillance Society: Monitoring Everyday Life*, Buckingham: Open University Press.

Lyon, D. (2007), *Surveillance Studies: An Overview*, Cambridge: Polity.

Massey, D. (2007), *World City*, Cambridge: Polity.

Mathiesen, T. (1997), 'The viewer society: Michel Foucault's "Panopticon" revisited', *Theoretical Criminology*, **1** (2), 215–233.

McGrath, J. (2004), *Loving Big Brother: Surveillance Culture and Performance Space*, London: Routledge.

Melo, D. (2010), 'Washed away', *Infosur*, available at www.infosurhoy.com/cocoon/saii/xhtml/en_GB/features/saii/features/main/2010/04/22/feature-01 (accessed 14 June 2010).

Mollenkopf, J.H. and M. Castells (1992), *Dual City: Restructuring New York*, New York: Russell Sage Foundation.

Moreno-Dodson, B. (2005), *Reducing Poverty on a Global Scale: Learning and Innovating Development*, Washington, DC: World Bank Publications.

MSAO (Massachusetts South America Office) (2008), *The Brazilian Security Industry*, available at www.moiti.org/pdf/Brazil Security Industry.pdf (accessed 14 June 2010).

Murakami Wood, D. (2009), 'The surveillance society: questions of history, place and culture', *European Journal of Criminology*, **6** (2), 179–194.

Murakami Wood, D. and K. Abe (2011), 'The spectacle of fear: anxious mega-events and contradictions of contemporary Japanese governmentality', in C.J. Bennett and K.D. Haggerty (eds), *Security Games: Surveillance and Control at Mega-Events*, London: Routledge, pp. 72–86.

Murakami Wood, D. and R. Firmino (2009), 'Empowerment or repression? Opening up identification and surveillance in Brazil through a case of "identification fraud"', *Identity in the Information Society*, **2** (3), 297–317.

Murakami Wood, D., D. Lyon and K. Abe (2007), 'Surveillance in urban Japan: a critical introduction', *Urban Studies*, **44** (3), 551–568.

Murakami Wood, D. and C.W.R. Webster (2009), 'Living in surveillance societies: the normalisation of surveillance in Europe and the threat of Britain's bad example', *Journal of Contemporary European Research*, **5** (2), 259–273.

Norris, C. and G. Armstrong (1999), *The Maximum Surveillance Society: The Rise of CCTV*, Oxford: Berg.

O Globo (2009), 'Mandante da invasão ao Morro dos Macacos utiliza câmeras para controlar favelas' [Instigator of the invasion of the Morro dos Macacos uses cameras to control favelas], *O Globo*, available at http://oglobo.globo.com/rio/mat/2009/10/20/mandante-da-invasao-ao-morro-dos-macacos-utiliza-cameras-para-controlar-favelas-769532516.asp (accessed 14 June 2010).

Ogura, T. (ed.) (2003), *Rojō ni Jiyu o [Freedom in the Streets!]*, Tokyo: Impact Shutsupankai.

Simon, M. and S. Feeley (1994), 'Actuarial justice: power/knowledge in contemporary criminal justice,' in D. Nelken (ed.), *The Future of Criminology*, London: Sage, pp. 173–201.

Smith, N. (1996), *The New Urban Frontier: Gentrification and the Revanchist City*, London: Routledge.

SSN (Surveillance Studies Network) (2006), *A Report on the Surveillance Society*, Wilmslow UK: Information Commissioner's Office (ICO).

Tajima Y., T. Saito and H. Yamamoto (eds) (2003), *Juki-net to Kanshi Shakai [Juki-net and Surveillance Society]*, Tokyo: Akashi Shoten.

Taylor, P.J. (2004), *World City Network: A Global Urban Analysis*, London: Routledge.

UOL.com.br (2008), 'Polícia estoura central clandestina de monitoramento de TV no RJ' [Police discover a hidden CCTV monitoring centre in RJ], available at http://noticias.uol.com.br/cotidiano/2008/09/12/ult5772u806.jhtm (accessed 14 June 2010).

Wacquant, L. (2008), *Urban Outcasts: A Comparative Sociology of Advanced Marginality*, Cambridge: Polity.

Webster, C.W.R. (2004), 'The diffusion, regulation and governance of closed-circuit television in the UK', *Surveillance & Society*, **2** (2/3), 230–250.

Zureik, E., L.H. Stalker, E. Smith, D. Lyon and Y.E. Chan (2010), *Surveillance, Privacy, and the Globalisation of Personal Information: International Comparisons*, Montreal: McGill-Queen's University Press.

31 Global cities and infectious disease
Harris Ali and Roger Keil

INTRODUCTION

Throughout history it may be said that cities have been global to some extent: they have always been provisioned from far-away places, they have always been refuge for scattered populations, they have always been centres of commerce and finance, geo-political hubs, imperial(ist) way stations, (post)colonial *entrepôts* and melting pots of (multi)cultures. Notably, in recent decades, however, a number of major metropolises have increasingly transcended their respective national urban systems and have come to articulate their localized economic, demographic and sociocultural processes into a broader, globalized configuration of capitalism. Hierarchized, networked or otherwise tightly interconnected, these 'world-city node[s]' (Friedmann, 2002, p. 9) arguably con-stitute an important part of the global economic architecture that has emerged since the economic crises of the 1970s, most notably through what has since been described as the emergence (and crisis again) of neoliberalization, globalization and a shift from Fordism to post-Fordism. With these developments, urban regions have become increasingly tied into networks that make the globalizing economy material and recognizable (Friedmann and Wolff, 2006, p. 58). In this light, a remarkable and distinguishing feature of today's urban–global relationships is the nature and extent to which the 'global city' localities are intertwined with each other in a myriad of ways to create a new and unique type of networked topology that essentially serves as the backbone of an integrated world economy. It is within this emergent networked topology that critical defining features of global cities and their associated relationships may be found – features, as we shall see, that have significant implications for the spread of infectious diseases today.

A crucial element in understanding what makes today's cities 'global' is to recognize that global cities are constitutive of a complex, multi-scaled and topologically connected network space. That is, global cities should no longer be conceptualized as bounded enti-ties that function in a relatively autonomous and independent manner like the walled cities of the past. Rather, today the borders between global cities are quite permeable, allowing flows of all sorts to tie together global cities in varied ways and over different scales, especially under political pressures for trade liberalization, privatization and deregulation. The resulting network of global cities that arises under such circumstances tends to be much more complex than in the past and it becomes difficult to parse out, delimit and compartmentalize the entering and exiting of flows of one global city to and from the next. That is, because of the increased volume and intensity of real time linkages that are an important dimension of contemporary globalization, we now have a situation where global cities, although they may be quite distant as measured through the tradi-tional metric of physical distance, are in fact quite close together if measured through the network metric of connectivity (Smith, 2003). Global cities now merge into one another because of their networked flows in a topological space where the degree or intensity of connectivity and not physical distance matters in terms of defining the nature and types of relationships between global cities.

Although facilitating the relations upon which the global economy now depends, the emergence of this globalized networked topology does not necessarily translate into better conditions for all world citizens. This is because the global cities network is hierarchically segmented as certain globalized cities articulate national and regional economies into the world economy to a greater extent than others (i.e. there are variations in the level of connectivity of a particular place with the rest of the world), and by performing a bundle of certain functions and not others (based on the different needs of the different fractions of capital – finance, mercantile, cultural, retail, etc.), as is reminiscent of world-systems core–periphery conceptualizations. In this manner, global cities are not only networked but they are arranged somewhat hierarchically, as a function of overall wealth and influence as well as in terms of their level of connectivity.

Today, it is worth noting that while some global urban networks are tangible and material – as would be described by traditional core–periphery models – others are virtual, in turn depending on the maintenance of advanced information and communications infrastructures for their continued existence (Graham, 2006, p. 119). Consequently different types of unevenness and inequalities develop based on the degree to which particular global cities are integrated or connected into the world economy on the basis of their respective material and virtual levels of flow (e.g. capital, labour, information, etc.). Such inequalities are in essence manifested in terms of differential access to goods and services. The consequences of this are two-fold. First, such inequalities due to differential connectivity with the world economy may create notable sites of social polarization and differentiation *within* these cities themselves, and in so doing exacerbate social problems within them – especially under post-Fordism and neoliberalization, such as for example divisions between a 'creative class' and the traditional proletariat, or between globally mobile fractions of capital that jet-set across the world while staying in hotels where global city hospitality and tourism service workers labour to ensure that another – often overlooked – dimension of the global cities network is maintained (Major, 2008). At the same time, such inequalities arising from the inability to access and connect to the global flows which undergird the world economy may lead to inequalities *between* different regions of the world that are, in turn, based on the differential influence of particular global cities on the regional, national and global economy. Yet, besides the general recognition that each city's level and type of integration into the global city network and hierarchy may entail polarization, the other downsides of this connectivity have garnered little analytical attention. Neither the boosterist nor the dystopian literatures say much about the pitfalls that lie in the network itself, nor do they pay much attention to other than economic connectivity, such as those involving the social, ecological and technological connectivity. That is, we have no sustained understanding of the dangers and opportunities that lie in being networked *per se*. It is to issues of networked vulnerability that this chapter speaks: the relationship of systemic networked connectivity with new forms of vulnerability in the global city system. To illustrate such new types of relationships we draw from the experience of the outbreaks of Severe Acute Respiratory Syndrome (SARS) in 2003 as a point of reference – bearing in mind that our discussion is also relevant for many other types of contemporary disease spread, including for example HIV/AIDS and the resurgence of (multi-drug resistant) tuberculosis.

NETWORKS, CONNECTIVITY AND VULNERABILITY

According to a networked approach, cities may be thought of as nodes that are connected to each other, either directly or indirectly, through various types of flows, such as: information bytes, the migration patterns of people, the trade in commodities, the flow of money in transactions, the flights of airplanes or the movement of viruses. By conceptualizing the relationships between cities in this way we can draw upon insights from the new and emerging interdisciplinary field of 'network science' (Buchanan, 2002; Barabasi, 2003; Watts, 2003). Research on networks and complexity has found that systems based on networked connections share certain defining characteristics, including: the systems' ability to self-organize (i.e. ability to adapt to local environmental circumstances and change), upheavals at the edge of chaos (such as cascades that occur once critical threshold tipping points are exceeded), the existence of feedback loops and, most importantly for our discussions, nonlinearity, that is, the idea that very small changes in the systems may have unpredictably large effects (Pearce and Merletti, 2006) – a phenomenon commonly referred to as the 'butterfly effect' in chaos theory where small differences in the initial conditions of a dynamical system produce large variations in the long-term behaviour of the system. If the connections amongst global cities do indeed lead to the formation of a hierarchical and segmented network, as noted by global city theorists, then some of the properties identified by complexity researchers will be useful for our understanding of how networked connectivity (i.e. interconnectivity) between global cities is related to infectious disease vulnerability.

The advantages of any network stem from its ability to effectively link up different elements, so that whatever flows through the links is able to efficiently go from any one node to another. In this light, much research in network science has focused on the network architecture – that is, the particular configuration through which nodes are linked[1] and how this influences the degree to which the nodes are linked together (i.e. their level of connectivity), thereby giving some indication of how efficiently the network operates in terms of transmitting flows. For many networks of interest to social scientists, the nodes are usually defined as individual persons and the links between these persons may take the form of ideas, such as the spread of rumours amongst a group of people at a party, or the adoption of a new technological gadget (e.g. fax machines, cell phones, etc.) in a population. Other human-based social networks that have been studied involve collaborations between scientists (that may be charted through citation indexes that reveal the co-authors of a given paper), the interlocking networks of the directors that sit on different boards of companies, and the network of Hollywood actors – as popularized by the 'Six Degrees of Kevin Bacon' game in which the challenge is to link any actor through his/her roles in movies to the actor Kevin Bacon within six linkages (i.e. two actors working in the same movie represent one link). Also studied have been various human-made networks such as the World Wide Web and infrastructure networks such as the electrical grid, sewage systems and the airport system (Buchanan, 2002; Barabasi, 2003; Watts, 2003).

A fundamental aspect of most networks is the role that hubs play in their maintenance. Hubs are essentially connector nodes that have an anomalously large number of links. As a result of the large number of connections that are made through them, the functioning of the overall network is very dependent on the proper functioning of hubs. In essence, through their connection to an unusually large number of nodes, hubs serve a critically important function in network operation by effectively creating shorter paths between any two nodes in the system, thereby increasing the efficiency of the flows that channel through the network. An important corollary of this dependency relation, however, is that the failure of a hub may lead to a crippling of the network. That is, since the contribution of a hub to the overall functioning of the network is much greater than that of other smaller nodes, the failure of the hub node will have a much more devastating effect on the proper overall functioning of the network. By the same token, the malfunctioning of smaller nodes in the network will have very little effect on the overall network functioning because their contribution to the overall integrity of the network is much less. Studies have found that in most real world networks in both the natural and social world, the number of smaller nodes far outnumber the hubs, and as a consequence, there is a greater likelihood that a smaller node rather than a hub will fail at any given time (all other factors being equal of course). This means that although a lot of smaller nodes may fail, this will not necessarily lead to overall network failure because the network will be able to compensate by developing alternative links/pathways/connectivities to keep the flows going. For example, in a roadway network a minor traffic mishap may force cars to follow alternative routes without necessarily leading to problems everywhere in the roadway network. Sometimes failure will however cascade and resonate throughout the network system. Why such catastrophic failure occurs on certain occasions and not others and how precisely it cascades through the system depend on the architecture of the network, particularly the ratio of highly connected to less well connected nodes (Graham, 2010; Little, 2010).

The type of network arrangement that we have been referring to thus far, that is, those consisting of a large number of smaller nodes with much fewer hubs, are known as scale-free networks (Barabasi, 2003). The natural advantage of scale-free networks is their ability to withstand complete network breakdown due to random failures – a property referred to as the robustness or resilience of the network. This type of resiliency however may be offset by the Achilles heel of the scale-free network alluded to above, namely the network's dependency on hubs. Thus although hubs contribute to flow efficiency within the network, thereby strengthening the integrity of the overall network, they also represent points of vulnerability, since failure of hubs will more likely lead to overall network failure. Thus non-random or deliberate targeting of hubs (such as through sabotage) will increase the likelihood of network collapse.

Another fundamental characteristic of scale-free networks is that they exhibit what is known as the 'small world' property (Barabasi, 2003; Watts, 2003). The term is used in the same sense as in situations where we are surprised to learn that a complete stranger we have just met knows someone that we know, at which time we declare 'wow, what a small world we live in'. Mathematically it has been proven that we are indeed linked to anyone else in the world through a maximum of six common acquaintances (Barabasi, 2003; Watts, 2003). On a more general level, applicable to all scale-free networks, mathematical work has proven that what accounts for making worlds small is the presence of long-range links that serve as crucial shortcuts that drastically shorten the average separation between nodes (Barabasi, 2003, p. 45). In today's interconnected world, it is clear that global city hubs serve as the facilitating mechanism for long-range linkages between all parts of the world. Let us now consider in more detail some of the implications of these characteristics of networks for understanding the relationship between infectious disease spread and global cities.

THE GLOBAL CITIES NETWORK AND VULNERABILITY TO INFECTIOUS DISEASE: THE CASE OF SARS

From a conventional epidemiological perspective, the nodes of the network in which a given disease spreads consist of individuals, and the links are the physical contacts. Physical contact links, in turn, need to be defined with reference to the contextually embedded characteristics of the disease in question, and will vary according to the specific factors involved: for example, physical proximity (i.e. the sharing of common space), level of intimate contact (i.e. conversation, sexual relations) or some other form of interaction (such as the sharing of needles); as well as the capability of the pathogen to survive in the physical environment for prolonged periods. Getting an idea about the specific connectivity between people is of great importance in epidemiological investigations and responses to outbreaks, and much attention and resources are directed by public health officials towards activities related to contact tracing. It is on the basis of contact tracing that social distancing strategies such as quarantine and isolation are adopted to break the chain of disease transmission. It will be argued now that such epidemiological orientations may benefit from a broader approach that takes into account some basic principles of global cities and network theory. It should be noted at this point that our approach to the application of network theory is based on a more broadened orientation that is intended to be much more sensitive to context, that is, the political and social dimensions of the settings in which networks operate, rather than more narrowly defined mathematical analyses that have thus far dominated network analyses. As we shall see, the ability to contain (or facilitate) the flow of infectious diseases within human networks will vary according to contextual factors, not the least of which include other networks – that is, *human-made* networks, such as information and communication infrastructures and political organizations.

The spread of SARS through the global cities network began at the Metropole Hotel in Hong Kong, where a physician from Ghuangzhou infected with the disease was staying in February 2003. From here the virus spread to 11 hotel guests who continued their respective travels to various cities around the world, including Toronto, Singapore, Taipei, and Hanoi, and to other parts of Hong Kong (Abraham, 2004). The exact mode of transmission in the Metropole Hotel has not been conclusively determined as some of the guests who became infected may not have had direct contact with the index case. The prevailing theories propose that the virus contaminated an elevator or travelled through the ventilation system (NACSPH, 2003). Such suspicions would be in line with another phenomenon observed during the SARS outbreaks, namely the phenomenon of 'superspreader', where an individual exhibits an unusually high tendency to infect others, possibly because of the production of higher viral loads or a greater amount of respiratory secretions that may linger in the surroundings (Centers for Disease Control and Prevention, 2003).

In considering the international spread of SARS, it was clear that a networked infection was involved with global cities serving as hub-nodes that were linked together through air travel (Ali and Keil, 2006, 2008; Bowen and Laroe, 2006). Indeed, it was on the basis of this implicit recognition that the World Health Organization (WHO) 'regard[ed] every country with an international airport, or bordering an area having recent local transmission, as a potential risk for an outbreak' (cited by Gostin et al., 2003, p. 3231). And it was also partly on this basis that the WHO, violating the long-standing Westphalian-based governance principle that public health actions should not interfere with international commerce, issued travel advisories to SARS-affected areas, thereby resulting in significant economic repercussions for those areas.

A question that arises in understanding the spread of SARS as a reflection of the network of global cities is why it was that certain global cities such as Toronto, Singapore and Hong Kong were affected while other more major hub global cities such as Tokyo, New York and London were not? The answer to this question lies in considering the human-based capillary networks that lie within each particular global city itself. Such capillary networks are quite unique and hard to capture because they reflect the diversity of human experience and individuality involved in their constitution. This diversity can be seen by comparing, for example, the social contact networks of the spread of SARS in Vancouver versus Toronto (Meyers et al., 2005). In Vancouver, the SARS patient zero returned from the Metropole Hotel with his wife to an empty abode, and was almost immediately hospitalized thereafter. In Toronto, the SARS patient zero, returning from the same epicentre Hong Kong hotel, was the matriarch of a large extended, multi-generational family who died at home as an unrecognized case of SARS (Meyers et al., 2005). Subsequently ten members of her family were infected, which in turn led to a chain of transmission involving 200 cases, including health care workers, patients and their families. These two very different situations highlight the fact that spread of disease requires the simultaneous consideration of two distinct kinds of structure – social structure and network structure (Watts, 2003, p. 116). According to Watts, a key notion in understanding the relationship between the two is the idea of affiliation network (2003, p. 118). Two nodes may be said to be affiliated if they participate in the same group or context. Thus we return to the important consideration of context in the spread of disease. The context for a given phenomenon may be conceptualized in many ways; the challenge is to identify the most salient for the particular phenomenon under study. And for the spread of SARS it was clear that the global cities context was important in network terms because global cities tend to form affiliation clusters based on various shared characteristics, including economic interests and migration settlement patterns of diaspora communities (Ali and Keil, 2006), such as, for instance, the affiliation network of Hong Kong and Toronto.[2]

Another dimension of context that is sometimes neglected is the role of various infra-structures, such as information, air travel and hospital infrastructures, in containing or channelling the flow of infectious diseases both within and between global cities. The maintenance and operation of such infrastructures, it is important to note, are influenced in significant ways by political (e.g. neoliberal) and cultural factors which inform the context in which disease spread takes place (Sanford and Ali, 2005; Salehi and Ali, 2006; Keil and Ali, 2007; Hooker and Ali, 2009). We will briefly turn to such considerations below, noting that fuller accounts are given elsewhere – see, for example, the following in relation to SARS and information, airport and hospital infrastructures, respectively: Ali (2009); Ali and Keil (2010); Ali and Keil (2009).

NETWORKS AND THE RESPONSE TO SARS

Prior to its global spread, the initial outbreaks of SARS occurred in various cities within Southern China over a period of several weeks starting from November 2002. The full extent of the burgeoning pandemic was not known to the global public health community during these early stages because the Chinese national government did not make any public announcements concerning the outbreaks (Saich, 2006). Indeed, under Chinese law, epidemics were defined as state secrets, thus barring local public health officials from commenting on the outbreaks until permission to do so was granted by national authorities. But this permission was not forthcoming for various political reasons, not the least of which related to fears that news of the outbreaks would disrupt the recent leadership transition occurring in the Chinese government at the time (Saich, 2006). Such nondisclosure actions were later interpreted as part of a systematic cover-up and denial concerning the extent of the outbreaks on the part of the Chinese government; actions which subsequently received admonishment from the global public health community and the WHO (Eckholm, 2006). Information about the outbreak nevertheless spread throughout the country and to the outside world through alternative channels as messages were exchanged via new technologies such as cell phones and the Internet (Heymann, 2006). What is noteworthy about these developments is that they illustrate the self-adaptive quality of networks. In the pre-Internet era, information flows could be more tightly controlled by local and national government agencies, as these would serve as hub nodes that formed the backbone of the information network. With the explosion of the Internet, the number of nodes and linkages likewise exploded, as anyone possessing Internet or cell phone technologies would now be nodes in an expanding network of newly possible, and previously unavailable, linkages. Thus the conveying of information through the network no longer depended on government hubs, as information flows between nodes could circumvent these hub nodes. What this meant was that the citizenry no longer had to rely on official government channels to receive information.

Recent changes in the architecture of the information network also had dramatic implications for surveillance and response by the global public health community. Most notably, knowledge of disease outbreaks could no longer be solely contained to and by the particular nation state affected. Previously, the WHO had to rely on outbreak information that was forwarded to them through official channels, namely from nation state governments. Disease outbreak information from non-governmental sources, if available at all, would not be considered. The WHO response to SARS illustrates how new types of networked relations have changed the way surveillance and response now take place. In the year 2000, the WHO recognized the potential for other source nodes of outbreak information to be accessed. In this light, the WHO established the Global Outbreak Alert and Response Network (GOARN) – a network of 120 partners (including national government agencies and scientific institutions having expertise in infectious disease) located across the world (Levy and Fischetti, 2003, p. 7). One of GOARN's members was the Health Canada based Global Public Health Information Network (GPHIN), a computer application that continuously and systematically trawls web sites, news wires, local online newspapers, public health e-mail services and electronic discussion groups in six languages (English, French, Spanish, Russian, Arabic and Chinese) for reports of infectious disease outbreaks using key words or phrases (Heymann, 2006, p. 350). And it was GPHIN that first alerted the WHO about suspected outbreaks of 'atypical pneumonia' in Southern China in late November 2002, which in turn served as the impetus for the subsequent requests by the WHO for information about the suspected outbreak from China on 5 and 11 December 2002 (Heymann, 2006).

Another information network of great significance in the SARS outbreak response was the network of scientists. Again, due to the introduction of new communications and information, laboratory scientists from around the world temporarily put aside their competitive interests in order to link up in virtual networks whereby satellite broadcasts, teleconferencing and Webcasts were used to share laboratory results (Levy and Fischetti, 2003, p. 14). It was on the basis of this rapid real-time information sharing and analyses that the viral agent and its genetic code were identified in the unprecedented span of several weeks (as opposed to the past experiences of at least several months) (Levy and Fischetti, 2003) – one of the greatest successes of the global outbreak response (Ali, 2008).

It is important to note that just as the global response to the spread of SARS was based on the spread of information through networks and was influenced by various domestic and international political and cultural machinations, so too was the local response within the global city. Consider for example the particular nature and functioning of local public health infrastructures in each global city and how this differed in comparing the Toronto, Hong Kong and Singapore contexts.[3] Toronto and Hong Kong experienced similar problems in their respective public health response to SARS. Many of the problems both cities faced involved information handling and communication difficulties. In the case of Toronto, such difficulties arose from the cumulative neoliberal-inspired disassembly of the public health infrastructure, especially in relation to a lack of investment in updating the computer platform required to share epidemiological data required to trace the contact pattern involved in the disease diffusion. This was coupled with a seriously inadequate level of surge capacity that resulted from recently imposed cost saving efforts to decrease the personnel involved in public health and the specialization of infectious diseases, as well as through the continual casualization of the nursing profession in Ontario (Affonso et al., 2004; Ali and Keil, 2009). In Hong Kong, the terse political relationship between the central government in China and the local government in Hong Kong led to a level of distrust and bureaucratic wrangling that severely hindered an effective and coordinated response to SARS (Ng, 2008). In contrast, the Singapore government's response was praised by the WHO for its high level of effectiveness (Teo et al., 2008). The successful Singapore response to SARS has been attributed to a uniquely defined global-city state governance style based on an unusual mix of authoritarianism and paternalism. That is, a governance style that arose from the particular historical and colonial circumstances of the island nation resulting in a strong emphasis on protection from outside threats (e.g. Britain, Malaysia). This was coupled with the development of an efficient bureaucratic organization based on an urban-national structure in which resources could be readily mobilized and deployed in response to emergencies such as disease outbreaks due to a lack of a provincial or middle layer of bureaucracy (Teo et al., 2008).

CONCLUSION

To understand the contemporary spread of infectious diseases requires an understanding of the uniquely interconnected nature of the globalized world in which we live. We have argued that the recent work on network analysis and its application to global-city theory is particularly well suited to this task. Pathogens spread through social networks of people, while the strategies used to combat their spread involve other types of network, such as the information networks we have discussed in this chapter. What is often missing from the analysis of networks and disease spread is the consideration of the context in which social and information networks implicated in the spread and response to infectious disease are embedded. It is in addressing this deficiency that the work of global cities researchers becomes paramount. Interestingly, the context in which social and information networks operate is situated or embedded within a network itself – the global cities network. Not only that, but each global city itself forms a complex capillary network of its own, and in turn is linked to other global cities networks through various flows, including, as the SARS experience has dramatically revealed – flows of pathogens. We are therefore dealing with a situation of embedded and cross-cutting networks, leading to a folding of time and space and therefore a new topology in which the degree of connectivity rather than distance is increasingly becoming the defining characteristic of not only the relationships between global cities, but the relationship between global cities and disease. For example, the spread of SARS has revealed how vulnerability to infectious disease is one consequence of the development of a 'small world' due to the connectivity of global cities through various flows, the most obvious of which is air travel. Not recognizing the developments and dynamics of modern networks is to ignore two major insights of the science of networks as related to life in our connected age. First, as Duncan Watts (2003, p. 301) notes, 'we may all have our own burdens, but like it or not, we must bear each other's burdens as well'. Secondly, the recognition that, in complex networks, cause and effect are often related in a complicated and quite misleading way. Consequently, at times small changes may have major implications, while at other moments major shocks can be absorbed with remarkably little disruption (Watts, 2003). The outbreak of SARS in the global cities network revealed both aspects. Thus, we see, for example, how the stay of only one individual at a particular global city hotel led to the international spread of a disease, while the potential disruption was far less than it could have been because of the international public health response facilitated by the rise of new types of extensive information sharing networks made possible by recent technological advancements in communications. What should not be forgotten, however, is that the (relatively) effective response that we saw in the case of SARS occurred because the disease affected those global cities that had in place the advanced technologies required to collect and share epidemiological and clinical information – at least to some level of adequacy. These global cities were well connected with the global flows of information; other global cities, however, especially the megacities of the Global South, may not be so well connected to the flows running through the developed world's global city network. Their ability to respond effectively to infectious disease spread will therefore be limited. Remembering however that in a 'small world' all nodes are connected to each other through a surprisingly small number of connections, the vulnerability of a major Global South city renders the whole global city network vulnerable to disease spread. This situation of networked vulnerability is exacerbated by the global inequalities resulting from the broader social and political forces that drove the emergence of the global cities network in the first place – namely colonialism, neo-liberalization, post-Fordism – which, somewhat ironically, constrain the very nature of the networks involved in the public health response to the spread of infectious disease in the contemporary era.

NOTES

1. Some examples of how nodes can be linked together (referred to as network topologies) include: a star shape where each node is linked to a central hub; a line model where nodes are linked to each other in a linear sequence; and nodes that have multiple linkages to each other forming a mesh.
2. See Keil and Ali (2008) for further elaboration on the implications of the connections of global city diaspora communities to issues of 'othering' and the racialization of disease in the context of Canadian multiculturalism.
3. For a full account of the SARS response in these three global cities, see Ali and Keil (2008).

REFERENCES

Abraham, T. (2004), *Twenty-First Century Plague: The Story of Plague*, Baltimore, MD: The Johns Hopkins University Press.
Affonso, D., G.J. Andrews and L. Jeffs (2004), 'The urban geography of SARS: paradoxes and dilemmas in Toronto's health care', *Journal of Advanced Nursing*, **45** (6), 568–578.
Ali, S.H. (2008), 'SARS as an emergent complex: toward a networked approach to urban infectious disease', in S.H. Ali and R. Keil (eds), *Networked Disease: Emerging Infections in the Global City*, Oxford: Wiley-Blackwell, pp. 235–249.
Ali, S.H. (2009), 'The local and global outbreak response to Severe Acute Respiratory Syndrome (SARS) in Toronto', in *Disaster and Emergency Management: The Canadian Context*, Canadian Risk and Hazards Network, available at www.crhnet.ca (accessed 16 December 2009).
Ali, S.H. and R. Keil (2006), 'Global cities and the spread of infectious disease: the case of Severe Acute Respiratory Syndrome (SARS) in Toronto, Canada', *Urban Studies*, **43** (3), 1–19.
Ali, S.H. and R. Keil (eds) (2008), *Networked Disease: Emerging Infections in the Global City*, Oxford: Wiley-Blackwell.
Ali, S.H. and R. Keil (2009), 'Public health and the political economy of scale: implications for understanding the response to the 2003 Severe Acute Respiratory Syndrome (SARS) outbreak in Toronto', in R. Keil and R. Mahon (eds), *Leviathan Undone? Towards a Political Economy of Scale*, Vancouver: UBC Press, pp. 195–208.
Ali, S.H. and R. Keil (2010), 'Securing network flows: infectious disease and airports', in S. Graham and S. Marvin (eds), *Disrupted Cities: When Infrastructure Fails*, New York: Routledge, pp. 97–110.
Barabasi, A.-L. (2003), *Linked*, New York: Plume.
Bowen, J.T. and C. Laroe (2006), 'Airline networks and the international diffusion of severe acute respiratory syndrome (SARS)', *The Geographical Journal*, **172** (2), 130–144.
Buchanan, M. (2002), *Nexus: Small Worlds and the Groundbreaking Science of Networks*, New York: W.W. Norton and Company.
Centers for Disease Control and Prevention (2003), 'Severe acute respiratory syndrome (SARS)', available at www.cdc.gov/ncidod/sars (accessed 3 June 2005).
Eckholm, E. (2006), 'SARS in Beijing: the unraveling of a cover-up', in A. Kleinman and J.L. Watson (eds), *SARS in China: Prelude To Pandemic*, Stanford, CA: Stanford University Press, pp. 122–130.
Friedmann, J. (2002), *The Prospect of Cities*, Minneapolis, MN: University of Minnesota Press.
Friedmann, J. and G. Wolff (2006), 'World city formation: an agenda for research and action', in N. Brenner and R. Keil (eds), *The Global Cities Reader*, London: Routledge, pp. 57–66.
Gostin, L.O., R. Bayer and A.L. Fairchild (2003), 'Ethical and legal challenges posed by Severe Acute Respiratory Syndrome: implications for the control of severe infectious disease threats', *Journal of the American Medical Association*, **290** (24), 3229–3237.
Graham, S. (2006), 'Global grids of glass: on global cities, telecommunications and planetary urban networks', in N. Brenner and R. Keil (eds), *The Global Cities Reader*, London: Routledge, pp. 118–126.
Graham, S. (ed.) (2010), *Disrupted Cities: When Infrastructure Fails*, London: Routledge.
Heymann, D.L. (2006), 'SARS and emerging infectious diseases: a challenge to place global solidarity above national security', *Annals Academy of Medicine*, **35** (5), 350–353.

Hooker, C. and S.H. Ali (2009), 'SARS and security: health in the new normal', *Studies in Political Economy*, **84**, 101–126.

Keil, R. and S.H. Ali (2007), 'Governing the sick city: urban governance in the age of emerging infectious disease', *Antipode*, **40** (1), 846–871.

Keil, R. and S.H. Ali (2008), 'Racism is a weapon of mass destruction: SARS and the social fabric of urban multiculturalism', in S.H. Ali and R. Keil (eds), *Networked Disease: Emerging Infections in the Global City*, Oxford: Wiley-Blackwell, pp. 152–166.

Levy, E. and M. Fischetti (2003), *The New Killer Diseases*, New York: Random House.

Little, R.G. (2010), 'Managing the risk of cascading failure in complex urban infrastructures', in S. Graham (ed.), *Disrupted Cities: When Infrastructure Fails*, London: Routledge, pp. 27–40.

Major, C. (2008), 'Affect work and infected bodies: biosecurity in an age of emerging infectious disease', *Environment and Planning A*, **40** (7), 1633–1646.

Meyers, L.A., B. Pourbohol, M.E.J. Newman, D. Skowronski and R. Brunham (2005), 'Network theory and SARS: predicting outbreak diversity', *Journal of Theoretical Biology*, **232** (1), 71–81.

NACSPH (National Advisory Committee on SARS and Public Health) (2003), *Learning from SARS: Renewal of Public Health in Canada*, Ottawa: Health Canada.

Ng, M.K. (2008), 'Globalization of SARS and health governance in Hong Kong under "one country, two systems"', in S.H. Ali and R. Keil (eds), *Networked Disease: Emerging Infections in the Global City*, Oxford: Wiley-Blackwell, pp. 70–85.

Pearce, N. and F. Merletti (2006), 'Complexity, simplicity, epidemiology', *International Journal of Epidemiology*, **35** (3), 515–519.

Saich, T. (2006), 'Is SARS China's Chernobyl or much ado about nothing?', in A. Kleinman and J.L. Watson (eds), *SARS in China: Prelude To Pandemic*, Stanford, CA: Stanford University Press, pp. 71–104.

Salehi, R. and S.H. Ali (2006), 'The social and political context of disease outbreaks: the case of SARS in Toronto', *Canadian Public Policy/Analyse de Politiques*, **32** (4), 373–385.

Sanford, S. and S.H. Ali (2005), 'The new public health hegemony: response to Severe Acute Respiratory Syndrome (SARS) in Toronto', *Social Theory and Health*, **3** (2), 105–125.

Smith, R.G. (2003), 'World city topologies', *Progress in Human Geography*, **27** (5), 561–582.

Teo, P., B.S.A. Yeoh and S.N. Ong (2008), 'Surveillance in a globalizing city: Singapore's battle against SARS', in S.H. Ali and R. Keil (eds), *Networked Disease: Emerging Infections in the Global City*, Oxford: Wiley-Blackwell, pp. 86–101.

Watts, D. (2003), *Six Degrees: The Science of a Connected Age*, New York: W.W. Norton and Company.

II D   World city divisions

32 Urban social polarization
Chris Hamnett

The concept of 'social polarization' has become widely used in recent discussions of social change, social divisions and inequality in global cities (O'Loughlin and Friedrichs, 1996; Moulaert et al., 2010). The term has become a convenient shorthand for a variety of social problems and has become part of the conventional discourse on cities, but it is often used without precise definition. In this respect, its rise to prominence parallels the term 'urban decline' which, as Beauregard (1993) has shown, has acquired a narrative power of its own independent of rigorous analysis or empirical evidence, and the existence of social polarization is often maintained irrespective of evidence to the contrary.

This uncritical acceptance of the existence of social polarization means that its existence is frequently assumed rather than demonstrated. This is not helpful for the development of theory, empirical analysis or policy. If social polarization is intended as a convenient catch-all shorthand term for urban social divisions or urban inequality, we cannot dispute its existence, as cities are clearly socially divided and unequal in a multiplicity of ways, but the question must be posed: why not use the simpler alternatives? If, however, the term is intended to be more precise and to specify the potential existence of particular processes and outcomes, we must be clear what these are.

The term 'polarization' is commonly defined in dictionaries as relating to 'the production or condition of polarity', 'the process of being divided into two opposing groups' or 'the condition of having or giving polarity'. In a social context it is commonly used to refer to economic and social processes which lead to widening social divisions or the splitting apart of society into distinct groups of the advantaged and disadvantaged at opposite ends of the social spectrum. The next section examines the origins and development of the term in relation to world and global cities.

SOCIAL POLARIZATION AND INEQUALITY IN WORLD/GLOBAL CITIES

The debates on social polarization in world or global cities began with the work of John Friedmann (Friedmann and Wolff, 1982; Friedmann, 1986), who advanced seven hypotheses based on the role of such cities in the global capitalist system, and the new international division of labour, focusing on their role as control and command centres for global capital. Friedmann (1986) argued that the role of such cities in the global system meant that they functioned as key centres for corporate headquarters' business and finance, and that changes in their employment structure generated changes in their occupational class and income structure. Specifically, he saw them as attracting large numbers of highly skilled workers. This, in turn, generated a need for a large army of low skilled service workers. As Friedmann and Wolff (1982, p. 322) noted:

> Transnational elites are the dominant class in the world city, and the city is arranged to cater to their life styles and occupational necessities. . .The contrast with the third (or so) of the population who make up the permanent underclass of the world city could scarcely be more striking.

Hence, '[t]he primary social fact about world city formation is the *polarization of its social class divisions*' (Friedmann and Wolff, 1982, p. 322; emphasis added). Friedmann (1986) also noted that:

> In terms of occupations, world cities are characterized by a *dichotomized labour force*: on the one hand, a high percentage of professionals specialized in control functions and, on the other, a vast army of low-skilled workers engaged in manufacturing, personal services and the hotel, tourist and entertainment industries that cater to the privileged classes for whose sake the world city primarily exists. (Friedmann, 1986, p. 73; emphasis added)

Friedmann's pioneering work has been of considerable value, providing the basis for the systematic study of the role and structure of world/global cities in the context of increasing economic globalization. He argued that the basic structural reasons for social polarization in world cities lie in the emergence of a dichotomized labour market, linked to growing immigration and growing inequality of earnings and incomes, and that this was linked to growing spatial segregation between rich and poor.

Friedmann's work was subsequently developed by Saskia Sassen (1991, 2001) in her book *The Global City*. Sassen argued that the evolving structure of economic activities in global cities, that is, those cities with a major role in the organization of the global system of production and finance, particularly the rapid growth of financial and business services and the sharp decline of manufacturing industry, has brought about 'changes in the organization of work, reflected in a shift in the job supply and *polarization* in the income distribution and occupational distribution of workers' (Sassen, 1991, p. 9; emphasis added).

Sassen (1991) also argued that two other developments in global cities have contributed to social polarization. The first is the large supply of low wage jobs required by high income gentrification, both residentially and commercially, and the associated need for low wage industrial services, even in financial and specialist services. The second is what she terms the 'downgrading of the industrial sector', specifically the development of sweat shop labour and home working (1991, p. 9). She summarized her thesis as follows:

> [N]ew conditions of growth have contributed to elements of *a new class alignment* in global cities. The occupational structure of major growth industries characterized by the locational concentration of major growth sectors in global cities in combination with the polarized occupational structure of these sectors has created and contributed to growth of a high-income stratum and a low-income stratum of workers. (Sassen, 1991, p. 13; emphasis added)

Sassen's key idea is straightforward. The decline of manufacturing industry is associated with a decline in the number of middle skill and middle income jobs, while the growth of the service sector is associated with growth both in professional and managerial jobs at the top, and with jobs in low skill and low wage service jobs at the bottom – such as hotel maids, waiters and waitresses, cleaners, security guards and so on. As she noted: 'Major growth industries show a greater incidence of jobs at the high- and low-paying ends of the scale than do the older industries now in decline' (p. 9). In this respect, her thesis reflects the earlier debate about the so-called 'declining middle' in the US occupational spectrum which is seen to have occurred as a result of de-industrialization and the loss of skilled manufacturing workers and their replacement by both high and low skilled workers in the service sector.

Similarly, Mollenkopf and Castells (1991) posed the question of whether New York has become a 'dual city', split into two distinctive parts, one of wealth and one of poverty. But they argued that while New York is an unequal city, it is *not* a dual city and that the dual city metaphor, while politically useful, is flawed as an analytical approach. As they noted:

> The dual city is a useful ideological notion because it aims to denounce inequality, exploitation, and oppression in cities. . .But, its underlying assumptions are rarely made explicit, because those who employ it tend to favour social critique over social theory. The political and emotional charge of a dualist approach and the failure to spell out its assumptions mean that it cannot comprehend the complexity of urban social reality, which is certainly not reducible to a simple dichotomy. (Mollenkopf and Castells, 1991, p. 405)

The idea of social polarization and other dualist notions has proved extremely attractive, both intellectually and politically. But, as Fainstein et al. (1992, p. 13) perceptively pointed out:

> The images of a dual or polarised city are seductive, they promise to encapsulate the outcome of a wide variety of complex processes in a single, neat and easily comprehensible phrase. Yet the hard evidence for such a sweeping and general conclusion regarding the outcome of economic restructuring and urban change is, at best, patchy and ambiguous. If the concept of 'dual' or polarising city is of any real utility, it can serve only as a hypothesis, the prelude to empirical analysis, rather than as conclusion which takes the existence of confirmatory evidence for granted.

Fainstein et al.'s observation that polarization is a hypothesis rather than a conclusion is crucial. There are also two important issues implicit in both Friedmann's and Sassen's work on polarization which require discussion. The first is the extent to which the trends and processes they identify are *inevitable* outcomes of the process of economic globalization, and the extent to which they can be modified by state policies regarding labour markets, immigration and welfare. The second concerns the extent to which these trends and processes are common across all global cities, irrespective of their culture, history and politics, and the extent to which they may vary from one city to another. Sassen (1991, p. 4) claimed that there were 'massive and parallel changes [occurring] in [the] economic base, spatial organization, and social structure' of global cities, but the empirical evidence suggests that this is not so clear cut. While there are a number of similarities, there are major differences in, for example, immigration experience and income inequality, with Tokyo experiencing very limited international immigration and much lower levels of inequality than either New York or London (Fainstein, 2001).

As used by Sassen, the term 'social polarization' involves absolute and proportional growth at the top and bottom end and a decline in the middle of the occupational skill distribution. There are related changes in the distribution of earnings and incomes, with growth in the *size* of both the top and bottom groups and a decline in the middle. It should be noted that this is not the same as an increase in earnings at the top or bottom, or the size of the gap, but the size of the groups themselves. Sassen (1991) argued that both occupational class distributions and earnings were tending towards a dumb-bell shape, with more workers at the top and bottom and fewer in the middle of the distribution. This idea of a 'squeezed middle' is very different from the analysis put forward by Ray Pahl (1988) where he argued that Britain was seeing the emergence of a more onion shaped distribution of occupational class, with a much larger middle and a shrinking lower end.

It is important also to note that social polarization is not the same as inequality, which is a measure of the gap between top and bottom of the earnings or income distribution. It is possible to have greater polarization and lower inequality, lower polarization and greater inequality or any combination of the two, although some combinations are more likely than others (Esteban and Ray, 1994). It is also possible to talk of spatial polarization between different groups, though we already have a useful term for this in 'segregation'.

SOCIAL POLARIZATION, INEQUALITY AND THE ROLE OF THE STATE

It is sometimes suggested that social polarization is an inevitable outcome of the changes in industrial structure and associated changes in occupation and migration of global cities. This is certainly the impression which is given in Sassen's work. It can be argued, however, that the existence and extent of social polarization in global cities are likely to be strongly related to the level of migration in these cities and the existence of a low skill and low wage migrant underclass (Hamnett, 1994). Sassen's thesis was largely based on her early research on New York and Los Angeles, both of which have very high levels of low wage international migration. However, May et al. (2007) and Wills et al. (2009) argue that in recent years London has also followed this trend and may thus be becoming increasingly socially polarized.

Secondly, it can be argued that social polarization needs to be examined in the context of different types of welfare state regime (Hamnett, 1994, 1996b). It is well known that different societies have very different welfare regimes, with some of the Scandinavian social-democratic countries having high levels of welfare provision and redistribution and other liberal capitalist countries, such as the USA, having considerably less. It would be expected from this that countries with extensive welfare regimes could have lower levels of inequality and polarization and vice versa.

This argument has been taken up in the context of South East Asia by Hill and Kim (2000), who have argued that there is a major difference between liberal capitalist states such as Britain and the USA and South East Asian developmental states such as Japan, South Korea and Singapore, and that it cannot simply be assumed that theories of social polarization which are based on liberal capitalist states will necessarily apply in developmental states. This generated a major debate (Hill and Kim, 2001; Sassen, 2001; Wang, 2003; Chiu and Lui, 2004; Tai, 2006) which suggests that Singapore, Seoul and Taipei are different from other global cities by virtue of a lower degree of occupational polarization and income inequality.

THE EMPIRICAL EVIDENCE

I have summarized the main theoretical positions and the definitional problems regarding social polarization, but what does the evidence suggest? The evidence on occupational class polarization is fairly easy to summarize in that the evidence based on official census and labour force statistics up until 2001 suggests that, within western developed countries outside the USA, there has *not* been a general process of occupational class polarization and where found it has tended to be asymmetric, with a greater growth at the top end than the bottom. A dominant trend in cities such as London, Paris, Amsterdam, Cape Town and Sydney has been the growth of the professional and managerial middle classes (Hamnett, 1994, 1996b, 2003a; Préteceille, 1995, 2007; Baum, 1997, 1999; Borel-Saladin and Crankshaw, 2009). Research by Butler et al. (2007) shows a continuation of this trend in London up to 2001 with the additional growth of a new lower middle class of routine white collar and administrative jobs. They are not lawyers, doctors or engineers but neither are they traditional working class occupations. This view is challenged by May et al. (2007), who argue that London is now characterized by a new division of labour in which growing numbers of overseas migrants occupy low skill and low wage jobs in the service sector. Others have argued that the reliance on official data such as the census or labour force surveys overlooks changes taking place in the informal and undocumented economy, whose members are unlikely to be captured in such data. This is a fair point but such arguments often rely on very small geographically specific qualitative surveys which are of limited general applicability. Burgers (1996) has argued that the growth of the unemployed in Dutch cities is evidence of polarization but, while there may be a growing polarization between the employed and the unemployed and economically inactive, Sassen's thesis focused on trends in the employed labour force (Hamnett, 1996a).

While it is indisputable that there are many new low wage jobs created in hotels, restaurants, security and cleaning, what is often overlooked in the context of developed countries by the proponents of social polarization is the scale of job losses in routine service jobs. In London, and in Britain as a whole, for example, railway porters, bus conductors and tube train guards, who were very common until 30 years ago, have almost totally disappeared in an effort to streamline the labour process and to cut costs and increase profitability. These losses are numerically very important but they are often far less visible than the growth areas. Thus while many new low wage service jobs have been created, many others have also been lost. We cannot simply assume that the growth of new low wage service jobs points to polarization, as some researchers do. Also, as Borel-Saladin and Crankshaw (2009) have shown for Cape Town, de-industrialization has been accompanied by the growth of middle class service sector jobs with middle incomes. As they note:

> the growth of service-sector employment can produce a large middle-income occupational class of clerks, sales and personal services workers. The growth of this class can offset the decline of middle-income jobs caused by the loss of artisans, machine operators and drivers in the declining manufacturing sector. (Borel-Saladin and Crankshaw, 2009, p. 645)

More generally, they argue that polarization researchers have tended to assume, following Sassen, that service sector jobs are either high skill and high wage or low skill and low wage, but they argue that in fact it is possible to have middle income service jobs.

In those countries with high levels of immigration into low wage jobs, occupational class polarization does seem to be occurring. Chiu and Lui (2004) show that from 1991–2001 Hong Kong experienced both a strong absolute growth of managers, professionals and associate professionals, and a decline of skilled jobs and growth of elementary occupations which they link to the growth of immigration from China. They thus conclude that Hong Kong has seen the growth of occupational polarization over this period (though Borel-Saladin and Crankshaw (2009) criticize their interpretation of data). Many large Chinese cities have also been characterized by a large inflow of temporary migrant workers from rural areas who occupy many of the low wage jobs in manufacturing, services and construction. These cities have seen growth of inequality and urban marginality (Wu, 2004). But in Taipei and Singapore the experience seems rather different (Baum, 1999; Tai, 2006). Singapore experienced clear occupational professionalization: an upward shift in class structure.

In contrast to occupational polarization, there is little doubt that both earning and income inequality has increased very significantly in many global cities over the last twenty years, partly as a result of the changes in industrial and occupational structure which generate more high paid jobs in finance and business services and partly as a result of very high growth of top earnings (Hamnett, 1994, 1996b, 2003a, 2003b; Préteceille, 1995; Warf, 2000; Fainstein, 2001). But the growth of income or earning inequality is not the same as an increase in polarization. Polarization usually implies growth in the absolute size of both top and bottom groups, whereas inequality refers to the gap between them. It is quite possible to have an increase in the size and proportion of professional and managerial workers combined with stability or decline in the number of low paid service workers and to have a major increase in earnings inequality, which is what has happened in London where the earnings of the top decile rose much faster than other groups from 1979 to 1993 (Hamnett and Cross, 1998; Hamnett, 2003b) and this has continued in recent years.

This corresponds to the data on New York (Mollenkopf and Castells, 1991; Warf, 2000) and Paris, where the earnings and incomes of the top deciles have grown much faster than those of other deciles, as have their shares of total earnings and incomes, and inequality is increasing. This group has been remarkably successful in gaining both higher earnings and a much larger share of the total cake. At the other extreme, the low wage and income groups have maintained their wages or seen a much lower rate of increase. Intermediate groups have seen a lower rate of earnings growth. Consequently, the most highly paid have pulled away from the rest.

However, it is noteworthy that several Scandinavian cities such as Stockholm, Helsinki and Oslo (Wessel, 2000; Vaattovaara and Kortteinen, 2003) have much lower levels of income inequality, largely as a result of the much stronger social-democratic welfare states (although Wessel shows that income inequality increased sharply in Oslo from 1986 to 1996). This highlights an important factor in the level of inequality, namely the role of the state and the degree of intervention and redistribution. Greater inequality appears to be common to many global cities as a result of the change in industrial structure but it is not inevitable or inexorable. Policy and state regulation and social expectations can make a difference. This is clearly shown by Wang (2003) and by Tai (2006) in his comparative analysis of social polarization in three developmental states, Singapore, Hong Kong and Taipei. Baum's (1999) research suggests that Singapore experienced an upwards shift in income distribution from 1986–96 but as his figures do not appear to be adjusted for inflation, it is difficult to know to what extent this upwards shift is simply a result of workers in low income groups slowly moving up into higher income groups as a result of wage inflation. Therborn (2011) has recently strongly emphasized the key role of the state on global cities in the wake of the financial crisis.

CONCLUSIONS

The concept of social polarization is an interesting and theoretically attractive one. It has the advantage, as Fainstein et al. (1992, p. 13) note, that it seems to summarize 'the outcome of a wide variety of complex processes in a single, neat and easily comprehensible phrase'. The problem, however, is that the concept has acquired a life of its own, and has become widely accepted as the conventional wisdom on urban social change largely independently of extensive conceptual debates and empirical work that have questioned its validity.

My conclusion is that occupational social polarization is not inevitable in global cities, and nor is an increase in earnings and income inequality (although this is more likely). While there is little doubt that the professional, managerial and technical middle classes have been growing, and the skilled manual groups have been shrinking, what has been happening at the bottom end is more uncertain and more problematic. While there has been a growth in low skill and low wage service work in some sectors, there have also been declines in other sectors such as transport which have been less well documented. There have also been increases in the size of the routine administrative sector in many cities, leading to the growth of lower middle class jobs.

The extent of occupational polarization, if it occurs at all, is likely to be related to the level of immigration, with cities experiencing high levels of low skill immigrants more likely to experience polarization than those with low levels of low skill immigration such as Singapore. This in turn is likely to be related to the role of the state and the extent of state control over migration and wage levels, and so on. The growth of earning inequality is more likely in global cities as a result of the transformation of the industrial and occupational structure and the growth of the high skill, high wage segment of the labour force who have seen their earnings increase much faster than other groups. The evidence suggests that inequality is far greater in liberal market economies than in economies with a higher degree of state intervention and control or those with a social-democratic policy.

REFERENCES

Baum, S. (1997), 'Sydney, Australia: a global city? Testing the social polarisation thesis', *Urban Studies*, **34** (11), 1881–1901.
Baum, S. (1999), 'Social transformations in the global city: Singapore', *Urban Studies*, **36** (7), 1095–1117.
Beauregard, R.A. (1993), 'Representing urban decline: postwar cities as narrative objects', *Urban Affairs Review*, **29** (2), 187–202.
Borel-Saladin, J. and O. Crankshaw (2009), 'Social polarisation or professionalisation: another look at theory and evidence on deindustrialisation and the rise of the service sector', *Urban Studies*, **46** (3), 645–664.

Burgers, J. (1996), 'No polarisation in Dutch cities? Inequality in a corporatist country', *Urban Studies*, **33** (1), 99–105.

Butler, T., C. Hamnett and M. Ramsden (2007), 'Inward and upward: marking out social class change in London, 1981–2001', *Urban Studies*, **45** (1), 67–88.

Chiu, S.W.K. and T.S. Lui (2004), 'Testing the global city–social polarisation thesis: Hong Kong since the 1990s', *Urban Studies*, **41** (10), 1863–1888.

Esteban, J.-M. and D. Ray (1994), 'On the measurement of polarization', *Econometrica*, **62** (4), 819–851.

Fainstein, S. (2001), 'Inequality in global city regions', in A.J. Scott (ed.), *Global City-Regions: Trends, Theory, Policy*, Oxford: Oxford University Press, pp. 21–25.

Fainstein, S., I. Gordon and M. Harloe (1992), *Divided Cities: New York and London in the Contemporary World*, Oxford: Blackwell.

Friedmann, J. (1986), 'The world city hypothesis', *Development and Change*, **17** (1), 69–83.

Friedmann, J. and G. Wolff (1982), 'World city formation: an agenda for research and action', *International Journal of Urban and Regional Research*, **6** (3), 309–344.

Hamnett, C. (1994), 'Social polarisation in global cities: theory and evidence', *Urban Studies*, **31** (3), 401–424.

Hamnett, C. (1996a), 'Why Sassen is wrong: a response to Burgers', *Urban Studies*, **33** (1), 107–110.

Hamnett, C. (1996b), 'Social polarisation, economic restructuring and welfare state regimes', *Urban Studies*, **33** (8), 1407–1430.

Hamnett, C. (2003a), 'Gentrification and the middle class remaking of inner London, 1961–2001', *Urban Studies*, **40** (12), 2401–2426.

Hamnett, C. (2003b), *Unequal City: London in the Global Arena*, London: Routledge.

Hamnett, C. and D. Cross (1998), 'Social polarisation and inequality: the earnings evidence', *Environment and Planning C: Government and Policy*, **16** (6), 659–680.

Hill, R.C. and J.W. Kim (2000), 'Global cities and developmental states: New York, Tokyo and Seoul', *Urban Studies*, **37** (12), 2167–2195.

Hill, R.C. and J.W. Kim (2001), 'Reply to Friedmann and Sassen', *Urban Studies*, **38** (13), 2541–2542.

May, J., J. Wills, K. Datta, Y. Evans, J. Herbert and C. McIlwaine (2007), 'Keeping London working: global cities, the British state, and London's new migrant division of labour', *Transactions of the Institute of British Geographers*, **32** (2), 151–167.

Mollenkopf, J.H. and M. Castells (eds) (1991), *Dual City: Restructuring New York*, New York: Russell Sage Foundation.

Moulaert, F., A. Rodriguez and E. Swyngedouw (eds) (2010), *The Globalized City: Economic Restructuring and Social Polarization in European Cities*, Oxford: Oxford University Press.

O'Loughlin, J. and J. Friedrichs (eds) (1996), *Social Polarization in Post-Industrial Metropolises*, Berlin and New York: de Gruyter.

Pahl, R. (1988), 'Some remarks on informal work, social polarization and the social structure', *International Journal of Urban and Regional Research*, **12** (2), 247–267.

Préteceille, E. (1995), 'Division sociale de l'espace et globalisation: le cas de la metropole parisienne', *Sociétés Contemporaines*, **22–23**, 33–67.

Préteceille, E. (2007), 'Is gentrification a useful paradigm to analyse social changes in the Paris Metropolis?', *Environment and Planning A*, **39** (1), 10–31.

Sassen, S. (1991), *The Global City: New York, London, Tokyo*, Princeton, NJ: Princeton University Press.

Sassen, S. (2001), 'Global cities and developmentalist states: how to derail what could be an interesting debate. A response to Hill and Kim', *Urban Studies*, **38** (13), 2537–2540.

Tai, P.F. (2006), 'Social polarisation: comparing Singapore, Hong Kong and Taipei', *Urban Studies*, **43** (10), 1737–1756.

Therborn, G. (2011), 'End of a paradigm: the current crisis and the idea of stateless cities', *Environment and Planning A*, **43** (2), 272–285.

Vaattovaara, M. and M. Kortteinen (2003), 'Beyond polarisation versus professionalisation? A case study of the Helsinki region, Finland', *Urban Studies*, **40** (11), 2127–2145.

Wang, C.H. (2003), 'Taipei as a global city: a theoretical and empirical examination', *Urban Studies*, **40** (2), 309–334.

Warf, B. (2000), 'New York: the Big Apple in the 1990s', *Geoforum*, **31** (4), 487–499.

Wessel, T. (2000), 'Social polarisation and socioeconomic segregation in a welfare state: the case of Oslo', *Urban Studies*, **37** (11), 1947–1967.

Wills, J., K. Datta, Y. Evans, J. Herbert, J. May and C. McIlwaine (2009), *Global Cities at Work: New Migrant Divisions of Labour*, London: Pluto Press.

Wu, F. (2004), 'Urban poverty and marginalization under market transition: the case of Chinese cities', *International Journal of Urban and Regional Research*, **28** (2), 401–423.

33 Gentrifying the world city
Loretta Lees

It is interesting that the process of gentrification that has been evident in London, New York City and Paris since at least the 1950s (Carpenter and Lees, 1995; Lees et al., 2008), in Toronto since the 1960s (Caulfield, 1994) and in Tokyo since the 1980s (Fujitsuka, 2005) has not been evident in that other 'world city' – Los Angeles – until very recently. Gentrification can be defined broadly as the social upgrading of a locale by incoming high income groups which includes the reinvestment of capital and results in both landscape change and the direct or indirect displacement of low income groups (Davidson and Lees, 2005). That not all world cities have been gentrified, nor have experienced gentrification at the same time, is important, for we have long assumed that gentrification and world city status go hand in hand (e.g. Sassen, 1991). In the gentrification literature there has been the beginning of work on the specifics of gentrification in global or world cities (e.g. Lees, 2003; Butler and Lees, 2006), yet such a research agenda has much further to go. So what do we know about gentrification in world cities and those cities which aspire to be world cities, what might the future of gentrification in world cities be, and what might a future research agenda look like?

GENTRIFICATION AND THE WORLD CITY

It is perhaps significant that the term 'gentrification' was first coined in London (Glass, 1964), at a time when London was emerging as a global or world city, slightly earlier than New York as a result of its milder regulatory climate which brought many financial operations from New York to London in the mid 1960s (Butler and Lees, 2006). London's gentrifiers turned their backs on suburbia at the same time as the city became the hub of a new fast-moving capitalism that was expanding across the globe. These new post-production world cities embraced new forms of consumption – one of which was old inner city spaces and places. In London, first wave or pioneer gentrification was superseded in some neighbourhoods by a quite different second wave of gentrification – led by more corporate types who worked in the private sector, especially the City, where jobs had expanded due to deregulation of the Stock Exchange in 1986. Sassen (1991) noticed these new 'City types' who were drawn from the upper professional strata:

> The most central areas of London have undergone a transformation that broadly parallels Manhattan's . . . We see a parallel increase in the stratum of what Brint (1988) has described as upper professionals, a group largely employed in corporate services, including finance. The sharp growth in the concentration of the mostly young, new high-income professionals and managers employed in central London represents a significant change from a decade ago. (Sassen, 1991, p. 265)

Deregulation of the Stock Exchange in London brought about a big expansion in City employment but deregulation had another effect too, one that led some years later to a process of super-gentrification (Butler and Lees, 2006). In the mid 1990s because deregulation had been insufficient to invigorate the rather conservative British finance houses, these firms were taken over, largely by foreign, mainly US based, financial mega-players. This led to large numbers of very high salaries (comparable to their New York counterparts) and to the increased internationalization of the workers in these firms, which made up about a third of City employment (Buck et al., 2002, p. 112). A new super-wealthy group of professionals working in the City of London, at the top end of the legal professions and financial services industries, looked for a neighbourhood from which they could commute quickly to the City, that was walkable so they could pursue face to face social interaction with 'people like themselves', already had symbolic status (e.g. had already been gentrified and was now considered to be an elite neighbourhood): in London, Barnsbury in Islington was one such example (see also Lees et al., 2008, pp. 150–153). In New York City a similar process, fed by the fortunes of Wall Street, also emerged in another mature gentrified neighbourhood – Brooklyn Heights (Lees, 2003). One super-gentrifier in Brooklyn Heights, an English woman employed on Wall Street as a broker specializing in Japanese bonds and securities, bought a brownstone for US$595,000, writing a personal cheque for the full amount. The woman did not move in immediately but spent nine months gutting and renovating the house, spending nearly what she had paid for it again in renovation costs. Like London, New York had a new generation of gentrifiers flush with the exorbitant rewards of the global finance and corporate service industries that were able to marshal previously unheard of sums to finance their domestic reproduction. It was not only the volume and source of the assets they mobilized that marked out these 'financifiers' from previous generations of gentrifiers, but their lifestyles and values as well (see Lees, 2003; Butler and Lees, 2006).

Other world cities, like Tokyo, were also identified as primary sites for gentrification because of the growth in service functions that administered to their global economic status. Authors such as Cybriwsky (1998) and Sassen (1991) discussed the in-movement of young professionals into traditional housing in the shitamachi or poor inner city areas of Tokyo. There has been little written on gentrification in Tokyo since, but it seems that a quite different context – less inner city/CBD decline, a less sharp decline in industry and manufacturing and a less sharp growth in financial services (in other words a less sharp transition to post-industrial society), a very tight and tenurially different housing market, and a more controlled economy and society – has led to less significant residential gentrification in Tokyo. By way of contrast there has been significant retail or commercial gentrification and it is here that social polarization is most noticeable as restaurants that sell a bowl of noodles for £70 sit a hundred yards from those that sell a bowl of noodles for £4 (*The Times*, 2010).

But these processes of gentrification were not readily found in that other global or world city – Los Angeles – until very recently. It is only as we entered the 21st century that there was anecdotal evidence that gentrification had finally taken off in Los Angeles. It is significant that the Los Angeles School of urbanism, that emerged in the mid 1980s as a challenge to the Chicago School of urbanism, re-visioned the future city (their prototype was Los Angeles) as one where the periphery of the city dominated a marginalized downtown. The process of gentrification did not feature in their keno game board urban model. If anything has discredited the LA School's urban model it is the emergence of gentrification in Los Angeles' downtown, in Bunker Hill and the older historic part of downtown. Los Angeles' downtown is one of abandoned movie theatres, large buildings that are vacant or used for manufacturing, grand hotels that are now welfare hotels, and retail for the poor; it also has huge open lots. Los Angeles' downtown is Neil Smith's (1987) rent gap par excellence. The *LA Weekly* has 'outed' gentrification in LA:

In Venice, old-timers are fuming over the oversize fences that are being erected around beach cottages, saying wealthy newcomers won't engage the community. . .Welcome to Gentrification City, where an overheated real estate market is dramatically reshaping neighborhood after neighbourhood. . . . (Zahniser, 2006)

Apartment buildings have been razed. Office buildings are being reinvented as housing. Construction craters occupy half a block. . . Koreatown is just one small section of Los Angeles being transformed by soaring real estate values. In Echo Park, apartment houses are being cleaned out, with speculators paying off – or forcing out – tenants who have lived in their homes 20 and 30 years. (Gold, 2008)

So why has gentrification come so late to LA? The answer probably lies in the fact that LA is a relatively young city, too young to have had the waves of gentrification that London and New York did in the 1950s, 1960s and 1970s. LA is somewhat exceptional; for example, it lacks the historic architecture (Victorian or Georgian properties) that London and New York first wave gentrifiers sought. Given that gentrification has been seen to be a search for authenticity (see Jager, 1986) it is perhaps not surprising that gentrification has not been found in LA until very recently, in a city famed for its *in*authenticity. Indeed, it is testimony to the mutation of gentrification into new forms/ types that we now find gentrification in LA; it demonstrates a process searching for ever more profit margins (often in more recent architectural forms), be they modernist ex-council tower blocks in London (see Davidson and Lees, 2010) or abandoned, kitsch, Hollywood movie theatres in LA.

Gentrification has Gone, and is Still Going, Global

Gentrification progressed well in cities that had gone global, then gentrification itself went global – as Neil Smith (2002) describes, gentrification became *the* leading edge of global urbanism; it became 'gentrification generalized'. Gentrification became a state-led, global urban strategy (Lees and Ley, 2008). In the Global North this involves:

an innovative race to create attractive, novel, and interesting – but also safe and sanitized – playgrounds for the wealthy residents and visitors who work for (or receive interest and dividends from) the institutions of global capital. (Lees et al., 2008, p. 166)

But in the Global South it is played out in more diverse ways:

Although urban thinking in much of Europe and North America is obsessed with the contours of postindustrial society, urbanization in the Global South is driven by the simultaneous expansion of 'old' and 'new' spatial economic shifts; cities are being reshaped by the expansion of manufacturing and heavy industrial activities, as well as the growth of high-tech off-shoring and outsourcing activities and smaller pockets of service sector innovation. (Lees et al., 2008, p. 166)

Increasingly, as I will show in my discussion of aspirant world cities, the class transformation of cities in the Global South involves the systematic and large scale redevelopment of large swathes of the urban fabric of central cities. This restructuring is supported financially by transnational investors and politically by the state. The state in the Global South has been at the forefront of 'defining' the indigenous poor as an undeserving population – this is very evident in cities like Mumbai and Shanghai. Gentrification is very much part of a world-wide neoliberal urban agenda that appeals to the role of the individual, the state and the private market.

Atkinson and Bridge (2005) suggest that contemporary gentrification – based as it is on wide differences in wealth and power – resembles earlier waves of colonial or mercantile expansion that exploited national and continental differences in economic development. In the same way, they argue that contemporary gentrification privileges wealth and whiteness and reasserts a white Anglo appropriation of urban space and historical memory. The universalizing of neoliberal principles of governing cities forces the poor and vulnerable to endure gentrification as a process of colonization:

> Those who come to occupy prestigious central city locations frequently have the characteristics of a colonial elite. They often live in exclusive residential enclaves and are supported by a domestic and local service class. Gentrifiers are employed in . . . new class occupations, and are marked out by their cosmopolitanism. Indeed, in many locations, especially in ex-communist European and east Asian countries, they often are western ex-patriots employed by transnational corporations to open up the markets of the newly emerging economies. (Atkinson and Bridge, 2005, p. 3)

Gentrifying Global Elites

Rofe (2003) and Atkinson and Bridge (2005) identify a transnational set of elite gentrifiers that have been created by the expansion of financial services in certain global cities and the real estate investment that exploits these changes in the labour market. An elite set of gentrifiers has been born; however, these elite gentrifiers are not a homogeneous group or class, for within this group are different types, some of which have been written about, some of which have yet to be researched. The transnational set of elite gentrifiers that Rofe (2003) identifies are cosmopolitans who show a willingness to engage with diversity, they are very mobile and not especially rooted. They reject a suburban-orientated identity, they are really the grown up version of the pioneer gentrifier – the 'cultural new class' that David Ley (1996) discusses. By way of contrast super-gentrifiers or financifiers are a different species; they have more suburban values, they are less interested in socio-cultural diversity, their investment in space (the neighbourhood) is more economic than cultural, and they are interested in fixity in their local neighbourhood and yet have the capacity to be very mobile on a global scale in work and play (see Lees, 2003; Butler and Lees, 2006).

The timing and context for gentrification are significant. In Moscow's gentrifying Ostozhenka neighbourhood, elite gentrifiers were given the label of 'the New Russians' because they were seen to have succeeded in the early stage of economic transition

(Badyina and Golubchikov, 2005). These gentrifiers were symbolic of change from the Soviet Union to the New Russia; promoters of Ostozhenka talked about the 'Europeanization' of the neighbourhood as a way of creating social distinction from the rest of Russian society. The new architecture was used to represent this value change:

> [New buildings] seem to be located not here, but sometimes in France, sometimes in Switzerland, more often in Finland. They have the elements unimaginable for Russian homes – well-groomed yards, elegant lawns, carefully paved paths, underground parking, impossible for Russia, luxurious terraces and lobbies. It is not the Moscow quality of life, it is rather a very prestigious, very bourgeois neighbourhood of top-managers in an old European capital city. (Revzin, 2003; cited in Badyina and Golubchikov, 2005, p. 124).

Ostozhenka's gentrifiers are the owners and CEOs of large and medium Russian businesses whether industry or financial groups, well to do artistic and media elites, and also foreign business people and diplomats working in Moscow. As Badyina and Golubchikov (2005, p. 124) state: 'in many respects this cohort shares its identity with the new upper classes colonizing the "elite" districts in the major world cities'.

Yet more recently the characterization of gentrifying global elites has been beginning to change. There is increased recognition that there are many different types of gentrifier, that their so-called hypermobility could also act as a stabilizing process and be used by them as a way of living and belonging to particular communities (see the discussion in Andreotti and Le Gales, 2008), and that many contemporary gentrifiers, especially those in world/global cities where gentrification has matured the most, are as suburban in their values as they are urban. There is important work to be done on how the lives of these different gentrifiers in different places, this gentrifying global elite, are the same or different. Wang and Siu Yu Lau's (2009) research into the cultural consumption patterns of Shanghai's new middle class is one piece of work that has already begun this task.

GENTRIFICATION AND ASPIRANT WORLD CITIES

As gentrification has gone global, as the status of world cities has increased, and as cities around the world scramble to get onto the world stage it is not surprising that aspirant world cities in both the Global North and the Global South have placed gentrification at the core of their urban strategies and policies.

In Miami, for example, the Mayor, politicians and big business are running after 'world city status' and in so doing they have sought to displace poor black populations from the downtown core. This is nowhere more evident than in Overtown, a historic and predominantly black community located adjacent to downtown Miami. More than 50 per cent of Overtown's residents live in poverty, the median family income is just over $14,000 a year, and approximately 90 per cent of residents are renters. Long neglected, it stands as a barrier to overall gentrification in downtown Miami. In the face of pressing affordable housing shortages the City permitted (in an uncompetitive, no-bid process) a politically connected developer to build luxury homes on publicly owned land in Overtown; land that had been vacant for over 20 years. Miami has one of the highest levels of vacant public housing in the nation yet has done little to fill these vacancies. It seems that the City would rather allow the empty units to fall into disrepair, condemn them and then redevelop/gentrify them as part of what some are calling a 'scorched earth' removal policy. In the United States, where blacks were once segregated in abandoned downtowns while whites lived in the suburbs, now black communities are expected to disperse to the peripheries as cities are reappropriated by white upper and upper-middle income groups (see Lees et al., 2008, on fourth wave gentrification in the United States). Nijman (2001) argues that many of Miami's wealthiest people, entrepreneurs, politicians and real estate owners, are recent immigrants, they are a footloose cosmopolitan elite like nowhere else. As a result of this cosmopolitanism he argues that Miami could be considered to be the 'first global city' because 'it is ahead of the curve'; yet strangely Nijman ignores the colonizing impact of gentrification. There is a need to reconcile these stories of the white Anglo appropriation of the black inner city and world city cosmopolitanism, especially in the United States.

Is the story of gentrification and aspirant world cities the same in the Global South? Following the 2008 Olympic Games the Mayor of Beijing presented a blueprint to the 13th Beijing Municipal People's Congress to remake Beijing into a 'world city' by 2050. Beijing is undergoing rapid redevelopment, many historic buildings have been bulldozed to make way for high rise towers, and Chinese preservationists are facing the threat of gentrification. The few ancient courtyard houses that survived destruction have become coveted status symbols for the country's growing upper class and for wealthy foreign investors:

> As more and more money is poured into elaborate renovations, the phenomenon is not only draining these neighborhoods of their character but also threatening to erase an entire way of life. (Ouroussof, 2008)

Chinese cities have come back to the network of the global economy, particularly after China's re-entry to the World Trade Organization (Wu, 2000, 2002), and they want to look and feel like other world cities. Among them is Shanghai, the largest city in China, a city that was once called 'The Paris of the East, The New York of the West'. In 2002, Shanghai won the bid to host the 2010 World Exposition, which the state hopes will solidify the city's reputation as a global hub, putting Shanghai back on the international map (Wasserstrom, 2003). In Shanghai state-sponsored gentrification under market transition is motivated by the pursuit of economic and urban growth at the cost of large scale residential displacement (He, 2007). Global and metropolitan styles of building are seen by China's new middle classes to represent modernity and change. Low rise traditional houses built pre-communism and declining workers' villages, factories and warehouses built in the socialist period are considered to be inappropriate for a global city image. As a result there has been massive new build gentrification in Shanghai that has displaced existing residents and demolished historic buildings and landscapes. The aspirant world city Shanghai is undergoing a fundamental class remake in a much more rapid and drastic way than its Western counterparts. Low income people have been pushed to the outskirts of Shanghai, nearly a million households have been relocated over the last 12 years and 51.02 million square metres of housing has been demolished. The displaced have been removed to new housing on the outskirts of Shanghai away from their employment and their social networks – their lives and livelihoods have often been destroyed (He, 2010).

Another rapidly developing city aiming to be a global/world city (like London) is Mumbai. The associated gentrification of Mumbai has a background in the liberalization of the Indian economy which began in 1991 and of the emergence of new middle class urban identities in India. Lower Parel at the heart of Mumbai's Island City was an area of former mill lands; it is now an area of residential high rises, converted mills and new office and leisure complexes. The gentrification of Lower Parel, however, did not just occur because of economic liberalization and a new middle class – there were concerted efforts by commercial and political elites to curtail union power in the working mills and to curtail opposition movements against gentrification. New planning rules sanctioned the conversion of the mills, then after 2001 allowed extensive redevelopment of the land in the face of massive opposition (Harris, 2008). Mumbai's Lower Parel has experienced intense socio-spatial inequality and a very sharp edged gentrification – enacted through harassment and the denial of basic services like water and electricity. Most of the former mill workers have moved to townships and shanties on the outskirts of the city; there is no place for them in Mumbai's world city image. Similar processes are operating in other cities striving for world city status, cities like Cape Town, South Africa, where a new class-based apartheid is emerging (see Visser and Kotze, 2008).

The global economic recession has impacted gentrification in world cities differentially. The future of gentrification may well be with those cities in the Global South, like Mumbai, Beijing and Shanghai, that are advancing rapidly in terms of world city status and whose governments are aggressively pushing gentrification to help them onto the world city stage. Back in the Global North gentrification in London and New York City continues and is creating new types. In an economically struggling Los Angeles gentrification has already slowed down significantly, warranting fears that it will return to being 'a Los Angeles version of flyover country' (Timburg, 2009). In Toronto, seemingly somewhat less affected by the global economic recession, gentrification is continuing through wholesale downtown 'condofication' that has a fascinating gender dimension to it (see Kern, 2010).

A RESEARCH AGENDA FOR GENTRIFICATION AND THE WORLD CITY

It is clear that more and more cities are battling for world city status. One weapon in that battle is state-led gentrification. In cities desperate to attain world city status quickly and with little welfare provision, or interest in welfare provision, the process of gentrification acts as a sharp knife cutting out the proletarian underbelly of inner cities and enacting plastic surgery with a newly emergent middle class. The impacts are:

1. The erasure of the proletariat in central cities (class change).
2. In some cities the whitening of the central city (racial/ethnic change).
3. The creation of a culturally homogeneous inner city population that, ironically, will damage creativity and the economy (the suburbanization of the central city).
4. The creation of a global inner city aesthetic that will make cities around the world all look and feel the same (placelessness – the 'ageographia').

Demonstrating that gentrification is a large scale, global 'problem' is one way forward in getting governments to create an alternative vision for their cities. Refocusing on the socioeconomic inequality that is inherent to world cities, as illustrated so effectively by gentrification, re-necessitates investigating the world city as a function of social class struggle (following on from, and indeed extending, Sassen, 1991). But we must branch out in the terms of comparative urbanism to investigate gentrification in world cities, and aspiring world cities, outside of the metropoles of London and New York. This means a re-grounding of comparative methods to support a more properly international urban study (in the vein of Robinson, 2006) of gentrification and world cities, and comparative research into the politics of city strategies to attain world city status.

REFERENCES

Andreotti, A. and P. Le Gales (2008), 'Middle class neighbourhood attachment in Paris and Milan: partial exit and profound rootedness', in T. Blokland and M. Savage (eds), *Networked Urbanism: Social Capital in the City*, London: Routledge, pp.127–146.

Atkinson, R. and G. Bridge (eds) (2005), *Gentrification in a Global Context: The New Urban Colonialism*, London: Routledge.

Badyina, A. and O. Golubchikov (2005), 'Gentrification in central Moscow – a market process or a deliberate policy? Money, power and people in housing regeneration in Ostozhenka', *Geografiska Annaler B*, **87** (2), 113–129.

Buck, N., I. Gordon, P. Hall, M. Harloe and M. Kleinman (2002), *Working Capital: Life and Labour in Contemporary London*, London: Routledge.

Butler, T. and L. Lees (2006), 'Super-gentrification in Barnsbury, London: Globalisation and gentrifying global elites at the neighbourhood level', *Transactions of the Institute of British Geographers*, **31** (4), 467–487.

Carpenter, J. and L. Lees (1995), 'Gentrification in New York, London and Paris: an international comparison', *International Journal of Urban and Regional Research*, **19** (2), 286–303.

Caulfield, J. (1994), *City Form and Everyday Life: Toronto's Gentrification and Critical Social Practice*, Toronto: University of Toronto Press.

Cybriwsky, R. (1998), *Tokyo: The Shogun's City at the Twenty-First Century*, Chichester: John Wiley and Sons.

Davidson, M. and L. Lees (2005), 'New-build "gentrification" and London's riverside renaissance', *Environment and Planning A*, **37** (7), 1165–1190.

Davidson, M. and L. Lees (2010), 'New-build gentrification: its histories, trajectories, and critical geographies', *Population, Space and Place*, **16** (5), 395–411.

Fujitsuka, Y. (2005), 'Gentrification and neighbourhood dynamics in Japan: the case of Kyoto', in R. Atkinson and G. Bridge (eds), *Gentrification in a Global Context: The New Urban Colonialism*, London: Routledge, pp. 137–150.

Glass, R. (1964), 'Introduction: aspects of change', in Centre for Urban Studies (ed.), *London: Aspects of Change*, London: MacGibbon and Kee, pp. xiii-xlii.

Gold, S. (2008), 'Gentrification divides Echo Park community in Los Angeles', *LA Times*, 27 June.

Harris, A. (2008), 'From London to Mumbai and back again: gentrification and public policy in comparative perspective', *Urban Studies*, **45** (12), 2407–2428.

He, S. (2007), 'State-sponsored gentrification under market transition: the case of Shanghai', *Urban Affairs Review*, **43** (2), 171–198.

He, S. (2010), 'New-build gentrification in central Shanghai: demographic changes and socioeconomic implications', *Population, Space and Place*, **16** (5), 345–361.

Jager, M. (1986), 'Class definition and the aesthetics of gentrification: Victoriana in Melbourne', in N. Smith and P. Williams (eds), *Gentrification of the City*, London: Unwin Hyman, pp. 78–91.

Kern, L. (2010), *Sex and the Revitalized City: Gender, Condominium Development, and Urban Citizenship*, Vancouver: UBC Press.

Lees, L. (2003), 'Super-gentrification: the case of Brooklyn Heights, New York City', *Urban Studies*, **40** (12), 2487–2509.

Lees, L. and D. Ley (2008), 'Special issue: gentrification and public policy', *Urban Studies*, **45** (12), 2379–2384.

Lees, L., T. Slater and E. Wyly (2008), *Gentrification*, New York: Routledge.

Ley, D. (1996), *The New Middle Class and the Remaking of the Central City*, Oxford: Oxford University Press.

Nijman, J. (2001), 'Miami's origins as a "world city" differ from L.A.'s', *World City Business*, **3** (21), 13–26.

Ouroussof, N. (2008), 'Lost in the new Beijing: the old neighbourhood', *The New York Times*, 27 July.

Robinson, J. (2006), *Ordinary Cities: Between Modernity and Development*, London: Routledge.

Rofe, M. (2003), '"I want to be global": theorising the gentrifying class as an emergent elite global community', *Urban Studies*, **40** (12), 2511–2526.

Sassen, S. (1991), *The Global City: New York, London, Tokyo*, Princeton, NJ: Princeton University Press.

Smith, N. (1987), 'Gentrification and the rent gap', *Annals of the Association of American Geographers*, **77** (3), 462–478.

Smith, N. (2002), 'New globalism, new urbanism: gentrification as global urban strategy', *Antipode*, **34** (3), 427–450.

The Times (2010), '£70 for a bowl of noodles? Only in Tokyo, gourmet capital of the world', 19 February.

Timburg, S. (2009), 'When the next wave wipes out', *The New York Times*, 25 February.

Visser, G. and N. Kotze (2008), 'The state and new-build gentrification in Central Cape Town, South Africa', *Urban Studies*, **45** (12), 2565–2593.

Wang, J. and S. Siu Yu Lau (2009), 'Gentrification and Shanghai's new middle-class: another reflection on the cultural consumption thesis', *Cities*, **26** (2), 57–66.

Wasserstrom, J. (2003), 'The second coming of global Shanghai', *World Policy Journal*, **20** (2), 51–60.

Wu, F. (2000), 'The global and local dimensions of place-making: remaking Shanghai as a world city', *Urban Studies*, **37** (8), 1359–1377.

Wu, F. (2002), 'China's changing urban governance in the transition towards a more market-oriented economy', *Urban Studies*, **39** (7), 1071–1093.

Zahniser, D. (2006), 'Welcome to gentrification city', *LA Weekly*, 24 August.

34 The privileged world city: private banking, wealth management and the bespoke servicing of the global super-rich
Jonathan V. Beaverstock

INTRODUCTION

> Of all classes, the rich are the most noticed and the least studied. (John Kenneth Galbraith, 1977, p. 44)

> geographers . . . seem to have little to say about the contemporary super-rich, despite their evidential role in shaping the global economy. (Beaverstock et al., 2004, p. 402)

The gap in understanding the super-rich is somewhat ironic given the widening disparity of world household income inequality. In 2000, about 2 per cent of the world's adult population possessed more than 50 per cent of total global wealth, with the richest 1 per cent holding 40 per cent of all global assets (Davies et al., 2008). In the United States of America (USA) and the United Kingdom (UK), on the back of the roaring bull market, a wave of neo-liberalism and muted income redistributive policies, the super-rich have swelled their numbers as never before (Thorndike, 1980; Lundberg, 1988; Haseler, 1999; Smith, 2001; Irvin, 2008). The *Forbes Billionaire* and *The Sunday Times Rich List* have made transparent the once secretive worlds of the rich. The super-rich are now an identifiable market in their own right. Those wealthy individuals with investable assets greater than US$1 million are now termed 'High Net Worth Individuals' (HNWIs) and these totalled 10.1 million in 2008, with wealth approximating US$40.7 trillion (Merrill Lynch Capgemini (MLCG), 2009). Given the global market value of this segment of the population, servicing the billionaire, multi-millionaire and 'meagre' millionaire has become a multi-billion US$ industry. Just as world cities are the 'basing points' for international capital (Friedmann, 1986), they are the places where the super-rich connect with a bespoke, exclusive and privileged circuit of economic relations in private banking and wealth management. The rest of this chapter will be organised in four main sections. The first section will conceptualise the identifiable traits of the super-rich. Section two defines, quantifies and locates the super-rich in global society, drawing on the new financial discourse of the high net worth market. Section three introduces one of the major privileged world city economies which services the requirements of the super-rich: private banking and wealth management. Finally, several conclusions are reported, which reflect on the super-rich being the *super-class* in global society.

CONCEPTUALIZING THE SUPER-RICH

Historically, there has always been an interest in the wealthy segments of society. Veblen (1899) mused about the existence of a 'leisure class' in the USA at the end of the nineteenth century, and Thorndike (1980) analysed family dynasties of the Gilded Age (e.g. Astors, Carnegies, Du Ponts, Gettys, Mellons). In the USA and UK, these socio-historical studies of the wealthy dwelt on the existence of wealth accumulated through 'old' money: inheritance, resource-based wealth, and the land and gentry (North, 2005). However, much has changed since the early 1980s. Increasingly, the source of individual private wealth has grown quickly from 'new' money and the advent of the 'self-made' millionaire, drawn from astronomical executive remuneration packages (share/stock options and salary bonuses), exorbitant returns from financial markets, alternative investments like hedge funds and real estate investment, and, significantly, entrepreneurial activity translated in stock-market flotations (Frank, 2007; Irvin, 2008). Since financial de-regulation in Wall Street and the City of London, aided by relatively low US and UK personal taxation regimes, a new breed, and significant number, of 'financial elites' (Hall, 2009) have personally benefited from instant wealth creation, from one of the longest bull markets in living memory (*The Economist*, 2009). Running in parallel to the 'self-made' multi-millionaire and billionaire, the 'West's' engagement with the rapidly expanding Russian, Chinese and Indian economies, coupled with major price gains in commodities, has also created 'a whole new batch of emerging market plutocrats' (*The Economist*, 2009, p. 4) and 'oligarchs' who quickly joined the ranks of the billionaire super-rich.

The super-rich are a slippery population to pigeonhole in a generic, let alone distinctive, homogeneous social stratum or 'class' like Sklair's (2001) transnational capitalist class. Collectively, the super-rich have traits of transnationalism, cosmopolitanism and living fast and hyper-mobile lifestyles, which are played out in exclusive circuits of social and capitalist relations. Bauman (2000) refers to the super-rich as the 'new cosmopolitans', who are the 'fast subjects' in global society (see Beaverstock et al., 2004). The super-rich occupy a world of exclusiveness, with multiple residences, family offices to run the household, private security, the use of penthouse suites in five, six, seven star hotels, private jets and bespoke luxury consumption. The life worlds of the USA's super-rich are very eloquently conceptualized by Frank (2007, p. 3), who suggests that they have

> formed their own virtual country . . . and with their huge numbers, they had built a self-contained world unto themselves, complete with their own health-care system (concierge doctors), travel networks (Netjets, destination clubs), separate economy (double-digit income gains and double-digit inflation), and language (Who's your household manager?) . . . The rich weren't just getting richer, they were becoming financial foreigners, creating their own country within a country, their own society within society, and their economy within an economy.

Frank named this virtual country Richi$tan, which is sub-divided into four distinctive virtual-spaces: Lower Richi$tan (net worth $1m–$10m, 7.5m households), Middle Richi$tan (net worth $10m–$100m, >2m households), Upper Richi$tan ($100m–$1b, thousands of households) and billionaireville (over $1b, 400+ households). Prior to Frank (2007), Beaverstock et al. (2004, pp. 405–406) noted that the super-rich are 'perpetually between nation-states, to the extent that they dwell in global space-time . . . as key actors in the articulation of the "network society"'. However, as I shall note later, an important tangible trait of the super-rich is that they are embedded in particular world cities, as places of multiple residences and centres of business interests and activities, and, importantly, expert banking, financial and professional service economies which manage and protect their wealth.

DEFINING AND LOCATING THE SUPER-RICH

1982 was the key moment for a rigorous 'scientific' identification of the wealthy as it marked the publication of the first *Forbes* list of the USA's 400 wealthiest individuals. As Smith (2001, p. 3) notes:

> Most of us were astonished to learn in 1982 that there were twelve American families worth more than $1 billion. There were also twenty-five between $500 million and $1 billion; nearly 100 between $200 [million] and $500 [million]; and 267 others among the richest 400 families with net assets (at approximate market value) above $100 million. In those days, billions were numbers that only governments dealt in.

The *Forbes* list at that time was dominated by 'old' money: inherited wealth, manufacturing industrialists, real estate tycoons, traditional bankers and financiers, and natural resource barons (oil, mining), but also included a list of people who were virtually unknown entrepreneurs (like Sam Walton, the founder of Wal-Mart), Philip Knight (Nike shoes) and Steve Jobs (Apple Computers). The *Forbes* wealthy lists (and later *The Sunday Times Rich List*, first published in 1988) provided new intelligence on an individual's wealth to a new and burgeoning private wealth management industry from the mid 1980s, which allowed for the refinement of many terms to describe the rich and super-rich and, ultimately, in the 1990s, frame a market for the HNWI. There are several definitional characteristics of the rich and super-rich that coincide with the established financial definitions of HNWIs. For example, Haseler (1999, pp. 2–3) noted three subcategories of the super-rich: (i) millionaires – who are 'by no means lavishly well off', but can maintain their lifestyle without the need to work (in 1996 it was estimated that there were approximately 6 million dollar millionaires, with 3.5 million residing in the USA); (ii) multimillionaires – these are 'at the very lower reaches of the world of the super-rich . . . [and] . . . their homes and pensions are included in the calculations'. In 1995 about 1 million US households possessed an average of $7 million, during the same period about 48,000 British households (the top half per cent) had on average US$2 million. The multimillionaires are highly mobile with homes around the world and the 'literal mobility' of private yachts and aircraft; and, (iii) mega-rich and billionaires – a distinction can be drawn between the mega-rich at the lower (<$50m) and upper (>$500m) end of the spectrum where the distinction is not necessarily lifestyle but economic power. The peak of the mega-rich are the billionaires (US$1000m+).

The wealth management industry began to define the rich and super-rich as a target market in earnest from the mid 1990s. MLCG (2009, p. 2), who published the *World Wealth Reports* annually from 1996, defined the high net worth (HNW) market as:

(i)   HNWIs are defined as those having investable assets of US$1million or more, excluding primary residence, collectables, consumables, and consumable durables.

(ii) Ultra-HNWIs are defined as those having investable assets of US$30million or more, excluding primary residence, collectables, consumables, and consumer durables.

(iii) Mid-tier millionaires are HNWIs having US$5million to US$30million.

Whichever definition is adopted to classify the wealth of the rich and super-rich, it is apparent that once the millionaires and multi-millionaires are identified, there exists a stratospheric gap in social relations and everyday lifestyles of these individuals in rela-

Table 34.1   The growth of HNWIs worldwide and the value of their wealth, 1996–2008

	Number (millions)	Change (%)	Wealth ($ trillions)	Change (%)
1996	4.5	–	16.6	–
1997	5.2	+15.6	19.1	+15.1
1998	5.9	+13.5	21.6	+13.1
1999	7.0	+18.6	25.5	+18.1
2000	7.2	+2.9	27.0	+5.9
2001	7.1	−1.4	26.2	−3.7
2002	7.3	+2.8	26.7	+2.7
2003	7.7	+5.5	28.5	+6.7
2004	8.2	+6.5	30.7	+7.7
2005	8.8	+7.3	33.4	+8.8
2006	9.5	+8.0	37.2	+11.4
2007	10.1	+6.3	40.7	+9.4
2008	8.6	−14.9	32.8	−19.4

Source: Merrill Lynch Capgemini (2008, 2009)

tion to the billionaires atop the Forbes' list (which in 2009 ranked: 1. William Gates $40b; 2. Warren Buffett $37b; 3. Carlos Slim Helu & Family $35b; 4. Lawrence Ellison $22.5b; and 5. Ingvar Kamprad & family $22b).

The Size and Composition of the High Net Worth Market

In 2008, the world population of HNWIs stood at 8.6 million, which was down 14.9 per cent from a year earlier due to the global financial crisis (MLCG, 2009). Referring back to 2007, since 1996 there has been more than a doubling of the number of HNWIs worldwide from 4.5 million to 10.1 million (+121.7 per cent) and almost a two and a half fold increase in the value of their private wealth (+145.2 per cent), from US$16.6 to $40.7 trillion (Table 34.1).

Turning to the definitional composition of the HNWI sector, the Ultra-HNWI category (>$30 million) has accounted for only about 0.9 per cent to 1.0 per cent of the total number of HNWIs since data collection commenced in 1996 (MLCG, various). In 2008, the ultra-HNWI group represented 0.9 per cent of the population of HNWIs (78,000) but accounted for 34.7 per cent of the total value of private wealth (MLCG, 2009). These data findings indicate very clearly that the global population of HNWIs is dominated by those persons in the 'millionaire next door' and mid tier millionaire categories (between $1 million and $5 million, and between $5 million and $30 million) (Table 34.2). At the individual billion level, in 2009 there were 793, a reduction of almost 30 per cent (−332 persons) since 2008, with a net loss of private wealth of approximately US$2.0 trillion (Forbes, 2009).

Table 34.2   The composition of the HNWI private wealth market, 2002–2008

Category	Percentage of the total population of HNWIs						
	2002	2003	2004	2005	2006	2007	2008
Ultra-HNWI	0.8	0.9	0.9	1.0	1.0	1.0	0.9
Mid tier millionaire and 'millionaire next door'	99.2	99.1	99.1	99.0	99.0	99.0	99.1
Total number of HNWIs (millions)	7.3	7.6	8.3	8.7	9.5	10.1	8.6

Source: Merrill Lynch Capgemini (2003 to 2009)

Table 34.3   The changing geographical coverage of HNWI and private wealth, 2000–2008

	HNWIs (millions)			Value of private wealth (US$tr)		
	2000	2008	% growth	2000	2008	% growth
North America	2.2	2.7	+23	7.5	9.1	+21
Europe	2.5	2.6	+4	8.4	8.3	−1
Asia-Pacific	1.6	2.4	+50	4.8	7.4	+54
Latin America	0.3	0.4	+33	3.2	5.8	+81
Middle East	0.3	0.4	+33	1.0	1.4	+40
Africa	0.1	0.1	–	0.6	0.8	+33
Totals	6.9	8.6	+25	25.5	32.8	+29

Source: Merrill Lynch Capgemini (2002, 2009)

Locating the High Net Worth Population

North America and Europe have had the highest share of the total number of HNWIs and value of global private wealth worldwide (by an average of approximately two-thirds for each grand total) (MLCG, various). In 2008, North America and Europe accounted for 5.3 million HNWIs and ultra-HNWIs (62 per cent of the total), and just over half of the distribution of private wealth ($17.4 trillion) (MLCG, 2009) (Table 34.3). Prior to the dot.com bust in 2001/02, there had been significant relative growth in the number of HNWIs and value of private wealth in the 'emerging markets' of the Asia-Pacific (e.g. Singapore, mainland China and India), Latin America and the Middle East (e.g. United Arab Emirates) (Table 34.3). However, all worldwide regions experienced large reductions in the number of HNWIs and value of private wealth in the fallout of the global financial crisis, with North America experiencing the highest reductions by −19.0 per cent (down 0.6m HNWIs, from 3.3m to 2.7m) and −22.8 per cent (down $2.6tr, from $11.7tr to $9.1tr) respectively, between 2007 and 2008 (MLCG, 2008, 2009).

The much publicized 2009 Forbes list of billionaires indicated that the US had the highest share representing 45 per cent (359 billionaires), followed by Europe (25 per cent, 196) and Asia-Pacific (16 per cent, 130). Forbes 2009 data also revealed that New York (55), London (28) and Moscow (27) were the homes to the most billionaires (Forbes,

Table 34.4   *The number and share of the top 1000 richest persons who were born, live or have their interests centred in London or the south-east of England*

	London	South-east of England
2002	NA	489 (48.9%)[1]
2003	NA	469 (46.9%)[1]
2004	NA	491 (49.1%)[1]
2005	NA	503 (50.3%)[1]
2006	NA	NA
2007	411 (41.1%)	534 (53.4%)[1]
2008	415 (41.5%)	554 (55.4%)[1]
2009	385 (38.5%)	506 (50.6%)[1]

Note: 1. Includes London; NA data not available

Source: *The Sunday Times Rich List* (2002 to 2009; except 2006)

2009). Five years earlier in 2004, London was the most popular home for the dollar billionaires with 40, followed by New York (31), Moscow (23) and Geneva (20) (Figure 34.1). During the 2000s, London and the south-east of England accounted for an average of 51 per cent of the UK regional distribution of *The Sunday Times Rich List* wealthiest 1000 (Table 34.4). However, according to *The Sunday Times Rich List* (2008, 2009) the number of UK billionaires fell by 43 per cent from 75 in 2008 to 43 in April 2009. The latest market intelligence from the Centre for Economics and Business Research (2009a) suggests that the number of UK millionaires has fallen 51 per cent from 489,000 in August 2006 to 242,000 in May 2009. Such has been the severity of the global financial crisis on the wealth of the UK's HNWIs, through the collapse of house prices, falling share values and plummeting City bonuses.

London's position as the premier international financial centre (Z/Yen, 2009) is a significant generator of personal wealth for its employees in banking, finance, insurance and professional service jobs. The much publicized remuneration and bonus packages for City workers, especially investment bankers, is a major factor which has contributed to the exponential growth of 'new' money and the location of the 'new' money super-rich in world cities. At the height of the bull market in 2007, an estimated 354,000 City workers (employed in City type jobs) received bonuses worth £10.241 billion, in 'stark' contrast to the allocation of 'only' £4.008 billion to 324,000 in 2008 (Table 34.5). A similar remuneration and bonus culture is associated with many of the leading international financial centres. For example, Wall Street's securities industry divided up $32 billion in bonuses in 2007 (which was down to $18 billion in 2008) (Goldman, 2009).

Other metrics can be used to locate the super-rich. For example, the wealth 'think tank' www.wealth-bulletin.com estimates that the most expensive streets in the world (per sq/m) are to be found in Monaco, New York, London, Paris, Hong Kong and Moscow (Table 34.6). As most geographers and urbanists seem to be allergic to studying the super-rich, there is a dearth of studies of places where we intuitively know the super-rich live or have their 'town' residences, for example: the London Boroughs of Westminster, Kensington and Chelsea; Mid-town and the Upper East and West Sides of Manhattan, New York;

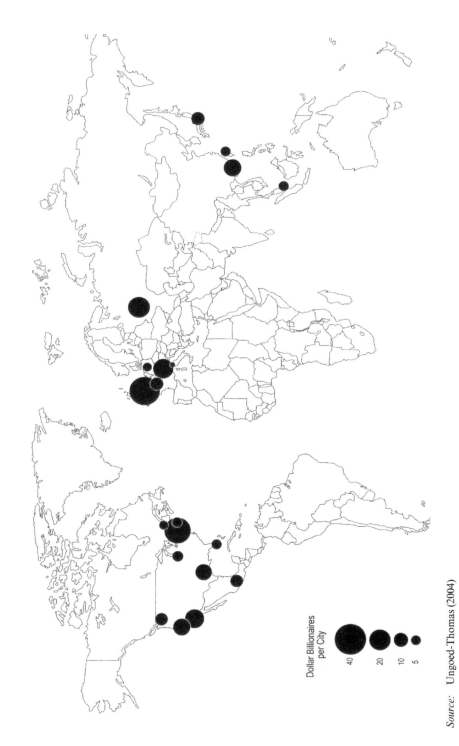

Source: Ungoed-Thomas (2004)

Figure 34.1   Dollar billionaires per city, 2004

Dollar Billionaires
per City

40   20   10   5

Table 34.5   City bonus payouts and employment in City type jobs, 2001–2009

Year	City jobs	City bonus (£billion)
2001	312,000	3.921
2002	308,000	3.329
2003	317,000	4.893
2004	325,000	5.695
2005	327,000	7.130
2006	343,000	10.059
2007	354,000	10.241
2008	324,000	4.008
2009	305,000	6.012

Source: Centre for Economics and Business Research (2009b, 2009c)

Table 34.6   The world's most expensive streets

Street	City	Price per sq/m (£)
Avenue Princess Grace	Monaco	115,000
Chemin de Saint-Hospice	Cap Ferrat, Nice	60,000
Fifth Avenue	New York	44,000
Kensington Palace Gardens	London	40,000
Avenue Montaigne	Paris	33,000
Via Survretta	St Moritz	27,000
Via Romazzino	Porto Cervo (Italy)	25,000
Severn Road	Hong Kong	24,000
Ostozhenka Street	Moscow	21,000
Wolseley Road	Sydney	17,000

Source: Wealth-Bulletin.com (accessed 6 January 2010)

Neuilly, Auteuil and Passy in Paris; Bel Air in Los Angeles; Moscow's 'Golden Mile' district; and Point Piper in Sydney. The super-rich have multiple residences, and anecdotal evidence from sources like *The Sunday Times Rich List* and Forbes indicates that they have these residences in world cities (e.g. London, New York, Paris, Los Angeles, Rome); offshore 'havens', like the Caribbean (e.g. Bahamas) and European Principalities (e.g. Monaco and Monte Carlo); the seasonal 'playgrounds' (e.g. St Moritz and Aspen; and Côte d'Azur; Isle of Capri; the Hamptons, Long Island); and isolated retreats (e.g. in the UK context, Scottish estates and isles, and country houses in rural counties).

WORLD CITIES SERVING THE SUPER-RICH: PRIVATE BANKING AND THE WEALTH MANAGEMENT INDUSTRY

Prior to the financial deregulation in the USA and the UK in the 1980s, the Anglo-American and European market for individual wealth was serviced almost exclusively

Table 34.7   The world's largest private banks, 2008

Bank	Global assets under management	
	US$billion	% share
Bank of Am/M Lynch	1501	12.9
UBS	1394	12.0
Citi	1320	11.4
Wells Fargo	1000	8.6
Credit Suisse	612	5.3
J.P. Morgan	552	4.8
Morgan Stanley	522	4.5
HSBC Group	352	3.0
Deutsche Bank	231	2.0
Other banks	4177	35.5

Source: International Financial Services London (2009, quoted in Scorpio Partnership, 2009 Private Banking Benchmark Study)

by European and American private banks, 'onshore' in London, New York, Paris, Amsterdam and Frankfurt, and 'offshore' in Geneva, Zurich, Basle, Lausanne, Luxembourg, St Helier and St Peter Port (Channel Islands), Douglas (Isle of Man), Hong Kong, Singapore and numerous centres in the Caribbean (e.g. Georgetown – Cayman Islands, Nassau – Bahamas) (Bicker, 1996). Many of these private banks were steeped in history, headquartered in London or Switzerland, and had office networks which spanned the major onshore and offshore jurisdictions (e.g. ANZ Grindleys (1828), Bank Sarin & Co. (1900), Citibank (1902), Coutts & Co. (1692), Lombard, Odier (1798), UBS (1865)). Competition to traditional private banking gathered pace from the mid 1980s, following financial deregulation as a new breed of private wealth management firms entered the market to serve 'new', self-made money, attracted by the rapidly growing HNWI market share (Maude, 2006). This new wealth management sector was established to service a much higher volume HNWI customer base, both on and offshore, offering more extensive services than private banking to accumulate, manage and transfer personal wealth between generations (International Financial Services London (IFSL), 2009). Today, the types of private wealth management service typically involve brokerage, banking, lending, insurance and protection products, advice (e.g. trusts, inheritance, tax planning) and concierge-type services (e.g. yacht broking, art storage). The private wealth management industry of the twenty-first century is a significant global industry, composed of private banks, which are still the major players in the wealth management market (Table 34.7), universal banks (e.g. UBS, Credit Suisse), financial advisors, investment banks (e.g. Goldman Sachs, J.P. Morgan) which service their own HNWI employees, family offices which serve the very ultra-HNWIs and billionaires in the US (there are around 4500 in the US and Europe), professional services ('magic circle' law and top accounting firms), and an array of specialist stockbrokers, asset managers and product specialists (e.g. in hedge funds) (Table 34.8).

London is one of the leading world cities for expertise in managing private wealth. Its world class reputation is founded on the UK's regulatory framework and close relation-

Table 34.8   Selected private wealth management firms, 2009

Private banks	Asset management	Law firms
Arbuthnot Latham & Co.	Aberdeen Asset Man.	Allen & Overy LLP
Adam & Company	AXA Fund Managers	Baker McKenzie LLP
Bank J. Safra	Cazenove Capital Man.	Charles Russell LLP
C. Hoare & Co.	Credit Suisse Asset Man.	Dawson Cornwell
Cater Allen	Fleming Family & Partners	Harcus Sinclair
Duncan Lawrie Ltd	Goldman Sachs Asset Man.	Herbert Smith LLP
Lloyds TSB Private	Lazard Asset Man.	Hughes Fowler Carruthers
SG Hambros Private Bank	Pictet Asset Man.	Macfarlanes LLP
R. Raphael & Sons	St James Place	May, May & Merrimans
Weatherbys Bank	Virgin Money Man.	Forsters LLP
Accountancy	Insurance	Investment banks
Baker Tilly Management	AIG UK Ltd	Barclays Wealth
BDO Stoy Hayward	AXA Art Insurance	Barings Wealth Man. Ltd
Deloitte	Abbey Life Assurance	Citi Private Bank
Ernst & Young Banking	Allianz Insurance plc	Credit Suisse Private
Grant Thornton	Brit Insurance Ltd	HSBC Private Bank
Horwath Clark Whitehall	Chubb Custom Insurance	J.P. Morgan Private Bank
KPMG Bank	DAS Legal	Kleinwort Benson Private
Moore Stephens Wealth	Hiscox Insurance Company	Morgan Stanley Private
PwC Ltd	Markel International	Rathbone Investment Man.
Shipleys	QBE Insurance	UBS AG

Source: Firm websites (various, accessed 7 January 2010)

ship with offshore jurisdictions (Switzerland, Channel Islands, Isle of Man, Hong Kong and Singapore), the range of its financial and professional services, the availability and quality of professional advice, expertise in global and regional financial products (e.g. Islamic finance), and, importantly, an international client (HNWI) base (IFSL, 2009). In 2008, London's private wealth management industry managed UK private client securities by banks, fund managers and stockbrokers valued at £335b, had over 300 family offices with assets over £100m, had the ability to manage both conventional (e.g. cash, bonds, equities) and alternative (e.g. hedge funds) assets, specialized in Islamic financial services, and had expertise in offering advice on trust and taxation matters (IFSL, 2009).

CONCLUSIONS . . . THE NEW *SUPER*-CLASS?

All world cities, as defined by both John Friedmann (1986) and Anthony King (1990), are playgrounds for the super-rich. These are the places where they live in luxurious accommodation, have their business interests, manage and protect their personal wealth, and engage in conspicuous consumption. In this chapter, the world city's private banking and wealth management industry has been discussed in relation to its coveted clientele, the super-rich. Three important conclusions can be drawn from this brief analysis of the super-rich and their engagement with such exclusive economic financial networks. First, the booming financial market performance of the last twenty years, coupled with the opening up of emerging markets and high rises in commodity prices, has created unprecedented conditions for significant growth in the ranks of the super-rich across the globe, especially the self-made, billionaire and multi-millionaire, from 'new' money sources. Admittedly, the fallout of the global economic crisis has put the brakes on this growth, especially for the ultra-HNWIs, but it will be interesting to note how fast the HNW market will recover in the 2010s. Early indications suggest that the HNWIs and billionaires are on their way back from the (relative) squeeze of 2008. MLCG's (2010) latest annual survey for 2009 reports a 17 per cent annual increase in the number of HNWIs, reaching 10 million worldwide, and a rebound in their net personal wealth of +21.5 per cent, which totalled $39 trillion. Furthermore, evidence from the 2010 Forbes list of billionaires suggests that their number had increased by 27 per cent, from 793 to 1011, and their net average wealth was up a staggering $500m to $3.5bn, from the previous year (Forbes.com; www.//news.bbc.co.uk/1/hi/business/8560731.stm, accessed 11 March 2010). Secondly, we have witnessed a sea-change in which the super-rich are serviced by banking and financial services. The millionaires, multi-millionaires and billionaires are now classified as an HNW *market* by a new private wealth management industry, reflecting the changing social composition of the super-rich from 'old' to 'new' money. Importantly, the information and intelligence provided on the rich by 'think tanks' like Merrill Lynch Capgemini are considerably useful in beginning to present a fine grain conceptual analysis of the super-rich. Thirdly, given the refined data on the size and composition of the HNWI market, it is now possible to make more informed explanations about where individuals of specific wealth bands may be placed in any conceptual schema which teases out the differentiation of the super-rich. For example, as significant numbers of individuals fall within MLCG's millionaire group, one could argue that these are more aligned to the characteristics of the 'new' middle classes (Butler and Savage, 1995). The same may not be appropriate for the mid-tier millionaires (US$5–30 million) who may show distinctive attributes of global- and super-gentrifiers and financial elites (Butler and Lees, 2006; Hall, 2009). But there is a cataclysmic gap between the ultra-HNWIs (over US$30m) and the billionaires identified by Forbes, who have wealth in tens of billions. Ultra-HNWIs, at the lower end (say less than US$100m), certainly show traits of being highly cosmopolitan, transnational, mobile and engaging in luxury consumption. These are certainly constituent members of the super-rich, unlike the millionaires and mid-tier, multi-millionaires. As for the billionaires, these are the global super-rich, with significant economic power, as noted by Haseler (1999) and Frank (2007).

But how should we try to conceptualize the super-rich (above say US$100m)? Perhaps an answer to this conundrum is to refer to the super-rich in global society as the *super-class*. Just as Sklair (2001) teases out the *transnational* as being the omnipresent trait of a certain class of capitalist society, the socio-economic and cultural characteristics, and reproduction of the truly global super-rich point to a distinctive and exclusive 'class' that is worthy of the *super* pre-fix. Drawing on Frank's (2007) thoughts about Richi$tan, it can be argued that the super-rich are a global super-class, creating their own global society within global society and their own global economy within the global economy. But at its core is a network of privileged nodes which have a multitude of connections and flows between them, such as Kensington and Chelsea and the City in London, the Upper West/East Side and Wall Street in New York City, and Moscow's 'Golden Mile'.

REFERENCES

Bauman, Z (2000), *Community: Seeking Security in an Insecure World*, Cambridge: Polity.

Beaverstock, J.V., P. Hubbard and J.R. Short (2004), 'Getting away with it? Exposing the geographies of the super-rich', *Geoforum*, **35** (4), 401–407.

Bicker, L. (1996), *Private Banking in Europe*, London: Routledge.

Butler, T. and L. Lees (2006), 'Super-gentrification in Barnsbury, London: globalization and gentrifying global elites at the neighbourhood level', *Transactions of the Institute of British Geographers*, **31** (4), 467–487.

Butler, T. and M. Savage (eds) (1995), *Social Change and the Middle Classes*, London: UCL Press.

Centre for Economics and Business Research (2009a), 'Number of millionaires in the UK falls from 489,000 in 2007 to 242,000 now', press release, 27 May.

Centre for Economics and Business Research (2009b), 'City bonuses bounce back by fifty per cent – but still far lower than 2007/08 peak', press release, 21 October.

Centre for Economics and Business Research (2009c), 'City jobs increasing in 2010 but will remain below peak levels for at least a decade', press release, 15 October.

Davies, J.B., S. Sandstrom, A. Shorrocks and E.N. Wolff (2008), 'The world distribution of household wealth', in J.B. Davies (ed.), *Personal Wealth from a Global Perspective*, Oxford: Oxford University Press, pp. 395–418.

The Economist (2009), 'Spare a dime? A special report on the rich', *The Economist*, 4 April.

Forbes (2009), *The World's Billionaires 2009*, available at www.forbes.com (accessed 6 January 2010).

Frank, R. (2007), *Richi$tan. A Journey through the 21st Century Wealth Boom and the Lives of the New Rich*, New York: Piatkus.

Friedmann, J. (1986), 'The world city hypothesis', *Development and Change*, **17** (1), 69–83.

Galbraith, J.K. (1977), *The Age of Uncertainty*, Boston, MA: Houghton Mifflin.

Goldman, H. (2009), 'Wall Street bonuses plummeted 44 per cent during 2008 (update3)', available at Bloomberg.com (accessed 6 January 2010).

Hall, S. (2009), 'Financialised elites and the changing nature of finance capitalism: investment bankers in London's financial district', *Competition & Change*, **13** (2), 173–189.

Haseler, S. (1999), *The Super-Rich: The Unjust New World of Global Capitalism*, London: St. Martin's Press.

International Financial Services London (2009), *International Private Wealth Management*, November, available at www.ifsl.org.uk (accessed 6 January 2010).

Irvin, G. (2008), *Super Rich: The Rise of Inequality in Britain and the United States*, Cambridge: Polity.

King, A.D. (1990), *Global Cities: Post-imperialism and the Internationalization of London*, London: Routledge.

Lundberg, F. (1988), *The Rich and the Super-Rich*, New York: Citidel Press.

Maude, D. (2006), *Global Private Banking and Wealth Management*, Chichester: Wiley.

Merrill Lynch Capgemini (2002 to 2010), *World Wealth Report*, available at www.ml.com (accessed 6 January 2010).

North, R.D. (2005), *Rich is Beautiful: A Very Personal Defence of Mass Affluence*, London: The Social Affairs Unit.

Sklair, L. (2001), *The Transnational Capitalist Class*, Oxford: Blackwell.

Smith, R.C. (2001), *The Wealth Creators: The Rise of Today's Rich and Super-Rich*, New York: Truman Books.

The Sunday Times (2002 to 2009, except 2006), *The Sunday Times Rich List*, April.

Thorndike, J. (1980), *The Very Rich: A History of Wealth*, New York: Crown.

Ungoed-Thomas, J. (2004), 'London: billionaire capital of the world', *The Sunday Times*, 7 March, 9.

Veblen, T. (1899) [1985], *A Theory of the Leisure Class*, London: Allen & Unwin.

Z/Yen (2009), *The Global Financial Centres Index 6*, September, available at www.cityoflondon.gov.uk/Corporation (accessed 6 January 2010).

35 Global workers for global cities: low paid migrant labour in London

Kavita Datta, Cathy McIlwaine, Joanna Herbert, Yara Evans, Jon May and Jane Wills

INTRODUCTION

Global cities have an uneasy relationship with migrant workers. There is a growing recognition that they are crucially dependent upon migrant workers, both those who work in top end highly skilled jobs which give global cities a competitive edge over their rivals, but also in bottom end service sector jobs such as cleaning, hospitality, care, construction and food processing which literally keep these cities working. Yet, those who are employed in these low pay sectors are often invisible – they clean our schools and offices before we arrive, our underground and trains while we are hastily exiting, and care for our children and elderly relatives while we are at work. As a result, their vital contributions to the functioning of global cities are largely unrecognized and certainly undervalued by the societies to which they have migrated.

Drawing upon a three year project, *Global Cities at Work*, this chapter has two aims: first, it identifies the processes through which London's low wage economy has come to rely upon migrant men and women originating from diverse parts of the world; second, it seeks to make these workers visible by highlighting their contributions and working conditions. The chapter draws upon original empirical data collected through the deployment of a mixed methods approach including a questionnaire survey of over 400 workers employed in five migrant dependent sectors of London's low pay economy: cleaning (offices and London Underground), hospitality (hotels and catering), domiciliary care, construction and food processing. These data were supplemented by 103 in-depth semi-structured interviews undertaken with migrant workers also drawn from these sectors, as well as 31 interviews with key informants including employers, employer associations and community organizations. The research further involved the development of new data sets based on the Labour Force Survey (LFS)[1] and an analysis of wages taken from the Annual Survey on Hours and Earnings (ASHE) (see Wills et al., 2010 for details).

GLOBAL CITIES AND MIGRANT WORKERS

> London is now the world's financial centre. [But] the world's financial centre would not exist if it weren't for migrant workers. Both to do the banking and the trading but also [the] cleaning.
> (Representative from the Institute for Public Policy Research)

The changing dynamics of the labour markets of global cities have been the focus of much academic debate. Largely developed within the context of cities in the US such as New York and Los Angeles, key theorists such as Saskia Sassen (1991) argued that the

Table 35.1   Total employment and the proportion of foreign born (FB) labour, by occupation, London, 1993/94, 1999/2000, 2001/02, 2004/05

Occupation	1993/94 (000s)	% FB	1999/2000 (000s)	% FB	2001/02 (000s)	% FB	2004/05 (000s)	% FB
Chefs, cooks	29	51	34	61	31	67	38	76
Catering assistants	27	42	25	52	38	55	39	62
Care assistants	22	n/a	41	48	36	38	35	56
Cleaners	64	41	55	46	52	61	51	69
All London	2,894	25	3,262	27	3,349	30	3,375	34
UK	24,449	7	26,687	8	27,114	9	27,599	10

Source: Wills et al. (2010, p. 42)

labour market of these global cities reflected a growth at the top end of the labour market (attributable to the rapid expansion of financial and associated services) as well as an increase in service sector job opportunities located at the opposite end of the spectrum in the low wage economy. In turn, she argued that a significant number of these bottom end jobs were filled by migrants. While Sassen's arguments were broadly accepted as an accurate representation of the US global cities, another global city – London – appeared to be an exception to these trends. Here, it was posited that even while the city had witnessed a phenomenal growth in its top end managerial and professional jobs, this had been paralleled by rising levels of unemployment and economic inactivity rather than an increase in size of the low paid workforce (Hamnett, 2003). These trends were explained by lower rates of immigration into the UK as compared to the US as well as a more generous provision of welfare. Taken together these factors had inhibited the growth of both a 'working poor' population as well as a foreign born workforce.

Arguably, while these arguments may have held some weight a decade or so ago, London's contemporary labour market exhibits professionalization and economic inactivity *as well as* the growth of the 'working poor'. Wills et al. (2010) argue that over the past decade, London's labour market has come to be characterized by polarization whereby the significant increase in the proportion of highly skilled workers employed at the apex of the city's labour market has been accompanied by a smaller but still significant rise in the proportion of workers labouring at the very bottom end. Perhaps even more significant is that this newly expanded low wage economy is dominated by migrant workers, leading to the emergence of what may be termed a 'migrant division of labour' (MDL) (May et al., 2007). In 2001 official statistics indicated that 46 per cent of London's low wage jobs were occupied by foreign born workers (Spence, 2005, p. 61). Indeed, this reliance on migrant workers is even more significant in certain sectors such as cleaning where the numbers of foreign born workers rose from 40 per cent in 1993–94 to almost 70 per cent in 2004–05 (see Table 35.1). Within the specific context of one employer, Transport for London, it is estimated that 96 per cent of all cleaners are foreign born. Similar rates are evident among chefs and cooks, catering assistants and care assistants such that it is increasingly evident that some parts of London's low wage economy could in fact no longer function without the labour of migrants (Wills et al., 2009).

What factors account for the emergence of this migrant division of labour in London? The *Global Cities at Work* research identified three key processes: labour market deregulation, a growth in global mobility and changes to the British welfare state. The British economy has been transformed in the last three decades as it has shifted from being dominated by heavy industry to services, with a concomitant transformation of 'jobs for life' to part time, flexible working as well as escalating polarization between male and female, skilled and unskilled, old and young, white and black and minority ethnic workers. Furthermore, the aggressive pursuit of sub-contracting – with an estimated 93 per cent of private sector workplaces now outsourcing at least one of their activities – has meant that wages at the bottom have been held down, conditions of work have generally deteriorated and bargaining power among workers who can no longer easily identify their employers has also been eroded (Evans et al., 2007; Somerville and Sumption, 2009).

Not surprisingly, London's employers have found it extremely difficult to attract native unemployed workers into these jobs (Wills et al., 2009). This is attributable to the fact that the supply of a foreign labour force (see below) has enabled employers to keep wages down, thus rendering these jobs unattractive to native workers who are – despite sustained attempts to reform the benefit system in the UK in recent years – eligible for welfare. As one manager in the cleaning industry explained to us, the role of the benefits system meant that those who were entitled – and especially those with young children at home – would be better off staying at home:

> Let's look at it this way. The English are used to a social security system . . . they're used to having that whereas the immigrants don't have that in their country. We've always had something to fall back on, so those English that are not educated – that, you know didn't go out and get themselves great jobs – could come out and do the cleaning, but they won't do it for a lower wage because they might as well sit indoors and get paid to look after the kids . . . To motivate them you'd need ten pounds an hour, definitely.

The export of neoliberal policies to poorer parts of the world has delivered a workforce that is filling these vacancies in an effort to try and improve their lives on the other side of the world. The outsourcing of lower value jobs to locations with an abundant supply of 'cheap' labour was a defining feature of the reconstruction of economies in the Global South in the aftermath of the so-called 'lost decade of development' of the 1980s. Engendering internal and regional migration to begin with, this migration has since expanded globally as people began to move from the Global South to the North – both in response to the hardships that were being unleashed by neoliberal economics but also somewhat contradictorily because of development (Datta, 2009; May et al., 2010). Following a slow-down in the 1980s, levels of immigration into the United Kingdom rose very significantly through the 1990s with 42 per cent of those who had arrived in the UK by 2001 settling in London (Spence, 2005, p. 17). Furthermore, in the last 20 years the proportion of London's population born abroad has doubled and, by 2006, just under a third (31 per cent) of the city's population and just over a third (35 per cent) of its working age population were born overseas (Spence, 2005, p. 31). Given that migrant workers have very limited, if any, access to welfare,[2] they have been transformed into an ideal flexible labour force which can theoretically be called upon at times of need and then disposed of when economies contract (Fix et al., 2009).

WORKING IN LONDON'S LOW PAY ECONOMY

> Life of a Pole in England looks something more or less the following way. I leave for work at 6.45, take some overtime and am back home at 7.30. After 11 hours of hard physical work I do not have much desire for sociability. (Mirek, Polish construction worker)

Having detailed the importance of migrant workers to London's low wage economy, this section turns to the working lives of low paid migrant workers, beginning with a brief discussion of who these migrant workers are. There is widespread consensus that London's migrant labour force is remarkably global or 'super-diverse' in terms of its national origins, immigration status, socio-economic composition and labour market outcomes (Vertovec, 2007). London is often referred to as a 'world within one city', a finding which was substantiated by the *Global Cities at Work* research, which recorded some 63 different nationalities with the majority of migrants from Eastern Europe, sub-Saharan Africa and Latin America. This in itself reflects the fact that where once migration to the UK was dominated by nationals from the Commonwealth (the Indian subcontinent and Caribbean), these flows are being diversified by migration from both an enlarged European Union as well as from parts of the world without strong historical colonial connections with the city or the country, especially Latin America (McIlwaine, 2007).

This super-diversity is also reflected in the immigration status of migrant workers. The last decade or so has seen the emergence of a 'managed migration' approach as the British state has sought to control immigration into the country, culminating in the implementation of a points based system. This system highlights three key immigration priorities: first, a cherry picking of highly skilled migrants from a global market which the British economy needs; second, a clamping down on so-called 'bogus' asylum seekers and third, an encouragement of European migration over and above migration from the Global South (Datta, 2009). The latter has particularly emerged following the expansion of the European Union in 2004 to incorporate the Accession 8 (A8) countries of the Czech Republic, Estonia, Hungary, Latvia, Lithuania, Poland, Slovakia and Slovenia and then again in 2007 when the Accession 2 (A2) countries of Bulgaria and Romania joined the Union. By 2008, the number of A8 Europeans in the UK labour force was reported at just under half a million (equivalent to 21.8 per cent of all foreign workers), with an estimated 1.4 million people arriving between May 2004 and March 2009. In turn, Poles had emerged as the UK's largest foreign national group by the end of 2008 (having been 13th at the end of 2003) (Fix et al., 2009). The right to live and work in the UK even among the A8/A2 migrants is differential in that while A8 nationals enjoyed the right to work in the UK without work permits, the unexpectedly large influx of these migrants, likened by some to an 'invasion from the East', led to more cautious welcome of A2 nationals whose rights to work are more proscribed.

Notwithstanding this, part of the logic of managed migration policies has been that European migrants would fill low skilled labour market vacancies leading to a declining reliance upon migrants from the Global South. Faced with an increasingly restrictive

Table 35.2   The wages of low paid migrants in London

Wages	Number	%
Up to and including the NMW	105	25
Between NMW and the LLW	289	68
Above the LLW	30	7
Total responses	424	

Source: Wills et al. (2010, p. 77)

migration regime, migrants from poorer parts of the world are faced with fewer options, limited to entering the UK as students, tourists, asylum seekers and as part of family reunification. In addition, entry under all of these routes has been considerably tightened in recent years. Arriving in London through these diverse channels, the migrant labour force therefore comprises those who have the right to live and work in the UK (the A8 migrants), those with limited rights to work (including for example, A2 migrants, students who can work what used to be 20 hours a week during term time and full time in holidays and what is now ten hours per week) and those with no right to work (including tourists), which has several consequences for their labour market experiences.

So, what were the working conditions encountered by migrant workers in our study? Our research from *Global Cities at Work* revealed very poor pay and conditions (see Table 35.2). Although the majority of employers adhered to the law and paid the National Minimum Wage (NMW) (which at the time of this research had risen from £4.80 per hour to £5.40 per hour), these wages were still below the level recognized as the minimum standard required to live adequately – with only 7 per cent of workers earning more than the London Living Wage (LLW).[3] Average annual earnings (for those working 36 hours a week) were just £10,200 a year (before deductions), less than half national average earnings (£22,412) and just a third of the London average annual salary (£28,912) (GLA, 2008). In turn, there was some variation in wage levels across the five sectors with highest levels of pay found in the care sector and the lowest in the hotel and hospitality sector, where processes of sub-contracting and the employment of agency staff are more entrenched. Compounding these very low wages was the lack of what may be termed as a 'social wage' with only 26 per cent of the workers having any guarantee of an annual pay rise and minimal entitlement to holidays and sick pay.

Not surprisingly, perhaps, workers reported struggling to survive on such low wages. Contrary to popular stereotypes about the preponderance of lone male migrants who arrive in Britain looking for work, our research highlighted the high proportion of migrant workers with families in London, with a third of respondents responsible for children aged 16 or under living in the UK. Not only were migrants financially responsible for dependants in the UK, the majority of them were also responsible for the upkeep of their families living in home countries, with over three-quarters of all migrants remitting money back home.

As such, we discovered numerous cases of migrant men and women who in a bid to survive in an expensive city were working overtime (43 per cent of our sample, of whom more than half worked an extra 8 hours while a further third worked an extra 16 hours overtime),[4] and/or taking on more than one job (18 per cent), usually also located in the low pay economy and often as cleaners. Several migrant workers reported that they sometimes did not go to bed at all, sleeping instead on buses and trains between jobs and courses. Describing her working life, Ellen, an agency nurse from Ghana, told us:

> Because sometimes they [the agency] book me for a shift, say 8 to 8, and that's a long day. Eight in the morning till 8 in the evening and . . . most of the shift in the City [hospitals] . . . this is very far from Thamesmead so even if I start the shift at 8 o'clock in the morning I have to leave my house by half 6.

Workers often moved frequently between jobs in response to even a small rise in wage levels, with 46 per cent of workers having been with their employer for less than one year. In turn, the culture of extremely hard working took its toll on migrants like Antonio, a construction worker, who described his working conditions as incredibly demanding and physical, admitting that 'sometimes I feel like giving everything up and going back home. I have even cried, I sat down on the pallets and cried, thinking "I am going home, I can't take it any longer."'

Many migrant men and women also made reference to the lack of respect for the work that they did and the contributions that they were making to British society. This sentiment was best summed up in an interview with a representative of the Central Association of Nigerians in the UK who said:

> You're [migrants] portrayed as all these criminals, and yet we actually hold the keys to all of these buildings, 'cause we are the cleaners. We are the guards. We lock up and we close down. And we are so untrustworthy? . . . If Africans went on strike, there'd be no security men, there'd be no trained nurses on the wards, there'd be no cleaners, there'd be . . . no traffic wardens. All the jobs that nobody else wants to do.

In concluding this section, it is important to also draw attention to the finding that while migrant men and women knew their jobs were undervalued and low paid by local standards, they often evaluated this in relation to the wages that they would have earned in their home countries as well as the cost of living there. As Janet, a carer from Jamaica, explained, 'Money-wise, you know here is better. If you compare the pay scale here to back home, it's better paid here.' Moving away from the world of work, other migrants commented on how being in London enabled them to acquire the goods they felt were necessary to enjoy a good life. As highlighted by Luis, a Brazilian cleaner: 'What I managed to achieve here in one year, I would achieve there [Brazil] in five or six. It sped things up a lot.' Living and working in London not only enabled (young) migrants to achieve long term financial independence, it also enabled them to live and work in a city which many saw as being at the heart of the world. Vijay, a Mauritian carer, summed this up best when he said:

> You get a lot of experience in London. You know people from around the world. You have an idea of how the world is . . . Perhaps you don't realize that when you come from another country like Mauritius, a small island but the fact that it is small gives you . . . a narrow perspective on life. . . . When you come to London you see the world as it is, large, big and [while] the difficulties are big, the prospects are also big. You get a new perspective on life.

These narratives highlight processes of uneven development and inequality across the globe as well as attempts by migrant men and women to make sense of their lives in

London by presenting their situation as a short term episode leading to a brighter future. The reality may be different for a significant number who find themselves trapped in low paid work.

CONCLUSIONS

This chapter has identified the emergence of a migrant division of labour in London where workers originating in the Global South and Eastern Europe work in low paid occupations. This is itself attributable to a complex interplay of global and local neo-liberal economic restructuring, the associated increase in transnational migration and changes to welfare provision in the UK. Despite their significance in low paid employment, the contributions of migrant men and women are often invisible and unacknowledged. As this chapter has shown through its exploration of migrant men and women's working lives, it is not only poor wage levels or working conditions which matter, it is also an urgent need to value the jobs that migrant workers do, as well as migrants themselves.

NOTES

1. The LFS provides a record of changes in employee numbers, the numbers of migrant workers and levels of pay across a number of occupational categories in the London labour market between the period 1993/4 to 2004/5.
2. Whilst workers from the European Union A8 countries have been given some grudging access to welfare (for which they have to be registered on the government's Workers' Registration Scheme, for a continuous 12 month period), low skilled workers coming to Britain from beyond the European Union or who are in Britain illegally have no recourse to public funds.
3. The London Living Wage is the low cost but acceptable income calculated for the city. Calculated annually by the Greater London Authority (GLA), the costs of a basic standard of living for different family types is constructed, compared to 60 per cent of median income, adjusted for family types in London and based on an assumption of full benefit take-up. In 2009, the LLW was £7.60 per hour while the NMW was £5.80 per hour (GLA, 2009).
4. Further, only a minority of these workers received a higher rate of pay for overtime (see Wills et al., 2010).

REFERENCES

Datta, K. (2009), 'Transforming South–North relations? International migration and development', *Geography Compass*, **3** (1), 108–134.
Evans, Y., J. Wills, K. Datta, J. Herbert, C. McIlwaine and J. May (2007), '"Subcontracting by stealth" in London's hotels: impacts and implications for labour organising', *Just Labour*, **10**, 85–98.
Fix, M., D.G. Papademetriou, J. Batalova, A. Terrazas, S. Yi-Ying Lin and M. Mittelstadt (2009), *Migration and the Global Recession*, Washington, DC: Migration Policy Institute.
GLA (Greater London Authority) (2008), *A Fairer London: The 2008 Living Wage in London*, London: GLA.
GLA (Greater London Authority) (2009), *A Fairer London: The 2009 Living Wage in London*, London: GLA.
Hamnett, C. (2003), *Unequal City: London in the Global Arena*, London: Routledge.
May, J., J. Wills, K. Datta, Y. Evans, J. Herbert and C. McIlwaine (2007), 'Keeping London working: global cities, the British state and London's migrant division of labour', *Transactions of the Institute of British Geographers*, **32** (2), 151–167.
May, J., J. Wills, K. Datta, Y. Evans, J. Herbert and C. McIlwaine (2010), 'Global cities at work: migrant labour in low paid employment in London', *The London Journal*, **35** (1), 85–99.

McIlwaine, C.J. (2007), 'Living in Latin London: how Latin American migrants survive in London', *Working Paper*, Department of Geography, Queen Mary University of London.

Sassen, S. (1991), *The Global City: New York, London, Tokyo*, Princeton, NJ: Princeton University Press.

Somerville, W. and M. Sumption (2009), *Immigration in the United Kingdom: The Recession and Beyond* (Equality and Human Rights Commission, March 2009), Washington, DC: Migration Policy Institute.

Spence, L. (2005), *Country of Birth and Labour Market Outcomes in London: An Analysis of Labour Force Survey and Census Data*, London: GLA.

Vertovec, S. (2007), 'Super-diversity and its implications,' *Ethnic and Racial Studies*, **30** (6), 1024–1054.

Wills, J., K. Datta, Y. Evans, J. Herbert, J. May and C. McIlwaine (2009), 'London's migrant division of labour', *European Urban and Regional Studies*, **16** (3), 257–271.

Wills, J., K. Datta, Y. Evans, J. Herbert, J. May and C. McIlwaine (2010), *Global Cities at Work: New Migrant Divisions of Labour*, London: Pluto Press.

36 Cultural diasporas
Caroline Nagel

INTRODUCTION

World cities are commonly distinguished from other 'ordinary' cities by the particular function they serve in the global economy. As concentrations of advanced producer services, world cities are the command-and-control centers of the global economy – nodes of power and connectivity where flows of communication, information and capital converge. World cities can also be thought of as particular social and cultural spaces characterized by high levels of human mobility and diversity. In many 'top tier' world cities, a fifth or more of the population is foreign born, and it is not uncommon to find neighborhoods, districts or boroughs where over half of the population is foreign born. Steve Vertovec (2007) speaks of these urban spaces as 'super-diverse', referring not only to residents' places of origin, but also to their legal statuses, their routes of entry and their insertion within labor markets. The world city, indeed, is home to skilled and unskilled workers, to sojourners and long-term residents, to documented and to clandestine migrants, and to the highly privileged and the abject. The differences and disparities among the residents of world cities have led some theorists to conceive of the world city as a polarized space of haves and have-nots where transnational elites are served by a transnational servant class (see Hamnett, 1994 for a critical discussion). Others, though, while not denying the inequalities within world cities, emphasize the unique forms of social and cultural production that take place within them. These social and cultural forms are often described as 'diasporic', a term that denotes persistent and multiple connections between 'here' and 'elsewhere' enacted by migrant communities.

As key gateways of migration, world cities can be thought of as paradigmatic diasporic spaces. The term 'diaspora' traditionally has referred to groups (Jews being the archetype) who have been exiled and scattered from homelands but who have maintained a degree of cohesion through dense communal ties and the collective remembrance of origins (see Safran, 1991; Cohen, 1997). In recent decades, the term 'diaspora' has been applied more broadly (some would say indiscriminately – see Brubaker, 2005) to any group that experiences displacement or placelessness, whether through exile or more 'voluntary' forms of migration. Diasporas are seen to engage in an array of transnational practices that bind them to places of origin; these include the sending of remittances, the participation in homeland politics, and the maintenance of emotional links with friends and family members through telephone calls, yearly visits and the exchange of gifts. At the same time, diasporas reproduce homeland in the places they settle through their consumption of cultural commodities, their construction of community spaces, and their performances of cultural identity in community rituals and celebrations (for a critical overview of these themes, see Blunt, 2007; also Mavroudi, 2008). Diasporas, in this regard, actively create world cities by enacting transnational connections and by anchoring these, so to speak, to actual physical spaces of the city.

But while we can think of diasporas as agents of globalization and as co-creators of the world city, we cannot think of them solely in these terms. As much as diasporas (like world cities themselves) are situated in spaces of flows, they are also situated in national spaces and, as such, are subject to the logics of nation-building and the technologies of state sovereignty. Their lives may transcend nation-state boundaries, but in the eyes of dominant groups they are 'immigrants' and 'minorities'. This chapter therefore situates the experiences of diasporas in localities and nation-states, as well as in global networks and transnational social spaces. It asks, what are the negotiations that take place between diasporas and host societies? And how do diasporic engagements with dominant groups help us to understand world cities?

DIASPORA AND ITS LIMITS

Many accounts of world cities are situated in a historical narrative that emphasizes momentous change or even rupture. While most scholars recognize that the processes we associate with globalization and the formation of world cities – geographically extensive trade and production networks, global markets and technologically enhanced communications networks – are not entirely unprecedented, there is a sense that contemporary globalization represents a step change in terms of economic integration, political-territorial reorganization, and the creation of new, hybrid and often commodified, cultural forms (e.g. Appadurai, 1996).

A similar analysis has informed discussions of migrant transnationalism. Most scholars of transnationalism and diaspora[1] recognize that migrants have always maintained connections with their homelands, but they suggest that these connections have become far denser and more persistent as a result of growing levels of mobility and the widespread availability of relatively cheap communications technologies, from cell phones to satellite dishes to the internet (Glick Schiller et al., 1992; Portes, 1999; Vertovec, 2004). Through their emotional, financial and political connections with places of origin, diasporas are seen to create social fields that, like global flows of capital, disrupt and transcend the boundedness of the modern nation-state. Many theorists, therefore, regard the language of diaspora and transnationalism as an alternative to notions of 'assimilation' and 'integration', both of which suggest a one-way process of cultural adaptation and change. As Glick Schiller et al. (1992, p. 1) argue:

> The word immigrant evokes images of permanent rupture . . . of the abandonment of old patterns and the painful learning of a new language and culture. Now, a new kind of migrating population is emerging, composed of those whose networks, activities, and patterns of life encompass both their host and home societies. Their lives cut across national boundaries and bring two societies into a single social field.

The concepts of transnationalism and diaspora have become ubiquitous in the field of migration studies, and there has been a growing recognition even among assimilation theorists that migrants' lives must be understood as taking place simultaneously 'here' and 'there'. Still, scholars continue to debate some of the key assumptions that underlie these concepts. One important topic of discussion and debate concerns the role of nation-states in the lives of diasporas.[2] In using concepts like diaspora and transnationalism, scholars have intended to disrupt the view of society as contained within nation-state boundaries. Yet diasporas in many cases are very much engaged in the nation-building projects of their places of origin (Glick Schiller and Fouron, 1999; Laguerre, 1999). Some scholars have therefore advocated that greater attention be paid to the nation-state and its role in structuring diasporas and transnational connections (Yeoh and Willis, 1999).

In bringing the nation-state back into analyses of diasporas, several authors have focused, for instance, on the 'recurrent and institutionalized interactions and exchanges between, on the one hand, immigrants and their social and political organizations, and, on the other hand, the political institutions and state apparatus of the country of origin' (Itzigsohn, 2000, p. 1130; also Levitt and de la Hasa, 2002; Smith, 2003). A major motivation for sending states to foster these interactions, scholars note, is the massive value of remittances earned by émigrés; indeed, in many countries of the Global South, remittances are the main source of foreign exchange, outweighing exports and foreign aid transfers. Whatever their exact reason (or reasons) for courting diasporas, sending states are increasingly inclined to extend the rights of citizenship to their communities abroad, in some cases granting representation to diasporas in national legislatures. Migrant communities, in turn, make demands on and pursue their own interests vis-à-vis nation-states of origin, sometimes using internet technologies to create a 'diasporic public sphere' through which they articulate particular political aims and agendas (see, for instance, Parham, 2004; Bernal, 2006).[3]

DIASPORAS AND HOST SOCIETIES

In contrast to these discussions of diasporas and countries of origin, other efforts to 'bring the nation-state back in' to discussions of transnationalism have focused on relationships between diasporas and host societies. Theoretical statements on transnationalism and diaspora generally acknowledge that migrants are inserted into the political systems, as well as the racial and ethnic hierarchies, of the countries where they have settled (Glick Schiller et al., 1992; Bauböck, 2003). Yet as a practical matter, most empirical accounts of transnationalism have emphasized homeland orientations, rather than migrants' negotiations of social membership and belonging in places of settlement. The privileging of 'homeland' reflects that this literature was conceived as an alternative to host-society-centered accounts of immigrant integration. The desire to break out of 'methodological nationalism', in effect, discredited the very notion of a monolithic host society and shifted attention away from the receiving contexts that had been the focus of migration literature throughout the 20th century. There is a growing body of literature, however, that attempts to bridge the gap that has developed between the study of transnationalism and the study of integration (Kivisto, 2001; Levitt and Glick Schiller, 2004) and to explore how processes of transnationalism and integration intersect and interact.

The relationship between transnationalism and integration has been approached in different ways. Some scholarship has shed light on the variability of transnational practices within and among migrant groups and the effects of transnational orientations on integration (and vice versa). Guarnizo et al. (2003) have shown that levels of transnationalism vary significantly between groups, and that the frequency and intensity of transnationalism '[affect] the way immigrants incorporate themselves and alters conventional expectations about their assimilation' (2003, p. 1239). Their findings highlight that transnational activism does not preclude 'successful' integration, insofar as those who are active transnationally are also better established in economic and social terms in countries of settlement.

Other work has highlighted the multiplicity and simultaneity of migrants' political engagements and identities (Levitt and Glick Schiller, 2004). David Fitzgerald (2004), for instance, attempts to unpack migrants' 'transnational' practices by examining the internal politics of a labor union in Los Angeles. Fitzgerald uncovers a plethora of political and identity-based claims being made by union members, some revolving around hometowns, others around membership in a transborder Mexican nation, and still others relating to American citizenship and local presence in Southern California. Similarly, in my own work with Lynn Staeheli on Arab activists in Britain and the United States, we have shown that our respondents see themselves as situated in multiple political spaces (locality, nation-state, home country, 'ummah') and as addressing multiple political communities. Our respondents, moreover, understand these spaces and communities to be interconnected: what is going on in the Arab world impinges on their experiences in Britain and the United States, and their engagements in 'homeland' issues are mediated by political structures and discourses situated in Britain and the US (Nagel and Staeheli, 2008a).

A key point highlighted by these discussions is the asymmetry in relations between 'hosts' and 'guests'. Understanding migrants' political identities, opportunities and aims, in this respect, requires that we understand how they are positioned in, and how they produce and reproduce, class, racial and gender hierarchies in receiving contexts (Anthias, 2001; Samers, 2003; Ehrkamp, 2005). This point is more fully developed in Yeh and Lama's (2006) account of Tibetan refugees in the United States. The Tibetan community's leaders, Yeh and Lama argue, in their efforts to gain support for the Tibetan cause, strive to appeal to white audiences, who are drawn to romantic Western images of Tibetan Buddhism. In doing so, leaders contrast the Tibetan community with 'less worthy' immigrant and minority groups, including other Asian refugees. They also reprimand second-generation Tibetans – most of them living in poverty – who have adopted African-American hip-hop culture as a way of undermining their elders' 'excessive subservience to "white society"' (2006, p. 822). An equally complex case can be seen in Jazeel's (2006) ethnographic account of an elite Sri Lankan women's organization in London. The organization's members, he shows, have acquiesced to performing the role of the exotic Other, as a way 'of being accepted as "raced" subjects in London' and of 'being rendered safe through the very lens of imperial, Orientalist knowledge-making' (2006, p. 27). Yet Jazeel also acknowledges that such highly gendered and classed performances have 'enabled these women to handle colonial power' and to 'side step the economic and psychological marginality assigned to . . . formerly colonized migrants trying to forge lives in post-imperial England' (2006, p. 30). These cases and others (Salih, 2001; Houston and Wright, 2003; Kosnick, 2004) demonstrate the interweaving of transnational linkages and host society relationships, and encourage us to think about the complex, and often ambivalent, ways that migrants experience and engage with multiple spaces and narratives of belonging in contexts of settlement.

THE WORLD CITY AS A 'DIASPORIC' SPACE

Having brought the complexities of diasporic lives to the fore, I want to return to the world city and to reconsider how we should understand the world city as a diasporic space. World cities, as described above, are often seen as crossroads through which multiple, trans-border flows of people, capital, commodities and cultural imagery inter-sect. The sheer level of diversity, mobility and interconnectedness in world cities makes them distinctive spaces – a 'space of flows', to use Castells' (2000) terminology, rather than a 'space of places'. As such, they are often viewed as spaces apart – urban nodes that are economically, politically and culturally divorced from their national hinterlands (Delanty, 2000; Sassen, 2000).

The many conversations I have had with British Arabs in London over the past decade of my research have mirrored this understanding of world cities as exceptional spaces. British Arabs, and especially young people born and raised in Britain, talk about London as fundamentally different from the rest of Britain and as a place where Britishness is not clearly definable, least of all in terms of Englishness. London, as they describe it, con-sists of a multitude of subcultures – black hip-hop culture, Asian culture, Arab culture, English culture – that encounter, mix and sometimes clash with one another in the spaces of everyday life. Participants in my research have spoken of a lack of cultural rigidity in the city, and they often describe their own social circles as 'multicultural' and 'diverse', comprising other Arabs, as well as Greeks, Turks, Europeans, and so on, whose con-nections to Britain are relatively recent and always partial and contingent. These young people seem to find commonality in their difference and in the sense that they feel 'at home' in multiple locales. For them, London is home, but the Arab world – their other home – is not far removed from their daily lives. Indeed, it is part of the social fabric of London itself.

Yet there are limits to understanding London (or any other world city) as a space apart – as diasporic, global, cosmopolitan and/or super-diverse, rather than as embedded in bounded, national territory and integrated within a more localized societal context. Like diaspora itself, the world city does not escape the boundary-creating logic of race, class and nation. In Britain, to illustrate, politicians since the early 1990s have been on a mission to define a more robust national identity and to build a more cohesive society. The impetus for this effort has been the perceived lack of integration among Britain's post-colonial immigrant communities, and especially among the 'British Muslim' com-munity, most of whom are of Pakistani origin. Following the outbreak of riots in 2001 between Asian and white youths in the economically depressed Northern mill towns of Bradford, Burnley and Oldham, investigators found Muslim and white Britons to be living 'parallel lives'; and while some of those investigators hesitated to assign blame to one group or the other, public discussion inevitably fixated on the 'self-segregating' ten-dencies of Muslim communities. Within this discussion, a host of cultural practices asso-ciated with Muslim communities, including arranged marriages and women's veiling, were held up as inimical to core British national values of liberalism, gender equality and tolerance (for a fuller discussion, see Kundnani, 2008). Simultaneously, Muslim space became a counterpoint to particular understandings of national space and identity. In public discourse since the 2001 riots, Muslim neighborhoods have served as evidence of self-segregation and community isolationism (rather than of poverty and housing market discrimination), and have been linked, in turn, to 'home-grown terrorism' (D. Phillips, 2006).

These sorts of discussions do not necessarily focus on London, but London certainly is not removed from them. For those criticizing the supposed excesses of British multiculturalism, London is not a cosmopolitan, diasporic space, but a seething cauldron of foreignness – 'Londonistan' or 'Londonibad', the capital of Eurabia – that requires re-nationalization through immigration restrictions and assimilationist policies (see, for instance, M. Phillips, 2006). The presence and visibility of otherness, in this sense, is as problematic in London as it is in Leeds. To be sure, not all representations of 'cultural diversity' are negative. As Vertovec (2007) notes, political leaders in London often treat the presence of so many foreign nationals speaking so many different languages as the city's main selling point; indeed, 'diversity' has been part of London's marketing strategy for the 2012 Olympics. And Muslim spaces, in some cases at least, are viewed as an important component of this diversity. For instance, 'Banglatown' in the Spitalfields area of East London – once the home of Huguenot and Jewish refugees and now a predominantly Bangladeshi Muslim neighborhood – is touted as a vibrant, colorful space in which locals and tourists can experience an exotic culture by eating at a local Balti house. The key point here is that migrant groups are constantly confronted by multiple discourses – some relatively inclusionary and others decidedly exclusionary – relating to the possibility of their membership in a host society. By virtue of its diversity, London is perhaps a more tolerant place than a 'provincial' city and more capable of accommodating cultural difference; but London's residents, and London itself, are nonetheless caught up in wider sets of debates about belonging to a national society and to national space.

This is the case even for those as privileged as British Arabs in London. In many respects, British Arabs, while predominantly Muslim, have been able to shelter themselves from the kinds of accusations that have been leveled against 'British Muslims' by virtue of their relatively high socio-economic status. But the fact that they are not targeted by discourses of 'social cohesion' does not mean that they are not implicated in them or affected by them. Some activists, especially of the older generation, are intent upon being recognized within Britain's official system of multiculturalism, which sets forth policies to accommodate cultural differences and to monitor discrimination against recognized groups. Such activists have tried for years to have Arab accepted as an official census category. Others with whom I have spoken view official multiculturalism as outmoded and irrelevant, but even these individuals must articulate and perform their difference in a way that grants them acceptance by dominant groups. As Lynn Staeheli and I have argued elsewhere (Nagel and Staeheli, 2008b), some British Arab activists gain this acceptance, in part, by avoiding association with much-disparaged British Muslims. Emphasizing a British *Arab* identity, in this sense, is not just about maintaining transnational links; it is also about avoiding stigmatization and asserting compatibility with dominant constructions of Britishness. This negotiation involves a wide variety of performances – and non-performances – in everyday spaces. While many, for instance, do not hesitate to speak Arabic in public, and are eager to create a more visible Arab presence in Britain, they may be less comfortable publicly expressing specifically religious identities which have become associated in the mainstream imagination with extremism. In this way, and despite their own frustration with dominant stereotypes of Islam, British Arabs often reinforce rather than challenge mainstream discourses about Muslims.

Thus, even as they live diasporic lives in the archetypal world city, the lives of British Arabs and other immigrant and minority groups are situated, quite literally, in national spaces, and they are subject to the scrutiny of more powerful groups who make decisions about the appropriateness or inappropriateness of their cultural identities and practices (cf. Cresswell, 1996). Clearly, nation-state-centered conceptions of migrant adaptation and assumptions about monolithic host societies are problematic, especially when we consider the cultural complexity of world cities. Yet dominant groups place migrants and other minorities within racial and class hierarchies that tend to operate at a national scale, and migrants and minorities, in turn, actively attempt to reconfigure – or to conform to – these boundaries through their strategic uses of space.

CONCLUSION

In writing this chapter, my aim has been to challenge the ways we think about both diasporas and world cities. We have come to understand contemporary migrant groups as creating globalized spaces by maintaining emotional and material connections with homelands, by re-territorializing homelands in places of settlement, and by destabilizing and perhaps subverting national boundaries. In short, they create social and spatial milieus that come up against the nation-building projects that are central to modern society. Diasporas, at the same time, are 'immigrants', and I have tried to convey that the politics of 'here' and 'there' are often layered and intertwined in complicated ways.

Rather than privileging one particular set of processes, connections or identities, it is useful, I think, to consider more broadly the complex spatiality of migrants' lives. Anthias (2001) offers an especially useful way of thinking about this spatiality. Using the term 'translocational positionality', Anthias highlights that individuals and groups are engaged in processes of, and struggles over, boundary formation within, and in relation to, different places. Anthias's conceptualization avoids focusing exclusively on any one kind of space (be it sending society, host society or world city) or any single social entity in which migrants may claim belonging. Instead, it highlights the ambivalences involved in the creation and negotiation of multiple social and spatial boundaries.

This conceptualization raises the question of whether we should think of world cities as exceptional spaces. The fact that there is a distinctive body of scholarly research and literature on world cities suggests that world cities are worthy of independent inquiry – that is, world cities are singled out for investigation precisely because they are not 'ordinary' cities. World cities, by definition, embody a level of connectedness that is found only in a few places on earth, and they cannot be appreciated solely in terms of their position in national urban hierarchies. I am reluctant, though, to view world cities as entirely exceptional spaces, just as I am reluctant to privilege diaspora and transnationalism as the defining characteristics of contemporary migrants' experiences.

I have tried to show in this chapter that neither diasporas nor world cities are completely divorced from the political and social structures of nation-states. Migrants *make* world cities, but migrants and the cities in which they live are embedded in national spaces and are subject to the rules and social norms that are formulated, in part, at a national scale. Diasporic and national space (and other kinds of space), in this sense, can be seen as simultaneous and intertwined. By the same token, while diasporic relationships (and other forms of globalization) may be more evident in world cities, they are certainly not exclusive to them. Migration scholars in the United States, for instance, have noted that the most rapid growth of migrant populations in the past two decades has taken place in cities and states that have never been 'immigrant gateways' in the past – in highly decentralized urban environments like Winston-Salem, North Carolina, Fort Worth, Texas and Memphis, Tennessee (see Singer et al., 2008). Migrants in these cities, no less than in New York and London, build transnational linkages while establishing a place for themselves in local and national narratives of membership. And no less than in New York and London, it becomes necessary for long-established residents and relative newcomers to negotiate identities and membership and to make explicit what it means to belong (see Trudeau, 2006; Winders, 2006; Nelson, 2008). It behooves us, then, to look beyond the 'world city' to understand the cultural and political change wrought by migration and diaspora and to think about the multiple spaces and locales in which insiders and outsiders produce, contest and reformulate social membership.

NOTES

1. Transnational and diasporic are not identical terms. As Dahlman (2004, p. 486) remarks, 'transnational-ism is not a sufficient condition for diasporas, which additionally imply a common sense of territorial identity among its members, nor are all transnational relations diasporic' (quoted in Blunt, 2007, p. 689). However, when speaking of migrant groups, these terms overlap a great deal, and I use them here almost interchangeably.
2. There are many other topics of debate, among them the issue of whether migrant transnationalism is, in fact, a historically novel pattern (see Kivisto, 2001; Brubaker, 2005).
3. While some accounts describe these patterns in celebratory terms, most of them are more ambivalent, sug-gesting, as does Itzigsohn (2000, p. 1146), that while 'transnational politics have opened spaces for participa-tion of previously marginalized groups, [they do] not subvert the current socioeconomic order' or 'constitute a challenge to the structures of power. . .that existed before' (also Mitchell, 1997; Guarnizo et al., 2003).

REFERENCES

Anthias, F. (2001), 'New hybridities, old concepts: the limits of "culture"', *Ethnic and Racial Studies*, **24** (4), 619–641.
Appadurai, A. (1996), *Modernity at Large: Cultural Dimensions of Globalization*, Minneapolis, MN: University of Minnesota Press.
Bauböck, R. (2003), 'Towards a political theory of migrant transnationalism', *International Migration Review*, **37** (3), 700–723.
Bernal, V. (2006), 'Diaspora, cyberspace, and political imagination: the Eritrean diaspora online', *Global Networks*, **6** (2), 161–179.
Blunt, A. (2007), 'Cultural geographies of migration: mobility, transnationality and diaspora', *Progress in Human Geography*, **31** (5), 684–694.
Brubaker, R. (2005), 'The "diaspora" diaspora', *Ethnic and Racial Studies*, **28** (1), 1–19.
Castells, M. (2000), 'Urban sustainability in the information age', *City*, **4** (1), 118–122.
Cohen, R. (1997), *Global Diasporas: An Introduction*, Seattle, WA: University of Washington Press.
Cresswell, T. (1996), *In Place/ Out of Place*, Minneapolis, MN: University of Minnesota Press.
Dahlman, C. (2004), 'Diaspora', in J. Duncan, N. Johnson and R. Schein (eds), *A Companion to Cultural Geography*, Oxford: Blackwell, pp. 485–498.
Delanty, G. (2000), 'The resurgence of the city in Europe? The spaces of European citizenship', in E. Isin (ed.), *Democracy, Citizenship, and the Global City*, London and New York: Routledge, pp. 79–91.
Ehrkamp, P. (2005), 'Placing Turkish identities: local attachments and transnational ties of Turkish immi-grants in Germany', *Journal of Ethnic and Migration Studies*, **31** (2), 345–364.

Fitzgerald, D. (2004), 'Beyond "transnationalism": Mexican hometown politics at an American labour union', *Ethnic and Racial Studies*, **27** (2), 228–247.

Glick Schiller, N., L. Basch and C. Blanc-Szanton (1992), 'Transnationalism: a new analytic framework for understanding migration', in N. Glick Schiller, L. Basch and C. Blanc-Szanton (eds), *Towards a Transnational Perspective on Migration: Race, Class, Ethnicity, and Nationalism Reconsidered*, New York: New York Academy of Sciences, pp. 1–24.

Glick Schiller, N. and G. Fouron (1999), 'Terrains of blood and nation: Haitian transnational social fields', *Ethnic and Racial Studies*, **22** (2), 340–366.

Guarnizo, E., A. Portes and W. Haller (2003), 'Assimilation and transnationalism: determinants of transnational political action among contemporary migrants', *American Journal of Sociology*, **108** (6), 1211–1248.

Hamnett, C. (1994), 'Social polarization in global cities: theory and evidence', *Urban Studies*, **31** (3), 401–425.

Houston, S. and R. Wright (2003), 'Making and remaking Tibetan diasporic identities', *Social & Cultural Geography*, **4** (2), 217–232.

Itzigsohn, J. (2000), 'Immigration and the boundaries of citizenship: the institutions of immigrants' political transnationalism', *International Migration Review*, **34** (4), 1126–1154.

Jazeel, T. (2006), 'Postcolonial geographies of privilege: diaspora space, the politics of personhood and the "Sri Lankan Women's Association in the UK"', *Transactions of the Institute of British Geographers*, **31** (1), 19–33.

Kivisto, P. (2001), 'Theorizing transnational immigration: a critical review of current efforts', *Ethnic and Racial Studies*, **24** (4), 549–577.

Kosnick, K. (2004), '"Speaking in one's own voice": representational strategies of Alevi Turkish migrants on open-access television in Berlin', *Journal of Ethnic and Migration Studies*, **30** (5), 979–994.

Kundnani, A. (2008), 'Islamism and the roots of liberal rage', *Race and Class*, **50** (2), 40–68.

Laguerre, M.S. (1999), 'State, diaspora, and transnational politics: Haiti reconceptualised', *Millennium: Journal of International Studies*, **28** (3), 633–651.

Levitt, P. and N. Glick Schiller (2004), 'Conceptualizing simultaneity: a transnational social field perspective on society', *International Migration Review*, **38** (3), 1002–1039.

Levitt, P. and R. de la Hasa (2002), 'Transnational migration and the redefintion of the state: variations and explanations', *Ethnic and Racial Studies*, **26** (4), 587–611.

Mavroudi, E. (2008), 'Palestinians in diaspora, empowerment and informal political space', *Political Geography*, **27** (1), 57–73.

Mitchell, K. (1997), 'Different diasporas and the hype of hybridity', *Environment and Planning D: Society and Space*, **15** (5), 533–553.

Nagel, C. and L. Staeheli (2008a), 'Integration and the negotiation of "here" and "there": the case of British Arab activists', *Social & Cultural Geography*, **9** (4), 415–430.

Nagel, C. and L. Staeheli (2008b), 'Being visible and invisible: integration from the perspective of British Arab activists', in C. Dwyer and C. Bressey (eds), *New Geographies of Race and Racism*, Aldershot: Ashgate, pp. 83–94.

Nelson, L. (2008), 'Racialized landscapes: whiteness and the struggle over farmworker housing in Woodburn, Oregon', *Cultural Geographies*, **15** (5), 41–62.

Parham, A.A. (2004), 'Diaspora, community, and communication: internet use in transnational Haiti', *Global Networks*, **4** (2), 199–217.

Phillips, D. (2006), 'Parallel lives? Challenging discourses of British Muslim self-segregation', *Environment and Planning D: Society and Space*, **24** (1), 25–40.

Phillips, M. (2006), *Londonistan*, London: Gibson Square Books, Ltd.

Portes, A. (1999), 'Conclusion: toward a new world – the origins and effects of transnational activities', *Ethnic and Racial Studies*, **22** (2), 463–477.

Safran, W. (1991), 'Diasporas in modern societies: myths of homeland and return', *Diaspora*, **1** (1), 83–99.

Salih, R. (2001), 'Moroccan migrant women: transnationalism, nation-states and gender', *Journal of Ethnic and Migration Studies*, **27** (4), 655–671.

Samers, M. (2003), 'Diaspora unbound: Muslim identity and the erratic regulation of Islam in France', *Population, Space and Place*, **9** (4), 351–364.

Sassen, S. (2000), 'The global city: strategic site/new frontier', in E. Isin (ed.), *Democracy, Citizenship, and the Global City*, London and New York: Routledge, pp. 48–61.

Singer, A., S.W. Hardwick and C.B. Brettell (2008), *21st Century Gateways: Immigrant Incorporation in Suburbia*, Washington, DC: Brookings Institution.

Smith, M.P. (2003), 'Transnationalism, the state, and the extraterritorial citizen', *Politics and Society*, **31** (4), 267–502.

Trudeau, D. (2006), 'Politics of belonging in the construction of landscapes: place-making, boundary-drawing and exclusion', *Cultural Geographies*, **13** (3), 421–443.

Vertovec, S. (2004), 'Cheap calls: the social glue of transnationalism', *Global Networks*, **4** (2), 219–224.

Vertovec, S. (2007), 'Super-diversity and its implications', *Ethnic and Racial Studies*, **30** (6), 1024–1054.

Winders, J. (2006), '"New Americans" in a "New South" city? Immigrant and refugee politics in the Music City', *Social & Cultural Geography*, **7** (3), 421–435.

Yeh, E. and K. Lama (2006), 'Hip-hop gangsta or most deserving of victims? Transnational migrant identities and the paradox of Tibetan racialization in the USA', *Environment and Planning A*, **38** (5), 809–829.

Yeoh, B. and K. Willis (1999), '"Heart" and "wing", nation and diaspora: gendered discourses in Singapore's regionalization process', *Gender, Place and Culture*, **6** (4), 355–372.

37 Suburbanization and global cities
Roger Keil

INTRODUCTION

Global city formation has been predominantly a narrative of centrality. It is about establishing urban primacy or hegemony at a variety of scales. Most of all, the idea of global cities was originally linked to the notion of globalization as a worldwide process of economic expansion in which cities play a major role as control centers and headquarters locations. In so far as this steering role in the world economy has been linked to the rise of financial capitalism after the 1970s, the focus of global city research has been predominantly on the advanced producer services, often located in the central business districts, that support the burgeoning, fast-changing and pace-setting financial industries at the core of the globalized urban region. Policies of expansion and renewal were recorded as in step with the rising spatial and service appetites of those industries and their high-flying white-collar workforce (to the detriment of dramatic social polarization and socio-economic segregation), leading to gentrification and creating, as Sassen (2000) notes, a 'narrative of eviction'. The formation of the built and social environment of global urbanity around the financial-producer services complex has itself gone through a series of material restructurings and ideological and discursive shifts. Cities' push for global relevance has often been accompanied by spectacular urban development through mega-projects and iconic cultural and architectural objects (museums, etc.); more recently the rise of creative class discourse has been used as the hegemonic frame for global city expansion. Whether it is transportation terminals or talent, the geographical and functional focus of any such strategy has usually been the central city. Even geographically peripheral developments such as expanded airports or ports were tightly linked in their functionality and logistical connectivity to the needs and logics of the central city economy. This narrative, sketched here in the most simple terms and with a lot of omissions and selective choices, eclipses an important trend that is often overlooked in global city research: the reliance of global city formation as a centralized process on the *accelerated suburbanization of the global city region*. This chapter will concern itself with this often overlooked process and aim for a more complete account of global city formation. I will not attempt here to talk about the economic coherence of the global city region. I rather occupy myself with the suburbanization of the global city region itself. I will revisit the story of global city formation in Los Angeles, Frankfurt and Toronto as a process of regional suburbanization. This entails the story of back-offices, regional infrastructures, residential dispersal, and so on which is not usually focused on in global city research but it will also mention the proliferation of ethnoburbs as a typical world city phenomenon. I end the chapter with a reflection on suburbanization as a global event which now defines the landscape of globalized urbanity overall.

Conceptually, this chapter concerns itself with a central omission from some work on global and world cities: the disregard, to some degree, for the rather important processes of political agency and strategic intervention that have had a hand in structuring the geographies of global city formation. This includes acknowledgment of the historical layers of urban form and function that precede the current phase of globalized urban restructuring and the multi-scale and topological relations in which such histories are currently reshaped. Theoretically, this builds on the insights of Henri Lefebvre on the notion of 'centrality' (see MacDonald (2008) for a good discussion of this in our present context). If centrality is what the world city is about, this article discusses the significance of the peripheral for the production of that centrality. Following Stanek (2008, p. 74), the so-called '"dialectic of centrality" consists not only of the contradictory interdependence between the objects but of the opposition between center and periphery, gathering and dispersion, inclusion (to center) and exclusion (to periphery)'. Such reasoning is fundamental to the understanding of the relationship of suburbs and global cities which, as I will argue here, constitute themselves mutually in a dialectical fashion. In turn, then, it can be argued that suburbanization is a necessary and integral, constitutive element of the global city's centrality.

GLOBAL SUBURBS

The very notion of a global city conjures up central places, central functions and concentrated urbanity. Much of this is justified as agglomeration economies in globalized cities have created easily recognizable built and social environments of centrality: not least the three cities I will focus on below have only started to display extensive and ever taller skylines of gleaming office and bank towers in this most recent period of financial-industry-based urban accumulation. If you look at picture postcards of Los Angeles, Toronto and Frankfurt up until the 1960s, the Los Angeles City Hall, Toronto's Royal York Hotel and the turning-top tower of the Henninger Brewery in Frankfurt marked the respective skyline. Hardly the built environment of global capitalism. The explosive expansion of the global appearance of centrality in those cities after the 1970s – towering skylines – eclipsed perhaps a more significant if surprising trend: the emergence of the suburban as a place of muted centrality on which such globalized importance could be erected. The pathways leading to the emergence of suburbanized globality are different historically and diversified geographically from place to place. Three cases will be discussed below: Los Angeles, whose Fordist past prefigured its globalized presence; Frankfurt, whose competitive success was predicated on a movement of the global city 'up the country'; and Toronto, whose globality is literally resident in its burgeoning ethnoburbs and edge cities.[1]

THE SUBURBAN GLOBAL CITY PROTOTYPE: LOS ANGELES

While most stories of the globalization of Los Angeles have concentrated on the heightened significance of the central spaces of Los Angeles, some have specifically noted the role of the urban region in the rise of Los Angeles to the top of the urban hierarchy in the 1980s (Soja, 1989; Davis, 1990). Steve Erie (2004), in addition, points out that the region was restructured to serve global needs through recalibrated and globally oriented infrastructure projects, most of which span the suburban expanse of Southern California. This landscape was built on the Fordist history of political fragmentation and functional division that characterized the modernist period. In Southern California, perhaps more pronouncedly than anywhere else in the United States, the class-stratified privatization of space at the basis of the social ecology of suburbanization (Hoch, 1984) coincided with the rise of big industry (from oil to consumer durables) and the interventionist force of the Keynesian welfare state. The main socio-spatial contradiction in Los Angeles during Fordism was the bi-polarity of urban center and suburbia. The Fordist landscape of Los Angeles was partly a product of local political decisions to support early automobile-based transit and decentralized homeownership, which divided the city's working class socio-spatially through industrial and residential suburbanization. Decentralization was primarily a consequence of dispersed industrial patterns. The extractive industry in particular was instrumental as oil discoveries led to an early incorporation of scattered 'black gold suburbs'. The industrialization of the suburbs stopped the annexation strategy of Los Angeles because it improved the economic basis of the suburban web of emerging municipalities (Viehe, 1981). Consequently, a new metropolitan configuration emerged in Los Angeles: 'Instead of developing an industrial urban core surrounded by residential suburbs, the city developed an administrative-residential core surrounded by an industrial suburban network' (Viehe, 1981, p. 14). Los Angeles was eventually fragmented into an inner city populated by people of color and a mainly white suburban belt. Neighborhood groups from affluent communities became very powerful on the local political scene in the 1970s, receiving their impetus from the 1978 Proposition 13 which severely restrained the spending powers of local government. Seeking to preserve a 'homogeneity of race, class and, especially, home values' (Davis, 1990, p. 153), a patchwork of suburban fiefdoms, the product of homeowners' associations, have been established to prevent the erosion of property values. In the 1990s, there was a plethora of community name changes led by homeowner associations resisting both pro-growth forces as well as the burgeoning low-income ethnic and immigrant populations which threatened to bust out of the ghettos and barrios into the low-density gentility of the suburbs. This scenario became the political backdrop to secessionist movements in the San Fernando Valley and San Pedro regions from the late 1990s.

As a world city, Los Angeles has built on the fragmented and increasingly privatized structure created in earlier decades. Largely suburban local states have been integrated into the spatial and political logic of the region's 'structured coherence' (Harvey, 1989) on the basis of distinct politics and policies which have granted them special status in the spatial division of labour. Southern California's fragmented, suburbanized and decentralized structure – which had helped to organize the regional space of a Fordist production/consumption complex – was retooled in a way that facilitated the integration of the region into the newly globalized economy. Dispersed suburban local governments have pursued the project of the world city by weaving the rhetoric of world city *grandesse* into a new political economy of place. Cities have attempted to deal with the pressure of internationalization on their communities with similar, yet significantly varied, policy responses and rhetoric.

West Hollywood, an enclave wedged between Los Angeles and Beverly Hills, incorporated into a separate municipality in 1984 on the strengths of a political coalition of an activist homosexual population with a majority tenant population, mostly elderly people. Subsequently, West Hollywood pursued an aggressive marketing and economic development strategy, deliberately attempting to integrate itself into the global economy and the global city region. In September 1987, West Hollywood began to market itself as an 'avant-garde, culturally sophisticated, creative city'. The concept of the 'creative city' as an advertising slogan intended to generate urban development was developed by the non-profit West Hollywood Marketing Corporation (see WHMC, 1988) whose director said at the time: 'Much of what people associate with Los Angeles – which is this newly self-conscious world capital – emanates from West Hollywood'. The 'creative city' campaign was intended to give the newly founded city high visibility in the local and global marketplace, articulating its own image production with the contextual rhetoric of the world-class city. The adjective 'creative' was derived from the fact that more than 40 per cent of the economic activity in the city took place in 'creative' industries: fashion, design, food, movies, and so forth. There were obvious cross-references to the construction of an urban and a gay identity in this process (Forest, 1995, pp. 143–144). Plugging itself into the regional process of world city formation, West Hollywood sold itself to the world with an 'innovative strategy' as a 'unique community'. The relevant aspect of this reincarnation of traditional boosterism is the self-confident evocation of uniqueness in an international and world-historic ambience.

The production of place in West Hollywood led to the concrete materiality of a suburban municipality in an emerging global city economy. The 'creative city' itself became a productive force in securing a niche in the global economic environment of Southern California. In this context, the 'creative industries' of West Hollywood were put to work: the City secured them a location in the chaos of the global economy and did not shy away from using its power in structuring the newly incorporated economic base of the municipality.

In a very similar fashion, in Santa Monica, a suburban seaside town of about 87,000 people (2008) west of Los Angeles, the combination of a large tenant population (80 per cent of residents) and a young, liberal middle class provided the basis for a 'progressive' majority on the city council in 1981. The success of the 'progressive' coalition in the municipal election was pre-dated by a referendum that had introduced a strict local rent-control law in 1979. The 'radical' program of the Santa Monicans for Renters Rights provided municipal services to a specific segment of the fragmented suburban society of world city Los Angeles. The municipality was forced into a paradoxical policy constellation in which middle-class politicians, conscious of the need to protect their privileges, continued to pursue alternative social policies. Next to rent control, the City's policies on homelessness were significant in this respect. Before harsh control policies were reintroduced, Santa Monica spent one third of its social service budget on care for the homeless, who were congregating on the City's beaches and streets.

The story is a different one in Carson, a suburban municipality of 85,000 (1993) in the South of the Los Angeles Basin. The city capitalized on the opportunities that sprung up through the northward expansion of the harbor economy along the Long Beach and Harbor Freeways. The operative logo the community has chosen for itself is 'Future Unlimited'. Carson's explicit development strategy – heavily influenced by the city's leading place entrepreneur, the Watson Land Company – was to provide a safe ground for international investment. Carson's development has been largely a product of the entangled interests of (inter-)national capital and of local real estate capital, specifically the oil and development companies. In the era of the global city Carson positioned itself as an important part of the sub-economy of the South Bay based on world trade and high technology and a headquarters site for Fortune 500 companies. High-technology 'clean' production has been considered desirable. The formation of an integrated 'glocal-ized' political economy was the program of the suburban local state. Yet Carson is also a residential suburb with one of the most ethnically diverse populations in the United States, with a population almost evenly distributed among the region's major ethnic groups: Hispanic, Black, Asian and White. This diversity is seen as congruent with the goal of economic growth as long as citizenship is defined as operating in the global marketplace of interurban competition.

Yet another set of circumstances has characterized the restructuring in the eastern working-class suburbs and industrial communities of Los Angeles. Globalization in the suburbs of LA's Eastside has not meant investment from Asia or Europe into glittering office complexes but massive immigration from the Third World, gambling casinos, and multinational crime. The Eastside has been under constant threat of becoming a giant garbage dump and sink for pollution as well as an emergency ward for the infrastructure crisis of the urban region. Cities in the old industrial belt of LA, also sometimes called 'hub cities', include the industrial communities Vernon and Commerce and the mixed, or residential, communities of Bell, Bell Gardens, Cudahy, Huntington Park, Lynwood, Maywood and Southgate.

These suburban communities have been losers in globally induced interurban competition in the world city region. They have taken the brunt of the deindustrialization, impoverishment and housing crisis encountered in the region overall. Deindustrialization and new immigration have been coupled with a visible tendency toward industrial restructuring, during which service industries, small office parks, small warehouses and light industry as well as mini steel mills and garment factories have emerged as indicators of a changing industrial base in a formerly heavy industrial area.

The insertion of the region's suburban communities into the global city was taken to an extreme in Compton, south of Los Angeles, one of the poorest suburbs in the United States. Compton owes its place in the global city to its economic success on the world market. Once a murderous center of gang activity where Crips and Bloods and other gangs were fighting for the control of territory and markets in the 1980s, Compton became, for a while, the unrivaled world headquarters of hiphop, particularly in its 'gangsta rap' version. When NWA from Compton sold half a million copies of its album 'Straight Outta Compton' in the summer of 1989, a flood of defiant self-stylization was triggered in the world-forsaken community. The creation of communal identity was achieved through a decidedly anti-establishmentarian attitude that expressed itself in blunt realist style and with an unapologetically capitalist sales strategy fueling an entire industry of inverted Compton marketing. In contrast to the conscious simulacra of the marketing strategies of West Hollywood and Santa Monica, and in contrast to the class-based community strategy of the hub cities, the rappers of Compton subscribed to an allegedly unmediated representation of stark reality and truth meant to give identity to the inhabitants and to the place of Compton. It is the inversion of Carson's strategy that targets global business investment with images of a peaceful multinational community. In Compton, distinction is achieved through claiming the suburban 'hood as the natural home territory of gangland. While other local states have marketed themselves as localities of innovation, stability and success, Compton's global music market handlers sold the city as the home of the drive-by shooting: 'It's the Compton Thang'.

FRANKFURT UP THE COUNTRY

The German global city of Frankfurt presents a markedly different but related story. Clearly, the differences between the American and German planning, constitutional, political and land use systems are stark. Yet functionally, Frankfurt's suburbs have also established their visibility in the global city region. Viewed from the center, there are two main thrusts of spatial peripheralization in Germany's financial capital. First, there are all kinds of displacement both of people and of industries. Traditional manufacturing (such as metalworking factories) and crafts industries were pushed to the spatial periphery. Simultaneously, the poor, the immigrants, the subcultures have been displaced into areas further away from the city center. Often, spatial peripheralization coincides with social marginalization. The hegemonic discourses of urbanity and centralization have largely ignored these sociospatial effects. Second, overspill effects of the core economy have created back-office and housing needs which have been increasingly filled in peripheral areas outside the municipality of Frankfurt. Suburban areas like Office City Niederrad and Eschborn were at times virtual 'flood control' devices for the booming inner city economy, sites of back-offices and routine functions of banks and other businesses located in the core. Not all development in the periphery can be credited to expansion in the core, however. The periphery became the staging ground for important sectors of the global city economy. The concentration of office towers in the downtown often eclipses the tendency of the 'real' economic center of Frankfurt to shift away from the downtown into the forest on the fringe of the city: Frankfurt airport, the second largest in Europe after London Heathrow, has developed into the crucial modem of the global flows of people, goods and information as air traffic-related infrastructures along with first class office, conference and hotel space have been continuously (re-)developed there. Recent plans for an additional runway in the northwest of the existing facility have led to considerable opposition in the region. Meanwhile, less desirable functions have been displaced from the actual airport area. This development mirrors a tendency visible in Frankfurt-Rhine-Main on the whole: manufacturing, waste management, supply industries like the slaughterhouse and the produce wholesale market as well as other industrial activities were shifted from the core to the periphery. This practice still coincides largely with a center-oriented real estate market. Yet with the growing significance of the airport (and possibly other subcenters) these markets become more nodal.

A regional ring of small and semi-autonomous suburban communities has become a significant target of foreign investments and the terrain of the peripheralization of globalization. Also, commercial and industrial parks housing consulting services and marketing outlets of domestic and foreign computer and electronics firms form a rim around Frankfurt. Housing construction both in the core and in the periphery has, in the meantime, hardly been able to keep up with the continuing office boom, putting considerable stress on the regional socio-economic situation.

The spatial form of the periphery is being produced by a series of often contradictory dynamics. The periphery has not just been colonized by the core but appears as the product of exchange processes both of core and periphery and of various subcenters on the fringe. Ambitious large-scale housing projects near old village cores reflect this urbanization trend as much as the often mannerist and pastiche 'reurbanization' of such cores, increase of density, and so on. Even in smaller communities, social housing has now become a ubiquitous issue while high-tech companies in newly designated industrial areas and cultural centers in medieval city halls have become part of the image we have of former country towns. Thus uniform 'urban sprawl' is, in fact, increasingly replaced by a multiplication of centralization effects. We are starting to find, in the periphery, a socio-spatial structure equally as complex as (or even more complex than) the center of the global city.

Poor immigrants still tend to live in or near the central city, in the working-class neighborhoods along the Main river where their share of the total population reaches up to 70 per cent. But as they are driven out of these neighborhoods by gentrification and conversion of affordable housing, they can be found increasingly in the peripheral social housing projects built since World War Two. It is actually in these peripheral districts that the increase in foreigners has been most pronounced since 1970. This marginalizing peripheralization in fact has meant that the suburbs have become the urban form of multicultural society. The crisis of the globalized outer city is now a prominent feature of European metropolises more generally.

TORONTO: CREATING THE GREATER GOLDEN HORSESHOE

The Toronto case, while still different from Los Angeles and Frankfurt, confirms the overall narrative we have presented here. The urban region has been a veritable testing ground for center–periphery re-regulation for at least a generation. Prompted by the urban region's dramatic demographic and economic growth after World War Two, suburban sprawl of residences and employment has been a major factor in Toronto's formation into 'Canada's global city'. While the urban economy is often seen as synonymous with the strong presence of a financial services cluster downtown, its strengths have also been regional manufacturing (such as automobile assembly and parts production), producer services, transportation, cultural production, media, education and tourism. Pearson International Airport, in the west of the city, has become a major – suburban – center of employment and economic activity. Around the airport as well as other suburban employment hubs, residential expansion has occurred.

The growth of the region overall has led to a re-segmentation of urban population and has redefined the traditional meanings of suburb and center (for a recent discussion see Harris, 2010). Two processes stand out. First, immigration has become a suburban process. Long thought of as dependent on the dense institutional and cultural structures of the inner city, immigrant settlement has increasingly shifted directly to areas peripheral to the urban region. Secondly, as gentrification of the inner city continues apace, the old and new suburbs of Toronto have increasingly become home to significantly poorer populations than in the core. They tend to be more composed of visible minorities, have a higher ratio of tenants versus homeowners and tend to have a higher percentage of new immigrants among them. In some of the outer suburbs, like Brampton, Markham and Mississauga, large minorities of South Asian or East Asian populations have recently arrived and become homeowners. The global city economy of Toronto, which is dependent not only on the high-tech- and transportation-related employment centers in Toronto's northern fringe but also on the warehouses and commercial infrastructures 'out there', has self-confidently embraced the urban region as the basis of its operations. The Greater Toronto Area has now been expanded conceptually to the Greater Golden Horseshoe, a sprawling suburban expanse that wraps around the western tip of Lake Ontario.

While inner city boosters and opinion makers continue to treat Toronto as a centralized urban landscape of creative economies and residential diversity, the reality of the urban region has long bypassed this image: the urban fringe is a bustling, emergent, surprising globalized area in its own right. By no means still dependent on impulses from the central global city economy or the finance and business services industry and not just inactive service space for the needs of the core, the urban periphery in Toronto is strongly developing a version of regional globalization that, like its counterparts Los Angeles and Frankfurt, is based on self-generated and vital economic and demographic internationalization. Equally, the political process and institutional developments have begun to reflect this reality as the Ontario government has introduced a binding Places to Grow Plan, which ascribes suburban growth centers a prime role in the overall structured coherence of the global city region. Meant to help manage explosive growth (in a region which now has 9 million people and is expected to have 11.5 million in 2031), the Places to Grow Plan redefines the often center-dominated and -driven expansion plans of the global city economy as a territorial and relational project in which cooperation of actors across a wide range of suburban municipalities and sectors is seen as vital to the survival of the plan to sustain Toronto's efficacy as a world economic center.

CONCLUSION

Rather than treating suburbanization as just an aspect of global city formation as we have done in the preceding three case studies, we can go one step further.[2] Clearly, the expansion of urban space is now a global phenomenon. It marks the moment of our shared experience as planetary citizens since more than half of us today live in cities. While often referred to as an 'urban revolution' (Lefebvre, 2003; Brugmann, 2009), most urban growth worldwide now takes the form of peripheral or *suburban* development. Urban planners and environmentalists oppose low-density sprawl for its disproportional environmental impact and find the 'explosion' of squatter settlements problematic. Global and creative city boosters and scholars of urban global economies have often displayed a bias toward the (gentrified) central and dense urban neighborhoods and production spaces that have triggered yearnings for widespread re-urbanization (see disP, 2010). Yet, despite normative preferences in planning and city building for a dense and centralized urban form, suburbanization remains the dominant mode in which cities are built. Whether by choice or by force, builders and inhabitants, rich and poor, construct and live in urban peripheries around the world. The universality of the suburban trend and the boundless divergence in its real processes and outcomes pose an encompassing yet particularized set of scenarios which need to guide our research.

Although the case studies discussed in this chapter are all from cities of the global

North, they help 'provincialize' the literature on the core global cities (Robinson, 2006) and create new geographies of globalization (Roy, 2009). Just as a 'worlding' of formerly 'peripheral' areas in the Global South has been observed in recent analyses (Roy, 2011), the tremendous presence of the global suburb in the intellectual domain of the global city can no longer be ignored. This is particularly so as the suburbs of the global city contribute more visibly and thoroughly to the galloping modernities and diversities one finds throughout the urban world around the globe that defy the common patterns of Western urbanization. Looking 'from the expanding edge of the global city' into the dynamic process that drives the urban revolution today (Brugmann, 2009), students of globalizing cities must now address salient suburban challenges.

Surprisingly, the universal character of suburbanization and its role in creating spaces of globality are, to date, unrecognized. Patterns and processes of urbanization in the developed and developing worlds are almost invariably examined by different people using different categories despite stunning recent developments in some countries – often those with the most dynamic global city formation such as China and India – which blur conceptual categories. By studying the suburbs of the global city, we can better understand emergent forms of urbanization and of urbanism around the world more generally but also specifically bring the suburban experience into view for global city research.

Diverse in histories, economies, institutions and spatialities, all suburbs have in common their difference from the central city. Suburbanization is no uniform phenomenon in all parts of the world, but includes all manner of peripheral growth: from the wealthy gated communities of the West, to the high rise-dominated old suburbs of Europe and Canada, the Westernized outskirts of Indian and Chinese cities, and the slums and squatter settlements in Africa and Latin America. They all articulate various modes of globalization in ways that had originally been hypothesized for the core global city. This points to *suburbanism* as the growing prevalence of qualitatively distinct 'suburban ways of life' that are indispensable to the formation of the global city region. These ways of life are now themselves entirely globalized and not the 'provinces' to the central city's global economic 'metropolis'.

In the future, we need to address both the ubiquity of difference between central city and suburbs and the diversity within the latter, including their hybrid, in-between forms (Sieverts, 2003). Suburbanism includes elements such as centrality/peripherality, scale, mix of land uses, population characteristics, power/control, governance, mobility modes, services and amenities. While one must consider their profound localized manifestation if transposing them across global suburbanisms, one needs to envision them as part of one world of the global city.

NOTES

1. These brief case study narratives build on previous work by the author in Keil (1998), Keil and Ronneberger (1994) and Boudreau et al. (2009).
2. I am building here on work under way in a Major Collaborative Research Initiative funded by the Canadian Social Sciences and Humanities Research Council on Global Suburbanisms which intends to subject peripheral growth around the world to scrutiny with a methodology of comparative (sub)urbanism. A brief description may be found at www.yorku.ca/city/Projects/GlobalSuburbanism.html.

REFERENCES

Boudreau, J.-A., R. Keil and D. Young (2009), *Changing Toronto: Governing Urban Neoliberalism*, Toronto: University of Toronto Press.

Brugmann, J. (2009), *Welcome to the Urban Revolution: How Cities are Changing the World*, Toronto: Bloomsbury Press.

Davis, M. (1990), *City of Quartz: Excavating the Future in Los Angeles*, London: Verso.

disP – The Planning Review (2010), Special Issue on Reurbanization, Issue 180.

Erie, S. (2004), *Globalizing L.A.: Trade, Infrastructure, and Regional Development*, Stanford, CA: Stanford University Press.

Forest, B. (1995), 'West Hollywood as symbol: the significance of place in the construction of a gay identity', *Environment and Planning D: Society and Space*, **13** (2), 133–157.

Harris, R. (2010), 'Meaningful types in a world of suburbs', in M. Clapson and R. Hutchison (eds), *Suburbanisation in Global Society* (Research in Urban Sociology No.10), Emerald Group Publishing Limited, pp. 15–47.

Harvey, D. (1989), *The Urban Experience*, Baltimore, MD: The Johns Hopkins University Press.

Hoch, C. (1984), 'City limits: municipal boundary formation and class segregation', in W.K. Tabb and L. Sawers (eds), *Marxism and the Metropolis*, New York: Oxford University Press, pp. 101–119.

Keil, R. (1998), *Los Angeles: Globalization, Urbanization and Social Struggles*, Chichester: Wiley.

Keil, R. and K. Ronneberger (1994), 'Going up the country: internationalization and urbanization on Frankfurt's northern fringe', *Environment and Planning D: Society and Space*, **12** (2), 137–166.

Lefebvre, H. (2003), *The Urban Revolution*, Minneapolis, MN: University of Minnesota Press.

MacDonald, I.T. (2008), 'The end of suburbia, or the return to centrality?', available at www.lepanoptique.com/sections/societe/the-end-of-suburbia-or-the-return-to-centrality/ (accessed 9 July 2010).

Robinson, J. (2006), *Ordinary Cities: Between Modernity and Development*, London and New York: Routledge.

Roy, A. (2009), 'The 21st-century metropolis: new geographies of theory', *Regional Studies*, **43** (6), 819–830.

Roy, A. (2011), 'Slumdog cities: rethinking subaltern urbanism', *International Journal of Urban and Regional Research*, **35** (2), 223–238.

Sassen, S. (2000), *Cities in a World Economy*, Thousand Oaks, CA: Sage.

Sieverts, T. (2003), *Cities Without Cities: An Interpretation of the Zwischenstadt*, London: Spon Press.

Soja, E.W. (1989), *Postmodern Geographies: The Reassertion of Space in Critical Social Theory*, London: Verso.

Stanek, L. (2008), 'Space as concrete abstraction: Hegel, Marx, and modern urbanism in Henri Lefebvre', in K. Goonewardena, S. Kipfer, R. Milgrom and C. Schmid (eds), *Space, Difference, Everyday Life: Reading Henri Lefebvre*, London and New York: Routledge, pp. 62–79.

Viehe, F.W. (1981), 'Black gold suburbs: the influence of the extractive industry on the suburbanization of Los Angeles, 1890–1930', *Journal of Urban History*, **8** (1), 3–26.

WHMC (1988), *'The Creative City': Promoting West Hollywood*, internal document, no p. nos.

PART III

WORLD CITY CASE STUDIES

38 NY-LON
Richard G. Smith

> London and New York are very special cities and in this sense they represent the two poles of a transatlantic metropolis.
>
> Sir Peter Hall (2003, p. 31)

The term 'NY-LON' is a descriptor, a simple (and simplifying) label, for how – through globalization – New York and London have become increasingly linked by a shared economic culture despite being separated by a distance of more than 3400 miles. The compound abbreviation 'NY-LON' was deployed by journalists around the turn of the millennium to capture the sense that, in many ways, the world's two premier 'global cities' are coming together, increasingly working hand in hand, to become not just one type of city (be it a global city, a post-industrial city, a creative city, a mega-city, a meta-city, or so on), but one city: a transatlantic metropolis that is the heart-beat of the global economy.

The notion of NY-LON as a trans-maritime 'unicity', an elite transnational urban network, was first coined by journalists writing in *Newsweek* magazine who observed a new trend whereby some of New York's and London's wealthiest people, entrepreneurs and financial 'whizz-kids' were 'resident of a place called NY-LON, a single city inconveniently separated by an ocean' (McGuire and Chan, 2000, p. 41). Observing the lifestyles of some of the two cities' 'rich and famous', they noted how an increasing number are 'working and playing in New York and London as if they were one city' (McGuire and Chan, 2000, p. 41). As two of the world's leading centres of culture and economy – Broadway and the West End, Manhattan/Wall Street and the City/Canary Wharf, NYSE and the LSE, and so on – the journalists noted how a number of high-earning 'yuppie' individuals are darting back and forth: residing, socializing, working and doing business across both metropolises to be in step with globalization.

The journalists noted the working lives of several high-income individuals that stride both New York and London. A middle-aged businessman, who owns both an apartment in the East Village and a flat in Wilton Crescent in Belgravia (London's wealthiest neighbourhood), is cited as evidence of 'how joined up New York and London have become'. He 'flies between the two cities up to five times a month' both through his capacity as a theatrical producer, 'he takes shows between Broadway and the West End, the twin capitals of the theater world', and the demands of his company that does specialized printing for investment banks, which 'quite naturally takes him to both Wall Street and the City, the world's two great financial centers' (McGuire and Chan, 2000, p. 41). Further anecdotal evidence for the NY-LON trend, a kind of 'transnationalism from above', was provided by a journalist writing in the *London Evening Standard*. In an article entitled 'We're the Nylons' she contends that 'Nowadays, every businessman, model, actress or young entrepreneur worth their salt wants the best of both worlds – a pad in New York and a pied-à-terre in London' (Johnson, 2003, p. 25). Through three brief biographical vignettes of the nomadic elite – the working lives of an investment banker, an entrepreneur and a newspaper journalist – Johnson gives a flavour, a fleeting sketch, of how a privileged few span both cities through their work and lifestyle.

In addition to the privileged urban lifestyles of a rich minority the *Newsweek* journalists also noted a larger analytical picture; namely, a certain hierarchy amongst the world's most famous great cities: 'In a world dominated by money and English-language-based information technology, NY-LON stands atop a lesser tier of second cities. Tokyo and Hong Kong are not in the same league' (McGuire and Chan, 2000, p. 43). However, journalists writing in 2008, in *Time Magazine*, suggest that as 'Asia's World City' Hong Kong has now joined New York City and London to stand apart from the world's other leading cities – such as Paris, Tokyo, Singapore, Los Angeles, Shanghai, Beijing, Berlin, and so on – with regard to their importance as examples and explanations of globalization as a whole: 'Connected by long-haul jets and fiber-optic cable, and spaced neatly around the globe, the three cities have (by accident – nobody planned this) created a financial network that has been able to lubricate the global economy, and, critically, ease the entry into the modern world of China, the giant child of our century. Understand this network of cities – Nylonkong, we call it – and you understand our time' (Elliott, 2008, unpaginated). Indeed, the validity of the claims in *Time Magazine* of a transition from a bipolar to a tripolar urban order has been lent some credence. A Chairman of HSBC gave a speech confirming *Time Magazine*'s vision of Hong Kong as China's Wall Street, joining New York and London to form the dominant axis across the global economy; a joining which he speculates will perhaps in the future lead to Hong Kong becoming first amongst equals in that triad of cities that rule the world: 'Hongnylon' (Cheng, 2008, unpaginated). What is more, the *Hindustan Times* (2009) also tacitly confirms the triad of cities as atop a hierarchy of the world's business cities. The journalist speculates as to whether one day, with the problems facing its regional rival Dubai following the global 'credit crunch', Mumbai might grow to such significance that it would be locatable on the same axis as New York, London and Hong Kong, 'with competition reducing between the London–Hong Kong time zone, the end of Ny-Lon-Kong-Dub could mean the rebirth of Ny-Lon-Kong-Mum' (2009, unpaginated). Indeed, a common opinion amongst many business commentators and economic experts is that the axis of power in the global economy is shifting from West to East, and more specifically toward the high-growth economies and cities of the so-called BRIC countries: Brazil, Russia, India and China.

The journalists – writing in such publications as *Newsweek*, the *London Evening Standard*, *Time Magazine* and the *Hindustan Times* – who have coined these hyphenated contractions have all noted, if only anecdotally, that a network of great cities is an increasingly important geographical fact that functions to bind together the fortunes of people living across the world's most wealthy economic zones: North America, Europe and Asia. Indeed, the term 'NY-LON' has been deployed by some urban researchers (Hall, 2003; Smith, 2003a, 2003b, 2005; Pain, 2009) precisely because it is an invented latitude that chimes with a shift in urban studies, one that began in the late 1990s, toward trying to understand how some cities can be increasingly described and identified by their links to one another, rather than just through their internal characteristics – as had been the focus of virtually all previous urban scholarship, radical or otherwise.

To further approach the idea of NY-LON the chapter is in two more parts. First, some writings on urban networks, published over the last decade, are discussed to demonstrate how they lend further empirical support for the NY-LON phenomenon that so many journalists have observed. Secondly, NY-LON's asymmetry with regard to the mega- and meta-cities of the developing world is noted to point to a certain irony with regard to the wider issue of the global development of transnational urbanism as a whole. For, whilst many settlements in the developing world are also coming together through globalization, they are not doing so to form cultural and financial transnational spaces like NY-LON or NY-LON-KONG with their comparable economies, cultures and 'circulating' high-earning elite migrants, but rather to become hugely populous metropolises that are 'transnational' in a completely different sense: because of their rapidly expanding slum settlements that sprawl across national boundaries paying scant attention to the boundaries of political geography.

NY-LON: THE ACADEMIC EVIDENCE

Studies of global cities are generally replete with information that facilitates evaluations of individual cities and comparative analyses of two or more cities. The data upon which such studies are based are overwhelmingly derived from measures of attributes. Such information is useful for estimating the general importance of cities and for studying intra-city processes but it tells us nothing *directly* about relations between cities, with how they are, for example, connected together through globalization (Beaverstock et al., 2000). Thus, there is very little publicly available information on the connections between New York and London because such networks are not researched and consequently not reported on. For example, published at the turn of the millennium a Corporation of London (2000) report on New York and London is typical in that it only highlights the two cities' common themes and issues. The study compared the general characteristics of the two cities with regard to: demography, labour force and income; major economic trends in the 1980s and 1990s; the metropolitan region; financial services; business and professional services; visitors and hotels; media; transport; economic development; and governance. Thus, the finding of the report that 'London and New York, despite striking differences in their historic past and with very contrasting forms of local governance, have developed economies that, at the century's turn, are at an extraordinary point of symmetry' (p. 8), is sound but also partial because the issue of how the two cities are joined together is not considered. An oversight that is important because the symmetry between the two cities may not be because the cities are in competition and therefore duplicate one another, but rather because the cities are in sync as they complement and collaborate with one another.

Decades of published research based on measures of city attributes has confirmed that both New York and London are the world's pre-eminent international financial centres; both are the world's leading centres for the provision of legal services; both dominate the market for international advertising; both are the leading centres for international accountancy and management consultancy (cemented over the years through Anglo-American mergers). Indeed, both cities have higher concentrations of international business services than are found in any other cities anywhere in the world. Furthermore, we know that in terms of cultural industries both cities are the twin capitals of the theatre world (buoyed by the successes of so-called 'mega-musicals'); both have significant fashion industries (aligned with Paris, Tokyo and Milan in this sphere of economic activity); both have significant film industries; and both are leading centres for the global publishing industry. Thus, it was in the face of such overwhelming attributional evidence as to the importance of New York and London that Taylor (2003, p. 31) could declare that 'there is no publicly available information about the most important inter-city relation [between New York and London] – the most significant geographical connection – in the world today.'

The NY-LON phenomenon was first presented in *Newsweek* as a lifestyle adopted by some of New York's and London's elite migrants. According to journalists increasing numbers of people were flying between New York and London. This observation is confirmed by subsequent research on international airline passenger data which show that in the period January to August 2001 some 1,609,337 passengers flew between London and New York, making it by far – if one considers passenger traffic between Hong Kong and Taipei as a national route – the busiest international passenger route in the world (Witlox and Derudder, 2007).

In identifying the NY-LON phenomenon *Newsweek* and *Evening Standard* journalists identified investment bankers as a key group of elite migrants making NY-LON a reality: '"In terms of our business," says Richard Corrigan of Merrill Lynch in London, "the cities are beginning to meld into one massive whole"' (McGuire and Chan, 2000, p. 42). This observation is confirmed by the research of Beaverstock (2007), whose empirical study of international mobility within the global investment banking industry 'unearthed a world city network characterized by . . . a New York–London dyad' (p. 69). Beaverstock found that movement (high-frequency business travel and commuting) of investment bankers between New York and London is the dominant global urban axis within that corporate service sector: 'the inter-connected high-value service economies of cities in globalization are founded upon highly-professional and knowledge rich expert staff, who are world city hyper-mobile . . . the "NYLONers"' (2007, pp. 68–69).

The wider picture of a global economy articulated through three financial centres, the joining of Hong Kong to NY-LON, proposed by *Time Magazine* in 2008 and confirmed by a Chairman of HSBC, is an observation that is not lent credence by Taylor's (2004) research on global services. Through a quantitative analysis of a data set of the 'worldwide' office locations of 100 firms across 6 business services (accountancy, advertising, banking/finance, insurance, law, management consultancy) Taylor identifies London and New York as by far the most important and connected 'global service centres' out of a macro-geography of some 316 centres. Taylor classifies those centres into ranked types – Mega, Major, Medium and Minor – showing that as a whole New York and London are potentially the most massively connected across these business service sectors, statistically way ahead even of those few cities ranked as 'major': Hong Kong, Paris, Tokyo, Chicago, Frankfurt and Miami.

Support for the NY-LON phenomenon has also been evidenced through the identification of a coming together of the two cities through the formation of a cross-continental office market (Jackson et al., 2008). The economic specialization of both cities through an inter-linked financial service sector produces two of the largest and most liquid international office markets in the world, a liquidity that attracts a substantial strategic international investment behaviour that has the consequence of binding the real estate fortunes of both cities together. In other words, the performance of the NYSE and the LSE stock markets play such a disproportionate role in the real estate markets of both cities that an investment portfolio spread across both cities is, whilst liquid, nevertheless a risk because it is not diverse: any investor is not spreading his bets because NY-LON is one market.

Overall, the academic evidence supports those suggestions in the popular press that New York and London are both highly symmetrical and increasingly connected together and interchangeable. However, this is viable only when the two cities are focused on through very particular lenses: as financial centres, producer service centres, gentrification 'hotspots', commercial real estate markets, and so on. In other words, NY-LON, *in nuce*, is an accurate descriptor only when it is referring to quite particular connections across New York and London; when it is identifying the dual urban geography of a wealthy elite: 'Even New York and London are not like each other. The only way you can think of these cities as being interchangeable is to focus on parts of the city – finance or commerce – at the expense of everything else' (Frug, 2005, p. 2).

A/SYMMETRY: THE PARALLEL WORLDS OF TRANSNATIONAL URBANISM

Some of them call me London,
I'm also known as New York.
Anywhere in the world you find me.

Faithless (1996)

It is the symmetry, the harmony, the synchronicity, of New York's and London's economies and business cultures which make 'NY-LON' (as a conflation of the two cities) a most viable descriptor of how these two cities mirror one another in striving to place themselves as the powerhouses at the centre of neoliberal globalization. In the financial and business press New York and London are often presented as an inter-urban connection that has a certain 'special relationship' and economic symmetry, and consequently as two 'sister cities' or 'sibling-cities' with a shared fortune and future that are based on collaboration as much as competition. Three examples from the business press will suffice to make my point. First, in 2006 the *Financial Times* pointed to how the quotidian movement of money and financial products between the two centres is the source of their mutual wealth: 'New York need not fear London. The competition spurs both of them on, and activity migrates between them during the trading day. They are the world's great financial capitals. Both of them can and will prosper' (2006, unpaginated). Secondly, in 2007 the *Financial Times* noted that the two cities must 'hang-together' through difficult economic conditions: 'the credit squeeze, and the fear not only of a US recession but also of a downturn in the financial services industry, has brought back into focus their [New York's and London's] close similarities – indeed their symbiotic relationship. There is nothing like a spot of common adversity to bring people together and that is what NyLon, as the twin cities are sometimes known, faces' (Gapper, 2007, unpaginated). Finally, *Newsweek* magazine in 2009 shunned all speculation about an eastern challenge to NY-LON's hegemony, to point to how their symmetrical dominance of globalization will continue: 'Financial crises tend to trigger overwrought predictions of major economic shifts – and then debunk them . . . it has become popular to predict that New York and London (or NyLon, as they're together known) will soon lose market share as cities in the emerging world use the crisis to wrest away dominance. But history suggests that the opposite is more likely: that New York and London will actually increase in importance over the decade to come' (Pettis, 2009, unpaginated).

The idea of a world economy articulated through certain 'super-star' or 'heavyweight' cities – such as Rome, Venice, Amsterdam, London or New York – is a longstanding one (Braudel, 1984; Hall, 1998). However, the present obsession with identifying and confirming the world's 'leading cities' is undoubtedly the defining characteristic of the academic and policy literature on global and world cities as a whole. Ever since Peter Hall (1966) singled out seven world cities, and Sassen (1991) three global cities, numerous authors working in all kinds of public and private institutions have advanced urban balance sheets for globalization of one kind or another. Little surprise, then, that there is a seemingly constant speculative interest, especially in the popular press and in policy circles, with foretelling those up-and-coming cities that might become like, or even surpass, New York and London as the 'upper crust' of contemporary globalization. Thus, and especially with the global financial crisis, there has been on-going speculation as to whether the 'gravity' of the global economy will shift in the twenty-first century away from the core cities of New York and London to cities such as Hong Kong, Shanghai, Mumbai and Dubai. However, whilst journalists, business commentators, think-tanks, consultants, academics, city mayors, and no-doubt most importantly, urban marketing professionals, have concerned themselves with identifying those cities that may match and join New York and London as the world's premium spaces of centrality (viewing NY-LON as a kind of urban prototype for advanced countries in the twenty-first century), the other 'transnational' urban story of the coming decades is not about whether this or that city will become economically symmetrical with NY-LON through growth, development and internationalization, but rather with how an increasing number of cities across the world – often because of their geographical propinquity – are literally joining together through a kind of 'transnationalism from below' to form mega- or even meta-cities that sprawl across international boundaries. In other words, whilst some residents of New York and London are treating the two cities as one place, elsewhere in the world a quite different story of transnational urbanism is unfolding. In the twenty-first century globalization is shaking itself out, in an urban sense at least, as a series of horizontal axes or plateaus, urban transects of different and distinct intensities, that whilst co-existent, are nevertheless parallel universes with alternate economic realities.

Around the world it is evident that a number of different 'circulations' are producing quite different forms of urbanization. In the developed world, 'elite migration' is a key factor in producing the NY-LON phenomenon, and is undoubtedly also bringing Paris and London (PAR-LON), London and Frankfurt (LONFURT) and Hong Kong and London, to name but a few cities, into closer symmetry – if only for the benefit of a limited, although still quite sizeable, elite. However, at the other extreme, in what used to be called the Third World, 'economic migration' often manifests itself as mass movement for little more than bare economic survival. The associated massive urban population growth means a lack of living space with basic infrastructure, so that even the most marginal spaces become occupied. For example, in Lagos more than a thousand people live in houses made of scrap on top of the Olusosun rubbish dump. Consequently, urban settlements are forever spreading out and joining up, coming together like spilt blobs of mercury, amalgamating into 'endless cities'. Sprawling across national borders as they grow together, self-organizing into a combination of extreme underdevelopment and development, to form the new trans-national 'mega-city regions' of the developing world. Along the western coast of Africa the cities of Accra, Ibadan, Lagos and Lomé are becoming a vast meta-city that stretches some 600 kilometres. A massively populated band of seemingly contiguous and never-ending urbanization that whilst driving a transnational regional economy, not only challenges the national integrities of Benin, Ghana, Togo and Nigeria, but also serves to feed the economies of global cities such as New York and London. Indeed, the unsettling truth of global capitalism and neoliberal globalization is that the raison d'être of NY-LON as a 'luxury city', as a place of blessed living, is to feed off the wealth generated 'elsewhere', to provide a luxurious gentrified stage that extends from Smith Street in Cobble Hill to Broadway Market in Hackney, an urban playground ('I ♥ NY-LON'), across which a privileged few (including the world's most influential citizens) can enjoy globalization's surplus.

REFERENCES

Beaverstock, J. (2007), 'World city networks "from below": international mobility and inter-city relations in the global investment banking industry', in P.J. Taylor, B. Derudder, P. Saey and F. Witlox (eds), *Cities in Globalization: Practices, Policies and Theories*, London: Routledge, pp. 52–71.

Beaverstock, J.V., R.G. Smith and P.J. Taylor (2000), 'World city network: a new meta-geography?', *Annals of the Association of American Geographers*, **90** (1), 123–134.

Braudel, F. (1984), *The Perspective of the World*, London: Collins.

Cheng, V. (2008), 'NY-LON-KONG – Hong Kong as Asia's financial centre', transcript of speech on 27 May, available at www.hsbc.com.hk/1/2/about/speeches/08may27e (accessed 29 November 2009).

Corporation of London (2000), *London–New York Study: The Economies of Two Great Cities at the Millennium*, London: Corporation of London.

Elliott, M. (2008), 'A tale of three cities', *Time Magazine*, available at www.time.com/time/magazine/article/0,9171,1704398,00.html (accessed 29 November 2009).

Faithless (1996), 'Dirty ol' man', *Reverence*, Sony/BMG Music Entertainment.

Financial Times (2006), 'The NY-Lon debate', *Financial Times*, available at www.ft.com/cms/s/0/0461b7ee-6d3b-11db-9a4d-0000779e2340.html?nclick_check=1 (accessed 29 November 2009).

Frug, G.E. (2005), 'Power: Shanghai, New York, London', *Urban Age*, Bulletin 2, Autumn, 1–3.

Gapper, J. (2007), 'NyLon, a risky tale of twin city states', *Financial Times*, available at www.ft.com/cms/s/0/7cd019f6-8247-11dc-8a8f-0000779fd2ac.html?nclick_check=1 (accessed 29 November 2009).

Hall, P. (1966), *The World Cities*, London: World University Library.

Hall, P. (1998), *Cities in Civilization*, London: Weidenfeld & Nicolson.

Hall, P. (2003), 'Londra, metropoli riluttante', *Urbanistica*, May–August, 21–31.

Hindustan Times (2009), 'Sandstorm at Dubai, or the rebirth of Ny-Lon-Kong-Mum', *Hindustan Times*, available at www.hindustantimes.com/business-news/columnsbusiness/Sandstorm-at-Dubai-or-the-rebirth-of-Ny-Lon-Kong-Mum/Article1-481364.aspx (accessed 29 November 2009).

Jackson, C., S. Stevenson and C. Watkins (2008), 'NY-LON: does a single cross-continental office market exist?', *Journal of Real Estate Portfolio Management*, **14** (2), 79–92.

Johnson, S. (2003), 'We're the Nylons', *London Evening Standard*, 16 June, 25.

McGuire, S. and M. Chan (2000), 'The NY-LON life', *Newsweek*, 13 November, 40–47.

Pain, K. (2009), 'Londres – the place to be', *Sciences Humaines, Les Grands Dossiers*, **17**, 30–32.

Pettis, M. (2009), 'Bigger than ever: why the crisis will only help NyLon', *Newsweek*, 1 June, available at www.newsweek.com/id/199100 (accessed 1 June 2009).

Sassen, S. (1991), *The Global City: New York, London, Tokyo*, Princeton, NJ: Princeton University Press.

Smith, R.G. (2003a), 'World city actor-networks', *Progress in Human Geography*, **27** (1), 25–44.

Smith, R.G. (2003b), 'World city topologies', *Progress in Human Geography*, **27** (5), 561–582.

Smith, R.G. (2005), 'Networking the city', *Geography*, **90** (2), 172–176.

Taylor, P.J. (2003), 'Generating data for research on cities in globalization', in A. Borsdorf and C. Parnreiter (eds), *International Research on Metropolises: Milestones and Frontiers*, Wien: Verlag der Österreichischen Akademie der Wissenschaften, pp. 29–42.
Taylor, P.J. (2004), *World City Network: A Global Urban Analysis*, London: Routledge.
Witlox, F. and B. Derudder (2007), 'Air passenger flows through cities: some new evidence', in P.J. Taylor, B. Derudder, P. Saey and F. Witlox (eds), *Cities in Globalization: Practices, Policies and Theories*, London: Routledge, pp. 37–51.

39 Shanghai, Beijing and Hong Kong within a financial centre network

Karen P. Y. Lai

INTRODUCTION

Since the early 1990s, Shanghai has been earmarked by the central government as the new flagship city to connect China to an increasingly integrated world economy, with particular emphasis on finance and trade sectors (Hertz, 1998; Wu, 2000; Yatsko, 2001; Yusuf and Wu, 2002; Green, 2004). This has raised increasing concern that it may overtake Hong Kong as the pre-eminent financial centre within China, if not the wider Asian region (Wild, 1997; Ng, 2000; Ogden, 2000; *Economist*, 2002; Wong, 2007). In addition, the development of *Jinrong Jie* (Finance Street) in Beijing with its agglomeration of regulatory institutions and headquarters of state-owned banks has thrown into question Shanghai's own trajectory to become the leading international financial centre (IFC) for China (Hu, 2008; Caijing, 2009). Based on these views, Shanghai's future as China's IFC seems far from assured and Hong Kong's position appears threatened by the development of IFC capacities on the mainland. However, the reality is that Hong Kong continues to be the dominant IFC in East Asia and a global leader in international banking and finance (Meyer, 2002, 2009).

This chapter focuses on the distinctive development of Shanghai as a commercial centre, Beijing as a political centre and Hong Kong as an offshore financial centre by analysing the decision making of large foreign banks and the different functional roles of their banking operations in each city, with all three financial centres performing complementary roles within the regional banking strategies of foreign banks. It is this network that enables them to capitalize on their respective advantages and perform different roles as banking centres in China. The case of Shanghai, Beijing and Hong Kong as networked financial centres thus illustrates the importance of a relational perspective on IFC geographies that places world cities within a network of complementarity, enabling their continued participation and success in the global economy (Faulconbridge, 2004, Bassens et al., 2011).

Since the early 1980s, urban scholars have explored the interplay between globalization and urban development and the emergence of a global urban hierarchy (Friedmann, 1986; Knox and Taylor, 1995; Sassen, 2000). This hierarchy divides cities into different tiers of importance according to their degree of integration into the global economy, and their roles as basing points of capital in the spatialization and articulation of global production, finance and markets. In the past decade, there has been a shift away from examining urban functions and hierarchies to exploring networks and flows between global cities (Beaverstock et al., 2000, 2002; Sassen, 2002, Taylor, 2004). This focus on inter-city relations and systemic linkages in a network society (Castells, 2000) emphasizes complementary forms of relations and alliances and the valourization of previously unconsidered nodes and networks in the global economy (Lai, 2009). By considering how places are enmeshed within a wider context and constituted through their relations with other actors or other places (Dicken et al., 2001), a relational perspective enables us to explain inter-city relationships not on purely competitive terms but in terms of how different urban centres perform different complementary roles as part of a wider strategy of global integration.

Using this relational approach, this chapter unpacks the network processes leading to the sustained dominance of Hong Kong and the increasingly influential but distinctive roles of Shanghai and Beijing over the past two decades. The analysis is based on 68 semi-structured interviews with foreign and Chinese financial institutions, Chinese government and planning officials, and foreign chambers of commerce, in Shanghai from 2005 to 2007 and in Hong Kong in 2009. The next section focuses on the development of a dual headquarters relationship between Shanghai and Beijing as differentiated markets in financial regulation and business operations of foreign banks. The chapter then examines how different regulatory structures and financial expertise between Shanghai and Hong Kong lead to their development as complementary banking centres. Taken together, results demonstrate inter-city relations that make these three Chinese world cities interdependent and complementary IFCs, functioning as differentiated markets within the regional network of foreign banks in China.

SHANGHAI AND BEIJING: DUAL HEADQUARTERS STRATEGY

As a financial centre, Beijing's most significant advantage lies in its role as the capital of socialist China and home to key political and economic institutions, such as the central bank – the People's Bank of China (PBOC), headquarters of all major financial regulatory institutions such as the China Banking Regulatory Commission (CBRC) and State Administration of Foreign Exchange (SAFE), along with the headquarters of almost all state-owned banks and state-owned enterprises. The agglomeration of these important institutions creates an environment rich in political and economic information that is crucial to the development of a financial centre (Thrift, 1994; Clark and O'Connor, 1997; Tickell, 2000). If the head offices of transnational corporations (TNCs) and financial institutions provide a good indicator for overall assessment and ranking of IFCs and global city status, the role and future development of Shanghai as a flagship IFC for China appear to be threatened by Beijing (Zhao et al., 2004).

However, this argument overlooks the fact that Shanghai and Beijing perform qualitatively different roles within the Chinese IFC network. Chinese government officials, and foreign and Chinese financial actors, recognize a clear distinction between Beijing as a political centre and Shanghai as a business and commercial hub that is rooted in their histories and social and cultural milieux. For example, interviewees highlight a focus on relationships, information gathering and exchange and politics in Beijing that is contrasted with an orientation towards commercial opportunities and action in Shanghai. While Beijing has an established historical role as China's political capital, Shanghai has an illustrious history as a regional commercial and financial hub in the early twentieth century (Howe, 1981; Wei, 1987; Wasserstrom, 2009), and this has led to the development of distinctive business and social environments in both cities. The differentiation has led to the development of different functional roles as financial centres within a regional network, as reflected in two aspects of IFC linkages: first, the roles of both cities in financial regulation and, second, the decision of large foreign banks to locate different types of financial institutions and branch operations in each world city.

In terms of financial regulation, there is a clear distinction in their roles as IFCs with Beijing being responsible for policy making and macroplanning while Shanghai is tasked with testing new products, developing new markets and financial innovation. Laws are passed by central authorities in Beijing but are implemented and enforced by local branch offices; this lack of specificity allows for adaptation to local needs by local branches in the context of a large country with wide disparities in regional and local political economies. Over the past five years, local regulatory offices in Shanghai have been given increasing authority in their operations, with former headquarters functions being delegated to branch offices. As Shanghai continues to have the highest concentration of foreign banks and host new financial markets in futures, derivatives and foreign exchange, the allocation of more responsibilities to local regulatory offices would improve regulators' market response to changing economic conditions and increase their sensitivity to the business requirements of foreign and domestic financial institutions based in Shanghai (CBRC official: #25, 16 April 2006; local vice-director of Chinese fund management company: #26, 18 April 2006; local analyst for Chinese securities company: #34, 17 October 2006).

This interdependent relationship within a regulatory financial network is illustrated by the establishment of PBOC's second headquarters in Shanghai on 10 August 2005 (*China Daily*, 2005b). With this dual headquarters structure, the Beijing headquarters continues to run policy-oriented operations related to monetary policy, financial research, note issuance and anti-money laundering while the Shanghai headquarters focuses on market-oriented and international activities such as financial supervision and analysis, and coordinating regional financial cooperation. Functions such as bureaus for payment, liquidation and national credit profiling have been transferred to the Shanghai headquarters to improve PBOC's efficiency (*China Daily*, 2005a). The Shanghai headquarters also plays a vital role in consolidating feedback from market actors in Shanghai to influence policy changes. The two headquarters therefore perform complementary roles in regulating China's finance:

> Shanghai focuses on financial innovation, new systems; Beijing focuses on regulation, macro adjustments. The operational aspects are in Shanghai; the macro aspects, elements of control are in Beijing. Making policies, macro planning, these are in Beijing. After planning, the details are then carried out in Shanghai [. . .] so its main functions as a financial centre are different from Beijing. (Local vice-director of Chinese fund management company: #26, 18 April 2006)

The complementary roles of Shanghai and Beijing as IFCs are also reflected in the locational strategies of foreign banks in China which have placed different types of business activities in the two cities. Following from the distinctive political, economic and social environments of both cities as highlighted earlier, a distinction between Beijing as an 'administrative capital' and Shanghai as a 'business capital' (foreign manager of foreign bank: #13, 7 March 2006) has emerged in the business strategies of foreign banks in China. Banking offices in Beijing mainly serve as 'diplomatic posts' (foreign president of foreign bank: #20, 11 April 2006) tasked with maintaining relationships with Chinese corporate clients, government and regulatory officials, and lobbying on specific issues; offices in Shanghai are responsible for the bulk of business transactions and focus on the provision of financial products and services to clients. Both cities perform vital roles in the business strategies of foreign banks as they have distinctive characteristics and advantages as financial centres; their branch networks in China are structured accordingly in order to take advantage of how both cities play complementary roles in their China business as a whole:

> Shanghai has its advantages and Beijing has its advantages. Shanghai's advantage is that you are closer to the market, closer to your customers. [. . .] Our head office is set in Shanghai so our branch manager at the Beijing branch has a special mission. His role is to maintain communication with the regulators in Beijing, [. . .] to look after official relations and not bank operations. On the other hand, for banks that have head offices in Beijing, they will not neglect the Shanghai market either. They will have representative offices and branch offices in Shanghai as well. So it's not just a matter of where the head office is; there is a dual strategy. (Chinese manager of foreign bank: #11, 6 March 2006)

The different roles of Shanghai and Beijing as IFCs can also be seen in the different types of foreign banks found in these cities. For political and historical reasons, the headquarters of Chinese regulatory bodies, state-owned banks and enterprises are almost all located in Beijing. This has influenced the decision of foreign investment banks such as Goldman Sachs, BNP Paribas, Morgan Stanley and Credit Suisse to locate in Beijing in order to be closer to their target clients of Chinese SOEs in the energy, telecommunications and utilities industry and state-owned banks. Due to the politically sensitive nature of business dealings with this clientele, maintaining good relations with government and regulatory officials based in Beijing is vital to business operations; thus the preference of foreign investment banks to locate their head offices in the 'administrative capital'. On the other hand, commercial banks such as HSBC, Standard Chartered, Citibank, ING and Deutsche Bank deem it more important to locate their China headquarters in Shanghai to better serve their foreign TNC clients and maintain business networks with other commercial banks in the 'business capital'. For banks with both investment banking and commercial banking divisions, their investment banking function tends to be in Beijing while their trading, financing and asset management functions are located in Shanghai to capitalize on its global linkages and agglomeration economies with its high concentration of foreign banks. This 'dual headquarters structure' (Shanghai government official: #28, 20 April 2006) reflects the different advantages of each city's distinctive political, economic and social environments. An analysis of the rationale and decision making of financial and regulatory actors therefore reveals how Shanghai and Beijing perform qualitatively different but complementary roles as IFCs within the business networks of foreign banks in China.

SHANGHAI AND HONG KONG: REGULATORY ARBITRAGE

As of 2006, there were more than 70 foreign banks with representative or branch offices in China, with the highest concentration in Shanghai (CBRC, 2007). Although the mainland banking sector has developed rapidly over the past two decades, major differences still exist between the regulatory structures of Shanghai and Hong Kong, resulting in very different business environments. In particular, foreign banks continue to face significant business restrictions on the mainland that limit the range of financial products and services that they can offer. While many foreign banks have opened branch offices in Shanghai to participate in the large mainland Chinese market, their offices in Hong Kong continue to play important roles in facilitating business transactions that are not permissible or inefficient on the mainland.

An example of this networked relationship between the two IFCs is the strategy of foreign banks in response to foreign currency restrictions on the mainland. The renminbi (RMB) is non-convertible and regulated by strict foreign exchange controls that effectively limit the business volume of foreign banks on the mainland. Theoretically, foreign banks could mobilize funding from their head offices or branches elsewhere in the region (such as Hong Kong or Singapore) to finance their China operations and plans for business expansion, but in reality they are subject to an annual foreign currency quota which limits the amount of business they can book on the mainland. For Chinese regulators, this serves the purpose of slowing down the business expansion of foreign banks so that domestic banks have more time to learn and improve on their banking standards and practices without being threatened by foreign competition. However, foreign banks are understandably frustrated at having to turn down business opportunities in order to stay within their quotas:

> If we get a short term deal, someone comes to me and says, 'Oh, we've got a brilliant deal, we'd like you to fund us for $10 million for 3 months', and he did it today, I can't do it because I've only got about $25 million [in my quota], $20 million already spoken for, and the other bits and pieces. So you're limited in terms of the amount of business you can do. [. . .] And that's it, that's the limit. A fantastic, huge deal comes along and you can't do it. (Foreign manager of foreign bank: #41, 27 October 2006)

To cope with this annual quota, many foreign banks choose to route business deals through their Hong Kong offices instead, where there are no such currency restrictions. With its geographical proximity, experience with China-related business and financial and legal expertise, Hong Kong is well positioned to provide such offshore services. As such, even if the actual business transaction is not conducted in Shanghai due to quota restrictions, the deal is not lost as it could be serviced out of Hong Kong to serve the China market. While the Shanghai offices of foreign banks are important for accessing and developing business opportunities in the Chinese market, their Hong Kong offices still perform crucial roles in facilitating business transactions and financial flows in order to circumvent restrictions on the mainland. In this way, both IFCs play complementary and interdependent roles in the business operations and strategies of foreign banks in China.

With the non-convertibility of the RMB and foreign exchange restrictions on the mainland, many financial products and services relating to capital markets are difficult if not impossible to operate out of a mainland IFC like Shanghai. The few foreign banks interviewed that had set up dealing desks in Shanghai admitted that they were underutilized, with their main treasury business still operating out of Hong Kong. The difference in regulatory space has led to Hong Kong's specialization in treasury and offshore financial services. While Hong Kong is a prominent IFC and centre for corporate headquarters in the wider Asia-Pacific region, it has also developed a distinctive role as an international capital intermediation centre for China since the mid 1990s. Its established finance and banking sector, sound regulatory framework, legal proficiency, agglomeration of financial experts and proximity to the mainland facilitate financial and knowledge flows that contribute to economic and financial development in China as well as sustain Hong Kong's success as an IFC. These inter-city networks are demonstrated by the large number of financial products that Hong Kong has developed for the mainland market in conjunction with the authorities of the People's Republic of China (PRC), such as the listing of PRC equities on the Hong Kong Stock Exchange, development of China-related venture capital and private-loan syndications. Growing financial needs and increased economic flows between Hong Kong and the mainland have also created demand for new financial products, with RMB deposits, remittances, exchange and credit cards introduced in Hong Kong in 2004, RMB cheques in 2005 and RMB bonds in 2007. More recently, the launch of a pilot RMB Trade Settlement scheme in July 2009 allows mainland companies to settle their trade accounts in RMB (instead of a foreign currency like US dollars) with their corresponding enterprises in Hong Kong, Macau and selected Southeast Asian countries. These developments are cementing Hong Kong's role in becoming the premier RMB settlement centre outside the mainland (Chan and Chiu, 2009; People's Daily Online, 2009a, 2009b). Therefore, even as Shanghai develops its banking sector and experiments with capital markets, restrictions on the mainland combined with the established financial expertise of Hong Kong mean that the latter still performs a vital role in providing offshore financial products to complement the growing financial needs of China. This interdependence and financial networks explain Hong Kong's continued pre-eminence as an IFC alongside the rapid growth and increasing importance of other Chinese financial centres such as Shanghai and Beijing.

CONCLUSION

The expansion of the Chinese economy and changing dynamics between Chinese cities have resulted in the continued pre-eminence of Hong Kong, the growing importance of Shanghai and the specific role of Beijing within the Chinese financial centre network. Financial and regulatory actors interviewed identified distinctive roles for each city, with Beijing as a 'political centre', Shanghai as a 'business centre' and Hong Kong as an 'offshore financial centre', that stem from their different historical backgrounds, social and cultural milieux and institutional environment. This regional division of labour is reflected in the strategy of foreign banks in locating representative offices and investment banks in Beijing, branch offices and commercial banks in Shanghai, and treasury business in Hong Kong.

Within this network of functional coordination, Hong Kong remains the dominant IFC because of its established administrative capability, stability, financial and legal expertise, and unique trading opportunities with its close economic ties to the mainland and deep linkages with global financial networks. The growing financial needs of the Chinese economy and (re)establishment of financial markets on the mainland have given Shanghai new opportunities as an IFC. Shanghai has grown rapidly over the last two decades based largely on the influx of foreign commercial banks and the establishment of equity and commodity markets oriented towards the large domestic economy. However, it is unable to provide the same level of services as Hong Kong because of regulatory restrictions, lack of financial expertise and lack of global connectivity; Hong Kong still performs a vital role for global trading and for the China and Asian financial activities of TNCs (Ritter, 2008). As a financial centre, Beijing has attracted foreign investment banks and other financial operations that benefit from proximity and regular interaction in political and regulatory circles. In recent years, it has relinquished some economic functions to focus on its political and macroeconomic role such as relocating more market-based functions of the PBOC to its second headquarters in Shanghai while maintaining policy-based and macroeconomic functions in Beijing.

For foreign financial institutions, these networks and relations between IFCs have become critical to their business operations in China as they enable different financial opportunities and activities in differentiated markets. As a result each Chinese city has specific roles that are reproduced by its interdependent relationships with other IFCs, with Hong Kong remaining dominant in this network due to its regulatory and financial expertise and unique global–local networks that other Chinese IFCs are dependent upon. It is this network that enables them to capitalize on their respective advantages and perform distinctive but complementary roles as financial centres in China. The case of Shanghai, Beijing and Hong Kong, therefore, lends further credence to the value of a relational approach in world city network and IFC research for understanding inter-city dynamics and contemporary globalization.

REFERENCES

Bassens, D., B. Derudder and F. Witlox (2011), 'Setting Shari'a standards: on the role, power and spatialities of interlocking Shari'a boards in Islamic financial services', *Geoforum*, **42** (1), 94–103.

Beaverstock, J.V., M.A. Doel, P.J. Hubbard and P.J. Taylor (2002), 'Attending to the world: competition, cooperation and connectivity in the world city network', *Global Networks*, **2** (2), 111–132.

Beaverstock, J.V., R.G. Smith and P.J. Taylor (2000), 'World city network: a new metageography?', *Annals of the Association of American Geographers*, **90** (1), 123–134.

Caijing (2009), 'Shanghai's new route to financial prestige', 10 April, available at http://english.caijing.com.cn/2009-04-10/110136921.html (accessed 1 March 2010).

Castells, M. (2000), *The Rise of the Network Society*, Oxford: Blackwell, 2nd edition.

CBRC (2007), *China Banking Regulatory Commission 2006 Annual Report*, available at http://zhuanti.cbrc.gov.cn/subject/subject/nianbao/english/ywqb.pdf (accessed 16 February 2010).

Chan, M. and N. Chiu (2009), 'Yuan trade payment could reach US$2tr', *South China Morning Post*, 8 July.

China Daily (2005a), 'PBOC Shanghai headquarters launched', available at www.chinadaily.com.cn/english/doc/2005-08/10/content_467852.htm (accessed 15 March 2010).

China Daily (2005b), 'Central Bank to open 2nd HQ in Shanghai', available at www.chinadaily.com.cn/english/doc/2005-08/10/content_467716.htm (accessed 15 March 2010).

Clark, G.L. and K. O'Connor (1997), 'The informational content of financial products and the spatial structure of the global finance industry', in K.R. Cox (ed.), *Spaces of Globalisation: Reasserting the Power of the Local*, New York: Guilford Press, pp. 89–114.

Dicken, P., P. Kelly, K. Olds and H. Yeung (2001), 'Chains and networks, territories and scales: towards an analytical framework for the global economy', *Global Networks*, **1** (2), 89–112.

Economist (2002), 'Rivals more than ever: which city, Hong Kong or Shanghai, will prosper most in the new century?', 30 March, available at http://www.economist.com/node/1056970 (accessed 14 July 2011).

Faulconbridge, J. (2004), 'London and Frankfurt in Europe's evolving financial centre network', *Area*, **36** (3), 235–244.

Friedmann, J. (1986), 'The world city hypothesis', *Development and Change*, **17** (1), 69–83.

Green, S.S. (2004), *The Development of China's Stockmarket, 1984–2002: Equity Politics and Market Institutions*, London: RoutledgeCurzon.

Hertz, E. (1998), *The Trading Crowd: An Ethnography of the Shanghai Stock Market*, Cambridge: Cambridge University Press.

Howe, C. (ed.) (1981), *Shanghai: Revolution and Development in an Asian Metropolis*, Cambridge: Cambridge University Press.

Hu, Y. (2008), 'Beijing's financial dream', *Beijing Review*, 24 March, available at www.bjreview.com.cn/business/txt/2008-05/24/content_122348.htm# (accessed 1 March 2010).

Knox, P.L. and P.J. Taylor (eds) (1995), *World Cities in a World-System*, Cambridge: Cambridge University Press.

Lai, K.P.Y. (2009), 'New spatial logics in global cities research: networks, flows and new political spaces', *Geography Compass*, **3** (3), 997–1012.

Meyer, D.R. (2002), 'Hong Kong: global capital exchange', in S. Sassen (ed.), *Global Networks, Linked Cities*, New York: Routledge, pp. 249–271.

Meyer, D.R. (2009), 'Hong Kong's transformation as a financial centre', in C.R. Schenk (ed.), *Hong Kong SAR's Monetary and Exchange Rate Challenges: Historical Perspectives*, Basingstoke: Palgrave Macmillan, pp. 161–188.

Ng, I. (2000), 'A clash of two cities', *Time*, 11 December, available at www.time.com/time/asia/magazine/2000/1211/hk.shanghai.html (accessed 15 March 2010).

Ogden, J. (2000), 'Shanghai ready to roll: Shanghai seems to be returning to its former glory as a world financial centre', *South China Morning Post*, 15 August.

People's Daily Online (2009a), 'HK looking forward to becoming RMB settlement center outside Chinese mainland', 20 June, available at http://english.peopledaily.com.cn/90001/90778/90857/90859/6689924.html, (accessed 15 March 2010).

People's Daily Online (2009b), 'RMB trade settlement pilot scheme new milestone for HK: HKMA chief', 3 July, available at http://english.peopledaily.com.cn/90001/90778/90857/90861/6692333.html (accessed 15 March 2010).

Ritter, P. (2008), 'Beijing's brokers', *Time*, 17 January, available at www.time.com/time/magazine/article/0,9171,1704395,00.html, (accessed 15 March 2010).

Sassen, S. (2000), *Cities in a World Economy*, London: Pine Forge Press, 2nd edition.

Sassen, S. (ed.) (2002), *Global Networks, Linked Cities*, New York: Routledge.

Taylor, P.J. (2004), *World City Network: A Global Urban Analysis*, London: Routledge.

Thrift, N. (1994), 'On the social and cultural determinants of international financial centres: the case of the City of London', in S. Corbridge, N. Thrift and R. Martin (eds), *Money, Power and Space*, Oxford: Blackwell, pp. 327–355.

Tickell, A. (2000), 'Finance and localities', in G.L. Clark, M.P. Feldman and M.S. Gertler (eds), *The Oxford Handbook of Economic Geography*, Oxford: Oxford University Press, pp. 230–252.

Wasserstrom, J.N. (2009), *Global Shanghai, 1850–2010: A History in Fragments*, New York: Routledge.

Wei, B. (1987), *Shanghai: Crucible of Modern China*, Hong Kong: Oxford University Press.

Wild, D. (1997), 'Revels in a new rivalry', *The Banker*, **147**, 62–64.

Wong, R. (2007), 'Shanghai: another Hong Kong?', *Harvard International Review*, available at www.hir.harvard.edu/articles/1479 (accessed 15 March 2010).

Wu, F. (2000), 'The global and local dimensions of place-making: remaking Shanghai as a world city', *Urban Studies*, **37** (8), 1359–1377.

Yatsko, P. (2001), *New Shanghai: The Rocky Rebirth of China's Legendary City*, Singapore: John Wiley & Sons.

Yusuf, S. and W. Wu (2002), 'Pathways to a world city: Shanghai rising in an era of globalisation', *Urban Studies*, **39** (7), 1213–1240.

Zhao, S.X.B., Z. Li and D.T. Wang (2004), 'Determining factors of the development of a national financial centre: the case of China', *Geoforum*, **35** (5), 577–592.

40 More than an ordinary city: the role of Mexico City in global commodity chains
Christof Parnreiter

INTRODUCTION

Accounts of big cities in poorer countries are commonly informed by the megacity discourse, whose first leitmotif is that megacities have, due to the size of their populations, more problems than other cities. They are, therefore, supposed to be 'major global risk areas, . . . particularly prone to supply crisis, social disorganization, political conflicts, and natural disasters' (Megacity Task Force, International Geographical Union, 2010). Mike Davis (2006, p. 138) simply contends that the poor megacities are 'stinking mountains of shit'.

Yet such assessments are problematic because authors expounding on the problems of megacities provide neither evidence nor compelling theoretical arguments for their claim that bigger cities face more or more serious problems than smaller ones. In fact, this notion is empirically difficult to sustain. Everybody knows, for example, that the megacity Mexico City does in many, if not all, aspects better than the non-megacity Ciudad Juárez on the Mexico–U.S. border, while it is equally recognized that the many disparities between the two megacities of Mexico City and New York do not stem from the difference in population size. Regarding the theoretical grounding of the claim that 'mass matters' (IGU Megacity Taskforce), it is striking that the mainstream literature on megacities has not seriously engaged either with Simmel's stimulating thinking that size makes a difference to the mental life of city dwellers (Simmel 2006 [1903]) nor with Jacobs' (1970) contention that cities are economically vibrant because of the necessity to resolve the many problems resulting from size and density. It remains, thus, unassessed whether crossing a certain quantitative threshold makes any qualitative difference in urban development or city life. I will therefore stick to the purely quantitative definition of a megacity given by the United Nations (2008), which establishes that megacities have at least 10 million inhabitants.

The second leitmotif of the megacity discourse is that big cities in poorer countries are of no relevance for the functioning of the world economy. At best, they are conceived as centres of national production (quite often they are, however, also dismissed as being unproductive parasites of national development). This allegation is commonly backed by the notion that megacities in poorer countries have no or only few headquarters of the world's biggest companies, or that they are barely integrated into global financial markets. From this – correct – observation it is deduced that megacities in poorer countries constitute a discrete type of city, analytically distinct from the category of global cities (Kraas, 2007, p. 876f). Yet a closer empirical analysis refutes this conclusion. According to the studies of the GaWC group, 18 of the world's 20 megacities (according to the UN definition) quality as world cities. The only exceptions are Dhaka and Osaka-Kobe – one poor and one rich megacity (GaWC, 2008).

Ironically, the notion of global economic insignificance of cities in poorer countries is (unwittingly) reproduced by postcolonial urban studies. Robinson (2006, p. 98f), for example, argues that '[m]illions of people and hundreds of cities are dropped off the map of much research in urban studies' because global city research focuses on producer services while ignoring the various ways in which cities in poorer countries can be connected to the world economy. It is, however, a misinterpretation to suggest that cities which are out of the game of global city-ness are 'excluded from global capitalism' (ibid., p. 102). On the contrary, Sassen's (1991) conceptualization of global cities as places wherefrom producer services are provided to manage and to control the world economy logically implies that the world city network is built upon ramifications that link global cities to the countless non-global, yet fully globalized cities where production for global markets is carried out. Low paid manufacturing work supplied in Ciudad Juárez is as vital to the reproduction of global capitalism as is the provision of high paid producer services. Global cities are therefore not only mutually constituted, as stressed by Taylor (2004), but also by their connections to Robinson's 'ordinary cities' (Parnreiter, 2003, 2010).

While it is true that most cities around the world are no direct subject for global city studies, this 'dropping off' results from uneven development itself. Core activities, which are necessary for running and controlling global commodity chains, are by definition located in the centres of the world economy, not in its peripheries. Thus the proposed shift of attention away from producer services to 'how "global" economic processes affect all cities' (Robinson, 2006, p. 102) would obscure the fact that there are places wherefrom rule-makers operate, and places where most, if not all, people are confined to be rule-keepers. Put differently: it is the focus on producer services that allows grasping the fundamental difference between the role of cities in *engendering* globalization and the impacts of globalization on cities. It is this difference that forms the core of reasoning in global city research.

Despite the fact that most cities are not direct subjects for global city studies, this research is much more inclusive than its opponents suggest, because it helps us to comprehend the multiple hinges between the relatively few global headquarters cities and the innumerable cities where production for the world market is carried out. Mexico City is an excellent example to counter the outdated notion of the megacity discourse that big cities in poorer countries are insignificant to the functioning of the world economy. Though the city had only three Fortune 500 corporations in 2009, accounting for 0.7 per cent of the revenues of the Global 500, and though its stock exchange comprised just 0.8 per cent of the worldwide market capitalization (Fortune 500, 2009; WFE, 2010), the city is a key place in the locational strategies of producer service firms. It is characterized as an alpha-world city – 'very important world cities that link major economic regions and states into the world economy' (GaWC, 2008). To back this claim, in what follows I provide both quantitative and qualitative information on global city formation in Mexico City, and I discuss the city's place in the geography of global economic governance. Finally, I sketch out the emergent new corporate geography within Mexico City.

GLOBAL CITY FORMATION IN MEXICO CITY

Since the key function of a global city is to articulate economic activities at various geographical scales into the world economy, the examination of global city formation in Mexico has to start with a brief outline of what is being articulated. Commodity chains in Mexico have gone through a rapid course of globalization since the end of import-substituting industrialization (ISI) in the early 1980s. While the yearly exports of goods and services have grown 9-fold (1980/85–2003/08; measured in current $US), imports have increased 12-fold (World Bank, 2009). An even more significant indicator for the globalization of economic activities is the profound change in the composition of the exports. Manufacturing now amounts to 81 per cent of exports (2007–09, up from 26 per cent [1980–83]), while the share of oil has decreased to 16 per cent (Banco de México, 2010). This reveals a changing integration of firms and cities in Mexico into global commodity chains, transforming them into production platforms designed chiefly to serve the US market. These export platforms were built up through a massive inflow of foreign direct investment, whose yearly inflows have grown ten-fold (1980/85–2003/08) (UNCTAD, 2010).

My central claim is that we should speak of global city formation in Mexico City, because this growing globalization of economic activities is partly organized from there. Empirical support for this contention comes, first, from data on the rise of the producer service sector. After the collapse of ISI, Mexico City's economy underwent a structural transformation, which was characterized a) by a partial deindustrialization (the share of manufacturing in Gross Regional Product (GRP) dropped from 24 to 19 per cent, while the city's participation in national industrial production fell from 47 to 17 per cent [1980–2003]), and b) by a strong rise of producer services. In 2003, they accounted for more than a third of Mexico City's GRP, with financial services alone comprising 25 per cent. As a consequence, Mexico City's share in the national production of producer services rose to 76 per cent (Sobrino, 2000; INEGI, 2004). This rise of producer services denotes that Mexico City has changed from a predominantly national production centre, catering to and integrating the domestic market, to a hinge between economic activities carried out in Mexico and the world market (Parnreiter, 2010).

My claim that the growing globalization of economic activities in Mexico is partly organized from Mexico City is also supported by data that show an increasing centralization of the headquarters of Mexico's biggest companies. While in 1993, the year before NAFTA was enacted, 255 of the Top 500 companies in Mexico were headquartered in Mexico City, 13 years later the number had risen to 352. Thus today the centralization of head offices is higher than in the time of ISI. It is remarkable that the bigger a corporation is and the more global links it has (in terms of foreign ownership and exports), the stronger the concentration of headquarters (Expansión, various years).

Yet it is neither the concentration of headquarters nor the growth of the producer service sector *per se* that makes a global city. In order to scrutinize the notion that global cities are nodes where commodity chains at the local, regional, national and global scale are articulated through the provision of producer services, the demand for these services must be confirmed. This can be done with an input–output analysis of the Mexican economy, which shows that in 2003 60 per cent of the producer services went to three strongly globalized economic sectors: the wholesale and retail trade (23 per cent),

Table 40.1 Share in value-adding activities in automotive industries, computer and electronic industries, and in producer services (selected municipios, 2003, %)

District	Share of value added in automotive industry	Share of value added in producer services	District	Share of value added in computer and electronic industries	Share of value added in producer services
Cuautlancingo	15.8	0.1	Juárez	26.2	0.6
Silao	11.5	0.0	Tijuana	14.8	0.5
Juárez	7.5	0.6	Mexicali	7.1	0.3
Ramos Arizpe	5.8	0.0	Aguascalientes	6.3	0.2
Toluca	5.3	0.2	El Salto	5.7	0.0
Nuevo Casas Grandes	4.0	0.0	Reynosa	5.6	0.3

Source: own calculations, based on INEGI (2004)

manufacturing (19 per cent) and the producer service sector itself (18 per cent) (INEGI, 2003). Though this input–output analysis cannot be broken down on a regional level, information on the strong geographical concentration of value-adding activities in producer services suggests, along with information provided in Table 40.1, that there are substantial flows of producer services from Mexico City to other parts of the country. Table 40.1 shows that the cities where most export manufacturing is carried out are not at all equipped to *manage* this production. The 11 *municipios* (districts), where half of the added value in the automotive industry and two-thirds of the added value in the computer and electronic industries come from, have together only 2 per cent of all added value in producer services. This suggests that the need to service export production in these cities is, at least partly, satisfied by producer services coming from Mexico City.

The demand for producer services by companies with global reach is also confirmed by an analysis of the client structure of producer service firms in Mexico City (Parnreiter, 2010). In auditing, for example, 91 per cent of the publicly traded companies (220 of the 300 biggest firms in Mexico) get their services from the Mexico City office of one of the 'Big Four' global accountancy firms (Deloitte, Ernst & Young, KPMG, PricewaterhouseCoopers). Among the Top 100 firms, which are listed at the stock exchange, only three have an auditor other than one of the 'Big Four'. Thus a considerable number of commodity chains obtain at least one producer service from Mexico City. The question as to whether Mexico City is a node from where producer services are fed into global production networks can be answered: for auditing this is clearly the case.

The same holds true for legal services. First, the 'Big Four' accountancy firms also offer legal services. Deloitte, for example, sells legal and tax services to 66 of the 100 biggest firms in Mexico. Second, some of the world's biggest law firms have offices in Mexico City, from where they service mainly foreign companies and Mexican firms with global operations. For instance, about 95 per cent of clients of the Mexico City office of Baker & McKenzie, the world's fourth biggest law firm (2008), have global reach. Foreign companies competing for the Mexican market make the biggest sub-group, followed by national firms catering to the world market and transnational corporations carrying out export production in Mexico. Comparably, the Mexico City office of Holland & Knight, worldwide the 51st biggest law firm, has worked for some of the most important firms in the country (e.g. the state-owned oil company PEMEX, the Grupo Financiero BBVA-Bancomer and the conglomerate Grupo Carso, which produces a range of commodities from cigars to autoparts). For law firms, one important aspect of servicing global operations of firms is the legal management of FDI. This includes decisions on the form of business organization of the investing company and its internal rules; adapting to the regulatory frameworks that vary across economic sectors and across the twelve free trade agreements Mexico has signed; making decisions on the labour union, with which the company is going to sign the collective bargaining agreement; buying or leasing a plant or a piece of property; dealing with tax issues, royalties and property rights; and attending to migration issues for professionals from the parent company.

In sum, the input–output analysis and the information on the clients of accountancy and law firms confirm links between Mexico City's producer service sector and companies that operate within global commodity chains that either emanate in Mexico (as, for example, in the case of petroleum), run through the country (e.g. automotive industry) or end there (as the products sold in Wal-Mart). This information constitutes, in addition to the expansion of the producer service sector and the increasing centralization of headquarters, the third empirical buttress for my claim that the growing globalization of economic activities in Mexico is, at least partly, organized from Mexico City. The city is thus *on* the map of both world cities and global commodity chains, making it one of those nodes where 'specialized services needed by complex organizations for running a spatially dispersed network of factories, offices, and service outlets' (Sassen, 1991, p. 5) are supplied.

MEXICO CITY IN THE GEOGRAPHY OF ECONOMIC GOVERNANCE

Underscoring that producer services are key activities for 'the production of management and control operations' (Sassen, 1991, p. 14), Sassen depicts global cities both as places for the management *and* the command of the world economy. Yet, it does not become clear how the provision of services for the running of global production networks translates into the capacity to govern them. This question is particularly relevant as regards global cities in non-core countries, which have a sizeable producer service sector but which are normally not considered to host decision-making capacities.

Contrary to this notion, my research indicates that the offices of producer service firms in Mexico City are places wherefrom some form of governance is exercised (Parnreiter, 2010). Interviewed auditors and lawyers acknowledged, for instance, that producer service firms are progressively more involved in influencing their clients' decision-making processes (though they frequently rejected this notion for the specific service they supply). As one lawyer at a global law firm put it: 'The way to make a deal, to take decisions, if it is not coming from the lawyer's office, I do believe that the one who makes the strategy, it's the partners of the law firm.' Frequently mentioned examples of this pre-structuring of decisions refer to real estate, tax and labour law issues. In addition, business lawyers quite often participate in the Board of Directors of big firms, which makes them part of their administration and allows them to influence the decision-making process. Thus producer service firms in Mexico City do handle issues which have an impact on how resources are allocated (or withdrawn) from the 'Mexican segment' of a global commodity chain. Supplying 'activities that need to be done for global firms to execute their operations without losing sight of the corporation's aims' (Sassen, 2010, p. 158), professionals in Mexico City exercise governance for commodity chains: 'It is a kind of embedded governance – embedded in the lawyering, the accounting and the investment choices of the firm' (ibid.).

Regarding the scope of global city functions in Mexico City, evidence suggests, first, that their geographical reach is basically confined to Mexico. The main pivot for the rest of Latin America is, according to Taylor (2000), Miami (compare also the GaWC Atlas of Hinterworlds [GaWC, 2010]). Second, the depth of influence that producer service firms in Mexico City have on the governance of production networks depends both on sector- and on firm-specific factors. Though the global organization of producer service firms tends to be rather flat, interviews in Mexico City also evoke that there is a specific hierarchy in doing business, which stems from the client's geography. What in legal, accountancy and real estate services defines the position of the Mexican office vis-à-vis other offices is the place where a client firm has its headquarters, because it is always the partner of the service firm with direct contact to the client who is in command. As one professional in a global accountancy firm in Mexico City stated: 'My global head is always the one from the country from where my client comes. . . . There is a lead partner who sends his instructions to all over the world' (quoted in Parnreiter, 2010, p. 47).

This structure helps us to understand the role and reach of Mexico City as a global city. The organizational model of the service firms' global networks implies that there is a chain of command: the 'big' strategies are made by the lead partners, who usually are located in an office close to the client firms. Because of this analogy between the geographies of lead partners and of headquarters of big companies, and because there are much fewer firms with origins in Mexico that compete successfully on the world market than foreign firms in Mexico, the Mexico City office of producer service firms will not often be in command. Put simply, the economic world order poses serious limitations to the development of far-reaching governance functions in Mexico City.

THE SPACES OF GLOBAL CITY FORMATION

The spread of high-rise office complexes is amongst the most visible imprints of globalization on cities. In Mexico City (like in many other cities), this transformation of the urban landscape is closely linked to global city formation (Parnreiter, 2009). Because of a construction boom, the supply in office space grew by 65 per cent between 1997 and 2007, totalling 5.6 million square metres in 2007 (data draw on reports of CB Richard Ellis, Colliers International, Cushman & Wakefield and Jones Lang LaSalle). Both the strong increase in market transactions and a very low vacancy rate (which amounted to 6 per cent in 2008 and which has not risen since) suggest that this increase of office space is demand driven.

In addition to the expansion, the inventory changed in two important ways. First, there is a marked upgrading of the supply – in the last decade, four-fifths of construction activity contributed to the first-class office market. Class A+ office space doubled its share in the total inventory, making up 30 per cent in 2008. Secondly, the geography of office space also changed considerably. The areas that during ISI constituted the CBD (the historical centre and its extension to the west, Paseo de la Reforma; Polanco; Insurgentes Sur and its neighbouring districts) lost importance, while new business areas in the west and south of the city were built (Lomas Palmas, Bosques de las Lomas, Santa Fe, Periférico Sur). These changes in the corporate geography are most visible if the focus is on prime office space, the fastest-growing segment of the market. By 2007, the share of the traditional CBD had fallen to a quarter of Class A+ office space, while Santa Fe alone has emerged as *the* dominant area of prime office space. There, more than 70 per cent of all office space belongs to the Class A+ segment, while 31 per cent of the city's inventory in A+ office space has been built in Santa Fe (see Figure 40.1).

The relationships between the production of new urban spaces and the processes of global city formation are striking. It has been the massive influx of foreign firms since the mid 1990s, the globalization of some Mexican companies, and the enormous growth of the advanced producer sector that have spurred *and* changed demand for prime office space. Since the enactment of NAFTA, the areas composing the new CBD have increased their share of major offices in Mexico City from 19 to 45 per cent (2007). Behind this increase lies a specific geography of the locations of the headquarters: Figure 40.1 reveals that foreign-owned and producer service firms are located mainly in the areas where most prime office space has been built. While the old CBD has only 30 per cent of the sales of the foreign-owned firms figuring in the list of Top 500 companies, the new CBD accounts for 47 per cent. In a similar vein, FIRE-sector firms in the new CBD make up 52 per cent of sales of the producer service firms, while the traditional CBD accounts for only 47 per cent. The outstanding submarket within the new CBD is Santa Fe, where firms are located that account for a third of the sales of foreign-owned companies and for 36 per cent of the sales of FIRE-sector firms. There is thus a spatially delimitable 'global city zone', where the cross-border networks of world cities and of commodity chains overlap.

CONCLUSION

The analysis presented offers comprehensive evidence of global city formation in a big city in a poorer country. The strong expansion and concentration of the producer service sector in Mexico City, the equally increasing centralization of the headquarters of Mexico's biggest companies, and the flows of auditing, legal and other producer services from firms in Mexico City to companies operating in the Mexican segments of global commodity chains confirm that the growing globalization of economic activities in Mexico is, at least partly, organized from Mexico City. Hence the city is changing from a national production centre, which integrated the domestic market, to a hinge between economic activities carried out in Mexico and the world market.

My research also proves that global city functions of Mexico City are not confined to supply services which are necessary for the smooth functioning of the world economy. Rather, producer service firms in Mexico City influence their clients' decisions in various

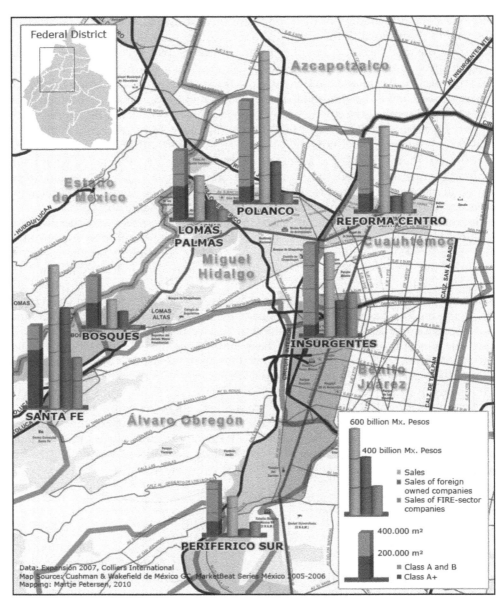

Source: author

Figure 40.1 Location of Mexico's largest companies and office markets in Mexico City

ways, and that is why Mexico City is a node wherefrom governance for global commodity chains is exercised. Yet the evidence also suggests that the scope of this governance is limited to secondary issues and, geographically, to economic activities in Mexico. Finally, global city formation in Mexico City has led to a massive restructuring of the urban landscape. In order to meet the demand of global (producer) firms for prime office space, a new CBD has been built in western parts of the city. In this delimitable 'global city zone', the intersections between the world city network and global commodity chains are located.

In sum, the research presented shows that Mexico City is a place wherefrom globalization is produced as well as that 'the urban' (e.g. the economy, the built environment) is strongly impacted by the processes of global city formation. The global city perspective thus proves to be more fertile for the study of big cities in poorer countries than the megacity discourse, because it relates 'internal' transformations to the 'external' role in the management and control of global commodity chains. The global city perspective is also better suited than postcolonial urban studies, because in underscoring the global city functions located in Mexico City it breaks with the all too simple divide into 'Northern' and 'Southern' cities, with the latter being 'victims' of uneven globalization.

REFERENCES

Banco de México (2010), 'Balanza de pagos', available at www.banxico.org.mx (accessed 28 January 2010).
Davis, M. (2006), *Planet of Slums*, London: Verso.
Expansión (various years), *Las 500 empresas más importantes de México*, México D.F.: Expansión.
Fortune 500 (2009), 'Global 500. Our annual ranking of the world's largest corporations', available at http://money.cnn.com/magazines/fortune/global500/2009/full_list/ (accessed 28 January 2010).
GaWC (Globalization and World Cities Research Network) (2008), 'The world according to GaWC 2008', available at www.lboro.ac.uk/gawc/world2008.html (accessed 28 January 2010).
GaWC (Globalization and World Cities Research Network) (2010), 'GaWC Atlas of Hinterworlds', available at www.lboro.ac.uk/gawc/visual/hwatlas.html (accessed 28 January 2010).
INEGI (2003), 'Matriz de Insumo-Producto de México para el año 2003', available at www.inegi.org.mx/est/contenidos/espanol/proyectos/scnm/mip03/default.asp?c=14040 (accessed 28 January 2010).
INEGI (2004), *Censos Económicos 2004*, Aguascalientes: Instituto Nacional de Estadísticas, Geografía e Informatica.
Jacobs, J. (1970), *The Economy of Cities*, New York: Vintage Books.
Kraas, F. (2007), 'Megastädte', in H. Gebhardt, R. Glaser, U. Radtke and P. Reuber (eds), *Geographie: Physische Geographie und Humangeographie*, München: Elsevier, pp. 876–880.
Megacity Task Force, International Geographical Union (2010), available at www.megacities.uni-koeln.de/ (accessed 28 January 2010).
Parnreiter, C. (2003),'Global city formation in Latin America: socioeconomic and spatial transformations in Mexico City and Santiago de Chile', *GaWC Research Bulletin*, 103, available at www.lboro.ac.uk/gawc/rb/rb103.html (accessed 28 January 2010).
Parnreiter, C. (2009),'Global-City-Formation, Immobilienwirtschaft und Transnationalisierung. Das Beispiel Mexico City', *Zeitschrift für Wirtschaftsgeographie*, **53** (3), 138–155.
Parnreiter, C. (2010),'Global cities in global commodity chains: exploring the role of Mexico City in the geography of global economic governance', *Global Networks*, **10** (1), 35–53.
Robinson, J. (2006), *Ordinary Cities: Between Modernity and Development*, London: Routledge.
Sassen, S. (1991), *The Global City: New York, London, Tokyo*, Princeton, NJ: Princeton University Press.
Sassen, S. (2010), 'Global inter-city networks and commodity chains: any intersections?', *Global Networks*, **10** (1), 150–163.
Simmel, G. (2006 [1903]), *Die Großstädte und das Geistesleben*, Frankfurt/Main: Suhrkamp.
Sobrino, J. (2000), 'Participación económica en el siglo XX.', in G. Garza (ed.), *La Ciudad de México en el fin del segundo milenio*, México D.F.: El Colegio de México, pp. 162–169.
Taylor, P.J. (2000), 'World cities and territorial states under conditions of contemporary globalization', *Political Geography*, **19** (1), 5–32.
Taylor, P.J. (2004), *World City Network: A Global Urban Analysis*, London: Routledge.
United Nations (2008), *World Urbanization Prospects: The 2007 Revision. Highlights*, New York: United Nations.

UNCTAD (United Nations Conference on Trade and Development) (2010), 'Foreign direct investment database', available at www.unctad.org (accessed 28 January 2010).
WFE (World Federation of Exchanges) (2010), 'Domestic market capitalization', available at www.world-exchanges.org/ (accessed 28 January 2010).
World Bank (2009), 'World development indicators online', available at www.worldbank.org (accessed 28 January 2010).

41 Mumbai as a global city: a theoretical essay
Jan Nijman

Mumbai is often viewed as South Asia's main global city. It is now included in most general representations of global urban networks and it is sometimes considered emblematic of world cities in the 'south'. Mumbai is a fascinating city in its own right, the kind of place that never fails to intrigue and that draws attention in myriad ways. It is, following the title of Suketu Mehta's (2004) book, a 'maximum city'. But Mumbai is also 'good to think'. It invokes comparison; it demands a place in a conceptual sense, vis-à-vis other cities. Upon closer inspection, Mumbai provokes essential questions about the notion of world cities, urban networks, the scale or reach of world city functions, geographic context, comparative urbanism and the history of globalization.

This chapter engages six critical issues in the treatment of Mumbai as a global city. The first concerns Mumbai's ranking in world city schemes. The second pertains to the significance of the global as distinct from local or regional effects in Mumbai's development. The third is about the delineation of Mumbai's hinterland. Fourth, in the inevitable comparing of Mumbai with other global cities we must consider historical trajectories and path dependency. Where does Mumbai fit? Fifth, matters of social stratification and polarization have been integral to world city debates ever since Friedmann's original hypothesis, but Mumbai presents a case that is fundamentally at odds with the situation in North American or European cities. Finally, it is important to say a few words about the 'world city trap': the notion of world city has a powerful policy appeal and raises the question of whether a place such as Mumbai can realistically aspire to be like London or Shanghai.

MUMBAI'S WORLD CITY STATUS

During a lecture at the Indian Institute for Technology in Mumbai, in 2000, this author was confronted with a question from the audience as to 'where Mumbai ranks among world cities'. This was just over a decade ago, and the city hardly figured in any of the existing studies at that point. I remember trying to bring the news gently but to no avail. The audience was taken aback by what they considered a striking lack of appreciation by world city scholars of Mumbai's 'obvious' significance as the economic capital of a country with nearly one-sixth of humanity. While I was not ready to submit to the biases of local city boosters, I vividly remember feeling compelled to rethink the validity of world city theory. As the audience would have it, surely something was wrong with it.

According to a wide range of measures, Mumbai is the leading city in India's urban hierarchy. For example, the city boasts the largest airport; it houses the biggest stock exchange; it is home to the headquarters of the Reserve Bank of India, the State Bank of India, and India's Western and Central Railway Zones; it has the largest share of bank deposits and income tax revenues; and Mumbai has the largest share of telephone and telex connections.

Perhaps most importantly, Mumbai is the country's main articulation with the global economy and the most globally connected city in India. For example, its airport has more international passengers than any other in India; the seaport registers more international cargo than any other in the nation; Mumbai houses more transnational companies than any other city; it has the largest share of foreign collaborations (joint ventures); it has the largest share of foreign direct investment as well as the largest share of international trade and customs duties; and it has more internet connections than any other city in India (Nijman, 2007, pp. 238–239).

But how important is Mumbai on the global scene, from a global perspective? Until recently, the city rarely showed up in rankings of any sort. It had (and still has) few headquarters of major transnational corporations and it seemed remote from leading centres such as New York and London. Things have started to shift since the early 1990s, when unprecedented liberalization measures facilitated the globalization of the Indian economy; gradually at first and at a faster pace in more recent years. The exposure of the national economy to forces of globalization was and still is highly uneven, and fragmentary, but there can be little doubt about the effects on Mumbai in particular.

The last 15 years or so have witnessed accelerating foreign investment in Mumbai and a rapid increase in the presence of transnational corporations, especially in the sphere of finance and producer services. This is vital because it is precisely the concentration of such activity that characterizes contemporary 'global cities' (Taylor et al., 2010). Empirical research on global urban networks shows that in the last decade Mumbai has strengthened its position in these sectors, especially in the area of management consulting (Grant and Nijman, 2002; Hanssens et al., 2011).

Mumbai's greater visibility can be seen as an integral part of the rise of some emerging markets. Other cities that have come to the fore during the past decade include São Paulo, Moscow, Buenos Aires, Shanghai and Beijing. The ascent of China and India in the global economy is unmistakable and Hong Kong seems to have taken the place of Tokyo in the triad that dominates the world city hierarchy, along with New York and London. In one recent comprehensive study, Mumbai was categorized in the third tier of the world city system along with cities such as Madrid, Seoul and Kuala Lumpur (Taylor et al., 2010).

This is still a debatable ranking if one considers the enormous reach of Mumbai as the most dominant city in all of South Asia – there may not be another city in the world that dominates such an enormous region. The reason for this 'under-valuation' is, of course, the emphasis in world city network analysis on *international* linkages and the relative disregard for the national role of some cities. In big countries, this can cause a notable bias. If Chicago is considered undervalued in this approach because of its predominantly domestic reach (ibid.), the bias towards Mumbai is considerably greater still. For all the efforts to sever world city research from state-centric thinking, it is held prisoner to it through the emphasis on inter-*national* connections.

THE SIGNIFICANCE OF THE GLOBAL IN MUMBAI

The theoretical premise is that a city's place in the global urban network is reflected in, and conditioned by, its internal socio-spatial structure. This means that our understanding of the space-economy of a particular city will hinge at least in part on an appreciation of that city's global functions. But it is possible that a city holds a significant position in the global system while being so large, so complex and so diverse that on the whole the global explains only a small part of its urban landscape. If one were to land in a randomly chosen spot on the ground in Greater Mumbai, there would likely be little evidence of global articulations in the surrounding landscape and globalization might be furthest from the mind of the local population – even in this most global of Indian cities.

Global articulations are highly concentrated in specific areas. Mumbai's corporate geography displays separate clusters of business activity with varying degrees of global engagement. South Mumbai, and especially the area around Nariman Point, has been dubbed the 'global CBD' (with mainly finance and producer services) as distinct from other, less internationally oriented, CBDs (Grant and Nijman, 2002). Particular upscale residential areas such as Cumbala Hill (in the south, as well) cater to the expat community and house most consular offices. But most urban areas, including those buzzing with economic activity, will show few signs of engaging the global.

It is hard to say, then, to what extent global city functions explain class dynamics, trends in the labour market, real estate developments, consumption patterns, economic restructuring or changes in the policy and political arena. Certainly, we can pinpoint specific global effects, such as the western consumption styles of the new urban middle class, but it remains quite unclear how much of the emergence of a new middle class itself is due to globalization as distinct from the domestic effects of liberalization policies.

At the same time, we must be careful not to *under*estimate the global: there is a great deal of international business activity, in a range of locations across Greater Mumbai, that does not show up in most empirical studies with an empirical focus on global networks. The reason is, of course, that most of those studies are based on a selection of large (often the very largest) global companies. Most of those are typically based in 'rich' countries and typically their main activities are in other highly developed regions of the global economy. If, instead, one studies Mumbai's role in the global network from the ground up, beginning with linkages that extend *from Mumbai*, we discover myriad connections of a great many smaller companies with international reach. The focus on large global companies, in many global network studies, is accompanied by an inevitable bias towards the most developed economies. Indeed, one could argue that the case of Mumbai underscores a tenacious underlying problem in world city research: the empirical unit of analysis is often the firm, not the city.

HINTERLAND AND EMBEDDEDNESS

Another theoretical assumption that is contentious in the case of Mumbai concerns the hinterland of world cities. The idea is that world cities are related more to other important nodes in the global network than to their immediate topographic surroundings. Thus London is more connected to Paris than to Leicester, for example. This may be debatable even in the example at hand and at least it would require specification of the nature of (comparing of) linkages that obviously differ among such very different pairs. But in the case of Mumbai and its hinterland, the question is particularly problematic.

In essence, the issue revolves around the geographic or regional embeddedness of Mumbai's space-economy. While Mumbai's particular world city functions (finance and producer services) involve connections to faraway places, most of the economy is linked to closer environs. There is no doubt that Greater Mumbai is tightly linked to the newly urbanized mainland across the Creek (Navi Mumbai, Vashi) and at a larger scale to the western industrialized region of Maharashtra that includes the cities of Pune and Nashik. These cities have recently been linked by a new highway system. The state government refers to the region as Maharashtra's 'Golden Triangle' (Maharashtra Economic Development Council, 2002).

It is the city's dominant *national* role, as indicated above, that firmly places it in the Indian and South Asian realm. Mumbai is an immigration centre at the national scale. Half of the urban peninsula's population of 12 million is estimated to live in slums and many of them are recent immigrants. It is well known that many urban slum communities hail from particular districts across the country and that their social fabric reflects their geographic origins (Nijman, 2010).

Hence Mumbai reveals effectively how questions of hinterland or more generally about geographic 'context' are a matter of scale. Mumbai has extremely important external economic linkages but at a wide range of scales from the regional to the national to the global. And it is embedded in each of these networks, in each of these 'hinterlands'.

The popular notion of the 'global south' is much harder to accommodate, as far as Mumbai is concerned. The scope and nature of the city's international networks do not suggest a pattern that might warrant such a label. Mumbai's linkages basically move between the South Asian and global levels without settling into any type of system that could be defined as a 'global south'. The historical grounds for such a category are shaky as well. The 'south' is much too broad a conceptual category, lumping together cities and regions with highly different colonial and, especially, post-colonial experiences. If we would have difficulty with the idea of a 'global north' (and we evidently do, as that term has not acquired currency anywhere), the notion of the 'global south', too, should be discarded.

PATH DEPENDENCY

History matters. The urban nodes in the global economic system vary greatly in their particular roles. The importance of any particular node and the nature of its position cannot be understood without due attention to historical origins. The current positions of London and New York and their actual global reach are predicated on their histories of hegemony. The present position of Hong Kong, similarly, is explained in 19th and 20th century developments; the city's separation from and rejoining of China, in particular.

World cities may be defined primarily in terms of their economic functions but their emergence is almost always a matter of political economy and, therefore, of political geography and political history. Mumbai has gone through four historical phases: the indigenous pre-colonial phase during which it had virtually only a local significance (a series of fishing villages without a major political role); the colonial/industrial phase during which it took on important international functions serving the British Empire; the national phase, immediately after Independence, that witnessed a profound reorientation in which Bombay became the main economic centre of a relatively sheltered national economy; and the current global phase in which the city has returned to the global stage but with much more diversified and less subservient connections. Each of these phases sets the stage for the next by way of institutional, cultural, political and economic legacies. And each of these phases is stored in the built environment of the city or, better put, each phase produces an urban space on top of that which is left behind by history (Nijman, 2007).

Today's world city functions must be accommodated in urban space. Cities can be remade, but only in the confines of their unavoidable continuities (Beauregard and Haila, 2000). Hence there are historical reasons for the diversity of roles among present-day world cities. To treat or rank cities one-dimensionally in terms of some singular measure of importance conceals more than it reveals. History would not allow such homogeneity. And nor would the global urban system itself. The nodes in the urban system compete with each other, in some ways, for capital and influence. But at the same time they exist by virtue of their interrelationships and complementarity (Taylor et al., 2010; Ward, 2010). There is, one could say, a division of labour among world cities that is regional and/or functional. That is the other reason why so-called 'convergence' among the world's major cities remains a long shot (Cohen, 1996).

If globalization is understood simply as a process of space–time compression, then the city bears clear marks of globalization's precursors, of a time at which Mumbai became the main node in a network that spanned South Asia from the mid 19th century. From a historical perspective, global connections are far from new to this city but 'Globalization I' was mainly a South Asian affair. Millions of immigrants from widely varying backgrounds came to Bombay and helped to create one of the world's most cosmopolitan cities, be it in a colonial context. It was reflected in residential patterns, the proliferation of languages spoken, architecture (from Victorian to Art Deco) and, of course, business connections. With Independence came a near half-century intermezzo, as far as exposure to the global economy was concerned. 'Globalization II' arrived in the early 1990s. In part it is attributed to the neoliberal ideological tide reaching the shores of South Asia. It was part of a global movement, to be sure, but the turn in India and in Mumbai was especially sharp. In the past two decades, the city has changed profoundly, along with its role in the global urban system.

SOCIAL POLARIZATION

The final theoretical premise in world city theory that deserves some attention in this chapter concerns the idea that world cities are characterized by trends of social and spatial polarization. This argument is mainly based in the experience of US cities (and to a lesser extent in that of Western European cities) that witnessed deindustrialization and an erosion of the middle classes from the 1960s to the 1980s. The consequences, in terms of job losses, were particularly painful to ethnic minorities and recent immigrants but also affected large numbers of other former middle class or lower middle class wage earners. The period since the 1980s witnessed an economic revival as the new information economy took its place. But this restructuring did not restore the middle class. Instead, the new urban economy and labour market are characterized by bi-modal income distributions separating highly educated high income earners (symbolic analysts, to use Robert Reich's (1992) phrase) from low educated low income service personnel. The corresponding trends of socio-economic polarization are often expressed spatially, in new kinds and more conspicuous forms of residential segregation, as in the proliferation of gated communities.

Contrary to western cities, urban India is said to have witnessed the emergence of a 'new middle class', some of it attributed to outsourcing and the relocation of jobs from the US and Western Europe to India. Could it be that different cities in the global urban system experience such opposite trends? A closer look at Mumbai's new middle class gives reason to pause. In actuality, Mumbai experienced similar developments in the past two decades to cities in the west – but the context, the existing socio-economic structure, was so different that the mediated result of these developments, too, has turned out to be quite different from that in western cities.

Mumbai did witness deindustrialization. From the 1970s to the early 1990s, the city's famous textile industry was decimated, causing enormous socio-economic disruption (D'Monte, 2002). In another parallel development to the western experience, a new economy evolved with an emphasis on finance and producer services, and information technology, creating new high end jobs (Grant and Nijman, 2002). In these respects, then, the same global (!) processes of economic restructuring seemed at work in Mumbai.

But the *pre-existing* labour market segmentation and class structure were completely different. Mumbai's textile workers could hardly be considered middle class in the same way as autoworkers in Detroit. The textile workers had nowhere near the income or benefits or opportunities for education, housing, and so forth. Most lived extremely modest lives with modest means. Mumbai's class structure prior to the 1970s is best described as bottom-heavy, dominated by the poor masses among whom the industrial workers were just slightly better off. The middle classes were much smaller than in US or European cities and consisted mainly of people with secure and better paying jobs in the public sector. The upper class was smaller still, comprising the political and economic elites.

In the past two decades or so, a new upper middle class has emerged in the private sector, mainly in finance, producer services and ICT. This new middle class is relatively small and their incomes are considerably higher than that of the old middle class that mainly worked in the government sector. This is why this new segment is better viewed as *upper* middle class. The income differences with Mumbai's toiling masses are enormous, and so are the consumption patterns (Nijman, 2006). Interestingly, the label 'middle class' is applicable mainly because of the similarities with the middle classes in western (US) cities in terms of purchasing power and consumption patterns. But in the context of income distributions in urban India, these new cohorts find themselves not in the middle but much higher up the ladder. It is an interesting case of globalization-induced confusion: the (new) Indian middle class is so labelled because of similarities to its shrinking namesake in the west – not because it actually occupies the middle stratum in India's class structure.

THE WORLD CITY TRAP

The notion of world city has a powerful policy appeal. Urban governments always seem interested in the highest possible rankings and put much weight on having or acquiring world city status, whatever it means exactly. The problem with most rankings is that all cities are ordered along one particular dimension; they are all measured the same way. The desire for higher rankings implies a willingness to compete specifically on a particular terrain. Bombay used to aspire to be like London. In the 1990s, the local chamber of commerce initiated a programme titled Bombay First, a straightforward copy of London First. Nowadays, the city to emulate is Shanghai, and at other times it is Hong Kong.

Can Mumbai realistically aspire to be like London or like Shanghai? Given the emphasis, in this essay, on geographical and historical context, the answer would be no. World city aspirations of this sort can be misleading and even dangerous. The obsession of city and state government and the 'establishment' with growth and with the new growth sectors, along with a more general neoliberal shift, tends to distract from the needs of Mumbai's impoverished urban masses, the great majority of Mumbaikars who have little or no connection to the new middle class (Nijman, 2008). This is not only a matter of politics. If Mumbai's millions of poor are not somehow included in the new economy and lifted out of their misery, their mere presence will impede the city's progress.

That does not mean, of course, that Mumbai should not aspire to become more like this city or that, or that it should not replicate particular practices that have proven successful in other places. It means one should avoid the normative connotation to the idea of the world city. World cities are mere nodes in the global urban system. They vary in centrality and even more in the nature of their particular functions in the network. Being a more important node in the network does not necessarily translate into being a better city. And there is no single world city model; there are many.

Gyan Prakash argues more generally that we should question 'the idea of the European metropolis, defined as a bounded unit by modernist theory, as the paradigmatic modern city'. We need to expand the focus 'beyond Europe and North America to include the experiences of urban modernity in Asia, Africa, and Latin America. It entails approaching the historical experiences of modern urban forms and transformations as ineluctably global, specific, diverse, and divergent' (Prakash, 2008, p. 2). Mumbai must follow its own path to prosperity and modernity. Mumbai can be its own kind of world city.

REFERENCES

Beauregard, R. and A. Haila (2000), 'The unavoidable continuities of the city', in P. Marcuse and R. van Kempen (eds), *Globalizing Cities. A New Spatial Order?*, Oxford: Blackwell, pp. 22–36.

Cohen, M. (1996), 'The hypothesis of urban convergence: are cities in the north and south becoming more alike in an age of globalization?', in M.A. Cohen, B.A. Ruble, J.S. Tulchin and A.M. Garland (eds), *Preparing for the Urban Future: Global Pressures and Local Forces*, Washington, DC: Woodrow Wilson Press, pp. 25–38.

D'Monte, D. (2002), *Ripping the Fabric: The Decline of Mumbai and its Mills*, Delhi: Oxford University Press.

Grant, R. and J. Nijman (2002), 'Globalization and the corporate geography of cities in the less-developed world', *Annals of the Association of American Geographers*, **92** (2), 320–340.

Hanssens, H., B. Derudder, P.J. Taylor, M. Hoyler, P. Ni, J. Huang, X. Yang and F. Witlox (2011), 'The changing geography of globalized service provision, 2000–2008', *The Service Industries Journal*, **31** (14), 2293–2307.

Maharashtra Economic Development Council (2002), *Maharashtra Vision 2005: Fast Track Development of Maharashtra – Strategy and Action*, Report submitted to the Government of Maharashtra, Mumbai: MEDC.

Mehta, S. (2004), *Maximum City: Bombay Lost and Found*, New York: Random House.

Nijman, J. (2006), 'Mumbai's mysterious middle class', *International Journal of Urban and Regional Research*, **30** (4), 758–775.

Nijman, J. (2007), 'Mumbai since liberalization: the space-economy of India's gateway city', in A. Shaw (ed.), *Indian Cities in Transition*, New Delhi: Orient Longman, pp. 238–259.

Nijman, J. (2008), 'Against the odds: slum rehabilitation in neoliberal Mumbai', *Cities*, **25** (2), 75–87.

Nijman, J. (2010), 'A study of space in Mumbai's slums', *Tijdschrift voor Economische en Sociale Geografie*, **101** (1), 4–17.

Prakash, G. (2008), 'Introduction', in G. Prakash and K.M. Kruse (eds), *The Spaces of the Modern City*, Princeton, NJ: Princeton University Press, pp. 1–18.

Reich, R.B. (1992), *The Work of Nations: Preparing Ourselves for 21st Century Capitalism*, New York: Alfred A. Knopf.

Taylor, P.J., P. Ni, B. Derudder, M. Hoyler, J. Huang, F. Lu, K. Pain, F. Witlox, X. Yang, D. Bassens and W. Shen (2010), 'Measuring the world city network: new results and developments', *GaWC Research Bulletin 300*, available at www.lboro.ac.uk/gawc/rb/rb300.html (accessed 19 July 2010).

Ward, K. (2010), 'Towards a relational comparative approach to the study of cities', *Progress in Human Geography*, **34** (4), 471–487.

42 Accra: a globalizing city
Richard Grant

Accra became the first African city to be visited by President Barack Obama. The president's inaugural visit followed his two US presidential predecessors, who also selected Accra for official Africa stops. For Obama's 2009 visit, West Africans were invited to welcome him by sending greetings as well as questions via short message service (SMS) so that the American president could respond via a 30-minute radio podcast. A Senegalese individual asked, 'Why [did] Obama choose to visit Ghana?' President Obama responded that he decided 'to go to Ghana, in part, because of the tremendous work they've done in developing a functioning democracy . . . Where you've got governments that work that aren't based on ethnicity and tribe, but rather based on rule of law, then they're better at fighting corruption, people have a greater commitment to making things work, and everybody prospers' (Americagov, 2009). There was a symbolic importance to the visit as a mark of respect. Of course, there was also a global teaching lesson in an African-American president visiting a globalizing city in Africa (Accra) and subsequently a remote former slave castle (Cape Coast) to peer through the prism of a gate 'of no return' where slaves had been carted off on ships to distant lands. This time around, though, the global power elite had returned to celebrate Ghana's achievements in the political and economic arenas. Obama's visit reflected the general phenomenon of states and companies now looking at Africa with a fresh eye: viewing it now for its prospects rather than problems. As such, the US president's visit must also be understood as a strategic move for open communication between Washington and Accra, specifically over an offshore oil discovery. One-quarter of US oil imports may come from West Africa after 2015.

Another achievement attracted attention: Ghana reached an urban milestone in 2010 when the majority of its population (51.5 per cent) became urban (as opposed to its former rural orientation). Urbanization will intensify: the urban share of population is expected to rise to 75.5 per cent by 2050 (Obeng-Odoom, 2010, p. 394). Within urban Ghana, Accra stands out as the most international city. Officially 'Greater Accra' refers to a broad administrative region of ten districts, but more commonly researchers conceptualize urban Accra as the built-up continuous area that centers on the Accra Metropolitan Assembly (AMA) and fans out into the adjacent areas of Tema and Ga districts (Figure 42.1).

Accra's official population in 2010 is estimated to be 2 233 000 (UN-HABITAT, 2008, p. 176), but local experts reason it is considerably higher (official figures rely on inadequate maps that are employed as the basis for determining census enumeration units). Data inaccuracies occur because there is no way to record those who do not want to be counted (many urbanites believe that the data will be used to increase taxes): slum dwellers, migrants and regular sojourners in particular are undercounted. Since the 1980s the city's spatial expansion has been spectacular. Administrative policies have not placed any limiting controls on sprawl. The urban frontier has been pushed farther and farther

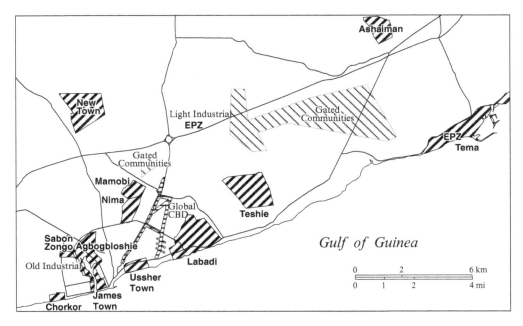

Source: Grant (2009, p. 146)

Figure 42.1   Globalizing Accra

away from the urban core. The growth of Accra is the confluence of migration streams, natural increase and more and more determined by in-situ urbanization (the absorption of smaller satellite settlements in the spatial growth of Accra). To put this in perspective, over the last ten years or so 'the number of urban residents has doubled . . . the areal size of the city has increased by over 300 per cent' (Yeboah, 2001, p. 68). The scholarly literature has documented and assessed Accra's physical changes that have overwhelmed urban managers and planners (see Grant, 2009). Researchers are still grappling with the socio-economic effects of these physical changes, such as the burgeoning informal economy, rapid land-use changes, the phenomenal growth of slums and the urbanization of extreme poverty (Obeng-Odoom, 2010).

Standard world city indicators (e.g., presence of Fortune 500 multinational corporations and presence of global service providers) do not register the substantial real-world changes in Accra (with the exception of significant presence of nongovernmental organizations [NGOs], which indicates an alternative globalization circuit). The city does not rate well on global buzz rankings: world city researchers locate Accra as isolated among the fourth tier of world cities (GaWC, 2008). This does not match evidence from the developing world that other international factors – for example, smaller foreign companies, migrants and remittances – now have a greater impact on these urban economies. Accra needs to be reconceptualized and reframed. Current international drivers of urban change require an understanding of the nexus between the local and the global and of the ways that urban geographic patterns are being reconfigured and transformed.

Accra is better understood through a globalizing city lens. Globalizing cities are different from global cities in that only points are articulated with the global economy. The entire city is not a node in the global economic system. Instead these are spatial entities where large amounts of economic activities are rooted in small-scale informal economic activities and only smaller proportions of higher-valued economic activities are directly connected to global circuits, but there are spillover effects and links among the informal and formal economies. As discrete urban entities, globalizing cities are characterized by rapid urbanization and intense transformation. As such, a globalizing city lens is sensitive to capturing more diverse ways that the urban arena is connected to the global arena. One way of assessing this diversity is to study globalization as being ushered in three ways: from above, from in between and from below. Full consideration of the simultaneity of these three avenues sheds a better light on the urban experience and provides some indication about possible urban futures.

Exploring the theme of Accra as a globalizing city, this chapter is divided into five sections. The next section provides a brief overview of Accra's development in time and space, and the three subsequent sections detail key elements in globalizing processes and examine globalizing from above, in between and below. The final section considers potential and probable urban futures for Accra and reviews a number of emerging geopolitical constellations.

ACCRA IN TIME AND SPACE

Not too long ago Accra was a sleepy fishing village. Its rise as an urban center dates from 1877, when the colonial headquarters were relocated from Cape Coast. Accra was selected as the site for colonial administration for a number of reasons: prominently health-related issues (building up a newer area was thought to protect Europeans from native-born diseases) and perceived locational advantages (a sheltered harbor and central location on the Gold Coast close to the prime meridian) (Grant, 2009). Turn-of-the-century historical accounts document a compact mass of thatched buildings arranged in a haphazard manner and separated by narrow crooked streets, but this was to change dramatically in time. With the arrival of the colonial machinery, political and economic power became focused on Accra for the first time. Until independence cocoa rather than government was the primary component in the economic base of the city. From Ghana's independence in 1957 until the mid 1980s Accra was shaped by nationalist economic policies, and the government promoted the city as a growth pole for the national economy, controlling the latter with import substitution policies and establishing it as the major shareholder in 400 different enterprises in manufacturing, financial, extractive and agricultural sectors. Certainly during the nationalist era, the pan-African political leadership role was invoked far more than its international economic role.

A major policy change was initiated with the introduction of liberalization policies in 1983, and policy measures to attract foreign companies (namely eliminating barriers to direct investment, upgrading of physical infrastructure, privatizing state-owned enterprises and reducing barriers to trade) were implemented. These policies promoted a gateway function for Accra and ushered in three globalization movements.

GLOBALIZING FROM ABOVE

Foreign direct investment (FDI) is a key international driver in urban development. Compared with economic powerhouses (e.g. Nigeria), investment levels are low, but the Ghanaian investment environment has considerably more room for foreign business growth (United Nations Conference for Trade and Development (UNCTAD), 2007). Ghana scores high on UNCTAD's inward FDI potential roster, especially in terms of natural resources and gateway markets, because its eastern border is within 150 miles of the larger Nigerian market (UNCTAD, 2007, p. 92). Furthermore, the launching of Ghana's and Nigeria's fast-track program in 2001 to spur economic integration has sent an important signal to investors. Ghana has generous incentives to attract FDI in the mineral sector and offers no cost interest, reduced royalty payments and low corporation tax rates. The country anticipates resource FDI to grow in coming years in line with trends in other African resource-rich countries. For instance, since 2007 Ghana has received more than 40 applications for oil exploration blocks. However, although policymakers embrace fully a market economy, capitalist traditions are quite recent and shortfalls in managerial skilled workers are FDI impediments.

A surge in FDI and the establishment of foreign companies occurred with the transition to democratic government in the 1990s. More than 2000 foreign firms were established in the liberalization era, accounting for approximately 75 per cent of the increase in export earnings and creating more than 73 000 jobs (Grant, 2009, pp. 138–139). India, China, the UK, Lebanon and the US have the largest international presence in Ghana. Significantly there is also an active presence of companies from the developing world. For example, Chinese investments have flowed into infrastructure, trade and minerals and China is loaning $10.4 billion to develop rail, road and mineral infrastructure (Bloomberg, 2010). The 2007 discovery of offshore oil in the Jubilee reserve has added a new economic dimension. Exxon Mobil's purchase of Kosmos Energy's stake for US$4 billion, which in turn accounted for a 23.5 per cent share of the total oil field, registered Ghana on global oil investment radar. The usual main oil players are well positioned but keen interest also comes from Asia. For instance, China was a bidder for the Kosmos stake and even loaned money to Ghana's National Oil Company for Jubilee Field infrastructural projects. Moreover India holds a strong interest in large hydrocarbon reserves and is in discussions with the Ghanaian National Petroleum Corporation about an acquisition.

There is a significant spatial imprint of this growing international presence on the urban landscape: a global central business district (CBD) (in addition to other competing CBDs) has emerged for headquarters of regional offices of foreign corporations (see Figure 42.1). The global CBD is away from the traditional city center (and the much smaller domestic companies) in the vicinity of the airport area. This global CBD has a high concentration of foreign firms engaged in the financial and producer services sectors. Another salient newer international feature in the urban landscape is a well-defined area with gated community concentrations of expansive housing in the airport vicinity. Gated communities primarily provide housing for expatriates, nonresident Ghanaians and domestic entrepreneurs (many of whom heavily engage with the international economy). More significant than the size of gated projects is their total market value of US$.5 billion (Grant, 2009, p. 51), and the broader implications of gated housing on community and segregation are being investigated (Asiedu and Arku, 2009).

GLOBALIZING FROM IN BETWEEN

The most visible change around Accra is the residential boom that has resulted in approximately 200 000 formal house structures in the last decade. Some of this building serves Ghanaians living abroad, but most can be accounted for by international transfers of monies into the housing sector and long-distance house building by three million diaspora wage earners (including 30 per cent of all highly educated Ghanaians) (Grant, 2009, p. 67). Yeboah (2001, p. 117) surmises that 'Ghanaians living abroad own half of the housing stock in Accra.'

Despite the intensity of this building, there is still a lot of vacant land in and around the city. Concerns have now turned to how the boom has impinged on land values and how this dynamic has exacerbated inequality (Obeng-Odoom, 2010). Significantly, the peculiar property rate system in Ghana, whereby rates fall on buildings rather than on land per se, has rung many alarm bells, particularly about equity and erratic spatial development. The property rate system provides incentives for landowners to leave their land bare to accumulate value resulting from public investment in road and other infrastructural investment improvements. A perspective gaining ground is that land titling (a World Bank focus) misdiagnoses the root causes of urban land and related poverty issues. It is underscored that the profits accruing from land are not reinvested to benefit the poor (Obeng-Odoom, 2010), and this has accelerated uneven development and a hyper-differentiation of space (Grant and Nijman, 2004). In essence this is the spatial accompaniment of the hyper-mobility of capital. It is expressed in increasing divergence among places and individuals within the context of reconfiguration and redivision of the global economy.

Remittances into Ghana have become another important driving force. Inward transfers grew steadily from US$179 million in 1994 to almost US$2 billion in 2004 but have shown a more recent decline (Grant, 2009). Remittances now register as a top foreign exchange earner after gold and cocoa. These funds are dispersed throughout the country, but the largest share is centered on Accra for obvious reasons. Remittances have traditionally been used to cover funerals, family emergencies and the like, but the evidence now indicates that these funds are flowing more into productive investments, for example housing and business start-ups.

Returnees are also regarded locally as key new players in the globalizing city. The government created a welcoming climate for members of the diaspora, hosting homecoming summits and introducing a Dual Citizenship Act. Bump (2006, p. 10) notes that 50 000 migrants have returned to Ghana, and most from wealthier European and North American countries. Returnees relocate primarily to Accra and their investments concentrate there. There are instances of high-profile returnees, for example Patrick Awuah, a Microsoft Corporation millionaire who established a private, western-styled institution of higher learning (Ashesi University), but for the most part returnees' contributions are not documented.

Some returnees' investments (in all kinds of entrepreneurial enterprises and new housing construction) may be facilitating a new episode in the development paradigm, complicating conventional understandings about the sources of economic growth and creativity. Furthermore, there are numerous examples of diaspora members organizing abroad to initiate development in Ghana from afar. Returnees have high participation rates in the urban economy, securing employment in foreign and domestic companies as well as operating entrepreneurial business enterprises (Grant, 2009). The frequency of their individual travel and/or business associates back and forth from Accra to other countries allows a stretching of the spaces of their economic activity. Although there is some information available, there is a dearth of research of return migrants, and huge knowledge gaps on returnees' societal roles exist. For instance, we do not know if their networks within Accra/Ghana are used benevolently or exploitatively.

GLOBALIZING FROM BELOW

There is modest evidence of civil society actors working with urban poor to facilitate a globalization from below. Obviously this is a complex relational topography that encompasses relationships among NGOs, local branch affiliates and members of the urban poor who constitute 'a community' of diverse identities, interests and goals. Furthermore, this sociopolitical terrain varies in context-specific situations. There is, however, some remarkable Accra evidence of particular slum communities organizing within this context to use the city as a platform to connect their housing issues with the global world beyond.

The flip side of the Accra building boom is a massive expansion in slum/squatter areas. The most controversial settlement is in Old Fadama/Agbogbloshie (Grant, 2009). This large slum abuts on the Korle Lagoon and contains 79 684 people within 1 km of the center of Accra (Housing the Masses, 2010, p. 2). Living conditions are severe, with unsanitary conditions and high-density living in wooden shacks and kiosks. This settlement has both residential and commercial functions and contains food markets, specialized e-waste markets, a commercial bus depot, and numerous shops and stalls. The government has made several (failed) attempts to evict the settlers, but several administrations have held onto an urban redevelopment vision that entails settler removal and the establishment of a green space for recreational use and tourism. Complicating the situation, the government obtained an international loan for US$73 million (from a range of Arab donors) in the early 1990s to restore the lagoon to its natural ecology, improve hydrological efficiency by increasing the throughflow of water and ultimately to better manage and beautify the area. Obviously, redevelopment is greatly hindered by the extensive settler occupation.

Ensuing struggles over evictions provide an important illustration of globalizing from below. Initially the settlers' modus operandi was survival and a combination of local legal action and local political pressures. After the High Court of Ghana's 2002 ruling that this occupation is illegal, the defense strategy of the settlers shifted to the international arena. The Swiss-based organization Centre on Housing Rights and Evictions (COHRE; an international human rights organization that campaigns for housing rights and against forced evictions) provided support. Through COHRE's involvement and briefings, another NGO, Slum/Shack Dwellers International (SDI), became heavily involved. SDI has considerable experience in organizing communities from the grass-roots and in this situation deployed its widely practiced methodology that pivots around daily savings, collections of these monies, and exchange visits with other slum communities in Accra as well as farther afield in Cape Town, Nairobi, and so on. By 2005 SDI had registered 3500 members in this settlement. The settlers' power in organizing and international NGO partnerships turned the tables on municipal authorities. Even though the issue is far from resolved, no forced removals have proceeded and redevelopment plans remain on hold. However, the emergence of a large e-waste site in Old Fadama within the last three years, labeled by the *New York Times* (2010, p. 1) as 'a global graveyard for dead computers', threatens to bring a different controversy into the urban, national and global optic.

The main lesson from this globalizing from below activity is that the urban poor and their support organizations are going forth into the world and consequently repositioning themselves within the local urban political context. In this new political landscape, locally rooted but globally connected groups have emerged to address issues of homelessness, housing for the poor and landlessness. Nonetheless, it is important not to extrapolate too much from this case. Many examples exist of grassroots globalizing efforts faltering.

ACCRA'S URBAN FUTURE(S)

Accra reveals much evidence of the increasing importance of the international dimension of urban change. Foreign company engagement is swelling, remittances are surging and investments into the housing sector are extensive. Even slum dwellers are participating in the international arena. Accra is a globalizing city because its circuits are fundamentally international. Accra is a globalizing city in transformation, but it may be in a permanent state of *becoming* neither a world city nor a traditional African city but rather a combination and integration of the two in ever more diverse and complex ways. Global enmeshment will continue and is likely to accelerate. West Africa with Accra as a pivot may become a more geostrategic region in three different ways: 1) as a military buffer in the war on terror, 2) as an emerging oil power and 3) as a gateway to an urban corridor that stretches from Accra to Ibadan, Nigeria.

Importantly, West Africa has become the latest front line in the United States' war on terror, with al-Qaeda in the Islamic Maghreb (AQUIM) becoming more active, and there are more frequent reports that Latin American drug cartels funnel cocaine through lucrative West African routes (Lyman and Morrison, 2004). *The Economist* (2010, p. 52) reports that AQUIM has a large role in the drug trade, linking narcotics trafficking and terrorism funding. A recent US-launched string of operations in Ghana and throughout the region uncovered evidence of AQUIM's role in the West African drug circuit. The global geopolitical consequences of AQUIM could be immense. Given Ghana's pre-eminence as the functionary democracy in the region, Accra could be the top candidate for a greater geostrategic role (if policymakers are so inclined).

The discovery of offshore oil has fundamentally altered Ghana in geoeconomic politics. The Jubilee oil field (Figure 42.2) is a significant discovery: estimates of this reserve

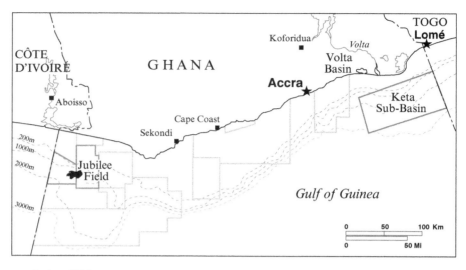

Source: Author, 2010.

Figure 42.2   Map of Accra in relation to Ghana's oil

are in the range of 600 million to 1.2 billion barrels (ISODEC, 2009, p. 20). Analysts now believe that the entire West African region from Sierra Leone to Nigeria could constitute a new oil frontier. The onshore oil pipeline will be operational toward the end of 2010. International Monetary Fund predictions reveal that Ghana could earn as much as US$20 billion between 2012 and 2030 (ISODEC, 2009). Analysts urge caution, noting that oil reserves are only one of the factors that affect profitability. The costs of getting deep oil onshore can be significant and Jubilee oil will trade on world oil markets against oil from lower-cost locations, for example Iraq. There are some speculative reports that Ghana's oil reserves in the Volta and Keta basins could be extensive, further adding to Ghana's oil power status.

Ghana's current oil resource is fraught with other controversies. First, the former National Patriotic Party government kept many of the detailed plans for the field secret, but it is believed that generous concessions were given to oil multinationals so that the state will only receive a modest return (10 per cent is reported) (ISODEC, 2009). Moves are afoot to restructure this initial deal in a more responsible way. A renegotiation will put Ghana at loggerheads with Exxon Mobil and the American government and other parties. Certainly, there is a lot of tension surrounding 'black gold' potential revenues, which are already putting a damper on current investment flows into Ghana, even beyond the global financial pullback. Second, Cote D'Ivoire has begun to make noises about a claim to the Jubilee field, complicating tensions in the region. Third, the history of oil resource-rich countries in promoting democracy and facilitating sustainable development is not good in Africa or elsewhere; an erosion of democratic accountability is more common. As such, a Ghanaian oil power could undermine progress already achieved in the political and economic arenas unless oil revenues and oil politics are used in responsible and democratic ways.

The emerging oil–urban Ghana nexus has not been well thought out (Obeng-Odoom, 2009). Predictably there will be considerable opportunities for construction and fuel. Oil resources will require towns, refinery and storage facilities, port extensions and various corporate and residential buildings. Accelerated urbanization along the west coast of Ghana is imminent that will connect the urban coastal cities to Accra in a linear axis: urban land values are increasing in anticipation. Most likely, Accra's role as a head-quarters city will be enhanced as more and more oil and related companies deepen their involvement in the region. Cheaper oil could have a disastrous effect on Accra, a city already overstretched by automobiles (Obeng-Odoom, 2010). It will likely lead to an even heavier reliance on autos and intensify urban sprawl as individuals locate farther from the urban core where land is available and lower in price. The peri-urban sprawl that has characterized contemporary Accra could be intensified. Unless Accra's urban sprawl is somehow held in check it will have disastrous effects on any future planning efforts.

A new urban spatial development in the opposite direction is the emergence of a linear urban corridor stretching from Accra to Ibadan, spanning four West African countries along a transportation highway. This corridor functions as an economic and demographic hub (with a combined population of 18.25 million), accommodating significant shares of clustered populations of the respective countries. This formation is based on transportation arteries that have unlocked peri-urban and rural areas between major cities as goods and people move within the corridor: importantly policy has not been a driver. Thus it remains unknown whether the corridor can develop into a coherent regional engine but this seems likely if growth continues to concentrate. Of course, any proactive solidification of the corridor could bring economies of scale but also result in even more unbalanced economic development for the respective countries. To date, city managers have not articulated an urban corridor vision and the corridor remains transnational in nature and under different national jurisdictions. Managers are pre-occupied with their respective city visions but there is now a need to establish a coordinated approach to manage the corridor.

Planning needs urgent attention. A promising start has been made with the partnerships among the AMA, the Earth Institute at Columbia University, University of Ghana, Legon and other development agencies such as the Cooperative Housing Foundation. In January 2010 they announced plans to design an effective development strategy to achieve the Millennium Development Goals (MDGs). The Accra Millennium City initiative is driven by the objective to design an urban plan that achieves sustainable development for the poorest populations by creating a broad consensus (among local government, scholarly, policymaking and NGO communities with citizens' active participation). This Millennium City initiative tackles the urban arena in a bold attempt to achieve eight development targets: 1) eradicate extreme poverty and hunger; 2) achieve universal education; 3) promote gender equality and empower women; 4) reduce child mortality; 5) combat HIV/AIDS, malaria and other diseases; 6) improve maternal health; 7) ensure environmental sustainability and 8) develop a global partnership for development. Given the enormous 'black gold' revenue possibilities for development, Accra could become the first African city to achieve the MDGs.

REFERENCES

Americagov (2009), 'Comments to president Obama', available at www.america.gov/obama_ghana.html (accessed 5 June 2010).

Asiedu, S. and G. Arku (2009), 'The rise of gated estates in Ghana: empirical insights from three communities in metropolitan Accra', *Journal of Housing and the Built Environment*, **24** (3), 227–247.

Bloomberg (2010), 'Ghana signs $10.4 billion infrastructure loan accord with China Exim Bank', available at www.bloomberg.com/news/2010-09-23/ghana-signs-10-4-billioninfrastructure-loan-accord-with-china-exim-bank.html (accessed 27 September 2010).

Bump, M. (2006), 'Ghana: searching for opportunities at home and abroad', available at www.migrationinformation.org/profiles/display.cfm?id=381 (accessed 6 May 2010).

The Economist (2010), 'Al-qaeda in west Africa. Desert menace', 15 May, pp. 52–53.

GaWC (2008), 'The world according to GaWC 2008', available at www.lboro.ac.uk/gawc/world2008t.html (accessed 4 June 2010).

Ghana Statistical Service (GSS) (2002), *2000 Population and Housing Census: Special Report on Urban Localities*, Accra: GSS.

Grant, R. (2009), *Globalizing City: The Urban and Economic Transformation of Accra, Ghana*, Syracuse: Syracuse University Press.

Grant, R. and J. Nijman (2004), 'The re-scaling of uneven development in Ghana and India', *Tijdschrift voor Economische en Sociale Geografie*, **95** (5), 467–481.

Housing the Masses (2010), *Final Draft Report on Community-Led Enumeration of Old Fadama Community, Accra. Ghana*, unpublished report, Housing the Masses/Peoples' Dialogue, Accra: Ghana.

ISODEC (2009), *Ghana's Big Test. Oil's Challenge to Democratic Development*, unpublished report, Washington, DC: ISODEC.

Lyman, P. and J. Morrison (2004), 'The terrorist threat in Africa', available at www.foreignaffairs.com/articles/59534/princeton-n-lyman-and-j-stephen-morrison/the-terrorist-threat-in-africa (accessed 2 June 2010).

New York Times (2010), 'A global graveyard in dead computers', available at www.nytimes.com/slideshow/2010/08/04/magazine/20100815-dump-2.html (accessed 17 September 2010).

Obeng-Odoom, F. (2009), 'Oil and urban development in Ghana', *African Review of Economics and Finance*, **1** (1), 18–39.

Obeng-Odoom, F. (2010), 'An urban twist to politics in Ghana', *Habitat International*, **34** (4), 392–399.

UNCTAD (2007), *Asian Foreign Direct Investment in Africa. Towards a New Era of Cooperation Among Developing Countries*, Geneva: UNCTAD.

UN-HABITAT (2008), *The State of African Cities 2008*, Nairobi: UN-HABITAT.

Yeboah, I. (2001), 'Structural adjustment and emerging urban form in Accra, Ghana', *Africa Today*, **7** (1), 61–89.

43 Geographies of power in the Indonesia–Malaysia–Singapore Growth Triangle

Tim Bunnell, Carl Grundy-Warr, James D. Sidaway and Matthew Sparke

INTRODUCTION

> Given the complexity and specificity of both the global and the national, their interlacing suggests the existence of frontier zones – from the perspective of research and theorization, these analytic borderlands are sure to require independent theoretical and methodological specificity.
>
> (Sassen, 2000, p. 216)

While Saskia Sassen and others have made many such arguments about the theoretical and methodological specificity demanded in studying the frontier zones of the global and national, there have been fewer examples provided of how to try and do this in practice. As we have argued elsewhere (e.g. Sidaway, 2002; Bunnell, 2004; Rajaram and Grundy-Warr, 2007; Sparke, 2009a and 2005), treating frontiers and borderlands as metaphors for other less spatial forms of intermixing runs the risk of ignoring critical geographies that profoundly shape how the global and national are interlaced. By way of an alternative, we chart some of the geographical specificities of the regional reterritorialization exemplified by the Indonesia–Malaysia–Singapore (IMS) borderlands (see Figure 43.1). Globally promoted as a Growth Triangle since the latter part of the 1980s, this cross-border region illustrates how the frontiers of the global and the national that pre-occupy so many theorists of globalization, global cities and so-called deterritorialization remain nonetheless sites in which spatial relations and territorial formations are particularly pertinent to explaining power relations. We sketch a complex regional geography of power relations that counterpoints the simplified trigonometry of the Triangle concept and contradicts attendant arguments about its embodiment of borderless world dynamics. Whereas Sassen's own critique of borderless world discourses underlined a need to examine an emerging 'geography of centrality' instantiated in world cities (Sassen, 1998), here we address the geographies of peripherality that in turn complicate decontextualized and ageographical accounts of world cities, city-regions and growth triangles as the simple spatial correlates of globalization and denationalization (Olds and Yeung, 2004; Sparke, 2009b).

The political commitment to tie together Singapore with the Malaysian state of Johor (sometimes romanized as Johore) and the Riau islands (principally Batam and Bintan) of Indonesia in the triangular relationship was formally constituted in a memorandum of understanding between the three states signed in Johor Bahru (Malaysia) on 17 December 1994. However, the project had a longer administrative history going back at least as far as the proposals of Singapore's Economic Development Board in the late 1980s that were made public by Singapore's Deputy

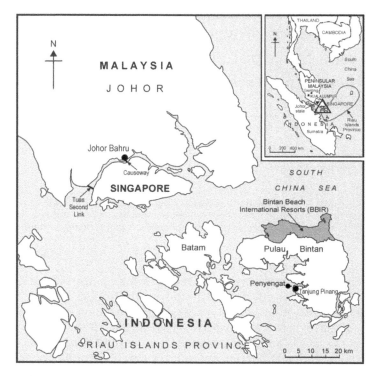

Figure 43.1   The Indonesia–Malaysia–Singapore Growth Triangle in Southeast Asia

Prime Minister Goh Chok Tong in December 1989 (Ahmad, 1993, p. 93). The basic vision was for Singapore to more effectively manage the cross-border hinterlandization of its economy, providing capital and strategic direction while securing access to the Malaysian supply of labour, semi-developed land and water, and while also accessing an abundant supply of undeveloped land and low-skilled Indonesian labour in Riau. Singapore, in short, was to supply the capital, and Johor and Riau were to provide the land and labour.

The vision of economic complementarity articulated in these proposals underpinned tall tales of anticipated cross-border regional growth. In ways that represented a contemporary simulation of Alfred Weber's simple triangular model of industrial location, the Asian Development Bank and other promotional groups scripted the Triangle as a three-way complementarity of capital, labour and land, an 'ideal triangle' of complementarities destined for growth in the midst of borderless trade (see Thant et al., 1994; Abonyi, 1996, p. 5). Moreover, insofar as the Triangle vision was also intended in part to assuage traditional concerns about Singapore's influence in the region, much stress was placed on the two-way reciprocal aspects of the complementarities, and related efforts were subsequently made to downplay Singapore's semiotic dominance in the Triangle with the abandonment of early names and acronyms such as 'the Singapore Growth Triangle' and SIJORI (Singapore–Johor–Riau) which placed Singapore first and signified the reality of Singapore's hegemonic economic role. Thus for both economic and political reasons the theme of economic complementarity became the dominant trope of writing on the region and it was readily rehearsed by academics as much as by policymakers.

This chapter is by no means the first to deal with such issues. Macleod and McGee (1996) early on pointed out the region's unevenness, arguing that, given the dominance of Singapore and the very limited ties between Johor and Riau, the Triangle is by no means 'equilateral' (see also Grundy-Warr et al., 1999). More recently, in a sustained ethnographic investigation of the experiences of 'development' in Batam, Lindquist (2008) contrasted the formal cross-border Triangle of the business planners and technocrats with the informal links and, more significantly, the many curtailed links of frustrated and exploited migrants. The non-equilateral aspect of the Triangle noted, there is no doubting the economic force of these so-called complementarities. In this region (unlike certain other concept cross-border regions (Sparke, 2000, 2002)) they are more than just a politically influential promotional story. The rent gaps – in terms of 'spatial fix' theory (Harvey, 1981) – are enormous. Land and labour are much cheaper in Johor, and cheaper still on the islands of Batam and Bintan. Such disparities have in turn unleashed all the forces of 'uneven development' (Smith, 1984), creating a classic economic geography of a regional scalar fix – involving transnational corporations (TNCs) and national and sub-national states along the lines of what Swyngedouw calls 'glocalization' (Swyngedouw, 1997). The theoretical challenge, therefore, is to adequately contextualize these economic imperatives and untangle the ways in which they are knotted together with other economic, political and cultural dynamics unfolding in interrelated but differently scaled contexts. In what follows, we consider them first in terms of capital and then in terms of land and labour.

CAPITAL

The Spatial Fix

Cost differentials between the three parts of the Triangle have had significant economic consequences. As *The Economist* surmised back in 1991, they have allowed Singaporean capital to escape the spatial limits and high costs of the island city-state by expanding to neighbouring parts of Malaysia and Indonesia. The peak of the Triangle investment hype was in the early 1990s when Singapore was booming with growth rates of 12.3 per cent in 1993 and 11.4 per cent in 1994, when unemployment was down between 1.7 per cent and 2.7 per cent, when skilled labour was in short supply, and when wages were rising (see Cunningham and Debrah, 1995; *Singapore Statistics*, 2003a). At the same time, new productive outlets for capital in Singapore were also increasingly limited by land shortages, and limits on water supply systems and other basic resources. These pressures towards reterritorialization were in turn combined with the facilitating capacity of Singapore's highly developed financial sector which was able to play a key role in financing developments in Johor, Batam and enclaves of Bintan (Guinness, 1992).

When the 1997–8 'Asian' financial crisis hit, the supposedly complementary quality of these patterns became increasingly eclipsed by rising concerns about competition (see Debrah et al., 2000). Unemployment levels in Singapore increased to as much as

4.6 per cent in 1999 and 5.2 per cent in 2002 (*Singapore Statistics*, 2003b), the upward pressure on wages was reduced, and new locales for external expansion elsewhere in Southeast Asia began to look cheaper for those holding US dollar-pegged Singapore dollars. In this new context, it was not entirely surprising that interest in local cross-border developments diminished. Overall, this uneven temporal development pattern of decline following expansion makes manifest the links between the growth of the Triangle and the ups and downs of the Singaporean economy. At least at this very extensive level, the pattern does seem to follow the classic spatial fix thesis, with re-territorialization developing in concert with the peaking of the high-growth/high-costs phase of the Singaporean business cycle. However, this bigger picture of a regional spatial fix needs to be nuanced by an acknowledgement of its uneven development on the ground.

While the significance of the developments for Singapore as a global city is not great in the economic aggregate (Rimmer, 1994, p. 1745), the same cannot be said of Johor and still less of Batam and Bintan. In Johor the state government had actively sought twinning with Singapore ever since 1988, and even before this the Malaysian Industrial Development Authority and the Singapore Economic Development Board had cooperated on facilitating cross-border industrial relocation and tourism development projects (Guinness, 1992; Parsonage, 1992). The Malaysian enthusiasm to engage with Singapore in this way (despite ongoing political tensions) was itself indicative of the potentially large amounts of Singaporean capital inflow that were possible. In 1988, as the prospect of the Triangle was being formulated, this inflow increased dramatically by 200 per cent (Parsonage, 1992, p. 309). With the consolidation of the official vision of the Triangle, these flows continued apace, and became part of a phenomenal period of growth for Johor which averaged GDP growth rates above 9 per cent through all of the 1990s up until the 1997 financial crisis. 'Within one decade Johor had developed into a largely export-oriented industrial economy. Manufacturing grew at about 14 per cent annually' (Van Grunsven, 1998, p. 184).

In Batam even more striking rates of growth were recorded during the 1990s. Again, the developments started before Goh Chok Tong's announcement of the 'Triangle of growth'. Back in 1978 the control of development in Batam was transferred to BIDA (the Batam Industrial Development Authority) under the chairmanship of B.J. Habibie (who went on to become President of Indonesia in the wake of Suharto's fall after the 1998 crisis). Habibie turned Batam into both a personal power base and a commercial-cum-national project of building an Indonesian mega-metropolis to vie with Singapore. Clearly, although the island is now home to over 500 foreign companies and its population had grown to 781,000 by 2009 (Azis, 2010), Batam is not even close to rivalling the levels of investment and urban development prized by Singapore. However, the plans that Habibie did make to invest in Batam and turn it into a duty free trade zone have led to remarkably rapid industrial development (Grundy-Warr et al., 1999). In 1990 private investment in the island reached US$2199 million per year, and by 1996 the same figure had more than doubled to US$4704 million (Van Grunsven, 1998, p. 189 (based on BIDA data)). Although it fell back in the aftermath of the Asian financial crisis to US$2818 million in 2000, by 2009 annual FDI had doubled again to US$5244 million (Azis, 2010). Eight industrial estates were completed during this time, amongst them the flagship project of Batamindo Industrial Park in the middle of the island that came to boast as tenants a host of TNCs including AT&T, CIBA Vision, Epson, Philips, Quantum, Sumitomo, Smith Corona, Seagate, Sanyo, Shimano, Siemens, TEAC and Thomson.

These global corporations noted, the bulk of the investment in Batamindo has nevertheless originated in Singapore. The same is true of the island as a whole, and in December 2000, BIDA documents recorded over $US 10 billion of investment from Singapore-based corporations, followed next by Japanese originated investment at just over $US 42 million (BIDA, 2000, p. 25). A decade later in 2009, 71.4 per cent of the investment in Batam still came from Singapore (Azis, 2010). Also indicative of the dependency of much of this development on Singaporean interest, 40 per cent of the joint venture ownership of Batamindo came from two Singapore government-linked companies (Grundy-Warr et al., 1999, p. 310). In parallel with these investments, Bintan island also became witness to the transformative influx of capital from Singapore. The same backers of Batamindo went on to create the Bintan Industrial Estate at Lobam and a consortium of Singaporean and Indonesian firms jointly developed the 'Bintan Beach International Resort' as a manicured tourist enclave in the north of the island (Bunnell et al., 2006; Hampton, 2010). Repeated articulation of the cost contrasts that drove these developments has effectively constituted a discourse of complementarity.

The Discourse of Complementarity

The performance of this discourse can be examined as a classic promotional form of geoeconomics. Analytically, it has led to the easy insertion of the Triangle as an example into broader discourses on growth triangles and cross-border regions as emerging global trends (e.g. Kumar, 1994; Wiemer, 2009, who draws lessons from Sijori for the Greater Mekong Sub-Region in a report commissioned by the Asian Development Bank). The hype around the region as a perfect embodiment of differential factor endowments nested around an easily accessible world city hub in Singapore speaks in this way to a larger set of comparisons: namely the comparisons made amongst the Singapore Economic Development Board and other local business elites that the region needs to position itself more competitively vis-à-vis other rival investment hubs in Asia. The diagramming of the Triangle based on the discourse of complementarity (see Figure 43.2) can thus be interpreted as doing the argumentative work of promoting the place of the Triangle amidst a wider geoeconomic competition for inward investment.

More recently Singapore has moved forward with other geoeconomic strategies for entrenching its brand of embedded exportism, including through a bilateral free trade deal with the US. Commentary in the Singapore *Business Times* drew out the place promotional demonstration point that 'the [Free Trade Agreement] should help re-focus investor attention on Singapore' (21 November 2003). To this it also added an open acknowledgement of the specific spectres of comparison driving the need to refocus: 'With north-east Asia – and China in particular – rising, Singapore is in danger of dropping out of the radar screen.' In these kinds of comments and comparisons the geoeconomics of place promotion through the Triangle have been harnessed to the new demonstration effect of bilateral free trade. But the performance has a very material side, too. Key products made in Batam and Bintan have been classified in the free trade agreement as subject to the same tariff reductions as those made in Singapore itself. Thus, for

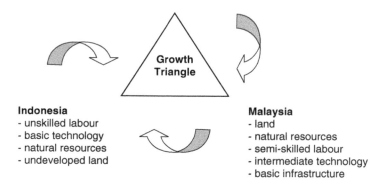

Singapore
- capital
- skilled labour
- advanced technology
- access to world markets
- advanced physical infrastructures
- advanced commercial infrastructure

Growth Triangle

Indonesia
- unskilled labour
- basic technology
- natural resources
- undeveloped land

Malaysia
- land
- natural resources
- semi-skilled labour
- intermediate technology
- basic infrastructure

Source: redrawn after Debrah et al. (2000)

Figure 43.2   The Triangle of Economic Complementarity

the purposes of the bilateral deal with the US, the borderless economy of appearances of the Triangle has become real: Batam-made and Bintan-made goods are treated by the US as if they actually originated in Singapore. As a result of the cost savings made available by Riau export processing, it is therefore again argued that 'Singaporean enterprises are better placed to compete against regional rivals' (Dhume and Saywell, 2002, p. 22). If such comments reveal the salience of the cost comparisons on both of the levels we have been discussing in this section – both in terms of the actual economic geography of export processing and the place promotional geoeconomics – they also underline once more the direct links and material fusions that result in practice. Thus in some sense, the bilateral free trade deal returns us to the place from which we began: the comparative geography of cost disparities. But we have not entirely turned full circle insofar as our argument has along the way introduced questions about the representation of the landscape of the Triangle and the politics of labour; themes that we take up next.

LAND AND LABOUR

The neat triangulation of complementarity conjoining Singapore's capital with Johor and Riau's land and labour not only licenses the geoeconomic landscaping of the Triangle as a place of borderless opportunity, it also overwrites and obscures a great deal of history, geopolitics and struggle (Bunnell et al., 2006). Today, this history of struggle continues to remain active and stirs just beneath the surface of the landscape, and any attention to land and labour brings it abruptly back into the story of triangular capital flows.

Another of Singapore's strategies for securing its growth trajectory – land reclamation – has further roiled relations with Malaysia and increased the geopolitical tensions. Land reclamation in Singapore began in 1962 with the creation of 0.2 sq km of new useable land for state housing development along the east coast. Much larger areas have since been reclaimed for infrastructure projects, most notably 11.6 sq km for various phases of Changi International Airport and the joining of seven islands off the south-west of the island to form Jurong Island for a vast petrochemical complex. In total, reclamation projects have resulted in Singapore growing from a land area of 580 sq km at independence to more than 710 sq km today. Over the past decade, this has repeatedly raised fears in Malaysia that Singapore's gains are Malaysia's and Indonesia's losses. With the sand, the raw material for the land being 'reclaimed', being removed from Indonesian and Malaysian territory and waters, the geography of land reclamation seemed to make explicit a zero-sum form of one-sided growth that the cant of complementarity in the Triangle was supposed to transcend. In 2002, the Malaysian cabinet announced that licences for the export of sand would not be renewed as the material was needed for Malaysia's own growth through reclamation. Two years later, when the issue arose again, those shifting sand to Singapore were described in the Malay language press in Malaysia as 'selling (out)' the nation (*menjual maruah negara*, literally 'selling the pride of the nation') (*Utusan Malaysia*, 10 March 2002).

Such nationalistic responses account in large part for a two-decade-long impasse over land in Singapore occupied by the Malayan Railway (KTMB – Keretapi Tanah Melayu Berhad) which the Singapore authorities wish to develop. It came as something of a surprise, then, when Singapore Premier Lee Hsien Loong and his Malaysian counterpart Najib Tun Razak reached an agreement on the railway land on 24 May 2010, in a deal which also included Singapore involvement in the Iskandar Malaysia township project in southern Johor. It is revealing that two Singapore-based political commentators expressed surprise that 'the KTMB deal did not bring about any new stirring of anti-Singapore sentiment in Malaysia' (Segaran and Pasuni, 2010, p. 2). The potential for further conflict remains however, including in the Iskander Malaysia project where there is evidence of competition as well as collaboration with Singapore (Wiemer, 2009).

Unsurprisingly, similar concerns come together with the spectres of comparison around direct economic competition, too. Thus *Utusan Malaysia* reports in 2002 both expressed and fuelled fears that Singapore's continued territorial growth plans threatened Johor's economic expansion. Reclamation projects around Pulau Tekong (northeast of Singapore) were reportedly resulting in a narrowing of the channel between the two countries (the Tebrau Straits), impacting upon ships' entry to Johor's eastern port at Pasir Gudang. More significantly given the heightened container port competition, reclamation on the west side of Singapore at Tuas was claimed to have narrowed access to Tanjung Pelepas Port. An area the size of ten football pitches around Tuas had been reclaimed using Indonesian sand from Riau, thus completing the decidedly asymmetrical triangulation (*Utusan Malaysia*, 10 March 2002). The English language Malaysian daily *New Straits Times* suggested that Singapore's growth plans were tantamount to economic sabotage of Johor: 'State authorities worry that the landfills have been cleverly designed to obstruct the smooth operations of Tanjung Pelepas Port, which is seen as a viable alternative to Singapore' (*New Straits Times*, 5 March 2002). Finally, it should be noted that the controversy over sand shipments itself became triangular with the Indonesian government reportedly giving authority to its navy to shoot and sink dredging barges illegally carrying sand from Riau to Singapore (*New Straits Times*, 3 July 2003). Seven years on, the theme cropped up again, with allegations of corruption chains involved in mining and shipping sand that found its way from islands of the Riau archipelago (some of which now had all their sandy soil stripped away) to building sites in Singapore. A recent article in the British newspaper *The Telegraph* (12 February 2010) notes that Singapore is being accused of launching 'Sand Wars'. The article quotes Nur Hidayati of Greenpeace Indonesia: 'It is a war for natural resources that is being fought secretly. The situation has reached critical levels and the tropical islands of Nipah, the Karimun Islands and many small islands off the coast of Riau are shrinking dramatically and are on the brink of disappearing into the sea.'

The tensions involved in the recent retriangulations of postcolonial land development are still more painfully evident in the landscapes of labour in the Triangle. In Batam, for example, the order of the official development schemes is everywhere flouted by the so-called *rumah liar* (literally, 'wild housing') settlements that represent the uncontrolled labour inflows onto the island. In much of Batam, striking juxtapositions proliferate, with smart (but very often half-empty) new housing standing right next to sprawling self-built *rumah liar*. Even around the perimeters of the tightly regulated (and multiply fenced) Batamindo Industrial Park, there are numerous ad hoc *rumah liar* built by migrants from all over Indonesia seeking opportunities in Batam. Many have been moved to make way for a reservoir and more industrial estates, and yet new settlements develop just as quickly, creating a series of stark juxtapositions between the manicured and controlled spaces of the estates and the workers' dormitories, nearby gated real estate developments (marketed to selected wealthy Indonesians and Singaporeans) and, around their edges, the sprawls of shanty housing, shops and services made out of corrugated iron sheets, planks and other improvised building materials.

Nonetheless, business spokespersons from Batam and Bintan are publicly voicing concerns that Chinese labour undercuts that in the Growth Triangle. At a recent meeting on the prospects for the Growth Triangle, a businessman from Bintan complained that the Batam Bintan Karimun free trade zone ('BBK FTZ' in the new vernacular – established by Indonesia public Law No. 44 in 2007) was never going to be able to compete well with Special Economic Zones (SEZs) in China, because there was still not a sufficiently pro-business climate and the full spectrum of 'freedoms' associated with SEZs! 'When will a SEZ be fully realized?' he asked to much applause (notes from a meeting on the Growth Triangle held at Traders Hotel, Singapore in March 2010): 'We need to catch up with the others in China. We are losing out and losing companies. We need tax holidays, tax concessions, and labour rules to be reset so the region can really compete in the world' (more applause from the Traders Hotel room). Another audience member at the meeting complained about the annoyance of having to renegotiate wage deals with labour unions in Batam and Bintan thanks to a new Indonesian law giving more rights to workers, and while Harry Azhar Azis, the Minister from Jakarta, diplomatically described a responsibility to balance labour wishes with management freedoms, a representative from Batam's Chamber of Commerce, Indina Fajar, more directly emphasized that: 'we are working so hard to sustain the cheap wage of the labour and to keep it a more conducive environment for business' (notes from a meeting held at Traders Hotel, Singapore in March 2010).

Others at the meeting talked about the long term dream of building a bridge from Singapore to Batam and Bintan. This, however, is not on the cards for the foreseeable future, for the 20–odd kilometres of water of the Selat Singapura now provide a convenient and relatively controllable barrier (Lindquist, 2008). Capital, tourists, investors and elites can move across it relatively freely: workers cannot. As 'wild' and disruptive as the landscapes of labour migration may appear, they represent a form of disruption that remains for the most part within the Indonesian and, to a much lesser extent, Malaysian corners of the Triangle. Despite the fears about HIV infection, Dengue fever-carrying mosquitoes and crime syndicates moving close to Singapore, the most fundamental feature of the Growth Triangle's labour geography remains – in every sense – in place: namely, that while capital can move relatively freely between Singapore, Johor and Riau, labour cannot. The hundreds of thousands of migrants coming to Batam and Bintan to find work depress wage rates very effectively, but they have little capacity to press over the Strait of Singapore onto the shores of the city-state.

CONCLUSIONS

A host of scholars have critiqued the banalities reproduced by the likes of Kenichi Ohmae (1995) about a looming borderless world. Far fewer have sought to examine the complex human geographies of transborder regional formations. This is precisely what we have attempted to do for the IMS Growth Triangle. What we have shown is that the Triangle is not borderless. It is transected by all kinds of divides and disjunctures that in fact represent an explosion of boundary drawing. Moreover, the national boundaries within the Triangle remain significant, not just for managing migrants but also for mediating the development plans such that only those dealing with free trade and investment schemes seem to find quick collaborative consensus. Meanwhile, what economists might call the negative externalities of the Triangle's development, including tensions over water, over migrants, over HIV and over sand dredging and land reclamation, endure. All of these tensions have cross-border ramifications, and what they show is that the economic abstraction of 'borderlessness' is actually instantiated in a complex human geography contoured by polymorphous problems and power relations which cannot be understood, let alone addressed adequately, in the geometric terms of the Triangle.

ACKNOWLEDGEMENTS

The authors are thankful for a National University of Singapore grant that supported their collaboration. An earlier version of this chapter was published as Sparke, M., J.D. Sidaway, T. Bunnell and C. Grundy-Warr (2004), 'Triangulating the borderless world: geographies of power in the Indonesia–Malaysia–Singapore Growth Triangle', *Transactions of the Institute of British Geographers*, **29** (4), 485–498. We are grateful to the publishers for permission to rework and update it here.

REFERENCES

Abonyi, G. (1996), 'The challenge of growth triangles for regional institutions', in I. Lim (ed.), *Growth Triangles in Southeast Asia: Strategy for Development*, Kuala Lumpur: SE Asia Roundtable on Economic Development.

Ahmad, M. (1993), 'Economic cooperation in the Southern Growth Triangle: an Indonesian perspective', in M.H. Toh and L. Low (eds), *Regional Cooperation and Growth Triangles in ASEAN*, Singapore: Times Academic Press, pp. 92–118.

Azis, H.A. (2010), 'The bridge of Batam, Bintan and Karimun to Singapore: FTZs and investment opportunities', speech presented 16 March 2010, at the Traders Hotel, Singapore by Chairman of the Budget Committee of the House of Representatives and Member of Parliament from Riau Archipelago, Republic of Indonesia.

BIDA (1996), *Development Data*, Jakarta: BIDA.

BIDA (2000), *Batam Industrial Zone and Tourist Resort: Development Data*, Batam: BIDA.

Bunnell, T. (2004), *Malaysia, Modernity and the Multimedia Super Corridor: A Critical Geography of Intelligent Landscapes*, New York: RoutledgeCurzon.

Bunnell, T., H.B. Muzaini and J.D. Sidaway (2006), 'Global city frontiers: Singapore's hinterland and the contested socio-political geographies of Bintan, Indonesia', *International Journal of Urban and Regional Research*, **31** (1), 3–22.

Colombijn, F. (2001), 'Of money and trees: a 19th-century growth triangle', *Inside Indonesia*, available at www.insideindonesia.org/edit49/freek.htm (accessed 27 December 2001).

Cunningham, B. and Y. Debrah (1995), 'Skills for managing human resources in a complex environment', *International Journal of Human Resource Management*, **6** (1), 79–101.

Debrah, Y., I. McGovern and P. Budhwar (2000), 'Complementarity or competition: the development of human resources in a South-East Asian Growth Triangle: Indonesia, Malaysia and Singapore', *International Journal of Human Resource Management*, **11** (2), 314–335.

Dhume, S. and T. Saywell (2002), 'Opportunity knocks', *Far Eastern Economic Review*, 19 December.

Grundy-Warr, C., K. Peachey and M. Perry (1999), 'Fragmented integration in the Singapore–Indonesian border zone: Southeast Asia's "Growth Triangle" against the global economy', *International Journal of Urban and Regional Research*, **23** (2), 304–328.

Guinness, P. (1992), *On the Margin of Capitalism: People and Development in Mukim Plentong, Johor, Malaysia*, Singapore: Oxford University Press.

Hall, R.B. (2003), 'The discursive demolition of the Asian development model', *International Studies Quarterly*, **47** (1), 71–99.

Hampton, M.P. (2010), 'Enclaves and ethnic ties: the local impacts of Singaporean cross-border tourism in Malaysia and Indonesia', *Singapore Journal of Tropical Geography*, **31** (2), 239–253.

Harvey, D. (1981), *The Limits to Capital*, Oxford: Blackwell.

Kelly, P.F. (2001), 'Metaphors of meltdown: political representations of economic space in the Asian financial crisis', *Environment and Planning D: Society and Space*, **19** (6), 719–742.

Kelly, P.F. (2002), 'Spaces of labour control: comparative perspectives from Southeast Asia', *Transactions of the Institute of British Geographers*, **27** (4), 395–411.

Kumar, S. (1994), 'Johor–Singapore–Riau Growth Triangle: a model of subregional cooperation', in M. Thant, M. Tang and H. Kakazu (eds), *Growth Triangles in Asia: A New Approach to Regional Economic Cooperation*, Hong Kong: Oxford University Press and ADB, pp. 175–242.

Lee, T.Y. (ed.) (1991), *Growth Triangle: The Johore–Singapore–Riau Experience*, Singapore: Institute of Southeast Asia Studies.

Lindquist, J. (2008), *The Anxieties of Mobility: Development, Migration and Tourism in the Indonesian Borderlands*, Honolulu: University of Hawaii Press.

Macleod, S. and T. McGee (1996), 'The Singapore–Johore–Riau Growth Triangle: an emerging extended metropolitan region', in F. Lo and Y. Yeung (eds), *Emerging World Cities in Pacific Asia*, New York: United Nations University Press, pp. 417–464.

Ohmae, K. (1995), *The End of the Nation-State: The Rise of Regional Economies*, New York: The Free Press.

Olds, K. and H. Yeung (2004), 'Pathways to global city formation: a view from the developmental city-state of Singapore', *Review of International Political Economy*, **11** (3), 489–521.

Parsonage, J. (1992), 'Southeast Asia's "growth triangle": a sub-regional response to a global transformation', *International Journal of Urban and Regional Research*, **16** (2), 307–317.

Poulgrain, G. (1998), *The Genesis of Konfrontasi: Malaysia, Brunei, Indonesia 1945–1965*, London: Hurst.

Rajaram, P. and C. Grundy-Warr (eds) (2007), *Borderscapes: Hidden Geographies and Politics at Territory's Edge*, Minneapolis, MN: University of Minnesota Press.

Rimmer, P.J. (1994), 'Regional economic integration in Pacific Asia', *Environment and Planning A*, **26** (11), 1731–1759.

Sassen, S. (1998), *Globalization and its Discontents: Essays on the New Mobility of People and Money*, New York: The New Press.

Sassen, S. (2000), 'Spatialities and temporalities of the global: elements for a theorization', *Public Culture*, **12** (1), 215–232.

Segaran, R. and A. Pasuni (2010), 'Malaysian reactions of the railway land deal', *RSIS Commentaries*, No. 60, electronic bulletin of S. Rajaratnam School of International Studies, available at http://www.rsis.edu.sg/publications/commentaries.asp?selYear=2010 (accessed 14 July 2011).

Sidaway, J.D. (2000), 'Postcolonial geographies: an exploratory essay', *Progress in Human Geography*, **24** (4), 591–612.

Sidaway, J.D. (2002), *Imagined Regional Communities: Integration and Sovereignty in the Global South*, New York: Routledge.

Singapore Statistics (2003a), *Official GDP and Growth Rates*, available at www.singstat.gov.sg/keystats/hist/gdp1.html (accessed 2 July 2003).

Singapore Statistics (2003b), *Official Unemployment Rates*, available at www.singstat.gov.sg/keystats/hist/unemployment.html (accessed 10 January 2003).

Smith, N. (1984), *Uneven Development: Nature, Capital, and the Production of Space*, New York: Blackwell.

Sparke, M. (2000), 'Chunnel visions: unpacking the anticipatory geographies of an Anglo-European borderland', *Journal of Borderland Studies*, **15** (1), 2–34.

Sparke, M. (2002), 'Not a state, but more than a state of mind: cascading Cascadias and the geoeconomics of cross-border regionalism', in M. Perkmann and N.-L. Sum (eds), *Globalization, Regionalization and Cross-Border Regions*, London: Palgrave, pp. 212–240.

Sparke, M. (2005), *In the Space of Theory: Postfoundational Geographies of the Nation-State*, Minneapolis, MN: University of Minnesota Press.

Sparke, M. (2009a), 'Triangulating globalization', *Journal of Historical Geography*, **35** (2), 376–381.

Sparke, M. (2009b), 'On denationalization as neoliberalization: biopolitics, class interest and the incompleteness of citizenship', *Political Power and Social Theory*, **20**, 287–300.

Swyngedouw, E. (1997), 'Neither local nor global: "glocalisation" and the politics of scale', in K.R. Cox (ed.), *Spaces of Globalization: Reasserting the Power of the Local*, New York: Guilford Press, pp. 137–166.

Thant, M., M. Tang and H. Kakazu (eds) (1994), *Growth Triangles in Asia: A New Approach to Regional Economic Cooperation*, Hong Kong: Oxford University Press and ADB.

The Economist (1991), 'Geography and geometry,' *The Economist*, 16 November, 9.

Van Grunsven, L. (1995), 'Industrial regionalization and urban-regional transformation in Southeast Asia: the SIJORI Growth Triangle considered', *Malaysian Journal of Tropical Geography*, **26** (1), 47–65.

Van Grunsven, L. (ed.) (1998), *Regional Change in Industrializing Asia: Regional and Local Responses to Changing Competitiveness*, IGU Commission on the Organisation of Industrial Space Series, Aldershot: Ashgate.

Vatikiotis, M. (1993), 'Chip off the block: doubts plague Singapore-centered "growth triangle"', *Far Eastern Economic Review*, 7 January.

Wiemer, C. (2009), *Three Cases of Cross-Border Economic Corridor Development with Lessons for the Greater Mekong Sub-Region*, Asian Development Bank consultancy report, 15 July, available at http://callawiemer.com/Documents/Wiemer%20Corridor%20Study.pdf (accessed 18 June 2010).

44 Randstad Holland: probing hierarchies and interdependencies in a polycentric world city region

Bart Lambregts and Robert Kloosterman

INTRODUCTION

It was Sir Peter Hall who halfway through the 1960s, in his seminal study of seven world cities, observed that next to the traditional 'highly centralised giant city' there exists a 'polycentric type of metropolis' as well (Hall, 1966, pp. 9–10). This polycentric metropolis, Hall proclaimed, consists of 'a number of smaller, specialised, closely-related centres' and should be understood as 'a perfectly natural form, which has evolved over a period of history quite as long as the single metropolitan centre'. Two such polycentric metropolises made it to Hall's selection of seven world cities: the Randstad Holland in the Netherlands and Germany's RheinRuhr region. Compared with their single-centred counterparts (e.g. London, Paris, New York), Hall assessed the polycentric metropolis to be 'a more viable form for the mid-twentieth century' (Hall, 1966, p. 157), as it supposedly offered better opportunities for coping with such problems as traffic congestion, competition for space, the availability of green spaces and other diseconomies of agglomeration. While Hall surely was not blind to the drawbacks associated with such metropolises (such as administrative fragmentation), he did consider regional planners in the Randstad Holland and RheinRuhr to be better off than their peers in London or Paris, for in addressing 'world city problems' the former, according to Hall, at least had a chance of achieving 'really satisfactory solution[s]' (Hall, 1966, p. 157).

Today, more than 40 years later, young Peter Hall's suppositions are basically still on the table. While the world has moved on and in many ways has become quite a different place, the polycentric 'metropolis' or 'world city region' and its, to a large extent, still hypothetical potential, continue to appeal to the imagination of planners, geographers and policymakers (both on the national level and on that of the European Union, for example) alike. The substantial literature on polycentric urban and regional phenomena that has emerged in recent years is testimony to this (see, for instance, the special issues of *European Planning Studies*, 6.4, 1998 and 12.3, 2004; *Urban Studies*, 38.4, 2001; *Built Environment*, 31.2, 2005 and 32.2, 2006; and *Regional Studies*, 42.8, 2008; as well as ESPON, 2006; Hall and Pain, 2006; Meijers, 2007a; Lambregts, 2009).

Polycentric 'world city regions' (to adopt the vocabulary used in this volume) have in common that they do not yield up their secrets easily. They constitute complex, multifaceted and multilayered spaces that, moreover, often lack clear boundaries in an administrative as well as in a functional sense (Kloosterman and Lambregts, 2007). Two of the questions that continue to fuel debate in many a polycentric world city region are first: to what degree does the polycentric world city region in question qualify as a coherent entity (as opposed to just an accidental coagulation of cities) and therefore merits to be labelled and treated as such; and second: how do such regions, that normally lack obvious 'world city candidates', create and/or maintain at least the impression that they belong to the same league as so regarded 'true' world cities such as London, Paris, Tokyo and New York.

Here, we show how these issues loom large in the Randstad Holland, where in spite of 50 years of – admittedly half-hearted – 'world city region-making', doubts about the legitimacy of conceiving the area as a single coherent regional entity continue, and where recent years have seen a bold solo effort by the city of Amsterdam to establish itself – together with a selection of neighbouring municipalities – as the 'genuine' metropolitan or world city region of the Netherlands. We take stock of these developments by looking into the dual role played by one of the Randstad's key categories of economic actors: international advanced producer services firms. We show how they are instrumental both in bolstering the impression that Amsterdam in comparison to other cities in the Randstad Holland is of a different class and in creating interdependencies between Amsterdam and the wider Randstad Holland. This assessment learns that to take things at face value in polycentric world city regions is a risky enterprise and may give rise to ill-conceived policies.

PICTURING A POLYCENTRIC WORLD CITY REGION

The Randstad Holland embodies the horseshoe-shaped urban configuration in the western part of the Netherlands. It roughly runs from Dordrecht and Rotterdam in the south, via The Hague and Leiden in the west to Amsterdam in the north and Utrecht and Amersfoort in the east (Figure 44.1). That Amsterdam, The Hague, Rotterdam, Utrecht and the medium-sized cities belong to the Randstad is widely accepted, but beyond that the demarcation is far from clear and largely depends on the perspective used. Using a more narrow definition, the Randstad Holland measures about 80 by 65 km, which equals 16 per cent of the Dutch land area. It houses about 42 per cent of the Dutch population, or 7 million people. These people live in a large number of mainly medium-sized cities and an even larger number of smaller towns and villages. In 2009, the area included 12 cities and towns with more than 100 000 inhabitants and another 12 in the 70 000–100 000 range. The most populous cities are Amsterdam (756 000), Rotterdam (587 000), The Hague (482 000) and Utrecht (300 000). The co-presence of so many distinct larger and smaller urban centres in a relatively small area seems to make the Randstad Holland the quintessential polycentric urban region (Kloosterman and Musterd, 2001; Lambregts et al., 2006).

The Randstad Holland is frequently rated among the world's 'world cities' (e.g. Hall, 1966; Shachar, 1994), 'global city-regions' (Scott, 1998; Simmonds and Hack, 2000; Fainstein, 2001) or 'mega-city regions' (Hall and Pain, 2006). The fact that it is one of Europe's top-five regional economies measured by Gross Regional Product (GRP) suggests it is deservedly so (Eurostat figures as cited in TNO, 2010). The area combines important, in part even world class, political, financial, cultural and international gateway functions and is home to a highly skilled, cosmopolitan labour force. These assets are, however, not located in just one city, as for instance in London or Paris, but are distributed over various, historically distinct cities. Among these, Amsterdam stands

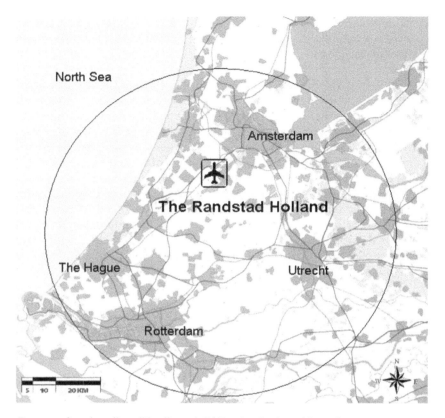

Source: Base map from http://en.wikipedia.org/wiki/Randstad, adopted by authors

Figure 44.1   The Randstad Holland

out as the financial and cultural capital, The Hague as the political and administrative centre, Rotterdam as the main logistics and industrial centre and Utrecht as a diversified logistics and producer services centre (Kloosterman, 2004; Engelen, 2007; Röling, 2010; Deinema and Kloosterman, forthcoming). Geographically in between these lies Amsterdam Schiphol Airport, Europe's fifth busiest airport in terms of passenger volume and nowadays a major economic centre of its own. The – in part – complementary profiles of the Randstad's main urban centres are often viewed as illustrating the reciprocity and parity that are thought to define the relationship between these centres (Kloosterman and Lambregts, 2001; Meijers, 2007b).

PLANNERS' PURSUITS

Since the Randstad Holland: 1) accounts for almost half of the Dutch economy; 2) constitutes the country's main (if not only) trump card in the so-perceived global, intermetropolitan competition for mobile resources; and 3) is characterized by a spatial layout that, in spite of young Peter Hall's optimistic remarks quoted above, comes with a number of profound challenges, it should be of no surprise that the area features large in Dutch strategic spatial and economic planning. Among the challenges that the Randstad Holland and its planners face are those related to transport (insufficient population density to render an extensive, finely grained mass transit system a viable option, with overburdened road networks as a result); relatively high levels of air pollution (partly as a consequence of the former); increased fragmentation of open space (linked to the polycentric character of the area and the tendency to seek to interconnect the various centres); and – so perceived – inefficient and ineffective spatial governance (see Lambregts et al., 2008 for a discussion). These issues are neither unique to the Randstad Holland, nor are they confined to polycentric urban regions alone.

Planners in the Randstad Holland, however, also have to confront two, interrelated key questions. These pertain more exclusively to polycentric world city regions in general and to the Randstad Holland in particular. The first one is 'to what degree does the Randstad Holland qualify as a *coherent region* – as opposed to just an accidental collection of cities?' The second question concerns 'how should the Randstad Holland, which arguably lacks an obvious world city candidate, be assisted to hold its ground on the world stage where it faces stiff competition from so-perceived "true" world cities such as London, Paris, Hong Kong, Tokyo and New York?' These questions constitute recurring themes in the region's strategic planning history (Lambregts and Zonneveld, 2004). More than that, they can be conceived as the main issue in a three-part 'geopolitical' struggle where frontlines simultaneously run between various Dutch regional coalitions (of which the Randstad Holland is just one), between Randstad-based authorities and the national government (see also Terhorst and Van der Ven, 1995; Van Duinen, 2004), and between Randstad-based authorities themselves (Lambregts et al., 2008). The state of the economy, the political balance of powers and national government's prevailing attitude towards the regions determine the intensity and the direction of the debate, with the tables being turned every once in a while (Lambregts and Zonneveld, 2004).

A NEW VISION FOR THE RANDSTAD

Currently, at the end of the first decade of the twenty-first century, the issue is highly topical again. The Dutch and the Randstad economies have not been spared by the global financial crisis (4 per cent contraction of GDP in 2009), worries about their competitive strengths are once more mounting, and the view that cities and notably metropolitan regions matter most in the international competition over mobile resources is still a popular one among planners and politicians. Typically, under such conditions, policy attention is directed towards the question of how the competitive strengths of the Randstad Holland can be fortified and how spatial policy can be put to use to bring to life the 'metropolitan' or the 'world city' qualities that are hidden in this region.

The government's latest views in this matter are documented in the *Structuurvisie Randstad 2040*, a regional plan, or rather, vision, drafted and published by the Ministry of Housing, Spatial Planning and the Environment (MINVROM) in 2008.[1] Compared with earlier government visions and plans, the *Structuurvisie Randstad 2040*

(*Structuurvisie* from hereon) gives a fairly elaborate analysis of the competitive conditions the Randstad is facing. Whereas previous documents would normally simply claim that 'the Randstad' competes with other Northwest European metropolitan regions such as the RheinRuhr, the Flemish Diamond, London and Paris, the *Structuurvisie* conveys the message that different cities in the Randstad, because of their different economic specializations, compete with different cities across Europe. For instance, Amsterdam, in its capacity as the region's financial and cultural capital, is understood to face competition from such peers as London, Paris, Brussels, Berlin and Frankfurt, while The Hague, profiled as a centre for international 'peace and justice' functions, is reported to compete with other international governance centres such as Geneva, Vienna, Bonn, Strasbourg and Brussels (MINVROM, 2008). This more subtle understanding obviously opens the door for the formulation of more specific and, arguably, even more effective spatial and economic policies. According to the *Structuurvisie*, such policies should depart from the strengths of the individual cities and aim at furthering these. In the view of the government this will help to diversify the Randstad economy and increase the attractiveness and the competitive powers of both the individual cities and the Randstad as whole. The government derives support for its view from several recent studies (e.g. RPB, 2006; OECD, 2007a) that argue and provide evidence that the bulk of the more elementary functional relationships (e.g. travel to work, travel for shopping, and firms' input and output relationships) in the Randstad is defined at the scale of the individual city-regions (i.e. greater Amsterdam, greater Rotterdam, etc.). Based on these, the government, for the time being and in contrast with previously held standpoints, considers it unproductive to develop policies aimed at fostering agglomeration economies at the scale of the Randstad as a whole.

As noted, however, polycentric world city regions are complex, multilayered constructs. Not every layer is equally easily unveiled. Below quite easily visible layers such as, for instance, those consisting of mobility patterns (travel to work patterns or other travel motives), we may also identify other, less visible ones. Visibility, in this respect, does not necessarily equal significance or meaningfulness. Less visible layers may be as indicative, for instance of spatial or functional coherence, as more visible ones. In the case of the Randstad it can be argued that the government in its *Structuurvisie* overlooks at least one important layer. It concerns a layer that strongly suggests that the individual cities derive competitive strengths not only from the assets that are theirs, but to a considerable degree also from the fact that they are part of the larger conurbation called Randstad Holland. Clarification follows below.

A SERVICE ECONOMY

The Randstad Holland has multiple faces indeed. However, from an economic perspective it is a services-oriented economy more than anything else. In 2009, commercial and non-commercial services together accounted for 87 per cent of the region's jobs, the commercial services alone for 53 per cent (CBS Statline, 2010). This service-based economy, moreover, is partly highly knowledge intensive and internationally oriented. The education level of the region's workforce is, on average, high (OECD, 2007a) and the share of knowledge-intensive service activities such as financial and producer services in total employment is substantial as well (27 per cent). The Randstad, in this respect, resembles most of the other world city regions in Northwest Europe.

The financial and producer services constitute an important category when the competitive qualities of the Randstad economy are concerned. They play an important role in the diffusion of knowledge in the regional economy. Their core business is to sell (mostly knowledge-intensive) services to third parties. Since it often concerns tailor-made products that may be partly or in whole produced at the client's office, the service production process usually involves intense interaction between the producer and the client (Bettencourt et al., 2002). In this process, the service producer transfers knowledge to his client. However, he is likely to gain knowledge himself as well: he may learn for example from the experience of fine tuning a service product to yet another client situation and obtain knowledge of the client's field of activity and working methods. Well-functioning services producers will internalize and possibly further develop this knowledge, and use it as an input in subsequent service production processes (Lambregts, 2008a).

Those service providers that operate internationally or belong to an international network or alliance represent a particularly interesting group in this. After all, through their international linkages these providers are very well equipped to gain access to knowledge that is generated and compiled elsewhere in the world. They are able to make this knowledge available to their clients in the Randstad swiftly and at relatively low cost.

The importance of this mechanism cannot be underestimated. For the Randstad Holland, as for any other world city region around the globe, today's reality is that knowledge carrying relevance for the local business community is produced in large measure 'elsewhere' in the world. For instance, of the global investments in research and development less than 1 per cent happens in the Randstad Holland. Even a massive world city region such as Southeast England (including London) does not account for more than 1.5 per cent of global R&D (OECD, 2007b). Of course, locally produced knowledge is more likely to suit local knowledge needs than knowledge that is produced somewhere at the other side of the world. Yet it is increasingly clear that in order to compete at the highest levels no city or city region can lean upon locally produced knowledge alone (e.g. Simmie, 2003). To have a sophisticated local knowledge base is crucially important, but at the same time not enough. Well-developed 'pipelines' that enable the exchange of knowledge between the region and others are another must (Bathelt et al., 2004). Internationally operating producer services firms, by means of their often worldwide office networks, provide such infrastructure for knowledge exchange.

EXCELLENCE ON THE BASIS OF BORROWED SCALE

The Randstad Holland is home to quite a number of such internationally operating producer services firms. Of the 97 most globally connected such firms that some time ago were selected by the Globalization and World Cities Research Network (GaWC), 80 per cent (78 in number) have a presence or multiple presences in the Netherlands (Lambregts et al., 2006). Almost all of these (94 per cent) have their main office in the Randstad area, with the bulk of them (over 70 per cent) concentrated in the Amsterdam city region (Lambregts et al., 2006; see also Table 44.1). The latter in particular is a remarkable concentration, both from a regional (i.e. Randstad) and from an international perspective.

Table 44.1   Spatial distribution of large firms, headquarters and international producer services firms

	The Netherlands	Randstad Holland	Amsterdam city region
Firms > 100 employees (2006)	7055 (100%)	3280 (47%)	670 (10%)
Headquarters of 96 largest Dutch companies (2004)	96 (100%)	73 (76%)	30 (31%)
GaWC top 97 global producer services firms (2004)	78 (100%)	73 (94%)	54 (69%)

Source: Lambregts and Van der Werff (2004); Lambregts (2008b)

Whereas in the polycentric Randstad Holland many functions are distributed quite equally between the four major city regions (if compensated for size) this is clearly not the case for the Dutch main offices of international producer services firms. Also from an international perspective Amsterdam seems to host significantly more such offices than one would expect it to on the basis of the city's rather modest size (Taylor, 2002).

At first sight these findings confirm the image that Amsterdam – once more – is rising above the in many respects fairly level playing field of the Randstad Holland, and they seem to support the national government's choice to encourage the individual city-regions to further develop their distinctive strengths and allow Amsterdam to parade as the country's real delegate on the world stage. A closer look into the motives of these firms, however, reveals that there is more to it.

Internationally operating producer services firms tend to open up shop in the Randstad not because they are footloose and able to land anywhere they want, but primarily because they see an interesting 'Dutch' market for their products (cf. Röling, 2010). Their target group primarily consists of the bigger enterprises and multinationals (the latter's headquarters notably). In 2006 (the most recent year for which such data have been compiled), the Netherlands was home to some 7000 enterprises employing 100 people or more. Almost half of these were located in the Randstad Holland (CBS Statline, 2010). In addition, of the headquarters of the country's 96 largest companies (of which many qualify as multinational corporations), roughly three-quarters are found in the Randstad (Regio Randstad, 2004). The 'Dutch' market, therefore, in practice is to a very considerable degree concentrated in the Randstad.

The intense producer–client interaction involved in the production and delivery of advanced producer services means that producer services firms prefer to be located within easy reach of their target group. Clearly, within the Netherlands the Randstad for them is the place to be. It has already been pointed out above that the bulk of the international producer services firms have their main office in the Amsterdam city region. This leads one to expect that the target group is concentrated in this area as well. The numbers (Table 44.1) suggest that this is true only to a limited extent. The Amsterdam city region does host a reasonable number of large firms and it has more than its fair share of headquarters indeed, but the concentration is not as marked as in the case of the international producer services firms. This means that international producer services firms located in the Amsterdam city region do find a reasonable number of potential clients in their immediate surroundings, but it also means that four times as many potential clients are to be found elsewhere in the Randstad area (notably in the city regions of Rotterdam, The Hague and Utrecht).

Interviews with 64 international producer services firms located in Amsterdam and elsewhere in the Randstad revealed that these firms tend to view the entire Randstad, and quite often even the entire country as their market (Lambregts, 2009). Amsterdam as a place of business is highly appreciated for its proximity to the airport, the attractiveness of the city centre, the worldly atmosphere, and the international character of its labour market, as well as for the simple fact that so many other international producer services providers are already located there. However, for many it is the potential provided by the Randstad market and, by extension, the Dutch market for advanced producer services that makes it worthwhile opening one or more offices in the area. Amsterdam in this respect 'borrows scale' as it were (Phelps and Ozawa, 2003), and it is especially because of a number of additional or secondary factors affecting the location choice of such businesses that it is able to emerge as the international business services centre of the Randstad. Without the support of the Randstad market, however, there would be much less to it.

CONCLUSION

The Randstad has been *the* template for polycentric urban regions for almost half a century. The close proximity and the finely articulated spatial division of labour between the four main cities seemed to show (as Peter Hall suggested many years ago) that different routes to the status of world city exist. Indeed, if we look at a few key indicators – for example, number of inhabitants, gross regional product, number of multinationals – the Randstad as a whole belonged and still belongs to the league of world cities. More recently, however, a more nuanced view on the Randstad as a world city has emerged. The impact of processes of deindustrialization and the accelerated shift to (producer and consumer) services as well as the arrival on the scene of young, highly educated, cosmopolitan, urban-oriented individuals and households have not only eroded the spatial division of labour between the four largest cities, but have also increased intra-urban socio-economic polarization. Notably, Rotterdam and its neighbouring cities have been hit hard by job loss in manufacturing and port-related activities, while Amsterdam, Utrecht, Haarlem and Leiden have clearly benefited from the combined (and interrelated) impact of the transformation of the production system and the inflow of highly educated urban dwellers (CBS Statline, 2010). Looking at the more recent election results, we observe that the different socio-economic fates of the cities within the Randstad have also been translated in the much higher support for populist parties in the cities that are doing less well (Deinema and Kloosterman, forthcoming).

Within the Randstad, Amsterdam (in conjunction with Schiphol) is becoming more important as the gateway to or interface with the global economy. Many important global flows – financial, knowledge, persons – start or pass through Amsterdam, land there and are transformed there. Some of the effects spread to nearby places (cf. Utrecht,

Haarlem and Leiden), but backwash effects can be noted in places such as Rotterdam and The Hague which have seen the departure of producer services firms to Amsterdam.

Notwithstanding the fact that Amsterdam is becoming more prominent as a window on the global economy, its attractiveness for international producer services providers is still inextricably bound up with the fact that this city is part of and gives access to the much larger market for inputs and outputs called 'Randstad Holland' (Kloosterman, 2010). The agglomeration effects defined at the regional scale form an essential part of the foundations for Amsterdam's growing prominence based on a highly diversified local economy historically geared towards international services, an attractive local atmosphere and a wide array of high-quality amenities for residents, workers, visitors and tourists alike. Other cities in the Randstad may also tap into the agglomeration economies generated at the level of the Randstad; many of the 'peaks' of the Randstad economy rest on foundations that cover the entire Randstad or more, but the larger Amsterdam region has become without doubt more of a *world* city than other components of the Randstad.

Several implications follow from this. First, polycentricity is to some extent in the eye of the beholder and depending on the spatial scale and the dimension(s) selected widely diverging conclusions may be drawn regarding the functional relationships between components of a (from a morphological perspective) polycentric urban region. Behind the obvious morphological patterns may lurk quite different relationships that may lead to contrasting understandings of a region's functioning and, concomitantly, to diverse 'most appropriate' policy scenarios.

The second lesson pertains to the Randstad in particular. The analysis has shown that in addition to patterns of relationships that are mostly defined at the level of city regions, there exist interdependencies that extend over the entire territory of the Randstad. As such the analysis contributes to the view that this particular polycentric world city region qualifies indeed as a coherent entity (as opposed to just an accidental coagulation of cities), and therefore merits to be labelled and treated as such. Within the Randstad region, however, we do see that agglomeration economies generated at the level of the region as a whole may intersect and interact with local qualities and lead to diverging socio-economic, cultural and political outcomes within one polycentric region.

The third and final lesson concerns the policymakers responsible for setting out the course of the Randstad. In their most recent policy paper they seem to have fallen for the view that the Randstad is a collection of separate cities and city regions. Competitiveness is pursued by encouraging the city regions to develop on the basis of their typical strengths. The fact that even such local strengths are at least partly derived from scale effects defined at the level of the Randstad is apparently overlooked. This renders the current policy strategy dangerously imbalanced, and in spite of its recent launch, already eligible for an overhaul.

NOTE

1. In the absence of a formal Randstad authority and given the importance of the area, formulating spatial visions and strategies for the Randstad is still a national government concern.

REFERENCES

Bathelt, H., A. Malmberg and P. Maskell (2004), 'Clusters and knowledge: local buzz, global pipelines and the process of knowledge creation', *Progress in Human Geography*, **28** (1), 31–56.

Bettencourt, L.A., A.L. Ostrom, S.W. Brown and R.I. Roundtree (2002), 'Client co-production in knowledge-intensive business services', *California Management Review*, **44** (4), 100–128.

CBS Statline (2010), Various tables (accessed between 4 and 8 November 2010).

Deinema, M.N. and R.C. Kloosterman (forthcoming), 'Historical trajectories and urban cultural economies in the Randstad megacity region. Cultural industries in Dutch cities since 1900', in J. Klaesson, B. Johansson, C. Karlsson and R.R. Stough (eds), *Metropolitan Regions: Preconditions and Strategies for Growth and Development in the Global Economy*, Berlin: Springer Verlag.

Duinen, L. van (2004), *Planning Imagery. The Emergence and Development of New Planning Concepts in Dutch National Spatial Policy*, Doctoral thesis, University of Amsterdam.

Engelen, E. (2007), 'Amsterdamned? The uncertain future of a secondary financial center', *Environment and Planning A*, **39** (6), 1306–1324.

ESPON 1.1.1/Nordregio (ed.) (2006), *ESPON 1.1.1 – Potentials for Polycentric Development in Europe*, Final Report, Stockholm/Luxembourg: Nordregio/ESPON Secretariat, available from http://www.espon.eu (accessed 10 July 2011).

Fainstein, S. (2001), 'Inequality in global city-regions', in A.J. Scott (ed.), *Global City-Regions: Trends, Theory, Policy*, Oxford: Oxford University Press, pp. 285–298.

Hall, P. (1966), *The World Cities*, London: Weidenfeld & Nicolson.

Hall, P. and K. Pain (eds) (2006), *The Polycentric Metropolis: Learning From Mega-City Regions in Europe*, London: Earthscan.

Kloosterman, R.C. (2004), 'Recent employment trends in the cultural industries in Amsterdam, Rotterdam, The Hague and Utrecht; a first exploration', *Tijdschrift voor Economische en Sociale Geografie*, **95** (2), 243–262.

Kloosterman, R.C. (2010), 'Building a career: labour practices and cluster reproduction in Dutch architectural design', *Regional Studies*, **44** (7), 859–871.

Kloosterman, R.C. and B. Lambregts (2001), 'Clustering of economic activities in polycentric urban regions: the case of the Randstad Holland', *Urban Studies*, **38** (4), 717–732.

Kloosterman, R.C. and B. Lambregts (2007), 'Between accumulation and concentration of capital: comparing the long-term trajectories of the Dutch Randstad and London urban systems', *Urban Geography*, **28** (1), 54–73.

Kloosterman, R.C. and S. Musterd (2001), 'The polycentric urban region: towards a research agenda', *Urban Studies*, **38** (4), 623–633.

Lambregts, B. (2006), 'Polycentrism: boon or barrier to metropolitan competitiveness? The case of the Randstad Holland', *Built Environment*, **32** (2), 114–123.

Lambregts, B. (2008a), 'Geographies of knowledge formation in mega-city regions: some evidence from the Dutch Randstad', *Regional Studies*, **42** (8), 1173–1186.

Lambregts, B. (2008b), 'Randstedelijke fundamenten voor stadsregionale pieken' [Regional foundations for urban centres in the Randstad], *Nova Terra*, **8** (1), 30–33.

Lambregts, B. (2009), *The Polycentric Mega-City-Region Unpacked – Concepts, Trends and Policy in the Randstad Holland*, Doctoral thesis, Amsterdam Institute for Metropolitan and International Development Studies, University of Amsterdam.

Lambregts, B., L. Janssen-Jansen and N. Haran (2008), 'Effective governance for competitive regions in Europe: the difficult case of the Randstad', *GeoJournal*, **72** (1–2), 45–57.

Lambregts, B., R. Kloosterman, M. van der Werff, R. Röling and L. Kapoen (2006), 'Randstad Holland: the multiple faces of a polycentric role model', in P. Hall and K. Pain (eds), *The Polycentric Metropolis – Learning from Mega-City Regions in Europe*, London: Earthscan, pp. 137–145.

Lambregts, B. and M. van der Werff (2004), 'Internationaal profiel van de Randstad in perspectief' [Putting the international profile of the Randstad into perspective], *Rooilijn*, **37** (6), 270–276.

Lambregts, B. and W. Zonneveld (2004), 'From Randstad to Deltametropolis: changing attitudes towards the scattered metropolis', *European Planning Studies*, **12** (3), 299–321.

Meijers, E. (2007a), *Synergy in Polycentric Urban Regions: Complementarity, Organising Capacity and Critical Mass*. Doctoral thesis, Delft: Delft University Press.

Meijers, E. (2007b), 'Clones or complements? The division of labour between the main cities of the Randstad, the Flemish Diamond and the RheinRuhr Area', *Regional Studies*, **41** (7), 889–900.

MINVROM (Ministerie van Volkshuisvesting, Ruimtelijke Ordening en Milieubeheer) (2008), *Structuurvisie Randstad 2040* (Structure Plan Randstad 2040), Den Haag: Ministerie van VROM.

OECD (2007a), *Territorial Reviews: Randstad Holland, The Netherlands*, Paris: OECD.

OECD (2007b), *Main Science and Technology Indicators (MSTI): 2007/2 Edition*, Paris: OECD.

Phelps, N. and T. Ozawa (2003), 'Contrasts in agglomeration: proto-industrial, industrial and post-industrial forms compared', *Progress in Human Geography*, **27** (5), 583–604.

Regio Randstad (2004), *Economische Strategie Randstad* [Economic Strategy for the Randstad], Utrecht: Regio Randstad.

Röling, R.W. (2010), 'Small town, big campaigns: the rise and growth of an international advertising industry in Amsterdam', *Regional Studies*, **44** (7), 829–843.

RPB (Ruimtelijk Planbureau) (2006), *Vele steden maken nog geen Randstad* [Many Towns do not Make a Randstad], Rotterdam/Den Haag: NAi Uitgevers/Ruimtelijk Planbureau.

Scott, A.J. (1998), *Regions and the World Economy: The Coming Shape of Global Production, Competition and Political Order*, Oxford: Oxford University Press.

Shachar, A. (1994), 'Randstad Holland: a "world city"?', *Urban Studies*, **31** (3), 381–400.

Simmie, J. (2003), 'Innovation and urban regions as national and international nodes for the transfer and sharing of knowledge', *Regional Studies*, **37** (6–7), 607–620.

Simmonds, R. and G. Hack (eds) (2000), *Global City Regions: Their Emerging Forms*, London: Spon.

Taylor, P.J. (2002), 'Amsterdam in a world city network', Loughborough University, available at www.lboro. ac.uk/gawc/rb/rm1.pdf (accessed 4 November 2010).

Taylor, P.J. (2004), *World City Network: A Global Urban Analysis*, London: Routledge.

Terhorst, P. and J. van der Ven (1995), 'The national urban growth coalition in the Netherlands', *Political Geography*, **14** (4), 343–361.

TNO (2010), *De Top 20 van Europese stedelijke Regio's: Randstad Holland in Internationaal Perspectief*, Delft: TNO, available at http://www.randstadregion.eu/actueel-0/nieuwsbericht/randstadmonitor-2010/#backlink (accessed 10 July 2011).

45 From national capital to dismal political world city: the politics of scalar disarticulation in Brussels
Stijn Oosterlynck

THE BRUSSELS PARADOX: ECONOMIC DYNAMISM AND SOCIAL POLARIZATION

Even a quick glimpse at the economic indicators for Brussels, officially the Brussels Capital Region (henceforth BCR),[1] suggests that it is one of the richest city-regions in Europe. In terms of the Gross Regional Product (GRP) per capita for example, the BCR is the third richest European city-region, after Inner London and Luxembourg, and scores 221 per cent above the average of the 27 European Member States (Eurostat, 2010).[2] In 2008, the BCR economy produced 679,889 jobs for a 'labour active'[3] population of 442,000 people (2007) (Corijn and Vloeberghs, 2009). This is an increase in jobs of more than 10 per cent compared with 1995. The BCR economy is heavily specialized in the public and private administrative sector (Deroo et al., 1998; Corijn and Vloeberghs, 2009). In 2001, only 11 per cent of salaried jobs were in the industrial sector, while 54 per cent of BCR jobs were in the government sector (16.2 per cent), business services (15 per cent), commerce (11.9 per cent) and financial institutions (10.7 per cent). BCR houses a large international public sector, with 41,000 people working for the European institutions, nearly 4000 for NATO and many more in activities related to the international public sector such as lobbyists (estimated between 15,000 and 20,000), journalists (estimated at 1400), lawyers, diplomats, and so on (Corijn et al., 2009). The Brussels city-regional service economy is hence strongly international in orientation (Swyngedouw and Baeten, 2001). According to Taylor, Brussels is a 'political world city', which has successfully turned its (international) political specialization as EU capital into a diversified and resilient urban niche economy that is strongly embedded in world city networks (Taylor, 2007).

The strong economic performance of Brussels does not however translate into an equally high socio-economic profile of its population. Despite its continued economic dynamism, the average family income in Brussels decreased from 160 per cent of the national average in 1963 to only 85 per cent in 2005 (Kesteloot and Loopmans, 2009). More than one-fifth of the Brussels population lives in poverty[4] (Beghin, 2006). In 2005, 30,828 inhabitants of Brussels (out of a total population of 1,012,258[5]) received the minimum income[6] of the Public Centres for Social Welfare, which is 24.22 per cent of the total number of Belgian beneficiaries (while the Brussels population makes up only 10 per cent of the total Belgian population). This poverty is mainly caused by the high unemployment in Brussels. In 2006, unemployment in Brussels was 18.2 per cent compared with 8.4 per cent for the whole of Belgium, increasing to 35.5 per cent for people aged between 15 and 24 (compared with 18.9 per cent for the whole of Belgium) (Corijn and Vloeberghs, 2009). Its youth unemployment puts BCR at twelfth place among the

EU 27 regions. Sixty-two of the unemployed had been unemployed for at least one year, a number which is still increasing. Thirty-two per cent of the children in BCR live in a family without labour income. In 2007, 25,020 BCR households (26 per cent of the total) were on the waiting list for social housing and condemned to look for housing in the private rental market, where housing often lacks basic quality features (e.g. 10 per cent of housing in the private rental market even lacks a toilet and individual bathroom) (Corijn and Vloeberghs, 2009). One in five people in BCR delays health care for financial reasons.

The immediate causes of this Brussels paradox between economic dynamism and social polarization are well known and not even specific to Brussels (see for example Sassen's (1991) argument about the social polarization in global cities and Friedmann's (1986) world city hypothesis). While many of the jobs in Brussels are highly skilled, a significant part of the Brussels population is low skilled. This leads to only 44.6 per cent of BCR jobs being occupied by BCR inhabitants (Brussels Observatorium van de Arbeidsmarkt en Kwalificaties, 2003). Some 55.4 per cent of the jobs are taken by Flemish (36 per cent) and Walloons (19.4 per cent), half of whom live in the green and residential Brussels periphery outside BCR (Corijn and Vloeberghs, 2009). The reverse movement, BCR inhabitants working in the Flemish or Walloon regions surrounding Brussels, is much smaller. As many BCR jobs are occupied by commuters, BCR misses out on a lot of income taxation. Indeed, the BCR proportion of the total Belgian government income via personal income taxation decreases every year. In 2005, the average taxable income of BCR inhabitants was 14.47 per cent lower than the Belgian average (Corijn and Vloeberghs, 2009). Four of the five Belgian municipalities with the lowest tax income per inhabitant lie within the BCR, while the two provinces surrounding BCR are the richest in Belgium.

However, this explanation referring to the spatial mismatch between the political-institutional demarcation of Brussels and its socio-economic dynamics still leaves much to be explained about the politics of the world city. Since articulating economic and social development is essentially a political activity, the deeper causes for the Brussels paradox have to be searched for in the political field. Why is the Brussels Capital Region politically incapable of mobilizing its economic dynamics and wealth to the benefit of large parts of its population? In this chapter, I focus on the spatio-political moment of Brussels' socio-economic development trajectory and argue that the glocalization of the city is the root cause of the persistence of the Brussels paradox over time. The scalar disarticulation underlying the Brussels paradox is the combined result of the internationalization of the city's political economy and the socio-spatial disintegration of the national–urban elite who ruled both Belgium and Brussels until the early 1960s.

THE 'NATIONALIZATION' OF BRUSSELS

To understand the current condition of scalar disarticulation, we need to go back to the 19th century, when Brussels was 'nationalized' as part of the Belgian francophone nation-building project. In the decades following the independence of Belgium in 1830, socio-political and economic power was centralized in the capital Brussels (Witte et al., 1997; Reynebeau, 2005). Although a majority of the national population spoke Flemish dialects, the French language was quickly adopted as an important cultural marker of the Belgian nation-building project. Language expressed social differentiation as much as it marked a geographical division.[7] The unitary Belgian state space was created through the institutionalization of social and political conflict-mediating mechanisms in the capital. Brussels was also the place through which the Belgian space economy was inserted in international circuits of capital (Quévit and Aiken, 1978). Belgian francophone holding capital, which over time came to control a large part of Belgian industry, acted as a crucial vehicle for the centralization of political–economic relations in the capital (Cottenier et al., 1989; Kurgan-van Hentenryk, 1996; Oosterlynck, 2007). As its members were predominantly drawn from the wealthiest Brussels bourgeoisie families, a financial elite residing in Brussels controlled Belgian industrialization. The Brussels urban elite was hence embedded in the national political–economic elite and its accumulation and regulatory strategies. The Brussels bourgeoisie was effectively a Belgian bourgeoisie, often occupying important political mandates at the local and national level. Because the interests of Belgium and Brussels were articulated by the national elite residing in Brussels, they converged.

The forging of a scalar articulation between political–economic processes in Brussels and Belgium by the national–urban elite implied that the political and economic success of Belgium also led to urban growth in Brussels. This elite, perhaps best embodied in the political figures of Brussels mayor Anspach and King Leopold II, made sustained efforts to make the success of the Belgian national–colonial project visible in the Brussels urban landscape (Demey, 1990). Between 1860 and 1880, they transformed Brussels into a modern national-imperial capital by demolishing parts of the old city and replacing them with a symmetric vision of space with straight lines, monumental perspectives, prestigious residences and ordered squares. The rapid industrialization of Brussels and the exploitation of Congo by King Leopold II provided the resources to finance the redevelopment of Brussels.

This national–urban elite further consolidated its position and political project in the first half of the 20th century. When the second industrial revolution, from the 1930s onwards, provoked a gradual shift of the centre of economic gravity from the French-speaking Walloon region to the Dutch-speaking Flemish region and Belgian holding capital further centralized, a truly integrated Belgian economy emerged, with the Brussels-based holdings as its private command centre (Vandermotten et al., 1990; Kurgan-van Hentenryk, 1996). The economic exploitation of Congo was equally administered and controlled from Brussels, with the Brussels-based holding Société Générale controlling 70 per cent of the colonial economy by 1930. The holding entertained close links with the colonial political structure, further tying the national, colonial and urban interests together.

THE GERMS OF DISINTEGRATION: THE TERRITORIALIZATION OF THE LANGUAGE STRUGGLE AND REGIONAL UNEVEN DEVELOPMENT

The first germs of the scalar disarticulation of the national–urban regime emerged in the first half of the 20th century. In the 19th century, a small Flemish movement fought a liberal struggle for the recognition of Flemish language and cultural rights (Reynebeau, 1995). For a variety of reasons, in the first decades of the 20th century, this became a struggle for territorial–linguistic integrity (Murphy, 1988). The aim was to root out every trace of francophone presence on the Flemish regional territory and safeguard its linguistic integrity. Once the language struggle was territorialized, language politics broadened to 'communitarian politics' as language and ideological disagreements between the Catholics and Socialists, respectively dominant in Flanders and Wallonia, became increasingly intertwined. From the 1950s onwards, political issues were increasingly framed through the prism of the territorial–linguistic communities (Huyse, 1980).

In the meantime, the regional uneven geography of socio-economic development in Belgium also gave rise to centrifugal tensions, which the national–urban elite would find increasingly difficult to contain in the post-war period (Moulaert and Willekens, 1984). The Walloon region was characterized by a pre-Fordist industrial structure and socio-economic relations steeped in confrontational class struggle, led by a militant socialist movement (Mandel, 1963). The Flemish region remained for the most part rural and underdeveloped all through the 19th century and only started industrializing in the 1930s, and much faster in the 1960s, and developed a Fordist industrial structure. Its socio-economic relations were, due to its late industrialization and the dominance of the Catholic trade union, more cooperative. After the Second World War these two diverging regional socio-economic development trajectories were gradually embedded in a national Fordist mode of regulation centred on Brussels. However, the socio-political struggles waged around the establishment of the different elements of this Fordist mode of regulation led to a definite change in the relations of power within the Belgian, and for that matter also the Brussels, political economy (Mommen, 1982; Witte et al., 1997; Oosterlynck, 2007). The francophone Belgian holding bourgeoisie, whose investment policy had grown increasingly conservative, favoured an extensive model of accumulation, based on low wages and the export-oriented production of basic and semi-finished goods. This strategy was criticized by the upcoming 'modernist' fractions of the Belgian bourgeoisie, supported mainly (but not exclusively) by politicians, technocrats and trade unionists from the Flemish region (Mommen, 1982). They called for wages tied to productivity increases, the establishment of neo-corporatist bargaining and an investment support policy. Although a whole range of piecemeal steps were taken before and after the war, it was not until the early 1960s that a full-blown Fordist mode of regulation could be established.

But before the linguistic and socio-economic cracks would become so big as to finally unleash their centrifugal forces and break the national–urban scalar articulation, Brussels was the scene for a last celebration of national unity. The organization of the 1958 World Expo in Brussels at once signalled Brussels' apogee as the socio-spatial core of Belgian political–economic space. Expo 58 became the emblematic embodiment of the socio-economic and cultural transformation of a city whose elites were still (but not for long) primarily articulated through national industrial–imperial–financial interests. It was set up as a moment of celebrating Belgian national unity, after the 1950s had witnessed the increasing but politically engineered convergence of the ideological and linguistic–territorial disagreements. The national–urban elite used Expo 58 to project the image of a modern and forward-looking, economically and technologically dynamic and unified nation to the world (Vanderwegen, 2003). At the same time, Expo 58 was used as a vehicle to expand the Brussels conference and hotel infrastructure and speed up the modernization of its road infrastructure, making sure it was at the core of the emerging Belgian and international highway system (Aron, 1978; Demey, 1992). This paved the way for the transformation of Brussels into an important hub for the emerging international service economy.

THE SCALAR DISARTICULATION OF THE NATIONAL–URBAN REGIME

The first crack in the unitary Belgian political–economic space appeared soon after Expo 58. The unexpected decolonization of Congo in 1960 hit the national–urban elite in Brussels extremely hard. Not only did it mean the end of their imperial ambitions, the francophone Belgian holdings also lost their main source of super profits. In 1955 the shares of the colonial companies made up 44 per cent of the total value of all stock-listed Belgian companies (Buelens, 2007). This event had knock-on effects on the position of Belgian holding capital in the Belgian economy. Soon after, they had to give up their resistance to the development of a Keynesian economic expansion policy, the last element of the Fordist mode of regulation that had not yet been put in place and that was necessary to overcome the tensions between the new Fordist norms of mass consumption and the outmoded pre-Fordist production structure. Holding capital suddenly found itself in a secondary role, with the modernist and largely Flemish-based fractions of the economic elite and multinational capital that increasingly invested in the Flemish region reshaping the Belgian socio-economic development trajectory along Fordist lines. Although Brussels remained the command centre of the Fordist national economy, the new political–economic leaders often did not originate or reside in Brussels. They consequently felt no special attachment to the city and in some cases, because of its history as the geographical centre of the francophone nation-building project, they even entertained latent hostility to it.

Apart from the weakening of its economic base, the position of Brussels at the socio-spatial core of the Belgian political economy was put under further pressure by the mainstreaming of federalism. In the early 1960s the Walloon regionalist movement, which emerged in response to the linguistic demands of the Flemish movement, was reinforced by large parts of the Walloon socialist movement who were frustrated about Walloon economic decline and felt marginalized in a Belgian state which they saw as increasingly dominated by Flemish interests. As Brussels-based holding capital disinvested from Wallonia, the Walloon regionalist movement turned its back on the unitary national–urban elite and fought for regional economic autonomy (Quévit and Aiken, 1978). This Walloon demand for economic regionalism was reinforced by the Flemish demand for cultural and linguistic autonomy. All this fed into the mainstreaming of federalism in the 1960s and signalled the end of the unitary Belgian francophone nation-building project. The position of Brussels as the preferred site for the symbolic and social reproduction of national unity equally came under attack, for example through the Flemish marches on Brussels in the early 1960s (Govaert, 2000). The combined erosion of the political and economic basis of the Belgian national political–economic elite residing in Brussels put the scalar articulation between Brussels and Belgian identity and interests under heavy strain. Consequently, as federalization proceeded, what was the erstwhile socio-spatial core of Belgium turned into its Gordian knot.

As the distinctively Belgian elite reproduced in the capital Brussels disappeared from the Brussels political scene, political–economic control over the Brussels space became initially strongly localized. A local elite coalition jumped into the political power vacuum and transformed Brussels into a centre for the international service economy, hence the urban expression of the national transition to Fordism. The Manhattan Plan to redevelop the Brussels Noordwijk into a central business district at the intersection of the two main European motorways was the most emblematic realization of this new localized elite (Demey, 1992; Vanden Eede and Martens, 1994). It was led by the bilingual Brussels Christian-Democrat politician Van den Boeynants and the local property developer De Pauw. Both were self-made men with extensive political and economic networks, but without membership of the Belgian Brussels-based holding bourgeoisie (Hirson, 1969; Willems and Ilegems, 1991). For almost a decade they were able to organize a consensus among relevant local public and private actors, including local corporatist networks, the press, the Belgian francophone nobility (important for financing purposes), construction companies and relevant national politicians, and mobilize the financial and political support to translate their urban vision into practice.

BRUSSELS IN THE INSTITUTIONAL FRIDGE

In 1970 an agreement was reached to decentralize the Belgian state (De Bruycker, 1989). However, this was only an agreement in principle and the position of Brussels as a separate region remained a major point of contention (Govaert, 2000). Many Flemish politicians did not consider Brussels as a separate cultural community, but as bilingual territory that was to be governed jointly by the two language communities. The Walloon movement at that time did not consider Brussels as an entity on equal terms with Wallonia and Flanders either. Apart from the socialist rejection of Brussels as the place of residence of the holding bourgeoisie, they conceived their relationship with Brussels mainly in terms of linguistic solidarity. The Gilson bills in 1962 and 1963 fixed the language border and installed linguistic homogeneity in every Belgian province, except for the Brussels area. These bills were highly significant for the position of Brussels, because of their determinate influence on Brussels' current spatial form. The 19 core municipalities of Brussels were designated as the bilingual area. This restricted what was later to become BCR to the 19 communities on the basis of linguistic arguments. Brussels was put into a 'spatial straightjacket' that problematized its growth dynamics and the spatial reach of its urban governance system. A similar evolution occurred in the field of socio-economic cooperation, where the economic conception of a larger Brussels also lost out against the more restricted political–linguistic conception of Brussels (Blaise, 1998).

The contested socio-spatial position of Brussels in the restructured Belgian political–economic space following the scalar disarticulation of the national–urban project led to a search for a new definition of its identity and interests. This search was reflected in the electoral instability that plagued Brussels for two decades after 1965, which stood in marked contrast to the electoral stability in the Walloon and Flemish region. Central to the electoral instability was the remarkable popularity of the Brussels political party

Francophone Front (FDF) (Govaert, 2000). FDF was the immediate response from Brussels to regionalist threats and signalled the emergence of an autonomous Brussels political current, be it still strongly attached to the unitary Belgian state and therefore distancing itself from both the Walloon regionalist and Flemish nationalist movement. FDF transcended ideological and corporatist divides to ward off the external threat. It reached its electoral peak in the 1970s, with close to 40 per cent of the vote in the 1974 elections, but started losing votes after 1978, when an institutional solution for Brussels came closer.

In 1980, a compromise was reached on the modalities of the reorganization of the Belgian state into a full-blown federal state, but only by excluding Brussels from the agreement. Whereas the Flemish and Walloon regions were allowed to create their own government and parliament, Brussels was kept in the institutional fridge and governed by a 'Brussels executive' that was embedded in the national government, thus also missing out on financial resources for regions. Now that the Flemish parties had secured an agreement, their point of view on Brussels as a third region radicalized. Because integration of Brussels in Flanders or Wallonia was not an option, there were only two alternatives: a third region with the same statute as the other two regions or a region with a special statute governed jointly by the two language communities, thus denying Brussels autonomy. The Flemish position during the 1970s and 1980s was close to the latter, whereas the Walloons were closer to the former. The Walloons hoped that linguistic solidarity between the Walloon and the Brussels region would help to counter Flemish power within the Belgian state.

It took another nine years before a definitive solution was found for Brussels. In 1989 the Brussels Capital Region was created as the third Belgian region, with a highly complex political configuration (for cultural and linguistic matters Flemish and francophone institutions remained responsible), but with the same financing mechanisms and responsibilities as the other two regions. The Flemish had to concede on the latter, but were able to permanently fix the territory of the 19 municipalities as BCR territory. In other words, the scalar and spatial basis for Brussels was definitively put into a straightjacket, which meant that a major part of the urban growth machine fell outside the political–administrative boundaries of the BCR institutions.

EPILOGUE: A DISMAL POLITICAL WORLD CITY

The historical process of scalar disarticulation described above has produced a fragmented and glocalized political configuration, which despite its political and economic internationalization remains spatially and institutionally 'embedded' – if not trapped – in the Belgian federal structure. The decentralization of the Belgian state clearly unfolded at the expense of Brussels political power. As a largely francophone (albeit officially bilingual but increasingly multilingual and cosmopolitan) city surrounded by Flemish territory, the BCR institutions have virtually no control over the city-region's most dynamic growth areas and its expansion is severely curtailed. Its complex scalar gestalt, with co-governance for cultural and person-related affairs by Flemish and francophone institutions, implies enduring and unproductive conflicts (played out in the BCR institutions) over the imagination and institutionalization of Brussels between actors with conflicting interests and strategies and often no real interest in the overall socio-economic development of Brussels.

The current BCR institutional configuration, and the political elite occupying it, are too much steeped in the scalar politics played out in the Belgian state space to be capable of unlocking the actual socio-cultural diversity that exists in Brussels. As many Belgian middle class residents suburbanized and were replaced by migrants and as corporate headquarters and European and other international political institutions set up shop in Brussels, its population effectively internationalized. Consequently, a growing number of Brussels residents have no Belgian roots and identify themselves neither as Flemish nor as francophone Belgian. The BCR institutions fail to tap into the political energies and skills of this internationally diverse population and channel them into the construction of a new political elite that can harness the economic dynamics of Brussels to the benefit of its own population. The political elite in Brussels, those occupying its formal governance institutions, are not ruling the city. They fail to form a coherent and locally embedded elite coalition that articulates a Brussels accumulation strategy with social development and a large-scale urban vision. To end on a more positive note, however, in recent years new attempts have been made to reimagine Brussels interests and identity and align them more closely with the actually existing diversity of urban life in Brussels. Several civil society initiatives, among them Aula Magna, Citizens' Forum of Brussels and Brussels Manifest, have emerged to do just that. Time will tell whether the city from which Europe is ruled will be able to nurture a new scalar gestalt that will help to overcome the paradox between its economic dynamism and social polarization.

ACKNOWLEDGEMENTS

This chapter is based on research carried out as part of the European FP6 financed project Demologos (Development Models and Logics of Socioeconomic Organisation in Space), coordinated by Frank Moulaert. I am grateful to Erik Swyngedouw for discussions on the content of this chapter.

NOTES

1. The Brussels Capital Region consists of 19 municipalities, but is only the core of a much larger urban agglomeration including at least 36 municipalities (Van Wynsberghe et al., 2009). In this chapter I will use 'Brussels' to refer to the larger urban agglomeration and 'Brussels Capital Region' (BCR) for the (smaller) institutional–administrative entity.
2. The position of Brussels is relatively stable over time. In 1986 and 1996 Brussels occupied the second position in the list of top performing regions in terms of GRP per capita in Europe (European Commission, 1999). In 2004 it occupied third place (European Commission DG Regional Policy, 2007).
3. The 'labour active' population is the number of people between the ages of 15 and 64 that are either employed or actively seeking employment. In 2007, 65 per cent of the Brussels inhabitants were labour active (Corijn and Vloeberghs, 2009).
4. In Belgium the poverty line is fixed at 775 Euro a month for a single person and 1.627 Euro for a family with two children (Beghin, 2006).
5. See www.briobrussel.be/ned/webpage.asp?WebpageId=39 (accessed 13 May 2010).
6. The 'minimum income' is the income Belgian citizens can receive from local Public Centres for Social Welfare if they have no other source of income or an income that is below that of the minimum income. In

the majority of cases, this 'minimum income' ('leefloon' in Dutch) is below the 'poverty risk line', which is determined at 60 per cent of median income in Belgium.
7. The language of the Flemish region in the North of the country is Dutch, whereas the Southern region, Wallonia, speaks French. Because of its role as capital, Brussels gradually frenchified. It became a largely francophone city surrounded by Flemish territory.

REFERENCES

Aron, J. (1978), *Le tournant de l'urbanisme Bruxellois, 1958–1978*, Brussels: Fondation Joseph Jacquemotte.
Beghin, J. (2006), *Armoede in Brussel*, Berchem: EPO.
Blaise, P. (1998), 'L'émergence de la concertation économique et sociale bruxelloise', *Courrier Hebdomadaire CRISP*, 1622–1623, 1–54.
Brussels Observatorium van de Arbeidsmarkt en Kwalificaties (2003), *Evolutie van de Brusselse arbeidsmarkt: tussen dynamisme en dualiteit*, Brussels: Brussels Observatorium van de Arbeidsmarkt en Kwalificaties.
Buelens, F. (2007), *Congo 1885–1960. Een financieel-economische geschiedenis*, Berchem: EPO.
Corijn, E., C. Vandermotten, J.-M. Decroly and E. Swyngedouw (2009), 'Citizens' forum of Brussels. Brussels as an international city', *Brussels Studies* (Synopsis nr. 13).
Corijn, E. and E. Vloeberghs (2009), *Brussel!*, Brussels: VUB Press.
Cottenier, J., P. De Boosere and T. Gounet (1989), *De Generale: 1822–1992*, Berchem: EPO.
De Bruycker, P. (1989), 'Bruxelles dans la réforme de l'Etat', *Courrier Hebdomadaire CRISP*, 1230–1231, 1–61.
Demey, T. (1990), *Bruxelles: Chronique d'une capitale en chantier 1*, Brussels: Paul Legrain/Editions C.F.C.
Demey, T. (1992), *Bruxelles: Chronique d'une capitale en chantier 2*, Brussels: Paul Legrain.
Deroo, R., A. Claes and E. Christiaens (1998), 'L'impact socio-economique des institutions europeennes et internationales dans la Region de Bruxelles-Capitale. Passe et avenir (resume)'.
European Commission (1999), *Sixth Periodic Report of the Social and Economic Situation and Development of the Regions of the European Union*, Brussels: European Commission.
European Commission DG Regional Policy (2007), 'Regional GDP per inhabitant in the EU27', available at http://europa.eu/rapid/pressReleasesAction.do?reference=STAT/07/23&format=HTML&aged=0&langua ge=EN&guiLanguage=en (accessed 4 March 2007).
Eurostat (2010), 'Regional GDP per inhabitant in 2007 GDP per inhabitant ranged from 26 per cent of the EU27 average in Severozapaden in Bulgaria to 334 per cent in Inner London', 18 February 2010, available at http://europa.eu/rapid/pressReleasesAction.do?reference=STAT/10/25&format=HTML&aged=0&lang uage=EN&guiLanguage=en (accessed 10 May 2010).
Friedmann, J. (1986), 'The world city hypothesis', *Development and Change*, **17** (1), 69–83.
Govaert, S. (2000), *Bruxelles en capitales. 1958–2000, de l'expo à l'euro*, Brussels: De Boeck Université.
Hirson, N. (1969), *Paul Vanden Boeynants: sa carrière*, Brussels: Editions Capitales.
Huyse, L. (1980), *De gewapende vrede. Politiek in België tussen 1945 en 1980*, Leuven: Kritak.
Kesteloot, C. and M. Loopmans (2009), 'Citizens' forum of Brussels. Social inequalities', *Brussels Studies* (Synopsis nr. 16).
Kurgan-van Hentenryk, G. (1996), *Gouverner la Générale de Belgique. Essai de biographier collective*, Brussels: De Boeck & Larcier.
Mandel, E. (1963), 'The dialectic of class and region in Belgium', *New Left Review*, No. 20, 5–31.
Mommen, A. (1982), *De teloorgang van de Belgische bourgeoisie*, Leuven: Kritak.
Moulaert, F. and F. Willekens (1984), 'Decentralization in industrial policy in Belgium: toward a new economic feudalism?', *Johns Hopkins European Center for Regional Planning and Research Working Paper*, 6.
Murphy, A.B. (1988), *The Regional Dynamics of Language Differentiation in Belgium: A Study in Cultural-Political Geography*, Chicago: University of Chicago Press.
Oosterlynck, S. (2007), *The Political Economy of New Regionalism in Belgium: Imagining and Institutionalising the Flemish Regional Economy*, Lancaster: Sociology Department, Lancaster University.
Quévit, M. and M. Aiken (1978), *Les causes du déclin wallon: l'influence du pouvoir politique et des groupes financiers sur le développement régional*, Brussels: Vie ouvrière.
Reynebeau, M. (1995), *Het klauwen van de leeuw. De Vlaamse identiteit van de 12de tot de 21ste eeuw*, Leuven: Uitgeverij Van Halewyck.
Reynebeau, M. (2005), *Een geschiedenis van België*, Tielt: Lannoo.
Sassen, S. (1991), *The Global City: New York, London, Tokyo*, Princeton, NJ: Princeton University Press.
Swyngedouw, E. and G. Baeten (2001), 'Scaling the city: the political economy of "glocal" development – Brussels' conundrum', *European Planning Studies*, **9** (7), 827–849.

Taylor, P.J. (2007), 'Brussels in world city networks', *GaWC Research Bulletin*, 223, available at www.lboro. ac.uk/gawc/rb/rb223.html (accessed 10 May 2010).

Van Wynsberghe, C., J. Poirier, D. Sinardet and F. Tulkens (2009), 'De politieke en institutionele ontwikkeling van het Brusselse Stadsgewest: bevindingen en perspectieven', *Brussels Studies* (Synopsis nr.10).

Vanden Eede, M. and A. Martens (1994), *De Noordwijk: slopen en wonen*, Berchem: EPO.

Vandermotten, C., P. Saey and C. Kesteloot (1990), 'België in stukken: bestaan Vlaanderen en Wallonië echt?', in Mort Subite (eds), *Barsten in België: een geografie van de Belgische maatschappij*, Berchem: EPO, pp. 11–65.

Vanderwegen, B. (2003), 'Over de Atoomstijl en zijn tijdsgeest. De hybride moderniteit van Expo 58', *ASRO*, Leuven, Leuven University.

Willems, J. and D. Ilegems (1991), *De avonturen van VdB: een biografie*, Antwerpen: Loempia.

Witte, E., J. Craeybeckx and A. Meynen (1997), *Politieke geschiedenis van Belgie van 1830 tot heden*, Brussels: VUB Press.

46 Las Vegas: more than a one-dimensional world city?

Robert E. Lang and Christina Nicholas

ORIGINS: BRIGHT LIGHT CITY

There are many routes to world city status. Most places get there by being financial, trade or manufacturing hubs, or, as is the case with the biggest and most connected world cities, have a concentration of all three. Las Vegas took a different path. It achieved world city status via one key sector – entertainment. Las Vegas is one of the newest world cities to emerge.

No one saw Las Vegas emerging as a world city. Even in the late 20th century few analysts predicted the region could ever achieve 1 million residents, let alone 2 million. One example of this is an analysis done by Jerome Pickard, a demographer at the Urban Land Institute in Washington, DC (Pickard, 1962, 1966). Pickard projected metropolitans expected to exceed 1 million residents by the turn of the millennium. His estimates were nearly perfect, but for one major exception – Las Vegas.

It is easy to see why Pickard failed to predict a major metropolis forming in Southern Nevada. Sure, the region was booming. Just a few years earlier, Elvis Presley and Ann-Margret had appeared in *Viva Las Vegas!*, a film that was essentially a booster's guide to the city. The movie was a hit and helped put the city on the map – at least Hollywood's map. By the 1960s even the mysterious but seldom miscalculating Howard Hughes had doubled down on Las Vegas, first taking up permanent residence and then buying the Desert Inn in 1967. Hughes soon became the largest land holder in the city. Despite investment by Hughes and others, the region remained home to just over a quarter of a million residents in 1970, whereas nearby Phoenix already had over a million people.

In the early 1970s Las Vegas was a one trick town and its industry – gambling (or 'gaming' in local parlance) – was so stigmatized that it existed only in Nevada. The city already had landmark hotels, and the famous 'Strip' was by then iconic enough to influence American architecture as in Robert Venturi and Denise Scott Brown's book, *Learning from Las Vegas*. But the idea that this overgrown honky-tonk could anchor a true world city seemed a stretch.

A generation later, the idea of Vegas as a world city exists firmly in the public mind. What changed? For starters, gaming spread throughout the US and worldwide. First Atlantic City, NJ allowed gambling in the 1970s and then the floodgates opened. Soon people could gamble on riverboats in the Mississippi and off the Gulf Coast. Then in 1988, the US Congress[1] passed the Indian Gaming and Regulation Act, providing a regulatory basis for Native Americans to build and operate casinos – and they did just about everywhere. Every time gaming expanded, some urban analyst or economist predicted the demise of Las Vegas. The logic seemed straightforward: why come to Las Vegas when one could gamble a state over, or even a city over? History proved that the widespread diffusion of gambling only induced a bigger appetite for even more gambling. In this socio-cultural–legal–lifestyle transition, Las Vegas became the epicenter of gaming. Many people who gambled in a nearby Indian reservation were really just warming up for Las Vegas.

The gaming industry in Las Vegas has matured in two key ways. First the city increasingly offered a host of complementary activities to go along with gambling. Las Vegas tied into Hollywood and live entertainment. Elvis might 'leave the building' at the end of the show, but in Las Vegas he always seemed to come back. The city quickly became one of the world's largest venues for entertainment, surpassing even New York City's Broadway by the 1980s, and has continued to add function after function related to tourism ever since – food, shopping and, perhaps most important of all, conventions.

Compounding economic expansion occurs when one industry facilitates the development of another. In the Silicon Valley, located outside of San Francisco, this happened when defense contracting led to electronics, which led to computing, which led to software, which led to the Internet, and to an explosion of web applications and technologies ranging from Google's search engine to Apple's iPhone. Each layer of new industry partly supplants the old ones, but also expands the regional economic base like a series of concentric rings. In Las Vegas, a similar economic ring expansion began from gambling.

Las Vegas emerging as a Mecca for gambling is a bit ironic considering its earlier history. In the 1930s Las Vegas was smaller and less well known than Reno, its rival gaming city in Northern Nevada. A 1930s Works Progress Administration (WPA) guide book[2] of Las Vegas described it as a smaller, sleepy alternative to Reno, NV that pushed health resorts and its Old West themed 'Helldorado Days' as its principal tourist identity. Two key changes occurred during this time which set in motion the eventual emergence of Las Vegas as the glitziest city in America. One was the building of Hoover Dam (finished in 1935), which provided Las Vegas with ample power and water. The second was a vastly improved Highway 91 to Los Angeles (also part of Roosevelt's New Deal public works projects), which would later be termed 'The Strip'. In 1941, on the eve of America's entry into World War II, the first hotel appeared on The Strip – Thomas Hull's El Ranch Resort.

The city's post-World War II modern origins are now the stuff of Hollywood legend depicted in such films as *Bugsy*, *The Aviator*, and *Casino*. The gangster/film star/visionary characters that populated mid 20th century Las Vegas made for compelling stories, but the more mundane and less documented tales of how these origins translated into a world city are not exactly what Hollywood calls 'high concept'. They are a series of complementary economic drivers that have transformed the city over several decades.

The casino and entertainment complex constructed in Las Vegas by 1970 allowed the city to reach a take-off scale in two other areas: airline connections and convention business. By 1963, at the time of its airport expansion and relocation, the city had enough tourist business to warrant non-stop links to most major cities in the US. To induce travel and tourism Las Vegas worked to keep landing fees among the lowest of any major American city. It is still relatively cheap and easy to fly to Las Vegas from anywhere in the US, and new routes are being added to Asia and Europe as McCarran Airport finishes its first dedicated international terminal.

The other advantage Las Vegas has is a lot of hotel rooms. In fact, 19 of the 23 largest hotels by room count in the world can be found on the Las Vegas Strip (which technically lies outside the city proper in unincorporated Clark County, NV). The presence of so many hotel rooms and the fact that their use is cyclical with high demands on weekends facilitated the emergence of the largest convention business in the US.[3] Most trade shows occur from Sunday to Wednesday nights and fill hotel rooms that would otherwise go empty had the city only catered to leisure travelers. Las Vegas' capacity for conventions is now so great that the largest trade shows have literally nowhere else to go, making the city a permanent annual feature in their industry. Such conventions include the Consumer Electronics Show, which is held every January and runs upward of 150 000 attendees.

The city is also a leading center of producer services specific to gaming. In essence, Las Vegas is to gaming what Houston is to energy – it is a command and control center in a global business. Las Vegas firms that specialize in building and managing mega-resort and entertainment complexes were often the first to build in the new gambling centers – from Atlantic City in New Jersey to Macau in China (which passed Las Vegas in total gambling revenue in 2006). In the current recession, as gaming revenue has plummeted in Las Vegas, properties in much of the rest of the world keep performing – especially in China. This geographic diversification strengthened the bottom line for such Las Vegas-based companies as MGM Resorts International and Wynn. Had these firms simply counted on their local market, they would have seen much greater declines in revenue in the last couple of years. While the Las Vegas regional economy may specialize in tourism, the geographic diversifications of the firms headquartered in the region have helped its leading industry weather the storm.

Even though Las Vegas now exports gaming technology and management techniques needed to run big resorts, Southern Nevada must still diversify its industrial mix to reach multi-dimensional world city status. Las Vegas' economic stability is hyper-dependent upon 'consumption'. Recent findings by the Brookings Institution indicate that 53 per cent of the Las Vegas metropolitan area private sector GDP is consumption, which includes food, drink, leisure, hospitality, construction and real estate. Orlando, FL comes in second with 46 per cent of its private sector GDP reliant on consumption (Brookings Institution, 2010).[4]

THE CONVENING CITY

Las Vegas may be the globe's leading convening space. According to one industry source, 'Las Vegas hosts the largest number of Tradeshow Week's top 200 largest conventions and rents more convention space than any other U.S. city' (Trade Show News Network, 2011). There are more face-to-face exchanges in Las Vegas during a major convention than key financial exchanges in New York or London. But unlike London or New York, these exchanges are ephemeral. Las Vegas, on any given week, may comprise the world's most expert cluster in a particular industry. Yet credit for performing this vital function in a critical industry and its ability to make permanent its temporary advantage have thus far mostly eluded the city. Steps are being taken to systematically capture at least part of this exchange capacity and fix it permanently in the Las Vegas economy.

The convening role Las Vegas plays in the world economy comprises perhaps the biggest opportunity for additional diversification, especially given the way business is evolving in sectors such as business services. Advanced producer service economies are environments in which information is rapidly changing and tacit knowledge is attained (Sassen, 2001). These global economies benefit from what some geographers and economists term 'buzz'. Buzz is:

> the highly efficient technology of communication; a means of overcoming coordination and incentive problems in uncertain environments; a key element of the socialization that in turn allows people to be candidates for memberships of 'in-groups' and to stay in such groups; and a direct source of psychological motivation . . . We speculate that there is a superadditivity in these effects, generating increasing returns for the people and the activities involved. Individuals in a buzz environment interact and cooperate with other high-ability people, are well placed to communicate complex ideas with them, and are highly motivated. (Storper and Venables, 2004, p. 365)

Buzz helped build Silicon Valley and is one reason most technology firms maintain at least some presence in the San Francisco Bay Area. Despite high costs, Silicon Valley provides workers with a dense network of contacts and membership in a creative milieu. In essence, companies pay a premium price to be part of this milieu with the expectation that their Bay Area-based staff will pick up on the latest trends in technology.

Convention environments also generate buzz. In fast moving fields such as alternative energy technology, biotech or telecom, they allow firms to efficiently acquire and exchange information and create strategic alliances, as well as provide access to regional, national or international networks. In Las Vegas these exchanges occur in a relatively compact urban area. The Las Vegas Strip is a short stretch of land hosting over 150 000 hotel rooms, the Las Vegas Convention Center (with 3.2 million square feet (msf) of convening space), Mandalay Bay's conference center (with 1.7 msf of space) and the Sands Expo and Convention Center (with 2.3 msf of space) according to the Las Vegas Convention and Visitors Authority (2009). Every major hotel on The Strip also contains significant 'in house' meeting space that would rival a convention center in a mid-sized city. For example, the newly completed 11 billion dollar City Center complex contains 300 000 square feet of deluxe, high-tech convention space that – while modest in size by Las Vegas standards – is bigger than the Charlotte, NC convention center.

In the most basic sense companies and trade associations put on conventions because they need direct face-to-face contact with customers. Executives and business travelers estimate that 28 per cent of their current business would be lost without in-person meetings. They also estimate that roughly 40 per cent of their prospective customers are converted to new customers with an in-person meeting compared with 16 per cent without such a meeting (Oxford Economics USA, 2009). Las Vegas' convention complex does more to promote face-to-face generated business than perhaps any other world city.

There is another dimension to business exchanges in Las Vegas absent in the industry or academic literature, but that may be the city's ace in the hole. Las Vegas is an adult playground, sometimes referred to as the adult Disney World. It has gambling, bountiful (and high quality) alcohol and food, and famously risqué entertainment. All of these elements would seem antithetical to the respectability needed for business, but on closer inspection it seems to work to the city's advantage. In American culture, Las Vegas is deemed a free fire zone where more edgy adult behavior is forgiven – hence the city's successful campaign 'What Happens in Vegas, Stays in Vegas'. The reason this campaign works so well is that it plays off how most American adults view the Las Vegas experience. It is a wide open, non-moralizing, libertarian place where grownups go to have fun. This is especially true in the afterhours of the conventions.

According to the Las Vegas convention officials, participants at Las Vegas trade shows spend more time on the convention floor than in any other US city. Contrary to President Obama's recent flip remarks that a trip to The Strip is a junket that wastes shareholder, and with the recent bailouts taxpayers' money, Las Vegas is really a place where trade show attendees work hard all day. The reward is the nights are fun, which is a big advantage over conventions held in, say, the actual Disney World of Orlando.

In a counterintuitive way, Las Vegas nights may be equally important to firming up trust between potential business partners than what transpires on the convention floors. People who make a night on the town in Las Vegas can really get to know one another quickly. It is often a chance to get to see people with their hair down. In certain business cultures – especially Asian – there is a premium placed on seeing how people behave away from the office or board room. Insight can be gained from observing how a potential business contact handles him- or herself placing bets at a blackjack table. The social bonding that occurs from a night partying in Las Vegas may provide an excellent basis for the kind of trust that leads to future business exchange. A night spent out on The Strip can provide a fuller picture of the person one may soon be doing deals with. Las Vegas is a place where business is mixed with pleasure.

WHAT HAPPENS IN VEGAS?

Las Vegas has done such an effective job of branding itself as a place where adults go for fun that it may overwhelm its function as a major business center. Paradoxically, the branding in essence helped establish Las Vegas as the most important business meeting space. The ad campaign 'What Happens in Vegas . . .' has been a Faustian Bargain. It ramped up the city's tourism by promising fun, yet it opened Las Vegas to criticism by neo-Puritan Americans or smug Easterners who see the city as either decadent or at best a trivial, unserious place. Las Vegas needs to tweak its branding in a way that signals its dual personalities as a play hard/work hard city.

This shift is already under way. The Las Vegas Convention and Visitors Authority now uses the tagline 'Only Vegas' as an omnibus identity for the city. Its website has two links: one for tourists which uses the tagline 'What Happens in Vegas, Stays in Vegas', and one aimed at the business community with the tagline 'Close the Deal and Make New Opportunities'. Leaders in Las Vegas are now taking a careful look at the convention business to see what aspects of these shows may become permanent fixtures in the local economy. One strategy seems to be the marketing of the city as a permanent trade show.

A key first step and an indicator of future potential for Las Vegas as a continuous world's fair is its new giant furniture mart – the World Market Center. This grew out of the city's role in hosting the largest furniture/homeware convention every year. High Point, NC had been the traditional home for many furniture manufacturers and was formerly the site for the nation's biggest furniture trade show. However, the event grew so big it permanently relocated to Las Vegas, even as High Point retains both an annual furniture show and a trade center. Las Vegas has developed a year-round trade show capacity in furnishing with big bi-annual events. The city is now poised to be a leading design center. Architectural and industrial design firms will follow. In this way Las Vegas could emerge as the Milan of the US, where design leads to industrial spinoffs.

Following the example of the World Market Center, Las Vegas is starting to systematically evaluate all its major conventions and to determine what trade shows can be turned into permanent industry. It would not take many of these leveraged opportunities to substantially diversify the Las Vegas economy and shrink the percentage of total gross regional product that comes from tourism.

The new strategy seems to be paying dividends as another industry has decided to develop a permanent trade show capacity in Las Vegas. The Consumer Electronics Association (CEA), an Arlington, VA-based trade association, announced it has acquired the rights to the title 'World Trade Center – Las Vegas' and plans to acquire a large facility for its convention. In the rollout for the project Gary Shapiro, President and CEO of the Association said, 'Las Vegas is an increasingly important city for international business, particularly because the city hosts so many conventions and trade shows of global interest' (Velotta, 2010). The CEA reasoned that so many people pass through the city that its new facility can display the latest in consumer electronics to a wider audience. The Association can also save the cost of constantly building and tearing down its annual show.

It is easy to imagine other associations following suit, with the effect being Las Vegas emerging as a permanent trade show. At Las Vegas' core would remain tourism and conventions. But now layered atop this original economy would be rings of trade, and perhaps even such sectors as design.

Because Las Vegas has such a capacity and talent for holding conventions it can even target new industries that do not currently hold conventions in the city. This is already happening in the energy sector as LV becomes the place for alternative energy conferences. The University of Nevada, Las Vegas has already hosted the two largest and most important national green energy summits to date. Meetings such as these can put a city on the map in a particular industry.

Consider the mid 1970s Asilomar Conference on the commercial use of DNA technology. Held just outside San Francisco at Monterey Bay, the event was attended by people from all over the US. Most biotech-related research at that point was based in the East, for example Harvard and MIT in Boston, Cold Springs Harbor Labs in Long Island, and the whole pharmaceutical research industry concentrated especially in central New Jersey. Despite this, the Bay Area researchers organized the 'Woodstock' of biotech, which succeeded in making key connections in academia, established rules for proceeding and set priorities for industry. In short, the conference set the frame for the entire biotech industry.

Clearly, the fact that Stanford University and the University of California, Berkeley had first rate molecular biology programs helped the Bay Area emerge as a major biotech center. But other regions – for instance, Baltimore with Johns Hopkins University – also had excellent capacity in life sciences yet never made the link to commercial biotech. Note that Asilomar was all about commercial application for technology and not an academic meeting covering basic research. In this way, the Bay Area made the leap into biotech ahead of other competing regions.

Sometimes a recurring meeting of national or international significance can establish a region as a leading center in a key sector. For example, the World Economic Forum in Davos, Switzerland has put the Swiss city on the map as a leading location for new ideas in a wide range of topics. Can Las Vegas become the Davos of alternative energy? Are there other key sectors the city can go after? What Las Vegas has is the world city status as a convening place and that means it can decide which high-profile events best match the city's plans for economic development.

LAS VEGAS AS THE INTERNET 'SWITCH'

One additional potential Las Vegas has for high-tech growth is so new and has hitherto been so purposely hidden that it appears almost nowhere in the academic literature. The industry is data storage and cloud computing. The story of how Las Vegas gained such advantage in this sector is telling in that the fate of so many places is often tied to accidents of history. It begins with the now defunct and disreputable Enron Corporation.

The Enron collapse was one of the most notable business failures in US history. The company was caught running an outright scam. It engaged in such practices as charging Californians high prices for electric transmission claiming it was due to energy shortages while actually holding back capacity. The result was a transfer of billions of dollars from California to Houston, TX where Enron was headquartered.

Enron's bigger corporate mission (or the legitimate one) was to capture futures and spot markets in areas such as energy and promising new technologies such as broadband transmission. To that end, Enron decided to construct the largest single junction box in the Internet from which it could deliver spot broadband services to the highest bidder. It picked Las Vegas as the best place to locate this capacity because the region turned out to be the safest based on an 18-point risk assessment and it is close to so many Internet users in California. The facility was constructed in the early part of the last decade – costing Enron billions.

Enron's corporate fate is well known. It went bust in 2001, but the fate of its giant Internet switch was the concern of just a few investors and some tech folks who understood what Enron was building. One entrepreneur – Rob Roy – found the capital to buy the switch and start a company around it. Switch Communications Group was born as an effort to fully utilize and repurpose Enron's big junction box. Roy reasoned the Enron switch could serve as a gateway into a vast data storage/server barn facility in Las Vegas. He also invented a new cooling method that allows tremendous and efficient data compression and built the world's most efficient server barn, which he dubbed the 'SuperNAP'. The SuperNAP storage/server facility is like no other in the world. It is literally thousands of times more efficient than competitors and has enabled the firm to land big data clients such as Fox and Disney. The first data barn (about the size of three super Wal-Marts) is rapidly filling up and three more are planned for Las Vegas.

Switch Communications Group is now attracting the technical staff from the firms it is servicing to work at its facility. Many more clients and technical people will arrive in the months and years ahead and they could form the core of a first rate tech workforce specializing in data storage. The other specialty that will emerge is cloud computing, which plays to Switch's strength as the fastest and densest storage capacity in the industry. Cloud computing is Internet-based computing, whereby shared resources, software and information are provided to computers and other devices on demand, like a public utility. Cloud computing thus constitutes a new form of supercomputing and is used in such computational-intensive industries as computer-generated images for film, or industrial design in fields such as autos or aircraft. Economic development researchers such as Heike Mayer have shown that a single dominant firm that gains a key toehold in a new industry can spin off an entire high tech universe. Mayer has documented this process in a number of cities such as Portland, OR. The process may or may not happen in Las Vegas, but the potential is there for the city to become a serious contender in the tech world because of the enormous data storage advantage now enjoyed by Switch Communications Group.

Finally, in the same vein as Switch, Southern Nevada may be able to use the Yucca Mountain giant underground facility, which was designed to receive all of the nuclear waste in the US, as a safety vault for America's most sensitive data. A new concern for those in the intelligence community such as Richard Clarke is a 'cyber war' on the nation's computing and data (Clarke and Knake, 2010). The Yucca Mountain facility is so deep underground and has such a high-level security that storing sensitive data there would make the US much less vulnerable to cyber war. This includes protection from electromagnetic pulses intended to bring down communications and wipe out stored data. If Yucca Mountain is repurposed in this way, it would be an enormous additional boom to the still vacant Las Vegas tech industry.

THE SOUTHWEST MEGAREGION – LOS ANGELES/PHOENIX/LAS VEGAS

Las Vegas is a globally connected city with a world-class airport. In 2008, McCarran ranked 15th in the world for passenger traffic, with 43,208,724 passengers passing through the terminal. The airport ranked 6th in the world for aircraft movements, with 578,949 takeoffs and landings (Airport Council International, 2009). Yet Las Vegas lacks good surface regional connections to its nearby neighbors of Southern California and the Sun Corridor (the new name for the Phoenix–Tucson metroplex).

The fact that Las Vegas now lacks a highway to the Sun Corridor and rail service to Southern California prevents the region from fully integrating into a larger Southwestern 'megaregion' economy. A megaregion, as defined by the Regional Plan Association of New York (RPA; Hagler, 2009), forms when proximate large-scale metropolitan areas share increasing amounts of business activity. The RPA is an advocate for improved transportation – especially high-speed rail – as a way to reduce friction of movement and tie smaller regional economies into globally important megaregions. With planned improvements to the other big regions in the Southwest, Las Vegas can join in what will become the second largest megaregion in the US.

A key surface connection is the proposed Interstate 11 to Phoenix. Phoenix and Las Vegas are the two largest US metropolitan areas that lie adjacent without a direct Interstate highway. The reason is that the Interstate routes were based on the 1950 census, when the two regions were tiny. Any recalibration of metropolitan connectivity would immediately green light a new Interstate between Phoenix and Las Vegas. The construction of Interstate 11 would be a proper recognition of the urban geography of the Southwest in the 21st century. It is likely that the Obama Administration will move Interstate 11 onto a priority list for infrastructure improvements of national significance in the next round of transportation authorization funding in late 2010. This road would also be part of the planned 'CanaMex Corridor' that links Canada to Mexico as part of the traffic generated under the North American Free Trade Agreement.

The other key surface transportation link is high-speed rail to Los Angeles. About a third of the visitors to the city are from Southern California. Many of these people arrive on short-haul flights that clog Las Vegas' airport. The energy used simply to lift a plane out of the airport represents the equivalent energy it takes to push a high-speed passenger train with the equivalent or even greater passengers from Las Vegas to Los Angeles. Moreover these flights take up capacity needed for more distant and international linkages with the rest of the world.

High-speed rail is used around the world as a high-capacity alternative to short-haul air travel. It is greener, more efficient and can go from city center to city center. Critics of high-speed rail argue that the US lacks the population density to support it. This is based on a complete lack of understanding of US urban geography. Large-scale American urban regions are as dense as those in Europe, and unlike Europe, most are still growing. The prevailing view in urban planning circles is that because of shifts in public policy, consumer preference, energy use and environmental impact, most large US metropolitan areas will become denser (Nelson and Lang, 2011).

Although the US is late to the high-speed rail game, this may prove to be an advantage which Las Vegas can gain. The benefits are two-fold. The technology is well established so Las Vegas will benefit from the latest rail design without having to upgrade from an older system. In one step, the Las Vegas–Los Angeles train can improve on the speeds seen in the Acela line between Boston and Washington DC – now the fastest rail in the US. Perhaps more importantly, high-speed rail represents an opportunity for an enormous technology transfer. The big European firms that build high-speed rail are eager to enter the US market. America is the last major and potentially the third biggest market for high-speed rail (after Europe and China). As a requirement to play in this market, the US should insist it is given the tools to locate some of the production within the country. Boeing is a prime example of this. The rest of the world demanded the US show them how to build aircraft, which is one way Boeing sells big orders of planes. As a key site for a major high-speed rail project, Las Vegas can grab some of this technology and manufacturing capacity and thus further diversify its economy.

URBAN DESIGN AND SUSTAINABILITY DEVELOPMENT

Finally, there is the issue of remaking Las Vegas' built environment. The city is in many ways highly urban. Las Vegas, along with Phoenix, is in the 'Dry Sunbelt' (Lang, 2002). The realities of aridity, steep mountainsides and large federal land holdings have served to constrain outward growth and produce more densely settled metropolitan areas than in the East. The average lot size for a single-family home in Las Vegas is a fraction of those found in the 'Wet Sunbelt' cities of Atlanta and Charlotte.

But so far Las Vegas has seen little benefit from its density. In fact, one can argue that the city really has 'dense sprawl' because it remains auto dependent. This is even true despite Las Vegas having one of the most concentrated and centralized major employment cores in the US.

This last round of growth saw the initiation of a new modern Las Vegas through style place making. The City Center project could be to Las Vegas what Rockefeller Center was to NYC: a city within a city that indicates a new urban form. Both projects were delivered during economic downturns.

In addition to better regional connections to Los Angeles and Phoenix, Las Vegas needs better intra-city transit. The new bus rapid transit system (BRT) is a first step in this process and comes as other major metros in the intermountain West are building light rail networks and commuter rail. If done properly, BRT can offer the benefits of light rail, including remaking the lower-density space.

Finally, despite some changes that will see Las Vegas shift to more traditional urban forms, it is not an Eastern city, nor is it some generic Sunbelt town. The city thrives on whimsy, and some elements of this should always remain or Las Vegas could lose what made it fun in the first place. But it is doubtful that the city will ever be boring.

NOTES

1. In 1987, the US Supreme Court ruled in *California v Cabazon Band of Mission Indians* that as sovereign political entities, tribes could operate facilities free of state regulation.
2. The WPA guides were a subset of the 'writer's project' begun in the administration of Franklin Roosevelt in an effort to provide relief to out-of-work authors during the Great Depression. The WPA guide books were done for every state and major city and capture America in great detail on the eve of World War II. These guides serve as an important historic resource for especially urban historians in that they vividly describe social conditions in nearly every city in the US circa 1939.
3. There is now over 10 million square feet of convention space in the Las Vegas Valley, including all of the space in major hotels on The Strip. The Las Vegas Convention Center, most recently expanded in 2002, accounts for about a third of the total.
4. The Orlando region shares many historical and economic elements with Las Vegas. After emerging as modest regional centers by the mid 20th century, both Las Vegas and Orlando became major metropolitan areas because of tourism. They differ in what niche they fill in the industry, with Las Vegas filling the adult theme casino market, while Orlando specializes in family–theme park tourism, but both cities share the risks and opportunities born of tourism. They have major airports and major convention sectors that tie them to the world, and likewise they are vulnerable to sharp contractions in consumer spending because of their failure to more fully diversify their economic bases.

REFERENCES

Airport Council International (2009), 'Passenger traffic 2008 final', available at www.airports.org (accessed 14 April 2010).
Brookings Institution (2010), 'Metropolitan Las Vegas: challenges and opportunities', *Blueprint for American Prosperity: Unleashing the Potential of a Metropolitan Nation*, Washington, DC: Brookings Mountain West.
Clarke, R.A. and R.K. Knake (2010), *Cyber War: The Next Threat to National Security and What To Do About It*, New York: ECCO Press.
Hagler, Y. (2009), *Defining U.S. Megaregions*, New York: RPA.
Lang, R.E. (2002), 'Open spaces, bounded places: does the American West's arid landscape yield dense metropolitan growth?', *Housing Policy Debate*, **13** (4), 755–778.
LVCVA (Las Vegas Convention and Visitors Authority) (2009), *Las Vegas 2009 Marketing Through Unprecedented Times*, Las Vegas, NV: Las Vegas Convention and Visitors Authority and R&R Partners.

Nelson, A.C. and R.E. Lang (2011), *Megapolitan America: A New Vision for Understanding America's Metropolitan Geography*, Chicago, IL: American Planning Association / Planners Press.

Oxford Economics USA (2009), *The Return on Investment of US Business Travel*, New York: Oxford Economics USA.

Pickard, J. (1962), 'Urban regions of the United States', *Urban Land*, April, 3–10.

Pickard, J. (1966). 'U.S. urban regions: growth and migration patterns', *Urban Land*, May, 3–10.

Sassen, S. (2000), *Cities in a World Economy*, London: Pine Forge Press, 2nd edition.

Sassen, S. (2001), *The Global City: New York, London, Tokyo*, Princeton, NJ: Princeton University Press, 2nd edition.

Storper, M. and A.J. Venables (2004), 'Buzz: face-to-face contact and the urban economy', *Journal of Economic Geography*, **4** (4), 351–370.

Trade Show News Network (2011), 'Top 250 US 2010 trade shows', available at http://www.tsnn.com (accessed 19 July 2011).

Velotta, R. (2010), 'World Trade Center to be established in Las Vegas', available at www.lasvegassun.com/news/2010/mar/09/world-trade-center-be-established-las-vegas (accessed 11 March 2010).

47 South Florida: world city, edgeless city
Robert E. Lang and Christina Nicholas

Known for its beaches, tourist attractions and retirees, South Florida has grown into a multicultural community of five million people. South Florida differs substantially from the northern parts of the state in that it is culturally and demographically apart from the American South. It is what cultural geographer Wilbur Zelinsky (1973) refers to as a 'voluntary region' in that it was settled late by migrants seeking a specific lifestyle and climate. The region has been settled by two major outside groups. The first one consists of domestic immigrants from the North, especially the New York region. The second includes international immigrants from Latin America, predominately Cuba, and recent arrivals from Haiti and the Dominican Republic.

Immigrants, many of whom are political refugees from Cuba, have positively impacted Miami's business community. As Castro rose to power over 50 years ago many of Cuba's middle class fled to South Florida. According to the US Census Bureau, Hispanics and foreign born residents account for over half the population in Miami-Dade County. The affluent and educated Cuban expatriate community quickly reestablished a business network to Latin America and helped South Florida become a major presence in the international economy – especially banking.

Geographically, South Florida is a three-county US census-defined region that includes Miami-Dade, Broward and Palm Beach Counties. The western parts of all three South Florida counties developed later than the coast in part because western lands were once part of the Everglades, which until recently covered most of Florida's southern tip. The newly developed parts of South Florida include the western parts of Broward and Palm Beach Counties that press up against the remaining Everglades. This western expansion has now ended because of a federally mandated growth boundary.

Much of the region is now built out, with some of the last new greenfield subdivisions popping up this past year in Broward County. 'Eastward Ho!' is a South Florida regional planning movement that emerged around the idea of encouraging new growth to stay to the east. In 2007, Lang and LeFurgy estimated that just 10 per cent of once-booming Broward County (in the middle of the region) remained buildable. They also argued that the region's development patterns would shift in the near future because it had run out of land. It is likely that future growth in South Florida will go up rather than out because there is very little 'out' left.

SOUTH FLORIDA'S GLOBAL ECONOMY

South Florida has benefited from the expansion of globalization by transforming its role within the United States and worldwide. Its greatest advantage has been the blending of Latin culture and language with the financial and legal stability of the US. Becoming an international city is not based solely on one factor, but a mixture of high levels of human capital, stability, favorable regulatory environment, communication and technology facilities, and taxes. South Florida compares favorably with Latin America in many categories (Jorge et al., 1992). Thus South Florida as the 'capital of Latin America' fully warrants its relatively high status in the world city network.

For Sassen (2001) major service cities become 'global cities' because of their 'strategic' placements in economic globalization. This means that their success is not a matter of separate city development; instead they function as nodes in a worldwide network of cities. Global cities have the capabilities to support, manage and finance global operations. Cities are not themselves the prime agents of world city network formation. It is advanced producer service firms that are largely responsible for creating and maintaining the network. These firms have offices in important cities across all world regions. Personnel, information, knowledge, intelligence, ideas, plans, instructions and advice flow freely among them. As such, these global service firms interconnect the cities in which they have a presence.

The service growth relative to manufacturing has led to an important economic shift of the twentieth century, and some services – those providing advanced knowledge products to multinational corporations – have become a cutting edge industry in the new globalizing economy. This new economy produces services for firms rather than individuals. A key feature of firms providing these services is their concentration in major cities, especially downtowns. Advance producer service firms utilize the knowledge-rich environs of these cities while themselves contributing to downtown development through their business practices. Not only is joint production possible, but these firms also reinforce each other and benefit from being in close proximity. Thus a central premise of global cities is the activity within the city as well as the connectivity to other cities.

In South Florida tourism is a major source of income. Florida is situated on a peninsula with the Gulf of Mexico to the west and the Atlantic Ocean to the east. Warm coastal weather and sunny beaches make Florida an attractive tourist destination year round. While central Florida hosts tourist attractions like Disney amusement parks, South Florida has a thriving cruise industry. In fact, Port of Miami has held the status as the number one cruise port in the world for more than a decade because of its close proximity to the Caribbean islands. In 2009, during one of the largest economic recessions in the US, the port served over 4.1 million passengers (Port of Miami, 2009). This is an increase of nearly a million passengers during a ten year period.

South Florida has also become one of the world's leading metropolitan areas for international markets. International trade and multinational corporations take advantage of South Florida's geographical position, which has proved vital in connecting the Americas as well as the rest of the world in commerce. According to the Beacon Council, Miami-Dade's economic development agency, the total number of global companies with offices in South Florida currently exceeds 1295. Multinational corporations such as FedEx, Hewlett-Packard and Samsung use Miami as their Latin American headquarters.

In 2004 Kraft Foods Latin America relocated its regional headquarters from Rye, New York to Coral Gables, Florida. Cristian Sainz, director of corporation affairs for Kraft Foods Latin America, summed up the company's rationale: 'Miami-Dade's cultural diversity and proximity to the nations where the division markets its products were key to the company's decision to relocate to Coral Gables. Even though we are based here, our business is in Latin America. Venezuela, Mexico, Brazil and Argentina are our biggest markets. There are several flights there and our office is only 10 minutes from the airport.' Sainz notes the environments of both South Beach and Coral Gables were additional draws. 'We bring people here from Latin America often and enjoy taking them out when they visit' (Perkins, 2005).

South Florida's well developed transportation network is vital in its connectivity to other global cities. The primary regional hubs, Miami International Airport and Port of Miami, make South Florida a valuable node in the world city network by managing the flow of goods. In 2008 the Port transited 7.4 million tons of cargo, while the airport accounted for another 1.8 million metric tonnes of cargo from around the globe (Port of Miami, 2009; Airport Council International, 2009a). This activity contributed well over 17 billion dollars to South Florida's local economy.

Miami's international airport is essential for tourist and service sectors. In 2008 the airport had over 34 million passengers in transit, which made it one of the busiest airports in the US (Airport Council International, 2009b). Taylor and Lang (2005) found Miami International has the highest Latin American service orientation among both US and EU cities – and among Miami's top 15 connections only 4 are US cities (Derudder et al., 2007). The remaining connections are to the capital cities of Venezuela, Argentina, the Bahamas, Colombia, Mexico, Peru, Haiti, Brazil and the Dominican Republic. This is where US preeminence to Latin America ends. EU cities have several medium-sized cities that are reasonably well connected to Latin American cities, while other US cities turn out to be weakly connected to Latin American cities. This reveals just how dense the connection between South Florida and Latin America is and how important South Florida is in connecting the US to the global economy.

REGIONAL GROWTH, EDGELESS SPRAWL

While South Florida shares many characteristics of other global cities, its built spatial structure remains distinct. This is due in part to the dramatic shift in location of office employment in metropolitan America over the last 40 years. This shift moved offices away from central cities into the suburbs. South Florida, in particular, has experienced rapid expansion and continued population growth. In fact, most of the building has taken place in the past half century, making it, along with such other Sunbelt boom metropolises as Phoenix and Las Vegas, one of the newest places in America.

Office density can be divided into four main segments varying by function and form. Primary downtowns and edgeless cities lie at the perimeters, while secondary downtowns and edge cities are in between. Edgeless cities are cities in function, in that they contain office employment, but not in form, because they are scattered, unlike traditional and even some suburban office development (Lang, 2003a, 2003b). The term 'edgeless city' captures the lack of a physical edge in suburban office areas.

Downtowns can be found throughout older parts of metropolitan areas. Often it is the original site of significant commercial development. The 'primary downtown', or central business district (CBD), lies at the center of the region. While downtowns vary in size and scale, they typically contain the largest single concentration of office space and have well defined boundaries. Such is the case in South Florida's primary downtown of Miami.

Referred to here as 'secondary downtowns' are the centers of major suburban and uptowns in central cities that developed a relatively modest commercial center early in the twentieth century. Fort Lauderdale is a secondary downtown – a scaled down, slightly less dense version of Miami's downtown. Secondary downtowns have their origin in the streetcar and early auto era and therefore support some pedestrian presence. They contain a modest amount of high density, low income residences and often replicated many of the CBD's features, including retail and commercial development.

In the literature on suburban office development, edge cities have a specific definition. Joel Garreau's 'edge city' used the same criteria that real estate consultant Christopher Leinberger used earlier to identify urban villages. As defined by Garreau, edge cities are places that have 5 million square feet or more of office space, have 600 000 square feet or more of retail space, have more jobs than bedrooms, are perceived by the population as one place, and were nothing like a 'city' as recently as 30 years ago (Garreau, 1991). In this chapter edge cities are defined only by total square feet of office space. The large number of edge cities varies depending on metropolitan area. Larger office markets typically contain several edge cities. Most edge cities are found along interstate beltways and major arterial roads which run through the mature suburban parts of metropolitan areas. The development around Miami International Airport is South Florida's only major edge city.

Edgeless cities are as elusive, diffuse and hard to define as urban sprawl, of which they constitute a major part (Lang, 2000). Edgeless cities, along with edge cities, identify a subset of non-CBD office space. As the term implies, edgeless cities lack a well defined boundary or edge. Edgeless cities capture all other non-downtown office space not in an edge city. They seldom strike a casual observer as unified in any meaningful way because they scatter far and wide across the region. Some ring the metropolitan edge, while others lie between edge cities or cover the outskirts of cities. Edgeless cities are so large and dispersed that it makes it difficult to refer to them individually. They may extend over tens and, in some cases, hundreds of square miles of urban space and their individual components often have a name ('So-and-so' office park). Consequently, unlike edge cities, edgeless cities are not perceived as a place. It is not always possible to say, 'Consider this particular edgeless city.' Because of their scale they have to be described in general terms: 'Edgeless cities constitute X per cent of a region's office space.' Using the term 'edgeless city' is in fact essentially the same as saying 'office sprawl'. In South Florida much of northern Broward County constitutes edgeless cities, specifically around Coconut Creek.

Perhaps most importantly, edgeless cities are not edge cities waiting to happen. Instead they represent a concurrent, competing and more decentralized form of office development. In fact, the office data indicate that edge cities and edgeless cities grew up more or less together (Lang, 2003a). Edge cities did experience a burst of growth in the mid to late 1980s at the time Garreau was observing them but this growth has since slowed. Edgeless cities, on the other hand, seem to have grown at a steadier pace.

GLOBAL CITY, EDGELESS CITY

Using Black's Guide, Cushman and Wakefield, and Costar office data (Lang, 2003a, 2003b; Lang and Sanchez, 2009), South Florida's development patterns were compared with 13 other US metropolitan office markets – Atlanta, Boston, Chicago, Dallas, Detroit, Denver, Houston, Los Angeles, Miami, New York City, Philadelphia, San Francisco and Washington DC.

Lang and his colleagues found that South Florida is perhaps the most centerless large office market in the US. Like much of the Sunbelt, South Florida's downtown centers have never been as big or dense as Northeast and Midwest downtowns. At the same time, South Florida has developed few edge cities, which are commonly found in other Sunbelt regions such as Atlanta, Houston and Dallas. Together the combination of modest downtowns and small dispersed suburban centers makes South Florida the nation's leader in office sprawl. This finding was consistant in three separate studies, using two different data sources (Lang, 2003a, 2003b; Lang and Sanchez, 2009).

Among the 13 cities compared, downtown Miami is the smallest primary downtown and Fort Lauderdale is the second smallest secondary downtown in terms of absolute square footage of office space. At only 14.7 million square feet, downtown Miami has less office space than the top dozen of the nation's edge cities (Lang and Sanchez, 2009). Moreover, South Florida also has the smallest share of all office space in its metro area located in its downtown. New York and Chicago maintain the largest regional shares of office space (57 and 54 per cent, respectively), while Dallas and Detroit have the smallest percentage of downtown space (21 per cent each). At 13.7 per cent South Florida has the smallest CBD relative to its metropolitan area market (Lang and Sanchez, 2009). South Florida comes in just below the median in terms of office space per capita. But compared to the other 13 metropolitan regions, South Florida has the largest disparity between its quantity of CBD and non-CBD office space.

In 1987 Miami's CBD had 11.1 million square feet of office space available and a 28 per cent vacancy rate. Two decades later in 2006, Miami's CBD had increased to 14.7 million square feet of available office space. During this time the vacancy rate fell 41.4 per cent to 12.4 per cent. This means that while very little office space was built in Miami's CBD, vacancy rates fell as businesses moved into existing office buildings or businesses upgraded their space by moving into new structures as their vacated offices were phased out of the market.

The vast growth in office space in Miami-Dade over the last two decades occurred in non-CBD markets. Disparity in growth rates between CBD and non-CBD office space explains the considerable decrease in the overall share of CBD office space in the metro area during this period.

The 1997 to 2006 data show that office space growth in Miami-Dade's non-CBD market continued to outpace growth downtown. Yet the Brickell Avenue submarket, a part of Miami's CBD which lies just south of the Miami River from downtown, actually gained over two million square feet since 1997. By contrast, downtown barely registered any growth. Changes in Miami-Dade's non-CBD submarkets are more complicated. Overall they grew by over 37 per cent but many submarkets are far off from the cumulative rate. Coral Way and Coconut Grove submarkets, for example, actually lost some office space (0.9 per cent and 10.5 per cent, respectively). The Biscayne Corridor, South Miami and East Airport submarkets only fared slightly better with modest gains. Kendall/South Dade and Miami Beach submarkets boomed with gains of 40 and 50 per cent, respectively.

Comparing the percentage of office space in South Florida using the categories downtown, edge cities and edgeless cities, the data indicate that of the nearly 40 million square feet of office space added in South Florida in the 1990s and the first half of the last decade, almost 60 per cent was located in edgeless cities. By 1999 two-thirds (66 per cent) of South Florida's current office space could be found in edgeless cities (Lang, 2003b). By 2006, the figure stood at 72.1 per cent (Lang and Sanchez, 2009). This shows that the majority of South Florida's office space is in edgeless cities. In fact, even by the mid 1980s, South Florida was the most edgeless metropolis of the 13 regions studied, standing in sharp contrast to core dominated areas like Chicago and New York, where edgeless office space made up less than 30 per cent of the area total.

POLICY IMPLICATIONS FOR EDGELESS CITIES

The policy relevance of these findings is so broad, a full explanation lies beyond the scope of this chapter. However, a number of general implications associated with the dominance of the edgeless city pattern of office growth cannot be ignored. The list below includes many major issues that have been at the center of South Florida's public policy debate over sprawl.

First there is a possible link between edgeless city expansion, lower density development and environmental concerns. To the extent that urban space sprawls into habitat areas, it increases the scale of environmental impact. In South Florida edgeless expansion has resulted in the loss of thousands of acres of Everglades and it is facing water quality issues due to the loss (Lang, 2002). There are those who argue, however, that when low density growth spreads its effects are not as intense as high density growth (Gordon and Richardson, 1997). A region must consider the trade-off – compact but intense environmental impact or more diffuse but less intense impact.

Edgeless cities fall short when it comes to transportation issues. They lack public transportation opportunities that dense, mature edge cities or downtowns have. Edgeless cities provide no prospect of being integrated into a bus or light rail system because operating public transportation between suburbs is too inefficient and costly. As the percentage of regional office space located in edgeless cities rises, the percentage of people commuting by mass transit drops. While some public transportation systems exist in South Florida, they have little benefit to most South Floridians who commute from one suburb to another.

Moreover, the reliance on private transportation grows as the percentage of regional office space and community distances expands. A recent study carried out by the Surface Transportation Policy Project (2005) ranked South Florida fourth in the nation among the regions with the largest percentage (19 per cent) of household income spent on transportation. There are proponents who argue that while office sprawl may add to commuting lengths, it reduces congestion, increases speeds and thereby reduces commuting time (Gordon and Richardson, 1996).

Another public policy issue is matching jobs to housing in order to reduce commuting distances. The jobs-to-housing balance may actually improve in many suburbs as edgeless city growth distributes offices deeper into residential areas. While office space is in fact widely distributed throughout South Florida this may not translate into significant reductions of commuting distances. The resulting paradox derives from the fact that local edgeless city building may not be the destination for a particular commuter. Given edgeless cities are neither concentrated employment centers nor destinations per se, it is doubtful the people living near them actually work there.

Edgeless cities have infrastructure costs as well as benefits. By their very nature edgeless cities have no centers; the cost in roads and other infrastructure may be higher than if such development were concentrated. These costs are often addressed at all levels of government. Since edgeless cities grow outside central cities, they can pull jobs and resources from the regional core. Orfield (1997) found that the metropolitan periphery has received far more investment than the center and the inner ring of suburbs. The entire region pays the public subsidies required for edgeless city infrastructure and road building projects. If edgeless cities capture a growing share of a region's office development, they may add to existing regional inequalities with regard to public infrastructure expenditures. In the case of South Florida, the west would draw resources away from the east as it develops.

With regard to municipal budgets, edgeless cities distribute office space so widely that they may help some suburban municipal budgets by adding ratable funds to the tax base. Office development, especially high tech research parks, enhances fiscal responsibility. If edgeless cities are built in less affluent municipalities their presence may even improve the distribution of the tax base across a region. Regional revenue sharing would likely prove a better method of distributing tax resources among municipalities than to have office development sprawl.

As noted earlier in the chapter, urban growth in South Florida is constrained by ocean to the east and Everglades to the west. This region has produced a much denser built environment than any other major metropolitan area in the Southern US (Lang, 2002). In many ways, the spatial form and urban densities in South Florida resemble cities in the US West – especially Los Angeles. Unlike other Southern city regions such as Atlanta, Charlotte and Nashville, South Florida has small lot sizes for single family detached homes, which often run below 10,000 square feet or a quarter acre. Los Angeles matches South Florida's residential pattern. The two also share a similar street structure, which is dominated by large grids of main arterial surface streets, overlaid by a freeway grid. In many respects, South Florida seems a lost colony of Los Angeles, including even its diversity and large Hispanic population.

Interestingly, the vast share of the edgeless city office space in both Los Angeles and South Florida is found in rather high density settings for suburban development. Almost two-thirds of this space lies in areas exceeding 3000 people per square mile in South Florida, while the figure for Los Angeles reaches 80 per cent. The 3000 person threshold exceeds the US census bureau definition for an 'urban' environment (really suburban) by three times the density. Thus Los Angeles and South Florida edgeless cities may be dispersed in terms of proximate office concentrations, but they are not exurban in form or setting. Rather, small office building clusters – and sometimes even standalone buildings – are threaded throughout densely built suburban areas in both regions. But unlike Los Angeles, South Florida does not have a major downtown or decent-sized edge cities. Even downtown Miami is no match for a major edge city such as Tysons Corner, Virginia outside Washington, DC.

The point of this analysis is not that edgeless cities are inherently good or bad. Instead we highlight that they exist and warrant analysis if we are to understand the development patterns in the past 40 years and to anticipate where growth will occur in the future.

No other region, even those with relatively dispersed patterns of office development, comes close to the percentage of office space that South Florida maintains in its edgeless cities. The ocean and the Everglades are borders which contain its sprawl, but within the urbanized space there are few major centers. This makes South Florida the most center-less region in the US and a prime location to study edgeless city growth.

Yet South Florida's edgeless city form has not held it back as a world city. As a global business center whose businesses connect to the world network of producer service firms, South Florida easily surpasses more traditional US metropolitan areas such as Minneapolis, Cleveland and St Louis. Most of the financial firms doing business with Latin America have at least some presence in tiny downtown Miami, but many of the support services and back offices for these firms are based in edgeless cities. South Florida shows that even a metropolitan area with a small downtown can be a world city and that the metropolitan-level structure of commerce may be less significant in determining global reach than the mix of businesses found in the region as a whole. This finding confirms Sassen's theory that the composition of a region's business community is more significant in establishing it as a world city than is any intrinsic quality of the region.

REFERENCES

Airport Council International (2009a), 'Cargo traffic 2008 final', available at www.airports.org (accessed 14 April 2010).

Airport Council International (2009b), 'Passenger traffic 2008 final', available at www.airports.org (accessed 14 April 2010).

Beacon Council, 'Global companies in South Florida', available at www.beaconcouncil.com (accessed 14 April 2010).

Derudder, B., F. Witlox and P.J. Taylor (2007), 'United States cities in the world city network: comparing their positions using global origins and destinations of airline passengers', *Urban Geography*, **28** (1), 74–91.

Garreau, J. (1991), *Edge City: Life on the New Frontier*, New York: Doubleday.

Gordon, P. and H.W. Richardson (1996), 'Beyond polycentricity: the dispersed metropolis, Los Angeles, 1970–1990', *Journal of the American Planning Association*, **62** (3), 289–295.

Gordon, P. and H.W. Richardson (1997), 'Are compact cities a desirable planning goal?', *Journal of the American Planning Association*, **63** (1), 95–106.

Jorge, A., R. Cruz and A. Diaz (1992), *Enterprise for the Americas Initiative: Its Impact on South Florida*, New Brunswick, NJ: Transaction Publishers.

Lang, R.E. (2000), 'Why are western metropolitan areas denser than eastern ones?', lecture given at the symposium *Metropolitan Frontier of the American West: Lessons for the East?*, Washington, DC National Building Museum, 17 April.

Lang, R.E. (2002), 'Open space, bounded places: does the American West's arid landscape yield dense metropolitan growth?', *Housing Policy Debate*, **13** (4), 755–778.

Lang, R.E. (2003a), *Edgeless Cities: Exploring the Elusive Metropolis*, Washington, DC: Brookings Institution Press.

Lang, R.E. (2003b), *Beyond Edge City: Office Sprawl in South Florida*, Washington, DC: The Brookings Institution (Survey Series).

Lang, R.E. and J. LeFurgy (2007), *Boomburbs: The Rise of America's Accidental Cities*, Washington, DC: Brookings Institution Press.

Lang, R.E. and T. Sanchez (2009), 'Beyond edgeless cities: a new classification system for suburban business districts', *Urban Geography*, **30** (6), 1–30.

Orfield, M. (1997), *Metropolitics: A Regional Agenda for Community and Stability*, Washington, DC: Brookings Institution Press.

Perkins, B. (2005), 'Kraft Foods Latin America', *South Florida CEO*, Jan.–Feb. CEO Publishing Group, Inc., available at http://findarticles.com/p/articles/mi_m0OQD/is_1_8/ai_n11843176/ (accessed 14 April 2010)

Port of Miami (2009), 'Port statistics', available at www.miamidade.gov (accessed 21 April 2010).

Sassen, S. (2000), *Cities in a World Economy*, London: Pine Forge Press, 2nd edition.

Sassen, S. (2001), *The Global City: New York, London, Tokyo*, Princeton, NJ: Princeton University Press, 2nd edition.

Surface Transportation Policy Project (2005), *Driven to Spend: Pumping Dollars out of Our Households and Communities*, Washington, DC: Surface Transportation Policy Project.

Taylor, P.J. and R.E. Lang (2005), *U.S. Cities in the 'World City Network'*, Washington, DC: The Brookings Institution (Metropolitan Policy Program, Survey Series).

Zelinsky, W. (1973), *The Cultural Geography of the United States*, Englewood Cliffs, NJ: Prentice Hall.

48 Marked by dynamics: Berlin and Warsaw in the process of functional change
Ewa Korcelli-Olejniczak

If you take a more Darwinian point of view, the dynamics of the universe are such that as the universe evolved in time, complex systems arose out of the natural dynamics of the universe.

Seth Lloyd (2002)

INTRODUCTION

Since the main dividing lines between the West and the East became dismantled, the urban systems in Europe have been in constant transition – the fluctuations within these systems being a reaction to transformation and globalization processes. The drive for high-order functions of international range, defining the position of Central European cities within national and transnational systems, rather than spatial policy, has allowed for a 'relative' growth of cohesion in the European urban system as a whole. Functional change, expressed by a shift to advanced services and a knowledge economy, indicated by competitiveness and attractiveness, has resulted in higher economic effectiveness, changes of supply and new quality of demand, all these being synergic processes, influencing one another on higher and higher levels in a spiral-like manner.

As predicted by Hall (2001), the absorbers of these processes were in the first place large cities, though not necessarily only the primary ones, as somewhat pessimistically hypothesized by Lichtenberger (1994). Still, in most cases, capital or otherwise leading cities were among the greatest gainers. According to the results of the ESPON 1.1.1. and 1.4.3. projects (ESPON, 2004, 2007), the Central European capitals of Prague, Bratislava, Budapest and Warsaw have qualified for the status of so-called potential 'MEGAs' that constitute the fourth level in a hierarchical scheme of European metropolitan areas. At the same time, they were the only representatives of this level in their respective countries. Berlin was assigned to the second level of MEGAs, together with the leading West German urban centres Rhein-Main, Hamburg, Munich-Augsburg and Stuttgart.

Cities of Central and Eastern Europe have each differently trodden the ground marked by systemic transformation. Functional change and the creation of new images have found a reflection in their evolving territorial position and shifting interrelations. In this chapter the focus is on Berlin and Warsaw – the two major capital cities of the region. Diverse as they are, they show evidence of parallel processes in their recent development. Their search for a new role in Central Europe and beyond has influenced the evolution of the region's urban system.

Since the beginning of the transformation process, Berlin's economic linkages were seen to extend to the East. Hall (1990), for instance, suggested that Berlin might to some degree recapture its former role as transnational traffic junction and centre of high-level service functions, thus filling a vacuum in this part of Europe. Kukliński (1999), in turn, saw Berlin as a world metropolis by the year 2010, one generating economic growth impulses along the main transportation corridors, the Western partner of a cooperative European spatial development project – the so-called Berlin–Warsaw trajectory (Domański, 1999). Although the concept of the trajectory has not been followed up, the question of interdependence of the two cities remains a pertinent one. Notwithstanding the early 1990 prognoses which saw Berlin as a global city of tomorrow, the intervening years have shown that it is not enough to be a beneficiary among those treated as latecomers in the drive for long-range metropolitan functions. The current and future positions of both Berlin and Warsaw in the European urban hierarchy result from a complex set of preconditions, potentials and interdependencies. It is claimed here that the most distinct mark of their transformation is its dynamic nature.

The present chapter has two objectives. The first is to look into the question of how the growth potential of Berlin and Warsaw has been evolving over time. This concerns the reshaping of the functional structure of the cities, as well as their position within Central European space. The second is to highlight the dynamics of change – a distinct mark of functional transformation of both Berlin and Warsaw. Drawing from these assumptions, an attempt is made to confront the expectations and forecasts related to the evolution of functional profiles of Berlin and Warsaw, as formulated in the early stages of the transformation process, with more recent developments and trends. In this context the results of the analysis of change of metropolitan functions of Berlin and Warsaw in the 1990s (Korcelli-Olejniczak, 2004, 2007) are reinterpreted in the light of newer empirical evidence. In the next section, focus is put on the question of continuity versus discontinuity of development trends. A retrospective view is taken concerning developments that occurred between 1990 and 2000 (mid-term evaluation), while the evaluation of the current state concerns the years 2005–2009. The subsequent section is devoted to the identification of more specific aspects of city dynamics, including population development, investment structure and functional profile, as well as patterns of spatial change. In the concluding section, the national positions of Berlin and Warsaw are briefly discussed and compared, and the '*quo vadis?*' question is posed concerning the future developments of the two cities in Europe.

CONTINUITY OR DISCONTINUITY OF DEVELOPMENT TRENDS?

The last decade of the 20th century to a certain extent defined the role of both Berlin and Warsaw in the European urban system. This role has mostly been identified with the performance of non-economic functions.[1] Results of the evaluation of development potential, as of 1990–2002 and prospects until 2015, are presented in Table 48.1 and Table 48.2. The data derive from a comprehensive study concerning the development of metropolitan functions in Berlin and Warsaw in the 1990s and early 2000s. The tables present a synthesis of the results of in-depth interviews with 30 experts from Poland and Germany, which analysed the state and prospects for the development of highly specialized functions of at least national importance (range) in Berlin and Warsaw (see Korcelli-Olejniczak, 2004). These results indicate that: (a) the main development potential of the

Table 48.1   Berlin and Warsaw: performance of functions 1990–2002

Metropolitan function	Berlin	Warsaw
Political centre	+	+
Transportation node	+−	−
Corporate control	−	−
Cultural centre	+	+−
Media and communication centre	+−	+−
Knowledge and innovation	+−	−+
Financial market	−	+−
Gateway city (political and economic aspects)	−+	−+

Note: ++ stands for global importance, + stands for positive, +− for national importance, −+ for poor performance and − for negative

Source: Korcelli-Olejniczak (2004)

Table 48.2   Berlin and Warsaw: prospects until 2015

	Berlin	Warsaw
Political centre	+	+
Transportation node	+−	−+
Corporate control	−	−+
Cultural centre	++	+
Media and communication centre	+	−
Knowledge and innovation	+	+
Financial market	−	−+
Gateway city (political and economic aspects)	+	+

Note: ++ stands for global importance, + stands for positive, +− for national importance, −+ for poor performance and − for negative

Source: Korcelli-Olejniczak (2004)

two cities builds on political, cultural and scientific aspects of gateway city functions; (b) the potential structure of their functions shows distinct parallels; (c) Berlin takes up a stronger position with respect to communication and circulation activities; and (d) relative to its size Warsaw shows somewhat greater potential with respect to economic functions.

It became clear by 2002 that, whereas Warsaw's national role was dominant and primary, Berlin, despite its newly established capital city position, has only partly succeeded to regain or win new advanced economic functions. Results of evaluations carried out around the year 2000 were unlike those drawn in the scenarios of the early 1990s, according to which Berlin would have developed globally with respect to economic functions and international connectivity. First of all, it became clear that the extreme losses

Table 48.3   Connectivity (2000) and connectivity change (2000–2008) for German cities and Warsaw

	Connectivity in 2000	Connectivity change between 2000 and 2008
Berlin	34.8	−0.51
Cologne	22.5	−1.61
Düsseldorf	37.8	−1.67
Frankfurt	57.5	−1.77
Hamburg	37.5	−1.08
Munich	36.5	−0.90
Stuttgart	23.8	−0.44
Warsaw	41.6	1.09

Source: Derudder et al. (2010)

of jobs in the manufacturing sector were not fully compensated by the growing services sector (Kujath, 2005). Secondly, Berlin did not experience any miraculous success in attracting new corporate-control functions. Its position in this respect has not met earlier expectations.

The international position of both cities – and its evolution over time – can be analysed by looking at their insertion in the office networks of globalized service firms. Based on data for the year 2000, it is clear that both Warsaw and Berlin were already well connected at that time (Taylor and Derudder, 2004; see Table 48.3). The connectivity measures in Table 48.3 are expressed as the proportion of the most connected city in the global economy in the year 2000 (i.e. London with a connectivity of 100). Warsaw's high connectivity is to a great extent due to the city's low intra-state competition, exemplified by the very small connectivity index for other Polish cities. Although slightly less connected than Warsaw, Berlin is also well connected in the office networks of globalized service firms. However, in contrast to Warsaw, Berlin is rivalled by other cities, with Frankfurt, Hamburg, Düsseldorf and Munich boasting higher connectivities.

Based on a new and comparable data set for the year 2008, the evolution of this connectivity can be tracked between 2000 and 2008 (Derudder et al., 2010; see Table 48.3). The connectivity change measures in the table are expressed as standard deviations from the average change across all major cities in the global economy: positive values point to rising connectivity, negative values point to declining connectivity. This analysis shows that Berlin's connectivity has declined in relative terms in this time period, albeit less so than for other German cities. Warsaw, in turn, has been one of the cities that have become more connected. Its primacy in the Polish urban system has apparently catapulted it into prominence on other scales, even to the degree that it now rivals Frankfurt in network connectivity at the global scale. Notwithstanding these indicators, Berlin has managed to develop its own specialization, related to scientific research and technology, based on transportation, medical and biological technologies, as well as in the field of cultural production (Kujath, 2005), which makes its position in Germany well defined and stable.

A recent study by Stein (2009) describes in detail the current functional structure of

Berlin, according to the job structure. The author makes an attempt to empirically check the actual professional specialization of the city which has been identified and promoted by urban policy (Enquete-Kommission, 2005) as its intrinsic development potential. The activities distinguished are science, culture, healthcare and transportation. The verification based on employment data concerning knowledge-intensive services and so-called transaction activities leads to the conclusion that only jobs related to culture are Berlin's indisputable specialization. With regard to scientific and innovative activities those connected with applied knowledge are underrepresented. The job ranking also shows indirectly that only a few headquarters of major corporations are located in the city. Also, Berlin's share of managerial jobs in private companies dealing with advanced producer services lies around the average for Germany, which is quite low for a city with metropolitan status. Warsaw, on the contrary, has shown progress with respect to its overall connectivity, as well as a considerable shift in the direction of economic function performance. At the same time, the city has managed to secure its position as an absolute leader in all pan-Polish urban classifications.

A recent ranking by the Nordea-Metrox research group (IKER, 2008), which measures the metropolitan position of 18 major Polish cities on the basis of three parameters (strength of the economy, quality of life and network connectivity) clearly shows that Warsaw is a leader with respect to all chosen criteria, while the competition from the next cities (Cracow, Poznań and Wrocław) will only become noticeable in a long-term perspective. By 2005 Warsaw was generating 13.3 per cent of the country's GDP, compared with approximately 3 per cent for Cracow and Poznań. This trend was not so obvious at the beginning of the present decade, when there were signs of approaching convergence at the upper level of the national urban system. At that time, notably the regional centres mentioned – Cracow, Poznań, Wrocław and also Gdańsk – were attracting increasing shares of new investment, while their functional distance vis-à-vis Warsaw was somewhat narrowing in this respect (Domański, 2004). However, Poland's entry into the European Union provided a powerful boost to Warsaw's economy. This is illustrated by the dynamics of formation of new firms representing the sector of advanced producer services (Śleszyński, 2009). The increase in their number in Warsaw, in relation to population number, was markedly higher between 2004 and 2007 than during 2001–2003, and the highest of all major urban centres. In this sector, which constitutes the core of metropolitan economic functions (Hall and Pain, 2006), Warsaw has clearly been leaving its national-level competitors behind.[2] Such tendencies also concern other economic functions. The on-going consolidation in the banking sector has again benefited Warsaw at the expense of other cities, and the Warsaw Stock Exchange has achieved the leading position in Eastern and Central Europe.[3] Similar changes are noted in the case of firms' headquarters location in general.[4] It may be of interest to trace here how the functional structure, as reflected by the occupational composition of Berlin and Warsaw, has been evolving over time, and what actual difference it shows in comparison with the early 1990s and the turn of the century.

Taking into account all limitations concerning the available data, some conclusions as to the overarching tendencies can clearly be drawn. Most characteristic is that the majority of trends have been sustained since the first half of the 1990s (see Figures 48.1 and 48.2). The most distinct growth by far can be observed for both cities in section K (property development, renting, business and research activities). This stands for the

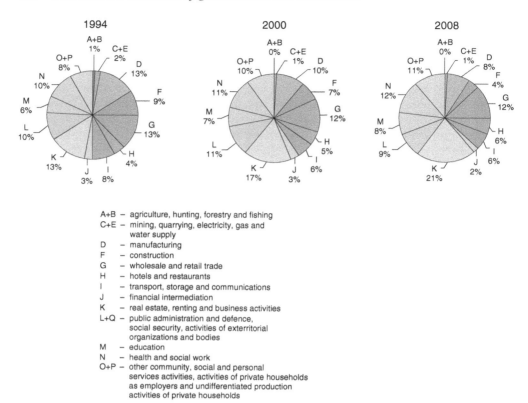

A+B – agriculture, hunting, forestry and fishing
C+E – mining, quarrying, electricity, gas and
        water supply
D   – manufacturing
F   – construction
G   – wholesale and retail trade
H   – hotels and restaurants
I   – transport, storage and communications
J   – financial intermediation
K   – real estate, renting and business activities
L+Q – public administration and defence,
        social security, activities of exterritorial
        organizations and bodies
M   – education
N   – health and social work
O+P – other community, social and personal
        services activities, activities of private households
        as employers and undifferentiated production
        activities of private households

Data have been aggregated according to Standard Industrial Classification Index 2003

Sources: Central Statistical Office, Warsaw (2003); Urząd Statystyczny Warszawa (2005); Amt für Statistik Berlin-Brandenburg (2009); own elaboration

Figure 48.1   Berlin: functional structure in 1994, 2000 and 2008

expanding positions of Berlin and Warsaw as centres of research, as well as business activities and the growing real estate markets. Berlin maintains a constant but relatively high position with respect to the share of the employed in this section in Germany (5.9 per cent in comparison to 6.6 per cent in 1991 and 5.9 per cent in the year 2000). A rise since 1994 is also observed in sections O and P, connected with social and personal service activities and activities in private households with employed persons. In this respect Berlin's position in Germany has been steadily growing since 1991 and has reached the share of 7.4 per cent of all employed. This also concerns Warsaw to an even greater extent since the year 2000 (8.8 per cent of the overall employment). Apart from that, in the case of Berlin there is an increase in sections related to education, social work and health, while Warsaw witnesses a distinct growth in section G, responsible for wholesale and retail trade; notably, the growth is even more visible after 2000.

With regard to the overall employment in services, the position of Berlin has slightly decreased (4.8 per cent of the total for Germany), when compared with 1991 (5.2 per cent), although the services sections actually witnessed a rise of the share of total employ-

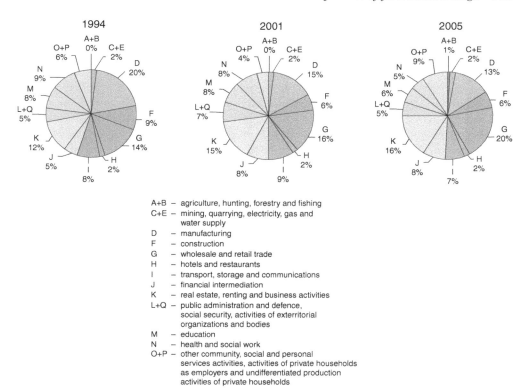

A+B   – agriculture, hunting, forestry and fishing
C+E   – mining, quarrying, electricity, gas and
        water supply
D   – manufacturing
F   – construction
G   – wholesale and retail trade
H   – hotels and restaurants
I   – transport, storage and communications
J   – financial intermediation
K   – real estate, renting and business activities
L+Q   – public administration and defence,
        social security, activities of exterritorial
        organizations and bodies
M   – education
N   – health and social work
O+P   – other community, social and personal
        services activities, activities of private households
        as employers and undifferentiated production
        activities of private households

Data have been aggregated according to Standard Industrial Classification Index 2003

Sources: Central Statistical Office, Warsaw (2003); Urząd Statystyczny Warszawa (2005); Amt für Statistik Berlin-Brandenburg (2009); own elaboration

Figure 48.2   Warsaw: functional structure in 1994, 2001 and 2005

ment from 71.2 per cent in 1991 to 86.4 per cent in 2008. In Warsaw the employment in sections related to services also grew from the middle of the 1990s, accounting for 70.4 per cent in 1995 and 78.5 per cent in 2005.

LOOKING FOR DYNAMICS

Urban transformation after 1990 has proceeded via institutional, functional and social change, as well as demographic fluctuations and the reshaping of physical space. These processes have occurred in constant reciprocity and interdependence. Spatial change derives – both conceptually (Castells, 1972) and in reality – from social and economic restructuring, as well as political and institutional change. Its progress is determined, directly and indirectly, by the investment policy of the public and private sectors. To some extent it can be assumed that spatial change is the most observable reflection of other types of change. It is, however, not always a faithful reflection.

Neither a conscious resident, a keen researcher nor a careful observer can deny that in major respects both cities are witnessing an extreme 'visual' reconstruction, the dynamics of which constitute a distinct characteristic of urban change. Taking into account how long it took for most Western European cities to create foundations for the development of their functional structure, the 20-year time span for the Central European urban centres seems short enough to describe their pace of development as imposing. Whereas changes concern all aspects of urban development, an interesting question to pose is, in which domain and to what degree can the processes observed be evaluated as truly dynamic? At the same time it should be stressed that, although parallel to a certain extent, the phenomena underlying these processes are somewhat different in the two cities.

Population Development

It is often stressed that the forecasts formulated at the beginning of the 1990s, which predicted a considerable growth of population in the major cities of Central and Eastern Europe, proved to be unrealistic. This hypothesis is however only partly true, as against a general stagnation or shrinkage of population numbers at a national level, as well as negative population balance for most large central cities throughout Europe, both Berlin and Warsaw exhibit relatively vigorous demographic dynamics. Their population numbers have been increasing since the 1990s, albeit at a slow pace, on account of in-migration. The rates of increase in the suburban rings have been markedly higher than in the cities proper. In the case of Warsaw the number of inhabitants grew from 1.69 million to 1.71 million between 2000 and 2007.[5] With respect to Berlin the increase was proportionally very similar. In the period mentioned, the number of inhabitants rose from 3.38 to 3.43 million, whereas the increase is more noticeable after 2004.

Investments and the Functional Structure

Figure 48.3 shows a comparison of trends in the total investment outlays in the two cities, that is, changes in the value of outlays during 2001–2008. The diagrams show that the investment outputs in Berlin were higher and more evenly allocated in time. In the case of Warsaw there was a visible reduction of investment outlays after 2001, and a slow but steady rise until 2007, when the total outlays amounted to 5.328 million Euros. In Berlin the changes were not as noticeable as in Warsaw, with two troughs, in 2003 and 2006. In 2007 the total investment outlays amounted to 7.197 million Euros.

When analysing the structure of investments in Berlin it is recognized that the outlays were the highest in the sections related to business, financial, property development and renting activities. Although the actual peak was in 1997, and in the later years the city experienced a steady fall of investment in these sections, in comparison with other sections the absolute numbers are still extremely high. This refers to most activities of the sector with the exclusion of financial services. Second place is occupied by transportation and media. The latter does not quite reflect the functional structure measured by employment.

Warsaw also presents a picture of a rather high concentration of outlays in sections related to transportation, real estate, renting and business activities. Since 2002 the value

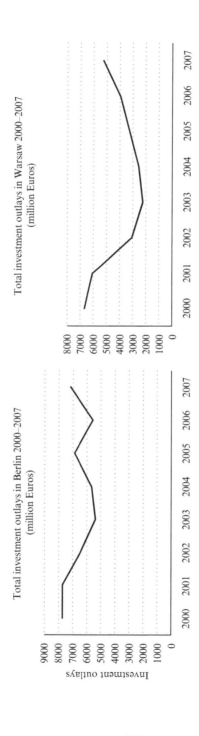

Sources: Urząd Statystyczny Warszawa (2008); Amt für Statistik Berlin-Brandenburg (2007); own elaboration

Figure 48.3   Berlin and Warsaw investment trend – outlays in the period 2000–2007

of outlays in section K has grown by around 20 per cent. This constitutes approximately 25 per cent of the total outlays in this sector in Berlin and around 14 per cent of all investment outlays in Warsaw in 2007.

In both cities the comparison of functional specialization, based on their occupational structure, with the structure of investment allocations shows some clear similarities, especially concerning the growth in research, the rental and real estate market, as well as other business activities. These seem to be the sections mostly invested in, which is the case for both cities. These are also growing sections with respect to employment. Concerning functional specialization and investment allocations in the transportation and media sector there seems to be no direct correlation. Whereas the financial outlays are rather high in the last few years, there seems to be no observable growth of employment in this section.

Functional versus Spatial Change

The above trends and processes lead to an interesting observation: the development of Berlin and Warsaw is reflected by change, not simply by growth. The cities are becoming metropolitan centres, not necessarily by gaining all resources that are ascribed to a metropolis. The change touches upon lifestyles, the quality of living, work and leisure, the variety and the quantity of activities, venues, institutions. 'Taking Berlin' in Germany is like 'taking Manhattan' in New York. It is observable that many Germans from the Old Länder take a decision to move to Berlin (Wegener, personal communication, 2009), as it is a place where 'things happen'. At the same time change is attributed to the reshaping of urban space and physical infrastructure. While in permanent transformation, this is being 'renewed', 'revitalized' and 'gentrified'. Prenzlauer Berg's return to nobility, Marzahn-Hellersdorf's new district centre and the almost extra-terrestrial BBI-International airport under construction are just a few examples of dynamic change. Change happens where spatial and social aspects meet, giving the city a truly metropolitan flair.

With respect to Warsaw, there is a clear spatial reflection of two phenomena: the city's transforming economic profile and the changes in lifestyle and quality of life. What carries weight in the overall picture are modern centres of commerce and business, as well as residential districts. But also public spaces have attracted more investments, which can be observed in most parts of Warsaw. Against the Asian urban model, which seeks spectacular shortcuts to what is metropolitan in the usual sense, by impressing the world with height and wealth, Berlin and Warsaw do not necessarily build their competitiveness and attractiveness on imposing parameters. Still, Berlin's Hauptbahnhof is one of the most spectacular objects of this kind globally, while the shopping mall *Arkadia* in the Polish capital is among the largest such centres in Central Europe.

BERLIN AND WARSAW IN BROADER TERRITORIAL CONTEXT: CONCLUDING REMARKS

As an effect of physical reconstruction, economic restructuring and restoration of its national capital functions, the position of Berlin in the urban system of Germany has advanced over the past decade, and the city has gained importance, as a scientific as well as cultural centre of at least European range (Aring, 2009, p. 10). The return of its primacy within the national urban system, however, does not seem likely, owing to the well-entrenched positions of regional metropolises – Munich, Hamburg, Frankfurt, Cologne, as foci of high-order, national-wide economic functions, but also due to structural weaknesses of regions that surround Berlin – the eastern Länder of Germany. The future growth of Berlin's importance may to a large extent be identified with its transnational role, to be gained by intensification of interaction and extension of the range of functions in Eastern and Central Europe. This, in addition to its role as a great cultural centre, is where its status as a world city may fully be confirmed.

At the same time, Warsaw will seek to maintain its present dominance within Poland's urban system with the gradual disappearance of barriers to inter-urban competition on a transnational scale. It will also aim at strengthening its function as a major financial market in this part of Europe. In order to reinforce its territorial position, Warsaw will have to overcome the existing infrastructural gap and develop knowledge-intensive economic sectors. Channels of intense interaction need to be established between Warsaw and the major regional centres, giving rise to a network which may evolve towards a polycentric metropolis (Ministry of Regional Development, 2008). Such a network might allow for decentralization of certain highly specialized functions, while augmenting the overall development potential of the urban system.

From the 20 years' (1989–2009) perspective it is justified to claim that the early expectations concerning the future positions of Berlin and Warsaw in the emerging European urban system have proved only partly true. In the case of Berlin, the spectacular reconstruction and integration of its urban fabric, together with the growing scope and magnitude of its symbolic functions (cultural in particular), have not been accompanied by a proportionate expansion of such activities as high-tech industry and corporate control. These functions have remained in the domain of major West German cities. Hence they are not the ones that define the role of Berlin as a European metropolis.

Conversely, Warsaw has succeeded in attracting a substantial segment of high-order services, as well as industrial activities generated in the process of growth and modernization of Poland's economy. By maintaining its dominance at the national level, Warsaw has also achieved a solid rank among the capital cities of Eastern and Central Europe – a position often attributed to Budapest in the 1990s (see, for example, Federal Ministry for Regional Planning, Building and Urban Development, 1994). While newcomers value Berlin for the richness of its cultural life and the range of its academic institutions (Wegener, personal communication), Warsaw acts as a magnet for those seeking career, or at least better job, opportunities.

A major problem that casts a shadow on Warsaw's development prospects is a deficiency of effective governance practices and a lack of an integrated city-region policy perspective. This results in a disorderly expansion of the city's suburban ring, which is a classical example of urban sprawl (Gutry-Korycka, 2005). Deficient transportation infrastructure and the related poor accessibility, by rail in particular, at the European level are other weak elements in the development potential of Warsaw.

Berlin is in a different situation in these respects, as it can profit from the well-established system of spatial planning and land management, including policy coordination between the city and the surrounding Land of Brandenburg. The city's major asset is its modern transportation infrastructure and its function as an international traffic node. Berlin's main weakness is a dwindling economy, social erosion and continuing depopulation of smaller towns situated in its hinterland (Kujath, 2005).

To conclude, the dynamics of change in urban space and urban functions of both Berlin and Warsaw have allowed the two cities to strengthen their positions in the European urban system. In spite of similarities with regard to their initial positions, the two cities have developed markedly different functional profiles. While the regional specializations of Berlin and Warsaw show signs of stability, their international roles are still in the process of formation.

NOTES

1. The Bundestag decision of 1991 on the status of Berlin as Germany's capital city was paralleled by confirmation of the role of Frankfurt am Main as a permanent seat of the German Federal Bank (Stoll, 1999).
2. The concentration of high-order economic functions in Warsaw, along with its dominance in other areas such as media, is evaluated by Polish planners as excessive from the point of view of territorial cohesion and the goal of maintaining the polycentric structure of Poland's urban system (Markowski, 2008).
3. In 2009 its capitalization surpassed that of the Vienna Börse, and was twice as big as the combined market value for Prague and Budapest.
4. Of the 500 largest enterprises operating in Poland 125 had their headquarters in Warsaw in 1993; by 2004 this number had increased to 192. Among those, financial services were represented by 10 firms in 1993 and 32 firms in 2004 and manufacturing by 36 and 54 firms, respectively (Śleszyński, 2007a, p. 118).
5. The remaining parts of the metropolitan area (1,379,000 inhabitants in 2007) have been gaining population at the rate of 1–2 per cent per year. According to several sources (Bijak, 2006) the size of the resident population of Warsaw is underestimated by approximately 0.25 million. The number of daily in-commuters is around 0.5 million.

REFERENCES

Aring, J. (2009), 'Europäische Metropolregionen – Annäherungen an eine raumordnerische Modernisierungsstrategie', in J. Knieling (ed.), *Metropolregionen: Innovation, Wettbewerb, Handlungsfähigkeit*. Metropolregionen und Raumentwicklung, 3. Hannover: Akademie für Raumforschung und Landesplanung, pp. 10–21.

Bijak, J. (2006), *Szacunek rzeczywistej liczby ludności Warszawy* [Estimation of actual size of resident population of Warsaw], Warsaw: Central European Forum for Migration and Population Research.

Castells, M. (1972), *La Question urbaine*, Paris: Maspero.

Derudder, B., P.J. Taylor, P. Ni, A. De Vos, M. Hoyler, H. Hanssens, D. Bassens, J. Huang, F. Witlox, W. Shen and X. Yang (2010), 'Pathways of change: shifting connectivities in the world city network, 2000–08', *Urban Studies*, **47** (9), 1861–1877.

Domański, B. (2004), 'Nowe międzynarodowe relacje Polski w świetle przepływów kapitału zagranicznego' [Poland's new international relations in the light of foreign capital flows], Mimeo, Kraków: Uniwersytet Jagielloński.

Domański, R. (ed.) (1999), *The Changing Map of Europe: The Trajectory Berlin–Poznań–Warsaw*, Friedrich Ebert Stiftung, Warszawa: Rewasz.

Enquete-Kommission (2005), 'Eine Zukunft für Berlin', Schlussbericht, Abgeordnetenhaus Berlin 15. Wahlperiode, Berlin, available at www.cdu-fraktion.berlin.de/ (accessed 10 July 2010).

ESPON (2004), 'ESPON 1.1.1. Potentials for polycentric development in Europe', Final Report, available at www.espon.lu (accessed 10 July 2010).

ESPON (2007), 'ESPON 1.4.3. Study on urban functions', Final Report, available at www.espon.lu (accessed 10 July 2010).

Federal Ministry for Regional Planning, Building and Urban Development (FMRPBUD) (Germany) (1994), *European Urban Network 1994. Spatial Planning Policies in a European Context*, Bonn: FMRPBUD.

Gutry-Korycka, M. (ed.) (2005), *Urban Sprawl: Warsaw Agglomeration Case Study*, Warsaw: Warsaw University Press.

Hall, P. (1990) 'Europe after 1992', in *Urban Challenges: Report to the Commission on Metropolitan Problems*, Statens offentliga utredningar, 33, Stockholm: Allmänna förl., pp. 176–185.

Hall, P. (2001), 'Global city-regions in the twenty-first century', in A.J. Scott (ed.), *Global City-Regions: Trends, Theory, Policy*, Oxford: Oxford University Press, pp. 60–77.

Hall, P. and K. Pain (eds) (2006), *The Polycentric Metropolis: Learning from Mega-City Regions in Europe*, London: Earthscan.

IKER (2008), *Pierwszy ranking metropolitalności miast polskich* NORDEA METROX.2008 [First ranking of the metropolitan level of Polish cities], Poznań: Instytut Konkurencyjnej Ekonomii Regionów.

Korcelli, P. and E. Korcelli-Olejniczak (2005), 'Warsaw: an evaluation of population trends and forecasts', in T. Markowski (ed.), *Regional Scientists Tribute to Professor Ryszard Domański*, Studia Regionalia, 15, Committee for Space Economy and Regional Planning, Warszawa: Polish Academy of Sciences, pp. 243–257.

Korcelli-Olejniczak, E. (2004), *Funkcje metropolitalne Warszawy w latach 1990–2002. Współzależność pozycji w systemie miast Europy Środkowej* [Metropolitan functions of Berlin and Warsaw in 1990–2002. Interdependence of positions in the urban system of Central Europe], Prace Geograficzne, 198, Warszawa: IGiPZ PAN.

Korcelli-Olejniczak, E. (2007), 'Berlin and Warsaw: in search of a new role in the European urban system', *Journal of Housing and the Built Environment*, **22** (1), 51–68.

Kujath, H.J. (2005), 'Restructuring of the metropolitan region of Berlin-Brandenburg: economic trends and political answers', *Geographia Polonica*, **78** (1), 117–136.

Kukliński, A. (1999), 'Berlin – the global metropolis of the 21st century', in R. Domański (ed.), *The Competitiveness of Regions in the Polish and European Perspective*, Studia Regionalia, 9, Warszawa: Polish Academy of Sciences, pp. 263–273.

Lichtenberger, E. (1994), 'Das metropolitane Zeitalter in Europa in West und Ost', *Mitteilungen der Österreichischen Geographischen Gesellschaft*, **136**, 7–36.

Lloyd, S. (2002), 'The computational universe', available at http://www.edge.org/documents/day2/day2_lloyd_index.html (accessed 10 July 2010).

Markowski, T. (ed.) (2008), *Koncepcja przestrzennego zagospodarowania kraju a wizje i perspektywy rozwoju przestrzennego Europy* [The Polish spatial development concept versus European visions of spatial development perspectives], Studia KPZK PAN, 122, Warszawa: Polska Akademia Nauk.

Ministry of Regional Development (Poland) (2008), *Experts' Project Poland's Spatial Development Perspective 2008–2033*, Warszawa: Ministry of Regional Development.

Śleszyński, P. (2007a), *Gospodarcze funkcje kontrolne w przestrzeni Polski* [Economic control functions in Poland's space], Prace Geograficzne, 213, Warszawa: IGiPZ PAN.

Śleszyński, P. (2007b), 'Szacowanie liczby i rozmieszczenia pracujących w dużym mieście na przykładzie Warszawy' [Estimation of size and distribution of employed in a large city on the example of Warsaw], *Przegląd Geograficzny*, **79**, (3–4), 533–566.

Śleszyński, P. (2009), 'Zmiany strukturalne i przestrzenno-funkcjonalne w rozwoju przedsiębiorczości po przystąpieniu Polski do Unii Europejskiej' [Structural and spatio-functional changes in the development of entrepreneurship following Poland's accession to the European Union], *Studia Regionalne i Lokalne*, **3** (37), 5–25.

Stein, R. (2009), 'Besondere und allgemeine metropolitane Spezialisierungen in Berlin: Kultur und Wissenschaft, Koordination und Transaktion' [Particular and general metropolitan specializations in Berlin: culture and science, coordination and transaction], *Raumforschung und Raumordnung*, **67** (4), 287–299.

Stoll, M. (1999), 'Berlin in the network of the European metropolises', in R. Domański (ed.), *The Competitiveness of Regions in the Polish and European Perspective*, Studia Regionalia, 9, Warszawa: Polish Academy of Sciences, pp. 251–261.

Taylor, P.J. and B. Derudder (2004), 'Porous Europe: European cities in global urban arenas', *Tijdschrift voor Economische en Sociale Geografie*, **95** (5), 527–538.

49 'The world city concept travels East': on excessive imagination and limited urban sustainability in UAE world cities
David Bassens

This chapter discusses the fast-growing United Arab Emirates (UAE) cities Abu Dhabi and Dubai, which, although emblematic of urban-centred growth, have attracted surprisingly little attention in world cities literature. Although the 2009 debt crisis in Dubai has raised questions about urban sustainability in the wider Gulf region, both cities have been prospering as nodes of global flows of money, people and goods. Perhaps most indicative of this is the fast and massive population growth both cities have experienced in recent decades. In Dubai, the population rose from ca. 40 000 in the 1960s to more than 1.6 million in 2008 (www.dubai.ae, accessed 10 February 2010), while Abu Dhabi's urban population reached ca. 800 000 in early 2010 (www.visitabudhabi.ae, accessed 10 February 2010), compared with a mere 25 000 in the 1960s. A lot of the initial population growth resulted from the discovery of oil in the early part of this period. As a consequence, earlier forms of subsistence such as pearl diving, smuggling and manual production lost their importance, while the influx of oil industry workers and windfall oil money transformed these formerly small settlements into a specific urban form which Khalaf (2006) identifies as 'oil cities'.

More recently, however, in a move to diversify their economies away from oil dependency, the ruling families (Abu Dhabi's al-Nahyan and Dubai's al-Makhtoum) have endorsed the development of cities within their realms as centres of business, trade and advanced servicing – quite successfully, so it appears, as even during the global financial crisis, both Abu Dhabi and Dubai were identified as 'winning' financial centres, with banks maintaining high levels of profitability and capital base (see Derudder et al., 2011). Also in terms of advanced producer services (APS) broadly defined (comprising accounting, advertising, finance, law and management consultancy), Gulf cities have become more important, as was illustrated in a longitudinal analysis of major APS firms between 2000 and 2008 (Derudder et al., 2010). In addition, Abu Dhabi and Dubai have become global transport nodes of goods and people, both in terms of seaports (Jebel Ali and Port Rashid in Dubai) and accompanying free trade zones and maritime service providers (Jacobs and Hall, 2007), and also large-scale airports and international airlines such as Emirates, Etihad and so on (O'Connell, 2006). These variegated but coherent growth trends echo a broader geographical 'reOrientation' (Frank, 1998) and geo-economic shift in the world economy, where 'the Orient' – China in particular – is becoming the 'emerging market' on which to keep a watchful eye. While 'traditional' world cities such as London and New York have been hit hard by the crisis, Chinese cities (most notably Beijing, Shanghai and Hong Kong) are booming, while Gulf cities are profiling themselves as hubs in between. But also in itself, the Gulf region, floating on oil money, remains a crucial source of global capital. Some of the world's largest sovereign wealth funds (SWFs), such as Abu Dhabi Investment Authority (ADIA), which holds a massive US$875 billion (Behrendt, 2008), and also high-net-worth private investors from that region have seized the opportunity to acquire assets in major key sectors and blue chip companies in 'the West'.

Accounts of Middle Eastern political economies have often been inclined towards an 'exceptionalist' reading of contemporary processes (see for instance Aarts, 1999 on Middle Eastern political and economic integration), which tends to explain the failure of external concepts of democracy, secularism or market-led transition as a consequence of internal – cultural or religious – resistance. However, the sheer growth of Gulf cities and their broad insertion into global circuits of capital, goods and people recall the very essence of Friedmann's (1986) seminal world city hypothesis, and suggest the world city prism of analysis as a *universal* category is relevant within the UAE's urban context. It is true, of course, that Gulf cities *can* be identified for their idiosyncratic political economies, notably their city-state character, the intermingling of state and corporate spheres, the role of Islam in urban development and finance, and so on. But instead of the simplistic view that the Middle East is 'not like any other region', there is a need for an analysis of the Middle East which at the same time addresses issues in terms of universal categories, while being sensitive to historical particularities. This is a need which has long been recognized (see Halliday, 1987, pp. 215–218, who elaborates on the essentialist and orientalist dimensions of Middle Eastern analyses). In this chapter, therefore, I map the idiosyncrasies of Gulf cities to inform a more 'global' perspective on world cities and aim to open up the particularities of Gulf city economies as an 'antidote' to analyses that leave out regional actors, ideologies, lifestyles and others. The resilience of the 'world city concept', both as an analytical lens and as a discursive field, lies precisely in its ability to 'travel' and to become regionalized and adapted to various political economic settings. The aim of this chapter, therefore, is to discuss the evolution of Abu Dhabi and Dubai as 'emerging' Gulf world cities from three interrelated perspectives. First the growth of Abu Dhabi and Dubai as a complementary evolution of city-states within the UAE's federation is discussed. Secondly, I explore how 'world city discourse' is being employed in the construction of Abu Dhabi and, especially, Dubai as 'emerging' world cities. The focus here is specifically on the role of financial elites in building Dubai, and the Gulf region more generally, as a market for mainstream and 'Islamic', that is, Shari'a-compliant markets. Thirdly and finally, I question the sustainability (broadly defined) of these cities and their future as post-industrial sites of production from city-level and regional perspectives.

THE UAE: A FEDERATION OF QUASI CITY-STATES

The rise of two booming cities along the Gulf in such close proximity – within a mere hour's drive from each other – reflects how under the conditions of the UAE's federal configuration, ruling Emirati elites have actively put 'the urban' at the centre of economic development of their territories. In fact, following an 'amalgamation' of previously autonomous emirates, a very idiosyncratic political economy of 'quasi city-states' (Sidaway, 2008) has emerged, characterized by great autonomy vis-à-vis other members of the federation, and by public/private entanglement of the ruling family and numerous government-related enterprises (GREs).

Regionally, the emergence of city-state entities can be framed within historical power relations among regional Emirati elites which mark processes of mutual political and economic cooperation and competition. In particular, when the British left the region in 1971, the emirates of Abu Dhabi, Dubai, Sharjah, Fujairah, Umm al-Qaiwain and Ajman (and from 1972 also Ras al-Khaimah) along the so-called Trucial Coast decided to form a federation (UAE) in order to counter what they feared would be imminent interference from their strong neighbours Iran and Saudi Arabia. Although the individual emirates thereby chose to transfer power to a higher echelon, from its inception the UAE was also the stage for conflicting interests and strife among its members, especially between Abu Dhabi and Dubai. As argued by Peck (2001, p. 150), much of this deep-seated rivalry can be traced back historically to the establishment of Dubai as a separate Sheikhdom in 1833 by the disaffected Al Bu Fasalah subsection of the Bani Yas tribe of Abu Dhabi. Following this 'schism', Dubai and Abu Dhabi developed along different lines: Dubai as a cosmopolitan outward-looking mercantile city-state, while Abu Dhabi remained a more traditional tribal federation. From the nascent federation's initial meetings in the late 1960s onwards, the charismatic Sheikh Zayed bin Sultan al-Nahyan of Abu Dhabi played an instrumental role in forging a federation, relying on the oil wealth of Abu Dhabi and its clear territorial dominance in what would later be the UAE (Davidson, 2006). This move to consolidate 'national' power around Abu Dhabi (which would be home to the federation's capital and provide the new nation's president) encountered resistance from the leader of Dubai, Rashid al-Makthoum, who, although lacking the oil wealth of his neighbour, was able to negotiate a relatively strong influence for Dubai in the newly forged federation, securing, for instance, the right of veto in the Supreme Council, provision of the federation's vice-president and an equal number of votes in the Federal National Council (Peck, 2001, p. 150). From its inception, then, the federal character of the UAE state and the actions and attitudes of geographically separated ruling families have allowed the development of multiple autonomous urban centres.

At the level of these individual emirates themselves, the lines between the emirate as a political entity (a 'city-state') and as a commercial/business enterprise have been substantially blurred. Especially in Dubai – so-called 'Dubai Inc.' – a highly centralized and autocratic state power, embodied in the emir (Prince Mohammad Al-Makhtoum) and his family, is combined with a quasi corporate style of administration (Davis, 2006). Both Abu Dhabi's SWFs, such as ADIA and Mubadala Development Company, and Dubai's GREs, such as Dubai Holding or Dubai World and its subsidiaries (Nakheel, Dubai Ports World, etc.), have become the prime vehicles for ruling elites to diversify the economy away from oil dependency. In contrast to SWFs, which are generally regarded as 'government-owned', GREs are more like 'semi-private entities' set up as independent companies, but which nevertheless embody the state's development strategies. Within this context, two modes of diversification can be identified.

On the one hand, both SWFs and GREs *channel and manage investments abroad*. Sovereign Gulf investors have become involved in the 'core' regions of the world economy, notably Europe and Northern America, both in terms of buying sovereign debt and acquiring corporate assets. Along with China and Japan, the Gulf Cooperation

Council (GCC) States have financed roughly a quarter of the United States' current-account deficit, by investing heavily in US treasury bills (Abdelal et al., 2008). In terms of corporate assets, Gulf investors have turned to key sectors in 'the West' such as finance, the automotive industry, cultural institutions (e.g. The Louvre) and others. With the global financial crisis lurking in 2007, ADIA acquired a 5 per cent share in Citigroup, while the Mubadala Development Company has bought itself into Ferrari, the Carlyle Group (a private equity firm) and the California-based chipmaker AMD. Generally, these numerous investments have a 'passive' character in the sense that they tend simply to hold assets to generate a stable flow of income. However, sometimes, as with the acquisition of the ports manager P&O by GRE Dubai Ports World in 2006, these investments generate suspicion about a possible underlying geostrategic agenda. In the aftermath of 9/11 the US Congress regarded the prospect of the UAE's presence in North American ports as a possible security breach and blocked the acquisition of the North American arm of P&O (Abdelal et al., 2008).

On the other hand, GREs (but not so much SWFs) operate within a highly competitive and entrepreneurialist atmosphere to *attract foreign investments*, feeding into the growth of the city-state. Dubai's GREs in particular have been the prime vehicles for enacting the ruling families' 'visionary' city-building projects. As such they are involved in the development of luxurious tourist resorts (for instance the Jumeirah Resort, Burj al-Arab), building a state-of-the-art business and service infrastructure (Dubai International Financial Centre), logistics and trade hubs (Jebel Ali Free Trade Zone, Dubai Logistics City), knowledge and media centres (Dubai Media City, Dubai Internet City), and so on. Often foregrounded by high-profile architecture, these projects carry the intention to physically engineer and construct post-industrial sites of production through the attraction of regional and global investors.

BUILDING UAE WORLD CITIES: THE ROLE OF GLOBAL FINANCIAL ELITES

Both the image and actual economic growth of UAE cities have been intensely related to their discursive constructions as attractive sites for global production and accumulation. In the efforts to make their city a node for global flows of capital, goods and people, UAE elites have operationalized world city discourses in their respective city-building projects. Mirroring examples of successful service-oriented urban economies (International Financial Centres (IFCs) such as Singapore and Hong Kong), or well-established 'global cities' (Sassen, 2001) such as New York and London, they have aimed to build instant world cities through rhetoric (city marketing), form (architecture) and function (port, IFC, etc.) (Davis, 2006; Bassens et al., 2010a). Dubai's strategy has subsequently served as a model for urban development – an 'urban growth machine' (Molotch, 1976) if you like – throughout the Middle East (for instance in Amman; see Parker, 2009). Paradoxically, its spirit of urban entrepreneurialism has given rise to a 'post'-industrial city-state in an emirate which lacks any substantial industrial history, and, as irony would have it, this model of urban development was soon copied by cities throughout the wider Middle Eastern region. Before the 2009 Dubai debt crisis, the Dubai model promised to generate a success story in itself, a unique safe haven for regional and international investments in the conflict-ridden Middle East. Dubai's ruling al-Makhtoum family itself has obviously played an instrumental role in the city's rapid development, creating the stage for international investments from a 'supply side' perspective. They have aimed to make Dubai a global 'brand' (Bagaeen, 2007), mainly through the above-mentioned high-profile architectural projects and infrastructure developments, intended as the 'tangible' base of Dubai's construction as a world city. In addition, the fiscal and juridical environment has been relaxed in order to attract regional and global investments: for instance, since 2002, non-UAE nationals have been allowed to purchase property within the emirate of Dubai. However, from a 'demand side' perspective, Dubai's growth does more than reflect the ambitions of its leaders alone. Actors operating at both global and regional scales have had an active interest in building an investor-friendly site for production and accumulation. The following two paragraphs explore these developments in greater depth.

First, on a global scale, business and financial elites within and around global APS firms, especially financial firms (such as large investment and commercial banks), have played a crucial role (Bassens et al., 2010b). Banking on both mainstream and 'alternative' (for instance, interest-free Islamic finance) 'emerging markets', financial elites in conjunction with the local ruling elite have discursively 'constructed' Dubai as an attractive investment market for property development, real estate, tourism, business, trade, and so on. The reason, then, why oil-depleted Dubai has been able to realize its gargantuan dream on vast amounts of borrowed money is because of the built-up 'credit' the Dubai rulers were given by transnational networks of financial elites, based in IFCs – London in particular – and the booming UAE cities themselves. Looking for profitable new markets in the affluent Gulf, investment bankers introduced themselves not only into mainstream debt-based finance but also into Shari'a-compliant financial circuits, as illustrated by the importance of *sukuk* (Islamic asset-based/asset-backed notes) in Dubai's finance strategy. Drawing on Islamic economics, which refrains from *riba* (literally 'growth', but usually interpreted as interest) and avoids *gharar* (contractual uncertainty) and *maysir* (gambling, speculation) (see Bassens et al., 2011), the Islamic financial services (IFS) sector has seen rapid growth (e.g. 22.8 per cent between 2008 and 2009, when its asset value amounted to US$822 billion; *The Banker*, 2009). As a result of windfall oil money in the 1970s oil boom, the initial growth of the IFS sector was mainly driven by Gulf-based fully fledged Islamic banks (Dubai Islamic Bank, Bahrain Islamic Bank), which set out to operate in national or regional markets. More recently, however, global banks have also entered Shari'a-compliant markets through 'Islamic windows' in order to tap into the rising demand for Shari'a-compliant financial products. Large UK banks such as the Royal Bank of Scotland, Barclays Capital, HSBC and Standard Chartered in particular have been heavily involved in establishing Dubai as a financial hub, not only through the setting up of well-staffed regional headquarters (mostly in the Dubai International Financial Centre) but also as creditors of Dubai's 'world city project' through Islamic and conventional debt-based structures (now leaving them exposed to an estimated US$19 billion in outstanding debt). By using the high credibility of the Islamic sector, 'mainstream' financial elites have developed Dubai as a prime 'emerging' market (compare with Sidaway and Pryke, 2000), while regional (Islamic) banks have mobilized Islam in an often orientalist discourse to attract Shari'a-compliant investment. Ironically, notwithstanding the Shari'a-base call for a return to the 'real' economy as a means of avoiding speculation and uncertainty – *sukuk* were designed to generate a steady flow of rent – all this 'imageneering' (compare with Lai, 2006 on the construction of Asian 'emerging' markets) has left Dubai extremely vulnerable to market bubbles, such as the collapse of property markets when the global financial crisis hit the region.

Second, the property bubble and the debt crisis which it induced when Dubai's GREs proved unable to redeem issued *sukuk* near the end of 2009 (see for instance the Dubai Palm developer Nakheel's US$3.5 billion looming default) have highlighted regional interests in sustaining Dubai's image as a haven for investment. With its government-run agencies faltering, and Dubai's elites being either unwilling or unable to uphold Dubai's status as an emerging Gulf 'world city', the al-Nahyan from oil-rich Abu Dhabi decided to bail out their neighbouring city-state, buying US$10 billion of its soaring debt and thus enabling some of the most pressing debts to be redeemed. However, it is clear that this bail-out does not amount to a blank cheque. For the al-Nahyan, here lies the opportunity to strengthen their regional influence and 'fuel' an Abu Dhabi-led state-building project, possibly bringing an end to Dubai's days as an 'autonomous' city-state. The current crisis elucidates how cycles of urban competition/decentralization and urban cooperation/centralization often alternate, reflecting the respective rising and diminishing importance of the UAE state for the cities within its borders. As long as Dubai was booming, the al-Makhtoum downplayed its status as member of the federation, portraying it as an autonomous city-state, while the state-representing al-Nahyan in Abu Dhabi found political 'consolation' in providing the federation's president. Now that Dubai is in trouble, apart from being eager to save the national image of the UAE as a safe haven for investments, the latter may very well use the bail-out as an opportunity to strengthen their position in the UAE state, discourage regionalist tendencies and keep Dubai's previous ambitions in check (Bassens et al., 2010b). The fate of the so-called Burj Dubai ('tower of Dubai') is perhaps most telling: although it had taken Dubai's rulers six years to build the highest tower in the world, just days before its opening the skyscraper was renamed 'Burj Khalifa', referring to Sheikh Khalifa bin Zayed al-Nahyan, the current ruler of Abu Dhabi. It is hard to imagine an event more symbolic of the region's underlying power configuration.

UAE CITIES: A HALLMARK OF LIMITED SUSTAINABILITY?

To conclude, as if we were dealing with real-life urban experiments, a focus on the UAE's 'instant world cities' (Bagaeen, 2007), which have emerged in a region lacking significant urban history, allows us to readdress the very premises of globalized urbanization, globalized urbanity, the global shift to post-industrial modes of production and rescaling processes towards the level of the city-state. Although strong in discourse and actual growth, the sustainability of the Gulf post-industrial city-state, which is arguably the dominant Gulf world city model, has never been without debate. Much of this chapter has elaborated upon the questionable economic sustainability of Gulf cities, which has been highlighted recently by Dubai's debt crisis. This particular focus, however, threatens to overshadow perhaps even more fundamental dimensions of the UAE's cities, namely their inability to somehow embed global flows of capital, knowledge and people into their fast-growing globalized urbanity in an ecologically and socially sustainable way. Ecologically, both cities are notorious for eyebrow-raising energy and water consumption, be it in the form of evergreen golf courses, indoor ski arenas, air-conditioned malls or massive desalinization programmes. In addition, the urban planning of both produces car dependency and generates excess commuting, as a result of a zone-based perspective on how cities are to function (e.g. Media City, Health City, Sports City). Yet here again is another paradox: it is the same Abu Dhabi, an exporter of old school carbon energy, which is building a 'visionary' zero-carbon emission city, MASDAR, within its territory – zero-carbon after it has been built of course. As a subsidiary of Mubadala Development Company, this project aims to produce sustainable neighbourhoods for as many as 40 000 residents and a site for research and development of new energy technologies (www.masdar.ae/en/home/index.aspx, accessed 4 March 2010). However, while this new development might bring ecological relief, high property costs and legal barriers will no doubt make this a place for 'the happy few', the Emirati, and perhaps the expat community. Similar to lots of other high-profile property developments in Abu Dhabi and Dubai, MASDAR will be yet another example of how urban inequality, and in particular a three-tiered society, in effect a 'set of cities' (Elsheshtawy, 2008), of Emirati nationals, Western expats employed in business and services and Asian low-skilled workers, is spatially reproduced.

In conclusion, this leads us to reconsider the UAE's urban sustainability from a social dimension, or as Elsheshtawy (2010, p. 968) has urged us to do, to look 'behind the urban spectacle'. In fact, the UAE's globalized urbanity – in infrastructure *and* lived experience – is the product of an army of low-skilled migrant workers, typically of South Asian origin, who constitute the majority of Abu Dhabi and Dubai's urban population. At the same time, recalling Smith (2001) and Robinson (2002), these Afghans, Bangladeshis, Indians, Pakistanis and others sustain myriads of economic, ethnic, ideological, religious and other transurban linkages that have remained largely understudied in much contemporary world cities research. In the end, then, this chapter aims to draw attention to emerging/existing forms of transnationality that have been less studied, but which originate in Gulf cities themselves (for instance the globalizing Islamic financial services sector). Opening up these and other kinds of Gulf-based agency as a (analytical) source of transnationalism and globalization would add to a more 'global' perspective precisely because they would regionalize urbanization and urbanity, most certainly so in regions where 'global' cities such as London and New York as world city models appear to miss out on current urban realities.

REFERENCES

Aarts, P. (1999), 'The Middle East: a region without regionalism or the end of exceptionalism?', *Third World Quarterly*, **20** (5), 911–925.
Abdelal, R., A. Khan and T. Khanna (2008), 'Where oil-rich nations are placing their bets', *Harvard Business Review*, **86** (9), 119–128.
Bagaeen, S. (2007), 'Brand Dubai: the instant city; or the instantly recognizable city', *International Planning Studies*, **12** (2), 173–197.
Bassens, D., B. Derudder and F. Witlox (2010a), 'Searching for the Mecca of finance: Islamic financial services and the world city network', *Area*, **42** (1), 35–46.
Bassens, D., B. Derudder and F. Witlox (2010b), 'The making and breaking of Dubai: the end of a city-state?', *Political Geography*, **29** (6), 299–301.

Bassens, D., B. Derudder and F. Witlox (2011), 'Oiling global capital accumulation: analysing the principles, practices, and geographical distribution of Islamic financial services', *The Service Industries Journal*, **31** (3), 327–341.

Behrendt, S. (2008), 'When money talks: Arab sovereign wealth funds in the global public policy discourse', *Carnegie Papers* (Carnegie Middle East Centre), 12, Washington, DC: Carnegie Endowment for International Peace.

Davidson, C.M. (2006), 'After Shaikh Zayed: the politics of succession in Abu Dhabi and the UAE', *Middle East Policy*, **13** (1), 42–59.

Davis, M. (2006), 'Fear and money in Dubai', *New Left Review*, **41**, 47–68.

Derudder, B., M. Hoyler and P.J. Taylor (2011), 'Goodbye Reykjavik: International banking centres and the global financial crisis', *Area*, **43** (2), 173–182.

Derudder, B., P.J. Taylor, P. Ni, A. De Vos, M. Hoyler, H. Hanssens, D. Bassens, J. Huang, F. Witlox, W. Shen and X. Yang (2010), 'Pathways of change: shifting connectivities in the world city network, 2000–08', *Urban Studies*, **47** (9), 1861–1877.

Elsheshtawy, Y. (2008), 'Transitory sites: mapping Dubai's "forgotten" urban spaces', *International Journal of Urban and Regional Research*, **32** (4), 968–988.

Elsheshtawy, Y. (2010), *Dubai: Behind an Urban Spectacle*, London and New York: Routledge.

Frank, A.G. (1998), *ReORIENT: Global Economy in the Asian Age*, Berkeley, CA: University of California Press.

Friedmann, J. (1986), 'The world city hypothesis', *Development and Change*, **17** (1), 69–83.

Halliday, F. (1987), 'The Middle East in international perspective: problems of analysis', in R. Bush, G. Johnston and D. Coates (eds), *The World Order: Socialist Perspectives*, Cambridge: Polity Press, pp. 201–220.

Jacobs, W. and P.V. Hall (2007), 'What conditions supply chain strategies of ports? The case of Dubai', *GeoJournal*, **68** (4), 327–342.

Khalaf, S. (2006), 'The evolution of the Gulf city type, oil, and globalization', in J.W. Fox, N. Mourtada-Sabbah and M. al-Mutawa (eds), *Globalization and the Gulf*, London and New York: Routledge, pp. 244–265.

Lai, K.P.Y. (2006), '"Imagineering" Asian emerging markets: financial knowledge networks in the fund management industry', *Geoforum*, **37** (4), 627–642.

Molotch, H. (1976), 'The city as a growth machine: toward a political economy of place', *American Journal of Sociology*, **82** (2), 309–330.

O'Connell, J.F. (2006), 'The changing dynamics of the Arab Gulf based airlines and an investigation into the strategies that are making Emirates into a global challenger', *World Review of Intermodal Transportation Research*, **1** (1), 94–114.

Parker, C. (2009), 'Tunnel-bypasses and minarets of capitalism: Amman as neoliberal assemblage', *Political Geography*, **28** (2), 110–120.

Peck, M.C. (2001), 'Formation and evolution of the federation and its institutions', in I. Al Abed and P. Hellyer (eds), *The United Arab Emirates: A New Perspective*, London: Trident Press, pp.145–160.

Robinson, J. (2002), 'Global and world cities: a view from off the map', *International Journal of Urban and Regional Research*, **26** (3), 531–554.

Sassen, S. (2001), *The Global City: New York, London, Tokyo*, Princeton, NJ: Princeton University Press, 2nd edition.

Sidaway, J.D. (2008), 'Globalising the geohistory of city/state relations: on "Problematizing city/state relations: towards a geohistorical understanding of contemporary globalization" by Peter Taylor', *Transactions of the Institute of British Geographers*, **33** (1), 149–151.

Sidaway, J.D. and M. Pryke (2000), 'The strange geographies of "emerging markets"', *Transactions of the Institute of British Geographers*, **25** (2), 187–201.

Smith, M.P. (2001), *Transnational Urbanism: Locating Globalization*, Oxford: Blackwell.

The Banker (2009), 'Banker survey shows the growth in Islamic finance', available at www.thebanker.com (accessed 15 December 2009).

50 Sydney: the wicked power-geometry of a greening global city

Michele Acuto

Sydney's newest urban strategy, the *Sustainable Sydney 2030 Vision*, sets out to create a 'green, global and connected' metropolis that wants to be capable of challenging urban giants like New York and London. *Green* is the centrepiece of this master plan, which seeks to situate sustainability at the core of Sydney's competitive and innovative edge. This chapter seeks to sketch the lifestyle imagineering that underpins Sydney's global growth, the move to a green theme in urban planning, the multiscalar governance process that defines Sydney politics, and the increasingly central urban entrepreneurialism of the city's governance. As I argue, the 'Harbour City' has indeed succeeded in improving its status as a world city, thanks to an increasingly entrepreneurial approach to urban governance which, in the long run, might set the city on a perilous 'wicked' path.

THE CONSCIOUS RISE OF THE HARBOUR CITY

Sydney has rapidly moved to a centre stage in both popular and academic discourses. It has firmly surpassed Melbourne, its long-standing national rival, to become Australia's core settlement (Searle, 1996; Connell, 2000; Elias, 2003; Tonts and Taylor, 2010). It has become the country's key mobility hub and primary link with the world economy (Hugo, 2008) and reached global recognition by hosting the 2000 Summer Olympics. At present, the city is an increasingly stable presence in the plethora of urban rankings that has sprawled amongst academic and journalistic publications. In GaWC's revised roster, Sydney now occupies an 'alpha+' position that is second only to the ever-dominant NYLON (New York and London) duo, and its rapid elevation to this status – along with Beijing and Shanghai – is considered to be the key finding of the 2008 survey (Taylor et al., 2009). Yet, if financial records and environmental rhetoric are set aside, there is more to the rise of Sydney as 'green' global city than meets the eye. However, Sydney's global fortunes cannot be explained by global processes alone. The city's ascent in world urban hierarchies is not merely a consequence of worldwide realignments, nor simply an Olympic legacy. Rather, Sydney's increasingly central positioning on global financial, information and mobility 'highways' is the result of a complex mix of flows and networks that have been consciously sown by the various actors involved in the city's governance. In an analogous move to several growing Asian world cities such as Hong Kong and Shanghai, the Harbour City has been built to compete on a global scale against other strategic sites of globalization, with the state (China and Special Administrative Region Government for the former, New South Wales in the latter case) taking the lead role in both political and physical construction of Sydney as a 'global' city.

Since the urban boom of the mid 1970s, and even more markedly from the mid 1990s with the growing importance of its CBD as financial hub, Sydney has been developed around a two-fold imagineering underpinning the policies of various governments. As Peter Murphy and Sophie Watson (1997) underlined, the Harbour City has centred its globalization on the twinned themes of tourism and business, linked by the strategic branding of a Sydneysider lifestyle that is rooted in cosmopolitan, modern and relatively inexpensive features. In this view, Sydney's characteristics are supposed to appeal to both the transient visitor in search of the Australian experience, or the corporate (middle-to-high) class looking for a livable but styled settlement. Tourist branding required the development and marketing of icons such as the Opera House and Bondi Beach, and the improvement of mobility infrastructures to house greater numbers of transient users, as well as an emphasis on special events like Mardi Gras, New Year's celebrations on the Harbour and mega-events like the Olympics (Spearritt, 2006). Along with these, Sydney has proved capable of sustaining the parallel growth of a business-pitched re-organization that has been pinpointed on similar, if not often analogous, developments: efficient mobility hubs to house global flows not just of people but also of capitals, information and goods, feature corporate spaces such as Aurora Place and 126 Phillip Street, and cultural institutions are in fact compatible and often contingent on much of the same complexes that form the visitor-oriented urban substrate. These configurations can coexist in the same Sydneysider lifestyle imagineering, selling the Harbour experience and commodifying the urban into a product to be consumed in either a short or a long term (Figure 50.1). Likewise they have both equally found fertile ground in the liberalization and demand-oriented approach that, as we will see below, the city has undergone throughout the last decade. As the lifestyle narrative has arguably been bearing some fruit, the Harbour City slowly integrated a third theme to its imagineering: sustainability. Although some movements towards environmentalism were present in the 1970s and in alternate phases in the mid 1980s (Christoff and Low, 2000, pp. 246–249), the increasing centrality of green solutions in Sydney has taken off more extensively only through the 1990s, inaugurated by the Australian Labor Government's 'Building Better Cities' plan in 1991, which prompted some *ad hoc* arrangements to growing sustainability questions such as the inner docks renovation in Ultimo (Hundloe and McDonald, 1997).

'Green' is nowadays a key element in the construction of Sydney's global image. It is, even before becoming actual urban planning, a re-problematization of the city's identity in the global imaginative geography. What this means in practice is that the city has to act accordingly both through the definition of a new urban narrative and through the reconfiguration of its features to suit the changing discourse. If this might equal a paradigm shift for some metropolises, especially in the East (Hong Kong, Shanghai, Seoul to name a few), greening Sydney is instead relatively easy: the city's identity is already substantiated by an environmentally prone image of the 'Harbour City' that is solidly rooted in its lifestyle branding, be it visitor- or business-oriented. Ever since the 1988 twin development of Darling Harbour and the First Fleet anchorage that now houses Circular Quay and the Opera House, Sydney's dramatic growth in tourism and corporate activities has been tied tightly to the 'café harbour society' (Bargwanna, 2006, p. 364) stereotype of a green and livable city open to all kinds of guests from the back-packer to the financial elite. This should, however, not downplay that there are some

Source: author

Figure 50.1   The Opera House and Harbour Bridge constitute the worldwide image of what Sydney is: a livable, ocean-oriented and vibrant metropolis

separate areas of urban and architectural development that do not overlap between these two categories. Business-oriented planning, for instance, requires interior space configurations and preferential pathways that have (and in most cases are *meant to* have) little connection to public areas. Nonetheless, Sydney remains one of the most striking cases of intertwining between the two. This intersection has in fact fuelled a demand for more natural attractions and green spaces such as Hyde Park, and greater connectivity with the various areas of Sydney Harbour National Park such as Watsons Bay in the far East end of the city. Arguably, the green theme has progressively acted as a linkage between the vacationer façade of the city and its corporate core, enhancing the attractiveness of that 'leisure dimension' that 'differentiates Sydney from other [globalizing] cities in the Asia Pacific region' (Dean, 2005, p. 52). In turn, the escalating prominence of green solutions to city planning and architecture has slowly modified the patterns of consumption of the city's major urban spaces, remodelling large central areas such as the CBD, Bondi or Manly, to fit the new dominant lifestyle. Yet, where does all of this *green* come from?

GREEN, GLOBAL AND. . . CONNECTED?

The question of governance is far more complex than it might seem to the outsider's eye, as the identity of Sydney in the popular imagination often hinders a full appreciation of the extreme intricacy of the cross-related political processes that underpin it. The City of Sydney Council is perhaps the most active green agent of the last few years. Its growing concern with environmental responses to climate change and urban livability is probably best epitomized by *Sustainable Sydney 2030* – a vision for a 'green, global and connected' metropolitan centre that originated in a series of public consultations and cooperation with various key local planners (such as Lend Lease property management corporation) which culminated in a policy document issued in 2008. This project sets out to revolutionize and revitalize the metropolis' core with environmentally oriented developments and emphasis on sub-local community improvement. As the document points out (City of Sydney, 2008a, pp. 6–7), Sydney's inner city is thus supposed to become 'internationally recognized for its environmental performance' (thus 'green'), 'Australia's most significant global city' (thus 'global') and networked within and without its boundaries (thus 'connected') (Figure 50.2). However, we should not mistake this as a Sydney-wide initiative, since this strategy refers only to this Council's domain, which covers little more than the CBD area. On the whole, the 12,000-odd square kilometres of Sydney's

Source: author

Figure 50.2 A slogan poster on Market Street promoting the Sustainable Sydney 2030 *initiative*

area lack a metropolitan-wide system of government that features in many other global or world cities such as the Greater London Authority. No analogous body exists in the case of Sydney, where the overall conurbation is split into 39 local government authorities (LGAs) with a relatively weak legal position (Painter 1997, p. 148; Christoff and Low, 2000, p. 257). Many of the administrative and policy functions are constitutionally devolved to the state level, with federal entities playing only minor parts. In this sense, Sydney has historically lacked a key local coordinating authority.

Many authors have underlined how, in this institutional void, the government of New South Wales has acted as *animateur* in order to produce metropolitan strategies and orientations (Searle and Bounds, 1999; McGuirk, 2007). Chiefly through Planning NSW and the Department of State and Regional Development, the state has shaped Sydney to become a strategic globalizing site through an increasingly neoliberal agenda oriented towards regulatory flexibility and attempts to attract international elites. Planning NSW has acted as facilitator to many of these initiatives and has, since December 2005, elaborated a metropolitan strategy known as *City of Cities*. With a substantial focus on urban consolidation, this scheme has envisaged differential development based on a classification of Sydney's LGAs in a set of 'strategic centres' with different functions. Thus the LGAs have been ranked as 'global Sydney, regional cities, major centres and specialized centres' (NSW Planning, 2005). Importantly, this view has outlined what parts of the overall conurbation 'have national and international significance' (North Sydney and the City of Sydney) and which are instead major logistic hubs (such as the Airport, Olympic Park-Rhodes or Randwick Education and Health precinct), diversifying these from 'regional' service centres (such as Liverpool and Parramatta) and other sub-local communities (such as Campbelltown). Likewise, the strategy has also indicated what areas have the potential, but are not presently developed, to acquire 'major centre' status (as for Cambramatta and Leppington).

While I do not wish to undermine the planning quality of this strategy, there are some daunting signs in this imagineering approach. Green solutions are, in fact, presented here not solely as necessities of an expanding metropolis faced with internal environmental problems and transnational climate change dangers, but also (if not predominantly) in a somewhat commodified form as accessory features of Sydney's lifestyle branding and accessory features to promote the Harbour City in the global marketplace. This can be tantamount to a move that, as Sharon Zukin (2009, p. 543) recently pointed out, leads to a selective urban 'upscaling' aimed at providing physical support and programmatic narratives to that 'universal rhetoric of growth' fuelling global city governance at large. In this sense, the political construction of the city as a 'space of governance' (McGuirk, 2007, pp. 179–180) has followed the path of many other cities in shifting from a top-down government to an open governance approach to urban politics, with the increasing prominence of a multipolar, rather than hierarchical, process (MacLeod and Goodwin, 1999). The NSW government itself has been a strong supporter of this participatory process, promoting coalition-building across local actors and rallying consensus for its initiatives, as in the case of the establishment of the Organizing Committee for the Olympic Games in 1993, or with the 1996 South Sydney Development Corporation set up to coordinate the city's industrial transition. Where Sydney's entrepreneurship has paid off, in particular, is in the aforementioned twin tourism–business branding, with many events being amalgamated into the package of Sydneysider experiences to be consumed by city guests – as profitably demonstrated by the Mardi Gras celebrations.

Key participants to the realignment of city governance now include authorities and agents organized at scales beyond the traditional presence of NSW and federal agencies. While this list of actors is quite dependent on the case observed, a few usual suspects can be identified in this process. Private lobbying coalitions, for instance, are playing an increasingly relevant role in the Harbour City. Amongst many, one of the key actors of this kind is the Committee for Sydney. As a policymaking group of business leaders established in 1997, the Committee seeks to tackle issues that concern the 'whole of Sydney' and in particular lobbies on all levels of government in order to promote the city's prosperity. Members of the group range widely across the urban corporate and culture spectrum, with representatives from, for instance, Macquarie Capital Group, Sydney Airport Corporation, Minter Ellison, Coca-Cola, the National Rugby League and the Museum of Contemporary Art. As attested by the *Sydney 2020* strategy paper released in 1998, the Committee developed a proactive role in Sydney's global positioning because its founding members perceived that the public sector alone was no longer capable of tackling this challenge by itself. Importantly, the Committee has been a key driver in the commodification of green features from environmental responses to market qualities. For instance, in its recent *Global Sydney: Challenges and Opportunities for a Competitive Global City* research paper, 'building a sustainable city' appears as only one of the 19 priorities, listed as a subset amongst other livability features as an attractive asset for Sydney's reputation (Committee for Sydney, 2009, p. 43).

Along with the Committee and NSW, a key player in the city's power-geometry is, as we noted above, the City of Sydney. Formally an equal amongst 38 LGAs present in the vast metropolitan region, and representing only 26.15 square kilometres stretching from Rosebery to the Rocks, this local government has become the catalyst of the city's globalization (Figure 50.3). Under the last two Mayors, Labor Frank Sartor between 1991 and 2003 and Independent Clover Moore since 2004, the City of Sydney has acquired a core spot in Sydney politics, thanks especially to the relevance of the CBD in the process of ascent of the city in global urban hierarchies. This central place has certainly not been hindered by NSW, which has made the City of Sydney the focal point of much of its 'Sydney-centric strategy' (O'Neill and McGuirk, 2005), to the extent that today the LGA is now considered – as one Planning NSW official put it – 'the driving force' of both New South Wales and Australia (in McGuirk, 2004, p. 1028). The City Council certainly does not dismiss such imputation as it is presently taking over core regulatory and service provision functions that presently sustain a conurbation far greater than its constitutional boundaries. As the Council described it in the last Annual Report: 'the City of Sydney has an important role as *caretaker* of Australia's global city' (City of Sydney, 2008b, p. 11, emphasis added). Thanks to its privileged location and proactive governance, this LGA has been a key driver in setting a tourist–business brand for the whole conurbation, and is currently the major actor in the 'greening' of the city.

However, it is important to point out that the ascent of the City of Sydney as key player in urban politics has been coupled with a growing strategic dependence of other actors (NSW, other LGAs as well as non-governmental actors) on the CBD's centrality. Rather than moving towards a polycentric-type conurbation (Hall and Pain, 2006), often hinted at in policy documents, Sydney has progressively embarked on a path towards

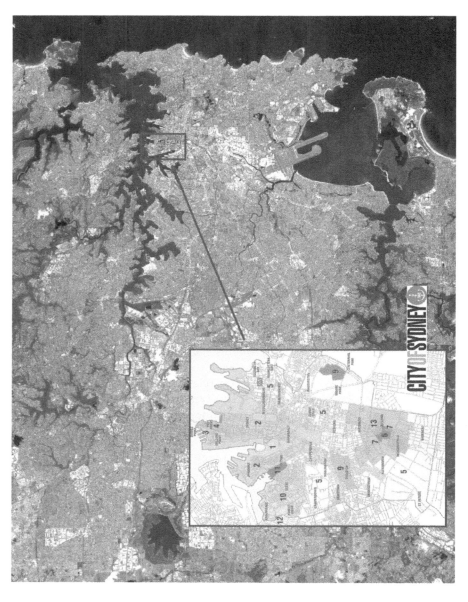

Source: City of Sydney Council and NASA Satellite image PIA 03498 (adapted by the author)

Figure 50.3   The City of Sydney Authority represents 27-odd sq. km within the vast conurbation of the greater Sydney metropolitan area

internal 'hierarchical differentiation' (Pumain, 2006), with both City of Sydney and North Sydney playing major roles in attracting global flows, mobility infrastructure secondary centres organizing the conurbation's physical connectedness to worldwide networks, and outer suburbs (especially in the West) becoming marginalized communities. This is not just the result of an indirect re-organizing prompted by the rise to global city status, but also a conscious project undertaken – at times with different goals – by state government and central LGAs. Of course, this has raised more than a few eyebrows.

THE PROBLEMATIC RISE OF ENTREPRENEURIAL SYDNEY

Ever since the 1990s, Sydney has followed an increasingly entrepreneurial governance path, shifting at a rapid pace from the management-style approaches of the 1970s and 1980s, to a more and more opportunistic, market-driven and outgoing edge (Lennon, 2000, pp. 149–150). Crucially, this approach is not just the result of global pressures, but a 'real and reflexive' shift representative of 'a purposeful aim' and substantiated by an urban narrative (the lifestyle imagineering described thus far) that attests its rationality (Jessop and Sum, 2000, p. 2287). In the context of this move, Sydney has progressively been the target of pro-entrepreneurial activities both from without (NSW and the federal government) as well as from within (City of Sydney and Committee for Sydney). The city has in fact been the object of aggressive liberalization, with a conscious agenda by the parties involved in order to promote, mostly through neoliberal policies, global competitiveness (Stillwell and Troy, 2000; McGuirk, 2004). Sydney has progressively been described as a 'golden egg' – as the Committee for Sydney put it in 2003 – capable of bringing benefits to all Sydneysiders and Australians (Committee for Sydney, 2003). However, as Doreen Massey's study of another famous golden treasure – London as a 'golden goose' – has pointed out, there are important differences between the rhetoric of these localities as 'global cities' and the actual benefit flows that generate and circulate through them (2007, pp. 97–113). Underlying interests and economic relations underpin their power-geometries, and inequality develops both across the conurbation, and between the city and other adjacent urban centres. Not everyone benefits from the goose, and the socio-spatial impacts of globalization on the Harbour (Searle, 2002; Baum, 2008) are a growing concern for scholars and planners alike.

First, there are serious physical downsides to growth without a clear lead to guide the city's orientation. While metropolises like Singapore, Hong Kong and London have a well-identified catalyst to the multiscalar governance process that underpins their entrepreneurship, Sydney is still too dependent on market-driven *ad hoc* strategies. Entrepreneurship, contrary to management, pushes towards liberalization and demand-oriented branding, while the forces of globalization (and those of neoliberal globalization in particular) pull the city in manifold directions as inspired by the ever-changing set of global networks and global realignments. The Harbour City also lacks the strong institutional texture that has allowed rising East Asian cities to avoid 'letting themselves be led like lambs to the slaughter of international competition' (Martin and Schumann, 1997, p. 143).

This has reflected on Sydney's planning rather substantially, resulting in what Penelope Dean has aptly termed 'deadline urbanism' (2005) which is demand-driven, surgical and oriented towards remedial solutions rather than planning for the long term. Sydney has become 'the accidental city' where liberalization, laissez-faire policies and global economic aspirations have driven the design and configuration of the city (Punter, 2005), leaving profound 'scars of socio-economic change' (Baum, 2008, p. 2) that define the locality's human geography. Some of these, importantly, can be the result of rational policies – as the *City of Cities* strategy shows. Lacking a catalyst capable of setting the pace and direction of urban restructuring, Sydney risks emulating the dangerous entrepreneurial edge that characterizes several newcomers to the highest echelons of the world city hierarchy such as Dubai (cf. Acuto, 2010).

With the rise of the City of Sydney as core entrepreneurial actor in metropolitan governance, and with the publication of both the *City of Cities* and the *Sydney 2030* strategies, it seems like the political process underpinning the ascent to global city status has elected the inner city as catalyst for action. The City of Sydney has been consciously talked into authority by the state government and by its own growing entrepreneurial edge. Yet the formal, legal and many of the consuetudinary practices are far from setting this rather limited LGA to the helm of the whole conurbation. Without a clear pecking order, or at least a widely acknowledged spokesperson for the entire Sydneysider community, these sustainability strategies remain unaccountable to most of the inhabitants of the Harbour City, thus allowing little or no accountability mechanism, and no overall guarantor of a universal right to the city.

Moreover, there is today an increasingly worrying trend in Sydney that shows social polarization processes with higher- and lower-income (or lower- and higher-deprivation) groups occupying increasingly differentiated areas. For example, it is particularly significant that if Scott Baum was able to dismiss this bimodal distribution thesis in 1997, his latest study now shows how Sydney is 'reflecting the polarized nature often associated with global cities' (cf. Baum, 1997, p. 1881 with Baum, 2008, p. 16). This 'two-Sydneys' (Healy and Birrell, 2003) thesis is sustained by a bimodal distribution trend in immigration patterns towards higher-end jobs for skilled migrants and low-income service occupations for others (Hugo, 2008). Likewise, this worrying path is largely complicated by the structural changes underpinning the city's re-styling, as the Harbour City's spatial segregation goes beyond a poor West/rich East dichotomy and becomes a 'splintering' and 'quartered' city with a strong internal hierarchical differentiation crowning the City of Sydney at the expense of the outer suburbs, and 'premium networked spaces' amongst the key globalizing areas (cf. Marcuse, 1989; Graham and Marvin, 2001). As journalist Debra Jopson (2002) wrote reporting a National Economics survey in 2002: 'Sydney has been described as Australia's only globalized city, but less than 2 per cent of the 12,138 square kilometers in the greater metropolitan area really deserve the title.'

WICKED ENTREPRENEURIALISM

Sydney's move to entrepreneurialism has meant an increasingly central focus on competitiveness. Since the 1990s, the governance process underpinning Sydney politics has been inspired by a 'global imperative of looking, acting and being governed as a competitive city' (McGuirk, 2004, p. 1019). The growing salience of global networks, the increasing importance of the advanced producer services industry and the key role of business elites in shaping the form and orientation of the city have all been essential factors in pushing towards the antagonistic element of entrepreneurialism, thus subjugating its other two features (innovation and the outgoing edge) to competitiveness. Even the 'greening' of the conurbation has increasingly become a matter of market competition: the *Sydney 2030* strategy, for example, is a foremost attempt to, in the words of Mayor Moore, 'position Sydney as one of the leading green cities in the race to address global warming and to become a city with strong green credentials to attract future business and investment' (City of Sydney, 2009).

This shift has been fed by the heightened popular and academic interest in city rankings, with a sprawl in urban measurements and up-to-date monitoring of urban performances that have provided even more justification for an emphasis on intercity rivalry (McNeill et al., 2005, p. 937). As recently pointed out by Peter Taylor (2009), discipline and policies have been affected by a 'categorising imperative' (Robinson, 2002) that has been fuelled by both the increasing popular attention and the ever-present policymaking beat on intercity competition. In an attempt to move away from listing pecking orders for the sake of singling out winners and losers, some authors – Taylor included – have thus far attempted to move beyond this simplistic account of urban relations as an antagonistic and finance-based race. Yet this is not just a question of scholarly evolution: as Mike Davis has fittingly pointed out in his *Dead Cities*, even if the academy has progressively accepted postmodern and critical approaches, when it comes to cities it is still 'vulgar economic determinism [that] currently holds the seat of power' (2002, p. 415). In this sense, Sydney planners and policymakers are the ones that should first and foremost understand the complexity of global city formation and the risky business of entrepreneurship.

Because of the lack of a clear authority and the multiscalar nature of urban governance, the city is raising serious social questions: the excessive focus on entrepreneurship (best represented by city imagineering) has put too much emphasis on competition at the expense of the possibilities for cooperation, both with other cities and with different levels of governance. Consequently, the city has turned too much towards tackling sustainability within its urban dimension as a source of global competitiveness, while social polarization questions are steadily advancing to the forefront as wicked challenges that cannot be solved without intercity teamwork.

Sydney is nowadays faced with a lack of a clear metropolitan-wide authority capable of prompting an approach that goes beyond mere deadline urbanism. There is a need to exploit more practically that 'strategic governance capacity' (Betsill and Bulkeley, 2003; Healey, 2004) that global cities have because of their key positioning as hinges of the present world-system. As climate change, social polarization, human rights, security and overpopulation emerge as transnational 'wicked problems' (Rittel and Webber, 1973) in a multilayered and multiscalar context such as the one depicted above, global cities require the concerted reaction of individuals at every social level.

However, this is at present an impracticable solution in the confused bureaucratic milieu of a Harbour without government. It is perhaps time to look at the possibility of establishing a Greater Sydney Authority: a workable and more sustainable alternative which can provide sustainable alternatives to the present rise of an intra-urban hierarchy dominated by the City of Sydney – a direct result of the progressive entrepreneurialism and polarization of the Harbour City. This is not, however, a call for a despotic internal pecking order but rather for a system capable of organizing the practice of governance evolved thus far, going beyond a tacit dominance of the City of Sydney. Such a structure is not incompatible with governance processes (as the case of London shows) and might be capable of managing a balanced entrepreneurship far better than the present alignments, while – and most importantly I would argue – offering an accountable voice for all Sydney's citizens to see their right to the city respected.

REFERENCES

Acuto, M. (2010), 'High-rise Dubai: urban entrepreneurialism and the technology of symbolic power', *Cities*, **27** (2), 272–284.
Bargwanna, S. (2006), 'From Brownfield to blue sky: Sydney Harbour's renaissance', in U. Mandler, C.A. Brebbia and E. Tiezzi (eds), *The Sustainable City IV: Urban Regeneration and Sustainability*, Southampton: WIT Press, pp. 353–366.
Baum, S. (1997), 'Sydney, Australia: a global city? Testing the social polarisation thesis', *Urban Studies*, **34** (11), 1881–1901.
Baum, S. (2008), 'Suburban scars: Australian cities and socio-economic deprivation', *Urban Research Program Research Paper* 15 (February), Brisbane: Griffith University & URP.
Betsill, M. and H. Bulkeley (2003), *Cities and Climate Change: Urban Sustainability and Global Environmental Governance*, London: Routledge.
Christoff, P. and N. Low (2000), 'Recent Australian urban policy and the environment: green or mean?', in N. Low, B. Gleeson, I. Elander and R. Lidskog (eds), *Consuming Cities*, London: Routledge, pp. 241–264.
City of Sydney (2008a), *Sustainable Sydney 2030: The Vision*, Sydney: City of Sydney Council.
City of Sydney (2008b), *Annual Review 2007/08*, available at www.cityofsydney.nsw.gov.au/Council (accessed 5 November 2009).
City of Sydney (2009), 'Sustainable Sydney 2030: one year on', Council media release, 12 August, available at www.sydneymedia.com.au/html/3951 (accessed 5 November 2009).
Committee for Sydney (2003), 'The golden egg', presentation on Sydney as the gateway to trade and development in Australia, available at www.sydney.org.au (accessed 5 November 2009).
Committee for Sydney (2009), *Global Sydney: Challenges and Opportunities for a Competitive Global City*, Sydney: SGS Economics and Planning Pti.
Connell, J. (2000), *Sydney: The Emergence of a World City*, Melbourne: Oxford University Press.
Davis, M. (2002), *Dead Cities*, New York: New Press.
Dean, P. (2005), 'The construction of Sydney's global image', in S. Read, J. Rosemann and J. van Eldijk (eds), *Future City*, New York: Spon Press, pp. 48–59.
Elias, D. (2003), 'Tell Melbourne it's over, we won', *Sydney Morning Herald*, 31 December, available at www. smh.com.au (accessed 5 November 2009).
Forrest, R., A. La Grange and N. Yip (2004), 'Hong Kong as a global city? Social distance and spatial differentiation', *Urban Studies*, **41** (1), 207–227.
Graham, S. and S. Marvin (2001), *Splintering Urbanism*, London: Routledge.
Hall, P. and K. Pain (eds) (2006), *The Polycentric Metropolis: Learning from Mega-City Regions in Europe*, London: Earthscan.
Healey, P. (2004), 'Creativity and urban governance', *Policy Studies*, **25** (2), 87–102.
Healy, E. and B. Birrell (2003), 'Metropolis divided: the dynamic of spatial inequality and migrant settlement in Sydney', *People and Place*, **11** (2), 65–85.
Hugo, G. (2008), 'Sydney: the globalization of an established immigrant gateway', in M. Price and L. Benton-Short (eds), *Migrants to the Metropolis: The Rise of Immigrant Gateway Cities*, Syracuse, NY: Syracuse University Press, pp. 69–96.
Hundloe, T. and G. McDonald (1997), 'Ecologically sustainable development and the Better Cities Program', *Australian Journal of Environmental Management*, **4** (2), 88–111.
Jessop, B. and N.L. Sum (2000), 'An entrepreneurial city in action: Hong Kong's emerging strategies in and for (inter)urban competition', *Urban Studies*, **37** (12), 2287–2313.
Jopson, D. (2002), 'The savvy sliver of Sydney that puts it among the world's heavyweights', *Sydney Morning Herald*, 4 March.
Lennon, M. (2000), 'The revival of metropolitan planning', in S. Hamnett and R. Freestone (eds), *The Australian Metropolis: A Planning History*, Sydney: Allen & Unwin, pp. 149–167.

MacLeod, G. and M. Goodwin (1999), 'Space, scale and state strategy: rethinking urban and regional governance', *Progress in Human Geography*, **23** (4), 503–527.

Marcuse, P. (1989), 'Dual City: a muddy metaphor for a quartered city', *International Journal of Urban and Regional Research*, **13** (4), 697–708.

Martin, H. and H. Schumann (1997), *The Global Trap* (transl. by P. Camiller), London: Zed Books.

Massey, D. (2007), *World City*, London: Polity.

McGuirk, P. (2004), 'State, strategy and scale in the competitive city: a neo-Gramscian analysis of the governance of global Sydney', *Environment and Planning A*, **36** (2), 1019–1043.

McGuirk, P. (2007), 'The political construction of the city-region: notes from Sydney', *International Journal of Urban and Regional Research*, **31** (1), 179–187.

McNeill, D., R. Dowling and B. Fagan (2005), 'Sydney/global/city: an exploration', *International Journal of Urban and Regional Research*, **29** (4), 935–944.

Murphy, P. and S. Watson (1997), *Surface City: Sydney at the Millennium*, Annandale, Sydney, NSW: Pluto Press.

NSW Planning (New South Wales Department of Planning) (2005), *City of Cities: A Plan for Sydney's Future*, Sydney: New South Wales Department of Planning.

O'Neill, P.M. and P. McGuirk (2005), 'Reterritorialisation of economies and institutions: the rise of the Sydney basin economy', *Space and Polity*, **9** (3), 283–305.

Painter, M. (1997), 'Reshaping the public sector', in B. Galligan, I. McAllister and J. Ravenhill (eds), *New Developments in Australian Politics*, Melbourne: Macmillan, pp. 148–155.

Pumain, D. (2006), 'Alternative explanations of hierarchical differentiation in urban systems', in D. Pumain (ed.), *Hierarchy in Natural and Social Sciences*, The Hague: Springer, pp. 169–222.

Punter, J. (2005), 'Urban design in central Sydney 1945–2002: laissez-faire and discretionary traditions in the accidental city', *Progress in Planning*, **63** (1), 11–160.

Rittel, H. and M. Webber (1973), 'Dilemmas in a general theory of planning', *Policy Sciences*, **4** (1), 155–169.

Robinson, J. (2002), 'Global and world cities: a view from off the map', *International Journal of Urban and Regional Research*, **26** (3), 531–554.

Sassen, S. (2001), *The Global City: New York, London and Tokyo*, Princeton, NJ: Princeton University Press, 2nd edition.

Searle, G. (1996), *Sydney as a Global City*, Sydney: Department of Urban Affairs and Planning and Department of State and Regional Development.

Searle, G. (2002), 'The demise of place equity in Sydney's economic development planning', *Australian Geographer*, **33** (3), 317–336.

Searle, G. and M. Bounds (1999), 'State powers, state land and competition for global entertainment: the case of Sydney', *International Journal of Urban and Regional Research*, **23** (1), 165–172.

Spearritt, P. (2006), 'Consuming Sydney', in R. Freestone, B. Randolph and C. Butler-Bowdon (eds), *Talking about Sydney: Population, Community and Culture in Contemporary Sydney*, Sydney: University of New South Wales Press, pp. 199–212.

Stillwell, F. and P. Troy (2000), 'Multilevel governance and urban development in Australia', *Urban Studies*, **37** (5–6), 909–930.

Taylor, P.J. (2009), 'Commentary: urban economics in thrall to Christaller: a misguided search for city hierarchies in external urban relations', *Environment and Planning A*, **41** (11), 2550–2555.

Taylor, P.J., P. Ni, B. Derudder, M. Hoyler, J. Huang, F. Lu, K. Pain, F. Witlox, X. Yang, D. Bassens and W. Shen (2009), 'Measuring the world city network: new developments and results', *GaWC Research Bulletin*, 300, available at www.lboro.ac.uk/gawc/rb/rb300.html (accessed 5 November 2009).

Tonts, M. and M. Taylor (2010), 'Corporate location, concentration and performance: large company headquarters in the Australian urban system', *Urban Studies*, **47** (12), 2641–2664.

Zukin, S. (2009), 'Changing landscapes of power: opulence and the urge for authenticity', *International Journal of Urban and Regional Research*, **33** (2), 543–553.

Index